Economics, Law and Intellectual Property

Economics, Law and Intellectual Property

Seeking Strategies for Research and Teaching in a Developing Field

Edited by

Ove Granstrand

Center for Intellectual Property Studies,
Department of Industrial Management & Economics,
Chalmers University of Technology, Göteborg, Sweden

KLUWER ACADEMIC PUBLISHERS
BOSTON / DORDRECHT / LONDON

A C.I.P. Catalogue record for this book is available from the Library of Congress.

ISBN 1-4020-7708-4

Published by Kluwer Academic Publishers,
P.O. Box 17, 3300 AA Dordrecht, The Netherlands.

Sold and distributed in North, Central and South America
by Kluwer Academic Publishers,
101 Philip Drive, Norwell, MA 02061, U.S.A.

In all other countries, sold and distributed
by Kluwer Academic Publishers,
P.O. Box 322, 3300 AH Dordrecht, The Netherlands.

Printed on acid-free paper

Printed in the Netherlands.

List of Contributors

Arrow, Kenneth, Professor of Economics (Emeritus), Stanford University, Department of Economics, Stanford, CA, USA

Adams, John, Barrister, Professor of Intellectual Property University of Sheffield, Department of Law, Sheffield, UK

Anawalt, Howard C., Professor of Law, Santa Clara University, School of Law, Santa Clara, CA, USA

Arora, Ashish, Professor of Economics and Public Policy, Carnegie Mellon University, Heinz School of Public Policy and Management, Pittsburgh, PA, USA

Barton, John H., Professor of Law (Emeritus), Stanford University, Law School, Stanford, CA, USA

Cohen, Wesley, Professor of Economics and Management, The Fuqua School of Business, Duke University, Durham, North Carolina, USA.

Domeij, Bengt, Associate Professor of Intellectual Property Law , The Royal Institute of Technology, Department of Industrial Economics and Management, Stockholm, Sweden

Foray, Dominique, Principal Administrator at Center for Education, Research and Innovation of OECD; Research Director at Centre National de la Recherche Scientifique (CNRS); Professor at the Institute for the Management of Research and Innovation (IMRI), University of Paris-Dauphine, Paris, France

Colyvas, Jeannette A., Ph.D. Candidate, Institute for International Studies, Stanford University, Stanford, CA, USA

Fosfuri, Andrea, Associate Professor of Management, Universidad Carlos III de Madrid, Department of Business Administration, Madrid, Spain

Gambardella, Alfonso, Professor of Economics and Management Sant'Anna School of Advanced Studies, Pisa, Italy

Gelijns, Annetine, Associate Professor, Columbia University, Department of Surgery, New York, NY, USA

Goto, Akira, Professor, University of Tokyo, Research Center for Advanced Economic Engineering, Tokyo, Japan

Granstrand Ove, Professor of Industrial Management and Economics, Chalmers University of Technology, Department of Industrial Management and Economics, Chairman of CIP – Center for Intellectual Property Studies, Göteborg, Sweden

Hall, Bronwyn, Professor of Economics, University of California at Berkeley, Department of Economics, Berkeley, CA, USA; National Bureau of Economics Research (NBER), Stanford, CA, USA

Harhoff, Dietmar, Professor of Innovation Research, Technology Management and Entrepreneurship, Ludwig-Maximilian-University Munich, Munich School of Management, Munich, Germany

Kingston, William, Research Associate, University of Dublin, Trinity College, School of Business Studies, Dublin, Ireland

Koo, Bonwoo, Research Fellow, Environmental and Production Technology Division, International Food Policy Research Institute, Washington, DC, USA

Nagata, Akiya, Associate Professor, Japan Advanced Institute of Science and Technology, Ishikawa, Japan

Nelson, Richard R., Professor of International Political Economy, Columbia University, Department of International and Public Affairs, New York, NY, USA

Petrusson, Ulf, Jur.Dr., Director, CIP – Center for Intellectual Property Studies, Chalmers University of Technology; Göteborg University, School of Law, Göteborg, Sweden

Radin, Margaret Jane, Professor of Law, Stanford University, Law School, Stanford, CA, USA

Rosenberg, Nathan, Professor of Economics (Emeritus), Stanford University, Department of Economics, Stanford, CA, USA

Scherer, Frederic M. Professor of Economics (Emeritus), Harvard University, John F. Kennedy School of Government, Cambridge, MA, USA

Towse, Ruth, Dr., Erasmus University Rotterdam, Faculty of History and Art Studies (KCW), Rotterdam, The Netherlands

Ullrich, Hanns, Professor of Law, Bundeswehr University Munich, Faculty of Economic and Organisational Sciences, Neubiberg, Germany

Walsh John P., Associate Professor of Sociology, University of Illinois at Chicago, Department of Sociology, Chicago, IL, USA

Verspagen, Bart, Professor of Economics, Eindhoven University of Technology, Eindhoven Center for Innovation Studies (ECIS), Eindhoven, The Netherlands

Vopel, Katrin Research Fellow at Centre for European Economic Research (ZEW), Department of Industrial Economics and International Management, Mannheim, Germany

Wright, Brian, Professor of Economics, University of California at Berkeley, Department of Agricultural and Resource Economics, Berkeley, CA, USA

ERRATUM

Economics, Law and Intellectual Property
Edited by Ove Granstrand

ISBN 1-4020-7708-4

On page 123 of the volume, footnote 1 needs to be

This chapter draws heavily on the paper by W.M. Cohen, A. Goto, A. Nagata, R.R. Nelson & J.P. Walsh, "R&D Spillovers, Patents and the Incentive to Innovate in Japan and the United States," *Research Policy*, Vol. 31, Nos. 8-9, December, 2002, pp. 1349-1367.

Foreword

Since its inception as the first engineering academy in the world, the Royal Swedish Academy of Engineering Sciences, IVA, has seen as its key role to promote both the exploring and exploiting facets of engineering. If one avoids the obsolete interpretation of engineering as simply applied science, engineering has a defining characteristic of sustaining influence upon as well as from the natural sciences, being at the same time immersed in economic considerations if not calculations.

As a corollary the Academy promotes the difficult but decisive two-way traffic between natural sciences and economic applications. To help build functional bridges for interdisciplinary communications then becomes inherent in the Academy as a pro-active learned society.

Integrating economic sciences into the span of disciplines of our Academy has seemed as justifiable as it is to integrate economics in engineering. As the pace of engineering and technological development of our society is continually increasing, social sciences as well as humanities appear ever more relevant to engineering, and thereby to the Academy.

One example is legal science in general, as laws and regulations both constrain and promote techno-economic developments. In particular the revived area of intellectual property provides a bridge to the field of law, although there are other sites such as the environmental and health areas.

The Academy has by tradition been active in furthering intellectual property studies. In 1992-1993 a large study was undertaken resulting in the report "Profit from Innovation" (IVA, 1993), a study which led to heightened awareness of intellectual property in Swedish industry. In the aftermath of this study an interdisciplinary center for studies of intellectual property was proposed, although not immediately materialized.

It is now with great pleasure – and great expectations – that I can see the development of such a center with a growing range of teaching and research activities. A first international symposium has been organized in collaboration with the Academy, from which the current book emanates as an early vehicle on a new bridge. I unreservedly recommend it for exploration and exploitation in the area of intellectual property.

Stockholm, Sweden, May 2003
Lena Torell, President,
The Royal Swedish Academy of Engineering Sciences

Preface

A new truth does not triumph by convincing its opponents and making them see the light, but rather because its opponents eventually die, and a new generation grows up that is familiar with it.

Max Planck,
"Scientific Autobiography and Other Papers",
Williams & Norgate Ltd., London, 1950,
pp. 33-34.

This book is an edited selection of revised research papers, which were originally prepared for an international symposium, entitled "Economics and Law of Intellectual Property – Seeking strategies for research and teaching in a developing field". The symposium was held in Göteborg, Sweden, June 26-30, 2000, organized by Chalmers University of Technology in collaboration with the Royal Swedish Academy of Engineering Sciences and the School of Economics and Commercial Law at Göteborg University.

The general purpose of this symposium was to convene internationally prominent and active researchers studying the interaction between economic, legal and technological changes in the field of intellectual property (IP). Since the advent of the "pro-patent era", triggered in the US in the 1980s, this old and traditionally minor field of study has been developing rapidly in many ways around the world, catching the interest of a much widened audience with new generations of researchers, teachers, students and practitioners searching for new knowledge and new paradigms. Therefore, in something of a "take-off" stage of the IP field, it was considered important to identify useful results of past research and seek fruitful strategies for future research and teaching, and then especially considering the international dimension of the field. A specific purpose of the symposium was also to produce a carefully edited volume, integrating material of interest for researchers, teachers, students and future decision-makers, and make it readable across disciplines.

The symposium tried to focus on issues that were broad and sustainably open and thus could serve themes and questions for continued research, such as:

1. **Incentive schemes for hard and soft investments in new technologies and innovations in general.** What determines soft and hard capital formation in different technologies in firms and nations? What are the nature and role of IPRs in R&D decision-making and technology strategies inside the firm? Inside the university? How can we make evaluations (ex ante/ex post) of different incentive schemes (patents, prizes, contracts, regulations etc) for investments in science, technology, arts and innovations?

2. **Diffusion and transfer of new technologies and the functioning of knowledge/information markets in general.** What is the role of old and new types of IPRs (e.g. database protection) in this context? What is the role of new technologies and new contractual forms? What is the role of Internet and e-business?

3. **Current and future issues, problems and possible remedies.** What are the issues related to specific technologies, like infocom technologies and biohealth technologies? What are the issues related to specific jurisdictions? What are the needs and prospects for international legal harmonization? Is the IPR system conducive or obtrusive to scientific, technological and economic progress?

4. **Methodological issues.** What are the possibilities and limits of econometrics, technometrics, jurimetrics, case studies, history studies, modelling, simulation etc? What are the methodological and statistical needs specific to the area? Which are the most fruitful levels of analysis and what are the problems of aggregation? What are the possibilities and limits of patent information in particular as technical and economic indicators?

5. **Issues regarding paradigms and theory formation.** What are the possibilities and limits of historicism, empiricism, formalism, positivism, utilitarianism, constructivism, eclectic theories, normative theories, general (unifying) or specific theories etc? What are the limits to causal reasoning and prediction? What are the theoretical needs and most promising advances? What are proper conceptualizations of intellectual property on the whole?

The symposium had over twenty scholars presenting papers containing original and important work in the fields of economics and law of intellectual property and intellectual capital. Contributions were empirically as well as theoretically grounded and represented the micro-level of industries, universities and firms and the idiosyncrasies of different technologies, as well as the macro-level of countries, legal systems and the international context in general. The symposium also focused on sectors exhibiting particularly strong interaction between economic, legal and technological changes, such as in infocom technologies and biohealth technologies.

The editorial work has given priority to quality and pluralism rather than to coherence within some narrow theme. An ambition has also been to view the collection of chapters as a sample of writings in the developing IP field, and to make a bit of comparative "case analysis" as part of an editorial method. The "sampling" of authors has also been stratified with authors sampled in the economics and law strata, which are quite separate as a bibliometric analysis shows in the opening chapter. Editorial efforts have therefore been made to characterize and compare the various contributions in the concluding chapter in an attempt to pave the way for future research and teaching in the IP field with more of an interdisciplinary outlook.

In organizing the symposium and editing this book, I want to mention and sincerely thank many persons and institutions that have helped me. I would first like to thank Prof. Lotta Vahlne Westerhäll and Jur. Dr. Ulf Petrusson at the School of Economics and Commercial Law at Göteborg University, and the Royal Swedish Academy of Engineering Sciences with former Acting President Enrico Deiaco, for co-organizing the symposium. The conscientious assistance of Jur. Cand. Ola Küller and Eva Burford in promptly catering to a wide range of matters, both in organizing the symposium and in supporting the editing of the book, is greatly appreciated. I would also like to thank Jur. Cand'.s Lars Andersson, Karin Hervéus and Jeffrey Johns as well as students at the School of Law – Emma Lorentzon and others – for handy and spirited assistance in various matters. Many thanks also go to Patent Attorney Thomas Ewing for his numerous valuable comments and contributions from a practitioner's perspective.

The financial support obtained from various sources is gratefully acknowledged. The major sponsors of the symposium were the Marcus Wallenberg Foundation for International Scientific Cooperation and Stiftelsen för Ekonomisk Forskning i Västsverige (the Western Sweden Foundation for Research in Economic Sciences). Additional funding was provided by the Technology Link Foundation, the National Swedish Board for Industrial and Technical Development (NUTEK), Eka Chemicals AB, Stena AB, Awapatent AB, and Awapatent's Stiftelse för Immaterialrättslig Forskning. The fund-raising assistance of Dr. Arne Wittlöv, Chairman of the Royal Swedish Academy of Engineering Sciences (IVA), and Mr. Jack Forsgren, member of IVA, is also warmly acknowledged.

In connection with producing this volume, my foremost thanks go to all contributors. Special gratitude is indeed due (and overdue) to the early responders in the revision process, who are not rewarded by any early-mover advantages. On the contrary, some are even penalized in the waiting game that not uncommonly develops behind editing a book. Thanks also go to Jon van Leuven, who assisted in checking the language, providing occasional comments on the contents, and thanks to Jakub Gubanski and Frank Tietze for their invaluable help with proof-reading. Last but surely not least to be thanked is Eva Burford for her indispensable editorial assistance throughout the entire undertaking, always readily provided with equanimity.

Göteborg, Sweden, March 2003
Ove Granstrand
Professor, Chairman, Center for Intellectual Property Studies

Prologue

The term, "intellectual property", represents a metaphorical extension of a straightforward concept, the ownership of physical goods. Ownership is now extended from entities that can be described with spatial coordinates to the much more impalpable area of knowledge, generally knowledge how to do something useful, to produce something valued in the market. The usual picture of "property" is that it is in scarce supply and that it can be alienated, that is, if ownership is transferred from one individual to another, the former doesn't have it in any sense while the latter does. Among other implications of these facts is that markets are a suitable way of transferring ownership. Given a legal framework which enforces sales contracts, the ownership is clearcut and practically self-enforcing.

It is by now a commonplace that intellectual property differs from other forms of property in these aspects. Knowledge cannot be undone. If one individual knows how to make a product, he or she does not cease to know on transferring ownership of the knowledge to someone else. A given piece of knowledge may thus be multiplied indefinitely in the population. (There are obstacles to transmission, but they are on the part of the receivers. The recipient may have to supply complementary inputs, such as other knowledge, to understand and use the information. But there are no obstacles to the supplier of the knowledge.) In short, knowledge does not satisfy the algebra of ordinary commodities, which is linear. If knowledge is transferred from A to B, A still has it; on the other hand, the same piece of information repeated is not twice as much, as it would be with steel, but the same (i.e., $1 + 1 = 1$, not 2).

The market system based on linear algebra no longer applies to knowledge. If knowledge were exogenously given, this would offer no policy problem. If the reproduction cost of knowledge is zero, that should be its price, and knowledge should circulate freely. Indeed, knowledge does circulate pretty widely, in spite of property rights, and this fact increases the efficiency of the economy. However, the policy problem arises when the production of knowledge is costly (research and development costs in some industries, such as pharmaceuticals, can be very high); the knowledge will not be produced at its efficiency price of zero. There are (at least) three resolutions of the policy dilemma: (1) making knowledge private property, through patents, copyrights, or protection of trade secrets; (2) providing new knowledge as a public good by the governments; and (3) private development of knowledge, either intentionally or as a by-product of production, because of its value to the firm, even though the knowledge cannot be made private property.

All three offer problems for policy, but it is the first that seems the most difficult in principle. The reward to compensate for the costs and risks of innovation is monopoly profit; and monopoly is of course in itself a source of inefficiency. Historically, a second-best solution has been limitation of the time period of the monopoly. Obviously, such a simple rule is far from optimal (even as second-best), since the time period of monopoly should vary with circumstances, but it does have the virtue of easing the problem of enforceability.

Still, in recent times, there has been renewed attention to the problems raised by the patent system. Many problems have emerged, but I will mention two. One is the interaction with anti-monopoly policy. In the increasingly numerous industries marked by network effects and other aspects of increasing returns, effective competition in the static sense is probably impossible. The main emphasis rather is on making sure that entry based on innovation is not blocked ("dynamic competition"). Monopoly by itself discourages innovation by the monopolist, since the innovation in effect competes with the previous product of the firm. Free entry means that other firms have an incentive to innovate, and the firm in being also has such an incentive to meet potential entry. But patents can be used to block entry. This is especially true when the later innovations build on the previous one, so that the earlier patent can be used to block entry by refusal to license (or by charging high license fees). This leads to a view by several analysts that the breadth of patents be restricted sharply.

A second problem relates more to distributional ethics and applies especially to pharmaceuticals. Maximization of monopoly profits frequently requires price discrimination across countries. One aspect is that the nationalized health services of many other countries have more market power than the dispersed United States market, so that the latter system or the individuals in it pay much higher prices. A second aspect is that price discrimination in favor of poorer markets may cause international shipments, since the markets cannot be separated very effectively.

These are not the only difficulties with the patent system as it exists today, but they are enough to suggest the need for the further research exemplified by this volume.

Kenneth J. Arrow

Chapter 1

INNOVATIONS AND INTELLECTUAL PROPERTY STUDIES

An introduction and overview of a developing field

Ove Granstrand

Chalmers University of Technology, Dept. of Industrial Management and Economics, Göteborg, Sweden

Chapter contents:

Abstract: The fundamental role of innovations and their economic and legal aspects are described as a starter before departure into the book. A number of illustrations of close interaction between economic, legal and technological changes related to IP are provided as a contrast to the long-standing separation of economics from law and IP studies, thereby indicating a need for further interdisciplinary research and teaching in the IP field. To help meet this need is the purpose of this book.

A bibliometric analysis is provided, showing that the IP field is rapidly growing, also relative to social sciences in general. US journals and authors dominate the field. Law and economics, with economics catching up from far behind, are dominant disciplines in the IP field but fairly separated, although showing signs of science convergence over time, with economists dominating cross-disciplinary works.

The end of the chapter outlines the book as a whole.

O. Granstrand (ed.), Economics, Law and Intellectual Property, 9-40.

There are three sorts of people in the world – those who can count and those who cannot count.

Once discovered, this joke was novel to the world. Being a joke it is also non-obvious, since otherwise it provides no humour. To the extent that a good laugh enriches life, the joke is also useful. It could then be seen as an invention, even a medical invention to the extent that it prolongs life. The invention becomes an innovation when successfully received by consumers of humour. This innovation then diffuses in society, becomes perhaps widely adopted, retold, modified, improved etc. During this process no real commercial transactions take place. What is more: there is not a single trace of any intellectual property (IP) notions – no copyright, no trade secret, no trademark, no business method patent etc. Still, a good joke could be claimed to fulfil requirements of being novel, non-obvious in relation to prior art, and useful. This teaches us that intellectual property rights (IPRs) are not (yet) everywhere, despite their pervasiveness, ancient historic tradition and current popularity.[1] Thus there are exchanges in the economy that are driven by special remunerations without involving trade and property rights. In fact, much exchange of information in general takes place in this way. However, as soon as costs of creating new information, data or knowledge become substantial or the benefits therefrom become substantial, adequate provision of new information and innovations in general is endangered. IPRs then constitute one out of several available approaches of private or public provision of costly or valuable innovations. The IPR approach is not perfectly tailored and by far does not fit all situations, however. It does not come free of charge, distortions and side-effects. Neither do other available approaches. Innovations are simple to welcome but difficult to invite. Attempts to do so involve a large portion of muddling through and scholars of innovation must count on uncountable difficulties. *Innovatio non-jocus est.*

[1] This is not to say that the whole area of jokes and humour is an example of an area of human needs free from any IP notions and commercial considerations. The comedian Bob Hope allegedly ran almost factory-like operations for joke production and built a large inventory (database) of them, and the comedian W.C. Fields became involved in a lawsuit with a submitter of joke ideas.

1.1 Innovations, Laws and Economies in Interaction

1.1.1 Innovations and progress

Innovation is usually defined as something novel and useful – be it technological, organisational, financial, institutional, cultural or whatever under the sun. Thus, innovation more or less by definition is the basis for progress in all areas of human endeavour. If progress is sought, it is then of central concern to find means to stimulate a proper flow of innovations, neither too few for desirable progress, nor too many for smooth adaptations. However, economic systems, regardless of type, have difficulties in generating such a flow of innovations. It is simply difficult to tailor proper incentives for individuals and organisations that are capable and willing to move ahead as innovators, and to find a scheme for sharing the accruing advantages of the innovations between innovators and others. Sometimes early mover advantages are so weak compared to late mover advantages that prospective innovators are better off awaiting the moves of others, resulting in a waiting game. Sometimes it is the other way around and individuals engage in a race to become first with an innovation. The resultant racing game could then be even more costly in total than the total advantages of the innovation.

Competition is usually seen as conducive to innovation, but it is neither necessary nor sufficient for a flow of innovations. Curiosity and necessity would induce innovations in the absence of competition, and e.g. induce a Robinson Crusoe to become an innovator. On the other hand, presence of competition from imitators could bring forth innovations but could also bring innovations to a halt. Moreover, innovations mostly require cooperation, so prospects and advantages (rewards) have to be shared from that point of view in some kind of cooperative game. Difficulties then arise since incentive structures differ among individuals, some preferring monetary rewards in the first place, some fame and social recognition, some satisfaction from achievement and so forth.

There are various ways or strategies for early as well as late movers to reap or appropriate the benefits from innovations. The innovator, being in fact the first mover, can create a lead time over late movers by being secretive about the innovation, relatively faster in exploitation, and more skilful in subsequent development (upgrading), production and marketing to various users of the innovation, and in forging durable links with users for sharing advantages.

There are also various ways or policy means for a society to foster flows of innovations in rates and directions thought to be proper. Thus a society can provide means for social recognition and/or financial rewards in the form of ceremonies, prizes, grants, subsidies, procurement contracts, property rights or some form of regulation with associated penalties etc. Most societies or cultures, primitive as well as advanced, also employ such means, e.g. for social recognition of creators and innovations. At the same time there are usually means for checking, if not punishing, the kind of deviant behaviour associated with innovations and creative work. Despite this ambivalence, most cultures seem basically to welcome innovations.

The use of property rights or privileges to induce innovations of various kinds through strengthening first mover advantages is an old institutional arrangement. It is now customary to refer to these rights as intellectual property rights (IPRs), comprising old types of rights such as patents for inventions, trade secrets, copyrights, trademarks and design rights, together with newer ones such as breeding rights, maskwork rights and database rights. These rights – although subsumed under the label IPRs, suggesting some coherence – in fact comprise a very heterogeneous set of rights with fragmented historical developments, hardly constituting what could be called an IPR system. It is not even clearly natural to view these rights as property rights.

1.1.2 Economic, legal and technological changes

Innovation is a special type of change, being cause and consequence of a multitude of other interacting changes of various types. IP studies, and innovation studies more generally, tend to be oriented around some discipline or type of variables, and the interaction across relevant disciplines tend to be much weaker than the real interaction across the types of variables they study. This will be illustrated below, first by simply listing a limited number of major changes, which also serve as a background, next probing a few of them in more depth and then describing the disciplinary structure of IP studies.

The many strong interactions between general economic, organizational and technological changes and more IP-specific legal changes can be illustrated by listing various changes and trends which clearly are intertwined and clearly interact with other types of changes as well – political, managerial, social etc. (In fact, difficulties of classifying them into different types indicate close interaction.) With usual reservations about the adequacy of selective listings of different types of changes and uncertain trends, the following examples are hopefully sufficiently illustrative:

Economic changes

1. Economic rise of Japan and Asian NICs in the 1980s and disintegration of the Soviet Union political empire and economic system in the 1990s, changes which in large part were innovation- and technology-related.
2. Gradual emergence of a new type of economy (more knowledge- and innovation-based, ICT-driven, IP-oriented, etc.) with more use of technology and information markets, firms and products.
3. Military R&D, still amounting to roughly half of the world's R&D, is shifting in character, including increase of IP relevance.
4. Increasing importance of dynamic innovation-based competition across nations, sectors, companies and markets (including markets for labour, knowledge/ideas and financial services).
5. Increasing gaps of technology and competitiveness between the USA and Europe, including the defence sector.
6. Perceived underinvestment in R&D in Europe has prompted the European Commission to adopt the goal that overall spending on R&D and innovation in the EU should be increased with the aim of approaching 3% of GDP by 2010.
7. Universities and public research organisations are becoming more economically focused, i.e. becoming more industrialised, commercial, competitive, international, alliance-prone, strategic, and IP-conscious.

IP legal changes

1. Increasing strengthening, widening, awareness, use and enforcement of the various IP systems around the world, with growth on average of patents, patent portfolios, IP values, IP disputes, damages etc.
2. Increasing interaction between IP policies and other economic policies, especially trade policies through TRIPs and the WTO.
3. Extension of patentable and IP-protectable subject matter and IPR types (e.g. database rights).
4. Increasing international harmonisation of IP laws and practices.
5. Increasing strategic role and use of IPRs in various industries.
6. Increasing protests against the IP system and disputes within the IP system, with increasing litigation costs.

7. Increasing interaction between various IPR types and between IP laws and other areas of law, especially contract law, trade law and competition law.

Technological/R&D changes

1. Emergence of new technological systems (families of interrelated technologies), in particular ICTs, biohealth technologies (BHTs) and material and energy technologies.
2. Continued build-up of in-house R&D and various forms of corporate innovation systems in industry, now controlling most of worldwide technology and an increasing share of worldwide science.
3. Increasing specialization and division of R&D labour, use of technology markets and external technology acquisition.
4. Increasing technology diversification of products and processes, leading to increasing interdependencies among technologies, companies, products and processes.
5. A continued transition from individually based research and invention (for which IPR laws originally and still cater) to intra-company team-based and further to inter-company team-based, i.e. to inter-organisational R&D collaboration. Scale, critical mass, scope, interdisciplinarity, and speed to market will make collaborations and networking an increasingly appealing governance mode over purely market-mediated coordination.
6. Internationalisation, globalisation and "glocalisation" of R&D and technology acquisition (i.e. global coordination of firm R&D with increasing concentration in certain technology-intensive regions around the world).
7. Technological changes in the production and distribution of new technologies. Emergence of what can be called "e-Research" in intra- and inter-firm R&D through use of various infocom technologies as research tools (Internet, multimedia conferencing, networked databases, artificial intelligence tools, distributed computing, data grids, large-scale simulations etc.).

The first four changes listed as economic changes (in the main) above will be explored in greater depth below. The first example about the rise and fall of specific nations will be commented upon more generally, however.

1.1.3 Innovations, IP laws and economies in interaction

Progress requires innovations, but it is not clear that innovations require IP laws. Nevertheless, when innovations require investments, as for most technological innovations, some laws for public or private provision of the investments are required. These laws could vary as the nature of innovations and their interaction with the economy vary. To what extent IP laws, as they have developed, actually have influenced the flow of innovations and economic developments has long been debated. From time to time the debate has been quite heated, indicating deep-running controversies about rationales, impacts and relative merits.

While there undisputedly is a strong interaction between innovations and the economy, especially regarding technological innovations, there seems to be a much weaker interaction between IP laws on one hand and innovations and the economy on the other, at least in the past. Focusing more narrowly on technological innovations, IP laws seemingly have been neither necessary nor sufficient for either technological or economic progress throughout history, indicating a weak form of interaction on average. Nevertheless, there are numerous examples from history of how IP laws have in fact been influential upon, as well as influenced by, technological and economic developments. For example, there is a long history of how IP laws and trade-related privileges (patents in particular) have been used for national protectionist purposes. Handing out privileges and property rights was (and is) simply a handy way for rulers and governments to influence the economics of innovation.[2]

Various countries have, in the course of their catch-up processes, switched from weak to strong IP regimes (but seldom the reverse). Many industries and technologies have emerged under weak IP regimes, which then for various reasons have become reinforced. The same could be said about many companies, but here reversals have also occurred in the sense that some companies have had their cumulated IP powers curbed by antitrust authorities.

The contemporary and perhaps largest example of close economic, legal and technological interaction is the emergence of a new type of economy based more on knowledge, new technologies, innovations and intellectual capital and the emergence of a generally strong IP regime (dubbed the pro-IP era). The new type of economy has emerged gradually for a long time, although recognition and debate grew rapidly in the late 1990s, culminating

[2] In fact this policy could be seen as a special use of taxation powers, in the sense that some of these powers are handed over under certain conditions to innovators who, at their discretion for a limited time, can tax consumers through higher prices on the innovations.

with the financial bubble. The latter burst and so did some of the surface talk about the new economy, but the undercurrent of the latter remains. The pro-IP era emerged much more rapidly from the early 1980s onward, triggered by legal changes (judicial and policy-based) in the US, then spreading almost globally. Although too early for historians to say conclusively, it seems as if the new type of IP regime was more a consequence than a cause of the new type of economy. To proceed with sweeping characterizations, the latter seems to be more a consequence than a cause of new technologies, new infocom technologies in particular. These in turn, and the industries that have emerged based on them (computer, software, semiconductor and modern telecom industries), have by and large not developed as a consequence of a strong IP regime, but have rather developed in a weak IP regime that has then become strengthened.[3]

Another contemporary major example is the military sector with its special economy, technologies and laws. (The exposition of this example here is also motivated by the limitation to civilian innovations in this book.) For a long time roughly half of the world's S&T and R&D activities have been defence-related. R&D activities have been performed in mostly national military-industrial complexes, led by super-powers in distinctive alliance structures. The "appropriation" and control of military S&T have formed a special military IP regime based on secrecy and various types of controls and sanctions, quite separate from the civilian IP regimes (regardless of type of economic system – market or planned). Military and civilian technology, R&D, industrial activities, and governance structures in general have in fact been quite separate from each other (even within firms). For various reasons (downfall of the Soviet Union, multi-polarisation of power, US hegemony, growing importance of China, terrorism, guerrilla warfare techniques, rising capital intensity in conventional warfare, rising R&D costs, new technologies, waning geographic borders and distances etc.) this situation is now subjected to far-reaching changes and trends (without completely changing the nature of military affairs, of course).

What are increasing, and already visible in the USA, are: integration of military and civilian technologies and markets (through dual use, lead/lag reversals, scientification etc.); outsourcing of defence R&D, production and services for firms, nations and even cross-national alliances; internationalisation and globalisation of defence R&D, defence services, defence procurement and defence industries; limited military/police international "ventures";

[3] For some further readings, see e.g. Coriat and Orsi (2002), Granstrand (2000 a,b) and Jaffe (2000).

cross-national trade of military technology; R&D and production collaborations.

The likely implications of this are increasing R&D collaboration across nations, sectors, firms and civilian-military borders, industrial restructuring (divestments, joint ventures, M&As) and global concentration. Defence R&D as well as defence services (based on surveillance, command and control, robots, unmanned vehicles, electronic warfare, network defence etc.) will increasingly be ICT-based, and probably with closer integration of military and civilian ICT systems. This is especially likely in the area of surveillance, with its vast possibilities to use ICTs for development, production and exploitation of databases. (Note the military role in developing e.g. the Internet, GPS and Echelon (as alleged).) Awareness and strategic use of IPRs beyond trade secrets are then also likely to increase in military industry as a consequence. A more speculative but still conceivable scenario is that some kind of joining of legal and military powers could accrue in some situations.

A fourth example, concerning competition, will be given in Section 1.2.3 below. Other examples of economic, legal and technological interaction becoming closer might be found in environmental protection and health care regulation.

1.2 The Need for Economics and Law in Interaction for Innovations

1.2.1 Purpose of this book

This book is about intellectual property and its role in innovation. Since the early 1980s interest in, and concern about, the IP system and its various types of IPRs have grown rapidly. This rapid change is accompanied by an increasing recognition of a need for further research and teaching. A main purpose of this book is to contribute to meeting this need and to stimulate a more comprehensive understanding of IP issues and how their associated economic, legal and technological changes interact in an international context. A corollary purpose is to further stimulate the growing interest in IP studies among new generations of researchers, teachers, students and practitioners, thereby stimulating growth as well as renewal of the field.

A special purpose is to present different disciplinary approaches to IP, mainly within economics and law, two disciplines that unfortunately have become quite separated in the field, as we will see. Thus, this book is also a call for more interdisciplinary approaches in IP studies, besides being a call for international and intergenerational approaches.

1.2.2 Separation of economics, law and IP

Sins of omission and commission are common accusations of every discipline. As to economics and IP, the declaratory judgement of Prof. Fritz Machlup could hardly be expressed more succinctly:

> "Judging from the share which the subject of patents has had in the literary output of economists of the last fifty years, and from the share which economists have had in the literature on the subject of patents, one may say that economists have virtually relinquished the field. Patent lawyers were probably glad to see them go; some said as much with disarming frankness."
>
> Fritz Machlup (in Penrose 1951, p.viz)

This judgement is supported by a bibliometric analysis in Section 1.3 and still holds half a century later, although decreasingly so. The dictum in the last sentence can be supported by the following citations:

> "...the competing [economic] theories provide an unwitting parody of what must be one of the least productive lines of inquiry in all of economic thought. What does the patent system give us, and at what cost?"
>
> "...The ratio of empirical demonstration to assumption in this [classic economic] literature must be very close to zero. ...and all related literature of which I am aware have consisted of little more than assumptions."
>
> "...The inability of economists to resolve the question of whether activity stimulated by the patent system or other forms of protection of intellectual property enhances or diminishes social welfare implies, unfortunately, that economists can tell lawyers ultimately very little about how to enforce or interpret the law of intellectual property. ...Personally, I believe there is little hope that economic analysis can resolve the question of the appropriate scope of the protection of intellectual property. ...As a consequence, I regret, the influence of the economist on the law of intellectual property will always be limited. The lawyer must look to other sources for guidance. "
>
> George L. Priest (in Palmer 1986, pp. 19-24)

Some confessions might be added to complete the case that economists have shown negligence in the upbringing of the family of IPRs, not only regarding patents but also regarding other IPRs.

> "Although the patent system has developed primarily to promote economic ends, economists have devoted very little attention to it and none at all to the international patent system."
>
> Penrose, E. (1951, p.xi)

> "Despite the practical importance of trade secrets to the business community, the law of trade secrets is a neglected orphan in economic analysis."
>
> Friedman, D., Landes, W., and Posner, RA. (1991, p. 61)

> "Trade marks are … significant business assets; … Yet, they have not … been systematically studied by economic or business historians, even though much has been written by other scholars on these intangible assets."
>
> Wilkins, M. (1992, p. 66)

Having established the economists' sin of omission of IP in this way through "hearings" of the literature, one could ask for explanations. This would lead beyond the scope of this chapter. Suffice to say that there has historically been a broader sin of omission of technology and innovation in general for various reasons (see Granstrand 1994, Ch. 1). A major reason, and in fact partly an excuse, is that economists committed themselves to more pressing problems of their times and to refining and applying tools of their times, which were mainly tools for static analysis.

Besides, technology and innovation were (and are) complex, dynamic and unpredictable, not easily taken care of by a fairly young and busy social science such as economics. In the static frameworks for resource allocation and competition analysis, only process technology could be fitted in and then only in a static sense, and innovation could hardly be fitted in at all. Thus, assuming static conditions made patents (as well as copyrights and designs) difficult to handle (except by comparative static analysis), assuming certainty (perfect information) and no information asymmetries made trade secrets impossible to handle, and assuming homogeneous products across firms made trademarks (as well as other IPRs) impossible to handle. These common assumptions in static analysis in fact assumed away IPRs. Still, IPRs were present in the economy after all (guarded by many lawyers, engineers, inventors, managers etc.), if not in economics. Applied economists then largely perceived them as a disturbance of competition and efficient resource allocation.

This perception and commitment to static competition analysis and resource allocation suppressed a wider positive interest among economists in IPRs for a long time, and probably still does so.

In all fairness it must be said that an increasing number of economists have made considerable contributions to IP studies in the 20th century (see Granstrand 2000a, Ch. 2-3 for a review). Also it must be said that IPRs have not traditionally accounted for a large share of legal studies either. Stretching the metaphor perhaps too far, one may venture to say that the father (economics) left the difficult and disturbing minors (the IPRs) – occasionally paying them some visits, but then mostly complaining about them – in the custody of a happy, understanding but elsewhere busy mother (law).

1.2.3 The need for economics, law and technology in interaction

Given a historical separation intellectually of economics and law in the IP area, compounded by the "ordinary" institutional separation of the disciplines of law and economics, one can argue for increased interaction and integration, and then on several grounds. (See also Chapter 21 for further discussion.)

Section 1.1 showed several major examples of close interaction between economic, legal and technological factors and changes, a level of interaction that could be expected to grow stronger. Lags in legal responses to technological changes might be a natural (economic) way to position law in general, but the cost of too slow and/or erroneous legal response probably grows with increasing scale and scope of technological changes. Legal control can also be lost or counterproductive if the speed of technological changes is not matched. A highly complicating circumstance is that technological changes also change the language and its underlying conceptualisations. This slows down and distorts legal analysis, preoccupied as it is with the use of existing language. Legal analysis in turn is an important part of the total time lag in legal responses, so the issue of how to speed up legal responses is magnified by an increasing speed (rate) of technological changes. Should then the law become more anticipatory and/or research-based? Should "legal R&D" be more integrated with technological R&D? Should the public goods delivered by court cases be increased by pro-active measures? Should technology be slowed down? Should the mode of legal analysis be changed? Should it be complemented or replaced in part by more economic analysis? Which type of legal system is most fitting?[4] The general answer here is that answers to these difficult questions can more easily be found with closer interaction between economics, law and technology, i.e. between economists, lawyers and engineers.

Take the competition area as an example. Competition is a powerful but double-edged tool for price control (static competition) as well as for generating innovations in a broad sense, giving enhanced performance of products and services (dynamic competition). Financing increasingly expensive R&D and innovations through related prices and/or taxes builds in counteracting tendencies between static and dynamic competition, thus calling for adaptive trade-offs in terms of pro/anti static/dynamic competition policies. Typically these trade-offs have to be made with different time frames and with different levels of economic, legal and technological uncertainty.

The uncertainty pertains e.g. to innovation returns, market shares and market structure, but also to the concept of what is a relevant market. Major innovations in the form of entirely new products could be regarded as creating entirely new markets ("innovation markets"). At the same time, markets can always be conceptualised at multiple levels of product areas (e.g. sugar, sweetener, foodstuffs), and functional substitutes (e.g. gas/electric heaters) with competition always taking place at some higher level of substitutes; hence the notion of multi-level competition.

In addition, an increasingly systemic nature of complex products and systems technologies creates product complementarities, and thereby markets with complementary demand. This in turn enables more market leveraging and the creation of market power across interdependent markets.

Moreover, there is no one-to-one relationship between technologies and products or industries as often assumed. Rather there is a growing many-to-many correspondence between technologies and products, with the emergence of generic ("general purpose") technologies, having a wide range of product applications, and multi-technology ("mul-tech") products, incorporating a wide range of technologies. With increasing R&D costs for new product generations, increasing division of R&D labour and increasing use of technology markets, competition in product markets is increasingly accompanied by competition in a web of technology markets, including competition between substitute technologies ("technological competition").

[4] Just as for economic systems, one could speculate on a certain convergence of legal systems, possibly driven by technological changes and internationalization. After all, the original divergence of the civil and common law systems was not contingent upon large, lasting differences – quite the contrary (van Caenegem 1988).

Finally, technological change and innovations in general tend to change basic conceptualisations of products, markets and industries (cf. calculator versus computer; typewriter versus word processor; palmtop computer versus handset telephone; copier versus printer). In the case of converging technologies (with computer and communication technologies as a standard example of macro-technological change) the concept of a relevant market is broadening. In the case of diverging technologies and product differentiation, the opposite may occur (e.g. cars historically differentiating into passenger cars and trucks).

In summary, the dynamic nature of competition and market definition, in connection with R&D and innovation, calls for adaptivity in competition and IP policies, with due concern paid to economic efficiency of static vs. dynamic competition on product and technology markets, definable and redefinable at multiple levels of substitutes and complements. How to accomplish this is obviously non-obvious, but novelty in interdisciplinary thinking about legal certainty vs. static and dynamic economic efficiency vs. technological dynamics and uncertainty is likely to be useful. This theme will be returned to in Chapter 21.

1.3 The Growth of IP Studies

As described above, the economic value of and strategic attention paid to IPRs has increased considerably since the 1980s (without actually any far-reaching legislative changes), and a need to more closely integrate the previously fairly separate areas of IP economics and IP law has arisen. How does this separation reflect in the structure of contemporary academic writings on IP? To probe this question a bibliometric analysis has been undertaken.[5]

As a first step, a simple search of articles in Social Science Citation Index (SSCI) containing "intellectual property" or "IPR" in title, keywords or abstract in the period 1975-2002 was performed.[6] This revealed 1,064 papers in total (ca. 99% of which were in English) with a clear growth trend. The annual number of published IP articles in social sciences was below 10 in the period 1975-1981, between 10 and 100 in the period 1982-1999, and exceeded 100 from year 2000 on. In rough terms, the number of IP articles grew over 7 times faster in the whole period than the total number of articles in SSCI.

---

[5] The help of Prof. Olle Persson, Inforsk, Dept. of Sociology, University of Umeå, Sweden is gratefully acknowledged.

[6] IP articles (defined in this way) also appear in Science Citation Index (SCI). However, journals in economics and law are by and large covered by SSCI.

In order to see the positions of economics and law in academic IP writings, the top-cited journals in the set of IP articles were identified. The top 10 were (ranked according to number of citations):

Yale Law Journal	(Law)
Harvard Law Review	(Law)
Columbia Law Review	(Law)
American Economic Review	(Economics)
Stanford Law Review	(Law)
Science	(General)
California Law Review	(Law)
Journal of Legal Studies	(Law)
Univ. of Chicago Law Review	(Law)
Rand Journal of Economics	(Economics)

As seen from this list all journals are US, and most journals are law journals, accounting for 73.6% of the citations collected by the top 10, while economic journals collected 17.9% and the general journal Science collected 8.5%. US law journals also dominate the top 50 list of journals cited by IP articles. In fact almost all of these top-cited journals are disciplinary journals in either law or economics, with over 30 law journals and over 10 economic journals. Exceptions are Science (no. 6), Research Policy (no. 12), Journal of Law and Economics (no. 15) – the only explicitly bi-disciplinary journal – and Nature (no. 45) and Strategic Management Journal (no. 47).

Now if the central journals on IP in social science are discipline-oriented and fall into economics and law, how much do articles in them co-cite various pairs of economics and law journals, and how much do articles in economic journals cite law journals and vice versa? In other words, how much cross-disciplinarity is there in these two types of disciplinary journals? Moreover, is there any convergence in some sense over time between IP writings in these two social sciences, i.e. is there any sign of "science convergence" (analogous to the phenomenon of technological convergence)?

As a second step, a co-citation analysis of the IP articles was performed for the period 1986-2001. A co-citation map of journals is shown in Figure 1-1, where the proximity between any two journals approximately corresponds to the extent to which they are co-cited, i.e. the number of articles that cite both of them. Figure 1-1 shows that the law journals and the economics journals form two distinct and quite separated clusters, with American Economic Review and the Journal of Law and Economics being the two closest from each cluster. The singular but fairly central position of the journal Science is also noteworthy, indicating a cross-disciplinary bridging role with fairly strong ties to both clusters.

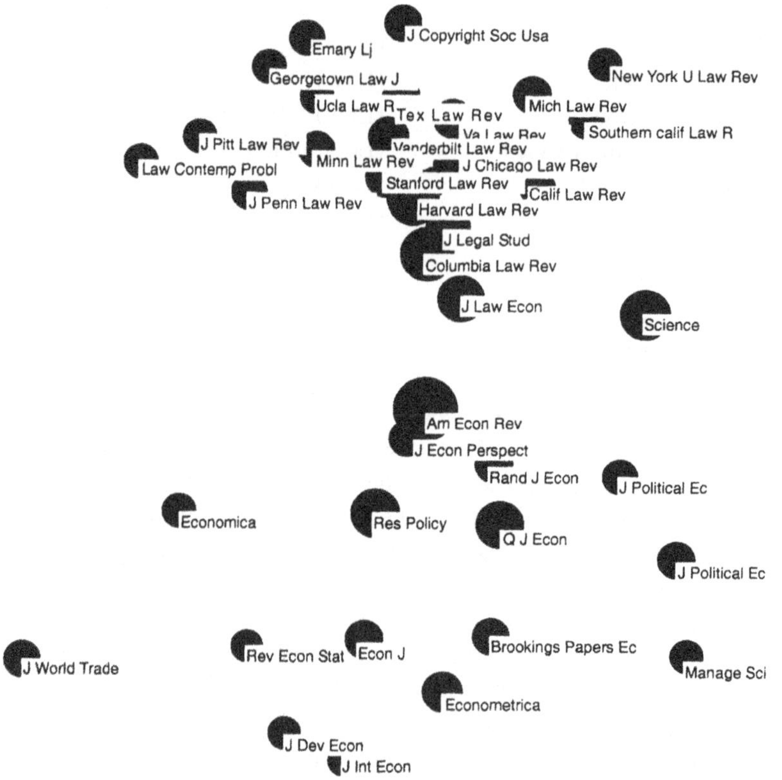

Figure 1-1: Most co-cited journals in articles on intellectual property in SSCI 1986-2001.

Figure 1-2 shows a co-citation map, now based on frequencies by which pairs of authors (rather than pairs of journals) appear in the same reference list of the various IP articles. Figure 1-2 shows a similar type of separated clustering of authors into economists and lawyers, with Kenneth Arrow and

[9] Since maps like the ones in Figures 1-1 and 1-2 are projections of positions in a "bibliometric space" of much higher dimensionality, the two-dimensional distances in Figures 1-1 and 1-2 are crude approximations and should consequently be interpreted with much caution.

Robert Merges as a close economist/lawyer pair.[9] The most frequently cited scholar is the economist Edwin Mansfield, however, followed by six lawyers (Samuelson, Merges, Reichman, Gordon, Landes and Goldstein).[10]

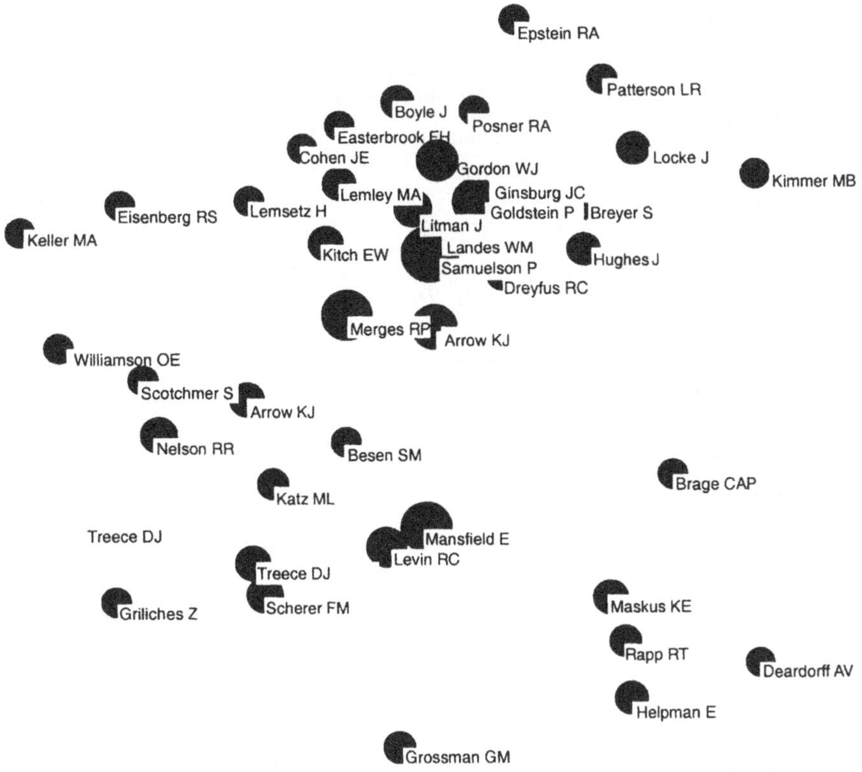

Figure 1-2: Most co-cited authors in articles on intellectual property in SSCI 1986-2001.

As a third step, Table 1-1 then shows a list of the 20 most cited authors, based on citations from **only** economics and law, with the citation shares of

[10] The areas of the black circles in Figures 1-1 and 1-2 are used to indicate the number of citations.

[13] Articles were classified into economics and law respectively on the basis of the department names associated with the authors.

these two disciplines.[13] Lawyers dominate the list by far and there are only three economists on the list (Mansfield, Maskus and Teece). As expected, authors get most of their citations from within their discipline. Almost half of the lawyers are collecting citations solely from within their discipline.[14]

Table 1-1: Top 20 authors on IP by citations from economics and law in SSCI 1986-2001.

Cited author	Percent citations from		Total no. of citations
	Economics	Law	
Gordon, WJ	0.8	99.2	118
Merges, RP	13.9	86.1	101
Samuelson, P	8.4	91.6	83
Reichman, JH	10.4	89.6	67
Litman, J	3.0	97.0	66
Mansfield, E	92.1	7.9	63
Lemley, MA	0.0	100.0	63
Ginsburg, JC	0.0	100.0	62
Maskus, KE	98.4	1.6	61
Landes, WM	8.3	91.7	60
Cohen, JE	0.0	100.0	48
Goldstein, P	4.7	95.3	43
Easterbrook, FH	2.8	97.2	36
Boyle, J	0.0	100.0	36
Teece, DJ	91.4	8.6	35
Radin, MJ	0.0	100.0	34
Eisenberg, RS	15.6	84.4	32
Dreyfuss, RC	0.0	100.0	32
Kitch, EW	3.2	96.8	31
Epstein, RA	0.0	100.0	31

An important question now is: Who are the most interdisciplinary-oriented authors? Table 1-2 shows those authors, among the 100 most cited ones in IP articles in SSCI 1986-2001, who have at least a 10% citation share in each discipline, ranked in order of increasing absolute difference between

[14] It is possible to design more accurate indicators of disciplinary inwardness, as well as of the correspondence to an "export/import ratio" in the cross-disciplinary "citation trade" (e.g. using diversification or concentration measures based on entropy or Herfindahl's index). Interdisciplinary composition of the education of the authors could also be taken into account, of course. All authors considered here have a single discipline as "theirs", however.

the two citation shares. These authors with strong interdisciplinary ties could be considered bridging persons, connectors or linking pins between economics and law.[15]

Table 1-2: Authors among the 100 most cited ones in IP articles in SSCI 1986-2001 with at least a 10% citation share in both economics and law.

Author	**Percent citations from**	
	Economics	**Law**
Arrow, KJ [1]	50.0	50.0
Scotchmer, S[1]	47.6	52.4
Nelson RR [1]	43.8	56.3
Klemperer, P[1]	36.4	63.6
Scherer, FM	65.2	34.8
Williamson, OE	66.7	33.3
Farrell, J	33.3	66.7
Coase, R.H.[1]	31.6	68.4
Braga, CAP	68.8	31.3
Besen, SM	69.2	30.8
Lerner, J	72.7	27.3
Katz, ML	72.7	27.3
Griliches, Z	78.3	21.7
McCarthy, JT	18.2	81.8
David, PA	83.3	16.7
Heller, MA	16.7	83.3
Eisenberg, RS	15.6	84.4
Merges, RP	13.9	86.1
Evenson, RE	87.5	12.5
Reichman, JH	10.4	89.6
Posner, RA	10.3	89.7
Demsetz, M.	10.0	90.0

Notes:

1) These are interdisciplinary cross-over authors in the sense that they collect more extra- than intra-disciplinary citations or equally many. Cross-disciplinary co-authoring contributes to such a status (e.g. the highly cited article by Merges and Nelson (1990), published in Columbia Law Review). It is notable that all interdisciplinary cross-over authors are economists (including two Nobel Prize Winners as of 2002), and mostly theoreticians.

[15] This does not mean that authors with weak interdisciplinary ties are unimportant from an interdisciplinary point of view. On the contrary, weak ties may have the strength that they link to otherwise disconnected parts of the citation network, thereby indicating interesting knowledge combinations or early-stage convergence. (Cf. Granovetter 1973.)

There are 22 such authors, meaning that about 4 out of 5 highly cited authors have their citations concentrated to more than 90% within their discipline. (Extreme "cross-over" authors with over 90% extra-disciplinary citations are not present.) As seen from Table 1-2, this set of 22 authors (all in the US) is dominated by economists, especially at the top.

Thus, these statistics indicate that, for academic IP articles, lawyers have a greater overall impact in terms of total citations, while economists have a greater cross-disciplinary impact in terms of citation shares. The question now is if there is any convergence of law and economics as the two dominating social sciences in academic IP-article writings. To probe this question as a fourth step, the number of shared references in articles from law and economics respectively was used as a measure of proximity between each disciplinary vintage of articles. A two-dimensional projection of the results is given in Figure 1-3. Although distances in figures like these must be interpreted with much caution, Figure 1-3 indicates a convergence over the years of economics and law when it comes to IP articles. Moreover, there seems to be a somewhat larger movement in economics than in law, and from more distant origins.

Thus, in summary, the bibliometric analysis indicates that the IP field in social sciences is:

1. Rapidly growing in absolute terms as well as relative to growth in general of social sciences

2. Dominated by US journals and authors

3. Dominated strongly by law, followed by economics, being fairly separated as disciplines, although showing signs of convergence

4. Dominated by economists when it comes to interdisciplinary citations from law and economics.

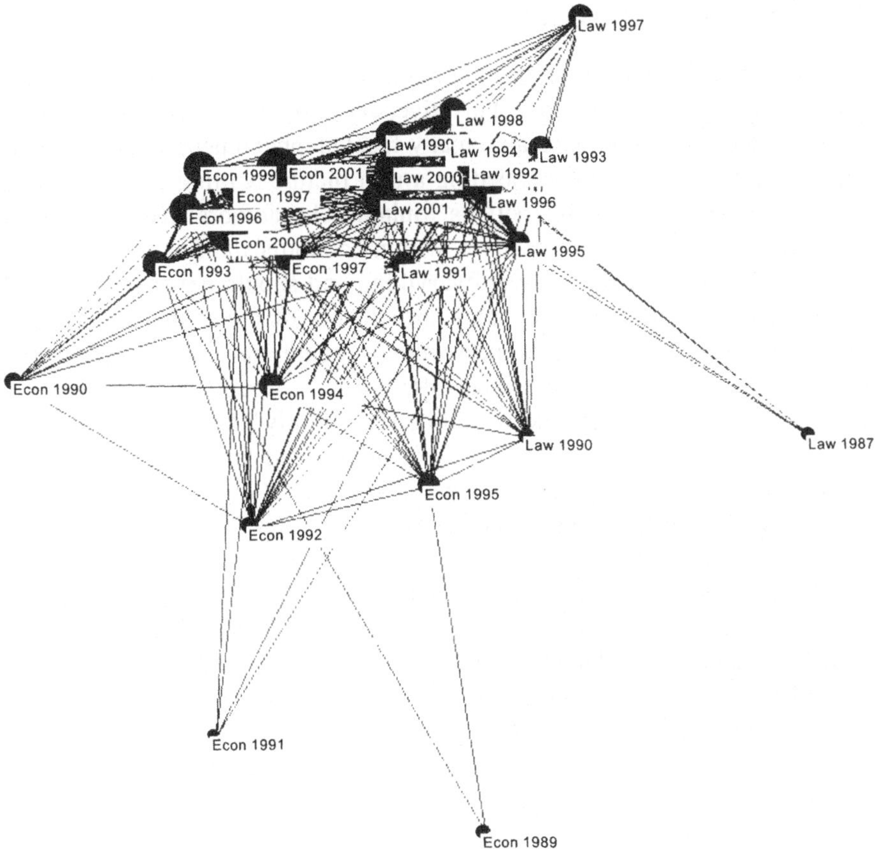

Figure 1-3: Projected proximity map over vintages of IP articles in economics and law in SSCI, based on shared references.

Finally, it must be emphasized that further research on IP studies is needed in the light of their rapid recent growth after a long period of minor existence. Some suggestions are to (1) study the history of IP studies and ideas in general, and in economics and law in particular; (2) make a thorough review of recent IP studies;[16] and (3) make a further bibliometric analysis of the structure and interdisciplinary relations in IP studies.

---

[16] Several surveys and review articles exist; see Granstrand (2000a). For a recent bibliography, see Granstrand *et al.* (2002). For surveys of IP-related theories, see Mazzeloni and Nelson (1998) for an economics perspective and Gutterman (1997) for a legal perspective. For literature on the new theme of university patenting, see Link *et al.* (2003) and Mowery *et al.* (2001). For

1.4 Outline of the Book

The authors and chapters in this book represent a wide variety of backgrounds, perspectives and foci. This diversity is by design as IPRs and innovation represent a complex and many-faceted phenomenon with recently rapidly growing proportions, needing a rich picture, calling for a variety of angles and lenses. Still diversity is limited. The authors mainly represent Western contemporary perspectives within economics and law. Needless to say a book like this cannot cover everything and should never pretend to do so. Thus many IPR relatated topics are still out of focus and several other disciplinary and international perspectives could have been represented. Then, however, commonalities and differences between the disciplines economics and law in the IP field would be less sharply focused. In fact the authors have been "sampled" from the economics and law "strata" (being the major ones in the IP field as described above), to allow for some comparative interdisciplinary analysis, as presented in Chapter 21.

The authors and chapters representing economics are Kenneth Arrow (Prologue); Ashish Arora, Andrea Fosfuri and Alfonso Gambardella (Chapter 4); Wesley Cohen, Akira Goto, Akiya Nagata, Richard Nelson and John Walsh (Chapter 6); Jeannette Colyvas, Annetine Gelijns and Nathan Rosenberg (Chapter 7); Dominique Foray (Chapter 9); Ove Granstrand (Chapter 10); Bronwyn Hall (Chapter 11); Dietmar Harhoff, Frederic M. Scherer and Katrin Vopel (Chapter 12); William Kingston (Chapter 13); Bonwon Koo and Brian Wright (Chapter 14); Richard Nelson (Chapter 15); Ruth Towse (Chapter 18) and Bart Verspagen (Chapter 20).

The authors and chapters representing law are John Adams (Chapter 2); Howard Anawalt (Chapter 3); John Barton (Chapter 5); Bengt Domeij (Chapter 8); Ulf Petrusson (Chapter 16); Margaret Jane Radin (Chapter 17); and Hanns Ullrich (Chapter 19).

Chapter 2 by John Adams sets out to discuss how problems of ensuring consumer protection in e-commerce are best approached. Most such problems essentially represent traditional types of problems with faulty products, faulty delivery and fraud. One issue is whether there are new types of problems, or whether some of the old ones are becoming so aggravated that they essentially should be looked upon as new types from a legal point of view. As is well known, e-commerce is subjected to rapid technological changes regarding forms of market communication among buyers and sellers, the

---

recent literature on IP and economic development, see Mansfield and Mansfield (2000). In general, various chapters in this book give further literature overviews.

appearance of pure information products, and the performance of various transactional steps in a mix of online/offline operations together with internationalisation. This leads to aggravated problems following from jurisdictional uncertainties, separation and mobility of buyers and sellers in space and also in time, distance e-contracting, e-payment and e-delivery (e.g. music, video, data, books or software on demand). Another issue is whether new solution approaches are needed, or whether old ones can be stretched to apply to new types of problems as well as to old but aggravated problems. John Adams then argues that market solutions are, after all, preferable to selective government intervention. The effectiveness of market solutions is in fact aided by internationalisation of trademarks together with extension of liabilities, in particular for intermediary financial institutions such as credit card companies. Thus, in this case, radical technological changes enabling e-commerce also enable existing institutions to provide solutions to old and new problems of consumer protection. No need for alarm by and large, that is. Far-reaching technological changes do not necessitate far-reaching legislative changes in the case of e-commerce.

In Chapter 3, Howard Anawalt addresses in a brief historic account the internationalisation of intellectual property rules, generally conceived of as international harmonisation. However, recent developments of international institutions in the form of TRIPs agreements and WTO represent a step beyond the traditional general principle of non-discriminatory treatment of foreigners in a given national legal culture. The step means making the acceptance of a fairly detailed legal framework, in no small measure rooted in US legal culture, the discriminatory condition for membership in WTO. Although some form of international harmonisation of IPRs is by and large conceived of as desirable, Howard Anawalt discusses its limitations and drawbacks. In national as well as global interests, there is a certain need to preserve national legal cultures in which intellectual property rules are embedded, and consequently a need for tempered international harmonisation. The chapter concludes with a fairly specific list of suggestions for IP guidelines and further research along this line of thought.

The author trio in the fourth chapter – Ashish Arora, Andrea Fosfuri and Alfonso Gambardella – presents an empirical study of the old but recently rapidly growing phenomenon of technology trade from an economics perspective. A growing importance of technology markets is an expected consequence of the emergence of the pro-patent era and the growing importance of IPRs. Well-functioning technology markets facilitate division of R&D labour and diffusion of new technologies. As a consequence there will be more attractive strategic options open to firms, small as well as large, for their acquisition and exploitation of new technologies. This in turn tends to reduce at least the relative importance of the traditional strategies of in-house R&D and product sales. The authors proceed even one step further and propose that the role of new technologies as a source of competitive advantage may thereby become reduced, relative to other resources with less well-functioning markets.

John Barton in the fifth chapter returns to the theme of changing IPRs in an international context, focusing on changes in the relation between IPRs and competition, static as well as dynamic. IPRs have traditionally been conceived of as presenting barriers to entry in order to foster dynamic competition, but there is also reason to be concerned over possible adverse impacts of IPRs on dynamic competition. In an international context with countries developing at different levels and paces, advanced ones may sustain their market power in various ways through utilising strong IPRs, and John Barton describes three contexts in which this may take place: (1) licensing, tying and leveraging; (2) research tools and broad patents; and (3) oligopolistic licensing. Thus, in these contexts anticompetitive behaviour is enabled by strong IPRs regarding both static competition and dynamic competition. Remedies, as suggested by John Barton, do not necessarily have to rely on an international antitrust body but rather on a redressed WTO code.

The author quintet in the sixth chapter – Wesley Cohen, Akira Goto, Akiya Nagata, Richard Nelson and John Walsh – presents another economically oriented empirical study, this one focusing on US-Japan comparisons of R&D and patenting and the role of patent information for coordinating R&D. A number of significant US-Japan differences were found across industries, such as Japanese firms having more R&D, having a larger share of product R&D, and having more emphasis on patents for appropriation, strategic use and information purposes. The latter in turn induce greater flows and spill-overs of R&D information, as well as greater cross-licensing propensities. The large cross-national differences compared to cross-industry differences suggest explanations to be found in national patent systems, policies and cultures, such as Japan having first-to-file priority, pre-grant opposition and lower infringement costs. The authors conclude by suggesting further research on the welfare costs and benefits of patent information disclosure.

The seventh chapter, authored by Jeannette Colyvas, Annetine Gelijns and Nathan Rosenberg, takes a close look, mainly with economics lenses, at the role of US academic health centers (AHCs) in the generation of new medical technologies and their related patenting and licensing. The approach comprises case studies of a handful of new medical technologies (DNA,

MRI, PET etc.), combined with historical and statistical analysis, with data from top universities (Columbia and Stanford in particular). The authors see AHCs as a dominant and growing source of innovations, patents and licensing revenues, with research tools being a critical output. The patenting and licensing of research tools is then addressed as an issue, calling for a variety of considerations, such as associated transaction costs, prospects for improvement, and development into diagnostic and therapeutic tools. In particular the authors suggest that universities ought to consider a more nuanced approach to licensing.

The eighth chapter by Bengt Domeij stays on in the medical field, and there addresses the very generic problem of how to design patent-based incentives for initial and follow-on inventions, in other words incentive design in the context of sequential innovation. Bengt Domeij's particular focus is patent breadth and patent claim structure for incentive design in pharmaceuticals. The approach is legal analysis of cases of pharmaceutical patents in a sample of European courts, thereby comparing case law with economic explanations in patent claim interpretations. Bengt Domeij finds a tendency in courts to make implicit economic valuations of follow-on inventions when limiting the patent scope of initial ones, which implies that courts take on a certain role of coordinating (or managing or governing) R&D. However, in order to increase consumer value and welfare from pharmaceutical R&D, courts ought to make economic considerations more explicit, substituting for the currently dominating technical analysis.

Chapter 9 by Dominique Foray re-raises the old standing issue of how to find the right balance between public and private domains in the new context of a pro-patent era and new infocom technologies. Public goods, being non-excludable and non-rival in use, typically with large fixed and small marginal costs, include knowledge as a special case, knowledge being in addition cumulative and interactive. Standard approaches to dealing with public goods in a market economy, such as private property, public procurement, public subsidies or private consortia, thus could be expected to apply in special ways to production and distribution of knowledge. Dominique Foray identifies and analyses special coordination problems resulting in tendencies towards overexploitation ("tragedy of commons") as well as underexploitation ("tragedy of anti-commons") of knowledge areas, plus a tendency towards a slow-down of cumulation. Finally, Dominique Foray discusses two remedies to the latter problem – a mixed private/public innovation system and a collective invention mechanism, e.g. in a consortium arrangement.

Chapter 10 by Ove Granstrand raises a question it cannot answer but just probe a bit: Are we on our way in the new economy with optimal inventive steps? This is a broad question that could be narrowed down in various ways. In granting patent rights to advances in technology space, the practice has for a long time been to require some form of minimal inventive step. The necessary assessment of size of invention by patent examiners is a difficult and subjective exercise, which nevertheless is carried out in patent offices and courts according to some de facto standards, varying somewhat across offices, courts and technologies and over time. The chapter sets out to explore how optimality can be specified in this assessment, especially in the light of transaction costs arising from congestion of patent rights and the increasing necessity for companies to assemble large packages of rights. The transaction costs associated with this IP assembly increase not only due to this congestion, but also due to the increasing interdependence between technologies and products. A narrow specification of optimality is illustrated in a model, which is kept as simple as possible to show that the question of existence of an optimum can be answered, at least in a stereotype way as a start. The chapter also discusses how a low minimal inventive step requirement can be used in particular by incumbents for "evergreening", i.e. for prolongation of effective patent protection. The chapter concludes with a brief discussion of patent rights viewed as a form of taxation rights and a decentralized form of governance.

Bronwyn Hall in Chapter 11 addresses some fundamental economic trade-offs when using IP protection to correct for markets failing to produce sufficient new information and innovations. She distinguishes between the case where pure new information is the main output and the case where physical products embody the new information. These two cases represent the output of university research and industrial R&D. She argues that the two cases are best served by different IP regimes, which have to be interfaced with each other on a boundary of increasing university-industry interaction. She surveys the situation in the US, which probably is a precursor in these respects, and finds that there are risks that the IP regime in industry, which increasingly finances university research although still at a low level, will dominate and impede university research. In particular she looks at software and databases which represent two vital product areas. These two cases involve two different but, since long ago, central types of IPRs – patents and copyrights – plus database rights as a new type of IPR, so far only in Europe.

The author trio behind Chapter 12 – Dietmar Harhoff, Frederic Scherer and Katrin Vopel – explore the nature of the top value distributions for samples of West German and US patented inventions. With the advent of the pro-patent era, the interest in patent valuation has grown considerably together with a variety of approaches. The authors use an asset value approach in a sound empirical way and find, not surprisingly, a strongly skewed top value distribution (with drug and surgical supply patents being most valuable). More surprisingly, the skewness was so strong that a distribution lacking finite mean and finite variance could not be ruled out as fitting the data. This is a disturbing but hopefully sobering result for all believers in patent counts for purposes of valuation and picking winners. Such distributions could also rule out, or at least limit, mean-variance approaches to financial risk management such as the CAPM.

Chapter 13 by William Kingston provides a thorough critique of the current IP system and the way it has evolved (especially in the US), too loosely connected to the nature of current R&D and new complex technologies, especially in software and biotech. This divergence increasingly creates misfits, and William Kingston proposes a radical *sui generis* type of protection. This approach builds on the ideas of providing to innovators economic rewards directly related to the investment for, and commercial value of, the innovation. The innovation is then subjected to compulsory licensing. In granting patent rights, neither investment effort nor commercial value explicitly enters the criteria for granting. Thus, this approach deviates from the private property approach and it comes closer to a mixed contract-prize approach. As such it certainly warrants serious consideration, at least in some areas. William Kingston finally pursues his constructivist endeavour with a proposal for compulsory arbitration of disputes.

Chapter 14 by Bonwon Koo and Brian Wright returns to the welfare aspects of patenting in sequential innovation, as addressed empirically by Bengt Domeij in Chapter 7. The authors present a theoretical approach with a two-stage model of an innovation process. Patenting in the first stage takes place without competition and is followed by a second stage with necessary follow-up patenting by competitors under competitive free entry. The results from this modeling exercise indicate that certain limitations in patent lifetimes induce follow-up patenting and reduce rent dissipation. This means that there may be other benefits accruing from patent lifetime limitation in addition to the traditionally recognised reduction of deadweight loss. This type of modeling approach to the proper designing or balancing of incentives in sequential patenting for innovation is still in its infancy. The actual importance of this difficult problem justifies a variety of empirical and theoretical approaches evolving over years to come.

In Chapter 15, Richard Nelson reviews the state of knowledge regarding the economic value added to university research by university patenting. With the emergence of universities as economic institutions and the emergence of the pro-patent era, the traditional open IP regime in universities not only clashes with the rather closed one in industry, but is also transformed into a more industry-like IP regime. The issue then is: Is this to the better or the worse? Are important complementarities between a public open IP regime and a private closed one thereby lost in the innovation system as a whole without sufficient gains from choosing just one IP regime, that is, the private closed one? Is complementary co-evolution to be preferred over competitive exclusion in this case? The American research university system has been a forerunner in this context, with the Bayh-Dole act as one palpable feature. Based on various studies of the US situation, and in particular of three top US universities (Stanford University, University of California and Columbia University), Richard Nelson finds a mix of tempered evidence about pros and cons. This ought to sober up the over-expectations held in many quarters, not least in Europe, regarding university patenting pay-offs. Thus, universities contribute increasingly to the flow of innovations, patents and licences, but mainly due to new technological opportunities and enlarged patentability, and less due to the Bayh-Dole act and university technology transfer offices. University patenting and licensing also incur costs, e.g. in the form of tensions in intra-university relations and in university-industry relations, and inefficiencies in fundamental research relative to a public open IP regime.

In Chapter 16, Ulf Petrusson challenges the fundamental nature of IP concepts in jurisprudence, looking at the IP system and its interaction with technological and industrial development. This is part of a grander view of how legal systems and their conceptualisations interact with an increasingly knowledge-based economic system. Ulf Petrusson's perspective draws on Scandinavian legal realism with the ambition of contributing to a constructionist approach to legal argumentation. With this perspective and ambition, the historical evolution of patent concepts is briefly described and analysed as social construction. Finally, Ulf Petrusson as a legal constructionist develops several new concepts for a better comprehension of patents as a type of structural capital.

Margaret Jane ("Peggy") Radin raises in Chapter 17 another set of fundamental issues, revolving around legal concepts and reconceptualisations in the face of new technologies, infocom technologies in particular. These have enabled commodification of a variety of information and communication-related "things", supported by a variety of physical embodiments. A particular example is a traditional contractual relation between a buyer and a seller being commodified into a contract-as-product in contrast to a traditional contract-as-consent relation. As technology leads and law generally follows in conceptualisations, this technological enablement of commodification is then reinforced by legal enablement through "follow-up" legal conceptualisations, analogies included. In particular, analogies to physical entities are stretched by interested parties (mainly industry) beyond what is reasonable, Peggy Radin argues, since there is an economic incentive to do so because physical property rights enable better rent control. In this process, commodification of information proceeds one step further towards tangibilisation of information and "physicalisation" of knowledge. To the extent that information and knowledge are embodied in human personhood, this physical tangibilisation of information and knowledge paves the way for its alienation from humans and alignment with property. A final question is whether legal concepts, once established in response to technological changes, then become outlived and start to obstruct change rather than facilitate it.

In Chapter 18, Ruth Towse focuses with the lens of a cultural economist on copyright and cultural industries, a concept which is far from an oxymoron. This focus fruitfully deviates from the common but increasingly narrow focus on manufacturing industries and patents in IP discourses. It is much needed as a complementary and mind-stretching focus, not least since it also throws light on the role of infocom technologies. The copyright system has been remarkably resilient or immune to radical technological changes and radical critique (not least creatively expressed by some writers), by and large retaining its basic economic and legal principles for centuries. The system has survived despite technological changes, and despite offering unbalanced incentives along the value chain. Thus, Ruth Towse argues, it has underincentivised artists and other creators in economic terms, while overincentivising intermediaries such as publishers and distributors. The former are perhaps less sensitive to monetary economic incentives, but not sufficiently so to render the imbalance optimal in any sense. In addition, the copyright system provides corporate actors with a higher rate of cumulation of market power. Technological changes "this time" in the form of new infocom technologies (enabling digitalisation etc.) have the potential to radically change this market structure. This in turn creates new challenges to copyright policies, and thereby to economic as well as cultural policies.

Hanns Ullrich in Chapter 19 delivers a fundamental critique of the IP system as we know it. The IP system interacts with competition law and economic policies, especially trade policies and technology and innovation policies. Based on a wide range of essentially legal cases and other sources, Hanns Ullrich argues that the IP system is misleading as a tool of contemporary economic policy. The system has traditionally been justified as an imperfectly designed but still functional tool for trading off (balancing) static and dynamic economic efficiency. However, in the course of functioning more or less well in this desired way, the system gives negative legal and economic side-effects, and perhaps increasingly so. Therefore it has to be fundamentally rethought, and Hanns Ullrich offers a list of extensive suggestions for further research. In summary, this is a quest for developing legal and economic principles that could better govern the legal and economic functions of institutions like IP laws and WTO. These principles should be based on theories of how to promote technological and economic progress, and should serve as unifying principles behind various forms of IPRs.

In Chapter 20, Bart Verspagen addresses a long-standing but increasingly important issue in the world economy – how a global IP system should be designed that is conducive to development in countries with widely differing levels and pace of development. Is there a "one size fits all" solution, or should IP systems differ as countries do? The problem of how to design or tailor IP systems to fit differing economic sectors, like the university and industry sectors, or differing industry sectors or technologies, like biotechnology and infocom technologies, thus appears for differing countries as well. The problem also has a parallel problem in tailoring free internationalised trade regimes. In his undertaking Bart Verspagen also makes a brief account of the main economic motives behind an IP system, and a patent system in particular, an account that should be useful reading for lawyers and other non-economists as well as students.

A particular feature of a patent system is the breadth or scope of a patent right. Verspagen focuses on this feature in particular as it influences technology spill-overs, which in turn are of crucial importance to economic growth, as demonstrated also by some of the new, endogenous growth models. This focus then gives a nice example of how specific detailed features of an IP system may have strong leverage on economic performance.

It is difficult to draw firm conclusions on such wide-reaching issues as IP impact on global welfare, especially since formal theorising is still highly abstract and stylised and empirical research is in an infant stage. However, Verspagen argues that – beyond some magnitude of country differences – differentiated IP systems could be better than an internationalised uniform one as pushed for in TRIPs. As countries catch up and converge, their IP systems could converge as well.

The concluding Chapter 21 summarizes the preceding chapters as to their main focus, key/novel concepts, approach/empirical data, main findings/arguments and suggestions for further research. The commonalities and differences between economics and law in the IP field are described and discussed. At one level of resolution, the commonalities among the chapters regarding focus, concepts and main findings are quite palpable. At a higher level of resolution, there is a wide variety of foci, approaches and suggestions for further research. Thus, one can say that there is a white elephant or a black box or a many-coloured cathedral out there that is coherent after all. The main differences between economics and law concern methodological approaches and mode of theorizing.

The final parts of the chapter reflect upon the need and prospects for further interdisciplinary research and teaching in the IP field. The chapter and the book end with some broad-brushed reflections and speculations about the future of the IP system.

1.5 Literature References

Coriat, B. and Orsi, F. (2002), 'Establishing a new intellectual property rights regime in the United States – Origins, content and problems', *Research Policy*, 31, pp. 1491-1507.

Friedman, D.D., Landes, W.M. and Posner, R.A. (1991), 'Some economics of trade secret law', *Journal of Economic Perspectives*, 5 (1), pp. 61-72.

Granovetter, M.S. (1973), 'The strength of weak ties', *American Journal of Sociology*, 78 (6), pp. 1360-1381.

Granstrand, O., ed. (1994), *Economics of Technology*. Amsterdam: North-Holland. Elsevier Science B.V.

Granstrand, O. (2000a), *The Economics and Management of Intellectual Property. Towards Intellectual Capitalism*. Cheltenham: Edward Elgar Publ.

Granstrand, O. (2000b), 'The Shift Towards Intellectual Capitalism – The Role of Infocom Technologies', *Research Policy*, 29, pp. 1061-1080.

Granstrand, O., Petrusson, U., Heiden, B. and Tärnström, M. (2002), *Previous Research and Literature on Economics, Law and Management of IPR and IC – A Survey*, Mimeo, Center for Intellectual Property Studies, Chalmers University of Technology, Göteborg, Sweden.

Gutterman, A. (1997), *Innovation and Competition Policy*. London: Kluwer Law International.

Jaffe, A.B. (2000), 'The U.S. patent system in transition: policy innovation and the innovation process', *Research Policy*, 29, pp. 531-557.

Link, A.N., Scott, J.T. and Siegel, D.S., eds. (2003), 'Economics of intellectual property at universities: an overview of the special issue', *International Journal of Industrial Organization* (in press).

Mansfield, E.D. and Mansfield, E. (2000), 'Intellectual property protection and economic development', Special Issue, *Intern. Journal of Technology Management*, 19 (1/2).

Mazzoleni, R. and Nelson, R.R. (1998), 'Economic Theories about the Benefits and Costs of Patents', *Journal of Economic Issues*, 32 (4), pp. 1031-1052.

Merges, R.P. and Nelson, R.R. (1990), 'On the complex economics of patent scope', *Columbia Law Review*, 90 (4), 839-916.

Mowery, D.C., Nelson, R.R., Sampat, B.N. and Ziedonis, A.A. (2001), 'The growth of patenting and licensing by U.S. universities: an assessment of the effects of the Bayh-Dole act of 1980', *Research Policy*, 30, pp. 99-119.

Palmer, J., ed. (1986), 'The Economics of Patents and Copyrights', *Research in Law and Economics*, Vol. 8, Greenwich, CT: JAI Press Inc.

Penrose, E.T. (1951), *The Economics of the International Patent System*. Baltimore, MD: Johns Hopkins University Press.

Priest, George L. (1986), 'What economists can tell lawyers about intellectual property', in Palmer (1986), pp. 19-24.

van Caenegem, R.C. (1988), *The Birth of the English Common Law* (2nd ed.), Cambridge Univ. Press.

Wilkins, M. (1992), 'The Neglected Intangible Asset: The Influence of the Trade Mark on the Rise of the Modern Corporation', in Harvey and Jones (1992), pp. 66-95.

Chapter 2

E-COMMERCE: THE CONSUMER, THE TRADE MARK AND THE CREDIT CARD

John N. Adams
University of Sheffield, Department of Law, Sheffield, U.K.

Chapter contents:

Abstract: In this paper it is argued that the problems of consumer protection in international e-commerce consumer transactions are insoluble either by national legislation, or even by EU legislation. I think, however, that the market will solve many of the problems. This will be facilitated by the effective protection being given to 'well-known' trade marks, and effective action being taken against those registering, without justification, confusingly similar domain names. Since the credit card is the almost invariable mode of payment for goods purchased on the Internet, the most effective legislation that governments could put in place would be an equivalent of section 75 of the United Kingdom Consumer Credit Act of 1974 which will give consumers effective remedies against the card companies, even for quite small claims.

2.1 Introduction

In this paper I would like to consider aspects of consumer protection for Internet buyers of goods. By 'goods', I mean what we think of traditionally as goods. Digital products such as software are not dealt with in this paper,

O. Granstrand (ed.), Economics, Law and Intellectual Property, 41-54.

because most jurisdictions are hesitant about classifying them as 'goods'[1] and in any case they raise special problems with which it is outside the purpose of this paper to deal. The relevance of this to the topic of this book is well put by the World Trade Organisation in their Report 'Electronic Commerce and the Role of the World Trade Organisation' ('WTO')[2]

These modern technologies [*computer, telecommunications and information technology*] are being combined, especially through the Internet, to link millions of people in every corner of the world. Communications are increasingly unburdened from the constraints of geography and time. Information spreads more widely and more rapidly than ever before. Deals are struck, transactions completed, and decisions taken in a time-frame that would have seemed inconceivable a few years ago.

With the Internet all elements of a commercial transaction can be conducted on an interactive basis with one or many people, unconstrained by time and space, in a multimedia environment with sound, image and text transmission, and at a relatively low (and still declining) cost.[3]

Goods are increasingly purchased through the Internet, and a great deal of thought is going into ways to achieve consumer protection for Internet buyers of defective goods. In a way, Internet transactions are much the same as traditional mail order transactions which have been with us for many years: the Internet is essentially just a more up-to-date means of distance selling. In traditional mail order, the buyer selects goods from specifications provided in advertisements or catalogues, and mails off an order form provided by the seller either in the advertisement or the catalogue, together with a cheque or card number. This technically constitutes an offer by the buyer to purchase the goods in question, in much the same way as you ask to purchase goods over the counter in a shop. The seller can either accept the offer and supply the goods to the buyer by post or carrier, or if for example stocks have run out, simply decline the offer and return the cheque to the buyer. E-sales are similar, except that the specification of the goods is provided via a website. The buyer who wishes to purchase goods places an order, almost invariably using a credit card. The seller may choose to accept the offer that the order constitutes and supply the goods using, as in traditional mail order, the post or a carrier, or when stocks run out simply inform the person placing the order that the goods are no longer available, and that will be the end of

[1] See Atiyah, *Sale of Goods*, 10th ed. Adams. Longman, 2001, p. 66 *et seq*.
[2] World Trade Organisation 1998.
[3] Ibid. p. 5.

the transaction.[4] The major difference between traditional mail order and Internet transactions lies in the fact that most mail order transactions occur within one jurisdiction, whereas e-commerce sellers[5] can be, and are, located anywhere, and the goods they supply can be sourced from many different countries. This makes it very difficult for a consumer to pursue a remedy in respect of defective products. It is not merely defective products about which buyers complain. Recent newspaper reports suggest that there have been quite a lot of complaints about the poor quality of after-sales service provided by Internet sellers. There is also the more serious concern about remedies for physical injuries caused by defective products.

I believe that most of the solutions proposed are a waste of time, because the value of most goods purchased in the course of e-commerce is small, and litigating to remedy product defects is not worthwhile, especially bearing in mind the complexity added by the fact that the e-seller may be in a jurisdiction which does not recognise, or will not apply, these measures, and may in any case have taken care that there are no available assets against which a judgment can be enforced. I would like to suggest that there are two things that will help to resolve these problems: a 'market' solution deriving from the role of trade marks on the Internet, and a legislative solution modelled on a United Kingdom legislative provision.

I think the first likely solution to these problems will be market-driven, rather than government-driven, simply because consumers will increasingly prefer to deal with e-sellers upon whom they can rely. In this, the international protection afforded to 'well-known' trade marks[6] has a crucial role. It is likely that the global Internet market will come to be dominated by such e-sellers' global 'well-known' trade marks. The problem is, however, that trade marks are national (or in the European Union acquired pursuant to the Regulation[7] through the Office for the Harmonisation of the Internal Market ('OHIM')). Thus, protection of well-known trade marks depends on national (or regional) laws. This obviously has the potential to lead to different de-

---

[4] This at any rate is the way in which properly set up commercial websites operate. It is possible to set up the site so that the goods are offered through the seller's website so that each buyer accepting this offer would become entitled to be supplied with the goods, but there would be obvious problems with this in practice for sellers, so that this would not be a normal way of conducting business. Even Internet auction sites require the 'auctioneer' to indicate by the equivalent of the fall of a virtual hammer that the buyer's bid is being accepted.

[5] I include in this term for present purposes p-commerce sellers using the wireless application protocol ('WAP') because the legal problems are identical.

[6] The nature of this protection is explained below.

[7] 40/94/EC.

grees of recognition and protection around the world. Attempts to deal with this problem are considered below. Furthermore, consumer trust requires that persons *other than* the owner of a well-known trade mark should not be able to pass themselves off as the owner of the well-known mark. A key economic function of trade marks is the reduction of search costs.[8] It is in this context that I consider current proposals for strengthening the law on well-known marks. The special problem for the Internet of closely resembling domain names has also received attention recently, and I deal with this also. Finally, I suggest a possible solution to the problem of consumer remedies for defective products supplied, modelled on United Kingdom law.

2.2 What is a Well-Known Trade Mark?[9]

Since 1925 Member States of the Paris Convention on Industrial Property[10] have been required to recognise well-known trade marks, and to take certain protective measures in relation to them. Article 6*bis* of this Convention provides –

> (1) The countries of the Union undertake, *ex officio* if their legislation so permits, or at the request of an interested party, to refuse or to cancel the registration, and to prohibit the use of, a trademark which constitutes a reproduction, an imitation, or a translation, liable to create confusion, of a mark considered by the competent authority of the country of registration or use to be well-known in that country as being already the mark of a person entitled to the benefits of this Convention and used for identical or similar goods. These provisions shall also apply when the essential part of the mark constitutes a reproduction of any such well-known mark or an imitation liable to create confusion therewith.
>
> (2) A period of at least five years from the date of registration shall be allowed for requesting the cancellation of such a mark. The countries of the Union may provide for a period within which the prohibition of use must be requested.

---

8 See Posner, *Economic Analysis of Law*. Little Brown & Co, 4th ed., pp. 43-45.

9 The definitive work on this subject is Mostert, Frederick W., *Famous and Well-known Marks*. Butterworths, 1997.

10 Paris Convention for the Protection of Industrial Property of March 20, 1883 as revised at Brussels on December 14, 1900; at Washington on June 2, 1911; at the Hague on November 6, 1925; at London on June 2, 1934; at Lisbon on October 31, 1958; at Stockholm on July 14, 1967; and as amended on October 2, 1979.

(3) No time limit shall be fixed for requesting the cancellation or the prohibition of the use of marks registered or used in bad faith.

What this provision is silent on is what a 'well-known' trade mark actually is. Indeed, in everyday usage a number of terms are in use which may or may not be synonymous:

'notorious marks';
'exceptionally well-known marks';
'highly reputed marks';
'highly renowned marks';
'marks with a high reputation';
'marques de haut renommée'; and
'famous marks'.[11]

These terms are not necessary absolutely interchangeable. It can be argued, for example, that while all famous marks are well-known, not all well-known marks (in the legal sense) are famous.[12] To add to the uncertainty, the European Trade Marks Regulation[13] and Directive[14] distinguish between well-known marks and marks with a reputation, which, the European Court of Justice has recently held, need not be so well-known.[15]

---

[11] See David Tatham, OBE, WIPO Resolution on Well-Known Marks – a Small Step or a Giant Leap. Intellectual Property Quarterly 2000; 2:. 127. 'WIPO'' is the World Intellectual Property Organisation. WIPO administers 23 treaties (two of those jointly with other international organizations) and carries out a program of work, through its member States and secretariat, that seeks to: harmonize national intellectual property legislation and procedures; harmonize national intellectual property legislation and procedures; provide services for international applications for industrial property rights; exchange intellectual property information; provide legal and technical assistance to developing and other countries; facilitate the resolution of private intellectual property disputes; and marshal information technology as a tool for storing, accessing, and using valuable intellectual property information – information supplied by WIPO website <http://www.wipo.org/ about-wipo/en/index.html> visited 29 December 2001.

[12] See Tatham, *loc. cit.*

[13] Reg. 40/94/EC.

[14] 84/104/EEC.

[15] See *General Motors Corporation v Yplon SA 'Chevvy' TM* Case C-375/97, [1999] European Trade Mark Reporter 122, in which the mark at issue was 'Chevy' which is a common abbreviation for 'Chevrolet' for automobiles in the USA and many other countries, whilst 'Chevy' was registered and used mainly in the Benelux countries as a brand name for washing powder etc. 'Chevy' thus had a reputation in a limited part of the world for washing powder etc., whilst Chevrolet is well-known for automobiles in most parts of the world, and the word 'Chevy' commonly used to refer to such automobiles.

Trying to do something about this unsatisfactory situation has been on WIPO's agenda since its programme of 1994/5.[16] Meanwhile, the scope of Article 6*bis* has been extended significantly by Article 16 of the TRIPs Agreement ('Trade Related Aspects of Intellectual Property Agreement'). It extends Article 6*bis* in three ways:

(1) well-known service marks are also to benefit from the provisions of Article 6*bis*;

(2) knowledge of a well-known mark in the relevant sector of the public is normally sufficient for a mark to qualify as well-known; and

(3) the protection of Article 6*bis* extends to marks being used on goods or services which are not similar to those for which the well-known mark is registered, provided that the use of the mark indicates a connection in the course of trade with the owner of the well-known mark and provided that such use would damage the proprietor's interests.

Unfortunately, Article 16 does not clarify what is meant by 'well-known'. However, in 1999, WIPO put forward a Resolution to be put before the member states of the Paris Union, and the WIPO Assembly, to clarify when a mark is to be regarded as 'well-known'. Article 2 of the Resolution says the factors to be considered are the following:

(1) the degree of knowledge of the mark;
(2) the duration and extent of its use;
(3) the duration and extent of any publicity associated with it;
(4) the number of registrations of it worldwide;
(5) the diligence with which its owner can prove that he has defended it against copiers; and
(6) the value of the mark.

This list is not intended as a check-list; it is for illustrative purposes only. This Resolution also settles a matter which has been controversial for many

---

Examples of well-known trade marks protected under 6*bis* of the Paris Convention are 'Kodak', 'Coca-Cola', 'Pepsi-Cola' (though in relation to the latter two marks the 'cola' part is purely descriptive and can be used by other traders as it was by 'Virgin'). 'Virgin' is itself a well-known mark, of course. There are other well-known marks largely known only to specialists. Examples are the marks used for their products by the pharmaceutical companies and producers of products used in diagnostics, which are largely known only to physicians.

[16] A useful history of this will be found in Tatham, *loc. cit.*

years, in that it makes it clear that it is not a pre-condition to a mark being well-known for the mark to be registered (or at least registration applied for) in the Member State concerned, or for it to be well-known to the public at large either in that Member State or anywhere else. Given that trade mark registrations are national, or at best European in the case of marks registered by the OHIM, whereas the Internet is global, this is a matter of some importance to our theme. Article 3 of the Resolution provides that a mark becomes a well-known mark from the time it becomes well-known under the criteria laid down in Article 2. Conflict with a well-known mark occurs when either the mark itself, or an essential part of it, 'constitutes a reproduction, an imitation, a translation, or a transliteration' of the well-known mark.[17]

The significance of the WIPO Resolution to marks used on the Internet, a global phenomenon, will be immediately apparent. The Internet has the potential to turn a mark into a well-known mark almost overnight, and from being a well-known mark it is an easy step for marks that have become well-known over the Internet to transform into famous marks within Article 6*bis* of the Paris Convention. I think that this development will be in the interests of the consumer. Unfortunately, there is one feature of the Internet which is unsatisfactory from the point of view of trade mark law and the economic justification for it, namely the nature of domain names.

2.3 Domain Names

The basic requirement for action to be taken to protect a well-known trade mark is the likelihood of confusion with the defendant's mark. Confusion is not an issue in the case of domain names; provided the name is unique, it need only differ from an existing domain name in a single characteristic. Many problems have been experienced by owners of well-known trade marks, and the phenomenon of 'domain name grabbing' i.e. registering domain names resembling well-known marks with a view to selling them to the proprietor of the well-known mark. To meet this problem, the Uniform Domain Names Dispute Resolution Policy ('UDNRDP') was promulgated by the Internet Corporation of Assigned Names and Numbers ('ICANN'). ICANN accredits bodies as dispute resolution service providers under UDNRDP, and early decisions suggest that the Policy is working.[18] Of

---

[17] Art. 4.

[18] Decisions of the three dispute-resolution service providers can be viewed on their websites. The three are the World Intellectual Property Organisation, Arbitration Forum, and eResolu-

course, nothing can be done about the situation where two companies have legitimate claims to similar domain names. In the UK Sun Computers and Sun Newspapers have closely resembling domain names.[19]

2.4 Consumer Protection Legislation

2.4.1 Introduction

The Federal Trade Commission of the USA issued a Notice on Consumer Protection in the Global Electronic Marketplace, inviting comments. In its response to this of 21 April 1999 the European Commission stated that in the European Union a body of law and policy on consumer protection already exists that facilitates cross-border trade in products and services, which is generally applicable to electronic commerce and covers all stages of the business-to-consumer commercial relationship, including advertising, promotion and marketing, pre-contractual information and disclosures, contract formation, payment, delivery, guarantees and after-sales services and ultimately redress.[20] It pointed out that the core elements of consumer protection must be co-ordinated at an international level. Accordingly, it welcomed the work in this area being done by WTO, the Organisation for Economic Co-operation and Development ('OECD') and the United Nations Committee on International Trade Law ('UNCITRAL').

Where then e-commerce takes place between buyers and sellers within the European Economic Area there is already a raft of legislation which will regulate the transactions. It is now necessary to look briefly at that.

(i) Directive of the European Parliament on the protection of consumers in respect of distance contracts[21]

This Directive, which is not yet implemented in the UK, has as its object the approximation of the laws of member states concerning distance contracts between consumers and suppliers. The Directive applies to 'distance contracts' which are contracts which make exclusive use of one or more means of 'distance communication', that is, any means which, without the simultaneous physical presence of the supplier and the consumer, may be

---

tion. The latter itself had its name grabbed – see *3636275 Canada, t/a eResolution v eResolution* in which eResolution secured the transfer to it of the domain name eresolution.com

[19] And see Pitman Training Ltd v. Nominet UK, [1997] FSR 797.

[20] Id. paras. 7 and 8.

[21] 97/7/EEC OJ 1997 L144.

used for the conclusion of a contract between those parties.[22] The Directive applies to sales of goods effected through the Internet.[23] There are certain exemptions, the most important of which for present purposes are auction sales, and contracts for the supply of foodstuffs.[24]

Article 4 of the Directive requires the consumer to be provided with the following information prior to the conclusion of the contract:

(a) the identity of the supplier and, in the case of contracts requiring payment in advance, his address;
(b) the main characteristics of the goods...;
(c) the price of the goods...including all taxes;
(d) delivery costs, where appropriate;
(e) the arrangements for payment, delivery or performance;
(f) the existence of a right of withdrawal...;
(g) the cost of using the means of distance communication, where it is calculated other than at the basic rate;
(h) the period for which the offer or the price remains valid;
(i) where appropriate, the minimum duration of the contract in the case of contracts for the supply of products...to be performed...recurrently.

Timely, written confirmation in a *durable* medium of the matters referred to in (a)–(f) above must be received by the consumer, and in any event not later than at the time of delivery.[25] This confirmation must provide in addition:

- written information on the conditions and procedures for exercising the right of withdrawal;
- the geographical address of the place of business of the supplier to which the consumer may address any complaints;
- information on after-sales services and guarantees which exist;
- the conclusion [sic] [conditions?] for cancelling the contract, where it is of unspecified duration or a duration exceeding one year.

---

[22] Id. Art. 2.
[23] Art. 2(4) and Annex 1 provide the Directive covers telephone means of communication with or without human intervention and e-mail.
[24] Art. 3.
[25] Id. Art. 5.

The consumer is given a minimum of seven working days to withdraw from the contract without penalty, without giving any reason.[26] The only cost which may be imposed on the consumer is that of returning the goods.[27] Provided the obligations laid down by Article 5 have been complied with, this period begins from the day of receipt of the products by the consumer.[28] If the obligations laid down in Article 5 have not been complied with, the period for withdrawal is three months from receipt.[29] If during the three-month period the Article 5 information is supplied, the seven-day withdrawal period starts to run from the time of such supply.[30] Within 30 days of the exercise of the right of withdrawal, the supplier must reimburse all sums paid by the consumer free of charge.[31] There are certain exclusions from the right of withdrawal, the most important of which for present purposes are in relation to products customised for the consumer, audio and video recordings and software where the packaging has been unsealed by the consumer, and contracts for the supply of newspapers periodicals and magazines.[32] Any credit arrangements made in connection with the supply must be cancelled without penalty.[33]

A particular problem with some mail order houses has been that they have tided themselves over difficult periods by taking the consumer's money and delaying delivery of the products. A similar problem could arise in relation to transactions effected through the Internet. Accordingly, under Article 7 suppliers are required to execute orders within 30 days. If they are not, the consumer is entitled to a refund as soon as possible, and in any case within 30 days.

The Directive covers other matters such as inertia selling,[34] but the above are the most important provisions for present purposes.

This Directive had to be implemented by member states by 4 June 2000. Its provisions would appear to be mandatory so far as buyers and sellers in the European Economic Area are concerned. However, it would appear gen-

---

26 Art. 6 (1).
27 Art. 6 (2).
28 Art. 6 (1).
29 Ibid.
30 Ibid.
31 Art. 6 (2).
32 Art. 6 (3).
33 Art. 6 (4).
34 I.e. the supply of goods or services to a consumer without their being ordered by the consumer beforehand, where such supply involves a demand for payment Directive 97/7/EC Article 9 (see also ibid. Recital 16).

erally not to be so where the supplier is not situated in a member state. Article 12 (2) provides:

> Member states shall take measures needed to ensure that the consumer does not lose the protection granted by this Directive by virtue of the choice of law of a non-member country as the law applicable to the contract if the latter has a close connection with the territory of one or more member state.

Effective implementation of this is difficult, however, because Member States cannot legislate for non-Member States, and courts of non-Member States do not necessarily have to recognise and enforce judgments given by the courts of Member States. I will return to this problem shortly.

(ii) Other EU measures

As noted by the Commission in their response to the Federal Trade Commission, there are other consumer protection measures which are applicable to e-commerce, such as the Products Liability Directive; but these are of limited value, for the reasons suggested above, where the seller has taken steps to limit its exposure to liability.[35]

2.4.2 What happens if the seller is outside the EU?

The problem with this excellent raft of legislation in the context of e-commerce is that it is easy for sellers to avoid its application. As I pointed out above, an Internet seller can locate itself in any country of the world, and source goods from various locations around the world. Moreover, in deciding the applicable law, it is the seller who calls the shots initially, because a well-set-up site will make the buyer accept the seller's conditions of business. Although many countries have a rule that it is not possible to contract out of mandatory domestic legal rules,[36] and most consumer-protection legislation like the distance-selling directive is mandatory, this rule can only bite if the suit can be brought in the courts of a country with such laws. As I pointed out above, most consumer claims are not worth litigating, and where they are, under the seller's standard conditions of business, it will usually be the courts of the seller's jurisdiction in which action has to be brought.

---

[35] 85/374/EEC.

[36] In the case of the UK the leading case is *The Hollandia*, [1983] 1 AC 565 – not possible to avoid the application of the Hague/Visby Rules by choosing Dutch law.

Moreover, even if a case can be brought to a successful conclusion in the consumer's jurisdiction the courts of the seller's jurisdiction will not necessarily recognise and enforce the judgment.

For these reasons, I think that consumers as rational economic actors will, as they gain more experience of e-commerce, increasingly gravitate to sites of sellers who deliver goods that conform to the contract (i.e. are of satisfactory quality etc) promptly, and who, if the goods turn out to be defective, remedy defects without delay. In consequence, the likelihood is that sites operated by sellers who give consumer satisfaction will grow, and the marks under which they operate will come to qualify as well-known marks under the criteria of the WIPO Resolution. Since that makes it clear that a well-known mark does not have to be tied to a national registration, the proprietors of such sites will be able to protect themselves through the national courts of member states of the Paris Union against those using confusingly similar marks.[37]

At the present stage of development, new websites providing niche markets for goods and services are appearing all the time. However, I believe that in the longer term the likelihood is, for the reasons given above, that the e-commerce market will come to be dominated by a few large players identified by their well-known marks. This, in practice, will solve many of the problems, as the preservation of goodwill requires some reasonable attention to consumer demands.

2.4.3 Credit cards

The almost invariable mode of payment over the Internet is the credit card. The disadvantage that this confines the use of the Internet to those who own credit cards is offset in the United Kingdom by a particular advantage. Under section 75 of the United Kingdom Consumer Credit Act 1974 the creditor and the supplier are jointly and severally liable.[38] The application of the Act to e-commerce transactions entered into with overseas suppliers is problematic, however. The supplier may well have been recruited to the credit card network (Visa/Mastercard or whatever) by a different company, or merchant acquirer. There is also the problem that the Act by its terms does

[37] See e.g. Marks & Spencer plc v. One-in-a Million Ltd, [1998] FSR 265.

[38] This provision is reinforced by s. 56 (2) which provides: 'Negotiations with the debtor [*antecedent negotiations*] shall be deemed to be conducted by the negotiator in the capacity of agent of the creditor as well as in his actual capacity'. See *Jarrett v Barclays Bank*, [1997] 2 All ER 484.

not apply to contracts entered into outside the United Kingdom (we will leave aside the very difficult question as to where e-commerce transactions are entered into).[39] However, in *Jarrett v Barclays Bank*[40] which involved claims against various United Kingdom banks[41] arising out of the purchase of timeshare properties in Spain and Portugal from, at least in one case, sellers in Portugal,[42] the Court of Appeal interpreted section 75 in a way that preserved the jurisdiction of the English courts (notwithstanding Article 16(1) of the Brussels Convention).[43] The agreements in question were held to be debtor-creditor-supplier agreements within the meaning of the Act, so that the credit card banks were liable under section 75. This precedent would appear to be of relevance to sales of goods over the Internet, where in any case the problem of Article 16 does not arise.

This is not merely a UK 'one-off'. There are also US state court decisions to the effect that connected lenders, i.e. lenders having a pre-existing relationship with the seller, are liable for the seller's breach of its duties.[44]

Since, as noted above, most consumer protection is mandatory, the fact that only the card company is within the jurisdiction should not matter. It is jointly and severally liable with the seller.

---

[39] Difficult, because the rules on the formation of contracts differ from jurisdiction to jurisdiction, and in some jurisdictions the *lex loci contractus* is considered relevant in determining the law applicable to the contract.

[40] Above.

[41] It should be noted that a licence is required to carry on a consumer credit business in the UK – Consumer Credit Act 1974 s. 21. An exception to this is 'European Institutions' authorised to carry on 'listed activities' in another Member State of the EU can carry on those activities in the UK without a licence – Directive 89/646/EEC implemented by SI 1992/3218.

[42] It is not clear from *Jarrett v Barclays Bank* (above) exactly why the claim against the Portuguese seller was a 'like claim'. The Court of Appeal construed these words as meaning essentially similar cause of action (ibid p. 495), but the relevant provisions of Portuguese law were not considered. A possible explanation is that since these were consumer claims, the Court treated the application of the relevant provisions of *English* law as mandatory (see *The Hollandia* above).

[43] Which provides: '...in proceedings which have as their object rights in *rem* in immovable property or tenancies of immovable property' the courts of the state in which the property is situated have exclusive jurisdiction. This restrictive interpretation is consistent with the view expressed in the Jenard Report, which is the main source of guidance other than court decisions on the interpretation of the Brussels and Lugano Conventions.

[44] See e.g. Smith v. Navistar International Transport Corp 714 F Supp 303 (N.D. Ill.) (1989); Christinson v. Venturi Const. Co. 109 Ill.App.3d 34, 64 Ill.Dec. 674, 440 N.E.2d 226 (5th Dist.1982).

2.4.4 Conclusion

I think that the market will solve many of the problems of consumer protection in e-commerce. This will be facilitated by the effective protection being given to well-known trade marks, and effective action being taken against those registering, without justification, confusingly similar domain names. This will provide a market solution to the problem, in that consumers will tend to gravitate towards sites whose owners have a valuable goodwill to protect. Obviously, such market solutions are imperfect, and something more is required.

In addition, I would suggest, since the credit card is the almost invariable mode of payment for goods purchased on the Internet, the most effective legislation that governments could be put in place would be an equivalent of section 75 of the United Kingdom Consumer Credit Act 1974 that would give consumers effective remedies against the card companies, even for quite small claims.[45] There is no reason, other than political will, that would make this solution inapplicable to other jurisdictions, and as noted above, some US decisions have resulted in a similar position being reached at common law.

[45] The current limits are goods costing more than £100 and less than £30,000 including VAT – ibid. s. 75. It may be noted that the US Federal Trade Commission Rule of 1975 reflects similar thinking.

Chapter 3

INTELLECTUAL PROPERTY SCOPE:

International Intellectual Property, Progress, and the Rule of Law

Howard C. Anawalt
Santa Clara University, School of Law, Santa Clara, California, USA

Chapter contents:

Abstract: Intellectual property plays an increasingly important role in the international economic arrangements.[1] Intellectual property rights are part of the fabric of commercial law. They create monopolies, which constitute exceptions to generally preferred norms of free access to ideas and freedom to engage in trade. Industrially developed nations and corporations engaged in international trade favor international rules concerning intellectual property. Indeed, these nations and entities have recently preferred rules that strongly protect intellectual property owner rights, without regard to whether these rules contribute directly to social progress, for example innovation.

The process of creating common or similar international intellectual property rules is generally referred to as "harmonization". Efforts to harmonize intellectual property law are part of a larger context which includes national legal cultures[2] and processes of global change. Through most of their relatively brief history, international intellectual property rights have been established primarily on the principle that the claims of foreign citizens should be judged

[1] The author may be reached by Email at h@anawalt.com.

[2] "Legal culture" refers to the fact that particular legal institutions grow up in response to the demands of particular societies and their cultures. As used here the term insists that the society follows a "rule of law" in the sense of effective restraint on sheer exercise of power by rulers.

O. Granstrand (ed.), Economics, Law and Intellectual Property, 55-75.

on the same basis as those of a nation's own citizens. The Agreement on Trade-related Aspects of Intellectual Property Rights (TRIPs) departs from this general pattern. Instead, TRIPs makes detailed and extensive intellectual property right laws a condition for membership in the World Trade Organization (WTO). These requirements include both substantive and procedural laws. These requirements unjustifiably interfere with national legal cultures and have other undesirable consequences.

The discussion concludes that tempered harmonization of intellectual property rules can benefit the world and its cultures. That benefit accrues when the international intellectual property norms are limited to those that clearly serve humanity at large and allow preservation of national cultures. Suggestions for future action are set forth which include proposals for further study, proposed intellectual property guidelines, and items concerning WTO/TRIPs.

Key words: access, copyright, cultures, harmonization, harmonize, history, innovation, monopoly, patents, progress, protection, trade, TRIPs, WTO.

3.1 Development of Intellectual Property

Intellectual property is part commercial law, comparable to laws that concern negotiability of instruments, banking, security interests, or interpretation of contracts. National commercial law can be contrasted with laws that prohibit dangerous or antisocial conduct, like murder, environmental pollution, or civil rights. The same contrast exists in international law. Intellectual property and other commercial treaties facilitate economic activity. Human rights treaties, environmental treaties and the laws of war seek to impose basic norms for protection of humanity and our world.

Intellectual property rights grant monopoly control over certain practices to the "owner" of certain classes of rights.[3] The function of a patent law is to prevent anyone but the owner from using a given process. The function of a trademark is to provide exclusive control over identifying marks, so that others may not use them at all. In general, intellectual property divides into two main branches. One branch protects the variety of inventive works through doctrines such as patents and copyrights. The other protects the identification

[3] It is important to emphasize that it is the owner who possesses these rights, rather than the developer or innovator. Often intellectual property laws end up denying claims of the originator of a new process. Furthermore, these laws often end up paying almost no attention to whether the current owner has contributed any innovative activity to society.

of goods and the "goodwill" value associated with that identification or branding.[4]

The history of intellectual property laws manifests a balance between freedom to trade items and creation of limited monopoly rights. In England, concern with the free flow of goods is traced back to the Magna Carta of 1215 which provided: "All merchants shall have safe and secure exit from England, and entry to England, with the right to tarry there and to move about as well by land as by water, for buying and selling by the ancient and right customs, quit from all evil tolls, except (in time of war) such merchants as are of the land at war with us".[5] That charter and its language emphasize the antimonopoly nature of commercial laws. Individuals and groups should remain free to practice their professions and trades without domination by others.

The creation of specific intellectual property laws, patents and copyrights occurred some four centuries later. The first of these laws, the Statute of Monopolies, was created as a specific reaction against monopoly powers exercised by certain individuals and entities. The operation of English law and royal practices had granted monopolies to various importers and producers. For instance, Queen Elizabeth's court favorite, Lord Darcy, appears to have been granted a monopoly over importing and selling playing cards in England. "When Mr. Darcy attempted to enforce his monopoly against a new entrant, his monopoly was found to be illegal at common law. ...Darcy's Case signaled the beginning of the end of the Monopoly System. As abuses mounted, Parliament was compelled to take action, and in 1628 enacted the Statute of Monopolies. The statute declared void all monopolies, commissions, grants, licenses, charters, and letters patent 'for the sole buying selling making working or using of any thing within this Realm or the dominion of Wales'."[6] The statute created an exception allowing the creation of a short-term monopoly (fourteen years) "to the true and first inventor and inventors" of new processes.

About a century later came the Statute of Anne, which granted qualified protection to the printing monopoly of the royally chartered Stationers' Company against "pirates", that is, those who would have the temerity to

---

4 See H. C. Anawalt and E. F. Enayati, *IP Strategy – Complete Intellectual Property Planning, Access, and Protection* (West Group 2001) §1.01.

5 Magna Carta, P 41, version prepared by Paul Halsall Feb 1996, http://www.fordham.edu /halsall/source/mcarta.html.(1215); see also 70 *University of Colorado Law Review*, 1051, 1055.

6 Letters To The Editor: "Playing Cards In The Hashemite Kingdom Of Jordan", Richard C. Wilder, 2 *University of Baltimore Intellectual Property Journal*, 237.

print materials on their own.[7] The act set up the first copyright regime, granting authors a fourteen-year monopoly term which might be renewed for a second fourteen-year term. The statute also contained a consumer protection provision that allowed relief against a printer or bookseller who might sell a book "at such a Price or Rate as shall be Conceived by any Person or Persons to be High and Unreasonable..."

As the markets of the world have become closely knit, harmonized commercial law, including intellectual property rules, offers advantages. Businesses can plan better, and they can expect the same laws to prevail in most places. On the other hand, nations may differ on the objectives they wish to achieve through intellectual property. Treaties creating internationally guaranteed intellectual property can have major impacts on national legal cultures and practices.[8]

International intellectual property law has grown up on the basis of individual national choice. For example, the Paris Convention covering "industrial property" requires that each nation grant foreign nationals the same treatment protection of industrial property that it grants to its own nationals.[9] Under the convention, "industrial property" includes patents, utility models, industrial designs, trademarks, and indications of source such as regional production. The convention grants to union members the reservation that member states may grant compulsory licenses to patents to prevent patent abuse.[10] The Convention preserves national independence with regard to

---

[7] Statute of Anne, 8 Anne c. 19 1710. See Gorman and Ginsburg, *Copyright for the Nineties*, 4th ed. p. 1.

[8] Treaties establish obligations between or among the states that enter into them. Usually the treaty itself does not provide the rule of decision in a given controversy between private parties. The law of the nation must be changed to incorporate the rules. Whether the treaty will create private rights depends on the intention expressed in the treaty and upon the expressed legislative will of the nation having jurisdiction over the particular piece of private litigation. See H. C. Anawalt and E. F. Enayati, *IP Strategy – Complete Intellectual Property Planning, Access, and Protection* (West Group 2001) §1.03 [17].

[9] Paris Convention for the Protection of Industrial Property of March 20, 1883, as revised. Text available at http://www.wipo.org. "Nationals of any country of the Union shall, as regards the protection of industrial property, enjoy in all the other countries of the Union the advantages that their respective laws now grant, or may hereafter grant, to nationals; all without prejudice to the rights specially provided for by this Convention". Paris Convention Art. 2 (1). Such reciprocal treatment is referred to generally as "comity".

[10] "Each country of the Union shall have the right to take legislative measures providing for the grant of compulsory licenses to prevent the abuses which might result from the exercise of the exclusive rights conferred by the patent, for example, failure to work". Paris Convention Art. 2, A, (1). The legal professions are accustomed to breaking law into two halves – substance and procedure. This is comparable to the distinction between content and form. "Sub-

procedural aspects. "The provisions of the laws of each of the countries of the Union relating to judicial and administrative procedure are expressly reserved".[11]

The Berne Convention on copyrights also obliges its member nations to accord similar protection to foreign works as they do to ones protected directly by their laws. It also requires certain minimum standards of copyright protection concerning the broad categories of copyrightable works. It goes into detail with regard to the kinds of works protected and the substance of the protection. However, as with the Paris Convention, the Berne Convention leaves the means of enforcement entirely to the national laws.[12] It states that "apart from the provisions of this Convention, the extent of protection, as well as the means of redress afforded to the author to protect his rights, shall be governed exclusively by the laws of the country where protection is claimed". The Convention does provide for one mandatory procedure, seizure of infringing copies. However, that remedy shall "take place in accordance with the legislation of each country".[13]

3.2 WTO/TRIPs

In 1995 the World Trade Organization (WTO) was established.[14] By 2001 the WTO had 134 members. Membership in the WTO has become a practical necessity for international trade today. The Agreement on Trade-related Aspects of Intellectual Property Rights (TRIPs) is a mandatory part of the WTO system.[15] TRIPs reaffirms the principle that a nation must pro-

---

stantive" refers to the *content* of a right or duty. "Procedure" refers to *how* the substantive law is carried into effect.

[11] Paris Convention Art. 2, A, (1).

[12] Berne Convention, Article 5 (2). Text available at http://www.wipo.org.

[13] Berne Convention, Article 16.

[14] The WTO is the successor to General Agreement on Tariffs and Trade (GATT). "The World Trade Organization came into being in 1995. One of the youngest of the international organizations, the WTO is the successor to the General Agreement on Tariffs and Trade (GATT) established in the wake of the Second World War". WTO Web site, http://www.wto.org/wto. The WTO's membership is 134 countries (as of February 1999).

[15] Agreement on Trade-related Aspects of Intellectual Property Rights (TRIPs), http://www.wto.org/wto/intellec/1-ipcon.htm; 33 *International Legal Materials* 81 (1994). The TRIPs agreement is Annex 1 C to the WTO treaty, one of the annexes which constitute "integral parts of this Agreement, binding on all Members" of the WTO, Article 2. Agreement Establishing the World Trade Organization (WTO Treaty), available at http://www2.law.cornell.edu/cgi-bin/foliocgi.exe/gatt/query= */doc/{@1}?. The North Ameri-

vide the same degree of protection of intellectual property for foreigners as it does for its own nationals.[16] However, its primary thrust is to mandate the content of intellectual property laws and to require particular enforcement mechanisms.[17] A salient feature of TRIPs is that comprehensive intellectual property right obligations are linked to membership in the worldwide trade system. TRIPs is part of a more general movement to standardize both the substance and procedure of intellectual property rights on a worldwide basis. This movement represents a departure from the predominant approach which had been to leave substance and procedure primarily up to the various nations.

The scope of mandatory intellectual property rights includes copyrights, trademarks, geographical indications, industrial designs, patents, integrated circuit layouts, and trade secrets. The TRIPs preamble states that "intellectual property rights are private rights". The agreement requires substantive laws and procedures to enforce these private rights, which are unprecedented in their detail and in their demand for commitment of national legal resources.

TRIPs requires all member nations to give effect to its provisions. The treaty states that members are free to determine the appropriate method of implementing its provisions.[18] Yet the context of the treaty combines with the economic force of the trade system to constrain member nations to be thorough in implementation of these obligations. Furthermore, the law of treaties binds nations to fulfill their obligations in good faith and denies that a nation may "invoke the provisions of its internal law as justification for its failure to perform a treaty".[19]

Here are some examples of the substantive and procedural requirements of TRIPs:

Substantive law.[20] TRIPs establishes broad categories of obligatory protection of intellectual property. In addition to these board mandates, it creates specific obligations, sometimes in excruciating detail.

TRIPs requires member nations to provide basic protections of copyrights and patents and other forms of intellectual property. In particular,

---

can Free Trade Agreement (NAFTA) slightly predates TRIPs and contains many similar provisions. 32 *International Legal Materials* 612, signed Dec. 17, 1992.

[16] TRIPs Article 1.

[17] The enforcement or procedural requirements are set forth in Part III, Articles 41 through 61.

[18] TRIPs Articles 1 and 3 (1).

[19] Vienna Convention on Treaties, Articles 26 and 27.

[20] Substantive law refers to the content or subject matter of laws. For example, the substantive law of patents defines what a patent right is and in a general sense how it is acquired.

TRIPs provides that "patents shall be available for any inventions, whether products or processes, in all fields of technology, provided that they are new, involve an inventive step and are capable of industrial application".[21] It also requires that "computer programs, whether in source or object code, shall be protected as literary works under the Berne Convention (1971)".[22] It also requires that with regard to computer programs, nations "shall provide authors and their successors in title the right to authorize or to prohibit the commercial rental to the public of originals or copies of their copyright works".[23]

These requirements dictate a very specific approach to protection of software. Legal control of software presents a deeply controversial subject matter. Computer programs lie on a boundary between information and function. A piece of software is in one sense pure information, like the word "twenty", or a communication, like the greeting "hello". At the very same time the data "twenty" or "hello" in a program may control an operation in the same way that wheels and gears control a machine. Data in software constitutes information and function at the very same time.

Legal control of software presents perplexing problems for courts and legislatures. What monopoly control should be granted to works whose functioning depends on the configuration and use of information? Monopolies in this area allow control of information and business practices, matters which law has often sought to assure will be free for use by all.

In the United States, for example, protection of computer programs by copyright and by patent has presented some of the most sensitive and difficult issues ever to arise. Many commentators have criticized the computer copyright and patent rules, and United States federal courts have wrestled with the problems for decades.[24]

TRIPs requires its members to provide trade secret protection. Protection of trade secrets was not previously not covered in multilateral treaties. The TRIPs Agreement explicitly requires that 'undisclosed information' benefit

---

[21] TRIPs Art. 27 (1).

[22] TRIPs Art 10 (1).

[23] TRIPs Art. 11.

[24] H. C. Anawalt and E. F. Enayati, *IP Strategy – Complete Intellectual Property Planning, Access, and Protection* (West Group 2001) sections 1.03 [1], [8], and [10]. There may now be hundreds of articles on the problems raised by technological copyright. See one of the most comprehensive critiques, Pamela Samuelson, Randall Davis, Mitchell D. Kapor, J. D. Reichman, "A Manifesto Concerning the Legal Protection of Computer Programs", 94 *Columbia Law Review* 2308 (1994).

from protection".[25] Identification of what should be considered a "trade secret" presents a very difficult problem for courts. Sorting out who deserves control over particular ideas is very difficult to do. Far more often than not, the claim of one party to a right to control a "secret" is counterbalanced by some other valid concern, such as freedom to engage in a business practice or profession. Equally often, trade secret claims are simply greatly exaggerated. It takes a very large commitment of legal resources to resolve trade secret cases.

TRIPs also contains specific requirements with regard to trademarks and protections for labelling of regional goods, "where a given quality, reputation or other characteristic of the good is essentially attributable to its geographical origin".[26]

Procedure. TRIPs requires member nations to create comprehensive and detailed enforcement mechanisms. Procedural requirements cut even more deeply into national legal systems than substantive requirements, because they dictate how a nation's courts and administrative bodies shall behave. Courts and administrative agencies are extremely expensive for all but the most wealthy of nations. Here is a survey of selected articles of the enforcement part of TRIPs:

Article 41 establishes a general obligation to ensure enforcement provisions are available to "permit effective action against any act of infringement of intellectual property rights".[27] The article also states that these "procedures shall be applied in such a manner as to avoid the creation of barriers to legitimate trade..." This insists that trade, not innovation or advancement of public interest, is the primary purpose for enforcing intellectual property rights. It should be noted that by contrast, the development of intellectual property rights has usually been based on their advancement of the broader interests of the public.

Article 43 dictates a specific result regarding availability of evidence. If a party who controls evidence fails to produce it, then judicial authorities shall have the authority to order that such evidence be produced. Such a provision can be appropriate, but why is it that intellectual property cases should be singled out for this particular treatment? Such a preference may constrain a

---

[25] Laurinda L. Hicks and James R. Holbein, "Convergence of National Intellectual Property Norms in International Trading Agreements", 12 *American University Journal of International Law and Policy* 769, 788-9. TRIPs Art. 39.

[26] TRIPs, Art. 15 through 33.

[27] Other provisions include damages and attorneys' fees (Art. 45), destruction of items (Art. 46), abuse of process (art. 48). See TRIPs, Part III.

nation that wishes to give priority to cases involving domestic violence or environmental pollution.

Article 44 provides that nations give their courts authority "to order a party to desist from infringement". Such a remedy is available in many industrialized countries, but administration of such jurisdiction is expensive. It also tends to favor the party who makes the intellectual property claim, whether that claim is strong or weak. TRIPs does not insist on some equivalent right that would assist the defending party. For example, nothing assures that a defendant will have the right to challenge the scope or validity of a copyright or patent claim.[28]

Article 50 requires powerful "provisional measures". These grant intellectual property right claimants powerful remedies before a trial is actually held. In practice in the United States, such preliminary orders often become in effect the final orders that decide the case. This is because provisional orders create heavy obstacles for a defending party to raise money, hire employees, and continue to market products. These obstacles exist for all parties, including those defending parties strong and valid defenses. Provisional orders favor intellectual property monopoly claims over claims of access or freedom to engage in trade and industry. This is especially true in cases where the intellectual property claimant has ample ability to spend money in court, and the defendant does not.

3.3 TRIPs' Relation to National Legal Culture

Intellectual property protection can provide value to commerce, to innovation, and to the society at large. However, when intellectual property claims receive too much protection or become viewed as ends in themselves, they erode the public interest. Overprotection also undermines the interests of traders and industry. As has been noted, the first English intellectual property laws, the patent laws, emerged as an exception to a general condemnation of monopoly power. As a general rule, "intellectual property laws stand as exceptions to major legal policies favoring free exchange of ideas

[28] One might contrast the broad scope of a right claimant's protections with the skimpy protection of a defendant in a patent case provided in article 34. That section allows a very crabbed defense to one accused of infringing a process patent: the accused infringer must rebut a presumption in favor of the patent claimant when the claim shows that it was substantially likely that the product was obtained by use of the patent and the claimant has "been unable through reasonable efforts to determine the process actually used".

and freedom to compete".[29] The historical perspective of intellectual property favors moderate degrees of protection that fit into national legal structures.

A balanced approach to intellectual property protection should facilitate innovation, assure wide dissemination of advances, and allow cultures to continue their development. The approach currently pursued under the WTO/TRIPs presents three major problem areas related to achievement of those goals. These concern property, legal resources, and innovation.

Let us begin with a few observations. First, the peoples of the world need progress under what is generally referred to as a "rule of law". The world and its cultures need to substitute a widespread use of reason authority for the sheer use of force. Second, the value of a stable legal order is best realized when the culture assimilates the notion of law. Law becomes a reality when the culture accepts it. Finally, economic theories and practices constitute means, but not ends in themselves. One cannot choose what is good or valuable based on economic considerations standing alone. These major premises color the analysis that follows.

Property. Property constitutes a means of exercising power. Claiming such things as "my coffee cup" or "my home" does not impose much on others. Assertion of ownership over methods to produce coffee cups or over large tracts of land do control other people. Property rights cut deeply into how communities and cultures structure themselves. Thus one needs to ask: "Who shall define property, rights, and their limits? Shall people who live outside our culture decide them, or shall we?"

Professor Francis Philbrick made the following useful observations about property. First, property is a legal concept which is constantly subject to change. "It is self-evident that neither the things recognized as the object of property rights nor the nature of these rights themselves could possibly be the same under a land economy of 1700 and our industrial economy of today".[30]

---

[29] H. C. Anawalt and E. F. Enayati, *IP Strategy – Complete Intellectual Property Planning*, Access, and Protection (West Group 2001) §1.01.

[30] F. Philbrick, "Changing Conceptions of Property in Law", 86 *U. Pa. L. Rev.* 691 (1937). In the same immediate context, Philbrick observes that intellectual property should be recognized as property "on Locke-ian principles, since it is a product of labor (and of genius)..." Id. p. 692. The 1930s inspired some careful legal scholarship in the United States on the nature of property as a legal institution. At that time the nation was experiencing the enormous problems of a great depression. The administration of President Franklin D. Roosevelt was pressing ahead with programs intended to remedy the economic ills that led to this collapse. The administration considered remedies that would cut into expectations that had firm legal groundings in two of the most deeply ingrained areas of American law – contracts and property.

Philbrick's second major point is that social conditions create the meaning of property as a legal institution.[31]

Intellectual property rights represent particularly forceful forms of social power. These rights grant control over valuable processes or expressions and deny others the capacity to use them unless the owner's consent is obtained, or unless some legal privilege of use is established that grants access. From its preamble forward, TRIPs insists that intellectual property of a whole range of substance and form must be treated not only as property, but as "private property rights".

Private property is not the only form of property. A range of other property options exists. If nations are constrained by trade considerations they may be foreclosed from useful choices of how to handle the "property" aspect of intellectual creations. These options include:

- Private property. This form of property means that a person, group, or entity, such as a corporation, owns the property. Examples include owning a car, a piece of land, or a patent. The private property options can include distinctions between corporate ownership and that of actual human beings or associations.
- Community property. This is a form of property in which a community, rather than an individual or a group of separate persons, owns the property. Examples include kibbutzim and the civil law institution of familial community property.
- Public property. In this form of property a political entity owns the property. Examples include public parks, roads, military facilities, and such things as government-owned patents or copyrights. These examples demonstrate the fallacy of conflating all property rights into a category of "private rights" as the WTO/TRIPs agreement does.

Since the United States has promoted the obligatory standards of TRIPs, it should be noted that the American Constitution steps very cautiously into the arena of intellectual property. The Constitution does not provide for federal definition of property rights, but leaves this to the constituent states of the Union. This is true even though the Constitution, unlike a treaty, created a government responsive to a people.

The Constitution does provide that the federal government may create patents and copyrights if Congress decides to do so. That clause does not

[31] Id. p. 696.

grant any rights itself. Nor does it oblige the constituent states to create such protection in the absence of an act of Congress. It simply grants to the federal legislature a power to act. The rights created by Congress must be limited in duration.[32] Once granted, due process (a separate constitutional norm) protects particular items of intellectual property, e.g. a patent already granted, from governmental taking without compensation.[33]

Another example from American experience is community property. This is a property institution which many West Coast states and Louisiana have borrowed from the European civil law culture. Community property is an institution that deeply affects the marriage relationship. All earnings and resulting property acquired during the marriage vest in the community of spouses. This is radically different from non-community property states, where the earning party owns the earnings and property purchased with the earnings.[34] The majority of states do not have community property. It remains up to each state to decide what form of spousal property rights exist, even though the United States is one nation.[35]

Legal resources. Legal institutions such as courts, libraries, processing, and legal professions create a large social expense, even for a highly developed economy like that of the United States. The TRIPs requirements of sub-

---

[32] The patent and copyright clause, Article I, section 8, clause 8, contains only a grant of power to the national legislature. Congress is not obliged to create any patent or copyright laws. The clause speaks of creating "exclusive rights" for inventors and writers, but since Congress need not create any rights, there appears to be no reason that it may not condition the rights heavily. For example, copyright ownership under the modern U.S. copyright law specifically allows others to also use the copyrighted material when the use is "fair use". 17 U.S.C. 107. American constitutional scholars dispute about every assertion made about the United States Constitution. At the risk of sparking such a dispute among American colleagues, I note that this is the only occasion in the Constitution which deals with the creation of a property right. Creation of property rights was apparently viewed as entirely beyond the scope of the central, i.e. federal, government. The institutions of property are left to the fifty states that comprise the nation. An example of divergence among the states is community property discussed in the text. Several western states provide for spousal community property, a continental European system. Under community property, all earnings and resulting property acquired during the marriage belongs to the community of spouses.

[33] United States Constitution, 5th and 14th Amendments guaranteeing due process; the 5th specifically assures that property may be taken by the federal government only for public purposes upon just compensation.

[34] The title vests in the community. However, the effect is much like creating a kind of joint title on behalf of both spouses.

[35] States having community property include Arizona, California, Idaho, Louisiana, Nevada, New Mexico, Texas, and Washington. The west coast states form a nearly solid block, but one can note that Oregon, a Pacific coast state, has opted not to have community property.

substance and procedure of intellectual property law create large demand on legal resources. Intellectual property cases are notoriously expensive in the United States. "The American Intellectual Property Law Association reports, based on a survey of its members, that the median cost of patent litigation to each side is $799,000 through the end of discovery, and $1,503,000 through trial and appeal".[36] Often parties will find that they must give up a good claim of right or a defense and settle a case, due to the expense of the litigation itself.

It is not clear why intellectual property claims should be singled out from other matters for mandatory legal procedures as the TRIPs agreement does. Many matters demand attention within a given legal order: divorces, domestic property disputes, claims of loss or injury to person or property, crimes, environmental protection, reduction of domestic violence, to name a few. It would seem that a nation itself should determine the priorities within a legal system, unless some established international human rights or other compelling legal norm intervenes. Are intellectual property rights among the compelling legal norms? If so, why?

Innovation and free trade. Trade should be an end in itself. Trade is a means for delivering needed or desired goods and services. Innovation constitutes a means of providing people with things that satisfy needs and wants. Innovation occurs without any special laws to assist it. The progress of science and engineering before recent centuries took place without patent and copyright laws to guide or channel ownership claims. Even pioneering discoveries in the twentieth century were made without an eye to whether the subject at hand would be patentable. Einstein did not consult with patent attorneys on his way to developing his theories.

Intellectual property rights do provide incentive for innovators to devote effort and capital to solving problems. The incentive function is one of the primary reasons for creating intellectual property rights. Freedom to engage in trade and incentives for innovation have a strong historical link in intellectual property law. Intellectual property rights, such as patents, have become permissible legal monopolies because they encourage innovation.

It is one thing to assert that intellectual property rights are permissible. It is quite another to make such monopolies mandatory, as TRIPs does. If a national government creates intellectual property rights, it will be responsible to its people. The WTO is not responsible to any people. The trade representatives who negotiate the trade-related treaties are not elected by con-

---

[36] 95 *Northwestern University Law Review* 1495, 1502, "Rational Ignorance at the Patent Office", Mark A. Lemley.

stituents. Such an organization has very little ability or incentive to assess the innovation needs of constituent nations.

Intellectual property rights can play a role in stimulating economic development and innovation when they are framed based on the actual innovation needs of the communities that they serve. Intellectual property rights can also frustrate innovation. For example, a large semiconductor chip producing corporation can use a patent portfolio to block the development of a pioneering new semiconductor technology. Suppose a newcomer to the semiconductor industry has developed a revolutionary chip that can operate in three states. Rather than being limited to either/or operations, the new chip can process "maybe" states. The newcomer, however, will face the fact that many relatively minor yet customary devices and processes make up the basic structure of a chip. A number of these may be covered by patents held by the large semiconductor producer. That large producer may assert its monopoly power through court processes to block development of the new chip, or may decide to charge excessive license royalties.[37]

In general, a legal order should assure that intellectual property rights are fully balanced by access rights. Since intellectual property rights operate as exceptions to freedom to use ideas and engage in productive activity, such rights need to be coupled with adequate legal assurances that others will not be unduly burdened in adapting new discoveries or practicing their established professions.[38]

Adequate incentives for innovation do not depend on mandatory international intellectual property rules. Traditional intellectual property economics has been satisfied with providing incentives that operate within a country's own national boundaries. The English and American development of intellectual property laws has proceeded from the assumption that one can achieve an incentive by rewarding inventions within one's own borders. Infringing goods may be stopped at the border. The patent, copyright, or trademark holder does not lose any return on its innovative or goods identification within the intellectual property-protecting nation so long as infringing good do not enter that market. Of course, stopping offending goods at a border impedes trade. However, that block is removed when the exporter or the

---

[37] See *Motorola Inc. v. Hitachi Ltd.*, 14 *United States Patent Law Quarterly* 2d 1769 (Tex. 1990) for an example of how such a case would develop.

[38] United States law provides for such assurances in, for example, the doctrine of "fair use" in copyright (17 U.S.C. 107) and the requirement that patents must not preempt customary knowledge and practice ("non-obviousness", 35 U.S.C. 103).

exporter's nation decides that it is too costly to continue to disregard the rules of the market nation involved.

The over-used term "piracy" should be reserved for those instances where an activity violates the laws of the nations having proper jurisdiction over the claim presented. That is, it should not apply to instances where a nation does not protect intellectual property rights by its own laws.[39]

Let us consider the example of the United States. That nation has been a very aggressive promoter of international intellectual property in recent decades. It has pursued this policy to serve its national interests and those of corporate powers.[40] When nations do not follow the same intellectual property rules as the United States they are often accused by the press and the government as engaging in "piracy". The United States has not always pursued this policy. "For a century (after 1790), the United States was exceptionally parochial in copyright matters, not only denying protection to the published works of nonresident foreign authors, but actually appearing to encourage piracy". American attitudes and actions began to turn around in the 1830s, but it was not until 1891 that an Act of Congress created a degree of international protection. Foreign authors could achieve protection in the United States only if they deposited two copies of the work before the date of publication anywhere, and the two copies had to be manufactured in the United States. The United States did not become a member of the Berne Convention until nearly a century later.[41]

---

[39] "...Thus, the frequent refrain in news media that actions taken in foreign countries 'violate intellectual property rights' must be taken with a grain of salt. If the law of the nation in question does not prohibit the copying, it is not wise to make such an accusation. Such propaganda misleads and tends to poison the atmosphere of discussion. It is far better to create an atmosphere of intelligent interchange and avoid power politics when intellectual property issues are raised internationally. The questions of what should be protected even within the United States are and remain difficult ones to answer. They are vastly more complicated in our world made up of many cultures, with its attendant difficulties of creating equitable distribution of the world resources, including intellectual property. Furthermore, the basic rule is that even treaties do not alter local intellectual property rules, unless enforcement legislation is adopted by the country in question". H. C. Anawalt and E. Enayati Powers, *IP Strategy – Complete Intellectual Property Planning, Access, and Protection*, (West Group 2001) §1.03 [17], footnote 567.

[40] See Pamela Samuelson, "The Digital Agenda of the World Intellectual Property Organization", 37 *Virginia Journal of International Law* 369, 373-4, Winter 1997.

[41] H. C. Anawalt and E. Enayati Powers, *IP Strategy – Complete Intellectual Property Planning, Access, and Protection*, (West Group 2001) §1.03 [17].

One needs to be careful about economic assumptions. For example, in an examination of the economics of international intellectual property, Professor R. Carl Moy states:

> "In essence, because the parties to an international sale of a patented item each belong to a different national economy, their private costs and gains become social costs and gains for the countries involved. For example, where a national of the country under consideration holds a foreign patent, the sale of goods under that patent transfers wealth out of the foreign country into the hands of the patent-owning national. The national's private gain is thus a social gain for the national's own country. "[42]

The direction of the economic transfer noted is not necessarily true. It is true that wealth is transferred whenever a patentee receives a royalty or enjoys an element of control due to his, her, or its patent. It is also true that such a transfer takes some portion of the wealth from the nation where the royalty is paid. It is not clear where that wealth actually ends up. For example, a powerful Swedish patent holder may receive a royalty from, say, Denmark or South Africa. That Swede, however, may have moved to Monaco, and the wealth may end up there. Or, what is even more problematic, a multinational corporation may enjoy the royalty (or element of control). In that case, its main economic beneficiaries will be major stockholders or corporate managers. These beneficiaries may be resident or otherwise rooted anywhere. Indeed, these beneficiaries may even be located primarily in the nation paying the royalty.

Intellectual property rights constitute a very powerful form of capital. They allow control over important advances in computers, biotechnology, and other areas. They also tend to control the directions that innovation may take, since intellectual property rights holders can use legal processes to interfere with progress made by competitors and even with their ability to do effective research. In the immediate past, one could summarize the international effects of patents as follows:

Patent systems are large-scale governmental intrusions into the free-market economy. They involve manipulating social costs and benefits to increase the national wealth. Perhaps the most significant cost of such systems is the higher prices imposed on consumers of the patented advance.[43]

---

[42] R. Carl Moy, "The History of the Patent Harmonization Treaty: Economic Self-Interest as an Influence", 26 *John Marshall Law Review* 457 (1993).
[43] Id.

What is said about government intrusion into the market and the impact of higher prices is true, but now one must consider additional consequences beyond higher prices to consumers. Intellectual property rights determine who will enjoy advances.

Intellectual property rights allow control of communications capacities in some instances. For example, if a means of communication depends on use of a patented or copyright-protected technology, an intellectual property right holder may enjoin uses of that technology. In effect, the intellectual property right holder may dictate how or whether people will engage in a very fundamental action – communication. Copyright owners can control the flow of valuable types of information and works over the Internet. A holder of rights in a prevalent system of software may often exercise a degree of control that extends far beyond any original monopoly granted by a copyright or patent.

The control offered by intellectual property rights can be exercised without regard to whether the right-holder has contributed any significant innovative activity to the intellectual property right. This divorce between ownership and innovative activity occurs in several ways. One can purchase an innovative technology. In that case the right-holder has simply obtained an existing technology. The holder of a very popular copyright or trademark-protected technology may exercise either of these intellectual property monopolies without contributing innovation. Such an entity may even stifle the entry of new technologies into the market.

The emergence of multinational businesses and concentration of corporate power constitute an important factor in the potential for use or abuse of intellectual property rights. They have the ability to influence governments and international negotiations leading to such treaties as TRIPs. They can engage in expensive processes such as litigation or pursuit of patent applications in a multiplicity of countries.[44] Large intellectual property right portfolios give such entities powerful leverage in negotiation of licenses or development agreements. It is a relatively minor expense for a large corporation to pursue a patent application, even when that requires filing and its related fees in many different countries.

---

[44] Prosecuting a patent application is *not* a minor expense for an individual or small company. Filing even in one's own country requires filing expenses, attorneys' fees and the like. When one seeks protection in more than one country these fees multiply. In addition, one must undergo the considerable expense of translations. Multiple-nation filings can easily mount into the hundreds of thousands of dollars per patentable invention.

3.4 Directions for the Future

Intellectual property rights can be helpful legal means when they are constrained to serve human and environmental needs. They cannot become ends in themselves. They must not be permitted to distort other essential elements of legal systems. International intellectual property rights must not become mere instruments creating or protecting private rights or capital, but must remain incentives to such things as innovation and necessary name identification.

When seeking harmonization of intellectual property rights, it is important to assure that international rules do not interfere unduly with national legal cultures. Intellectual property rights lack the compelling necessity of human rights covenants and rules on the use of force that might justify setting aside national legal cultures. The WTO/TRIPs approach fails to recognize these legal realities. Instead, it imposes mandatory substance and procedure linked to membership in a nearly essential world trade community. Such an approach commends itself to progress.

The question arises: What should be done for the future of international intellectual property rights? In response to that question I wish to offer a series of questions for further analysis and study, a set of proposed intellectual property rights guidelines, and a course of action for dealing with the trade/intellectual property rights regime created by WTO/TRIPs.

Questions for study and analysis:

1. Exactly what purposes do international intellectual property rights serve? To what degree are they necessary for human progress and protection of the planet? Do mandatory international intellectual property rights serve purposes other than commercial advancement?
2. To what degree are international intellectual property rights necessary? Do they rank with such things as human rights or control of military force?
3. To what extent do national and international intellectual property rights protect mere ownership, as opposed to providing incentives for achieving such goals as valuable innovation? Is it appropriate to encourage intellectual property rights to solidify into a form of capital?
4. What property institutions serve well in the intellectual property rights arena? Should inventive processes be viewed solely as "private property rights", or should they also include such forms of property as community property and public property?

5. To what extent do given intellectual property rights provide incentives for innovation? To what extent do they interfere with innovation? Under what circumstances do intellectual property rights become abused?
6. Should international intellectual property rights be accompanied by international intellectual property access rights? For example, should harmonized patent and copyright norms include such access rights as reasonable non-selective licensing requirements or fair use rights?
7. Is it advisable to link intellectual property right requirements to membership in international communities, such as trade organizations? If so, exactly why?

Proposed Intellectual Property Guidelines. Both international intellectual property and national intellectual property should be guided by useful principles, rather than be adopted at the behest of interest groups unguided by principles. The following are some proposed guidelines:[45]

Guideline 1. The community of nations should insist that international agreements on intellectual property do not interfere unduly with the flourishing of national legal cultures.

Guideline 2. International agreements on intellectual property should not be linked to trade and taxation policies.

Guideline 3. Intellectual property laws should be limited to providing incentives for innovation and appropriate name protection.

Guideline 4. Intellectual property incentives should be based on reasonable compensation to actual inventors, rather than on agglomerating property rights to the intellectual property owner. The sale or transfer of intellectual property rights from the actual inventor or author to other owners should be tailored (when possible) to assure that the transferee will not enjoy compensation in any form beyond the fair value of the original innovation in the hands of its creator.

Guideline 5. In general, intellectual property laws should observe the following pattern of norms:

- protection should be for limited purposes only,
- access rights (to technology) should be preferred,
- functional works (as distinct from e.g. expressive ones) should enjoy shorter duration of monopoly coupled with assured monetary compensation.

---

[45] These proposed guidelines find support in the development of intellectual property laws. See Howard C. Anawalt, "Control of Inventions in a Networked World", 15 *Computer & High Tech. Law Journal* 123 (1999), and 8 *Information and Communication Technology Law* 121 (1999). They should be subjected to study and critique along with the proposed questions for further study.

Dealing with WTO/TRIPs. The WTO is firmly ingrained in the international legal system. The WTO and its predecessor GATT have been part of the world order for a little more than a half a century and have become established economic institutions. However, the linking of trade and tariff policies to intellectual property right requirements constitutes a departure from the history of international intellectual property reflected in earlier treaty arrangements. The TRIPs requirements appear to interfere unduly with national legal cultures.

One immediate approach to TRIPs is to seek interpretations that ameliorate its interference with national legal cultures. The enforceable text of the TRIPs requires that "Members shall give effect to the provisions of the Agreement". Nevertheless, the TRIPs agreement offers some avenues for interpretation. The Preamble of TRIPs states that its intentions are "to reduce distortions" in international trade and "to ensure that measures and procedures to enforce intellectual property rights do not themselves become barriers to legitimate trade". Legitimate trade should not embrace trade which gives undeserved economic power to corporate owners (not innovators) or which frustrates the effective development of national legal systems by commandeering courts. The Preamble also recognizes that "the least developed" countries need great flexibility "in the implementation of laws and regulations in order to enable them to create a sound and viable technological base".

Article 8 provides that nations may adopt measures "necessary to protect public health and nutrition, and to promote public interest in sectors of vital importance to their socio-economic and technological development".[46] Nations, whether industrialized or least developed, can surely present cogent explanations of why overly demanding substantive or procedural rules concerning intellectual property rights should give way to other national legal needs. The orderly development of a culture under its version of the rule of law surely qualifies as a "sector of vital importance". Article 8 also provides that members adopt measures needed to "prevent the abuse of intellectual property rights by right holders…".

More ambitious approaches involve dealing directly with the linkage of trade and intellectual property mandates in the WTO/TRIPs treaty. The linkage of WTO membership to mandatory intellectual property rights and procedure should be ended, if that is politically feasible. If that cannot be accomplished, then over time the nature of the linkage between trade member-

[46] TRIPs, Article 8, 1. Article 8 also provides that members adopt measures needed to "prevent the abuse of intellectual property rights by right holders…".

ship and protection of intellectual property should be modified. The TRIPs agreement should be amended to require, with modest exceptions, only national reciprocity on the substance of intellectual property protection. In general, the TRIPs agreement should be amended to eliminate required procedures for enforcement, again with some exceptions.

Substantial change of WTO/TRIPs will require patience and long-term effort. However, all nations should study this matter conscientiously and afresh. This certainly includes those powerful and industrially developed nations that have so far promoted TRIPs. The suggestion that TRIPs be changed to revert to less onerous requirements is not, however, revolutionary or radical. To the contrary, it represents a return to the long history of intellectual property rights development on the international scene. TRIPs itself represents the radical departure.

3.5 Conclusions

International intellectual property rights will undoubtedly play a growing major role in the world economy. These rules will have major effects on innovation and progress. These rules can play a very positive role, but to do so, the nations must place intellectual property and its legal control mechanisms in proper perspective. The obligatory intellectual property norms of WTO/TRIPs represents a departure from the history of international intellectual property and an undue burden on national legal cultures. TRIPs takes economic policy to be the major, if not sole, determinant of how much of national legal policy and resources must be devoted to protection of intellectual property rights.

The future of useful international intellectual property rights lies in placing those rights in proper perspective. That perspective can best be achieved by careful analysis of essential policy questions, by pursuing future treaties through application of sound general principles, and by taking immediate steps to ameliorate any undue interference with national legal cultures by the WTO/TRIPs agreement. With these measures in mind, the future of harmonization will indeed be positive.

Chapter 4

MARKETS FOR TECHNOLOGY AND CORPORATE STRATEGY

Ashish Arora*, Andrea Fosfuri**, and Alfonso Gambardella***
** Carnegie Mellon University, Heinz School of Public Policy and Management, Pittsburgh, PA, USA*
*** Universidad Carlos III de Madrid, Department of Business Administration, Madrid, Spain*
**** Sant'Anna School of Advanced Studies, Pisa, Italy*

Chapter contents:

Abstract: Although market transactions for technologies, ideas, knowledge or information are limited by several well-known imperfections, there is increasing evidence that they have become more common than in the past. In this paper we argue that these markets change the traditional mindset in which the only available option for a company wishing to introduce an innovation is to develop the technology in-house, or for a company developing the technology to own the downstream assets needed to manufacture and commercialize the goods. This affects the role of companies both as technology users (they can "buy" technologies) and as technology suppliers (they can "sell" technologies). The implications for management include more proactive management of intellectual property, greater attention to external monitoring of technologies, and organizational changes to support technology licensing, joint-ventures and acquisition of external technology. For entrepreneurial startups,

O. Granstrand (ed.), Economics, Law and Intellectual Property, 77-108.

markets for technology make a focused business model more attractive. At the industry level, markets for technology may lower barriers to entry and increase competition, with obvious implications for the firms' broader strategy as well.

Keywords: markets for technology, intellectual property, technology strategy

4.1 Introduction

In the past two decades or so, there has been a rapid growth in a variety of arrangements for the exchange of technologies or technological services, ranging from R&D joint ventures and partnerships, to licensing and cross-licensing agreements, to contract R&D. Although we lack comprehensive empirical measures over time, all the available evidence suggests that, especially in high-tech industries, the trade in technologies has become more common than in the past. Recent studies have documented an increase in licensing revenues earned by US firms (Dengan, 1998) and the upsurge in patenting activities, possibly reflecting the increased opportunities for technology licensing (e.g. Kortum and Lerner, 1999; and Hall and Ham, 2001). (See also Teece, 1998; and Grindley and Teece, 1997.)

Elsewhere (Arora, Fosfuri and Gambardella, 2001) we have developed a comprehensive study of the nature and functioning of markets for technology. In this paper, we focus on the implications for corporate strategy.

Markets for technology affect the role of companies both as technology users (they can "buy" technologies) and as technology suppliers (they can "sell" technologies). This changes the traditional mindset in which the only available option for a company wishing to introduce an innovation is to develop the technology in-house, or for a company developing the technology to own the downstream assets needed to manufacture and commercialize the goods. Thus, for example, entrepreneurial startups may be able to focus more narrowly on developing technology rather than on its application, by relying on licensing and other arrangements to appropriate the returns to their innovative efforts. Given that manufacturing and commercialization require substantial resources, which smaller firms may be unable to mobilize, markets for technology may be critical for the very existence of high-tech startups. Moreover, markets for technology can undermine privileged access to technology that incumbent firms in an industry may enjoy, because competitors and entrants may acquire the technology from alternative sources of supply in the market. At an industry level, markets for technology lower entry barriers, increase competition and compress product lifecycles. These are all changes that require appropriate strategic responses.

We begin the next section by clarifying what we mean by markets for technology, and by briefly reviewing some evidence of the rise of such markets in recent years. Section 3 analyzes the consequences of "missing" markets for intangible assets. Section 4 focuses on large, established firms. Section 5 examines the different challenges faced by the smaller firms, especially technology-based startups. Section 6 deals with the external acquisition of technology. Section 7 discusses the implications on entry and competition. Section 8 summarizes our main conclusions.

4.2 Markets for Technology: Definition and Suggestive Evidence

Technology comes in very different forms, and no general definition will fit. For instance, it can take the form of "intellectual property" (patents) or intangibles (e.g. a software program, or a design), or it can be embodied in a product (e.g. a prototype, or a device like a chip designed to perform certain operations), or it can take the form of technical services. We will not attempt to define technology, treating it instead as an imprecise term for useful knowledge rooted in engineering and scientific disciplines, which usually also draws from practical experience from production. In turn, this means that technology transactions can take different forms, from pure licensing to complicated collaborative agreements, R&D partnerships and contracts, etc, which may well include the further development of the technology, or its realization "from scratch".[1] These transactions may involve full technology packages (patents and other intellectual property and know-how), or knowledge that is not patentable or not patented (e.g. software, or the many non-patented designs and innovations).

Markets for technology are not a new phenomenon. Lamoreaux and Sokoloff (1997; 1998) documented the existence of an active market for patents in the US during the 19th century. However, it appears that these markets declined after the 1920s, and have become reinvigorated only in the last couple of decades. For example, a study by a consulting company, British Technology Group (BTG, 1998), concluded that most large firms in the industrialized countries have unused technologies that they have not licensed in the past but would like to do so. This points to the under-development of a

[1] Transactions in technology can also occur through mergers and acquisitions, and through the mobility of people. However, we shall ignore these cases here.

market for technology. Supporting evidence also comes from an estimate by the European Union that, in Europe, 20 billion dollars are spent every year to develop innovations and technologies that have already been developed elsewhere. (See www.european-patent-office.org/patinfopro/index.htm.) Moreover, in recent years we have seen a number of examples of "strategic alliances", ranging from R&D joint ventures and partnerships, spin-offs, corporate venture capital, licensing deals, and a variety of "outsourcing" deals, signaling the increasing importance of transactions for intangible technology.

In Arora, Fosfuri and Gambardella (2001), we provided rough aggregate estimates of the size and scope of markets for technology for recent decades. Using systematic data on technology transactions we found that the extent of technology trade has grown in the 1990s, and high-tech industries like software, chemicals, and electronics lead the growth of such markets. Table 4-1a and Table 4-1b show the total number and value of such transactions, by industrial sector, between 1985 and 1997.[2] The value of a transaction is calculated here as the sum of licensing and royalty payments, and equity investments and R&D funding provided in return for licensing rights.

These tables show that there have been over 15,000 transactions in technology with a total value of over $330 billion, implying an average of nearly 1,150 transactions worth $27 billion per year. To put these numbers in perspective, note that the total R&D spending in the US, Japan, Germany, UK, France, Italy and Canada was about $340 billion, and non-defense R&D spending was about $300 billion in 1995. Thus, the value of the total technology transactions is about 9% of total non-defense R&D spending in the developed countries.[3] Although markets for technology are still in their infancy in many cases, the value of the transactions is already substantial.

---

[2] The data are from a commercial database provided by the Securities Data Corporation, the leading commercial provider of such data The SDC data are constructed from SEC filings (10-Qs), financial journals, news wire services, proxies and quarterly reports. We read through each transaction to verify that technology transfer was involved. From the description of the agreement, we also coded the granter or recipient of the technology, or whether there was a two-way flow of technology, such as a technology cross-licensing agreement.

[3] There are a number of possible biases going in both directions. We exclude outright acquisitions. Further, the figures for equity purchase may include payments for non-technology assets. Excluding these would reduce the value to about $15 billion per year. On the other hand, our database probably does not include a large number of smaller value transactions, and we are probably undercounting transactions from 1985-87, as well as 1996 and 1997. Based on other studies, using IRS data on licensing and royalty fees, we estimate the value of these flows to be of the order of $50 billion per year.

Table 4-1a. The market for technology: number of technology transactions, 1985-97, by sector

Year	1985-89	1990	1991	1992	1993	1994	1995	1996	1997	Total Number
28	439	310	461	395	486	596	351	208	222	3496
35	129	115	210	188	195	192	164	63	69	1360
36	234	190	310	316	366	415	326	135	151	2479
73	143	207	360	334	363	610	770	405	424	3689
87	11	9	45	253	156	73	34	22	17	707
All Others	174	209	468	523	560	540	545	289	293	3858
Total	1130	1040	1854	2009	2126	2426	2190	1122	1176	15073

Table 4-1b. The market for technology: value of technology transactions, 1985-97, by sector (millions of 1995 dollars, all countries)

Year	1985-89	1990	1991	1992	1993	1994	1995	1996	1997	Total Value
28	5809	4102	6101	5227	6431	7887	4645	2753	2938	46264
35	6280	5599	10224	9153	9493	9347	7984	3067	3359	66211
36	10971	8908	14534	14816	17160	19457	15284	6329	7080	116227
73	1740	2518	4380	4063	4416	7421	9368	4927	5158	44881
87	171	140	701	3939	2429	1137	529	343	265	11009
All Others	2781	2901	5471	6373	6549	6354	6658	3342	3156	48240
Total	27753	24169	41410	43571	46479	51604	44469	20761	21956	332831

Note: SIC28 = Chemicals; SIC35 = Industrial Machinery & Equipment; SIC36 = Electronic & Other Electric Equipment; SIC38 = Instruments & Related Products, SIC49 = Electric, Gas, and Sanitary Services; SIC 50 = Wholesale Trade – Durable Goods; SIC73 = Business Services.

Source: Our computations based on SDC datafiles. See Arora, Fosfuri and Gambardella (2001) for details.

Table 4-1a and Table 4-1b also show that the transactions are concentrated in few sectors, notably chemicals, software, electrical and non-electrical machinery, and engineering and professional services. These sectors together account for the bulk of transactions (both source and recipient of technology), and as expected, are also a net source of technology for other sectors. Table 4-2 lists some of the leading licensors in these sectors. As the table indicates, the list includes both large established firms, as well as small, high-tech startups. Our data also show that the number of these transactions has been steadily increasing over time, with the exception of the last two years in our sample (possibly reflecting incomplete reporting of transactions for these years).

Specific industry case studies provide possibly the most compelling evidence of the increasing importance of technology markets. The chemical industry for instance is one in which technology licensing, of both products and processes, has been quite widespread for many years. (See Arora and Gambardella, 1998; and Arora and Fosfuri, 2000.) Similarly, technology trade is becoming extensive in leading high-tech industries such as software, semiconductors, and biotechnology. In semiconductors there has been a significant growth of the so-called "fabless" or even "chipless" companies, which specialize in the design of self-contained, independent chip "modules" and sell their designs to other companies that design and manufacture the complex chip in which the individual modules are embedded (Linden and Somaya, 2000). Further evidence about technology trade in semiconductors is provided by Hall and Ham (2001), who find that licensing and cross-licensing deals have risen significantly in this industry and that the propensity to patent has increased during the last decade in response to the greater need to protect intellectual property in such deals.

Table 4-2 Leading licensors, by sector, selected sectors, 1985-1997

	Licenses Given	Licenses Taken	Cross-Licenses	Sector
Company				
IBM	34	48	69	Business Services
Apple Computer Inc	25	18	15	SIC 73
Sun Microsystems Inc	24	16	16	
Novell Inc	17	17	22	
Hewlett-Packard Co	13	24	28	
AT & T Corp	11	22	21	
Oracle Corp	10	9	35	
Digital Equipment Corp	8	20	21	
Fujitsu Ltd	6	11	34	

Table 4-2 Leading licensors, by sector, selected sectors, 1985-1997 (cont.)

Company	Licenses Given	Licenses Taken	Cross-Licenses	Sector
Qualcomm	15	0	1	Communication
AT & T Corp	4	3	5	SIC 48
Motorola Inc	3	1	2	
Pacific Telesis group	3	0	1	
Cable & Wireless PLC	2	0	1	
Kokusai Denshin Denwa Co Ltd	2	0	2	
Bell South Corp	1	0	1	
IBM Corp	0	2	5	
Sprint Corp	0	1	3	
General Motors Corp	4	2	3	Instruments and Related Products
Honeywell	4	0	4	SIC 38
Baxter International	3	4	1	
Eli Lilly & Co	3	4	3	
Daimler-Benz AG	2	0	4	
Hewlett-Packard Co	2	1	5	
Philips Electronics NV	2	2	1	
Eastern Kodak Co	1	3	1	
Siemens AG	1	3	4	
Johnson & Johnson	0	7	2	
	23	15	33	Electronic & Other Electric Equipment
Intel Corp	19	8	20	SIC 36
IBM Corp	18	9	38	
Texas Instruments Inc	18	14	39	
AT & T Corp	11	11	36	
Philips Electronics NV	7	8	35	
Siemens AG	7	7	26	
Toshiba Corp	5	23	30	
Samsung Group	4	39	15	
NEC Corp	0	21	27	

Table 4-2 Leading licensors, by sector, selected sectors, 1985-1997 (cont.)

Company	Licenses Given	Licenses Taken	Cross-Licenses	Sector
Apple Computer Inc	7	6	6	Industrial Machinery and Equipment
Hewlett-Packard Co	7	4	15	SIC 35
Digital Equipment Corp	6	0	6	
AT & T Corp	5	5	7	
Fujitsu Ltd	5	8	10	
IBM Corp	5	10	22	
Hitachi Ltd	2	8	9	
NEC Corp	2	9	8	
Matsushita Electric Industrial	0	12	2	
Toshiba Corp	0	8	12	
Roche Holding AG	29	32	21	Chemicals and Allied Products
American Home Products Corp	21	19	7	SIC 28
Monsanto Co	14	14	16	
Dow Chemical Co	13	20	11	
Rhone-Poulenc	10	15	11	
Hoechst AG	7	34	14	
Merck & Co Inc	7	16	10	
Eli Lilly & Co	5	25	12	
Johnson & Johnson	3	22	8	

Source: Our calculations from SDC database on Joint Ventures and Alliances.

4.3 The Effects of "Missing" Technology Markets on Corporate Decisions

In order to understand the implications of markets for technology for corporate strategy, it is useful to begin with a more general discussion of missing markets for assets that distinguish a firm from its competitors. These assets include technology, production expertise and facilities, strong brand-name reputation, human assets, supplier networks and established marketing channels. Porter (1985; and 1990) argues that a competitive advantage arises when the firm can find ways for creating more value than its competitors do (see also Barney, 1991). The resource-based theory of the firm (Penrose, 1959; Grant, 1991) suggests that, to be sustainable, a competitive advantage must be underpinned by resources and capabilities for which well-functioning markets do not or cannot exist. Thus, the firm builds a sustainable competitive advantage by having access to assets that its competitors cannot access. Barney (1986) notes that ultimately, the possession of assets that provide sustainable competitive advantage must be rooted in imperfections in the resources used to create such assets, and these imperfections ultimately arise from differences in the expectations that firms hold about the future value of the assets. Cool and Dierickx (1989) argue that not all the resources or assets required to sustain competitive advantage can be bought and sold. Instead, such assets must be developed in-house, often over a period of time. Much of the thinking on technology strategy has approached the problem by implicitly or explicitly assuming that technological assets cannot be directly bought and sold. In this sense, our paper builds on the resource-based view of the firm by analyzing what happens when some assets that were not tradable become tradable.

What are the consequences of such a missing market for technology? The immediate consequence is that the innovator must exploit the technology in-house. That is, in order to extract the value from the technology, it (or rather its services) must be embodied in goods and services which are then sold. Such goods and services must have lower costs or command higher prices, to deliver returns that are greater than the competitive rate of returns – firms earn "quasi-rents".

Consider a case where a firm has developed a new cost-reducing technology for the production of a certain good. In order to extract value from the technology, the firm must use it to produce the good. Not only does this require the firm to have access to the complementary factors (such as land and physical equipment, marketing channels and so on), but the returns would also depend on the volume of output that the firm can produce and sell. If these complementary factors are themselves not traded in a competitive market, or if firms differ in their access to them, then firms that have superior access to these complementary capabilities will be able to derive greater value from the technology. Similarly, firms that can exploit the technology on a bigger scale will be able to derive greater value (Cohen and Klepper, 1996; Klepper, 1996).

Following this logic further, larger firms or firms with superior access to complementary capabilities will have a greater incentive to invest in the technology in the first instance. Taking this one step further, firms investing in technology would be well advised also to invest in the complementary capabilities that cannot be easily and efficiently acquired from the market. In other words, as Teece (1986) put it, firms have to invest in creating co-specialized assets to maximize their returns from developing new technology. In sum, lacking a market for technology, a firm must often incorporate other, complementary, assets in order to extract profits from the technology. Thus, large, well capitalized and integrated firms have greater incentives to invest in developing new technologies (Nelson, 1959). Conversely, smaller firms face major hurdles in developing and commercializing technology.

The situation is quite different when the asset can be sold or rented. In this case, the relative importance of complementary assets that exist within the boundaries of the individual firms diminishes in comparison to the existence of such complementary assets at the level of industries or markets as a whole. Clearly, as we shall also note below, transaction costs may increase the cost of acquiring the complementary assets externally compared to owning them in-house, even when such markets exist. In Arora, Fosfuri and Gambardella (2001) we discuss cognitive factors (such as context dependence and absorptive capacity), contractual problems and other market imperfections that can limit the ability of firms to access external complementary assets. As these imperfections become less important, then, the existence of co-specialized assets at the level of markets or industries may offset the lack of such complementary assets at the level of the firm.

Ultimately, a market for the asset provides the innovator – a firm that has developed new technology – with more options. Instead of embodying a newly developed technology in goods and services, a firm may choose to sell or license it to others, or may choose to buy it from external providers rather than develop it in-house. This does not mean that companies would only acquire technologies from external sources. Leading companies would probably choose the right balance between external acquisition and in-house development of technologies, even though for companies with lower in-house technological capabilities the existence of external technology sources may be critical to enhance their ability to produce and sell more innovative goods. Similarly, a market for technology assets does not mean that innovating firms will become pure licensing companies, although several small (and not so small) firms have been successful as specialized technology suppliers. Rather, the appropriate strategy in the presence of markets for technology depends on the efficiency of markets for other types of assets, including finance.

4.4 Licensing and IP Management in Large Firms

4.4.1 Revenue vs. rent-dissipation effects in the licensing strategies of the large firms

The decision by a large established company of whether or not to license its technology is the result of two main forces pushing in opposite directions: the "revenue effect" and the "profit dissipation effect" (see Arora and Fosfuri, 2003). Licensing forces a trade-off. Licensing and royalty revenues net of transaction costs (the "revenue effect") have to be balanced against the lower price cost margins and reduced market share that the increased competition (the "profit dissipation effect") from the licensee implies. Although the licensor has many different strategies to limit the extent of this latter effect (for instance, the contract might impose quantity restrictions or exclusive territories, unit royalties might be fixed so as to control the licensee's output), an entrant is nevertheless a potential threat to the licensor's market share. This implies that firms with a large product market share (and by implication, possessing the required complementary capabilities) are better off exploiting the technology in-house. On the other hand, if the product market share is small, the firm may be able to increase profits by licensing in addition to in-house exploitation. Similarly, licensing is more attractive when the licensee operates in a different market and is unlikely to compete very strongly.

This is exemplified by the different ways in which BP Chemicals has approached acetic acid and polyethylene. In acetic acid, BP Chemicals has strong proprietary technology and a substantial market share. It licenses very selectively, typically only licensing to get access to markets it would otherwise be unable to enter. By contrast, in polyethylene, BP's market share is small. Although it has good proprietary technology as well, there are a dozen other sources of technology for making polyethylene. Thus, BP has licensed its polyethylene technology very aggressively, competing with Union Carbide, which was the market leader in licensing polyethylene technology. Even here, BP initially tried not to license in Western Europe, where it had a substantial share of polyethylene capacity. However, other licensors continued to supply technology to firms that wished to produce polyethylene in Western Europe, with the result that BP found that it was losing potential licensing revenues without any benefits in the form of restraining entry.

BP is not alone in choosing to appropriate rents by licensing its technology. As discussed in Arora, Fosfuri and Gambardella (2001), several other firms, including companies such as Dow Chemicals, Procter & Gamble, Du-

Pont, Boeing and Monsanto, which have traditionally neither licensed their technology nor acquired technologies from the outside, have embraced technology licensing as an integral part of their technology management strategy. Table 4-3 reports information from the web sites of some leading corporations wherein they advertise internal technologies available for licenses. Some of these companies have even created special internal divisions that focus on the licensing of their technologies.

Table 4-3. Selected web pages advertising the licensing of intellectual property

Company	www address	Available for licensing
Boeing	http://www.boeing.com/assoc products/mdip/home.htm	Algorithms, laser technology and manufacturing, coatings, material processing, composite technologies, materials, factory hand tools, measurement system, fasteners, placement systems, video display, fiber optic sensors and demodulation systems
IBM	http://www.ibm.com/ibm/licensi ng	Processes used in integrated circuit, hard disk storage technology, device designs, source code
DuPont	http://www.dupont.com/corp/ science/ technologies.html	Fibers related, composites, chemical science and catalysis, analytical, environmental, electronics, biological
Union Carbide	http://www.unioncarbide.com/ business/busprgde.html	Ethylene oxide/ethylene glycol, industrial performance chemicals, polyolefin resins and compounds, solvents, intermediates and monomers, coating materials, specialty polymers and products
Philips	http://www.licensing.philips. com	CD, DVD, SACD, MPEG, AC3
Procter & Gamble	http://www.pgtechnologytrans fer.com	It is P&G's own online market for technology
Yet2.com (several founding members)	http://www.yet2.com	All types of technology. It is an online market for technology backed by several large US corporations (e.g. 3M, Allied Signal, Boeing, Dow Chemical, Ford, Honeywell, Polaroid, Procter & Gamble, Rockwell)

The recognition of the potential of the licensing market has been prompted by several related factors. First, the growing demand for technologies has increased the opportunities for selling technologies. Moreover, globalization, along with the low transportation costs of technologies, has meant that large companies with sizable technological portfolios, have the potential to exploit their technology on a very large scale, provided they license. Second, the better functioning and the increasingly better organization of markets for technology have eased the opportunities for this type of trading. As a result, several leading large companies have recognized the opportunities for incrementing their returns on R&D by selling out technologies rather than focusing only on their internal exploitation. Moreover, as noted earlier, there is a huge potential for this strategy, as corporations have a large share of technologies that they do not use themselves. These factor have prompted many of these companies to organize their technological portfolios, and to focus more forcefully on the effective management of their technologies and intellectual capital.

Clearly, there are many reasons why firms license, and not all of them can be ascribed to the specifics of markets for technology that we are trying to advance here. For instance, firms may license to create demand, to deter entry by stronger rivals or to dissuade rivals from launching their own R&D projects in the area. Most importantly, in certain sectors like electronics and software, firms may license their technology to create *de facto* market standards which they control and can exploit. However, in Arora, Fosfuri, and Gambardella (2001) we have collected examples which show that many large firms are refocusing their technology strategy to seek additional returns from their R&D efforts by selling their technologies disembodied from products.

4.5 Increasing Importance of "Intellectual Property" Management

The discussion above also points to the need for firms to take the management of their intellectual property seriously. Recent work by Granstrand (1999 and 2000) and Rivette and Kline (1999) details how patent data can be used for competitive intelligence, to identify potential licensees, to identify potential research staff as well as to understand where the firm should focus its research efforts. Grindley and Teece (1997) also note that in some firms the management of intellectual property has moved from the licensing of "non-core" technologies to become a central element in technology strategy. They recognize that, in industries like semiconductors and electronics, licensing and cross-licensing have become a means for generating revenues in alternative to direct production. In turn, this implies that management needs to undertake a more active and positive stance towards licensing and intellectual property in general. A related implication is that firms should be more careful about managing efficiently their intellectual property. In particular they should identify technological areas to apply more forcefully for patent protection. Since both applying and maintaining a patent can be costly, firms might be selective in their patenting strategy.

Firms are still experimenting with how best to manage their intellectual assets and no single organization scheme will suit all firms. However, what is clear is that the old system of leaving patenting and licensing decisions largely under the control of the general counsel's office is likely to change drastically.

For instance, Xerox is often seen as an example of a firm that has mismanaged its intellectual property, having invented but failed to profit from a number of pathbreaking developments such as the PC and the graphical user interface. The new CEO of Xerox, Rich Thoman, has clearly focused on IP management as a top priority. In 1997 Xerox had 8,000 patents, earning only $8.5 million in revenues, not covering even the maintenance costs. Xerox set in motion a systematic process for cataloguing and evaluating its patent portfolio, pruning and giving away (often to universities) patents it did not wish to keep, and monitoring the use of the rest. To guide the use of intellectual property, a Xerox Intellectual Property Office, XIPO, was also set up as a separate profit center headed by a vice president level officer, reporting directly to the top management of the firm, and oversees all patent and licensing decisions. Lucent has adopted a similar structure, creating an intellectual property business unit as a profit center, responsible for managing intellectual property on a corporate-wide level (Rivette and Kline, 1999).

Dow Chemicals has taken a somewhat different approach. Dow used to have two people to manage its licensing business. Individual business units made their own decisions, independently of each other. The recession in the early 1990s, and the need to cut costs, brought the over $1 billion R&D budget under close scrutiny. In 1994, Dow Chemicals significantly restructured the management of its intellectual property. Each of the 29,000 patents was valued and assigned to one of 15 major business units. A new structure was put in place under which intellectual property managers from each business unit would meet regularly to review patent activity on an enterprise-wide basis. Dow Chemicals now earns $125 million in patent licensing, up from $25 million in 1994 (Rivette and Kline, 1999).

4.6 The Different Challenges Faced by the Smaller Firms

Smaller firms face a different set of trade-offs compared with leading corporations in choosing between licensing and self-exploitation. Typically, small firms, and particularly the technology-based startups, have to acquire the complementary assets should they choose to exploit their innovation by commercializing it themselves. For startups the choice often amounts to a fundamental choice of the business model itself.[4] The choice depends not only on the efficiency of a market for technology, but also on the efficiency of the markets for the complementary assets. In other words, in deciding how to exploit their technology, small firms and startups must trade off the costs of acquiring capital and building in-house production, distribution and marketing capability against the rents that would be lost or shared with their partners in a licensing deal.

A commonplace about technology licensing, particularly from the perspective of small firms, is that the technology owner does not get the full return from the technology (e.g. Caves *et al.*, 1983). There are two main reasons for the failure of innovators to capture more fully the rents from innovation: inefficiency of contracts for technology and differences in bargaining power. A related potential problem is that with a royalty-based contract, the innovator's earnings depend on the effort and investment that its licensees make in commercializing the technology. Thus the firm is unable to control its own fate, increasing the chances of failure. For instance, Rambus, which has developed a highly successful architectural interface that speeds up data transfer, depends critically upon manufacturers of semiconductor devices, notably Intel, for its survival.[5] In many instances, this leads entrepreneurs to adopt a strategy where they try to acquire the complementary capabilities themselves to avoid having to share rents.

There are some potential pitfalls in such a strategy. The obvious one is that small firms also have limited bargaining power when it comes to acquiring capital required to build or acquire the complementary assets they need

[4] However, many start-ups adopt a business model where they begin by licensing technology and doing contract research for others and using those earnings to acquire the required complementary assets.

[5] Rambus licenses its technology to all firms that make microprocessors, DRAMS, ASICS, or PC controllers and chip sets. Rambus does not itself produce any semiconductor devices. It lacks any special advantage in the manufacture of semiconductor devices, which requires large investments in fabrication facilities in addition to a great deal of tacit knowledge. By not producing any semiconductor device, Rambus also steers clear of any potential conflict of interests and avoids competing with its customers.

to exploit the technology themselves. Further, to the extent that many of the complementary assets are themselves not readily accessible through a market mechanism, and to the extent that the entrepreneurial startup may not be very efficient at building those assets in-house, in-house exploitation is probably a much riskier and possibly less efficient strategy.

As with the market for technology, the markets for the other assets are also developing. The clearest example is the tremendous growth in angel and venture capital. As well, the great success that small startups have had in attracting financing through the equity market has reduced the cost of technology development as well as the cost of acquiring some of the complementary capabilities. Another example is the growth of merchant fabricators in semiconductors, such as TSCM and several such firms, which are developing for instance in countries like Taiwan. These firms have invested in large semiconductor foundries, and manufacture application-specific integrated circuits (ASICs) and other types of semiconductor devices for other firms. A startup firm that has developed new semiconductor technology can outsource production to a foundry, and market its devices itself by developing a marketing and distribution organization. Whether it ought to develop a marketing organization or appropriate the rents from its technology through licensing the technology to others depends in part on whether it is likely to be able to develop and manage a marketing operation efficiently.

As the case of Cambridge Display Technologies (CDT) indicates, an innovative startup firm often may not be able to manage downstream activities efficiently. CDT, a Cambridge University spin-off in Britain, specializes in conjugated polymer technologies, with light-emitting polymers being a key application. This can lead to the production of light-emitting plastics, for application in a wide range of businesses, from calculator, cellular phones and similar displays to laptop computer screens.

When the technology was first developed in the early 1990s, the CTD founders, mainly Cambridge University researchers, tried to develop and manufacture the technology. The result was that the company nearly went bankrupt. When professional managers were brought in, they changed the business model so that the key CTD business is to license the technology to established manufacturers. CDT has entered into licensing and co-development and manufacturing deals with companies like Philips Electronics, Seiko-Epson, Hoechst AG, and DuPont. This recognizes that although CDT has world-leading ability in the light-emitting polymers area, it does not have the developed manufacturing and marketing skills which are also essential to be a world-class display manufacturer. Through licensing out patents and performing technology transfer, CDT can enable its partners to apply their complementary skills to the technology to develop specific products for their markets.

There are other important considerations involved that militate against self-exploitation as well. Even if the firm can develop and manage the complementary assets efficiently, these assets may be much longer lived than the technology itself. This puts the innovator in the position of having to develop new technologies to "feed" these complementary assets. Failing which, the firm will be left with under-utilized manufacturing facilities or marketing network. Unless these assets, or their services, can be traded on the market, at least a part of the value of these assets will be lost.

The case of Syntex illustrates the risk involved when an innovative firm chooses to build up firm-specific complementary assets to exploit an innovation in-house. Syntex was founded in 1944 in Mexico City and relocated 20 years later to Palo Alto, California. During the early 1980s, the firm became extremely successful thanks to a non-steroidal anti-inflammatory drug based on the compound naproxen, Naprosyn, first marketed in 1976. In 1981 Syntex listed on the New York Stock Exchange and in 1987 it reached $1 billion in annual sales. However, when the patents on Naprosyn expired in 1993 and generic products started to flood the market, Syntex became financially distressed. Its stock price plummeted from $54 a share in January 1992 to $18 a share 18 months later. In late 1993, Roche Holding AG, the Swiss pharmaceutical firm, acquired Syntex in a deal valued at more than $5 billion. Syntex's operations in Palo Alto, after some restructuring, were transformed into a research facility with support and strategic marketing planning staff.

The proximate cause of Syntex's failure was its inability to discover a new blockbuster, when the patents on Naprosyn expired. Indeed, Syntex's strong research abilities notwithstanding, pharmaceutical innovations still depend a great deal upon serendipity. Bad luck associated with large fixed costs took Syntex into a huge financial distress which triggered the acquisition by Roche.

Leaving aside the question of whether Syntex's research productivity had declined, consider the role of the business model. Had Syntex not built up a substantial downstream manufacturing and marketing capability, it might have been able to ride out the lean periods, because it would not have to find the revenues to support its downstream operations. Moreover, this business model also implied that Syntex had to invest in the extremely costly drug development and clinical trials to find its potential blockbuster drugs. The problem is not that Syntex had to exit the market. Had Syntex failed because its research ceased to be productive, exit would be both privately and socially desirable. Syntex's research capability continued to be valuable, as evidenced by how Roche repositioned Syntex after the acquisition. In sum, the problem was that Syntex failed as a pharmaceutical firm, destroying some of the value of the downstream assets that it had invested in. Put differently, even if integration did not hurt its research productivity, the failure of research destroyed the value of the Syntex brand name plus the value (partially) of other firm-specific assets that Syntex had built up.

Finally, and perhaps most important from a long-run perspective, integration may reduce the innovative potential of the firm, because the acquisition of the complementary assets inevitably increases the size of firms and induces important changes in the culture of the firm and in the speed and fluidity of information flows. As Levinthal and March (1993) note, organizations divide attention and resources between two broad groups of activities. They engage in the pursuit of new knowledge, exploration, and in the use and development of what is known, exploitation. Although not identical, exploration is similar to the notion of research and development, while exploitation is closer to the more downstream activities of production and marketing. A blend of exploration and exploitation is desirable, but as March (1991) and Levinthal and March (1993) note, dynamics within organizations may lead exploitation to drive out exploration. For instance, learning processes driven by experience, as is typically the case in manufacturing and marketing, tend to favor exploitation, because exploitation provides clearer, earlier and closer feedback.

These dynamics are hard to resist in larger organizations. Large organizations are unable to provide high-powered incentives for exploration. Contrast that with the incentives that the threat of bankruptcy and stock options provide for exploration in small startups. Further, as Stiglitz and Weiss (1981) have demonstrated, limited liability implies that smaller organizations, with fewer fixed assets at stake, will be willing to undertake more risks. Large organizations can try to encourage exploration by forming and nurturing small sub-units that are isolated from the rest of the organization. "Corporate ventures", however, have inherent limitations and, as Levinthal and March (1993) note, they tend to yield modest returns at best. In sum, there are reasons to believe that as a research-intensive company converts itself into an integrated firm, with in-house manufacturing and marketing units, its research productivity is likely to decline.

4.7 The External Acquisition of Technology and the "Not-Invented-Here" Syndrome

Markets for technology also affect the firm in its role as a user of technology (e.g. Granstrand *et al.*, 1992.) The objective is not only to maximize the revenues from the firm's actual stock of technologies, but also to identify technologies that are available at a reasonable price and that will increase the value of existing assets. This does not imply that firms can simply rely on outside technologies and need not invest in R&D itself. Evaluating technologies and being able to use them requires substantial in-house scientific and technological expertise (Arora and Gambardella, 1994; Cohen and Levinthal, 1989). As Mowery (1984) has pointed out, a firm is far better equipped to absorb the output of external R&D if it is also performing some amount of R&D internally.

The ability of the firm to evaluate and use outside technology may be conditioned by its existing organizational structure, which limits information flows, and how opportunities are framed (e.g. Henderson and Clark, 1990.) Sometimes, firms tend to disregard external technology options completely. The "not-invented-here" syndrome often has legitimate roots, as corporations attempt to instill pride in the achievements of their researchers. It may also serve to motivate the firm's researchers. Rotemberg and Saloner (1994) develop a model in which a "not-invented-here" type of corporate culture may serve a valuable role of committing the corporation to develop the technologies invented by the firm's in-house R&D departments, thereby providing the appropriate incentives to the researchers. However, in a world where R&D capabilities are widely diffused, such a commitment device is likely to be very costly.

Put simply, markets for technology increase the penalty of the "not-invented-here" syndrome. In the first place, the wide diffusion of new technology producers (other firms, smaller technology suppliers, universities, etc) makes R&D duplications likely. Even in a specialized field, several research units may be working on similar problems, or there could be units that have already solved problems that other units are facing. By relying only on internally developed solutions, companies can end up "reinventing the wheel".[6]

This also points to the importance of systematic monitoring of external technological developments on a worldwide basis. By using and building upon basic or generic technologies developed elsewhere, companies can focus on developing specialized applications that better suit the needs of their local markets. "Global" markets for technology can improve the innovation potential and the competitiveness of companies in technologically and possibly economically less dynamic regions. These markets permit an effective division of labor between technology producers located in areas that are more efficient in the production of technology, and local producers which have greater comparative advantages in understanding the needs of their customers.

4.8 Industry-Level Effects: Vertical Specialization, Entry and Competition

At the industry level, markets for technology provide the classical Smithian and Stiglerian advantages of division of labor. The story of the SEFs (specialized engineering firms) in chemical processing is a natural example. (See Arora and Gambardella, 1998, and Arora, Fosfuri and Gambardella, 2001.) SEFs are firms specialized in the design, engineering, and construction of chemical plants. Although some of them were founded as early as the 1920s, SEFs arose in the aftermath of World War II following the rapid growth of demand for chemical products. SEFs reaped the advantages of specialization. By working for many clients, they benefited from learning by doing, and by repeatedly selling their expertise (through licenses or engineering services) they could spread the cost of accumulating that ex-

[6] To provide some anecdotal evidence, one of us participated in 1998 in a Commission for the evaluation of R&D projects submitted for government support funding in Italy. Most of the projects were submitted by large Italian companies, or consortia of firms and other institutions. Even though the government program did require a state-of-the-art report for the proposed technology to be enclosed with the application, most projects charged costs for internal R&D activities that involved several early steps before the development of the ultimate technology. Few projects mentioned costs for acquiring externally developed technologies (e.g. licensing costs) which their innovation could build upon. A casual search from existing patent databases revealed that in a number of cases the applicants could have exploited existing technologies to build their innovation, or at least they could have found specialist individuals or institutions that could potentially offer valuable technical consultancy services in the specific domain of their project.

pertise over a larger output. As with any division of labor, the advantages of vertical specialization then translated into greater efficiency in the downstream industry as well. (See also Freeman, 1968.) Over time, the advantages that specialized engineering firms enjoyed in design and construction of certain types of chemical plants made them the preferred source for such services. In many cases, these specialized firms also provided in-house proprietary technology, often on very attractive terms. This reinforces our earlier point that that when markets for technology exist, the penalties from not monitoring the opportunities that are created by them, or from not using these markets, or even worse, from persisting with the "not-invented-here" syndrome, can be substantial.

Markets for technology lower barriers to entry, especially when they give rise to an industry of specialized technology suppliers. For instance, while the SEFs originated as an American phenomenon, during the 1950s and the 1960s the US SEFs became a source of technology for the European and Japanese chemical industry. This enabled the European and Japanese chemical producers to rise and grow, and to compete with the US chemical companies in the international market. Similarly, as Table 4-5 shows, SEFs from the advanced countries nowadays supply technologies to the chemical producers in the less developed countries, and these companies compete with the chemical industry of the First World in the developing country markets largely thanks to the availability of Western technologies. More generally, in the international context, markets for technology can lead to a dramatic shortening of the product life cycles.[7]

---

[7] The pattern just described is not different in several high-tech industries today. Specialized suppliers in biotechnology, software or semiconductors accrue typical advantages of specialization in their areas of technological expertise. Moreover, while many of these specialized technology suppliers originated in the US, and they are still largely US-based, their services and technology are available to the European and Japanese companies as well, which have entered into a number of licensing agreements and other types of alliances with US technology-based firms.

Table 4-4 Technology transaction of the leading participants in the market for technology, 1985-97, by sector

SIC	Firm	Total Deals	Licenses Given	Licenses Taken	Cross Licenses	R&D Agreements	Cross-border Deals	Sector
87	AT & T Corp	13			1	13	5	Eng. & Mgmt Services
87	Baxter International Inc	9	1	4	3	7	3	Eng. & Mgmt Services
87	Bristol-Myers Squibb Co	10		4	1	10	5	Eng. & Mgmt Services
87	IBM Corp	17	1		3	15	10	Eng. & Mgmt Services
87	Monsanto Co	10	2	4	1	9	6	Eng. & Mgmt Services
87	Motorola Inc	8		1	1	7	6	Eng. & Mgmt Services
87	Roche Holding AG	21	2	5	11	21	17	Eng. & Mgmt Services
87	Sandoz AG	10	0	1	1	10	10	Eng. & Mgmt Services
73	AT & T Corp	97	11	22	21	79	16	Business Services
73	Digital Equipment Corp	83	8	20	21	64	15	Business Services
73	Fujitsu Ltd	62	6	11	34	54	58	Business Services
73	Hewlett-Packard Co	132	13	24	28	104	27	Business Services
73	IBM Corp	277	34	48	69	222	78	Business Services
73	Microsoft Corp	204	44	45	55	140	39	Business Services
73	Apple Computer Inc	86	25	18	15	58	20	Business Services
73	Novell Inc	100	17	17	22	73	13	Business Services
73	Oracle Corp	88	10	9	35	73	18	Business Services

SIC	Firm	Total Deals	Licenses Given	Licenses Taken	Cross Licenses	R&D Agreements	Cross-border Deals	Sector
73	Sun Microsystems Inc	105	24	16	16	73	17	Business Services
48	AT & T Corp	18	4	3	5	13	5	Communication
48	Bell South Corp	8	1	0	1	8	2	Communication
48	Cable & Wireless PLC	8	2	0	1	7	6	Communication
48	IBM Corp	9	0	2	5	6	2	Communication
48	Japan	7	0	0	4	7	6	Communication
48	Kokusai Denshin Denwa	7	2	0	2	7	7	Communication
48	Motorola Inc	14	3	1	2	8	6	Communication
48	Pacific Telesis group	7	3	0	1	7	5	Communication
48	QUALCOMM Inc	17	15	0	1	3	8	Communication
48	Sprint Corp	9	0	1	3	8	6	Communication
38	Baxter International Inc	9	3	4	1	4	1	Instruments
38	Daimler-Benz AG	10	2	0	4	9	10	Instruments
38	Eastern Kodak Co Inc	13	1	3	1	10	5	Instruments
38	General Motors Corp	11	4	2	3	11	6	Instruments

SIC	Firm	Total Deals	Licenses Given	Licenses Taken	Cross Licenses	R&D Agreements	Cross-border Deals	Sector
38	Hewlett-Packard Co	11	2	1	5	9	4	Instruments
38	Honeywell Inc	14	4	0	4	7	8	Instruments
38	Johnson & Johnson	10	0	7	2	10	4	Instruments
38	Eli Lilly & Co	10	3	4	3	6	1	Instruments
38	Philips Electronics NV	13	2	2	1	7	10	Instruments
38	Siemens AG	14	1	3	4	9	11	Instruments
37	Boeing Co	15	1	1	3	14	5	Transp. Equip.
37	Daimler-Benz AG	27	0	0	10	27	22	Transp. Equip.
37	Fiat SpA	14	1	0	2	13	13	Transp. Equip.
37	Ford Motor Co	26	1	1	7	26	14	Transp. Equip.
37	France	20	0	0	7	20	18	Transp. Equip.
37	General Electric Co	13	0	0	3	13	10	Transp. Equip.
37	General Motors Corp	25	2	1	3	25	9	Transp. Equip.
37	Siemens AG	14	1	0	1	14	12	Transp. Equip.
37	United Technologies Corp	22	3	1	6	19	12	Transp. Equip.

SIC	Firm	Total Deals	Licenses Given	Licenses Taken	Cross Licenses	R&D Agreements	Cross-border Deals	Sector
36	AT & T Corp	83	11	11	36	63	32	Electronic Equip
36	Intel Corp	70	19	8	20	52	21	Electronic Equip
36	IBM Corp	104	18	9	38	87	37	Electronic Equip
36	Motorola Inc	113	23	15	33	84	51	Electronic Equip
36	NEC Corp	66	0	21	27	51	60	Electronic Equip
36	Philips Electronics NV	72	7	8	35	56	72	Electronic Equip
36	Samsung Group	62	4	39	15	22	62	Electronic Equip
36	Siemens AG	56	7	7	26	46	57	Electronic Equip
36	Texas Instruments Inc	88	18	14	39	42	49	Electronic Equip
36	Toshiba Corp	75	5	23	30	56	69	Electronic Equip
35	AT & T Corp	24	5	5	7	17	9	Ind. Mach. & Equip
35	Digital Equipment Corp	26	6	0	6	22	4	Ind. Mach. & Equip
35	Fujitsu Ltd	32	5	8	10	19	27	Ind. Mach. & Equip
35	Hewlett-Packard Co	37	7	4	15	28	14	Ind. Mach. & Equip
35	Hitachi Ltd	27	2	8	9	19	22	Ind. Mach. & Equip
35	IBM Corp	75	5	10	22	63	32	Ind. Mach. & Equip

SIC	Firm	Total Deals	Licenses Given	Licenses Taken	Cross Licenses	R&D Agreements	Cross-border Deals	Sector
35	Matsushita Electric Industrial	21	0	12	2	10	19	Ind. Mach. & Equip
35	NEC Corp	29	2	9	8	23	28	Ind. Mach. & Equip
35	Apple Computer Inc	27	7	6	6	17	16	Ind. Mach. & Equip
35	Toshiba Corp	28	0	8	12	18	28	Ind. Mach. & Equip
28	American Home Products	56	21	19	7	31	20	Chemicals
28	Dow Chemical Co	67	13	20	11	40	32	Chemicals
28	Hoechst AG	72	7	34	14	42	69	Chemicals
28	Johnson & Johnson	42	3	22	8	25	11	Chemicals
28	Eli Lilly & Co	58	5	25	12	38	14	Chemicals
28	Merk & Co Inc	47	7	16	10	33	19	Chemicals
28	Monsanto Co	55	14	14	16	38	35	Chemicals
28	Rhone-Poulenc	48	10	15	11	31	43	Chemicals
28	Roche Holding AG	94	29	32	21	53	92	Chemicals
28	SmithKline Beecham PLC	65	10	38	9	41	60	Chemicals

Table 4-5. Buyers of chemical process technologies by source of technology

Technology Buyer	Total number of plants	Share of licenses from SEFs	Share of in-house technology	Share of licenses from other producers
Third World Companies	4068	43%	3%	54%
First World Companies	4905	28%	37%	45%
Large First World Companies (*)	2836	22%	52%	26%
Small First World Companies	2069	37%	16%	45%

(*) This is a sample of 153 first-world chemical firms that have reported a chemical turnover of more than 1 billion US dollars in 1988

Source: Arora and Fosfuri (2003)

The example also highlights a closely related point. Markets for technology may reduce the importance of technology as a source of competitive advantages. The point is not that technological superiority in chemical processing is unimportant. Technologically less sophisticated chemical companies (such as those in the developing countries) were likely to be less effective in taking advantage of the SEF technologies, and gaps between technologically advanced and less advanced firms (or countries) did not disappear. Moreover, the absorptive capacity argument (Cohen and Levinthal, 1989) does underscore that even if technology is more widely available, there are differences in the ability of using it according to the internal technological capabilities of the companies. However, to keep with our example of the chemical industry, the presence of the SEFs meant that the gap between technologically advanced and less advanced companies (and countries) was reduced, and entry by newcomer chemical firms with no significant technological expertise became possible. One implication of this role played by the SEFs has been that many chemical firms exited products which they innovated and in which they had a great deal of experience in production.[8]

A natural response to the increase in competition produced by markets for technology is that firms have to cut costs, possibly by exiting businesses in which they lack a clear source of advantage. Another response is that they have to look for other distinctive competitive assets. As we have discussed in

[8] For instance, ICI, which first commercialized polyethylene and polyester, has virtually exited from these markets (Arora and Gambardella, 1998).

section 3, the resource-based theory of the firm argues that a competitive advantage is sustainable only if it is underpinned by resources and capabilities that are scarce and imperfectly mobile. The heterogeneity of demand can be an important source of such distinctive capabilities. In the first place, demand heterogeneity implies that companies can extract greater value from their customers by specifying products or services that better suit their special requirements. At the same time, customers are often unable to articulate their needs in ways that can be readily transferred to the producing firms. This information can only be acquired through close relationships with them; moreover, once established, these relationships are difficult to replicate by the competitors. Finally, the ability to highlight the specificities of demand (e.g. by customizing products, services, etc) can only be enhanced by a greater availability of a crucial complementary asset for this scope like technology.[9]

Thus, while knowledge about basic technologies could circulate to a greater extent, the tacit component of the knowledge bases in industry may shift towards information and expertise about what the individual customers want. This information is less tradable, and therefore it is likely to become a prominent source of competitive advantages. With markets for technology, companies could then take advantage of the lower cost of acquiring technologies, and focus on the combination of internal and external technologies to provide distinct solutions to their markets, customers and users. This has to be based on solid understanding of their needs, along with substantial investments in relationships with their customers and markets.[10]

4.9 Conclusions

There is growing evidence that trade in technology has become an important phenomenon in recent years. This paper has analyzed how markets for technology affect the technology strategies of companies.

The most direct implication is that leading companies can now sell technologies that they do not use in-house, thereby increasing their potential

---

[9] For example, platform or general-purpose technologies (like many information and communications technologies today) often provide a basis for further specifications of basic designs.

[10] For example, since the 1950s the chemical companies have paid significant attention to product differentiation by developing a range of different grades of their materials to suit the specific requirements of different markets or users. Similarly, control of the production of basic feedstock, through direct investments in oil-producing countries, has been for many years a relatively more important source of competitive advantages than technology for the leading oil and petrochemical manufacturers.

returns to R&D. For small firms and technology-based startups, markets for technology increase the effectiveness of strategies based on the specialization of such firms in technology development. Since markets for technology also involve firms as technology buyers, the growth of such markets increases the importance of external monitoring of technological developments, and it increases the penalty of insularity and the "not-invented-here" syndrome. In addition, markets for technology may reduce the relative importance of technology as a source of distinctive advantage, because the advantage of possessing some critical knowledge or technology may be limited by the ability of the competitors to acquire it from other sources. The natural consequence is that companies have to focus on other internal assets that may provide them with distinctive advantages. Investment in the idiosyncratic needs and characteristics of specific markets and buyers is an obvious candidate. Thus, markets for technology may increase the importance of downstream strategies for differentiation.

Markets for technology also have direct implications for intellectual property rights. A well-known paper by Merges and Nelson (1990) argued that large firms have many ways to protect their inventions (downstream and financial assets, etc). This implies that the additional effect of stronger property rights on their incentives to innovate is small. In fact, if the world were populated only by the larger firms, stronger property rights could lead to undesired consequences for welfare, as they would induce little additional incentives for innovation, while seriously undermining its diffusion.

But small firms and startups have fewer opportunities to appropriate their inventions other than a legal stake on them. Other things being equal, stronger intellectual property rights can make a difference for them. Two advantages could arise. First, more small firms and startups would engage in the production of new technologies, as they would now be able to profit from this activity even if they are unable to mobilize the costly assets to develop, produce and sell them. The degree of exploration in the economy increases. Second, to the extent that the smaller firms have some sort of comparative advantage (organizational or else) in upstream creative research activities, the implied division of labor with the larger firms, or with whoever is going to undertake the more costly developments of the technology, would be socially desirable.

In sum, stronger intellectual property rights can have serious social costs. In Arora, Fosfuri and Gambardella (2001) (see in particular Chapter 10), we discussed for example the tensions that they may create on the social norms of open science or the problem associated with the so-called fragmentation of intellectual property rights, which may forestall the development of systemic innovations when many parties have property rights on key complementary components. These costs, however, have to be assessed against their potential advantages. One of them is that stronger intellectual property rights may encourage the development of markets for technology, with implied benefits in terms of greater strategic options by the firms (whether small or large), advantages of specialization and division of labor, greater downstream competition because of wider diffusion of the technologies, and greater technological experimentation because of the entry of many potential technology suppliers.

4.10 Literature References

Arora A. and Fosfuri A. The Market for Technology in the Chemical Industry: Causes and Consequences, *Revue D'Economíe Industrielle* 2000; 92: 317-32.

Arora A. and Fosfuri A. Licensing the Market for Technology. *Journal of Economic Behavior and Organization* 2003, Vol. 52, Issue 2, pp. 277-295.

Arora A., Fosfuri A. and Gambardella A. *Markets for Technology: The Economics of Innovation and Corporate Strategy.* Cambridge MA: The MIT Press, 2001.

Arora A. and Gambardella A. The changing technology of technological change: General and abstract knowledge and the division of innovative labour. *Research Policy* 1994; 23: 523-32.

Arora A. and Gambardella A. "Evolution of Industry Structure in the Chemical Industry". In *Chemicals and Long Term Economic Growth,* Arora, A., Landau, R. and Rosenberg, N., eds. New York: John Wiley and Sons, 1998.

Barney J.B. Strategic Factor Markets: Expectations, Luck and Business Strategy. *Management Science* 1986; 32(10): 1231-41.

Barney J.B. Firms' Resources and Sustained Competitive Advantage. *Journal of Management* 1991; 17: 99-120.

British Technology Group (BTG). 1998. www.btgplc.com

Caves R., Crookel H. and Killing J.P. The imperfect market for technology licensing. *Oxford Bulletin of Economics and Statistics* 1983: 249-267.

Cohen W. and Levinthal D. Innovation and Learning: The Two Faces of R&D. *Economic Journal* 1989; 99: 569-96.

Cohen W. and Klepper S. Firm Size and the Nature of Innovation within Industries: The Case of Process and Product R&D. *Review of Economics and Statistics* 1996; 78(2): 232-43.

Cool K. and Dierickx I. Asset Stock Accumulation and Sustainability of Competitive Advantage. *Management Science* 1989; 35(12): 1504-13.

Dengan S.A. The Licensing Payoff from U.S. R&D. *Journal of the Licensing Executives Society International* 1998; 33(4).

Freeman C. Chemical Process Plant: Innovation and the World Market. *National Institute Economic Review* 1968; 45: 29-51, August.

Granstrand O. *The Economics and Management of Intellectual Property*. UK: Edward Elgar, 1999.

Granstrand O. The Shift Towards Intellectual Capitalism – The Role of Infocom Technologies. *Research Policy* 2000; 29: 1061-80.

Granstrand O., Bohlin E., Oskarsson C and Sjöberg N..External Technology Acquisition in Large Multi-technology Corporations. *R&D Management* 1992; 22 (2): 111-33.

Grant R.M. The Resource-Based Theory of Competitive Advantage: Implications for Strategy Formulation. *California Management Review* 1991; 119-45.

Grindley P.C. and Teece D.J. Licensing and Cross-Licensing in Semiconductors and Electronics. *California Management Review* 1997; 39(2): 8-41.

Hall B.H. and Ham R. The Patent Paradox Revisited: Determinants of Patenting in the US Semiconductor Industry, 1980-1994. *Rand Journal of Economics* 2001; 32 (1): 101-28.

Henderson R. and Clark K. Architectural Innovation: The Reconfiguration of Existing Product Technologies and the Failure of Established Firms. *Administrative Science Quarterly* 1990; 35 (1): 9-30.

Klepper S. Entry, Exit and Innovation over the Product Life Cycle. *American Economic Review* 1996; 86(3): 562-83.

Kortum S and Lerner J. What is Behind the Recent Surge in Patenting. *Research Policy* 1999; 28: 1-22.

Lamoreaux N and Sokoloff K., *Location and Technological Change in the American Glass Industry during the Late Nineteenth and Early Twentieth Centuries*. NBER WP 5938. Cambridge MA: NBER, 1997.

Lamoreaux N and Sokoloff K. ".Inventors, Firms, and the Market for Technology: US Manufacturing in the Late Nineteenth and Early Twentieth Centuries". In *Learning by Firms, Organizations, and Nations*, Lamoreaux, N., Raff, D. and Temin, P., eds. Chicago: The University of Chicago Press,. 1998.

Levinthal D.A. and March J.G. The Myopia of Learning. *Strategic Management Journal* 1993; 14: 95-112.

Linden G and Somaya D. *System-on-a-Chip Integration in the Semiconductor Industry: Industry Structure and Firm Strategies*. Draft. Berkeley, CA: University of California, 2000.

March J.G. Exploration and Exploitation in Organizational Learning. *Organization Science* 1991; 2: 71-87.

Merges R and Nelson R. On the Complex Economics of Patent Scope. *Columbia Law Review* 1990; 90 (4): 839-916.

Mowery D. Firm Structure, Government Policy, and the Organization of Industrial Research. *Business History Review* 1984; 58: 504-31.

Nelson R.R. The Simple Economics of Basic Scientific Research. *Journal of Political Economy* 1959; 67 (2): 297-306.

Penrose E.T. *The Theory of Growth of the Firm.* Oxford: Blackwell, 1959.

Porter M. *Competitive Advantage: Creating and Sustaining Superior Performance.* New York: Free Press, 1985.

Porter M. *The Competitive Advantage of Nations.* New York: Free Press 1990.

Rivette K.G. and Kline D. *Rembrandt In The Attic: Unlocking the Hidden Value of Patents.* Boston, MA: Harvard Business School Press, 1999.

Rotemberg J.J. and Saloner G. Benefits of Narrow Business Strategies. *American Economic Review* 1994; 84 (5): 1330-49.

Stiglitz J.E. and Weiss A. Credit Rationing in Markets with Imperfect Information. *American Economic Review* 1981; 71(3): 393-410.

Teece D.J. Profiting from Technological Innovation. *Research Policy* 1986; 15(6): 285-305.

Teece D.J. "Technological Change and the Nature of the Firm". In *Technological Change and Economic Theory*, Dosi, G. *et al.*, eds. London: Printer Publishers, 1988.

Teece D.J. Capturing Value from Knowledge Assets: The New Economy, Markets for Know-How, and Intangible Assets. *California Management Review* 1998; 40 (3): 55-79.

Chapter 5

NEW INTERNATIONAL ARRANGEMENTS IN INTELLECTUAL PROPERTY AND COMPETITION LAW

John H. Barton
Stanford University, Law School, Stanford, California, USA

Chapter contents:

Abstract: Intellectual property plays an increasingly important role in the international Intellectual Property[1] (IP) law and antitrust law can no longer be viewed separately. Technology has become so important that IP incentives to research must be maintained in order to benefit the consumer. There will be no investment in research unless there is a chance of recouping the investment through supranormal profits, i.e. profits based on sales at prices above marginal cost. At the same time, this dynamic efficiency goal must be balanced against a more traditional static efficiency goal, in order to ensure appropriate allocation of non-research resources and to avoid the inflation of prices to the consumer. The balance between these dynamic and static goals must be reflected in the supporting bodies of IP and competition law. It may today be among the most important issues in antitrust law, both because of the growth in the scope of intellectual property, especially of patents,[2] and because of the fundamental im-

[1] The term "intellectual property" or IP is used here quite broadly to denote all proprietary positions include ownership of a patent, trade secret, or copyright, or control of a standard, that permit appropriation of the benefits of innovation.

[2] See T. Maris (Chairman, U.S. Federal Trade Commission), "Competition and Intellectual Property Policy: The Way Ahead", before American Bar Association, Antitrust Section Fall Forum, Washington, D.C., Nov. 15, 2001.

O. Granstrand (ed.), Economics, Law and Intellectual Property, 109-121.

portance of technology to the future of the economy. If this is true domestically, it is even more true internationally. Because economic growth is heavily dependent on technology,[3] encouragement of technology can only accelerate the global consumer benefits of free trade.[4] Moreover, nations often attempt to compete through encouraging their technologically-advanced industries. By negotiating the TRIPS Agreement, the world has now chosen to recognize the importance of IP in world trade. At a static level, TRIPS implies that the developing nations will pay royalties to developed nations, who are the current leaders in technology. This, of course, is a broadly discussed phenomenon, particularly with respect to pharmaceuticals.[5] But, of far greater importance to the future, the dynamics of the new system may be likely to favor the industries of developed nations. The IP rights which these developed-world industries hold may sometimes prove anticompetitive by enabling these industries to slow entry of others into the market and thus prolong their period of market dominance. Evaluation of this possibility requires a much deeper analysis of the way that intellectual property rights are used. A response to it is likely to require the definition of certain specific antitrust principles, and possibly their harmonization, as in the form of a World Trade Organization (WTO) Code.[6] This paper explores three specific contexts in which IP rights may prolong developed-world market dominance, and generally describes the IP/competition law principles likely to be helpful. It concludes by exploring whether these principles need to be harmonized through an international code and defining first steps to be taken.[7]

---

[3] R. Solow, "Technological Change and the Aggregate Production Function", 39 *Rev. Econ. & Stat.* 312 (1957).

[4] There are, of course, arguments that infant industry protection can favor innovation and dynamic competition at the expense of static competition. This is generally true only in certain circumstances. The argument in text is much broader – that free trade and dynamic innovation work in parallel.

[5] See, e.g., J. Lanjouw, "The Introduction of Pharmaceutical Product Patents in India: "Heartless Exploitation of the Poor and Suffering?", Yale University, Economic Growth Center, Center Discussion Paper No. 775 (Aug. 1997); and the papers presented at the Høsbjør WHO/WTO Workshop on Differential Pricing and Financing of Essential Drugs, 8-11 April 2001, available at www.wto.org/english/tratop_e/trips_e/tn_hosbjor_e.htm.

[6] The parties to the Doha Ministerial Conference in November 2001 agreed to steps towards antitrust negotiations as part of the new round of world trade negotiations. World Trade Organization, Ministerial Conference, Ministerial Declaration, WT/MIN(01)/ DEC/W1, 14 Nov. 2001. Almost certainly, however, these negotiations will concentrate on more traditional trade-antitrust issues such as cartels.

[7] See R. Anderson, "Intellectual Property Rights, Competition Policy and International Trade: Reflections on the Work of the WTO Working Group on the Interaction between Trade and Competition Policy" (World Trade Forum, 2001, Vol. 3, Ch.17). There is of course a much broader international antitrust agenda that includes, for instance, procedural responses to national monopolies, export cartels, and the taming of anti-dumping law. See generally, e.g.,

5.1 Licensing and Leverage

The first example to consider is that of the use of IP (or other monopoly power) in one market to achieve control of another market, as exemplified by Microsoft's efforts to use its market power in Windows to obtain market power in browsers.[8] This is what economists traditionally analyze as "tying". Contemporary economic arguments generally favor such behavior, on the grounds that tying normally serves only as a way to price-discriminate.[9] Such price discrimination enables the IP holder to obtain a greater portion of the area under the demand curve, and thus provides greater research incentive while serving those who are willing to pay a range of prices. For example, contemporary tying analysis permits a firm to require that its patented machine be used only with its complementary materials. The logic is that this permits the firm to charge less for the machine and more for the complementary materials, and thus allows the seller/licensor to charge a higher net price to the heavy user than to the light user. Although this logic is relatively new, and replaces an earlier contrary perception,[10] it is today generally accepted by economists and lawyers in both the United States and Europe.[11]

The logic, however, fails in markets with network externalities (and such externalities are typical of contemporary high-technology markets). The Microsoft case provides a good example. Microsoft's power in the Windows market is a proprietary right and, for all practical purposes, a form of IP right. Because Windows is a standard and Microsoft can legally prevent direct copying, Microsoft has substantial power in the Windows/operating system market and other firms can't enter readily with competing operating sys-

---

Report (2001) of the Working Group on the Interaction Between Trade and Competition Policy to the General Council, World Trade Organization, WT/WGTCP/5, 8 October 2001; *Report (2000) of the Working Group on the Interaction Between Trade and Competition Policy to the General Council*, World Trade Organization, WT/WGTCP/4, 30 November 2000; and the earlier reports in the same series. Although most of the discussion in these reports is about cartels, the issues of IP and competition policy are raised in ¶ 104 of the 2000 report.

[8] United States v. Microsoft Corp., 253 F.3d 54 (DC Cir 2001).

[9] The key articles urging a "new" antitrust approach to IP are W. Baxter, "Legal Restrictions on Exploitation of the Patent Monopoly: An Economic Analysis", 76 *Yale L. J.* 267 (1966) and L. Kaplow, "The Patent-Antitrust Intersection: A Reappraisal", 97 *Harv. L. Rev.* 1813 (1984).

[10] See, e.g., International Salt v. United States, 322 U.S. 392 (1947), for the earlier contrary perspective.

[11] E.U. Commission Regulation 240/96 on the application of Article 85(3) of the Treaty to certain categories of technology transfer agreements, OJ L31/96; U.S. Department of Justice and Federal Trade Commission, *Antitrust Guidelines for the Licensing of Intellectual Property* (1995).

tems. Most of the application software is written for Windows, because most computer users use Windows, and most computer users use Windows because most of the application software is written for Windows. Now, when Microsoft ties its browser to Windows, it is not attempting to achieve the kind of price discrimination in the Windows market that was discussed in the previous paragraph. Rather, Microsoft is attempting to establish power in the new market, and to benefit in that market from exactly the same kind of network externalities that it benefits from in the Windows market. If all goes well for its strategy, it will displace others from the browser market, just as it has displaced them from the operating system market, and it will have enough unique aspects in its browser that its browser becomes the standard.

Not all such activity can be bad, because every firm in a high technology industry must recognize that its markets will constantly be changing and must constantly strive to use its current competitive advantages as a basis for moving into the new markets. At the same time, where there is the possibility of a "market tipping" of the type just described (i.e. the possibility that by acquiring enough of a market, a firm obtains the benefit of a network externality that enables it to dominate the market), a firm with a dominant position in a near-by market may have an especially strong ability to move into the new markets. From the perspective of maintaining a reasonable incentive to innovate (as well as of protecting against monopoly pricing), we want the market leader to have an optimal risk of not winning the battle. Although the exact standard certainly requires a balance, competition should almost certainly prohibit a firm with substantial market power from using its licensing rights (as distinguished from, say, technological linkages) to exclude competitors from the new emerging market. Firms in dominant positions should not be permitted to use contracts like those Microsoft used to prohibit computer suppliers from including competing software among that preloaded on the computer.[12]

This is an international issue because more and more high-technology industries operate on a global scale – certainly Microsoft's network externalities arise on such a scale. Moreover, these global industries more and more involve information, standardization, and software, in which the markets are

---

[12] Such contracts are significantly restricted in the provisions of the Microsoft consent decree, as agreed by the United States and Microsoft, but not accepted by all States that are also party to the litigation, or, as of early 2002, approved by the U.S. District Court, United States v. Microsoft, Revised Proposed Final Judgment, submitted to the court on Nov. 6, 2001, available at www.doj.gov/atr/cases/9400/9495.htm.

likely to have the kinds of externalities just described.[13] Indeed, the organization of standards by groups of leading firms – often from a combination of nations – poses very similar issues, for these standards may place other firms at a disadvantage.[14] United States, European, and Japanese information technology firms can arguably use their IP to slow entry by developing nations' firms – and the U.S. firms clearly have a lead over all others. Thus, depending especially on the way the law is applied in the United States, the world (including the U.S. consumer) may fail to receive the benefit of the technology of the new firms that might arise were there no inappropriate leverage by the technology leaders. The issue will be intensified by the extension of U.S. patents to business methods,[15] under which firms are patenting consumer interfaces, business models, and forms of calculation. These patents will affect a variety of forms of business, some of which seem likely to have network externalities.[16]

We therefore need a realistic set of standards for defining anticompetitive licensing behavior in these cases. If we can trust national antitrust authorities to apply such law on their own, no more is needed than perhaps consultation to deal with situations in which different nations reach different judgments. Realistically, however, the nation hosting an offending company may not have the incentive to control the company. After all, that nation benefits from the industrial leadership of its company, and, in the information industry context, from the export sales of information products that can be produced at essentially zero marginal cost. Although Microsoft actually was prosecuted, the settlement proposed by the Department of Justice in the United States is weaker than a number of individual states chose and may be

[13] An interesting example is presented in Re British Interactive Broadcasting/open, E.C. Comm. 1999/781/E.C., [2000] 4 *C.M.L.R.* 901. Among the relevant markets, several of which seem likely to have network externalities, are those for digital interactive television services, pay television, wholesale supply of films and sport to pay television, technical services, and for customer access infrastructure for telecommunication.

[14] See, e.g. letter from Joel I. Klein to Carey R. Ramos, Esq. (June 10, 1999), http://www.usdoj.gov/atr/public/busreview/2485.htm (DVD pool); R. Bekkers, G. Duysters, and B. Verspagen, "Intellectual Property Rights, Strategic Technology Agreements and Market Structure, the case of GSM" , *Research Policy,* vol. 31, pp. 1141-1161.

[15] State Street Bank & Trust Co. v. Signature Financial Group, 149 F.3d 1368 (Fed. Cir. 1998).

[16] Note that there may be significant effects even if other nations do not follow the U.S. lead in patenting business methods. U.S. courts might give a broad extraterritorial reading to the locus of infringement of such patents in the Internet context. The international implications of these patents have yet to be realized.

weaker than Europe is willing to accept in parallel litigation.[17] The risk of failure to prosecute is still a real issue. It will be discussed, along with other issues affecting the need for international action, in the final section of this paper.

5.2 Research Tools, Broad Patents, and Preemption

A second set of contemporary concerns arises from efforts by IP holders to extend the effective power of their IP rights to preempt a major area of research or product development. This has become a major theme in many areas of IP law,[18] and can be described here with a few examples. First, a firm identifying genetic sequences seeks patent rights on partial gene sequences, with the scope of the patent right intended to reach any product that relies upon the entire gene. Thus, the genomics firm seeks a legal bargaining chip against a firm that commercializes the gene, whether or not the genomics firm's partial sequence was actually used in developing the product. Second, a firm "licenses" (sells?) seed with a label-based license containing a provision purporting to permit the use of the seed only for growing a crop and to prohibit its use for breeding purposes. Third, a firm "licenses" (sells?) a computer program with a provision prohibiting any form of reverse engineering of the program (even prohibiting those actions that are permitted under the EU Software Directive). Finally, a firm sells an automobile containing a computer for engine control, with the computer program encrypted in a way that restricts repair activity or marketing of spare parts by other than authorized dealers.[19]

These examples all show use of an IP right to try to control a broad formation available to follow-on innovators. The initial innovator is staking out a claim to a share of the monopoly rent available from subsequent innova-

---

[17] See European Commission Press Releases: Commission initiates additional proceedings against Microsoft, IP/01/1232, 30 Aug. 2001; Commission opens proceedings against Microsoft's alleged discriminatory licensing and refusal to supply software information, IP/00/906, 3 Aug. 2000; Commission examines the impact of Windows 2000 on competition, IP/00/141, 10 Feb. 2000. The theories appear quite similar to those of U.S. antitrust, except that the Commission's August 2000 Statement of Objections may go somewhat further toward requiring Microsoft to provide access to its source code than would U.S. antitrust authorities.

[18] See, e.g., *Report of the NIH Working Group on Research Tools* (1998), available at http://www.nih.gov/news/researchtools/index.htm; J. Barton, "The Balance between Intellectual Property Rights and Competition: Paradigms in the Information Sector", [1997] 7 *E.C.L.R.* 440.

[19] See Motor & Equipment Manuf. Assoc. v. Environmental Protection Agency, 142 F.3d 449 (D.C. Cir. 1998).

tion. In defining the appropriate law, there must, however, be a balance between the incentives available to the initial innovator and those available to the subsequent innovator.[20] The current IP law trend has been to expand the rights of the initial innovator and there have been IP-based pressures favoring the initial innovator in all four cases just described. Most coming at the balance from an antitrust perspective would probably give a contrary response.

Of the three contexts discussed in this paper, this one is likely to give rise to the sharpest international conflict. The developed nations, and especially the U.S., have been responding to those lobbies that would benefit from stronger rights of the type discussed here, seeking, for example, to persuade developing nations to accept software protection regimes that prohibit all reverse engineering.[21] It is the developed nations whose industries would most benefit from an extension of such rights, and therefore be least likely to want to limit these rights in the name of competition. This U.S. perspective is intensified by the nation's enormous public investment in basic research, much of which is commercialized under provisions that favor the grant of rights to national firms rather than foreign firms.[22] Other nations are likely to take a contrary perspective, for they can benefit from the opportunity to adapt and improve existing technologies without obtaining permission from current rights holders – and they will be joined by many firms within the United States. In short, we will need a global understanding as to the effective limits to be put on the scope of intellectual property rights.

5.3 Oligopolies, Cross Licenses, and Market Entry

The last of the three examples is probably the most common and probably also the most intellectually difficult. This is the situation in which the various leaders of an industry each hold an IP portfolio, much of which is regularly infringed by competitors. But none of the firms usually brings suit on those patents, because each knows that the defendant would respond with a counterattack based on those of the defendant's patents that it itself is infringing. Litigation is too much like a nuclear weapon, and the relation becomes one of mutually assured destruction. Each firm must therefore maintain an IP portfolio for bargaining-chip, i.e. defensive, purposes. But, and here is

[20] See J. Barton, "Patents and Antitrust: A Rethinking in Light of Patent Breadth and Sequential Innovation", 65 *Antitrust L.J.* 449 (1997).

[21] See, e.g., U.S. Trade Representative Press Release 96-99, Acting Trade Representative Barshefsky Announces Results of Special 301 "Out-of-Cycle" Reviews, December 20, 1996 (Hong Kong software protection legislation).

[22] 35 U.S.C. §§ 204 (Bayh-Dole Act).

the point important for industrial structure, there is no reason not to use the portfolio against possible new entrants who might affect the oligopoly rents available to the industry leaders.

This is probably the most typical actual use for patents (outside the pharmaceutical industry, where they work in the way generally modelled by economists). This pattern is certainly typical in the semiconductor industry and may arise in others such as financial services and agricultural biotechnology. This pattern frequently arises in an oligopolistic context. There are several reasons – one is that there must be some form of monopoly rent to incent research and patents can be used to slow entry into the community. Second, mergers may often be an appealing way to avoid a patent fight. A merger is the ultimate cross-license and contributes to industrial concentration. And third, where there is already an oligopoly, it is essential to each member to build the patent portfolio needed to ward off litigation by its competitors.

There are also three situations in which litigation is likely in this context; their character should give rise to real concern about the effective workings of the IP system. One situation is that in which the plaintiff is doing less well than its competitors in the marketplace, so it has nothing to lose by converting the market battle into a legal battle. This is probably exemplified by some of the Texas Instruments suits of the 1980s.[23] A second is when a firm has such a big patent portfolio that it can obtain net revenues from its competitors; it may then use the threat of litigation as part of the process of bargaining over a cross-license rate and terms.[24] And the third is when the defendant is someone from outside the oligopoly, seeking to compete with the community.[25]

What is the appropriate patent-antitrust analysis in this situation? Clearly, this is an extremely difficult question, for the oligopoly may be maintained by IP rights and provides an economic return on research. At the same time,

---

[23] See Warshafsky, *The Patent Wars* (1994).

[24] There is sometimes substantial asymmetry in such cross licenses. See, for example, the license attached as Exhibit F to the License Development and Marketing Agreement of May 9, 1997, between Microsoft Corp. and Citrix Systems, attached as Exhibit 10 to Citrix System's 8-K filed with the SEC on June 20, 1997. Under this agreement all Citrix patents are licensed to Microsoft, while only some Microsoft patents are licensed to Citrix. Another example is posed by the various licenses that IBM obtained from Taiwanese computer manufactures during the 1980s. See, e.g., Bermar *et al.*, "IBM nears patent accords with many Taiwanese makers", *PC Week*, Sept. 12, 1988, p. 133; March and Burke, "Cloners feel patent pressure", *PC Week*, Dec. 5, 1988, p. 53.

[25] E.g. Cyrix v. Intel, 77 F.3d 1381 (CAFC 1996); Intel v. ULSI, 995 F.2d 1556 (CAFC 1993).

that return is so indirectly associated with the research that we reasonably question the role of the IP as a research incentive. For relations among the oligopolists, there is generally no reason to worry about cross-licenses if the relations are roughly symmetrical. (The licenses may be explicit, or tacit, through mutual decisions not to bring suit.) However, if the relations are asymmetrical, so that one firm can restrain others, we may have grounds for concern. We may also have grounds for concern about mergers or pools, if the arrangements decrease incentives to research.

But the more difficult issues, especially in the international context, involve when it is or is not legitimate for members of the inner oligopoly to use their IP to deter others from entering the inner circle. Arguably, such use of the IP simply protects the monopoly right inherent in the IP. But there is an economic counterargument: unless there is a threat of entry, the inner circle may become lazy, and it seems likely that a smaller, more cozy oligopoly would spend a smaller share of its monopoly rent on research. It is again essential to maintain an optimal level of threat to the insiders.

Hence, there may need to be a form of license to give outsiders access – perhaps a dependency license in the pattern of French law, where a subsequent inventor of a significant improvement can obtain, of right, a royalty-bearing license to the underlying invention.[26] One could provide legal justification for such an economic argument by the essential facility principle under which certain facilities are deemed so important that they must be shared among competitors. The doctrine developed in very specific situations including, for example, traditional sharing of a particular facility, and its possible application to intellectual property is quite controversial.[27] In a sense, it is a compulsory license, strongly opposed by many. Another legal approach is to recognize that the practical effect of the tacit or explicit cross-licenses may be to create a pool that is not open to outsiders and is thus a combination in restraint of trade.[28]

This form of industrial structure is very significant from the international perspective. The leaders of the various technology-based oligopolies are, today, generally from the developed world, with the oligopolists typically

---

[26] Code de la Propriété Intellectuelle, Loi 92-597, art. L. 613-15 (July 1, 1992).

[27] See T. Cotter, "Intellectual Property and the Essential Facilities Doctrine", 44 Antitrust Bull. 211 (1999). The European analogue of the doctrine is applied in Radio Telefis Eirann v. Commission of the European Communities, [1995] ECR 1-743 (Magill) and later reviewed, but not applied, in Oscar Brommer GmbH & Co. v. Mediaprint Zeitungs-und Zeitschriftenverlag GmbH & Co., Case C-7/97 (ECJ 1998).

[28] For careful analysis of the pool concept, see S. Carlson, "Patent Pools and the Antitrust Dilemma", 16 *Yale J. on Reg.* 359 (1999).

comprising firms from several different nations, e.g. the US and Japan in the case of semiconductors and the US and Europe in the case of agricultural biotechnology. Mergers within the industry are likely to be cross-national among developed world entities. But the challengers are perhaps especially likely to be from the developing world – and may be especially likely to bring different kinds of ideas and technologies. In the face of an oligopoly with strong IP portfolios, the challengers, however, may have only the opportunity to supply technology to or be acquired by the oligopolists – it will be very difficult, if not impossible, for them to grow to become full members of the oligopoly.

Thus, although the appropriate standards are again a subject on which substantial analysis is needed, it seems possible that firms outside the oligopoly should sometimes have a form of license or an antitrust-type defense to an infringement suit. The circumstances favoring such a right are that the oligopolist's patent portfolios are so substantial that no new firm can enter with the oligopolist's permission, that the patents are not enforced against oligopoly members but only against outsiders, that the number of oligopoly members is small enough that there is reasonable basis to fear that the members will not be aggressive in developing new technologies, and perhaps that the firm seeking the rights has made a substantial intellectual contribution.[29]

5.4 Structural and Institutional Issues

In all three of the contexts just discussed, there is need for a competetion-law principle to balance overly-broad use of IP. In all three, application of the competition-law principle would contribute to an industrial structure evolution more likely to be favorable to at least the more advanced developing nations – and of course more favorable to the advance of technology and to all the world's consumers, whether in developed or in developing nations. And in all three, there is incentive for developed-world competition-law enforcers to shade the application of the law in a way that favors their own industry.

Two levels of response deserve consideration. First, the Microsoft case indicates that the technological merchantilist pressure is not always dominant. Moreover, the intellectual subtlety of the area often leaves room for reasonable differences over what is economically or scientifically best from

[29] For a model of the likely incentives to innovate among oligopolists, the way these incentives vary with the number of firms, and the implications for the law, see J. Barton, "Antitrust Treatment of Oligopolies with Mutually Blocking Patent Portfolios", *69 Antitrust Law Journal*, 69 (3), 2002, pp. 851-882.

any individual nation's or the world's perspective – and there have been substantial differences even within one nation on issues such as the Microsoft case. Hence, a first, and minimalist, approach is to encourage joint thinking and analysis among the competition law and IP communities of different nations and regional groups, so as to make it possible for national and regional law to be enforced in a way that serves both the local consumer and the global interests. For this, what is needed is discussion and joint analysis.

It is this discussion and analysis that define the key agenda for research. What are the best answers, nationally or globally, for each of the three types of IP competition conflict identified in this paper? What actually is happening empirically? Are there other types of conflicts likely to become important? Are there genuine differences in perspective and analysis among different nations, as might be exemplified in the Microsoft case? Are there genuine differences in the interests of different nations as suggested here?

As a stronger response, we may need agreed standards for each of the contexts. Such a version is probably essential in order to overcome national reluctance to prosecute in these situations. At most, the need is for a WTO-type code – there is no need for creation of a separate international competition organization (although there may need to be arrangements to ensure appropriate expertise on any WTO panel). The code would serve several functions, beyond possibly clarifying the relevant legal standards. First, it would put pressure on national governments and regional organizations to live up to the competition law demands, even when these may cut against short-term national interest. Second, it would provide a basis for a WTO-type panel process, through which other governments could pressure a nation that failed to live up to its competition law commitment. Third, it would provide a set of standards by which third nations can reshape or create license arrangements imposed from abroad. For example, even if the US hadn't prosecuted Microsoft, a European OEM manufacturer might have been allowed, by EU competition law, to ignore Microsoft's restrictions against including competing browsers in preloaded software.[30]

Such a code may also be needed to resolve the impact of differing antitrust interpretations on trade. Consider a plausible example. Suppose, under a broad U.S. interpretation of patent law, a U.S. genomics firm obtains a patent right to any gene that contains a particular partial sequence (which it actually discovered). Suppose also that Europe refuses to grant such broad claims, and gives the US firm rights on only the shorter sequence it actually

[30] In this sense, the Code would elaborate on Article 40 of TRIPs, which specifically authorizes controls on "Anti-competitive practices in contractual licenses," and creates a consultation obligation to protect the interests of a nation alleging that anti-competitive practices are affecting it.

discovered, relying either on a less broad interpretation of the patent laws or on a competition law principle that such a broad patent would be anticompetitive. Assume a European company identifies the entire gene containing the sequence (without using the genomics firm's sequence as a research tool), and develops a pharmaceutical based on the gene. Can the new pharmaceutical be excluded from the U.S.? As a matter of US patent law, the answer may be yes, but the U.S. patent in this case has arguably become a trade barrier that fails to recognize appropriate competition-law concerns. Such issues will be posed as well by international Internet transactions in which U.S. firms seek to protect their position by requiring foreign governments to prohibit anti-encryption devices. In the future, there may be many such cases; they will have to be dealt with by some form of international understanding, or perhaps judicial recognition of global competition law concerns as a defense in infringement actions.

The possibility of achieving such an international antitrust code is anything but clear. Indeed, one of the authors in this book argues elsewhere that the chance of agreement is so small that no effort should be undertaken.[31] The United States has not generally been supportive of an international antitrust code, perhaps because of concern that a code would be more protective of small traditional distributors than of full competition in the distribution sector or that it would threaten the United States anti-dumping laws.[32] This position was taken in the context of traditional international antitrust issues such as export cartels and barriers to distribution. The new technology issues pose quite different issues. Even Europe, which has supported discussing antitrust issues at the WTO, may, along with the United States and possibly Japan, be very concerned about an arrangement that threatens their technological dominance with greater competition. Nevertheless, there is a very strong argument that a proper balance between competition concerns and IP is, like free trade, beneficial to all, at least in the long run.[33] Moreover, a competition code that reaches IP-antitrust issues may be part of a global tradeoff in which the technologically dominant nations wins in other dimensions. Clearly, the economic analysis to evaluate the effects of such a code

[31] H. Ullrich, "Antitrust Law Relating to High Technology Industries – A Case for or Against International Rules", in *Towards WTO Competition Rules* (R. Zäch, ed. 1999).

[32] See the discussion in D. Tarullo, "Norms and Institutions in Global Competition Policy", 94 *American J. of International Law* 478 (2000).

[33] Note that this cannot be said of intellectual property agreements such as TRIPs. Because of the actual flow of rents and the differences among nations in their balancing of short and long term interests, such an agreement is not necessarily in the interest of all. See J. Barton, "The Economics of TRIPS: International Trade in Information-Intensive Products", 33 *George Washington L. R.* 473 (2001).

on different nations is also an important academic task, as are evaluations of particular designs for institutional responses.

In all three contexts discussed above, the first diplomatic need is for understanding of the economic and industrial structure issues – and for realization that these issues pose important questions for the future of technologically based development. That understanding should be sought. There are at least two plausible fora. One is the OECD, or perhaps some form of working group that might be set up by the OECD in collaboration with a developing-nation oriented entity such as UNCTAD. A second is the WTO Working Group on the Interaction between Trade and Competition policy, perhaps working in collaboration with WIPO. And the United States has certainly indicated an interest in building such understanding. It is planning to include comparative analysis in the hearings being set up jointly by the Department of Justice and the Federal Trade Commission to be held in early 2002 on *Competition and Intellectual Property Law and Policy in the Knowledge-based Economy*, and it would be surprising if intellectual property issues did not come up in the "International Competition Network" (ICN) launched in the fall of 2001 to encourage cooperation among competition officials of different nations.[34] As that understanding is achieved, the basis can be laid for integration of the principles into national antitrust and IP law and possibly for international agreements.

[34] W. Kolasky, "U.S. and EU Competition Policy: Cartels, Mergers, and Beyond", Address Before the Council for the United States and Italy Bi-Annual Conference, New York, Jan. 25, 2002. Deputy Attorney General Kolasky specifically noted differences between the United States and Europe over the essential facility doctrine. See also Final Report, International Competition Policy Advisory Committee, February 28, 2000, available at www.usdoj.gov/atr/icpac/4272.htm. Although the key issues discussed in this report are the traditional ones involving cartels etc., there is a short discussion of the IP-antitrust issues as part of the discussion of e-commerce questions at pp. 287-293.

Chapter 6

R&D INFORMATION FLOWS AND PATENTING IN JAPAN AND THE UNITED STATES[1, 2]

Wesley M. Cohen,[a] Akira Goto,[b] Akiya Nagata,[c] Richard R. Nelson,[d] and John P. Walsh[e]
[a] *The Fuqua School of Business, Duke University, Durham, NC, USA.*
[b]*University of Tokyo, Research Center for Advanced Economic Engineering, Tokyo, Japan*
[c]*Japan Advanced Institute of Science and Technology, Ishikawa, Japan*
[d]*Columbia University, Department of Internationl and Public Affairs, New York, NY, USA*
[e]*University of Illinois at Chicago, Department of Sociology, Chicago, IL, USA*

Chapter contents:

---

[1] This paper draws heavily from a paper, entitled "R&D Spillovers, Patents and the Incentives to Innovate in Japan and the United States", by the same authors, to be published in Research Policy.

[2] Acknowledgments: For comments, we thank Anthony Arundel, Setsuko Asami, Ashish Arora, Marco Ceccagnoli, Jesper Christensen, Rebecca Henderson, David Hounshell, Steven Klepper, Rob Kneller, Mariana Mazzucato, Ichiro Nakayama, Manny Schechter, members of the Institute of Intellectual Property (Tokyo), participants in the DRUID Nelson and Winter Conference of June 2001, the White House Working Group on Intellectual Property, the NBER Workshop on R&D and Productivity, the Innovation Survey Data Conference (Ministry of Industry, Paris), the University of Chicago's Law and Economics Seminar, and the Wharton and UCLA strategy seminars for commentsand the Purdue University economics seminar. Principal research support was provided by the Alfred P. Sloan Foundation, the Center for Global Partnership, the National Institute for Science and Technology Policy of Japan, and Grant No. 99-76384 of the U.S. National Science Foundation. Supplemental support was provided by the Carnegie Bosch Institute of Carnegie Mellon University and Hitotsubashi University Institute of Innovation Research. Authors are listed alphabetically.

O. Granstrand (ed.), Economics, Law and Intellectual Property, 123-154.

Abstract: National surveys of R&D labs across the manufacturing sectors in the U.S. and Japan show that intraindustry R&D knowledge flows and spillovers are greater in Japan than in the U.S. and the appropriability of rents due to innovation less. Patents in particular are observed to play a more central role in diffusing information across rivals in Japan, and appear to be a key reason for greater intraindustry R&D spillovers there, suggesting that patent policy can importantly affect information flows. Uses of patents differ between the two nations, with strategic uses of patents, particularly for negotiations, being more common in Japan.

Keywords: Patents, R&D, Spillovers, Innovation, Appropriability

6.1 Introduction

The ability of firms to appropriate at least some of the value created by their innovations is essential if there is to be incentive to innovate. On the other hand, the economy-wide benefits from an innovation depend to a considerable degree on the extent to which the new knowledge associated with it becomes available to others to use and build on. This article reports the results of a survey research study that compares the ability of U.S. and Japanese firms to appropriate the returns to their innovations, how these firms protect their innovations (by using, for example, secrecy, patents, lead time advantages) and the magnitude and channels of intraindustry R&D information flows in the two nations. We focus particularly on the role of patenting since it is both a key policy instrument affecting appropriability and an object of growing managerial attention.

Our comparison of appropriability conditions and spillovers between Japan and the U.S. builds on prior research that shows that, in most industries, firms rely predominantly on mechanisms other than patents to protect their innovations, including secrecy, first mover advantages and the exploitation of complementary capabilities (Scherer, *et al.*, 1995; Mansfield, 1986; Levin, *et al.* 1987; Arundel, 2001; Taylor and Silberston, 1973). In some industries, such as drugs, patents are, however, quite important. A comparison between Japan and the U.S. should add to these insights by showing whether appropriability conditions depend on cross-national differences in policy and institutional environments, or factors, such as technology, that should vary little across nations.

The role and effectiveness of patents is of central concern to this study. We will explore whether differences between the U.S. and Japan in patent law, judicial and administrative practice affect the degree to which patents protect innovation. We also will examine whether the two nations' different patent policies affect the diffusion of technical knowledge, as suggested by Ordover (1991) and Granstrand (2000).

In brief, although R&D spending as a percent of GDP is higher in Japan than the U.S., intraindustry R&D information spillovers appear to be greater in Japan for almost all industries, and the appropriability of rents due to innovation appears to be less. In contrast to the U.S, Japanese respondents report secrecy as a minor appropriability mechanism and patents as comparably effective to other major mechanisms. A key reason for less appropriability and greater intraindustry R&D spillover in Japan appears to be that patents diffuse information across rivals more readily than in the U.S., yielding more information on rival R&D activities. We suggest that this cross-national difference is not only due to the policy differences highlighted by Ordover (1991), but also due to the different ways in which patents are used in the two nations.

In Section 2, we review our sampling and survey methods. Section 3 compares intraindustry R&D information flows and spillovers. Section 4 compares the appropriability of rents due to innovation. Section 5 considers how the two patent systems influence intraindustry R&D spillovers. Section 6 examines other factors that may affect intraindustry R&D spillovers in the two nations. Section 7 concludes the paper.

6.2 Method, Data and Samples

The data come from a survey of managers of R&D units of manufacturing firms in the U.S. and Japan. We asked respondents to answer questions in terms of the *focus industry* that represented the bulk of their R&D effort.[3] Where possible, our surveys employed objective response scales, which tend to be both more interpretable and more readily compared across respondents, which is especially useful for comparisons across nations where language and culture differ. First drafted in English, the questionnaire was translated into Japanese and then independently back-translated into English to assure accuracy. While most questions were identical between the two surveys, a small number of questions differed. The surveys were mailed during the summer of 1994. Both the American and Japanese teams conducted follow-up mailings and phone calls to increase response rates (cf. Dillman, 1978). To help interpret our findings, we also conducted 18 interviews with R&D managers and intellectual property officers at nine U.S. firms, and 12 interviews at nine Japanese firms, as well as with representatives of the Japanese Patent Office (JPO).

The population sampled in the U.S. included all R&D units belonging to R&D performing manufacturing firms located in the U.S. The U.S.

[3] By obtaining answers for a firm's activities and experience in a given product market rather than the firm as a whole, we reduce the measurement error associated with differences in conditions across the several industries in which a firm might be active.

sample was drawn from a frame consisting of eligible labs in the Directory of American Research and Technology (Bowker, 1994) or, if not included there, labs attached to firms listed in Standard and Poor's COMPUSTAT tapes. We surveyed 3240 labs located in the U.S. and received 1478 responses, for a raw response rate of 46% and an adjusted response rate of 54% of the eligible sample.[4] The U.S. survey data are supplemented with published data on firm sales and employees from COMPUSTAT, Dun & Bradstreet and similar sources.

The population sampled in Japan included R&D performing, manufacturing firms with capitalization over 1 billion yen. The sample was drawn from a list of 1219 firms amassed by Japan's Science and Technology Agency, or 71% of the 1722 firms estimated to meet the population definition (NISTEP, 1997). We received responses from 643 firms, yielding a response rate of 52%. On the basis of each respondent's self-reported principal market focus of its R&D, our observations are grouped into comparably defined ISIC industries, typically defined at the 3-digit U.S. SIC code level.

In order to make the two national samples as comparable as possible, we restricted our samples to respondents from firms with annual sales of $50 million or more.[5] Foreign-owned labs were also dropped in order not to confuse our cross-national comparisons. In this truncated sample there are 826 observations from the U.S. and 593 from Japan. Because the two national samples can contain very different numbers of observations for a given industry, we constructed weights that correct for the differences in industry mix in each country, and use these weights when comparing national aggregate results in order to rule out the possibility that country differences are due to variations in industry mix. When we make comparisons between these country averages, we use either weighted least squares or weighted logistic regressions as appropriate (see below). For comparisons across survey item averages within a country, we use paired t-tests or non-parametric tests (Agresti and Agresti, 1979).

Presenting summary statistics on firm and business unit sizes for the two samples, Table 6-1 shows that the U.S. sample contains substantially larger firms, though the business units (reflecting firms' activities in a given market) are more comparable in size. Consistent with public sources, our data indicate that Japanese firms spend more on R&D relative to sales than comparable U.S. firms. For our sample, the comparison means for own-financed R&D expenditures divided by sales are 2.26% for

[4] A nonrespondent survey found that 28% of the nonrespondents in the U.S. were not in the target population (for example, they did no manufacturing). After correcting the sample size accordingly for ineligible cases, the U.S. response rate was adjusted upward to 54%.

[5] We reran the analyses for the firms in the U.S. sample with sales revenue of less than $50 million. The results are not qualitatively different from the results reported in this paper.

the U.S. and 3.70% for Japan (t=6.89, p<.0001).[6] Our survey data suggest that the overall Japanese sample R&D intensity exceeds that of the U.S. largely because the Japanese R&D intensities in the least R&D intensive (i.e. below 2% in the U.S.) industries tend to be considerably higher. In contrast, in the most R&D intensive industries such as drugs or semiconductors, the average U.S. and Japanese R&D intensities tend to be comparable.[7]

Table 6-1: Firm and business unit size in U.S. and Japanese samples

	Sales ($Mil.)		Employees	
	U.S.	Japan	U.S.	Japan
Firm Size				
Median	1245	558	8600	1476
Mean (unweighted)	6067	1956	30009	3720
Mean (weighted)	6020	1793	29272	3462
Business Unit Size				
Median	300	361	1000	850
Mean (unweighted)	2403	1264	6282	2229
Mean (weighted)	2813	1122	6791	1945

Notes: 1 US$=102.8 ¥ , March 1994 exchange rate
*p<.05; **p<.01; ***p<.001; ****p<.0001

The composition of R&D activities appears to be comparable across the two samples. For example, most of the R&D effort in both nations is directed toward product rather than process innovation. Contrary to the Mansfield's [1988] earlier findings, we do not find that Japanese firms dedicate the majority of their R&D effort to process innovation. On the basis of a much larger sample and broader industry coverage than Mansfield's earlier survey, we observe that 80% of our Japanese respondents' R&D is dedicated to product innovation and only 16% to process, indicating that Japanese firms conduct relatively more product R&D than their American counterparts who report 66% of their R&D effort is dedicated to product innovation and 30% to process innovation.[8] After normalizing to control for the differences in question framing, we also find that U.S. and

[6] Our sample data excludes outliers, defined as business units with R&D intensities greater than 100% or more than 3 interquartile ranges from the median.

[7] Public data show that over the last 20 years, Japan has consistently spent more on non-defense R&D as a percent of GDP than has the U.S. Over the last five years, the Japanese average has been between 2.6% and 3.0%. During this same period, the U.S. average has been between 1.9% and 2.2% (National Science Foundation, 2000). We believe our aggregate results exceed the public data largely because we sampled only R&D-performing firms.

[8] The cross-national difference is significant: for product, t=11.98, for process, t=13.57, both p<.0001

Japanese firms spend comparable amounts on basic research, about eight to nine percent. Japanese firms, however, appear to spend relatively more on development and less on applied research.[9]

With regard to the types of responding R&D labs in our sample, the two samples are comparable. About 30% of the labs are located in the corporate headquarters, 40% at production facilities and 30% are stand-alone facilities in both samples. The organizational location of the responding labs is also similar in the two samples. In each case, about 60% of the R&D labs report to the corporate office or headquarters, about 30% report to a division, subsidiary or business unit office, and the remaining 10% report to another R&D unit or a production facility.

6.3 Intraindustry R&D Information Flows and Spillovers

In this section, we compare the extent of R&D-related information flows across rivals in the U.S. and Japanese manufacturing sectors. We begin by comparing responses to a question in the survey about the importance of information originating from a broad range of information sources, of which rival firms are one. Respondents report whether, over the prior three years, information from competitors either suggested new R&D projects or contributed to the completion of existing projects. Figure 6–1 shows clear differences between the U.S. and Japan. In Japan, information from rivals suggests new R&D projects for 48% of the respondents, exceeding the 41% figure for the U.S. (χ^2 [1 d.f.]=6.9, p<.01). This difference, though a relative one of almost 20% and statistically signifi-

[9] The difference between the two surveys is that the U.S. survey permitted firms to allocate their R&D to "technical service" as well as to basic and applied research and development. We compare the U.S. and Japanese figures for the composition of their R&D spending by dropping the allocation in the U.S. data to technical service and renormalizing as shown in the table below.

Allocation of R&D across Basic and Applied Research and Development

Adjustment to Data:	None	Drop Tech. Svc. in US
UNITED STATES		
Basic	8.0%	9.3%
Applied	27.7	33.7
Development	47.2	57.0
Technical Service	17.1	--
JAPAN		
Basic	9.2%	9.2
Applied	21.8	21.8
Development	69.1	69.1
Technical Service	--	--

cant, is dwarfed by the difference in the frequencies with which respondents in Japan and the U.S. claim that information from competitors contributes to the execution of existing R&D projects. In Japan, 51% of the respondents claim that information from rivals contributes to project execution versus only 13% in the U.S. (χ^2 [1 d.f.]=213.9, p<.0001).[10] These results suggest not only that intraindustry flows are more extensive in Japan than in the United States, but that they play a different role in the two nations. In the U.S., these flows predominantly guide R&D project selection, whereas they affect project selection and project completion comparably in Japan.

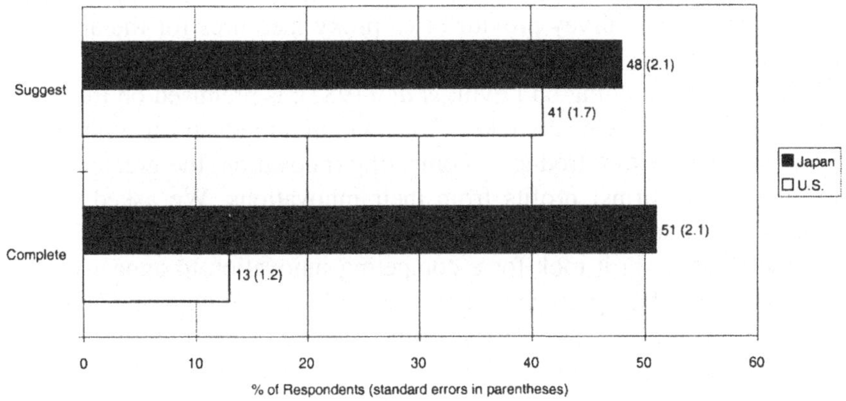

Figure 6-1: Competitors as information sources for suggesting new projects or contributing to completion of existing projects, for Japan and U.S.

Our survey data thus suggest that R&D-related information flows among rivals are greater in Japan than in the U.S. Does this difference correspond, however, to one in intraindustry (nonpecuniary) R&D spillovers, which Griliches (1992) and others identify as a major source of productivity growth? The key is whether the observed information flows are largely the outcome of market-mediated transactions or not. Our analysis of the different channels through which firms might learn about the R&D activities of rivals (discussed below) show that of the five channels that are the most important in both countries, four – namely publications, public meetings or conferences, informal information exchange and

[10] The industry-level results show little deviation from the aggregate patterns. For 25 of the 26 industries for which we have more than five observations for both samples, the percent of respondents indicating that information from rivals contributes to R&D project completion is greater in Japan than in the U.S. For 20 of 26 industries, the same comparison holds for the percent of respondents indicating that information from rivals suggests new projects.

competitors' products (via, for example, reverse engineering) – are not market-mediated, and the fifth, namely patents, is only partially so. We conclude, therefore, that not only are intraindustry R&D information flows greater in Japan, but intraindustry R&D spillovers as well.

6.4 Appropriability

While factors other than intraindustry R&D spillovers might condition the appropriability of profits due to innovation, such spillovers are a key determinant. Thus, if the extent of intraindustry spillovers are indeed greater in Japan than in the U.S., we should expect, ceteris paribus, that Japanese firms appropriate less of the returns to their R&D activities than American firms. Our survey provides two proxy measures for the appropriation of profits due to innovation.

Our first measure, building on Levin, *et al.* (1987), is premised on the notion that the longer it typically takes rivals within an industry to imitate a firm's innovation or to introduce a competing innovation, the greater will be the innovating firms' profits from their innovations. We asked each respondent, separately for patented and unpatented product and process innovations, how long it took for a competing innovation to appear after they had introduced a significant innovation.[11] Consistent with our finding of greater intraindustry spillovers in Japan, we find that the "imitation lags" for all four types of innovation are much more compressed in Japan than in the U.S. Presenting the results for the two national samples, Figure 6-2 shows much longer lags in the U.S., ranging from 40% longer for unpatented product innovations to about 80% longer for patented process innovations (all country differences significant, $p<.0001$). These qualitative patterns apply to all the industries except computers, where the imitation lags associated with patented processes and unpatented products and processes are longer in Japan.

[11] The response categories for this question were less than six months, six months to one and a half years, one and a half to three years, three to five years and more than five years. To compute aggregate and industry averages, midpoints were employed, except for the last, open-ended category to which we assigned a value of eight years.

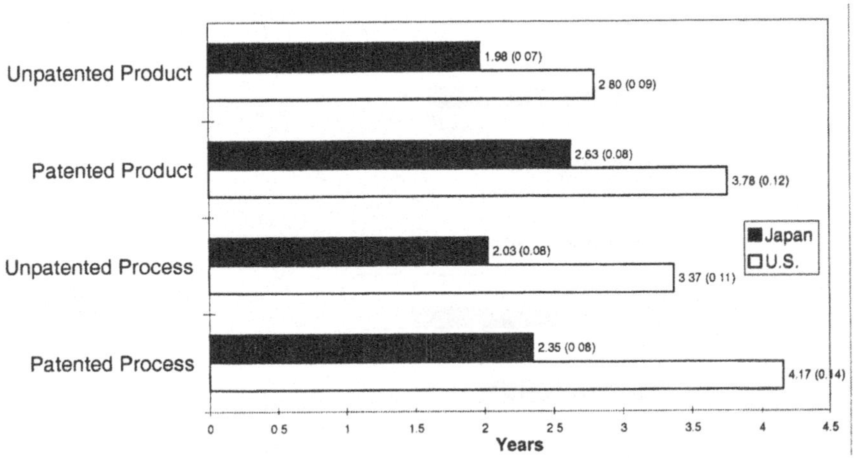

Note: Average Lags computed using midpoints of following categories: less than 6 mos., 6 mos. - 1.5 years, 1.5-3 years, 3 - 5 years, greater than 5 years. For top category, we assumed an imitation lag of 8 years. (Standard errors in patented innovations: Japan N=533; U.S. N=551. For unpatented innovations: Japan N=538; U.S. N0703)

Figure 6–2: Mean imitation lags for product and process innovations

To construct a second measure of appropriability, we asked each respondent to estimate the percent of their product and process innovations for which patents, secrecy,[12] lead time, complementary sales and service, and complementary manufacturing facilities and know-how were "effective" in protecting the "competitive advantage" from those innovations. Figure 6–3 shows the average percent of product and process innovations (based on category midpoints) for which each mechanism is judged to be effective.[13] With the exception of patents, which appear to be comparably effective in Japan and the U.S. in absolute terms, U.S. respondents report all mechanisms to be more effective, scoring every mechanism, on average, at least twenty percent higher (all country differences, except patents, significant, p<.01). Thus, consistent with the finding of more compressed imitation lags and greater intraindustry spillovers in Japan, the comparison of absolute scores suggest that the effectiveness of all appropriability mechanisms except patents is greater in the U.S.[14]

---

[12] Note that "secrecy" is not limited to formal trade secrecy protection, and that secrecy and patents are not exclusive. Firms, for example, may try to maintain secrecy about a project or a result until the patent is published. Also, firms may patent some aspects of the innovation while trying to keep other parts secret. More generally, Cohen *et al.*'s (2000) analysis of the U.S. data show that the different appropriability mechanisms considered are often used together, sometimes in quite systematic ways.

[13] The response categories were 0-10%, 11-40%, 41-60%, 61-90%, 91-100%.

[14] The pro-patent policy and legal changes in the US raise the question of whether the reported effectiveness of patents and other appropriability mechanisms has changed since

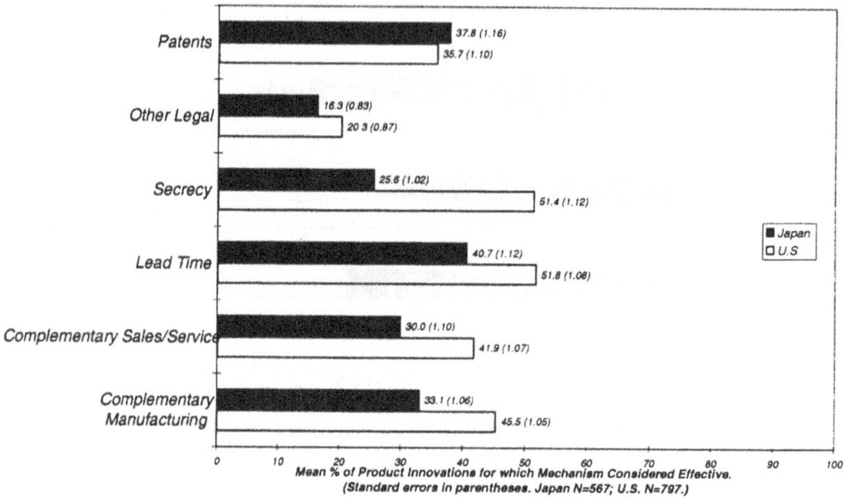

Figure 6-3: Effectiveness of appropriability mechanisms for product innovations

In addition to permitting an evaluation of overall appropriability, the data presented in Figure 6–3 also allow a comparison of the degree to which the different appropriability mechanisms are featured in the appropriability strategies of firms in the two nations. Figure 6–3 shows clear differences in the reported absolute and relative effectiveness of secrecy. For protecting product innovations in the U.S., secrecy is pervasively ranked as one of the most effective mechanisms across industries, and reported to be the most effective mechanism along with lead time in the aggregate sample. In contrast, of all the major appropriability mechanisms, secrecy is judged to be the least effective mechanism for protecting product innovations in Japan. For process innovations, U.S. firms report se-

Levin, *et al.* (1987), collected their data in 1983. After controlling for the different firm size distributions of the CMS and Levin *et al.* samples (the latter was limited to larger, publicly traded firms) and differences in the response scales, patents appear to occupy a somewhat more central role in larger firms' efforts to protect their product innovations in a larger number of industries than before (see Cohen, *et al.* 2000). For example, for 33 identically defined industries with at least four observations in each sample, patents were ranked first or second among the appropriability mechanisms seven times in the Yale survey versus twelve in the CMS. Reflecting a sharper difference, however, secrecy jumps from last place in the Yale survey to tie for first (with lead time) in the CMS. Secrecy is never ranked first or second for the protection of product innovations in the Yale survey versus 24 times in the CMS. The CMS findings on the limits on patent effectiveness differ from the Levin, *et al.* (1987) findings in one key way (cf. Cohen, *et al.* 2000). Consistent with the increased emphasis on secrecy noted above, concern over information disclosure has grown.

crecy as the most important mechanism, over lead time and complementary manufacturing capabilities (both significant, $p<.0001$). For Japan, in contrast, secrecy protects process innovations only about as well as lead time ($t=1.06$, $p>.25$) and a little better than patents ($t=3.15$, $p<.01$), with complementary manufacturing as the dominant mechanism (significantly above secrecy, $t=6.35$, $p<.0001$).[15] In absolute terms, the U.S. aggregate scores for product and process secrecy are approximately double those for Japan ($p<.0001$). Thus, we conclude that secrecy is more central to the appropriability strategies of U.S. firms.

Contrary to our initial conjecture that patents would be similarly evaluated in Japan and the U.S., we observe a difference in the relative standing of patents against other appropriability mechanisms. Consistent with the findings of Levin, *et al.* (1987), Scherer, *et al.* (1959) and Mansfield (1986) for the U.S., American respondents report patents to be less important than other major mechanisms in protecting product innovations (significantly below sales/service, $t=4.35$, $p<.0001$). In contrast, Japanese respondents report patents to be about as effective as any other mechanism for protecting product innovations, ranking slightly below lead time ($t=1.27$, $p>.20$) and a bit above complementary manufacturing capabilities ($t=3.75$, $p<.001$).[16] The almost identical absolute scores on patent effectiveness between the two nations suggest caution, however, before concluding that patents are stronger in Japan. Patents may not be more effective in Japan than in the U.S. in any absolute sense. Rather, other mechanisms may be weaker. Nonetheless, patents appear to be more heavily featured in the appropriability strategies of Japanese firms.

6.5 Patents and Intraindustry R&D Spillovers

Ordover (1991, p. 48) argued that "The Japanese patent system is a complex web of policy choices more or less consciously structured to affect R&D diffusion while maintaining overall incentives for R&D investment. The Japanese patent system subordinates the short term interests of the innovator in the creation of exclusionary rights to the broader policy goals of diffusion of technology". In the prior sections, we see that intraindustry R&D spillovers are greater and appropriability is less in Japan than in the U.S. In this section, we build on Ordover (1991) to consider

[15] Based on the Community Innovation Survey, Arundel (2001) reports secrecy to be relatively more important than patents in Europe, but not nearly as important as lead time, suggesting that it figures more prominently in the appropriability strategies of European than Japanese firms, but less than in those of American firms.

[16] Similar to our U.S. respondents, European respondents report patents to be the least effective appropriability mechanism for protecting product and process innovations (Arundel, 2001).

whether the two nations' distinct patent systems could affect the observed cross-national difference in intraindustry R&D spillovers.

6.5.1 Contrasting Features of the Japanese and U.S. Patent Systems

Originally established in the 19th century not only to encourage domestic inventors, but to facilitate technology transfer from the West, the Japanese patent system emphasized the disclosure function of patents.[17] This emphasis on diffusion is partly reflected by the Japanese requirement that all patent applications be disclosed 18 months after the applications are filed.[18] Since only 17% to 30% (Westney, 1992; Okada, 1997; JPO, personal communication) of the patent applications in Japan are approved, the preponderance of patent applications in Japan are disclosed with no ultimate benefit of intellectual property protection. In the U.S., in contrast, until November 2000, patent applications were only disclosed upon issuance, with somewhere between 10% and 30% never issuing (Westney, 1994, p. 162; Quillen and Webster, 2001).[19] Moreover, since the average pendency period in the U.S. was 20 months (U.S. GAO, 1997), a substantial fraction of the published applications were published later than 18 months.

Ordover (1991) also argues that patents tend to be applied for earlier in the innovation process in Japan due to a first-to-file rule of priority as opposed to the first-to-invent rule of priority that applies to the U.S. (cf. Scotchmer and Green, 1990). A procedural difference may also affect the disclosure function of patents. At the time of our survey, Japanese patents were still subject to "pre-grant opposition". For three months after a patent examiner gave notice that he intended to grant a patent, competitors or anyone else could challenge the validity of the prospective patent, and the examiners often relied heavily on the evidence provided during this period of pre-grant opposition in making their final determination.[20] No analogous opposition process applies to the U.S. Rather, the validity of a U.S.

---

[17]Until recently, the Japanese patent policy has followed what the Japanese refer to as "the conventional catch-up style patent system". Since the late 1990s, policymakers see Japan as beginning to adopt a "pro-patent policy" that realizes 'speedy, strong and broad' protection of rights". (JPO Annual Report, 1999, p.2).

[18] Reflecting interviewed Japanese patent officials' view that even 18 months is too long to effectively achieve the disclosure function in fast-paced technologies, the JPO recently implemented a system of pre-18 month disclosure where firms can opt to have their application published once it passes the formality check (usually 5 months after submission), or any time after that up to 18 months later. Current (February, 2001) estimates are that only 20-30 applications per month are published early.

[19] With the American Inventors Protection Act of 1999, the U.S. will publish applications filed after November, 2000, 18 months after filing. Strictly domestic patents are exempt.

[20] In 1996, pre-grant opposition was replaced in Japan with a system of post-grant opposition. Third parties now have six months from the JPO's announcement of their intent to grant to challenge the validity of the patent.

patent is more typically challenged in the courts after a patent is issued. Thus, the Japanese patent system places more information in the public domain sooner, induces the filing of a patent application sooner in the innovation process, and the opportunity for pre-grant opposition strengthened incentives to monitor competitors' patent filings early on.

In addition to different rules of priority and disclosure and the presence of a pre-grant opposition system, the analysis of Cohen, Nelson and Walsh (2000) suggests yet another dimension of policy and patenting practice that may make patents in Japan more effective vehicles of information disclosure than in the U.S. Specifically, they argue that the number of patentable elements in a commercializable new product importantly affects the way patents are used and, possibly, in turn, the degree to which patents contribute to information diffusion. They distinguish between "complex" versus "discrete" product industries[21] on the basis whether a new, commercializable product or process is comprised of numerous separately patentable elements versus relatively few. In the U.S., for example, new drugs or chemicals typically are comprised of a relatively discrete number of patentable elements. In contrast, electronic products in the U.S. tend to be comprised of a larger number – often hundreds – of patentable elements and, hence, may be characterized as complex. Consequently, in complex product industries, firms rarely have proprietary control over all the essential complementary components of the technologies they are developing. Firms hold rights over technologies that others need, and vice-versa, creating a condition of mutual dependence that fosters extensive cross-licensing, related negotiations and information sharing. As compared to discrete product industries, patents are used less often to enforce exclusivity and more to secure market access (by conferring access to key technology owned by others) and freedom of operation (by conferring an ability to countersue if sued, thereby discouraging suits).

While Cohen, *et al.* (2000), distinguish complex from discrete product industries largely on the basis of technology and the physical character of the products, policy and administrative practice can also play a critical role. For example, the recent ruling in the U.S. that gene fragments are separately patentable suggests that the commercialization of a single biotechnology drug product may now require rights over numerous patents (Heller and Eisenberg, 1998). In Japan, it is conceivable that almost all products are "complex" per our definition because, in Japan, patents encompass fewer claims, and the claims themselves tend to be interpreted more narrowly, generating more patents per product and, in turn, wide-

[21] Kash and Kingston (2000) and Kusunoki, Nonaka and Nagata (1998) make a similar distinction; the latter use the terms "materials" and "systems" industries.

spread technological interdependence (cf. Granstrand, 2000). For example, in Japan in the mid 1990's, the average number of claims per patent was less than five (Japan Patent Office, 1998), whereas in the U.S. it was approximately 15 (Allison and Tiller, 2001).[22] Regarding the scope of claims, one former Japanese patent examiner said he felt compelled to narrow the claims to those spanned by the enablements, rather than broadly interpret the claims, as is U.S. practice (see also Helfgott, 1990).[23] Our survey finding that the average number of patent applications per million dollars of R&D expenditure to be 0.6 in the U.S. versus a much higher 2.8 in Japan ($p<.0001$) is also consistent with the notion that there are more patents per commercializable innovation in Japan than in the U.S.[24] Thus, with a greater number of patents per product and consequently greater interdependence across firms' technology holdings in Japan, we would expect greater use of patents (as in U.S. complex product industries) to protect market access via cross-licensing and less use to enforce exclusivity. Reinforcing the impact of greater interdependence, there is also less incentive to enforce exclusivity in Japan due to the lower expected payoff to filing infringement suits there.[25]

A central question for our purpose is whether policies that increase the number of patents per commercializable innovation stimulate uses of patents such as cross-licensing that lead to greater information sharing, or do such uses largely reflect cross-industry (but not cross-national) differences in product technology and characteristics. To compare the effects of national policy versus technology on the uses of patents, we divide our sample into discrete and complex product industries. Lacking direct measures

---

[22] Sakakibara and Branstetter (2001) explore the effect on R&D and patenting of the 1987 reform where Japan moved away from a one claim per patent requirement.

[23] This was particularly the case in pharmaceuticals (and perhaps chemicals more generally), where Japanese firms had lobbied for stricter interpretations of claims in order to create space for domestic patenting around European and American pharmaceutical company patents. Recently, however, there have been attempts to broaden claims in Japan by requiring examiners to justify in writing their narrowing of claims. In addition, a 1998 Supreme Court ruling introduced the doctrine of equivalents, further broadening patent scope.

[24] A small portion of this difference may be due to the higher propensity to patent observed in Japan. Our two surveys collected data on firms' propensities to patent, defined as the reported percentage of product or process innovations for which a respondent applied for patents. The overall propensities to apply for product and process patents in Japan are, respectively, 62% and 42%, and in the U.S., are 54% and 32%, implying that the different national propensities to patent account for at most a tenth of the observed differences in patents per R&D dollar. While the difference in patents per R&D dollar may also partly reflect different R&D productivities between the two nations, there is little evidence of such enormous differences in R&D productivity.

[25] Plaintiff success rates in infringement suits are much less in Japan (Hylton, 1993) and, when the plaintiff is successful, payouts tend to be less. Until 1998, for example, the highest payout in a Japanese infringement suit was approximately $3.2 million as compared to almost $900 million in the 1990 Polaroid v. Kodak decision in the U.S.

of the number of patents per product or process, and following Kusunoki *et al.* (1998) and our interviews, we operationalize the distinction between complex and discrete product technologies by assigning industries with ISIC codes less than 2900 (e.g., food, chemicals, drugs, metals and metal products) to the "discrete" product technology category and those with ISIC codes of 2900 or above (e.g., machinery, computers, electrical equipment, instruments, and transportation equipment) to the "complex" category, and exclude ISIC 3600 (other manufacturing). We conduct a series of comparisons of the uses of patents between the two industry types, across the two countries. While uses of patents within each of the two groups of industries are surely heterogeneous, such heterogeneity provides for a conservative test of group differences by biasing the differences toward zero.[26] Our expectation is that the uses of patents that reflect mutual dependence will be more common in complex than in discrete industries. Also, we expect such uses to be more common in Japan than in the U.S. Finally, and this is the critical test of the effect of difference in patent policy, the gap between the uses of patents in discrete versus complex product industries should be smaller in Japan than in the U.S.

To develop data on the uses of patents in the U.S. and Japan, we asked respondents to report the reasons motivating their decision to file their most recent patent application and to report which of these was the most important. The reasons considered include: to measure the performance of their firm's researchers, to obtain licensing revenue, to improve their position in negotiations (e.g., cross-licensing negotiations), to prevent patent infringement suits, to prevent copying, to prevent other firms from patenting a related invention, and to enhance the reputation of the firm. The aggregate (patent application-weighted) results are presented in Figure 6-4.

---

[26] To compare the uses of patents between the two industry types and two countries, we use a weighted logistic regression where: the weights are each respondent's country-standardized number of patent applications, the dependent variable is a specific reason for patenting, and the independent variables are two binary variables (COMPLEX and JAPAN) and their interaction. We then report the means for each cell of the two by two table, and the analysis of variance estimates for the effects of each variable and the interaction term. Analogous to a t-test for differences in group means, this method permits us both to account for the dichotomous (yes/no) character of the reasons to patent and, at the same time, weight those reasons by the number of country-standardized patent applications to better reflect how the "average" patent is used.

Since some firms account for many more of the patent applications in an industry than others, using unweighted responses would give small firms' patents relatively greater influence on the totals. In addition, because of the very different average number of patent applications between Japan and the U.S., the Japanese scores overwhelm the U.S. scores in the cross-industry comparisons. To reduce this gap, we created a country-standardized patent application measure to weight our regressions. We begin with each country's unadjusted mean and standard deviation (U.S. mean=29, s.d.=84; Japan mean=438, s.d.=1220), and then transform the scores by country for each respondent to create a country standardized variable with a mean=100 and s.d.=250.

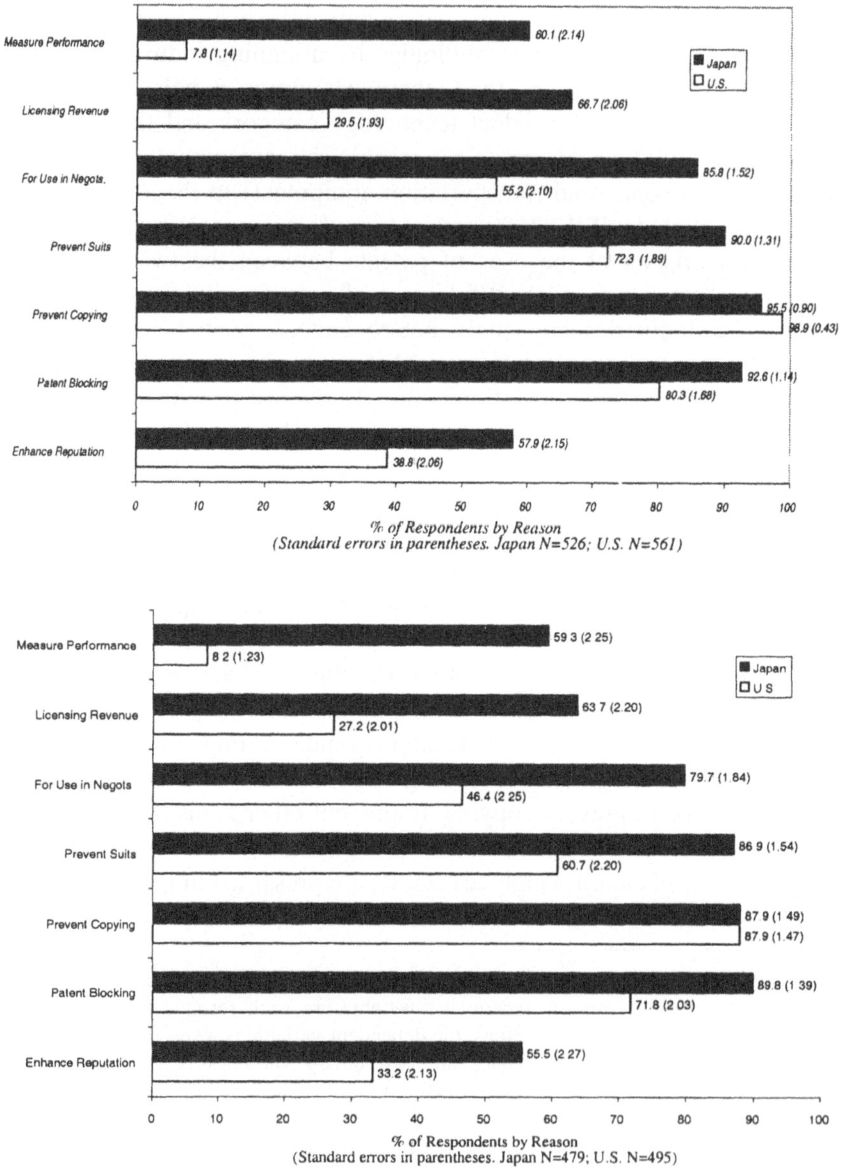

Figure 6-4a-b: Reasons to patent process innovations

Aside from the cross-industry differences, we find sharp cross-national differences. Generally, we find what might be called "strategic" uses of patents (e.g., to block others' patents, use in negotiations, to prevent infringement suits) to be common in both nations but more prevalent in Japan. For example, in the U.S., preventing rivals from patenting related inventions – what we call "patent-blocking" – was almost as pervasive as the prevention of copying as a motive for patenting.[27] For product innovations, 80% of U.S. respondents report blocking as a motive, second only to the prevention of copying which was reported by 99% of U.S. respondents (and significantly above preventing suits, $t=3.72$, $p<.01$). We see a similar result for process innovations (also significantly above preventing suits, $t=3.97$, $p<.0001$). And yet, while this use of patents is common in the U.S., Japanese firms rated patent blocking even higher (country difference is significant, χ^2 [1 d.f.]=3581, $p<.0001$), with 93% of respondents reporting blocking as a reason for applying for a patent on a product innovation.[28] For process innovations, patent blocking in Japan is more important still (country difference significant, χ^2 [1 d.f.]=5628, $p<.0001$). Defensive patenting also looms larger in Japan. The prevention of suits, listed by 90% and 87% of Japanese respondents for product and process inventions, respectively, is comparable in Japan to patent blocking as a reason for patenting (neither the product nor process scores differ significantly, $p>.05$). The Japanese figures also far exceed the comparable U.S. numbers of 72% and 61%.[29] Use of patents in negotiations is substantial in Japan at 86% and 80% for product and process inventions, respectively, greatly exceeding the U.S. figures of 55% and 46% (both country differences significant, $p<.0001$).[30]

We now consider our conjecture that greater mutual dependence in complex product industries and in Japan leads to greater use of patents for negotiations. Figure 6–5 shows for each country the weighted averages for discrete and complex product industries for various reasons to patent product innovations. As noted above, the use of patents to "improve your

---

[27] Since publication of a patent application after 18 months places the technology in the public domain, the published application alone, prior to any grant, can also prevent rivals from patenting identical or closely related inventions. Thus, it is not surprising that applicants do not request examination for a sizable share of applications. For example, of the 341,095 applications submitted in 1987, requests for examination were submitted by 1994 for only 47.6% of them (JPO, personal communication).

[28] The industry level results also show the motive of patent blocking to be at least as pervasive in Japan as in the U.S. in 18 of 26 industries.

[29] The country differences are significant (for product, χ^2 [1 d.f.]=107.2, $p<.0001$; for process, χ^2 [1 d.f.]=98.6, $p<.0001$).

[30] There is one other contrast between the two national samples with regard to reasons for patenting. Our data indicate that U.S. firms rarely (i.e., less than ten percent of respondents) rely on patents as a measure of the internal performance of their firms' researchers. In contrast, over half of the Japanese respondents report using patents in this way (country differences significant for both product and process, $p<.0001$), although they almost never cite it as the most important reason. Westney (1994) claims that it is this measurement of internal performance that mainly explains why firms patent so prolifically in Japan. Our investigation suggests that while performance measurement motivates Japanese firms to patent, the other "strategic" rationales for patenting highlighted above are more central to the way that patents are regarded in both countries.

position in negotiations with other firms, for example, in cross-licensing agreements" (labeled "Negotiate") is more common in Japan than in the U.S. Use of patents in negotiations is also more common in complex product industries than in discrete product industries. The overall averages for each country (not shown in Figure 6–5) are 82% "yes" for complex product industries, but only 49% "yes" for discrete product industries (p<.0001).[31]

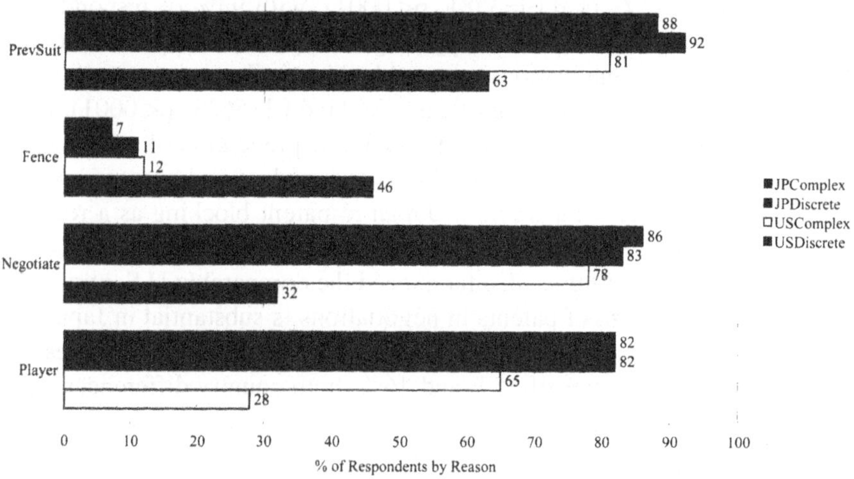

Figure 6-5. Reasons to patent product innovations, by country and by discrete and complex product industries

This confirms our expectations about the role of industry type on uses of patents. However, Figure 6–5 shows that this gap is primarily among U.S. firms because Japanese firms are equally likely to patent for use in negotiations *in complex and discrete product industries*. For the U.S. respondents, 78% of those in complex product industries report using patents for negotiations, while only 32% do so in discrete product industries. In contrast, in Japan, the percent reporting use in negotiations as a reason to patent is not only higher overall than in the U.S., but also nearly the same across the two groups of industries, about 85%. Thus, across the two groups of industries, Japanese firms are more similar than American firms in their use of patents for negotiations.

[31] The differences for process innovations are similar (73% for complex vs. 44% for discrete, p<.0001). In general, we are less certain about our predictions for process patents, because it is more difficult to know about the nature of the manufacturing process, and, thus, whether commercializable process innovations tend to be "discrete" or "complex" in a given industry.

As noted above, patent blocking is another common motive for patenting in both nations, though more prevalent in Japan. Cohen *et al.* (2000) identify two forms of patent blocking, though only one of these tend to foster information sharing. In the first form of patent blocking – which does not promote information sharing – firms patent numerous substitutes for some core invention, adopting what we call a "fence" strategy.[32] Alternatively, in complex product industries where a given innovation is comprised of numerous complementary elements, firms hold rights over technologies that others need to compete, and vice-versa, creating a condition of mutual dependence. Exploiting this mutual dependence, blocking in this case takes the form of patenting complements (in contrast to substitutes in the "fence" strategy) to preclude rivals' commercial use of their patents. By preventing other firms from controlling all the rights necessary to commercialize products, a firm will assure itself of "player" status in an industry in the sense of assuring itself access to the technology of rivals via cross-licensing – or, at least conferring the "freedom of operation" that comes from the ability to countersue if sued.[33]

To identify the use of patents for such a "player" strategy, we create a variable, "Player", which is "yes" if the firm uses the same patent *both* to prevent others from patenting related inventions *and* for negotiating cross-licensing agreements, and "no" otherwise. In other words, we are identifying respondents who use patents to block in order to compel other firms to cross-license with them and to strengthen their power in such negotiations. We expect the player strategy to be more common in complex product than in discrete product industries and more common in Japan than in the U.S. The row labeled "Player" in Figure 6–5 shows by country and industry type the percent of respondents who report using a patent for blocking

---

[32] For example, in the 1940's, du Pont patented over 200 substitutes for Nylon to protect its core invention (Hounshell and Smith, 1988).

[33] In addition to the work of Hall and Ziedonis (2001) for the U.S. semiconductor industry and Granstrand (2000) for selected Japanese firms, our interviews confirm the importance of this "player" strategy. One American R&D manager from the communications equipment industry (a "complex" product industry) stated: "Mostly, your patents are used in horse trading. You come together and say, 'Here's our portfolio'. In our industry, things all build on each other. We all overlap on each other's patents. Eventually we come to some agreement: 'You can use ours and we can use yours'." Japanese firms echoed this sentiment, noting that products tended to span patent portfolios and that patents were often used in cross-licensing agreements to secure "freedom of operation", the ability to make a product without interference from rival patent holders. These firms further confirmed that patents are traded largely to gain access to information and freedom of operation. One Japanese office equipment manager states, "Patents are not a good tool to get money. We always consider shaking hands (royalty-free cross-license). This cross-license gives us more freedom of design. Money is not so important as getting the other's technology when we license to other companies". Similarly, an IBM publication states: "The IBM patent portfolio gains us the freedom to do what we need to do through cross-licensing—it gives us access to the inventions of others that are key to rapid innovation". (Think, 1990, no. 5, pp. 10, 11).

and for negotiations (but not for licensing revenue). The overall averages across both nations (not shown in Figure 6–5) show that the use of the player strategy is indeed significantly higher in complex than in discrete product industries (73% vs. 46% for product innovations, 60% vs. 42% for process innovations, with both differences p<.0001). Figure 6–5 shows, however, that this result is driven by the difference across industry type only in the U.S. In Japan, the player strategy is used equally across complex and discrete product industries. Moreover, this strategy is employed more intensively in Japan than in the U.S., with discrete and complex product industries in Japan both scoring higher than the U.S. average for even complex product industries (the interaction effect is significant, p<.0001).[34]

As described above, a "fence" strategy entails a second form of patent blocking. In this case, firms patent substitutes for core inventions in order to maintain exclusivity over the technology. To the degree, however, that protecting some "core invention" patent requires it to be surrounded by numerous other patents, the transaction costs of licensing increases and the likelihood of licensing declines.[35] Also, since the goal is exclusivity, these patents tend not to be used for cross-licensing negotiations. To estimate how commonly the fence strategy is employed, we create a variable, "Fences", that is "yes" when firms report using a patent for patent blocking (i.e., to patent to prevent others from patenting related inventions), *but not* for licensing nor for use in negotiations, and "no" otherwise. We expect the fences strategy to be most common in discrete product industries, where the relatively low number of patentable elements per innovation makes fence building feasible. We also expect this strategy to be more common in the U.S., with a patent system that, as noted above, provides greater incentive to enforce exclusivity given higher expected payouts in infringement cases.

The row labeled "Fence" in Figure 6–5 shows patent application-weighted percentages of respondents reporting blocking as a motive for patenting, but not use in negotiations or licensing. The overall averages for product innovations (not shown in the figure) for discrete product industries is 34%, but for complex is only 10% (p<.0001). Figure 6–5 shows, as conjectured, that the use of patents to build such "fences" to be much less common in Japan no matter the industry (both the country effect and the interaction effect are significant, p<.0001).[36] Thus, while in discrete product industries in the U.S., patent blocking is a mechanism to

---

[34] We find similar results for process patents.

[35] Note that to the degree that patents are extremely effective in preventing copying, as is especially true in pharmaceuticals, then fence-building is not necessary since one or two patents can confer control of the market.

[36] We find a similar result for process patents.

generate appropriability through building patent fences, such fence building in Japan is rare across either kind of industry.

Our results indicate that Japanese, compared to U.S., firms, are much less likely to use their patents to achieve exclusivity (via, for example, a fence strategy), and much more likely to use them as a means of gaining market access, information from rivals and freedom of operation and design (the player strategy). By fostering technological interdependence across rivals and diminishing the returns to the enforcement of exclusivity, the Japanese patent system spawns a patent strategy across its entire manufacturing sector that is largely confined to the complex product technologies in the U.S. Pervasive interdependence across Japanese firms' patent holdings also encourages more patenting because successful execution of the player strategy requires the bargaining power that comes, in part, with having many patents.

We conjecture, therefore, that by encouraging cross-licensing and aggressive patenting, the Japanese patent system generates more disclosure and exchange of information. We suggest these impacts on information flows of the greater number of patents per product reinforce the effects of the Japanese system's rules of patent priority and disclosure and patent opposition discussed above.

6.5.2 Patents as a Channel of Information Flow

In this section, we consider whether patents are indeed a more important channel of intraindustry R&D knowledge flow spillover in Japan than in the U.S. as conjectured.

In our survey, we asked respondents to report the most important reason for *not* applying for a patent on the most recent invention which they decided not to patent. The reasons include: difficulty in demonstrating the novelty of the invention, the ease of legally inventing around, the information disclosed in a patent application, and the costs of applying for or defending a patent. The findings confirm that patents more effectively serve the information disclosure function in Japan than in the U.S. Specifically, Japanese firms are much more likely to report concerns over disclosure as the most important reason not to apply for a patent (46% vs. 26% in the U.S., χ^2 [1 d.f.]=54.0, p<.0001).

In our survey, we also examine the importance of different channels of R&D information flow across rivals. We asked both Japanese and U.S. respondents to score on a four point Likert scale the importance to a recently completed, "major" R&D project of each of the following sources of information on rival R&D: patents, informal information exchange, products (via, for example, reverse engineering), publications, public meetings and conferences, recent hires, licenses, joint or cooperative ventures, contracts with other firms and trade associations. Presenting the percent of respondents reporting that a given information source was "important" or "very important" (i.e., scoring at least a "three" on the four-point scale), Figure 6–6 provides comparisons for the aggregate samples.

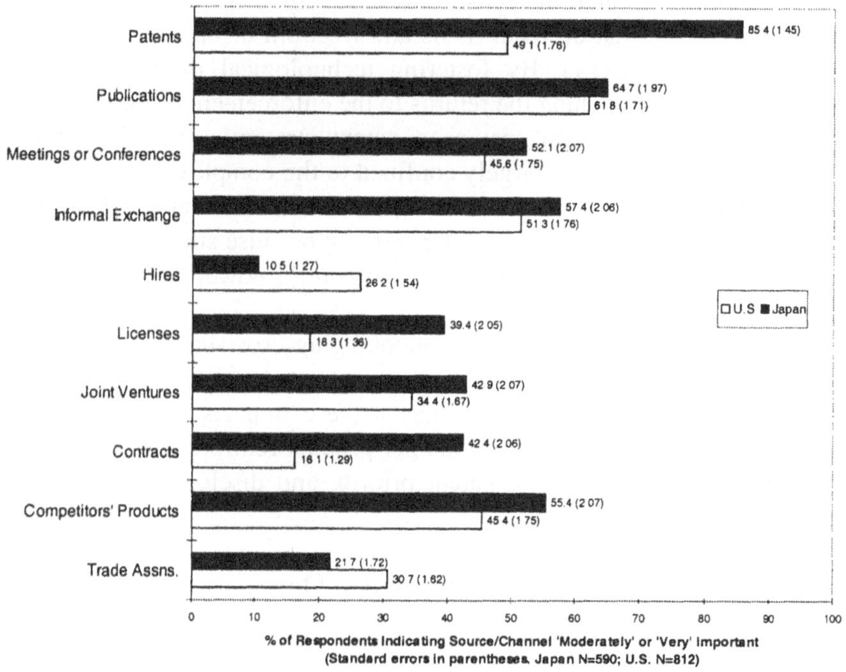

Figure 6-6. Importance of sources/channels of information on rivals' R&D

First, we find the same five sources of information on rival R&D – namely publications, public meetings or conferences, patents, informal information exchange and competitors' products (via, for example, reverse engineering) – to be the five most important sources in both nations.[37] A comparison of these five information sources shows the major difference between the two countries is in the importance of patents. The absolute score for patents in Japan exceeds that of the U.S. by 70% (χ^2 [1 d.f.]=175.7, p>.0001). In addition, patents are the most important channel in Japan, scoring over 30% higher than the next most highly ranked chan-

[37] Figure 6–6 also supports conclusion of Section 3 above that overall intraindustry R&D information flows are greater in Japan by showing that eight of the ten sources are rated more highly in Japan than in the U.S. (The country differences are significant (p<.05) for all but publications.) Moreover, the only two sources that are rated in absolute terms more highly in the U.S., namely recent hires and trade associations, are relatively unimportant in both nations as sources of information on rival R&D. Recent hires are easily the least important channel in Japan which is consistent with the convention of lifetime employment in Japan.

nel in Japan, publications (t=9.25, p<.0001). In the U.S., patents are ranked third behind publications and informal information exchange, and quite close to the sources of public meetings and conferences, and competitors' products (none of these are significantly below patents).[38] While patents play a role in diffusing information across rivals in the U.S., they appear to be the dominant channel in Japan.[39] Moreover, while some of the information conveyed by patents is conveyed via licensing, Figure 6–6 shows that licenses are a much less important source of information than patents generally, suggesting that a considerable portion of the information contained in patents is conveyed via public disclosure.[40]

These findings suggest that differences in the two nations' patent systems provide an important explanation for the differences in intraindustry R&D information flows and spillovers.[41]

---

[38] Two other sources score significantly higher in Japan, licenses and contracts. However, these two sources are relatively unimportant sources of information in both nations. They are the two least important information sources in the U.S. (significantly below the next lowest, hires, t=4.30, p<.0001) and are ranked only seventh and eighth in Japan (a little below joint ventures, t=1.8, p<.10). The higher ranking of licenses and contracts in Japan, and particularly their much higher absolute scores, is consistent with an environment where patents play a more important role in information diffusion since licensing typically requires a technology having been patented, and contracts often involve patented technologies.

[39] Some interview respondents noted that, while publications and meetings may be more important than patents as an information source in the U.S., firms may be willing to disclose information through publications or meetings only after they apply for a patent to protect that information. While we could not test this conjecture directly, we did examine the industry-level correlations between the mean importance of publications or meetings/conferences as an information source and the amount of patenting in an industry (measured as either the percent of respondents who had patented in the prior three years, the percent of product innovations patented, the percent of process innovations patented or the mean of the patent applications applied for among our respondents). These eight correlations range from -.14 to +.30. The only two significant (p<.10) correlations are between publications as an information source and either the propensity to patent process innovations (r=.24) or the mean number of patent applications (r=.30). If we control for the "generic" quality of information in an industry (which might increase both patenting and publications) by controlling for the importance of university research (measured as either the percent of projects that build on research findings, the percent of respondents for whom university research suggested new projects, or the percent for whom university research contributed to the completion of existing projects), these relationships weaken and become insignificant. Thus, while patenting may be a prerequisite for some publishing or meeting activities, we find only limited industry-level evidence suggesting a link between patenting and the disclosure of research via publications or presentations.

[40] The difference between the scores for patents and licenses are significant in each country (the paired t-test results for the U.S. are t=14.87, p<.0001; for Japan, t=18.90, p<.0001).

[41] Our argument that the role of Japanese patents in diffusing information across rivals is a key reason for the difference in R&D spillovers between the U.S. and Japan assumes that the patent filings of U.S. firms in Japan are not a major source of information to U.S. firms on the R&D activities of their American rivals. Although one might believe that U.S. firms have strong incentives to patent in Japan, only a fraction of U.S. patent applications are

6.6 Other Explanations

In addition to differences in the patent system, there are surely other possible explanations for greater intraindustry R&D spillovers in Japan. These might include, for example, cross-national differences in the significance of innovations ("major vs. incremental"), managerial practices regarding the monitoring of extramural information, the role of R&D consortia, geographic proximity, and market structure. To the extent that our data permit, we consider each of these in turn.

We begin with differences in the significance of innovations. The literature has long suggested that innovation tends to be more incremental in Japan than in the U.S. Consequently, R&D information spillovers may be more easily exploited by rivals. While Japanese innovation may have been more incremental in the past, that was not necessarily true by the 1990's. Rosenberg and Steinmueller (1988), for example, claim that R&D in the U.S. tends to be much more incremental than commonly thought. Our U.S. and Japanese questionnaires posed a question that partially addresses the point. In response to a question on the percent of R&D projects initiated with the goal of improving the performance or quality of existing products (as distinct, for example, from creating altogether new products), Japanese respondents overall reported 37.9% while U.S. respondents reported 40.3% (χ^2 [1 d.f.]=3.73, $p<.10$). Thus, our limited data do not support the notion that, as of the mid-1990s, Japanese R&D is any more incremental overall than is U.S. R&D.

The literature also suggests that Japanese firms are more aggressive than U.S. firms in exploiting extramural knowledge (e.g., Mansfield (1988)). Consequently, Japanese firms may report greater use of rivals' R&D findings because they expend more effort on monitoring and exploiting extramural information, not because there is more information

filed there. For example, American firms filed about 89 thousand patent applications in the U.S. in 1991. In contrast, they filed less than 16,000 applications in the same year in Japan (Science and Technology Agency, Japan, 1995). Moreover, those 16,000 applications in Japan are not equivalent to the same number of U.S. patent applications since, as noted above, Japanese patents tend to bundle about three times as many claims per patent than U.S. patents, suggesting that U.S. corporate patent applications in Japan may be equivalent to only about 6% of the number of patents filed in the U.S. The absence of aggressive filing of patents in Japan by American firms may reflect the skewed distribution of the value of patents, a focus on the domestic U.S market of many U.S. firms, concern over early disclosure per the Japanese system, and problems associated with the filing and enforcement of their patents in Japan, including the length of time involved, the cost and the scope of patent protection granted (US GAO, 1993). Also, though patent abstracts have been available since 1990, the official language of Japanese patents is Japanese, reducing the availability of the details of the disclosed patent application to most U.S. R&D personnel.

that "spills out". [42] Our survey questionnaire poses two questions on the subject of firms' attention to extramural information. First, we asked the respondents in Japan and the U.S. to estimate the amount of time their R&D personnel devote to monitoring and gathering information on new scientific and technical developments. Japanese respondents report that they devote, on average, 12.5% of their R&D effort to monitoring and gathering information, in comparison to 12.1% reported by the U.S. respondents ($t=0.75$, $p>.45$). We also asked respondents to indicate the percentage of their R&D projects that are at least partly initiated to keep up-to-date with new developments, which again can be viewed as one measure of effort dedicated to exploiting extramural information. Again, there is no striking difference between the U.S. and Japanese respondents. Japanese respondents indicate that this reason for initiating projects applies to 32% of their projects on average, while U.S. respondents report 33% on average (χ^2 [1 d.f.]=0.2, $p>.65$).[43]

Another possible explanation, based partially on interviews with Japanese firms, is that the geographic concentration of Japanese industry, and particularly Japanese R&D labs, in the Tokyo region generates greater spillover. We have evidence that bears indirectly on the influence of geographic proximity in the two countries. We start with the assumption that of the major sources of information on rival R&D (patents, publications, conferences, reverse engineering and informal information exchange), informal information exchange is the one most likely to be structured by proximity. A second source that may also be heavily conditioned by proximity is recently hired technical personnel. We compared the importance of each of these sources by country. We find that informal information exchange is greater in Japan than in the U.S. (57% vs. 51% scoring it at least "moderately important", $p<.05$), consistent with the geographic proximity argument. However, the gap (6 percentage points), while statistically significant, is relatively small, particularly compared to the 36 percentage point difference in the scores for the importance of patents as an information source on rival R&D. Also, in terms of relative ranks, informal information exchange is the second most important source in the U.S.,

[42] Of course, the "information availability" versus "effort" explanations are not mutually exclusive. The notion of an endogenous "absorptive capacity" (Cohen and Levinthal [1989]) suggests that the more potentially useful information there is in a firm's environment, the more effort the firm will expend to evaluate and exploit it

[43] As further evidence that there are not systematic differences in the level of monitoring, we note that, while Japanese firms report greater use of information from rivals, they do not uniformly report greater use of outside information generally. We find, for example, that while inflows from public research appear to be greater in Japan, those from customers are not obviously so, and those from suppliers appear to be less. This suggests that the greater intraindustry information flows observed in Japan do not necessarily reflect some broader Japanese managerial practice that affects flows from all information sources generally, but are due to factors that affect especially intraindustry information flows.

and only the third most important in Japan. In the case of new hires, as noted above, U.S. firms score this well above the Japanese (26% vs. 11%, p<.0001), although in both countries this is a relatively low ranked information source.[44] Thus, although very indirect, the evidence that we can marshall does not lead us to believe that the patterns we observe are due principally to geographic proximity.

Another explanation for the higher spillovers in Japan is the greater use of government-sponsored research consortia (e.g., Branstetter and Sakakibara (1997). We were not able to test this directly, since we do not have any measure of participation in such consortia. We do find, however, that Japanese firms report joint or cooperative research projects to be a more important source of information on rivals. Figure 6-2 shows that 42.9% of Japanese firms compared to 34.4% of U.S. firms considered this an important source of information on rival R&D (χ^2 [1 d.f.]=111.3, p<.0001). But this source ranks only sixth in importance in both countries (significantly below the fifth highest in each country, p<.001). Thus, while such consortia appear to be relatively more important in Japan, they are not a key source for intraindustry information flows more generally, and thus are likely not a primary explanation for the substantial difference in spillovers across the two countries.

An additional source of difference in spillovers may be market structure, or, more precisely, the number of direct competitors. The argument is simple. To the degree that there are more direct competitors, appropriability will be less partly due to competition and partly due to a greater likelihood of a rival profiting from your R&D. Expressed with respect to R&D information flows, the latter point can be recast as suggesting that the greater the number of rivals working in a similar technological area, the greater the likelihood of any one firm picking up relevant information from another.

Allowing us to explore this argument for Japan and the U.S., we asked respondents how many firms, by region (e.g., North America, Asia, Europe), "are able to introduce competing innovations in time to effectively diminish your firm's profits from your innovations". Assuming that information from geographically proximate firms is most accessible, we compare the average number of domestic technological rivals identified in both nations. In Japan, the average number is 5.0 firms, while the average in the U.S. is 3.9 firms and significantly less (t=3.64, p<.001), which is consistent with the possibility that less concentrated market structures in

[44] Also note that while the population of firms is more geographically dispersed in the U.S. than in Japan, the U.S. economy is characterized by many industry-specific geographic clusters (Porter 1998). Thus, while firms overall may be dispersed, firms in particular industries are often quite concentrated, with Detroit and Silicon Valley being two famous examples.

Japan may partially explain the difference in intraindustry R&D spillovers between the two nations.

Thus, we find little evidence for the claims that the difference in R&D spillovers is due to more incremental innovation in Japan, Japanese firms' expenditure of more effort on monitoring rivals or greater geographic proximity of rivals. We find some evidence for the impact of Japanese R&D consortia on information flows, and some evidence in behalf of a role for market structure. Nonetheless, our findings suggest that patent policy plays an important role in generating intraindustry spillovers, and, one might conjecture, the efficiency of innovative effort as well.

6.7 Conclusion

Our comparison of appropriability conditions and R&D-related information flows in the U.S. and Japan suggest some similarities, but mostly differences between the two nations. In both countries, the use of lead time advantages and complementary manufacturing and sales capabilities figure prominently in the way firms protect their inventions. Differences are, however, numerous. Secrecy, for example, is prominent in the appropriability strategies of U.S. but not Japanese firms. Though comparably rated in absolute terms, patents are reported to be the least effective among the major appropriability mechanisms in the preponderance of U.S. industries, but among the most effective in Japan. Notwithstanding the relative effectiveness of particular mechanisms, our data – especially our measures of imitation lags – also suggest that it is more difficult to protect rents due to invention in Japan than in the U.S. in almost all manufacturing industries (except computers). Consistent with this observation, we observe that R&D-related information flows across rivals and, we infer, R&D spillovers as well, are significantly greater in Japan.

Our cross-national, within-industry comparisons suggest that not only industry characteristics differentiate appropriability conditions and R&D spillovers, but also factors that cut across industries, such as the institutions, policies, cultures or norms that are distinctive to nations. Building upon the work of Ordover (1991), Granstrand (2000) and others, we proposed that one difference between the two nations, namely their respective patent systems, may at least partly account for the differences we observe, especially in intraindustry R&D information flows. These scholars argue that differences between the two nations in rules of patent priority, disclosure and patent opposition strengthen the contribution of patents to information flows across firms in Japan. Our data showing that patents are a more important channel of R&D information flow across rivals in Japan support this claim. In fact, we find that patents are *the most important* channel for such information flow in Japan.

Building on our analysis of appropriability conditions and the role of patents in the U.S. (Cohen *et al.*, 2000), we suggest that yet another difference between the U.S. and Japanese patent systems might further explain this finding. We argued that the lower number and narrower construction of claims per patent that yield a greater number of patents per product in Japan should spawn greater mutual dependence across the technological holdings of rivals, and, in turn, a greater tendency to use patents for mutual blocking, cross-licensing and negotiations – uses that tend to promote greater information sharing across rivals. We find that this "player" strategy, which in the U.S. is concentrated in complex product industries, applies equally across discrete and complex product industries in Japan, suggesting a policy impact on a behavior that Cohen *et al.* (2000) conjectured to be driven largely by physical differences between products. This pattern of use of patents also implies that Japanese firms tend to use patents more to assure their inclusion and freedom of operation even in discrete product markets where U.S. firms tend to use patents more for exclusion. The use of patents in Japan for maintaining market access and freedom of operation rather than for exclusion is reinforced by the comparatively low payoffs to infringement suits in Japan.

In addition to strengthening R&D spillovers, the technological interdependence induced by the Japanese patent system also likely stimulates patenting activity. A firm's successful execution of the player strategy depends in part on the bargaining power that comes with possession of a larger patent portfolio. Patents become weapons in mutually reinforcing, noncooperative strategic interactions where firms feel increasingly compelled to patent either because they need to protect themselves from suits or from being blocked, or they want to block rivals or use patents as bargaining chips in negotiations (cf. Cohen, *et al.*, 2000; Hall and Ziedonis, 2001; Granstrand, 2000). Consequently, firms in complex product industries in the U.S. and across the entire manufacturing sector in Japan may be accumulating more patents, and incurring more related litigation and other costs than what is collectively optimal. Our results suggest that if patenting is excessive, however, the associated social costs may be offset more in Japan to the degree that patents, ceteris paribus, diffuse information more effectively and the incentives to litigate are less.

An important limitation to our study is that we are observing similarities and differences in R&D spillovers and appropriability conditions between the U.S. and Japan at a point in time. Patent law and administrative and judicial practice have been changing in both nations, however, even since our survey was administered in 1994. Since differences in the patent systems impact the way patents are used and the degree of protection they afford, the patterns we observe today may not endure. Policy changes also raise the question of the degree to which differences in institutional environments across nations are exogenous, reflecting nations' cultures and unique histories, or are endogenous to global economic competition. In the case of patent policies, there appears to be an important endogenous component, stimulated by high profile infringement suits between U.S. and Japanese firms, trade disputes and, more generally, competition between the two nations' industries and firms.[45]

Mazzoleni and Nelson (1998) point out that the academic literature and much of the policy debate on patents have focused on the impact of patents on appropriability (an exception is Aoki and Spiegel (1998)). By showing that patents can have important and pervasive effects on information diffusion and R&D spillovers, and perhaps, in turn, on the efficiency of innovative effort, our results imply that the information diffusion effects of patents deserve at least equal time from policymakers and academics. The U.S. has recently adopted a policy of automatic disclosure of (most) patent applications after 18 months. One may question whether automatic disclosure will significantly affect R&D spillovers in the absence of the other judicial and administrative practices and policies that conditioned Japanese firms' incentives of when to patent, what to patent and how to use patents – all in ways that foster technology diffusion.[46] The first-to-file priority rule induces firms to patent earlier in the innovation process. The opposition process strengthened firms' incentives to monitor rivals' patents. Narrow construction of claims and fewer claims per patent (and, hence, more patents per product) foster interdependence and cross-licensing, while low infringement awards further diminish the returns to a strategy of exclusion.

Although we would like to see policymakers and academics pay more attention to the impact of patents on technology diffusion, we are not arguing that a patent system that promotes diffusion to the extent observed in Japan is, on balance, socially desirable.[47] A key question is how more disclosure affects R&D investment incentives. To the degree that disclosure does not dampen incentives to conduct R&D itself, a patent regime that strongly supports disclosure yields an unambiguous social welfare

---

[45] Ironically, some of the differences between the two nations' patent systems may reflect different responses to the same interactions. For example, Japanese firms have aggressively embraced patents partly in reaction to prominent infringement suits filed by American against Japanese firms over the prior ten to fifteen years. At the same time, American firms may have drawn a different lesson from the same events, namely that patents provide only partial protection and must be supplemented when possible by other ways of protecting their inventions, such as secrecy.

[46] In a theoretical treatment, Aoki and Spiegel (1998) consider the impacts on R&D spending and patenting of adoption of an 18 month automatic disclosure rule alone. Their model predicts that such a move would discourage patenting in industries where patents are only moderately effective, and that R&D would decline. As we note above, however, Japanese R&D intensities and patent propensities are on average higher than those of the U.S.

[47] One possibility is that different patent systems may be better suited to some industries versus others.

benefit, and, indeed, Japanese firms' R&D intensities and patent propensities exceed U.S. firms' overall. Before we can conclude, however, that a patent system that aggressively promotes diffusion yields a net social benefit, we require a more complete empirical analysis that considers the offsetting incentive and complementarity (or efficiency) effects of intraindustry information flows on R&D,[48] the mutual determination of R&D and patenting, as well as the other factors conditioning R&D.

6.8 Literature References

Agresti A. and Agresti B., *Statistical Methods for the Social Sciences.* San Francisco, CA: Dellen, 1979.

Allison J.R. and Tiller E.H. Statistical Analysis of Internet Business Method Patents. Draft report to the National Academies' STEP Board; 2001 October 7.

Aoki R. and Spiegel Y. Public Disclosure of Patent Applications, R&D, and Welfare. Tel Aviv University, Working Paper No. 30-98, 1998.

Arundel A. The relative effectiveness of patents and secrecy for appropriation. *Research Policy* 2001; 30: 611-24.

Bowker Press, *Directory of American Research and Technology.* New York: Bowker Press, 1994.

Branstetter Lee and Sakakibara Mariko. *Japanese Research Consortia.* Mimeo, UCLA, 1997.

Cohen W.M. and Levinthal D.A. Innovation and Learning: The Two Faces of R&D - Implications for the Analysis of R&D Investment. *Economic Journal* 1989; 99: 569-96.

Cohen W.M., Nelson R.R. and Walsh J.P. *Protecting their Intellectual Assets: Appropriability Conditions and Why U.S. Manufacturing Firms Patent (or Not).* NBER Working Paper #7552, 2000.

Cohen W.M., Nelson R.R. and WalshJ.P. *R&D spillovers, patents and the incentives to innovate in Japan and the United States.* Carnegie Mellon University, mimeo, 2001.

Cohen W.M. and Walsh J.P. *R&D Spillovers, Appropriability and R&D Intensity: A Survey-Based Approach.* Report to the Economic Assessment Office, NIST Advanced Technology Program, 2000.

Dillman D.A., *Mail and Telephone Surveys: The Total Design Method.* New York: Wiley-Interscience, 1978.

Granstrand Ove, *The Economics and Management of Intellectual Property.* London: Edward Elgar, 2000.

Griliches Z. 'The Search for R&D Spillovers. *Scandinavian Journal of Economics* 1992; 94 (3, Supplement): 529-47.

[48] Studies that have considered the offsetting effects of intraindustry information flows on R&D productivity and incentives include Spence (1984), Levin and Reiss (1984), Cohen and Levinthal (1989) and Cohen and Walsh (2000).

Hall B. and Ziedonis R.M. 'The patent paradox revisited: an empirical study of patenting in the U.S. semiconductor industry, 1979-1995. *Rand Journal of Economics* 2001; 32: 101-28.

Helfgott S. 'Cultural differences between the U.S. and Japanese patent systems. *Journal of the Patent and Trademark Office Society* 1990; 72: 231-8.

Heller M.A. and Eisenberg R.S. 'Can patents deter innovation? *Science* 1998; 280 May 1: 698-71.

Hounshell D.A. and Smith J.K., *Science and Corporate Strategy*. Cambridge: Cambridge University Press, 1988.

Hylton K. 'Asymmetric Information and the Selection of Disputes for Litigation'. *Journal of Legal Studies* 1993; 22: 187-210.

Kash D.E. and Kingston W. *Patents in a World of Complex Technologies*, Mimeo, George Mason University, 2000.

Kusunoki K., Nonaka I. and Nagata A. 'Organizational capabilities in product development of Japanese firms. *Organization Science* 1998; 9: 699-718.

Levin R.C., Klevorick A.K., Nelson R.R. and Winter S.G. *Appropriating the returns from industrial R&D*. Brookings Papers on Economic Activity 1987; 783-820.

Levin R.C. and Reiss P.C. "Tests of a Schumpeterian Model of R&D and Market Structure". In *R&D Patents and Productivity*, Z. Griliches, ed. Chicago: University of Chicago Press for the NBER, 1984.

Mansfield E. Patents and Innovation: 'An Empirical Study. *Management Science* 1986; 32: 173-81.

Mansfield E. 'The Speed and cost of Industrial Innovation in Japan and the United States: External vs. Internal Technology. *Management Science* 1988; 34 (10): 1157-68.

Mazzoleni R. and Nelson R.R. 'The Benefits and Costs of Strong Patent Protection. *Research Policy* 1998; 27: 273-84.

National Science Foundation, *National Patterns of R&D Resources*: 2000.

Data Update. http://www.nsf.gov/sbe/srs/nsf01309/

NISTEP (National Institute of Science and Technology Policy). *Technological opportunities and appropriating the returns from innovation - Comparison of survey results from Japan and the U.S. Tokyo*. Report no. 48, 1997.

Okada Y. "Patent System and R&D in Japan" In *Innovation in Japan*, A. Goto and H. Odagiri, eds. Oxford: Clarendon Press, 1997.

Ordover J. 'A Patent System for Both Diffusion and Exclusion. *Journal of Economic Perspectives* 1991; 5(1): 43-60.

Porter M.E., *On Competition*, Boston: Harvard Business School Press, 1998.

Quillen C.D. and Webster O.H. 'Continuing Patent Applications and Performance of the U.S. Patent Office. *Federal Circuit Bar Journal*, 2002.

Rosenberg N. and Steinmueller W.E. 'Why are Americans Such Poor Imitators?. *American Economic Review* 1988; 78(2): 229-34.

Sakakibara M. and Branstetter L. 'Do stronger patents induce more innovation? Evidence from the 1988 Japanese Patent Law Reforms. *Rand Journal of Economics* 2001; 32: 77-100.

Scherer F.M. *et al., Patents and the Corporation.* 2nd edn, Boston: privately published, 1959.

Scotchmer S. and Green J. 'Novelty and Disclosure in Patent Law. *Rand Journal of Economics* 1990; 21: 131-46.

Spence A.M. 'Cost Reduction, Competition, and Industry Performance. *Econometrica* 1984; 52: 101-21.

Taylor C.T. and Silberston Z.A., *The Economic Impact of the Patent System: A study of the British Experience.* Cambridge: Cambridge University Press, 1973.

U.S. G.A.O. *Intellectual Property Rights: U.S. Companies' Patent Experiences in Japan.* GAO/GGD-93-126. Washington, DC: General Accounting Office, 1993.

U.S. G.A.O. *Intellectual Property: Comparison of Patent Examination*, 1997

Statistics for Fiscal Years 1994 and 1995, GAO/RCED-97-58, Washington, D.C.: General Accounting Office

Westney E. "Country Patterns in R&D Organization: The United States and Japan". In *Country Competitiveness*, B. Kogut, ed. New York: Oxford University Press, 1992, pp. 36-53.

Westney E. "The Evolution of Japan's Industrial Research and Development". In T*he Japanese Firm*, M. Aoki and R. Dore, eds. New York: Oxford University Press, 1994.

Chapter 7

INTELLECTUAL PROPERTY RIGHTS AND ACADEMIC HEALTH CENTERS

Jeannette Colyvas*, Annetine Gelijns**, and Nathan Rosenberg*
**Stanford University, Stanford, California, USA*
*** Columbia University, New York, NY, USA*

Chapter contents:

Abstract: Academic Health Centers have become an increasingly important locus of inventive activity in biomedicine. The observed increase in patenting and licensing activity taking place at AHCs has called attention to this phenomenon but has also raised questions about the impact on the creation and diffusion of important technologies and research tools. This paper explores the contributions of academic health centers in generating new medical technologies, addressing the ways in which intellectual property rights affect technological innovation and diffusion. The paper underscores the relevance of understanding important features of the innovative process, namely the nature and degree of uncertainty in technological change. The paper draws on patent data and case studies from Columbia and Stanford University to illustrate these issues and raises questions about the costs and benefits of various commercialization strategies and university patenting approaches.

O. Granstrand (ed.), Economics, Law and Intellectual Property, 155-176.

7.1 Introduction

Patents constitute a valuable source of information on the contributions of U.S. universities to technological innovation and to the subsequent commercialization of these innovations. The authors share an interest in academic health centers (AHCs) in terms of the specific roles that they play with the university community in generating new medical technologies. For us, therefore, a particular form of intellectual property rights, i.e., the patent system, serves as a window into the contributions of AHCs to technological innovation. We should add, right away, that we are also interested in examining the contributions of AHCs that are *not* reflected in the patent data. There is the familiar pitfall here, of which we are very acutely aware, of focusing research attention on the variables that are readily quantifiable and neglecting those that are not, even though the latter may be far more important than the former. (The analogy here of course is to the drunk looking for his house keys under the corner street light. He knows that that's not where he lost the keys, but that's where the light is best.) One can make a strong case that, in the long run, the economic and social payoffs to basic research, which we cannot measure very well, are likely to be much greater than the payoffs to research of a more applied nature, where we do at least have some very useful patent data. This concern remains valid even though the American patent office has extended its patent coverage to certain forms of scientific knowledge of a quite fundamental nature.

Secondly, we have already devoted much time to looking at research tools in medicine, and this has raised in our minds the question of whether the patent system ought to treat research tools differently from innovations that do not perform a research function. This is, in fact, our main policy concern, and the burden of our discussion of it so far, regretfully, is that the issues involved are really even more complex than they have so far been made out to be. This concern is further exacerbated by the great uncertainty that usually exists concerning the eventual future uses of new technological capabilities. This uncertainty has important implications in developing a special patent policy for research tools, because it has been a frequent occurrence, as we will see, that new research technologies have become both diagnostic tools and tools of therapy.

Given these research interests of ours, then, it is interesting to note that the patent system *itself* has become a powerful research tool in very recent years; i.e., we will be exploiting the data, thrown up by the patent system, as a research base to provide evidence on the complex policy issues involved in the patenting of research tools. In doing this, we are engaging in what Robert

Merton (the Elder) has termed a "self-exemplifying phenomenon". That is to say, we are using the patent system *itself* as a research tool.

7.2 AHCs and Technological Change

The data on university patenting and licensing revenue identify a recent institutional development of great economic and, more generally, human significance: the AHC is now the dominant contributor, within the university research community, to technological innovation. "In 1970, one-eighth of the patents issued to universities were for biomedical inventions; by 1990, the percentage had doubled... Presently, over sixty percent of all university licenses are based upon biomedical inventions...."[1] Invention disclosure, patent, and licensing data of our two universities, Columbia University and Stanford University, also documents the overwhelming importance of AHCs as contributors to university inventive activity today and in recent years. Figure 7-1, for example, shows the growth of inventive activity at Columbia, as measured by the number of invention reports that faculty fill out when they believe they have created something of commercial value. Figure 7-2 depicts licensing activities at Columbia, which shows that the medical school is responsible for nearly 85% of all licensed inventions. At Stanford, 4 patented medical inventions (rDNA, the CT scanner, the fluorescence-activated cell sorter, and fluorescent conjugates) are among the 5 highest revenue earners in Stanford's history. In fact, these 4 technologies alone accounted for nearly 70% of all Stanford OTL reported revenue from 1976 up through 1994-95.[2]

---

[1] 'Biomedical' is here defined to include medical devices; Association of University Technology Managers (AUTM), "Licensing Survey, FY 1999: Full Report".

[2] Stanford University Office of Technology Licensing.

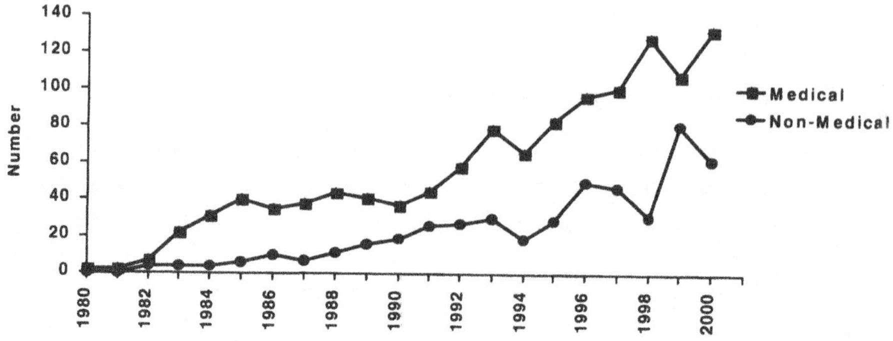

Figure 7-1. Annual Columbia invention reports

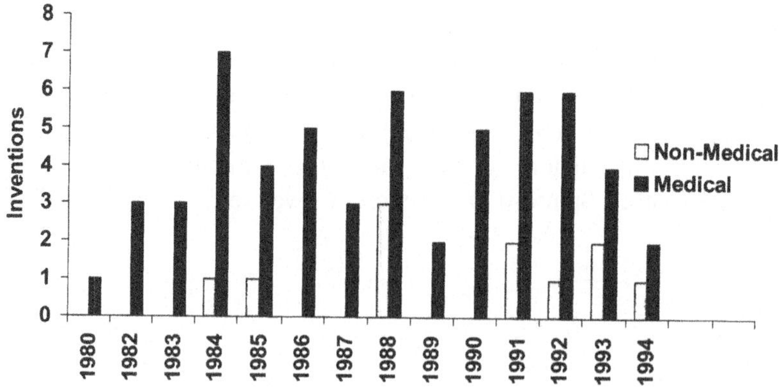

Figure 7-2. Columbia inventions resulting in licenses, 1980-1994

Academic health centers are among the most complex institutions in modern societies. They are multi-functional organizations that have a three-pronged mission: (1) they provide advanced specialty and tertiary care, and thus are early adopters of the "latest" in technology, as well as providers of care for the indigent; (2) they train biomedical researchers and clinicians and thereby shape the distribution of medical skills and specialties; and (3) they conduct a wide range of biomedical research activities ranging from fundamental bench research in such fields as molecular biology and genetics, to translational research, development of technology, and clinical testing in small groups of individuals and large populations. There is another dimension of diversity within AHCs: their research output includes clinical procedures, pharmaceuticals, medical devices, and a new subclass of medical technology, that of biotechnology, which did not even exist 25 years ago.

These medical technologies are manufactured by several extremely research-intensive industries, with distinct organizational characteristics, in terms of the number of firms and their size distribution. The oldest is the pharmaceutical industry, emerging in late nineteenth-century Europe as an offspring of the dye and chemical industry. The pharmaceutical industry today is multinational in scope, and is undergoing significant consolidation. In the past few years, there have been more than a dozen major acquisitions or mergers involving world-class, research-based pharmaceutical firms, including Novartis, Glaxo Wellcome, and Pfizer Warner Lambert. The pharmaceutical industry is highly competitive (none of the companies holds more than an eight percent share of the market), and extremely research-intensive (investing 18% of annual sales in R&D). The modern medical device industry is essentially a post-WW II phenomenon. In the U.S.A, it is comprised of some 16,000 firms. The firms are small (80% have less than 50 employees), and the industry is also highly research-intensive (investing over 12% of annual sales in R&D, with the most innovative firms investing up to 18%).[3] The biotechnology industry is the youngest addition to AHCs, emerging in the past quarter century. In the United States, it involves numerous start-up firms, although most of the more than 2,000 firms are not operating companies but investor-funded R&D ventures.[4] It too is highly research-intensive (investing $8 billion in R&D in 1999), and has very strong university ties, as well as many collaborative arrangements with pharmaceutical firms.

Biotech is a new industry that was actually invented in AHCs. The industry began with the revolution in genetics and molecular biology nearly half a century ago with the discovery of the function and, ultimately, the structure of DNA and continued with the discovery of techniques of genetic engineering. From its inception, this industry has been intimately tied to academic

[3] The Lewin Group, *Outlook for Medical Technology Innovation. The State of the Industry.* Washington DC: Health Industry Manufacturers Association, 2000.

[4] National Research Council, Intellectual Property Rights and Research Tools in Molecular Biology: Summary of a Workshop Held at the National Academy of Sciences, February 15-16, 1996 (Washington DC: National Academy Press).

scientists. Stanford filed its Cohen-Boyer patent on recombinant DNA technology in 1974, and Boyer, then at UCSF, and Swanson, a venture capitalist, founded the first successful biotech firm (Genentech) in 1977. Genentech engineered human insulin (marketed as humulin by Eli Lilly) which was the first commercial recombinant DNA product.[5] The geographic distribution of the industry in close proximity to research universities is evidence of the value of "star" scientists who have made significant contributions to biotechnology.[6] Audretsch and Stephan observe that "firms are geographically concentrated in three primary regions (the San Francisco-Bay Area, San Diego and Boston), two secondary regions (Philadelphia and New York), and a number of smaller clusters".[7] Harvard, Stanford, and the University of California at San Francisco have been the major producers of "scientific contacts" in the realm of biotechnology.[8]

Biotechnology accounts for an important share of the research output of Academic Health Centers. A breakdown of all invention reports, patents, and licenses at Columbia University between 1980 and 1995 also confirms the dominating importance of biotech agents. In fact, 60% of all invention reports and over 50% of all patents at Columbia were classified as biotech agents.[9]

Another major research output of AHCs is medical devices. At Columbia, 22% of all medical invention reports and 25% of all medical patents can be classified as medical devices.[10] The nature of the innovation process of medical devices, however, is substantially different from that of biologicals and pharmaceuticals. University departments, both within the medical school or outside of it (especially physics or electrical engineering),

---

[5] Niels Reimers, "Tiger by the Tail". *Chemtech*, (August 1987): 464-471; reprinted in *The Journal of the Association of University Technology Managers*, Vol. 7 (1995): 6.

[6] Lynne G. Zucker, Michael R. Darby, "Star Scientists and Institutional Transformation: Patterns of Invention and Innovation in the Formation of the Biotechnology Industry". *Proceedings of the National Academy of Sciences of the United States of America*, Vol. 93, No. 23 (Nov. 12, 1996): 12709-12716. Audretsch and Stephan hypothesize that "[w]hen university-based scientists are actively involved in knowledge transfer, their knowledge is more easily tapped if the firm is located in the same region as the scientist. But when the scientist plays other roles geographic proximity is considerably less important". David B. Audretsch and Paula E. Stephan, "Company-Scientist Locational Links: The Case of Biotechnology". *The American Economic Review*, Vol. 86, No. 3 (Jun., 1996): 644.

[7] Audretsch and Stephan, 642.

[8] Audretsch and Stephan, 644.

[9] These calculations were made using Columbia Innovation Enterprise (CIE) invention reports 1980-1994.

[10] CIE invention reports 1980-1994.

may generate new scientific insights or improved technological capabilities. Device innovation, therefore, is much more interdisciplinary in nature than pharmaceutical innovation. Moreover, devices – unlike pharmaceuticals – undergo extensive modification and refinement before and after introduction into the marketplace. Patents for medical devices are less important, in that they are easier to invent around, and product life cycles are shorter. Consider for example the lithotripter which was first developed and introduced by the firm Dornier in 1984 in the US.[11] Dornier's patent rights could be circumvented relatively easily because the basic technological principle by which shock waves were generated in the Dornier device, the "spark-gap" principle, could be realized in several other ways.[12]

The development of a device, its modification, and refinement of indications of use are often intricately linked to a specialized user group – i.e., clinicians in AHCs. Consider the field of computer tomography X-ray (CT) scanning. "CT scanning relies on X-rays but uses mathematical techniques and computer technology to produce images from which one can derive three-dimensional information".[13] Combining important scientific insights and improvements taking place at universities in such disciplines as neurology, computer science, mathematics, and nuclear physics, the first commercial CT scanner was introduced by Electrical and Musical Industries Ltd. (EMI) and installed in the Mayo Clinic in 1973.[14] Product modification and improvement in this imaging field moved rapidly, and radiologists played a particularly important role both in the development of new device prototypes and providing feedback to industrial firms about the necessary improvements. In the mid-1970s, for example, a collaborative research team of radiologists and physicists at Stanford University developed important patented technologies in CT scanning, most notably the xenon gas detector patent, which became fundamental to subsequent generations of CT scanners and earned Stanford nearly $8.4 million in royalty revenue. Between 1973 and 1976, four generations of CT scanning machines were introduced to the

[11] The device had first been introduced in Europe. The first patient was treated in 1980 and it was approved by the FDA in 1984.

[12] Annetine Gelijns, *Innovation in Clinical Practice: The Dynamics of Medical Technology Development* (Washington D.C.: National Academy Press, 1991).

[13] Annetine Gelijns and Nathan Rosenberg, "Diagnostic Devices: An Analysis of Comparative Advantage", in Gelijns, AC and Rosenberg, N., eds. *Sources of Medical Technology: University and Industry* (Washington, D. C.: National Academy Press, 1996), 321.

[14] Gelijns and Rosenberg, "Diagnostic Devices".

commercial market.[15] In the course of a small number of years, the industry came to be dominated by a few US firms and involved important collaborations between university and industry.

7.3 The Importance of Research Tools

The creation of new research tools, such as automated protein and DNA sequencing instruments, is an important research output of universities. In fact, we have estimated that nearly 40% of Columbia's medical inventions, nearly 40% of its medical patents, and over 50% of its medical licenses can be classified as research tools. By far, its most lucrative patent is a research tool: the co-transformation technology developed by Richard Axel. The "co-transformation" invention is a variant on "transformation", which refers to changing the genetic constitution of a receptor cell by introduction of selected pieces of foreign DNA. Co-transformation allows for the introduction of multiple genes.[16] Co-transformation was licensed widely and non-exclusively. Over time, 34 license agreements were signed. Columbia followed the strategy set by Stanford in Cohen-Boyer and provided reduced license fees to early users. Currently, annual sales on products using co-transformation amount to $7 billion; the cumulative sales over time are about $30 billion.

At Stanford, all four medical inventions of the top five patent revenue earners have a significant function as a research tool: (1) recombinant DNA technology (Cohen-Boyer), (2) fluorescent conjugates for analysis of molecules and cells (Stryer, Glazer, and Oi), (3) computer tomography X-ray scanner (Boyd and colleagues), and (4) the fluorescence-activated cell sorter (Herzenberg and colleagues). Of note in these cases is an important distinction between the types of research tools that are generated at AHCs, and the licensing strategies associated with their implementation in the commercialization process. Whereas, for example, the recombinant DNA technology was initially a process, or technique for DNA cloning, and was immediately accessible in the scientific and commercial communities, the fluorescence-activated cell sorter was an actual machine for automating cell research that

---

[15] William Mitchell, *Dynamic Commercialization: An Organizational Economic Analysis of Innovation in the Medical Diagnostic Imaging Industry* (Ph.D. Dissertation submitted to the University of California, Berkeley, 1988), 116, footnote 5. There was technical uncertainty related to these machines and it was not until General Electric emerged as the dominant firm in the early 1980s that the design of the third-generation machine came to dominate.

[16] Bhaven Sampat, "Development of Co-Transformation Technology", working paper, 2000

required further development before its dissemination would become feasible. A recent NRC report[17] makes a distinction between (1) research tools that become useful only if they are commercialized and (2) research or "discovery" tools, such as genes or receptors, that need no further development. With regard to the former category (1), patenting may be an inducement to commercialization, but this rationale may not hold for patenting the latter category (2) of research tools. We will elaborate below on these cases with a special focus on recombinant DNA and the FACS, keeping in mind these important variations in the characteristics of the technologies, the search process that generated them, and the industries that license them.

7.3.1 Recombinant DNA Technology

The Cohen-Boyer recombinant DNA discovery was the result of the collaboration of two scientists working at AHCs. Herbert Boyer developed his work on restriction enzymes "which 'cleave' DNA at a particular site", at the University of California at San Francisco, and Stanley Cohen developed his work on plasmid DNA at his laboratory at Stanford University in Palo Alto. The two scientists came together at a conference, discussed the possibility of combining their work, and were successful in DNA cloning in 1973.[18] In 1974, the two scientists agreed to filing a patent application that would be administered through Stanford University's Office of Technology Licensing, and shared jointly with the University of California.[19]

The recombinant DNA technique essentially had to do with being able to "insert foreign DNA into a plasmid, insert that plasmid into a living organism, and have that living organism replicate and produce expression products as directed by the foreign genetic information".[20] At the outset of the discovery, scientists were well aware of the enormous potential of the recombinant DNA technology, although there were as yet no commercial or "practical applications of the techniques".[21] As a research tool the technology held promise in "understanding of fundamental biochemical processes" particu-

---

[17] NRC, 41.

[18] Reimers, 1.

[19] Not coincidentally the first successful biotech firm, Genentech is located in South San Francisco, an easy drive to both UCSF and Stanford.

[20] Reimers, 1.

[21] Paul Berg, David Baltimore, Sydney Brenner, Richard O. Roblin III, and Maxine Singer, "Asilomar Conference on Recombinant DNA Molecules", *Science*, New Series, Volume 188, Issue 4192 (June 6, 1975): 991-994.

larly in pro- and eukaryotic cells.[22] A 1976 article in *Science* provided an overview of the research underway, emphasizing that molecular cloning was making possible the investigation and analysis of the overall structure and function of genes.[23]

Yet at the time of the discovery and patent application, there had emerged great controversy in matters such as safety[24], university conflict of interest, and the potential danger that a patent would hinder scientific communication. Even the inventors initially refused the idea of patenting this discovery.[25] Indeed the very notion of patenting living subject matter had reached the national policy level with the Supreme Court case of *Diamond vs. Chakrabarty* in 1980. The Chakrabarty decision allowed that "a living, manmade micro-organism is patentable subject matter" based on the notion that "the patentee has produced a new bacterium with markedly different characteristics from any found in nature and one having potential for significant utility". As for safety, the scientific community initially called for a voluntary research moratorium and in 1975 gathered for a conference in Monterey, California to address their concerns over potential human or ecological biohazards.[26] The result was a series of strict guidelines adopted by the NIH in the US, and comparable institutions abroad.[27]

---

[22] Paul Berg, David Baltimore, Sydney Brenner, Richard O. Roblin III, and Maxine Singer, "Summary Statement of the Asilomar Conference on Recombinant DNA Molecules", *Proceedings of the National Academy of Sciences of the United States of America*, Volume 72, Issue 6 (June 1975): 1981-1984.

[23] Jean L. Marx, "Molecular Cloning: Powerful Tool for Studying Genes", *Science*, New Series, Volume 191, Issue 4232 (March 19, 1976): 1160-1162.

[24] The safety concerns had to do with the speculation that "experiments which involve the tying together of genes from different species into recombinant molecules might produce a new agent that would cause a serious epidemic in humans or somehow harm the environment". Marx, Jean L., "The New P4 Laboratories: Containing Recombinant DNA", *Science*, New Series, Volume 197, Issue 4311 (September 30, 1977): 1350-1352.

[25] NRC, 41 citing Beardsley, T., "Big Time Biology". *Scientific American* (November 1994): 90-97.

[26] "In particular there were speculations that normally innocuous microbes could be changed into human pathogens by introducing genes that rendered them resistant to then-available antibiotics, or enabled them to produce dangerous toxins, or transformed them into cancer-causing agents". Berg, Paul and Maxine Singer, "The Recombinant DNA Controversy: Twenty Years Later", *Proceedings of the National Academies of Science*, Vol. 92 (September 1995): 9011

[27] Paul Berg and Maxine Singer, "The recombinant DNA controversy: Twenty Years Later", *Proceedings of the National Academies of Science*, Vol. 92 (September 1995): 9011. See also Berg, Baltimore, Brenner, Robbin, and Singer, 1981-1984.

The use of recombinant DNA technology has come to dominate research in biology and has had an enormous impact in many fields from chemistry to plant science to forensics and beyond.[28] "The most profound consequence of the recombinant DNA technology has been our increased knowledge of fundamental life processes. No longer is the gene an abstract notion, nor is it as enigmatic as interstellar dark matter or black holes. Genes, and chromosomes of which they are a part, are describable in precise chemical terms". Moreover, through the ability to synthesize, manipulate and reintroduce genes "into the cells of living organisms", recombinant DNA techniques have enabled scientists "to link genes with specific physiological functions".[29]

The Cohen-Boyer discovery ultimately yielded a total of three patents, the first on the actual process, and the second and third on the products.[30] The process patent was issued in December 1980, and the product patent application was divided into an application covering prokaryotic hosts, issued in August 1984, and an application covering eukaryotic hosts, issued in August 1988.[31] As the technology was the first of its kind, was easy and inexpensive to use, and held promise for a broad scope of applications and industries (e.g. biotechnology, pharmaceuticals, chemical, agricultural, mining, and oil), the patents were licensed non-exclusively and for a moderate fee.[32] The Stanford University OTL decided on four categories to determine the royalty structure of the discovery: basic genetic products, process improvement products, bulk products, and end products. Initially, "[t]he royalty rates ranged from 10% for the basic genetic product to 1/2% for the end product".[33] [34] As mentioned earlier, Stanford also provided a discount for early entrants to the licensing agreements.[35]

---

[28] Berg and Singer, 9011.

[29] Berg and Singer, 9011.

[30] The purpose of this process-product division had to do with the initial concern that although the patent examiner would be willing to "allow process claims that described the basic method for producing biological transformants", he would be unwilling to "allow claims on biological materials per se". Reimers, 3.

[31] Reimers, 4, 8.

[32] The NRC report identifies three key elements to the Cohen-Boyer discovery: "First, the technology was inexpensive and easy to use; from a purely technical standpoint, there were only minimal impediments to widespread dissemination. Second, there were no alternative technologies. Third, the technology was critical and of broad importance to research in molecular biology". NRC, 41.

[33] Reimers, 5. Royalty rates increased over time as reported in 1995 by Stanford OTL licensing agent Floyd Grolle.

The Cohen-Boyer technology is among the most remunerative patented discoveries in the history of AHCs. In total, 478 companies became licensees with total cumulative gross royalties of $256 million.[36] At the time of the patent's expiration, there were 369 licencees, 332 US companies and 37 non-US companies.[37] The top five royalty-paying licensees included Amgen, Genentech, Johnson & Johnson, Lilly, and Schering. 19% of the total royalties were attributed to the top licensee; 78% of the total royalties were attributed to the top 10 licensees. The total number of products that were based on the Cohen-Boyer patents in 1993 was 860; in 1997 the number had reached 2,442. Genentech's human growth hormone (marketed by Eli Lilly) and Chiron's hepatitis B vaccine (distributed by Merck) are two of the most successful products.[38]

7.4 FACS

Another of Stanford's most remunerative technological developments is the Fluorescence Activated Cell Sorter (FACS). The FACS is a medical device that has the capacity to rapidly sort cells by "tagging" each cell with

---

[34] An example of a "basic genetic product" is the "transformed organism that makes the basic genetic product of insulin" and it had a royalty rate of 10%. An end product would be a product considered for "ultimate consumer" use, "such as an insulin injection, vaccine, or pharmaceutical", and would have a royalty rate from 1% to 1/2% depending on the volume of annual sales. Reimers, 5. "Bulk products are products that will be processed further by a manufacturer and not used or consumed by the end user. An example of a bulk product is the disaccharide sweetener that will be used in soft drink and diet foods. Based on annual sales volume, the royalty ranges from 3% down to 1%". "Process improvement product is a material developed for or by a manufacturer to improve an existing process. An example is an enzyme that catalyzes a reaction. If an enzyme is genetically engineered and improves an existing process, the royalty is 10% of the costs savings or other economic benefit". Reimers, 5.

[35] As for licensing terms, Stanford specified that "if a licensee sells to another licensee, the two parties could agree among themselves as to which would pay the royalty", which generally worked out to be the producer of the end-product. Reimers, 5. Also, "to reduce incentives for overseas manufacture, the license provides for a flat royalty of 1/2% on end product made in the United States but sold outside the US". The fear was that as a US patent covers "the making, using, and selling of a technology", a manufacturer could choose to make the product offshore, in a country where Stanford/UC did not have patent protection, and pay royalties only on products sold back in the United States. This would avoid any infringement on the process patent. Reimers, 5.

[36] $107 million went to the University of California from Stanford. Stanford University Office of Technology Licensing Annual Report 1997-98.

[37] Stanford University Office of Technology Licensing Annual Report 1997-98.

[38] Reimers, 6.

specific surface markers on the basis of fluorescence and then diverting the desired cells into a collecting tube. The apparatus also has the capacity to count the number of cells that have been diverted with the particular marker, detecting a single tagged cell among millions and screening up to 10,000 cells per second.[39] A transforming technology in flow cytometry, the FACS enables researchers and clinicians to work with functional subpopulations of living cells in applications ranging from basic research on understanding the maturation of bone marrow cells to diagnostic work on the rapid detection of certain types of leukemia. It began as a critical research tool in pushing out the envelope of the science of cell biology and has also come to serve as a powerful clinical instrument in cell counting for diagnostic purposes including leukemia, various forms of cancer, and HIV.

The development of the FACS was the result of a multidisciplinary collaboration in the lab of Professors Leonard and Leonore Herzenberg, immunologists in the Department of Genetics in the Stanford School of Medicine. The machine combined the expertise of biologists (including immunologists and geneticists), electrical and mechanical engineers, computer scientists, and technicians with state-of-the-art instrumentation capabilities. The first article describing the apparatus was published in *Science* in 1969[40] and subsequently Leonard Herzenberg and his colleagues were awarded funding by the NIH to build their machine.[41] A request to patent the cell analysis technology was sent to the NIH,[42] and Herzenberg's group, working together with engineers and technicians from Stanford's Applied Electronics lab and later from the Stanford Instrumentation Research Lab, brought the FACS machine to the prototype stage in 1972.

While the prototype FACS machine had already been implemented for research purposes at Stanford's Department of Genetics, additional development was necessary to bring this expensive machine, which took up an

[39] Cynthia Robbins-Roth.

[40] R. H. Hulett, *et al.* "Cell Sorting: Automated Separation of Mammalian cells as a function of Intracellular Flourescence". *Science* 166 (1969): 747-749.

[41] Initial exploratory work in the development of the FACS was undertaken with permission under a previous NIH grant to the Herzenberg Lab. The NIH funding came initially in the form of a contract to build two machines, one to remain in the Herzenberg Lab, the other to be delivered to the NIH.

[42] At that time, which was before the Bayh-Dole act, universities that wished to take out a patent on federally funded research had to make a special request that the agency assign the invention to the university and specify the terms of the licensing being sought as well as the rationale for doing so. The reasoning was that patenting would be an inducement to commercialization.

entire room, into an affordable instrument that could sit on a desktop and thus be more widely disseminated.[43] Herzenberg and his colleagues sought a commercial partner with the technical capability and willingness to make the investment to accomplish this task. Varian was among the first companies to come forward with an interest in commercializing the FACS. However, shortly after taking out a contract with Stanford, the company abandoned the project due to budgetary concerns. Becton-Dickinson (BD Biosciences, Milpitas, CA USA) then entered into an agreement with Stanford in 1972 and by 1974 delivered the first-generation FACS machine.

Determining what portion of the FACS prototype machine would be patentable under US laws was not initially clear to the inventors or the Stanford Office of Technology Licensing. Ultimately, however, the cell analysis technology developed at the Herzenberg lab became a single patent titled a "particle sorting method and apparatus.[44] Stanford University entered a limited-term, exclusive licensing agreement with Becton-Dickinson in 1972 to develop and market instruments embodying this cell analysis technology.[45] In terms of royalty structure, the arrangement was that Stanford would receive an annual flat fee from B-D as well as a small percentage on each machine sold once commercialized. This percentage also applied to machines sold by companies to which B-D would sublicense. An important part of this licensing agreement was that, in addition to the patent, B-D was explicitly licensing "know-how" related to designing and developing this machine which would be transferred verbally and by demonstration. Overall, the patent yielded nearly $4.8 million dollars in revenues to Stanford.

The development of the FACS involved extensive modification and refinement before and after the introduction into the marketplace. In this process, there were many other mechanisms of knowledge transfer beyond the actual patent documentation and license agreement that played an important role in the development and refinement of the FACS. Leonard Herzenberg himself became an immunology consultant to the firm upon signing the licensing agreement and spent a significant amount of time with his staff

---

[43] The NIH had specifically requested a machine for their own purposes and suggested that Herzenberg find a commercial partner to develop the machine.

[44] The patent was the result of two consecutive invention disclosures to Stanford. The first was an "improved cell volume analyzer" developed by Russell Hulett and Nicolas Veizades. The second was an "improved fluorescence activated cell sorting instrument", developed by William Bonner, Richard Sweet, and Russell Hulett which combined with the first to make this patent.

[45] Exclusive rights to these patents was cited in the request to the NIH as a necessary incentive for a firm to make the high risk capital investment to develop this machine.

working directly with the B-D team. This process was also intricately tied to the *users* back at the Herzenberg lab who were regularly utilizing the apparatus to run experiments.[46] Biologists and engineers met regularly both within the lab and at the B-D site to identify need and further modify the machine based on their experimental work. The conceptualization and prototypical development of computational capabilities for the management and analysis of data principally took place at the university-based Herzenberg lab and were not made commercially available until the fourth generation of the machine. The Herzenbergs and their colleagues maintained regular contact with B-D for many years as consultants, as collaborators in research teams, and in training scientists. It was one of the Herzenbergs' postdoctoral students, for example, who in 1981 founded the B-D monoclonal research laboratory in Mountain View, California to accelerate the development of reagents used in this cell analysis technology.

Becton-Dickinson has sold several generations of increasingly sophisticated FACS machines, expanding parameters to identify cells and combining the machine's cell-sorting capability with increasingly powerful computation capability. The market for this technology was unexpectedly large,[47] especially with the development of fluorescent dyes (in this case, phycobiliproteins) that "extend the spectrum usable by FACS", and the development and introduction of monoclonal antibodies as FACS reagents.[48] Of note is that the phycobiliprotein technology mentioned above was also a patented technology (fluorescent conjugates), shared with UC Berkeley and earning Stanford over $12.5 million by 1995.[49] B-D sublicensed the FACS patented technology to other firms as well. Within a year of the first introduction of the commercial FACS machine, the Coulter corporation entered the market, and by the end of the decade, Ortho Diagnostic Systems (formerly Bio/Physics Systems until acquired by Johnson & Johnson) joined the market to com-

[46] The Herzenberg lab established a FACS facility to provide a broader access to the technology for research purposes which provides trained technicians on-site 24 hours per day.

[47] In an interview with Leonard Herzenberg, he reported that he initially estimated that approximately 100 machines would be sold. The B-D representative at the time thought that was far too high an estimation.

[48] The ability to produce monoclonal antibodies is considered a major breakthrough as a complementary tool for the FACS. For a detailed discussion of the significance of monoclonal antibodies and the FACS, see Leonore Herzenberg, Steve De Rosa, and Leonard Herzenberg, "Monoclonal Antibodies and the FACS: Complementary Tools for Immunobiology and Medicine", *Immunology Today*, Vol. 21, No. 8, (August 2000): 383-390.

prise the "big three" manufacturers in the U.S.[50] Over the next decade, the market expanded to include a few new commercial players as well as alternative apparatuses with varying capabilities and characteristics to serve a broader spectrum of clinical and research needs.[51] A recent paper written by the Herzenbergs and De Rosa states that, in 1999, FACS instrument and monoclonal reagent sales are together estimated to have reached $500 million in annual sales.[52]

7.5 Uncertainty in Technological Change

We would now like to emphasize a particular feature of major technological innovations that comes to be of special importance in the realm of patenting. We refer to the very high degree of uncertainty surrounding emerging major innovations. A case in point are the questions about the commercial significance of the Cohen-Boyer invention that were raised by its inventor immediately after the initial breakthrough. Stanley Cohen, although recognizing the scientific potential of the Cohen-Boyer breakthrough, expressed a reluctance to patent the discovery, indicating that significant commercial applications would not occur for twenty years.[53] In the case of Stanford's lucrative CT scanner "xenon gas detector" patent (issued in 1978), many people at the time, including the inventor himself, anticipated that xenon gas detectors would be replaced by solid state detectors, which were smaller and less expensive. However, reliance on xenon gas detectors lasted as long as the patent and accounted for most of the $8.3 million in revenue income to Stanford. It is only in the last 3-5 years that solid state detectors have come to replace xenon gas detectors in CT scanners.[54] Clearly, there is a high degree of uncertainty regarding the time it takes to commercialize, the rapidity of change in alternative technologies, and the size of the market. Beyond these uncertainties, however, there is another major source of uncertainty and that is that new indications of use are often discovered only a number of years after the initial introduction of the technology.

---

[50] Howard M. Shapiro, *Practical Flow Cytometry* (New York: Wily-Liss, Inc. 1995), 349.
[51] Shapiro, 349.
[52] Herzenberg, De Rosa, and Herzenberg, 385.
[53] Reimers.
[54] The higher-end models have been using solid state detectors for the last decade. Interview with Douglas Boyd, the inventor behind the detector patent.

A consequence of such uncertainties is that the value of a patent is extraordinarily difficult to determine in advance, when the invention is being patented. Or, to put it differently, it has often proven to be exceedingly difficult to forecast the range of applications of a new technology, including the time frame for the development of applications. This point is often obscured by the fact that historical studies are written at a later point in time, when the eventual value of the invention has, typically, long been established. Historical studies are, by definition, retrospective and not prospective, although an historical approach could indeed identify what contemporaries regarded as the future prospects for a particular technology.[55] It is important to emphasize that the difficulties in determining the market value of an invention are compounded when the invention is not to be sold directly in the form of some final product but, rather, is to be used primarily as an input to further inventive activity.[56] The point applies with particular force to the research tools with which we are presently concerned.

In considering the applications of important innovations, we may think of medical technologies as consisting of three categories: (a) research tools, (b) diagnostic and screening tools, and (c) therapeutic and preventive tools. Although we may readily distinguish among these three separate categories, there is abundant empirical/historical evidence that a tool may begin life in one of these categories, but later on evolve into one or both of the other two categories. We have recently been studying some of the major tools of diagnostic technology – the catheter, magnetic resonance imaging (MRI) and positron emission tomography (PET). We find striking the extent to which these technologies started as research tools, then became diagnostic tools, and, as they mature and experience performance improvement, evolve into indispensable components of therapy.

Consider the cardiac catheter. This tool was developed in the 1950s to examine the physiology of the heart. In the 1970s, they were moved from bench to bedside and became important diagnostic tools. In the 1980s they

[55] Nathan Rosenberg, "Uncertainty and Technological Change", in *The Mosaic of Economic Growth*, eds. Ralph Landau, Timothy Taylor, and Gavin Wright (Stanford, CA: Stanford University Press, 1996) and Annetine Gelijns, Nathan Rosenberg and Alan Moskowitz, "Capturing the Unexpected Benefits of Medical Research," *New England Journal of Medicine* 339 (September 3, 1998): 693-698.

[56] Kenneth Arrow, "Economic Welfare and the Allocation of Resources for Invention", in *The Rate and Direction of Inventive Activity: economic and social factors.* A conference of the Universities National Bureau Committee for Economic Research and the Committee on Economic Growth of the Social Science Research Council (Princeton: Princeton University Press, 1962), 609-626.

were transformed into therapeutic tools, also known as balloon catheters, used for opening clogged coronary arteries. MRI had its origins as magnetic resonance spectroscopy, an important research tool in experimental physics and chemistry. This led to the development of MRI – an increasingly important diagnostic instrument in a wide range of clinical conditions, ranging from the heart to the brain. More recently, MRIs have become part of therapeutic procedures; that is, they have been built into the operating room and become part of complex neurosurgical procedures. Positron emission tomography (PET) scanners are powerful tools for providing a quantitative analysis of certain physiological functions, unlike CT or MRI, which are valuable for anatomical observations. PET scanners play an important role as research tools, for example, in studies of the functioning of the brain by injecting radioactive "tags" to identify high-energy phosphates, blood sugars, or neurotransmitters (such as dopamine) and then observing associated changes in metabolic activity in different portions of the brain. PET not only has potential as a research tool, but PET has also turned into a diagnostic tool for detecting malignancies and assessing the viability of the myocardium.

This process works in reverse as well. There is also a high degree of uncertainty concerning the likelihood that new medical technologies – but especially diagnostic ones – will eventually become research tools. The channels through which this occurs, however, are sometimes more indirect. Any innovation that improves observational capabilities is, virtually by definition, a potential research tool. Thus almost all improvements in diagnosis hold out some prospect for being useful in research – and for therapy. Observing something that had not been previously observed may raise new questions or challenge old conceptualizations.

Consider the CT scanner. The CT scanner was developed as a diagnostic instrument for the early detection of tumors. Its subsequent use as a research tool provided important insights (e.g. in neurology it was a unique way to display neuroanatomy in living beings), but it also became embedded in therapeutic procedures; e.g. CT scanners are now used to guide surgical instruments in real-time surgical procedures. Another example is the endoscope. The endoscope was first developed as a diagnostic instrument. Later on it became a research tool used in numerous medical disciplines. As these scopes matured and experienced performance improvement, they eventually turned into therapeutic technologies – where they transformed the profession of surgery from using major, open procedures to minimally invasive ones. Flexible endoscopes, for example, were developed to visualize the GI tract, and provided important new knowledge about gastrointestinal disorders.

With the development of instruments that could be used through the channel of the endoscope, these devices were transformed into therapeutic technologies; e.g. to remove cancerous or precancerous polyps. In the case of rigid scopes, these technologies were extensively used by gynecologists in the 1950s for diagnostic procedures. With the development of instruments that could be moved through the operative channel of the endoscope, gynecologists began to undertake therapeutic procedures in the 1960s. However, it was only in the late 1980s that general surgeons began to adopt these tools and transformed gall bladder surgery from an open procedure into a minimally invasive one. In view of the time lag that was involved in crossing disciplinary boundaries (from gynecology to general surgery), the rate of adoption was breathtaking: more than 50% of U.S. practicing general surgeons learned to perform these laparascopic procedures in an 18-month period.[57]

These transformations may lead to substantial benefits. The transformation of the catheter from a research tool into a diagnostic tool into a therapeutic modality has supplanted coronary bypass surgery for particular patient groups. This has led to major progress in pain reduction, shorter recovery times, and, therefore, higher productivity levels. If restrictive intellectual property policies were to have discouraged or prevented such transformations from occurring, the social and economic costs would have been significant.

7.6 Some Concluding Observations

AHCs have become an increasingly important locus of inventive activity within American research universities, which is reflected in the patenting and licensing data that we have discussed so far. The research output of AHCs consists of many different types of technology classes including drugs, biologicals, devices, surgical and clinical procedures and systems of care. However, discussions of technological change in medicine have often been confounded by the notion that innovation is a more or less homogeneous activity. The truth, of course, is that innovation is not one thing, but many things. In medicine we have to keep in mind that the innovation processes of biologicals and pharmaceuticals on the one hand, and medical devices on the other, are substantially different. Intellectual property protection is much more important in the former category than in the latter.

Research tools are a critical output of AHC research, whether these tools are biologicals or devices. In thinking about patenting or licensing research

[57] White, J.V. "Laparascopic Cholecystectomy: The Evolution of General Surgery". *Annals of Internal Medicine* 115 (1991): 651-653.

tools, two important characterizations have to be kept in mind. First, we need to distinguish between two distinct categories of research tools: (a) instruments and devices that require further development, such as the FACS machine; and (b) research "materials", such as receptors or genes, that may not require further development. This point of view is also represented in a recent NIH guidelines report on research tools.[58]

Second, we have to distinguish between small firms and large firms, which might have very different interests in intellectual property. Well-established, large multinational pharmaceutical companies, for example, may want certain research tools, such as receptors or genes, to be placed in the public domain. By contrast, small firms or new start-ups may want strong intellectual property rights, which they may need in order to obtain access to venture capital, or to arrange to be bought out by a large pharmaceutical firm.

In terms of university patenting strategies and policies, we need to examine more carefully the tradeoffs between the benefits and costs of various approaches. The social benefits of intellectual property rights, aside from their obvious incentives to potential inventors, will often reside in their role in facilitating technology transfer, especially for those technologies that require substantial private sector development or that might be taken up by small firms. The costs are a more complicated story. Any serious restriction of access to research tools can only be damaging to the overall research enterprise. Moreover, even if these types of inventions are widely licensed, patenting could substantially increase the transaction costs of doing research, especially in the realm of biotechnology; i.e., in raising the administrative burden of gaining access to materials technologies. But we have made an even broader argument about potential costs, which is related to the dynamic nature of technological change and the high degree of uncertainty surrounding new technologies at their introduction. In other words, technologies may have uses that were entirely unanticipated at the time of their introduction. If through our approaches to intellectual property, we restrict access to research tools, this could not only hamper the development of particular areas of science, but it could also prevent the transformation of these tools into important technologies for the diagnosis and treatment of disease. The social and economic costs in such cases might be enormous.

---

[58] Report of the National Institutes of Health (NIH) Working Group on Research Tools, June 4, 1998. http://www.nih.gov/news/researchtools/. Also "Sharing Biomedical Research Resources: Principles and Guidelines for Recipients of NIH Research Grants and Contracts". http://www.nih.gov/od/ott/Rtguide.htm

Finally, there is a whole host of ways in which one can approach intellectual property, but our view is that there are various characteristics of the technologies themselves, and of the search processes that generate these technologies, and of the industries that license them, that need to be prominently kept in mind when balancing the costs and benefits of patenting policy. In particular, it is possible for universities to take a more nuanced approach in their licensing strategies, including exclusive rights but for a limited-term, narrowing patents or licenses by their field of application, or limiting them to particular areas of geography. We need to start thinking more creatively about how to use these various approaches, depending on particular sub-classes of technologies and particular characteristics of the industries involved.

7.7 Literature References

Arrow, Kenneth. "Economic Welfare and the Allocation of Resources for Invention", in *The Rate and Direction of Inventive Activity: economic and social factors. A conference of the Universities National Bureau Committee for Economic Research and the Committee on Economic Growth of the Social Science Research Council,* 609-626. Princeton: Princeton University Press, 1962.

Association of University Technology Managers (AUTM). Licensing Survey, FY 1999: Full Report.

Audretsch David B. and Stephan Paula E. Company-Scientist Locational Links: The Case of Biotechnology. The American Economic Review 1996; 86 (3): 641-52.

Berg, Paul; Baltimore, Brenner, David, Sydney; Roblin III, Richard O. and Singer, Maxine. Asilomar Conference on Recombinant DNA Molecules. Science, New Series. 1975; 188 (4192): 991-4.

Berg, Paul; Baltimore, David; Brenner, Sydney; Roblin III, Richard O. and Singer, Maxine. Summary Statement of the Asilomar Conference on Recombinant DNA Molecules. Proceedings of the National Academy of Sciences of the United States of America; 1975 June; 1981-1984: Volume 72, Issue 6.

Berg, Paul and Singer, Maxine. The Recombinant DNA Controversy: Twenty Years Later. Proceedings of the National Academy of Sciences USA; 1995 September; Volume 92: 9011.

Ernst and Young. "Biotech 99—Bridging the Gap". http://www.ey.com/global/gcr.nsf/US/Library-Health_Care-Ernst_%26_Young_LLP.

Gelijns, Annetine, *Innovation in Clinical Practice: The Dynamics of Medical Technology Development.* Washington D.C.: National Academy Press, 1991.

Gelijns, Annetine, Rosenberg, Nathan and Moskowitz, Alan. Capturing the Unexpected Benefits of Medical Research. New England Journal of Medicine 1998; 339: 693-8.

Gelijns, Annetine and Rosenberg, Nathan. "Diagnostic Devices: An analysis of Comparative Advantage". In *Sources of Medical Technology: University and Industry,* AC Gelijns and N. Rosenberg, eds. Washington, D. C.: National Academy Press, 1996.

Hulett R. H., Bonner W.A., Barrett J. and Herzenberg L.A. Cell Sorting: Automated Separation of Mammalian cells as a function of Intracellular Fluorescence. Science 1969; 166: 747-9.

Herzenberg, Leonore, De Rosa, Steve and Herzenberg, Leonard. Monoclonal Antibodies and the FACS: Complementary Tools for Immunobiology and Medicine. Immunology Today 2000; 21 (8): 383-90.

The Lewin Group. *Outlook for Medical Technology Innovation. The State of the Industry.* Washington DC: Health Industry Manufacturers Association, 2000.

Marx, Jean L. Molecular Cloning: Powerful Tool for Studying Genes. Science, New Series. 1976; 191 (4232): 1160-2.

Marx, Jean L. The New P4 Laboratories: Containing Recombinant DNA. Science, New Series. 1977; 197 (4311): 1350-2.

Mitchell, William. Dynamic Commercialization: An Organizational Economic Analysis of Innovation in the Medical Diagnostic Imaging Industry. Dissertation submitted to the University of California, Berkeley, 1988.

National Institutes of Health. Sharing Biomedical Research Resources: Principles and Guidelines for Recipients of NIH Research Grants and Contracts. http://www.nih.gov/od/ott/Rtguide.htm

National Institutes of Health, Report of the National Institutes of Health (NIH) Working Group on Research Tools, June 4, 1998. http://www.nih.gov/news/researchtools/.

National Research Council, Intellectual Property Rights and Research Tools in Molecular Biology: Summary of a Workshop Held at the National Academy of Sciences; 1996 February 15-16; Washington DC: National Academy Press, 1996.

Reimers, Niels. Tiger by the Tail. Chemtech 1987; 464-71. Reprinted in The Journal of the Association of University Technology Managers, Volume 7, 1995.

Rosenberg, Nathan. "Uncertainty and Technological Change". In *The Mosaic of Economic Growth,* Ralph Landau, Timothy Taylor, and Gavin Wright, eds. Stanford, CA: Stanford University Press, 1996.

Sampat, Bhaven, Development of Co-Transformation Technology. Working paper, 2000.

Shapiro, Howard M., *Practical Flow Cytometry.* New York: Wily-Liss, Inc., 1995.

Stanford University Office of Technology Licensing Annual Report 1997-98.

White, J.V. Laparascopic Cholecystectomy: the Evolution of General Surgery. Annals of Internal Medicine 1991; 115: 651-3.

Zucker, Lynne G. and Darby, Michael R. Star Scientists and Institutional Transformation: Patterns of Invention and Innovation in the Formation of the Biotechnology Industry. Proceedings of the National Academy of Sciences of the United States of America; 1996 November 12; Volume 93, Number 23: 12709-12716.

Chapter 8

INITIAL AND FOLLOW-ON PHARMACEUTICAL INVENTIONS IN EUROPE

Bengt Domeij[1]

The Royal Institute of Technology, Department of Industrial Economy and Organisation, Stockholm, Sweden

Chapter contents:

Abstract: This chapter examines how European courts have determined the scope of pharmaceutical patents. The author argues that the legal considerations in the different cases can be rationalized as attempts to promote both initial and follow-on inventors. Courts do this by interpreting the patent claims depending on the achievement made by the accused infringer. If a competitor to the patentee has made an important follow-on technical achievement, courts tend to interpret the claims narrowly and make a finding of non-infringement. If, on the other hand, the accused product is of no particular value compared to the initial invention, the claim interpretation is stretched so as to find the follow-on product infringing. This legal approach enables the patent system to maintain incentives at a high level for valuable follow-on inventions, even after the grant of a first patent. The economic advantages of using this approach to claim interpretation offer an explanation for why the scope of protection in a

[1] Associate Professor of Law, LL D, The Royal Institute of Technology, Industrial Economy and Organisation, Stockholm, E-mail: bengt.domeij@lector.kth.se. I would like to thank for valuable comments, in particular, Howard Anawalt (Santa Clara University Law School), John H. Barton (Stanford Law School) and Koichi Sumikura (University of Tokyo).

O. Granstrand (ed.), Economics, Law and Intellectual Property, 177-197.

patent may have to be left without a definitive technical boundary. By allowing courts some discretion in interpreting claims, through e.g. the doctrine of equivalence, they may be able to create extra incentives for especially valuable, but for the time being, unknown follow-on inventions.

8.1 Introduction

It is believed that the English patent system was the first intellectual property regime to introduce a verbal definition of the monopoly granted. In the early 18th century the grant of English patents routinely carried a statement that the patentee within a certain period – usually 6 months – was obliged to "particularly describe and ascertain the nature of said invention and in what manner the same is to be performed".[2] Today the use of patent claims is indispensable: it increases greatly the legal certainty for third parties. Nevertheless it must be kept in mind that verbal definitions also pose a danger. Infringement assessments in patent law may sometimes be practiced with no more sophistication than a verbal analysis of the claims. This may sacrifice socially valuable goals that can be achieved in the claim interpretation exercise.

In this chapter it is argued that a secondary function of claim interpretation is also relevant, beside the much-heralded legal certainty. Sequential inventions – which is more or less the only kind of inventions, since all inventors build on what their forerunners have done – can be facilitated through a practice of claim interpretation in which the value of follow-on inventions is specifically assessed. A coordination of research is achieved if particularly valuable follow-on inventions are considered non-infringing, while the not very valuable follow-on inventions are considered infringing.

A focus on the relationship between initial and follow-on inventions is not novel in today's patent literature. The legal mechanisms that control the dynamic between pioneer inventors and improvers have been studied extensively already, in particular by Robert Merges.[3] He has proposed that even a modest legal threat that a follow-on inventor will be let go, free of liability, would have a salutary effect on pioneer-improver bargaining where the pioneer's patent is used as a "holdup" right to extract significant rents from a

[2] E.C. Waltershied, The Early Evolution of the United States Patent Law: Antecedents, 77 *Journal of the Patent and Trade Mark Society* p. 771 (780-781) (1995).
[3] R.P. Merges, A Brief Note on Blocking Patents and the Reverse Doctrine of Equivalents in Biotechnology Cases, 72 *J. Pat. & Trademark Off. Soc'y* 870 (1991): cf. R.P. Merges, R. Nelson, On the Complex Economics of Patent Scope, 90 *Columbia Law Review* 1990, 839.

"radical improver".[4] The theory argued here is similar. The main novelty in this chapter therefore lies in the legal material that will be discussed: the cases all originate from Europe and the pharmaceutical industry. It seems that the problem of accommodating both initial and follow-on inventions is particularly important in the research-intensive pharmaceutical field. Cases on initial and follow-on inventions are also relatively easy to find in this field due to the litigatious environment.

8.2 Incentives for Initial and Follow-on Pharmaceutical Inventions

The pharmaceutical research process is particularly long and expensive.[5] For that reason it is important that patents can be awarded at an early stage in the process. The patentee will then know that only he may take advantage of subsequent investments made in a group of compounds. The patent position will increase his economic incentives. The merit of this has been much emphasised.[6]

> "With the selection of the lead compound, the chemist and biologist embark on an extensive program to improve its potency, the specificity of biological effect with concomitant reduction in toxicity, oral absorption, duration of action, metabolic pattern and pharmacokinetic pattern. This will involve extensive structure-activity (SAR) studies. Needless to say, the lead structure series must be patentable.[7]"

From a social point of view, early patenting allows companies to do parallel research efforts, rather than duplicative studies (on the same com-

---

[4] R.P. Merges, *Intellectual Property Rights and Bargaining Breakdown: The Case of Blocking Patents*, 62 Tenn. L. Rev. 75 (1994) (arguing that reverse doctrine of equivalents can be used to influence reluctant pioneers looking to exert "holdup rights" on radical improvers). See also R.P. Merges, *Who Owns the Charles River Bridge? Intellectual Property and Competition in the Software Industry*, 1999 available at http://www.law.berkeley.edu/institutes/bclt/pubs/merges/criver.pdf.

[5] The special circumstances applying in the pharmaceutical research process have been addressed in most areas of the world through extensions of the life of pharmaceutical patents beyond the usual 20 years. In Europe through the EC Regulation 1768/92.

[6] It is specially associated with Kitch and his prospect theory of the patent system, see E.W. Kitch, *The Nature and Function of the Patent System*, 20 Journal of Law & Economics 1977 265.

[7] G de Stevens, *Lead Structure Discovery and Development*, 261 (266), in C. Hansch, and C. Dayton, (eds.), Comprehensive Medicinal Chemistry, Oxford 1990.

pounds). Good opportunities for patenting and a low threshold of industrial applicability – a European patentability requirement which is similar to the US counterpart of utility – has become increasingly important over the last years as pharmaceutical companies try to move away from animal test towards more *in vitro* test.[8] *In vitro* tests are in the early research stages more cost-effective, reliable and also do not cause the same public protests as animal tests sometimes do. The current acceptance by the European Patent Office (EPO) of *in vitro* tests as confirmation of compound patentability is important and does not generally result in premature patenting.[9]

At the same time, the present-day low initial thresholds in the patent systems are creating a situation where almost everything can be patented, and this may come expensive to society. It has been said that:

> "Today, patents are avidly pursued all along the lengthy road from the most basic science through to the market-place for pharmaceuticals. Because every step along the way draws another patent application, the path towards public possession of real benefits is increasingly observed by dense thickets of intersecting, overlapping, and cross-blocking patents. Those operating at the beginnings of the road are most insistent on their right to nail down leverage that will remain formidable despite marketplace rejection of the uses to which they saw their inventions may be put. The frank aim of these early stage workers is to control ultimate applications discovered by others.[10]"

If early patenting is essential for the pharmaceutical industry but, at the same time, it is increasingly difficult to do pharmaceutical research without constantly being hindered by granted patents, one feature of the patent system leaps into the forefront: the scope of granted claims. How can claims be drafted and the scope of protection determined, so as to strike a proper balance between initial and follow-on inventors?

A discussion of the effects that occur in the pharmaceutical industry due to broad claims can be found in a decision by the German Federal Supreme Court, the Bundesgerichtshof. There was a product patent for human recombinant immuninterferon. A competitor to the patentee carried out clinical

---

[8] P. Ducor, *New Drug Discovery Technologies and Patents*, 22 Rutgers Computer & Technology Law Journal 1996, 388. *In vitro* = traditionally in test tubes, more generally, all experiments not carried out on animals or humans.

[9] B. Domeij, *Pharmaceutical Patents in Europe*, 19 ff, The Hague, London, Boston 2000.

[10] T.D. Kiley, *Patents on Random Complementary DNA Fragments*, 257 Science 1992, 915.

tests in order to search for possible new indications for the interferon, e.g. treatment of cancer, AIDS, allergies, leukemia, asthma, etc. The court described the effects that this research would have on the initial patentee in the following manner:

> "Die Möglichkeit, daß klinische Versuche zur Erkenntnis neuer Indikationen des geschützten Stoffs und zu einem entsprechendem Verwendungspatent führen können, gefärdet nicht den wirtschaftlichen Wert des Erzeugnispatents. Das Stoffpatent behält vielmehr infolge der Abhängigkeit des Verwendungspatents seinen wirtschaftlichen Wert, weil der Inhaber des jüngeren Patents zu dessen Benutzung die Zustimmung des Inhabers des älteren Patents benötigt und das ältere patent gegenüber Dritten auch bezüglich der durch das jüngere Patente geschützten Verwendung seine volle Feltung behält. ... Die Erschließung neuer Verwendungsmöglichkeiten durch weiterfürenden Versuche Dritter führt grundsätzlich zunächst sogar zur Steigerung des Wertes des Sachpatents und des davon bestehenden ausschließlichen Nutzungsrechts des älteren Erfinders.[11]"

The Court in its judgment stretched the research exemption to allow the competitor to carry out this kind of research within the scope of the initial patent. One explanation furnished was that any success in the research would increase the value of the first patent. If the follow-on inventor received a patent of his own, it would be a dependent patent that could not be utilized by the follow-on inventor without a license from the initial inventor. The initial inventor had to accept the research because he would get a share of the value of any new finding. But this patent law dependency will also reduce the incentives for third parties to do research within the scope of protection of the initial patent. This indicates that the problem with broad patents, that reach-through to second-generation uses, is that they have chilling effects on competitors to the first patentee. Their research efforts may be stifled. Lord Hoffman pointed to this in the case *Biogen v. Medeva*, decided by the House of Lords:

> "It is inevitable in a young science, like electricity in the early nineteenth century or flying at the turn of the last century or recombinant DNA technology in the 1970s, that dramatically new things will be done for the first time. The technical contribution made in such

[11] Bundesgerichtshofs, X ZR 99/92 of 11 07 1995, GRUR 1996, 109: [1997] RPC 623.

> cases deserved to be recognised. But care is needed not to stifle further research and healthy competition by allowing the first person who has found a way of achieving an obviously desirable goal to monopolise every other way of doing so.[12]"

An illustrative example of initial and follow-on pharmaceutical inventions, and also of the considerable complexities involved in determining justifiable patent scope, is a dispute between Bristol-Myers-Squibb Company and Aventis (formerly Rhône-Poulenc Rorer). It concerned the allowable scope of a patent claim related to one of the most effective anti-tumor agents currently known: Taxol® ($C_{47}H_{51}NO_{14}$: international non-proprietary name: paclitaxel). Aventis was the proprietor of European Patent 336 840, the object of which was a process that permits Taxol to be prepared much easier than had previously been possible. The novel and inventive part of Aventis' claims to the new process was the use of a particular protective chemical group, which prevented an unwanted reaction from occurring in the process. An additional feature of the claim to the process was an "esterification". Esterifications are among the most important and most frequently employed reactions in synthetic organic chemistry. To implement such a process the skilled worker under normal circumstances not only has a whole range of standard methods available, but in the extensive chemical specialists literature new methods for this purpose are continually being indicated. However, at the time of filing the patent application, Aventis had only developed one such esterification method: it formed the third step in the preparation of Taxol: in the description a number of necessary aspects to it were specified. Subsequently to the filing of the application it was discovered that developing new esterification methods was exceptionally difficult. But due to the unspecific and unrestricted nature of the claim feature "esterification", all present and future esterification methods were covered by Aventis' patent, as long, of course, as the particular protective group discovered by Aventis was also used in the process.

A few years after the –840 patent was filed a new esterification method was developed and patented. Bristol-Myers-Squibb acquired this second patent and then sued Aventis in Germany and claimed that the first patent was unduly broad, because it covered esterification processes that could not, on the filing date, be used by the skilled person. In 1997 the German Federal Patent Court, the Bundespatentgericht, ruled in favour of Bristol-Myers-Squibb. The patent was partially invalidated and Bristol-Myers-Squibb was

[12] House of Lords, *Biogen Inc v. Medeva* Plc [1997] RPC 1.

allowed to employ the newly developed esterification process, together with the protecting group that had been discovered by Aventis, for the production of Taxol. The Court ruled in translation:

> "When the plaintiff in the annulment demonstrates that the patent at issue is in parts non-performable, then account must be taken of the corresponding ground for annulment by a declaration of annulment. This is true in any case for process claims whose subject-matter and scope of protection comprise both performable and non-performable process variants. Patent protection for non-performable process variants is unjustified because to that extent the art has not been enriched".[13]

The Bundespatentgericht found that the art had not been enriched in respect of the non-performable esterification-process-variants. But the difficulties involved in finding an appropriate scope for the claims, can be appreciated from the appellate decision from May 2001 in the same case. The German Federal Supreme Court, the Bundesgerichtshof, reversed the lower court's finding of invalidity, stating in translation that:

> "[A] feasible route was sufficiently described, and the esterification problem was solvable, with the disclosure in the patent at issue ... In fact, in the case of a patent for a chemical synthesis process, it is possible to claim in general terms a specific process step in the form of a reaction which is familiar per se and is designed in general terms even when known possibilities of accomplishing this reaction fail but the patent reproducibly discloses a performable route to accomplishing the reaction. The plaintiff's interpretation, which differs from this, and which the Federal Patent Court adhered to, would if taken to its logical conclusion mean that the scope of protection of a process patent would always have to embrace, besides the procedures familiar to the person skilled in the art, only the specific path disclosed in the patent. In those situations at any rate when a particular process is first made available to the public, this does not in principle constitute any appropriate reward for inventive effort".[14]

Decisions like these, on the allowable breadth of claims and the appropriate reward for an inventive effort (in this case, the protective chemical group

[13] Bundespatentgericht, case 3 Ni 51/95 (EU) of August 21, 1997.
[14] Bundesgerichtshof, case no. X ZR 168/97, pronounced on May 3, 2001.

found by Aventis), have immediate consequences for the relationship between initial and follow-on inventors and therefore important policy consequences. The crafting of the details of the monopoly is also a part of the daily work with patents. It is a contentious issue debated intensely between the patent agent and the examiner. Nonetheless the legal rules are vague and uncertain. The difficulties encountered in formulating a legal regime for pharmaceutical patent claim scope, are to a large extent due to the fact that the two most straightforward legal alternatives are both quite inadequate. It would be unreasonable if it were only permitted to patent the compounds or processes that had been tested by the applicant on the filing day. The scope would become too narrow and the patents easy to escape. Some minor changes by a competitor would result in an alternative that was free to market. The Bundesgerichtshof referred in the *Bristol v. Aventis* case quoted above, to the lack of appropriate reward for inventive effort which would be the result of this approach. It would also mean that applicants would try to compensate for this by making a large amount of tests before a patent application was filed. The tests would usually be of little technical or commercial value. The other obvious legal solution is equally unreasonable. It would not work to allow applicants to include all conceivable solutions in the claims, provided the solutions satisfy the novelty requirement. The probability that a certain solution will work can definitely be too remote. Taken to the extreme, the applicant could assert that it is only a routine experiment to test whether any claimed compound has the effect stated in the description. That practice could soon render competition impossible.[15]

The appropriate legal rule must come somewhere in between these two extremes. But the problem one then confronts is that it is very difficult to formulate distinctly an intermediate situation. In the EPO Guidelines for Examination the following statements are directed to the question of generalisations in claims:

> "Most claims are generalisations from one or more particular examples. The extent of generalisation permissible is a matter which the examiner must judge in each particular case in the light of the relevant prior art. Thus an invention which opens up a whole new field is entitled to more generality in the claims than one which is concerned with advances in a known technology. A fair statement of a claim is one which is not so broad that it goes beyond the invention

[15] T. Roberts, *The Prospects of Success of the National Institute of Health's Human Genome Application*, [1994] EIPR 30.

> nor yet so narrow as to deprive the applicant of a just reward for the disclosure of his invention.[16]"
>
> "As a general rule, a claim should be regarded as supported by the description unless exceptionally there are well-founded reasons for believing that the skilled man would be unable, on the basis of the information given in the application as filed, to extend the particular teaching of the description to the whole of the field claimed by using routine methods of experimentation or analysis. Support must however be of a technical character; vague statements or assertions having no technical content provide no basis".[17]
>
> "In many cases a single example or single embodiment will suffice, but where the claims cover a broad field the description should not usually be regarded as satisfying the requirements of Art. 83 unless it gives a number of examples or describes alternative embodiments or variations extending over the area protected by the claims. However, regard must be had to the facts of the particular case. There are some instances where even a very broad field is sufficiently exemplified by a limited number of examples or even one example...".[18]

The EPO Guidelines seem rather vague on the question of allowable claim scope. One thing, though, is that it is stated that inventions that open up a whole new technical field should be granted wider protection than inventions pertaining to minor advances in established technical fields, on the principle that whoever creates opportunities for further inventive input should gain some of the value of the later developments. This is a common thought in analyses of patent scope.[19] An EPO Board of Appeal (case T 292/85) has also voiced it:

> "Unless broad, yet proper terminology is allowable, subsequent investigations by third parties might be encouraged to concentrate on finding alternatives outside the claims instead of trying to pursue progress through dependent inventions. The lack of recognition of

[16] EPO Guidelines for Examination C III 6.2.

[17] EPO Guidelines for Examination C III 6.3.

[18] EPO Guidelines for Examination C II 4.9.

[19] Green and Scotchmer have argued that it is an economic advantage for a later invention to become dependent on an earlier invention, if the later invention could not have been done without knowledge of the earlier one. See J.G. Green, S. Scotchmer, *On the division of profit in sequential innovation*, 26:1 RAND Journal of Economics Spring 1995, 25.

> the full significance and the interdependency of technical contributions could adversely affect progress in the area of microbiology and biochemistry".[20]

The Board motivated broad claims by the stimulating effect that one invention may have on further developments, refinements etc, of the invention. This may appear reasonable. If it is clear that one inventor has benefited from an earlier invention some reward to the first inventor appears warranted. But its truthfulness becomes more doubtful if one avoids a retrospective approach, where a further development has already been made. It is not certain that further developments will occur, at all, if the claims are excessively broad. To make follow-on inventions dependent on a previous invention has a chilling effect on the research that may lead to follow-on inventions. This was mentioned in the quote above from the House of Lords. If one studies the incentives available after the initial patent is granted, the question is whether new inventions within the scope of the initial patent will be made at all if the incentives are limited for all but the first patentee. That is the practical effect of broad claims on further research, nothing else. It does not seem to create any extra incentives for the first patentee to have an initial patent that covers further inventive developments. He can always file for a new patent for such a subsequent use, if his first patent does not already cover it.[21]

With this perspective, i.e. focusing on the need for further developments, the material factor is how the incentives for achieving new inventions can be kept on a high level. The first patentee has had access to all the information that may have facilitated subsequent inventions by others. If someone still has used that information in a manner that the first inventor did not, then this must mean that the second inventor used the available research opportunities better and that competition proved advantageous. The – no doubt, very real – technical interdependence of inventions does not override the conclusion that someone who has made a further inventive input has proved the value of competition in the search for new inventions. Therefore, avoiding or limiting broad claims do not necessarily lead to unjustified advantages for competitors to the initial patentee, but rather maintains an equal footing and competition between possible later inventors.

---

[20] T 292/85, OJ EPO 1989, 275.

[21] This is regularly done, even if the first patent covers the subsequently developed use, e.g. so called selection patents. One reason for this is that the new patent will last longer than the first patent (20 years from filing).

The Board stated in T 292/85 that it would be a problem if inventors were encouraged to find alternatives outside the claims rather than trying to pursue progress through dependent inventions. But this is a questionable description of the problems that occur when broad claims are allowed. At issue is not so much to prevent research being done outside the scope of patents granted. There are unlimited opportunities for research outside the scope of patents granted and such research will always be carried out. A genuine problem with broad claims is, however, that there may be too little research done within, or close to, the scope of granted patents. This may be a problem if there are valuable untapped technical opportunities available there. Whether new further technical opportunities are located inside or outside the scope of granted patents is, as such, irrelevant from a social point of view. It is their discovery that matters. This being so, the real problem seems to be the possible unknown production opportunities existing within the scope of patents already granted, not the possibilities of research being done outside the scope of granted patents. When considering the scope of protection, therefore, care must be taken to ensure that there will not be a lack of incentives to search for yet unknown production opportunities within the scope of already granted patents.

To summarize, the technical interdependence of inventions does not in itself seem to be a convincing justification for allowing broad claims, i.e. patents that reach-through to future but for the time being unknown uses. Broad claims reduce the incentives for all competitors to the patentee, but they do not necessarily enhance the incentives of the patentee: the initial patentee with a narrow first patent would still be able to get a new patent on any new discovery subsequently made. At least as long as we remain quite ignorant about what the *ex ante* socially optimal amount of research incentives are for initial inventions, that would also take into account the value of subsequently developed further dependent inventions, the patent system, I believe, should primarily focus on how the incentives for achieving new inventions within granted claims can be maintained. What matters then are not who has created certain technical knowledge (a first invention), but how further search for new information can be made efficient. It may be that one invention has been essential for a later one. But the fact remains that in such a case the junior inventor has made better use of the impetus for further research than the senior inventor. Therefore it appears that broad claims that incorporate unknown medical uses cannot solely be justified by the technical interdependence of inventions. A different justification for determining the scope of claims will be put forward here.

8.3 Co-ordination of Initial and Follow-on Research

Co-ordinating wealth-creating activities is a classic economic problem.[22] It was referred to already in the writings of Adam Smith (The Wealth of Nations, 1776). One aspect of the patent system is that it works to co-ordinate scientific research, an activity otherwise normally carried out in secret by competing firms.[23] In this chapter it will be endeavored to show that European patent courts have in pharmaceutical patent infringement cases, fulfilled a co-ordinating function with respect to pharmaceutical research. Courts have adjusted the granted patent scope, depending on the kind of contribution made by the follow-on inventors (i.e. the defendants in the infringement suits). Through this practice they may co-ordinate research in laboratories of pharmaceutical companies throughout the world. A follow-on inventor that has made a valuable further development is not usually seen as an infringer, because courts tend to narrow the technical scope of the patent or, at least they refrain from expanding it through the doctrine of equivalence. Extra incentives are made available for the radical improver, so as to prevent him being held up by an earlier patent.[24] On the other hand, if the defendant has only made a cosmetic, unimportant modification in relation to the claims of the initial invention, courts tend to stretch the scope of the claims in order to encompass the defendant's product. Courts engaged in claim interpretation, through this practice, fine-tune the incentives for further research into new production opportunities located on or close to the boundaries of claims already granted. Extra incentives are created for the kind of research that society truly values, i.e. that which adds some value. By added value in this respect I mean an additional market value in the attacked product, typically in the form of a therapeutic advantage, as compared to the value of the initial patent. If an initial patentee has not exploited such possible further valuable developments, the competitors that have, are usually favored in infringement disputes.

A need for co-ordination occurs because there will always be inventors who find new production opportunities on or in close approximation to the boundaries of granted patent claims. This may be because the engaged in-

---

[22] See e.g. the chapter in this book by D. Foray, Excess of Intellectual Property Rights, Tragedies and Possible Remedies.

[23] B. Domeij, *Pharmaceutical Patents in Europe*, 259 ff, The Hague London Boston 2000.

[24] See R.P. Merges, *Intellectual Property Rights and Bargaining Breakdown: The Case of Blocking Patents*, 62 Tenn. L. Rev. 75 (1994) (arguing that reverse doctrine of equivalents can be used to influence reluctant pioneers looking to exert "holdup rights" on radical improvers).

ventors have not noticed that a patent has been granted. It may also be that an inventor by pure coincidence, i.e. without doing systematic research, finds a new production opportunity close to a granted patent. In addition, there will be inventors who do research simply in a bid to escape, or further develop, granted patents ("inventing around"). An inventor, who has made a new development close to an already granted patent, has a choice to make between four main alternatives. He can end his research project and abandon the finding: he may change the direction of the project in order for the result to be propelled clearly outside the scope of the already granted patent: he may seek a licence from the proprietor of the patent or, finally: he may carry on with the project and argue that the new product does not infringe. In order to make a rational choice between the alternatives, the follow-on inventor will have to decide how the claims in the initial patent are to be interpreted. It is in this situation that the legal rules on claim interpretation play an important role for the incentives created by the patent system and thereby for the total research efficiency of the industry. It is at this point that courts can co-ordinate the research efforts by fine-tuning the scope of protection.

If the scope of protection hinges on the relationship between the value of the attacked product and the value of the technical information in the patent in suit, and this mode of interpretation is generally known, there will be special incentives for competitors to carry on with precisely those projects that society values. If there is no added value in a follow-on product and therefore courts make a broad interpretation of the claims, such competitors will be forced to reach an agreement with the patentee. Thereby courts do not create the same incentive for projects that add no extra value to consumers. These projects will either be abandoned or the competitor may seek a licence if he e.g. can produce and market the product more efficiently than the patentee. By using the available discretionary scope between a narrow and a broad interpretation of the claims, courts can thus guide the research effort of an industry to create especially valuable products, i.e. a favorable co-ordination through the incentives in the patent system.[25]

This proposition will now be compared to European cases on pharmaceutical patent infringement. The study turns to infringement cases adjudicated by European courts, because until one actually knows what further developments that were available close to the outer scope of a granted patent, it is not really possible to co-ordinate initial and follow-on inventors. The fine-

[25] In a similar vein see R.P. Merges, R.R. Nelson, *On the Complex Economics of Patent Scope*, Columbia Law Review 1990, 867 and R.P. Merges, *Intellectual Property Rights and Bargaining Breakdown: The Case of Blocking Patents*, 62 Tenn. L. Rev. 75 (1994).

tuning of the scope of protection must for practical reasons be done by the courts and not by the patent offices. The impossibility to know in advance what follow-on inventions that lie hidden offers an explanation for why the scope of protection in a patent may have to be left without a definitive technical boundary by the patent office.

8.4 Discussion of European Cases

The Oberlandesgericht in Düsseldorf has ruled that a recombinant protein was equivalent to a protein that was defined in the claims by being extracted from biological sources. One expert witness stated in the proceedings that a man skilled in the art would not have considered the differences between the claims and the contested product significant for the therapeutic use and the court therefore concluded that this was an infringement by equivalent means. Although the therapeutic use of the products did not differ as such in this case, it is difficult to reconcile the decision with the argument made above. When a protein for the first time can be manufactured recombinantly, it will be available at lower cost, in larger quantities and create less health risks for the patients. This probably amounts to a significant added value for consumers of the invention (the patients) and thereby also for the manufacturers.[26] One must therefore conclude that either the argument above regarding the importance of the added value is incorrect or the judgement from the German court is an exception. It appears as if the latter could be the case. The German court may have decided the case with too narrow a perspective. It only considered the nature of the therapeutic effect and found no difference between the two proteins. But if the court had taken into account all factors of significance for the use of the infringing product, it would have been clear that the added value was considerable. Therefore, strong incentives for development of this recombinant research project were warranted, even after the patent application on the protein derived from biological sources was published. One cannot be certain that the inventor of the recombinant protein could have negotiated a licence from the patentee, in any case it would have been costly and the negotiations would had created uncertainty in the recombinant research project. If this judgement is followed in similar situations, the danger is that new inventions of this kind, which consumers particularly value, will not be made or developed to marketable products.

---

[26] Oberlandesgericht Düsseldorf 2 U 52/89 of December 31, 1992, ref. by F. Hirsche, B. Hansen, *Protecting Inventions in Chemistry*, 329, Weinheim 1997: and by F. Lederer, *Equivalence of Chemical Product Patents*, IIC 1999, 280.

The House of Lords has ruled that a prodrug to ampicillin infringed the patent pertaining to the compound ampicillin. When the prodrug came into contact with water in the gullet it underwent a chemical reaction and became the active substance ampicillin. There was no therapeutic or other added value associated with the use of the prodrug. It was decided that this was an infringement, despite the existence of more than insignificant structural diversity between the claims and the infringing product. It was plainly important that the prodrug did not add any value to the known invention. Lord Diplock stated:

> "I have already expressed my opinion that the pith and marrow doctrine is applicable to claims for new products as well as to new processes; and I agree with the Court of Appeal that the relationship of hetacillin to ampicillin provides a clear case for its application. It was argued that what is claimed in the patent as an essential feature of the class of products to which ampicillin belongs is the presence of an amino group in the alpha position, and that this feature is absent in hetacillin. This is literally true at the time of importation and sale but it ceases to be true as soon as hetacillin is put to use for the only purpose for which it is intended. The substitution for the postulated amino group of the variant incorporated in hetacillin is evanescent and reversible and for all practical purposes of use can be regarded as the equivalent of the amino group in ampicillin. In the apt phrase used by the Court of Appeal, it is the reproduction of the substance ampicillin, albeit temporarily masked".[27]

It can be taken from Lord Diplock's statement that the absence of any "practical purposes of use" for the difference between the claim and the attacked product is crucial if the protective scope is to be stretched beyond the claims. The judgment can very well be explained by the argument that courts do not wish to create incentives for competitors who do not add anything of commercial value to a patented product.

Another interesting English case is the recent *American Home Products Corporation and Professor Roy Calne v. Novartis.* The patent was based upon the discovery made by Professor Calne that a product by the name of rapamycin, was useful to suppress transplant rejection. Rapamycin was at the priority date of the patent, June 6, 1989, known to have antifungal and antitumour properties. For that reason the main claims of the patent followed the form known as "Swiss type" which is a format used to claim an invention of

---

[27] House of Lords *Beecham Group v. Bristol Laboratories* of 30 03 1978, [1978] R.P.C. 153.

a second medical use. Claim 1 therefore claimed as inventive: "1. Use of rapamycin for the preparation of a medicament for inhibiting organ or tissue transplant rejection in a mammal in need thereof".

Novartis had produced an immunosuppressant which was referred to as SDZ RAD. It was a derivative of rapamycin. Chemically it retained a substantial part of the molecule rapamycin. But for it to come within the ambit of claim 1, the word "rapamycin" had to be construed as covering derivatives of rapamycin which retain the essential characteristics of rapamycin. In the Patents Court, Laddie J held the patent infringed and the allegation of insufficiency made by Novartis failed. He refused to make the declaration of non-infringement that was sought by Novartis:

> "I do not believe that any reasonable and objective person skilled in the art would read this patent as indicating that the inventive contribution was limited to rapamycin alone or that Professor Calne intended to restrict his monopoly simply to the use of that single chemical. ... To do that would have rendered the patent virtually valueless. It would have left out of its scope, for example, those closely similar molecules which could be derived by standard chemistry from rapamycin and which probably would have included many which those in the art would have expected to have equivalent or even better immunosuppressant properties. It would have disclosed to the art the novel seam of interrelated molecules but have claimed only one of them. In practice it was inevitable that the discovery of the activity of rapamycin would lead workers in the art to look for similar molecules derived from rapamycin which would have a better profile of properties".[28]

If the disclosure given to the world by Professor Calne included, not only the second medical use of rapamycin, but also the knowledge that derivatives of rapamycin would work as immunosuppressants, the technical contribution of the patent, as well as the scope of protection, could well be extended beyond the second medical use of rapamycin and included derivatives which had the same effect. On that view, a new class of compounds had been discovered which had the common characteristics that they contained the same core structure as rapamycin and worked in the same way as rapamycin.[29] There were statements in the description to that effect. The skilled person, who read the specification, would then be able to predict that

[28] [2000] RPC 547.
[29] P. Cole. Pioneering Pays – or Does it? [2000] E.I.P.R. 541.

derivatives would work and there would be no particular value in competitors finding them.

However, on appeal that reasoning was not followed. The Court of Appeal and Aldous L.J. on July 27, 2000, set aside the order of Laddie J. and the claim of infringement of the European Patent was dismissed. This was partly due to a different assessment of the technical contribution made by Professor Calne. The number of possible derivatives was found to be vast and whether any particular molecule derived from rapamycin would work at all was impossible to predict with certainty. It was pointed out by the Court that many derivatives would not exhibit immunosuppressant activity at all. Those which involved small changes to the side chain would be the most likely to work. Thus the skilled person could make up a list of possibles, with those believed to be the most likely at the top of the list. Even so, finding appropriate derivatives, if they existed, would involve a systematic and iterative process. Further, the Court of Appeal emphasized that when a derivative which had appropriate activity had been identified, it would be impossible to be certain that it did not exhibit unpredictable defects. To discover whether it did would require further tests which would take a long time. The very uncertainty and unpredictability meant that the skilled person was being required to carry out research, in the opinion of the Court of Appeal. With this assessment of the technical situation, it was more appropriate to consider the amount of work involved in finding useful derivatives of rapamycin, as something making a valuable contribution. It was not seen as an infringement of the claim.

It is not particularly difficult to reconcile the judgement by the Court of Appeal with the policy rationale presented in this chapter. One can even interpret it as a direct evaluation by the court of the best use of the research efforts of the two companies that were active in the field. Should Novartis, from a social point of view, have spent their resources on trying to find new follow-on derivatives or should they rather have done research in other fields? It was a question discussed in the evidence of Professor Acheson, one of Novartis' expert witnesses. He said:

> "I have been informed by Novartis that the aim of the SDZ RAD program within Novartis was to develop new and improved rapamycin derivatives. Such a project was clearly justifiable. There is no reason why a natural product, such as rapamycin, should be the best drug for treating a particular medical condition. There are known examples of synthetic derivatives, developed from a natural product, which show improved or advantageous functions and properties

> over the natural product itself. The production and screening of potentially useful derivatives is a huge task but vital. Because there is no sure way of predicting which derivatives of complex biological molecules, if any, will possess new and improved properties, it is, however, a high risk venture".

Professor Acheson suggested that American Home Products had not done enough in the search for follow-on inventions and therefore what Novartis did was justifiable and should not be seen as an infringement. It is, of course, difficult to judge whether the research done by Novartis in this case was warranted or should better have been left to the patentee. Such research may be in the interest of users of immunosuppressants, if the patentee did not efficiently tap the research opportunities. The claim interpretation made by the Court of Appeal – the finding of non-infringement – may gear research into avenues that are being insufficiently explored by patentees. But it may also lead to an inefficient duplication of research efforts, at least if the initial patentee is already exploiting the opportunities diligently. Perhaps the key issue in the case should have been, as it was in the ampicillin case, whether there were any practical purposes for users of immunosuppressants, to have at their disposal the SDZ RAD compound.[30] If yes, then the initial patentee had not taken full advantage of the research opportunities offered by Professor Calne's discovery. If, on the other hand, there were no additional advantages associated with SDZ RAD, compared to rapamycin, the best use for Novartis research resources would probably have been elsewhere. The question of an added value could perhaps function as a yardstick.

The Danish Supreme Court decided in 1993 that there was no infringement in a patent for an analogy process for manufacturing an ulcer drug.[31] The fact that the defendant had improved upon the patented process in a material and non-obvious manner was the elucidation furnished by the Court. The defendant in this case had established a new way of synthesis with advantages as to both yield and the environment. Hydrochloric acid did not have to be used, which meant that no special manufacturing equipment was needed. In addition, the purification process was less complicated. Together these differences added considerable value in relation to the patented manu-

[30] Cf. P. Cole. Pioneering Pays – or Does it? [2000] E.I.P.R. 540.

[31] Danish Supreme Court (Højesteret) *Allen Hanburys Ltd v. A/S GEA Farmaceutisk Fabrik* of 27 08 1993, Ugeskrift for Retsvæsen 1993, 859. An analogy process is a claim format that was used when compound protection for pharmaceuticals was not allowed. The novelty resided in the compound, but only the processes for manufacturing the compound could be patented. The analogy process claim format is today for all practical purposes obsolete.

facturing process. The decision therefore accords well with the argument that attacked embodiments representing an added value are non-infringing.

The City Court of Stockholm has also tried a case relating to a patented pharmaceutical manufacturing process. The Court found an infringement by equivalent means, because the modifications of the process made by the defendant were within the knowledge of the man skilled in the art. In this case that was a relatively far-reaching application of the doctrine of equivalence, because the practical effects of the differences between the processes, were considerable. The synthesis according to the claims took 24 hours, while the attacked process was almost instantaneous. Furthermore, the attacked process yielded 70 per cent more of the end-product than the patented processes. Finally, the infringing process produced pure cimetidine, while the patented process required a final purification step. These differences are of practical importance within the pharmaceutical business and of economic significance. One must therefore conclude that this judgement does not accord well with my argument. Some support for the added-value-argument can, however, be found in the fact that one of the judges has since stated that he questions the outcome of the case. The reason for his hesitation was the very fact of the differences between the invention and the infringing process being significant from a practical perspective.[32]

8.5 Conclusions

Any technique for claim interpretations must emphasize legal certainty because it reduces uncertainty for parties. But that does not hinder other consideration playing a role in the interpretation of claims. The additional justification, furnished above, for patent claim interpretation (i.e. that claim interpretation is important because it is a way to gear research into valuable avenues) has been compared to European pharmaceutical case law in this chapter. It has been found that courts attach importance to whether the contested embodiment adds any value to the information disclosed in the patent. Courts limit the reach of patents in the face of substantial improvements. This can usefully be seen as a process of co-ordination. The head of a research department within a pharmaceutical company would work in a similar manner, within the company, when he makes priorities between different projects. No definite conclusions can be drawn, however, regarding the poli-

[32] District Court of Stockholm case no. T 7-213-83 of 20 06 1985 and O. Westlander and L. Törnroth, *Patents – Case Law from the courts during the years 1983-1991*, p 213, Stockholm 1995.

cies adopted by the courts. It is difficult to determine whether the value added by the possibly infringing object is the most important factors in interpreting patent claims and in the determination of the scope of protection, especially since many judgments lack an explicit analysis of the economic value of the attacked product in relation to the invention. Many cases turn more or less exclusively on a verbal reading of the claims. This could of course be taken to indicate that courts do not consider the added value particularly relevant. However, I believe that case law shows that courts attach significance to the question. It affects the outcome, but is not always dealt with very explicitly in the legal reasoning.

One may perhaps conclude that the added value of the infringing product is one among the most important circumstances, when the scope is interpreted. It can, however, never be the only consideration. There must always be opportunities for competitors to design-around patent claims, without simultaneously having to improve upon the function of the patented invention. Considerations about the added value can therefore primarily be a defence against an application of the doctrine of equivalence or any other broad interpretation of the claims. A presence of economically significant differences between the contested embodiment and the claims could block a finding of infringement, even if the technical differences, taken as such, are marginal in relation to the claims. This would make competitors carry on research projects leading to valuable further developments of patented inventions. Legal considerations pertaining to "added value" create incentives for those technical developments that are especially valued by customers. Socially less important, but perhaps technically more remote, developments of a patented invention do not receive the same incentives. In the latter cases an agreement with the patentee will be needed, not in the former. But, it has already been pointed out, that these considerations must primarily be seen as a defence that can be made available by courts to follow-on inventors.

Legal certainty would perhaps benefit if courts more systematically discussed the added value of the attacked product. This is a factor that can be studied quite objectively by looking at the demand for the invention and the attacked product. Today the explicit analysis of patent scope in infringement cases is mainly of a technical nature. It is tested whether a man skilled in the art knew of the interchangeability between features in the claims and the contested embodiment. It is thereby considered to some extent, but more indirectly and implicitly, whether the contested embodiment has added some value to the patented invention. A linkage usually exists between the technical difficulties that have been overcome and the added value of the contested embodiment. If the contested embodiment was obvious to the man skilled in the art, this probably conveys a lack of economic value. But this grappling with the interpretation of patent claims has led me to the conclusion that courts would be well advised to investigate the added value of the attacked embodiment in a more direct manner. The important problem, seemingly inescapable in the patent system, that some valuable follow-on research results, of questionable ownership, may not reach consumers, is primarily related to the added value of the research results, not to the technical difficulties, as such, that have been overcome.

The interplay between initial and follow-on inventors is always played out in the shadow of the law, i.e. against the backdrop of patent law as perceived by the parties. In this article I have suggested a way for the law to provide broad initial patents, but still maintain incentives for valuable follow-on inventions, without sacrificing legal certainty. This has been attempted, because I believe that initial broad patents may have chilling effects on further research. They might therefore need to be pruned back, in certain situations. A different approach altogether to these situations would start from the proposition that the prospect of gaining dependent patents is incentives enough for companies to initiate new research projects. If a dependent patent is enough to instigate research, then the approach sketched here is less relevant. The question is if a granted patent is a more or less definitive foreclosure of further research by others into follow-on inventions or if the lure of dependent patents is enough? It would be valuable to have more legal/economic studies on this issue. A tentative answer to the role that dependent patents actually play in research would valuably illuminate the problems faced by both patent lawyers and patent examiners today.

Chapter 9

ON THE CREATION OF FUNDAMENTAL KNOWLEDGE: FINDING THE RIGHT BALANCE BETWEEN THE PUBLIC AND PRIVATE DOMAINS

Dominique Foray[1]

OECD, Center for Education, Research and Innovation (CERI), Paris, France

Chapter contents:

Abstract: This paper addresses the issue raised by the proliferation of patents on research tools and enabling technologies. In a first section, we explore the reasons for this new phenomenon. In a second section, we consider the economic consequences of patenting fundamental knowledge (transaction costs and innovation blockages) as well as some consequences for the legal system. We also discuss the effects of patenting fundamental knowledge on the organisation of scientific research. We conclude that the social costs imposed on the system are high because fundamental knowledge is by nature cumulative and generic, and probably higher than the expected benefits, due to the fact that private markets for basic knowledge function badly, even in presence of patents. In sections 3 and 4, the paper discusses various solutions including the revival of public property.

---

[1] The present version of this paper has benefited from comments received on an earlier draft from Ove Granstrand. I am grateful to him for very useful suggestions, as well as encouragement and great patience!

O. Granstrand (ed.), Economics, Law and Intellectual Property, 199-221.

Several authors (Nelson, 1959, Arrow, 1962, David, 1993,) have put emphasis on the complementary nature of different public and private institutions set up for the purpose of efficient resource allocation in the production and use of fundamental knowledge. This is due to the difficulties that private markets have in functioning efficiently, when the good in question is a public good. A recent book reminds us that the basic rationale of intellectual property law depends on an independent public domain containing a stock of freely accessible information (McSherry, 2001). That shared collection of basic knowledge provides the building blocks for new inventions. That was how the system functioned until the early 1990s. There was a clear division of effort between upstream not-for-profit institutions, which did curiosity-driven basic research, and downstream for-profit companies that did market-oriented applied research. The structure of this division appears clearly in the case of the pharmaceutical industry (Cockburn, 2002). It was an essentially binary structure with a clear distinction between upstream Open Science, and a downstream commercial sector dominated by large highly integrated firms. The modern era shows a somewhat different model. By the mid-1990s several thousand biotechnology ventures had been launched. This evolution was facilitated by a number of reforms and changes in the legal intellectual property right system, which resulted in a proliferation of patents granted for basic knowledge (Figure 9-1). Obviously, without patent rights in inventions such as DNA sequences, gene expression systems and other types of research tools, many biotechnology companies could not exist.

9.1 Unbridled Privatization of Basic Research

The use of intellectual property is thus becoming increasingly important in the domain of basic research, and within that general domain the use of the patent is growing rapidly. This general trend is also reflected in the increase in exclusivity rights over instruments, research materials, enabling technologies, research tools and databases[2]. All this contributes to the unprecedented expansion of the knowledge market and the proliferation of exclusive rights on whole areas of intellectual creation.

[2] Examples of research tools or enabling technologies include the Cohen-Boyer patent on the technology for inserting foreign genetic material into bacteria, the Genetech patent on a technology for getting foreign genes to "express", the PCR technology for replicating DNA in test tubes, gene guns, and recent suppression technologies that cause gene sequences to become inactive (these examples come from Shankerman and Scotchmer, 1999).

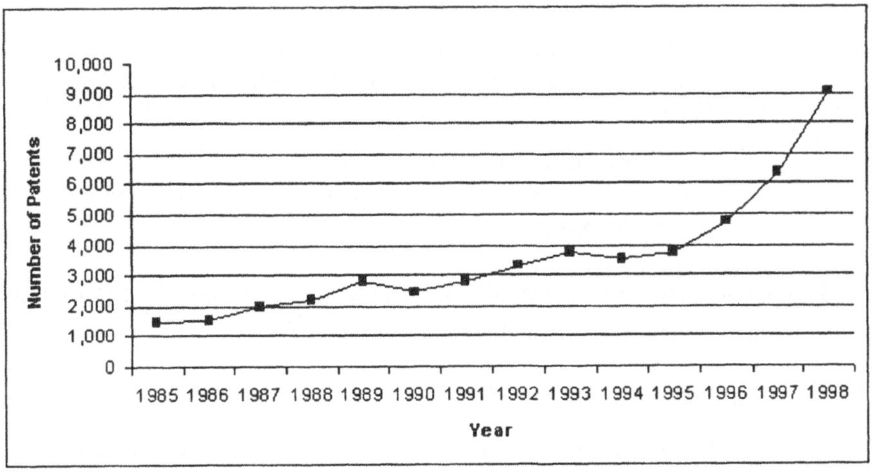

Figure 9-1. Upsurge in patenting in biotechnology

Source: BIO web page [Source: U.S. Patent and Trademark Office, Technology Profile Report, Patent Examining Technology Center, Groups 1630-1650, Biotechnology 1/1977 – 1/1998, April 1999]

Many factors explain this trend. We will consider two reasons as the immediate determinants of the upsurge in patenting[3].

9.1.1 The expansion of markets for basic knowledge

One main reason points out some important qualitative changes in the basic research system. It is, therefore, important to consider although it can explain only a very small fraction of the global increase of patents (which concerns almost all patent classes). This reason concerns the entry of new players into "basic knowledge markets". It includes:

> —The emergence of a new generation of firms which are specialized in fundamental research and are, therefore, in direct competition with the public research institutions. These new and/or small

[3] We are not considering here the more fundamental reasons, such as the shortening of the links between science and commercial markets in certain fields or the increasing problems of public budget in bearing the costs of science (which are themselves increasing). See Foray (1999) for a look at those broader issues.

> companies consider patent as the only reliable way to signal their value to the market (Cockburn, 2002).
>
> —The increasing orientation of public research institutions towards the promotion of their commercial interests (Henderson *et al.*, 1998).
>
> —The privatization of some of the activities of governmental civilian agencies, which become major players in the contractual research market (Jaffe and Lerner, 1999).

This triple evolution shows a general tendency towards the privatization of basic knowledge, as a public good.

9.1.2 Changes in the patent office

The second big reason deals with the institutional changes that have facilitated the first trend. The main aspect of changes concerns the fact that patent offices have completely given up their regulatory role. Until the 1970s, the general view of patent offices was that patents were anti-competitive and not good for the economy. Patent offices were considered more as "rejection offices" than as institutions for supporting innovators. They therefore played a significant regulatory role, blocking or slowing down private appropriation in certain fields. For example, the patentability criteria of "industrial application" (utility) were very effective in blocking patenting of the first genetic inventions in the late eighties. For several reasons patent offices have become extremely pro-patent since the early 1980s. The new view is that innovation must be helped and foreign investors attracted. The applicant, formerly considered with suspicion, has become a "client" whose needs must be satisfied, owing to quick, cheap procedures. The result is a total deterioration of examination procedures, for the office's role is confined to that of a registry office and a statistics bureau.

Thus, the pendulum started swinging away from rigorous examination, towards a cheap/fast process. Nowadays, patentability criteria have ceased to play their role of preserving the public domain. Pro-patenting policies of patent offices mean that patentability criteria have gradually been eased and extended to new subject domains. Many research results have now become patentable, as a result of both legal (court) and patent office decisions. The increasing ability to patent fundamental knowledge, research tools and data bases is part and parcel of a broader movement towards strengthening IPRs.

The consequence of this evolution is a sort of transfer of the responsibility for regulation from patent offices to the law courts. Since everything has become patentable and acceptable, most patents are legally fragile and therefore likely to be challenged by rivals. We clearly see this twofold tendency of deterioration of the patent offices' work, along with an increase in the efficiency of the legal system, especially in the US (Jaffe, 2000).

9.2 Consequences

These trends do not necessarily lead to an excess of privatization of knowledge. In many cases the establishment of intellectual property rights strengthens private incentives, allows the commitment of substantial private resources, and thereby improves the conditions of commercialization of inventions. Moreover, the establishment of private rights does not totally prevent the diffusion of knowledge, even if it does limit it. Finally, a large proportion of private knowledge is disseminated outside the market system, either within consortiums or by means of networks of trading and sharing of knowledge, the foundation of intentional spillovers discussed by several authors.

However, there is some concern when all these trends create a system with high transaction costs and some risks of blockage in knowledge exploitation and cumulativeness.

9.2.1 Economic consequences

Transaction costs

A large set of implications of this view involves various phenomena that can be grouped, for the sake of convenience, under the heading "transaction cost increases". Both qualitative trends (increasing fragility of patents) and quantitative changes (increase in numbers of patent applications and grants) are likely to increase transaction costs. Efforts and costs devoted to sorting out conflicting and overlapping claims to IPR will increase, as will uncertainty about the nature and extent of legal liability in using knowledge inputs. Again policy makers and academics are concerned with the increase of litigation costs, including indirect costs, which may distort the innovative behaviour of small companies (Lerner 1994). As John Barton (2000) put it, there is a problem when "*the number of intellectual property lawyers is growing faster than the number of researchers*". And this is exactly what has happened in the U.S., while similar trends in Europe show that it is no longer a purely American problem.

9.2.2 Blockage

It is possible that intellectual property-related transaction costs may increase so much that the result can be a deadlock in knowledge exploitation and accumulation. Basically, such situations stem from the fact that patents and innovations are two different realities that do not coincide. In some cases a single patent covers many innovations (especially when the field is too large or when the patent protects generic knowledge). In other cases, a single innovation is covered by many patents. This case is the anti-commons regime.

When a single patent covers many innovations: weakening of the cumulativeness of knowledge

The scope of a patent is a variable that can be the object of strategic choices by private agents, and that the legal authorities concerned will assess very differently, depending on the case. It is at the heart of the dilemma between protecting the first innovator and encouraging subsequent innovations (which is a form of the classic public good dilemma) (Scotchmer, 1991).

By staking a set of claims, inventors delimit the territory they want to have recognized as their property (the same principle as fencing off a field). If the field more than covers the territory of the innovation, subsequent innovations by other inventors, based on the first one, will be blocked. But if the field is too narrow the pioneer's efforts may not be rewarded at their full value. Note that a large field is not a major problem in the case of a discrete innovation. The metaphor of minerals prospecting is useful here. In a given territory where there is only one deposit surrounded by nothing else, whether the prospector closes off the territory very close to the deposit or far from it, creating a vast field, makes no difference since the additional space appropriated is of no value.

The problem is different in the case of interdependent and cumulative innovations. If an initial patent is too broad and generously rewards the pioneer inventor, it blocks possibilities for subsequent research by others. It thus reduces the diversity of innovative agents in the domain and the probability of cumulative developments taking place.

The case of a patent protecting a general result rather than the particular method used to obtain the result is a good example of a patent that is too broad. In this case, all subsequent research aimed at exploring other methods of obtaining the same result will be blocked. Patents on knowledge high upstream in the innovation process, particularly on research tools, can also hinder the cumulative dynamics of knowledge (Walsh *et al.*, 2000; Thomas, 1999).

A related case is the patent which covers all elements relating to the innovation and all imaginable applications, thus favouring the creation of extensive monopolies on exploitation.

After studying numerous cases, Merges and Nelson (1994) suggest that, in a context of interdependent innovations, an intellectual property policy that allows very broad patents leads to a number of deadlocks which impact on the general dynamics of innovation in the sector: "*In the cumulative systems technology cases, broad, prospect claiming, pioneer patents, when their holders tried to uphold them, caused nothing but trouble.... Nor is there reason to believe that more narrowly drawn patents would have damped the incentives of the pioneers and other early comers to the field.*"

When an innovation is covered by many patents: anti-commons regime and tragedy

The second type of problem is called "anti-commons" to indicate that its "structure" is the exact inverse of the common resources' problem (next chapter). It is a legal regime that has produced parcels of private property rights on "indivisible" goods (Heller, 1998) so that each party, being the owner of a portion of the indivisible good, has the right to exclude others from its share and no one has the effective privilege of use. The distinction between the private property regime and the anti-commons regime is represented in the following diagram where goods 1, 2 and 3 are represented by cells, and the initial property rights of individuals A, B and C are represented by lines in bold type.

The private property regime structures the material world vertically because A, B and C each own exclusive rights 1, 2 and 3 to an entire good (e.g. a piece of land). In other words, this regime does not prohibit exploitation of the resource. In the anti-commons regime the lines are horizontal since private rights fragment the goods.

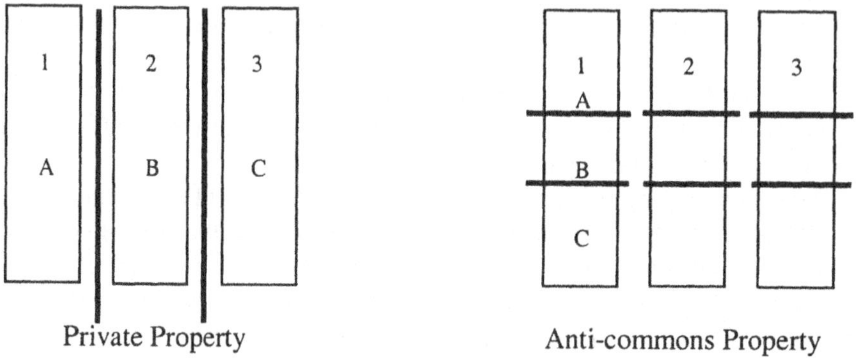

Figure 9-2 : The distinction between private and anti-commons property
Source: Heller (1998)

Tragedy results from the fact that multiple owners of "parcels" or "fragments" of a good each have the right to exclude others from their parcel, so that nobody can exploit the good in its entirety. This property regime thus breaks down and fragments objects. If too many owners have such exclusive rights (i.e. if there is too much fragmentation), there is a chance that the good will be under-utilized. The tragedy may then lead to exacerbated forms of non-distribution and under-utilization of the resource, due to the fact that rights on fragments or parcels are solely rights to exclude and can no longer be rights to exploit.

As in the case of common resources, the anti-commons regime does not necessarily lead to tragedy. First, the problem of under-utilization of resources can be solved through the trading of rights. In a world without transaction costs, owners can reorganize initial endowments through ex post exchanges, by gathering anti-common rights into property rights, that is, by recomposing the goods. Of course, the real world is one in which transactions are costly, but some problems of anti-commons – particularly those concerning a small number of agents – may nevertheless be reduced through transactions aimed at recomposing the goods. Another solution is similar to the one used for the problem of common resources: the adoption of informal norms for managing ownership.

Finally, to avoid the tragedy it is logical to try to eliminate the regime itself by endowing those concerned with more coherent initial rights.

How does this regime apply in the knowledge economy? It corresponds to excessive fragmentation of the knowledge base, due to intellectual property rights on parcels and fragments of knowledge that do not correspond to an industrial application. The result is a proliferation of blockages. The following two cases are particularly indicative of the problem (Heller and Eisenberg, 1998).

The first blockage results from the fact that knowledge is fragmented and rights are granted to portions of knowledge before the corresponding product is identified (whereas previously it was the genes corresponding to products that were patented, e.g. therapeutic proteins, diagnostic tests). The proliferation of patents on fragments of genes owned by different agents hugely complicates the coordination required by an agent wanting to develop a product. In particular, if the acquisition of all necessary licenses is too complicated or expensive, the product will never materialize. A good illustrative case is given by Kryder *et al.* (2000). The innovation known as "golden rice"[4] involves using as many as 70 pieces of IP spread over 31 institutions.

A second blockage results from procedures known as "reach-through licence agreements" which give the patent holder rights over future discoveries. These rights may consist of the payment of royalties on sales, of licences on future discoveries or of a priority option for obtaining licenses. The system was initially designed to enable researchers with few financial resources to use a patented discovery and to pay only if the research produced results. But in the end this kind of system gives the owners of first patents the right to be present at all stages of subsequent developments, even if they did not contribute to them. Once again, there is a risk of under-utilization of certain discoveries because of situations in which the rights of those concerned are entangled.

Certain situations in the domain of information technology also pose this type of problem.

Is the anti-commons regime described a transition or does it signal a tragedy? Theoretically, we can hope for the creation of appropriate institutions to help agents coordinate the trading of licenses (see Grindley and Teece, 1997, for numerous examples). Also theoretically, collective learning can lead to real decreases in transaction costs. In practice, however, it is difficult to see how mechanisms of natural correction could appear and put an end to these situations of deadlock. There is a huge degree of heterogeneity between actors, and transaction costs are enormous for those wanting to group together rights to recompose fragmented knowledge. To make it worse, cognitive biases cause everyone to over-estimate the probability of their own

[4] Beta-carotene enhanced rice

patent being a miracle patent – which leads everyone to want more than the probable value of that asset (Heller and Eisenberg, 1998).

Very few empirical evidences are now available to show whether anti-commons structure of private property is a real problem for innovation and knowledge cumulativeness. Although the conditions in certain fields appear conducive to a tragedy of the anti-commons, there is no clear case of project cessation and blockages due to those conditions. This is the main result of a preliminary survey carried out by Walsh *et al.*(2000): "*the vast majority of respondents say that there are no cases where valuable research projects were stopped due to IP problems*". However, addressing such an issue (dealing with the empirical validation of the anti-commons prediction) should require more systematic surveys based on highly sophisticated questionnaires and more theoretical work to get right interpretations of the results[5].

9.2.3 Distortion of the legal system

Introduction of new types of object into the patent system can introduce imbalances, for example by breaking the link between granting of exclusivity rights and the requirement of public description of the invention – a requirement which guarantees a balance between the general interest and that of the patentee. The requirement of a literal description of biotechnological invention harms the interests of applicants who cannot meet that condition. In order to bypass the obstacle, the requirement is relaxed somewhat ("*the description must be as complete as possible*" – meaning that a description which fails to allow reproduction of the invention will be tolerated, contrary to normal requirements in general). A whole series of distortions result. For example, exemption in favour of research (which allows use of the invention for research purposes) is no longer valid since an inadequate description no longer allows access to it. In short, there is a shift from a literal description to a deposit procedure so that third parties can obtain a sample of the invention (i.e. of the microorganism). This accentuates the distortion of the system. While the literal description is independent of the actual realization of the invention, a deposit procedure necessitates effective realization of the invention. Description is a "direction for use" which allows effective reproduction of the invention, whereas deposit is a copy of a given state of living matter which has evolving properties, implying that the following state will

[5] David (2002) in a short comment on the results of the survey points out the risk of highly biased answers, arising from the framing of the questions. He also develops some kind of sophisticated framework based on counterfactual arguments in order to avoid any naïve interpretation of the results.

not be accessible to the third party. The balance observed in patent common law between different interests is upset here (this point is brilliantly discussed by Clavier, 1998: 145-178). Thus, the system's adaptation to new objects can be obtained only by moving away from certain guiding principles in patent law.

9.2.4 Particular consequences for the organisation of scientific research

All studies show that this represents a real risk of irremediable alteration of modes of cooperation and sharing of knowledge in the domain of basic research. Restricted access to knowledge and the retention of knowledge produced by universities comes in several forms, e.g. delayed or partial publication and communication, secrecy, and patents. A significant form is the exclusive licence (new knowledge is sold exclusively to one firm). When there is nothing left but exclusive bilateral contracts between university laboratories and firms, we have forms of quasi-integration which undermine the domain of open knowledge.

Mowery, Nelson *et al.* (1998) study the impact of the US laws authorizing universities to grant exclusive licenses on the results of research financed by public funds (especially the Bayh-Dole Act). These laws aim at solving the problem of "post-invention" costs and risks in taking a new invention out of the laboratory and developing it into a successful commercial product. Firms would be unwilling to support these costs without some assurance of protection from competition. Patents and exclusive licensing thus facilitate the transfer of new technology to the private sector by providing exclusive rights to preserve the profit incentives of innovating firms. However, by focusing on exclusive licensing only, these laws are based on a narrow view of the channels through which public research interacts with industry. In reality these channels are multiple (publication, conferences, consultancy, training, expertise) and all contribute to the transfer of knowledge, while the incentives created by such laws promote only one channel (patenting and licenses), with the risk of blocking the others. The authors' conclusion is unambiguous: "*The Bayh-Dole Act and the related activities of U.S. universities in seeking out industrial funding for collaborative R&D have considerable potential to increase the 'excludability' of academic research results and to reduce the 'knowledge distribution' capabilities of university research*".

Another type of tragedy?

The famous case of Myriad Genetics is a good illustration of how detrimental the extension to Europe of a very broad patent in a field like health care can be. This case concerns patents granted to a private company that "discovered" the genes predisposing individuals to breast cancer. The patents are very broad, covering not only the structure of the genes but also a large range of diagnostic and therapeutic tools (Cassier and Gaudillère, 2001, Wadman, 2001). Extension to Europe of such a patent may have the potential of seriously hampering the system of therapeutic and diagnostic services provided by public hospitals in European countries. Since the US company has no intention of selling operating licences, European hospitals will be forced to send samples to the US for testing. The social cost imposed on the system would rise steeply and European researchers might be deprived of a powerful research tool (because a great deal of knowledge can be accumulated through tests). The prospect of such a transition is clearly explained by the company itself: *"The Company believes that the industrialization of diagnostics R&D now being catalyzed by genomics will transform the diagnostic industry from its current dependance on non-patented products generated sporadically by academic researchers into a market characterized by a steady flow of novel, proprietary tests protected by strong IP positions thereby achieving premium pricing and margins similar to those enjoyed by drugs and vaccines... The Company believes the diagnostics market is poised for a comparable value transition as a result of genomics and patenting",* (statement by Diadexus, a subsidiary of Incyte and SmithKline and Beecham, 2000). This kind of transition towards a market for diagnostic tests seems at least highly disputable in countries in which those services are provided mainly by public hospitals (e.g. France, Canada, Germany, UK, the Netherlands).

Institutional diversity in danger

A cause for concern is the fact that the diversity of institutional arrangements is threatened. Traditionally, IPRs are considered as one of the incentive structures society employs to encourage innovative effort. They co-exist with other incentive structures, each of which has costs and benefits as well as a degree of complementarity. The new view is that IPRs are the only means to commodify the intangible capital represented by knowledge, and should therefore be a common currency or 'yardstick' for measuring the output of activities devoted to knowledge generation and the basis for markets in knowledge exchange (Steinmueller 2002).

We consider such diversity (public-private-hybrid institutions) as being important because each institution fulfils specific functions and strong complementarities exist between them. But the space for public research (procurement and patronage) is shrinking and functions which were assumed by open science are no longer assumed at the same level[6]. This is a problem not only for the survival of open science *per se* but also for the sustainability of the system as a whole. Excessive privatization may undermine the long-term interests of industry itself (which will benefit from less public knowledge, less training and screening externalities). Finally, the scenario of a pure functional substitution (the private sector would simply carry out the functions which were formerly assumed by the public sector) is wrong. We know that private companies will never fund the same type of basic research that the public sector abandons (Brown, 1998). Similarly, the need for scientific training could be satisfied only very partially by market-based institutions. As argued by Cohen *et al.* (1998), spillovers from the downstream R&D conducted by firms engaged in basic research are not likely to entirely replace the information flows initially blocked for several reasons. First, firms will try to restrict spillovers to retain proprietary advantage. Secondly, there will typically be considerable lags between the time when the firm receives the valuable information and the time when information spills over to the other firms.

Of course, we can also count on academic researchers who are learning to negotiate their industrial contracts more and more advantageously in order to preserve areas of public knowledge (provided that the researchers themselves are not caught up in a sort of money-making frenzy). Industrial firms are often aware of the advantages of not completely undermining open and independent academic research and try to establish "good practice" so that universities work with and not for industry.

The fact remains that economic studies on the US model reveal a degree of concern. One of the conclusions of Cockburn and Henderson (1997) is that: "*policies which weaken these institutions (of open science), make public sector researchers more market-oriented, or redistribute rents through ef-*

[6] Lita (2001) provides striking evidence about the decline in the quality and focus of education as a direct consequence of the increasing orientations of universities towards commercialisation of research: (i) responsible mentoring is suffering due to conflicts of interest and simple limitations placed on time management; (ii) the time it takes to get the Ph.D. has increased over the last decade. On the second issue, Lita fears that entrepreneurial faculty members who must strike a balance between being a "boss" and "research advisor" might be more easily tempted into exploiting their students when business matters are involved.

forts to increase the appropriability of public research through restrictions in the ways in which public and private sectors work with each other, may therefore be counter-productive in the long run". This is a strong conclusion that prompts us carefully to examine this new model without being blinded by the brilliance of its undeniable short-term performance.

9.2.5 Private markets for basic knowledge function badly

Is the game worth the candle? Since fundamental knowledge and research tools are not sold to consumers, the profit on these inventions comes from licensing and profit-sharing arrangements with firms or other research institutions that want to use the research tools to create products. The idea underlying a private market for basic knowledge and research tools is, thus, that firms patent their inventions and then sell licenses to other researchers who develop products. But patents involve high social costs for the system, due to:

- Some cases of monopoly on the exploitation of a research tool. In such circumstances, the generic and cumulative value of the tool is lost and social costs derive from the fact that exclusive licenses and refusal to grant licenses deprive the system of potential benefits generated when several firms with different capacities and perceptions of a problem are mobilized.
- Increasing delays and costs involved in negotiation and litigation.
- Possible blockages (anti-commons) (see footnote 5).

On the other hand, the market has so many shortcomings in the area of basic research (uncertainty and difficulty in appropriating knowledge, despite the use of patents) that commercial success is rare. Anecdotal evidence and the relatively low stock market returns from research tool companies support this pessimistic view. This reflects what Nelson (1959) called "*the simple economics of basic research*". As argued by Cockburn (2002): "*patents or no patents, capturing the value that ultimately derives from fundamental early stage research is extraordinarily difficult for profit-oriented organizations*". In particular, the definition and observance of property rights on this basic knowledge are virtually impossible. The results of early surveys on researchers' behaviour as regards research tools protected by patents are surprising (Walsh *et al.*, 2000). First, the lack of awareness as to risks of infringement is dominant, for several reasons. At this stage of basic research each researcher is often guided by the "*do it yourself*" principle and is therefore unaware that application of a particular method is illegal. Use of the research exemption clause is naturally also widespread (even if it is legally more restrictive than most researchers seem to think)[7].

Secondly, the impression of impunity needs to be taken into consideration. Very often academics ignore (in the sense of failing to obey) the law and firms are reluctant to sue them. Infringement also corresponds to a logic of discovery in this sector: *"one has to try a million things for just one to work; it's only when you've found that one thing, that you think about property rights*" (quoted in Walsh *et al.*, 2000).

Hence the difficulty of making a private market function and of ensuring that property rights are respected when economic activity is centred primarily around the creation of scientific objects. Firms either anticipate bad appropriability of their knowledge, by granting licences on a large scale, or simply tolerate infractions, especially by academic researchers. Walsh *et al.* conclude: *"Universities and firms simply infringe and patent holders tacitly tolerate this.*"

We can rationalize positively this failure of patent holders to have their rights respected by considering it as a form of price discrimination of the Ramsey rule type. Economic theory suggests that such discrimination can enhance social welfare if the infringement which is tolerated does not reduce the value of the tool for users who are prepared to pay for access to it.

This conclusion suggests that the model of the small firm which invents a tool, patents it and hopes to obtain income by granting licenses to other researchers who will pay only in case of success, functions only very rarely. Thus, the game is not worth the candle.

[7] "Academic researchers are often shocked to discover that, except for some very limited statutory exemptions that do not generally apply to them, there is no general research exemption in the United States for using other people's patented technologies... As a rule, the Federal Circuit only found exemptions when use was for idle curiosity or purely philosophical pursuits. In this landscape, research at a university, even if performed without any profit motive, would be infringing, as it is difficult to imagine research that is outside the scope of business interests of an organization" (Nottenburg *et al.*, 2001).

9.2.6 Preliminary conclusion

In light of the above arguments, it is difficult to imagine that this privatization model can be reconciled with the goal of the UNESCO World Conference in June 1999, i.e. *"the identification of new principles for safeguarding the status of scientific knowledge as a public good."* We should note that the scientific revolution under way has unequalled potential to produce tools for development in the fields of agriculture, agri-food and health. But this scientific revolution is historically the first to be essentially private, a situation that generates problems of access to and acquisition of knowledge, as well as problems of priorities as regards research programmes (Foray and Kazancigil, 1999).

9.3 Patent Reform

Of course, the new system of knowledge production generates its own regulation, which can bring about a certain equilibrium in some instances. We can list three classes of solutions to the various problems developed below.

9.3.1 Facilitate access to private knowledge

Mechanisms are devised to support the fast dissemination and free exploitation of private knowledge, in certain circumstances or for certain classes of economic agents. There are three main mechanisms:

– Compulsory licensing (compulsory diffusion of private knowledge in the general interest): While the very idea of a compulsory licence was considered as an insult to the notion of property (since a basic right – that of not selling – is alienated), this practice is tending to take over and to spread to unexceptional circumstances. While most compulsory licences are applied for in the general interest (cf. the struggle between South Africa and the major pharmaceutical multinationals), it tends to become a last resort in the field of competition policy when the refusal to grant a licence can be interpreted as abuse of a dominant position.

– Patent buy-out: The state or an international foundation buying patents to put them back in the public domain (Kremer, 1997). To illustrate this mechanism Kremer uses the historical case of Daguerre, the inventor of photography who neither exploited his invention nor sold it for the price he wanted. In 1839 the French government purchased the patent and put the rights to Daguerre's invention in the public domain. The invention was developed very fast!

– Price discrimination: Ramsey's pricing rule suggests price discrimination between users whose demands are inelastic and those for whom the quantity purchased is extremely price-sensitive. The former category of buyer will therefore bear high prices without curtailing the quantity of goods purchased, whereas the low prices offered to those in the second category (e.g. scholars and university-based researchers) will spare them the burden of economic welfare reducing cutbacks in their use of the good (David, 2000). The clause of fair use for research or educational purposes is an interpretation of this rule.

Of course, the well-known problem involved in compulsory licencing and patent buy-out schemes has to do with valuation of the invention and with the likelihood of burdensome legal and administrative expenses that makes these schemes second-best solutions.

9.3.2 Navigating the patent thicket

Another type of solution to the anti-commons trap is offered by cross-licensing mechanisms (Grindley and Teece, 1997; Shapiro, 2000). Processes of learning on the trading of rights and systems of mutual concession can occur (for example within a consortium). This may keep transaction costs at tolerable levels and thus favour regulation of the anti-common regime to a certain extent. But it is a solution that can work only with a small number of companies. In that respect, the rapid growth of new kinds of firms does caution against over-confidence that anti-commons problems can be overcome. For example, the computer hardware industry had few problems with its cross-licensing arrangements until new kinds of semi-conductor companies emerged.

9.3.3 Actions directed at patent office practices

A great deal of action needs to be taken as regards the patent office if patent requirements are to be strictly enforced (utility requirement, non-obviousness, patent scope). Policy-makers should launch programmes to convince patent officers of the critical need to create initial endowments of property rights which are more coherent in so far as they respect the indivisibility of goods (avoiding the anti-commons trap).

One should note, however, that hybrid and complex objects – such as genes, DNA sequences, software, data bases – generate a lot of uncertainties about the appropriate intellectual property policy related to them, making the tasks of patent offices very difficult. It is difficult to provide non-ambiguous and clear answers to the question of whether these new objects should be privately appropriated and, if so, what class of IPR should be used. We are now living in a period in which these new objects are being put to the test.

This brings to mind a novel by the French writer Vercors, "*Les animaux dénaturés*." In the late nineteenth century, a new species, called the Tropis, was discovered by English anthropologists. Nobody in Victorian England could decide whether Tropises were humans or apes; neither the scientific academy, nor the church. The main theme of the novel is the search for legal truth. In the story a journalist kills a Tropis, simply to force the judicial system to qualify this act as murder or not. This is a good metaphor (developed by Clavier, 1998) to illustrate the perpetual necessity – in the presence of a new "object" – to proceed to a classification in order to infer a particular regime.

Under this kind of circumstance of great uncertainty, it might be useful to think about the creation of new categories of intellectual property such as the "common good"; a category which would match those situations in which "we don't know", meaning that society needs time to think about the legal status of the new object while the economy needs some legal certainty to go ahead with R&D investments. In this respect, lawyers think that certain new complex and hybrid objects (like genes) do not fit in the usual categories of private–public goods, and propose to work on a new category: the common good. Under a common good regime, innovation defies patrimonial and commercial appropriation. The private company that is in possession of it for industrial exploitation is not the owner of the good but serves as a sort of manager. Such a regime would allow for the emergence of an industry while avoiding private and exclusive rights.

9.3.4 Beyond intellectual property

In contexts in which reliance upon these mitigating devices is not feasible or not very effective, the alternative mechanisms for solving the public good problem based on public property may be superior to intellectual property rights as ways of stimulating innovation. We will turn to these mechanisms in the next section.

9.3.5 The changing nature of the IP system

To address these issues, the intellectual property institution is changing. It is shifting away from a system preserving the right of the inventor to "say no" (to refuse access and to keep the knowledge unexploited) to a system promoting systematic access right while preserving a right for the inventor to be remunerated. The increasing importance in policy discussion of compulsory licensing (beginning to be used not only in areas of public health and security but also for competition policy reasons), the new policy interest in price discrimination schemes, as well as the abundant literature on various ways to obtain a "freedom to operate" by bypassing or ignoring intellectual property, are signals of such an evolution (Nottenburg *et al.*, 2001). How far can the system go, and to what extent can the provision of this kind of tool help to solve the problems of knowledge access? Are these mechanisms sufficiently strong and enforced in domains where "essential human rights" are at stake (health, education, food)? Is, for instance, a system of compulsory licensing the solution to the problem raised by the broad patents covering diagnostic tests for breast cancer, as well as other similar problems in the health care and pharmaceutical area?

9.4 The Revival of Public Property: to keep the 3 E's!

But it is also a matter of a revival of public property. It is therefore important to restructure the rationale supporting public property in the domain of basic knowledge. We propose to restructure it under the three E's: externalities, equity, expertise.

Public intervention in such activities need not, of course, take the form of direct provision. Subsidies for commercially oriented private producers, or procurement contracting by the public sector, are important alternatives that can coexist with direct public production of public goods.

9.4.1 Externalities

One important part of basic research is carried out under an open principle: providing an effective mechanism for ensuring fast and extensive dissemination of new knowledge. The institution of open science has demonstrated its effectiveness as an incentive system. Thus, more than ever, standards of conduct regarding the disclosure and efficient distribution of knowledge should be top priorities in scientific research.

9.4.2 Equity

The second type of public action involves the optimal use of knowledge for the benefit of future generations and for protecting the well-being of certain non-solvent consumers, i.e., those without financial resources to purchase critical goods such as drugs to combat infectious diseases. Many issues related to finding "equitable solutions" to difficult problems of resource allocation among research "priorities" fall into this category. Private markets are as a rule short-sighted and tend to direct resources towards investment projects offering profit streams that have a high present value. The result is the tendency to under-fund not only projects with longer-term horizons, but also those targeted to the needs (or simply the tastes) of social minorities, as well as the low-income, developing economies. Generating and disseminating knowledge that is relevant to solving problems affecting the welfare of future generations is therefore an important societal objective. Future generations have the right to demand a "knowledge legacy", just as we currently benefit from knowledge produced by past generations. But these are not tasks that the private sector can be expected to perform unassisted.

9.4.3 Expertise

A final category of action involves the provision of conditions in society that nurture the formation of independent communities of "expertise" in complex scientific, technological and possibly also cultural matters such as historical studies and the arts. It is unrealistic to expect profit-seeking private entities that must survive in competitive markets to subsidize the work of communities of experts whose opinions cannot be controlled and who might reach conclusions that adversely affect an "altruistic" business sponsor, or benefit a rival company. An obvious difficulty in this area, however, is that the same mechanisms to control the pronouncements made by expert authorities on matters of a controversial political nature may exist in government circles as well. Sources of independent expertise are thus a form of public good that governments are unlikely to be able to supply by means of direct provision, and whose effectiveness can be vitiated if care is not taken to separate the receipt of subsidies from interested parties' assessments of the value of the opinions that the experts deliver.

9.5 Conclusion

There are some doubts about the fact that in the age of the knowledge economy, the new equilibrium (with intensive patenting activities, large amounts of cross-licensing, aggressive patent enforcement strategies and privatization of some basic research activities) is better than the preceding one which was characterized by a moderate level of patenting activities, firms allowing diffusion of their own knowledge in return for low-cost absorption of other's knowledge, and a large public research domain. The latter seems to be a system with lower transaction costs, while the former does not seem distinctly superior in terms of knowledge production.

9.6 Literature References

Arrow K. J., "Economic Welfare and the Allocation of Resources for Inventions". In *The Rate and Direction of Inventive Activity: Economic and Social Factors*, Nelson, ed. Princeton: Princeton University Press, 1962.

Barton J. Reforming the Patent System. *Science*. 2000; 287: 5460.

Brown K. M., *Downsizing science*. Washington D.C.: The AEI Press, 1998.

Cassier M. and Gaudillere J.P. La Recherche Biomédicale au coeur des Marchés Economiques. 2nd French Health Economists Conference, Paris: CNAM, 2001.

Clavier, J.P., *Les catégories de la Propriété Intellectuelle à l'Epreuve des Créations Génétiques*. Paris: L'Harmattan, 1998.

Cockburn I., *O Brave New Industry, that has such Patents in it! Reflections on the Economics of Genome Patenting*. Boston University and NBER, mimeo, 2002.

Cockburn I. and Henderson R. *Public-private interaction and the productivity of pharmaceutical research*. National Bureau of Economic Research, working paper series, WP 6018, 1997.

Cohen W., Florida R., Randazzese L. and Walsh J. *Industry and the academy: uneasy partners in the cause of technological advance*, draft, 1998.

Dasgupta P. and David P.A. Toward a New Economics of Science. *Research Policy*. 1994; 23 (5).

David P.A. Knowledge, property and the system dynamics of technological change. Proceedings of the World Bank Annual Conference on Development Economics 1992. World Bank, Washington DC, 1993.

David P.A. *Knowledge Spillovers, Technology Transfers and the Economic Rationale for Public Support of Exploratory Research in Science*. European Committee for Future Accelerators, 1998c.

David P.A. A Tragedy of the Public Knowledge Commons? Global Science, Intellectual Property and the Digital Technology Boomerang. Dept. of Economics, Stanford University, working paper 00-16, 2000.

David P.A. Digital Technologies, Research Collaborations and the Extension of Protection for Intellectual Property in Science: Will Building 'Good Fences' Really Make 'Good Neighbors'?, in IPR Aspects of Internet Collaborations, Final Report, Eur 19456, European Commission, 2001.

David P.A. Some Logical Tragedies in Seeking Evidence of the Anti-Commons Effect. Mimeo, 2002.

Foray D. *Science, Technology and the Market.* World Social Science Report, UNESCO. London: Publishing/Elsevier, 1999.

Foray D. and Kazancigil A. Science, economics and democracy: selected issues. MOST-UNESCO. Discussion paper, 1999.

Grindley P. and Teece D. Managing intellectual capital: licensing and cross-licensing in semiconductors and electronics. *California Management Review.* 1997; 39: 2.

Hall B. and Ziedonis R. The Patent Paradox Revisited: an Empirical Study of Patenting in the U.S. Semiconductor Industry, 1979-1995. *Rand Journal of Economics.* 2001; 32 (1).

Heller M. The tragedy of the anticommons: property in the transition from Marx to markets.*Harvard Law Review.* 1998; 111: 3.

Heller M. and Eisenberg R. Can patents deter innovation? The anticommons in biomedical research. *Science* 1998; 280.

Henderson R., Jaffe A. and Trajtenberg M. Universities as a source of commercial technology. *Review of Economics and Statistics*, February, 1998.

Jaffe A. The U.S. patent system in transition: policy innovation and the innovation process. *Research Policy* 29, 2000.

Jaffe A. and Lerner J. Privatizing R&D: Patent Policy and the Commercialization of National Laboratory Technologies. *NBER working paper*, no. 7064, 1999.

Kortum S. and Lerner J. *Stronger protection or technological revolution: what is behind the recent surge in patenting?* Harvard Business School, working paper, 98-012, 1997.

Kremer M. Patent buy-outs: a mechanism for encouraging innovation. NBER working paper no. 6304, 1997.

Kryder R.D., Kowalski S. and Krattiger A. *The Intellectual and Technical Property Components of Pro-Vitamin A Rice.* ISAAA Briefs, no. 20, 2000.

Lerner J., *Patenting in the Shadow of Competitors.* Harvard Business School, 1994.

Lita S. Debunking the Bay-Dole Myth: *Forgotten Contributors to the Rise of Academic Capitalism.* The George Washington University, mimeo, 2001.

Mcsherry C., *Who Owns Academic Work?* Cambridge: Harvard University Press, 2001.

Merges R. and Nelson R. On limiting or encouraging rivalry in technical progress: the effect of patent scope decisions. *Journal of Economic Behavior and Organization* 1994; 25.

Mowery, D.C., Nelson R.R., Sampat B. and Ziedonis A.A., *The effects of the Bayh-Dole Act on US University Research and Technology transfer: an analysis of data from Columbia University, the University of California, and Stanford University.* Harvard University: Kennedy School of Government, 1998.

Nelson R.R. The Simple Economics of Basic Scientific Research. *Journal of Political Economy* 1959; 67.

Nottenburg C., Pardey P. and Wright B. Accessing other People's Technology: Do Non-profit Agencies Need it? How to Obtain it? EPTD Discussion Paper no. 79, International Food Policy Research Institute, Washington DC, 2001.

Rose C. The Comedy of the Commons: Custom, Commerce and Inherently Public Property. *University of Chicago Law Review* 1986; 53: 3.

Schankerman M. and Scotchmer S. Damages and Injunctions in the Protection of Proprietary Research Tools. National Bureau of Economic Research, working paper 7086, 1999.

Scotchmer S. Standing on the shoulders of giants. *Journal of Economic Perspectives* 1991; 5 (1).

Shapiro C. Navigating the Patent Thicket: Cross Licenses, Patent Pools and Standard-Setting. NBER workshop on Innovation Policy and the Economy, 2000.

Steinmueller W. E. Networked knowledge and knowledge-based economies. International *Journal of Social Sciences*. 2002; 171.

Thomas S.M. Les brevets en surrégime. Biofutur 1999; 191.

Wadman M. Testing Time for Gene Patent as Europe Rebels. *Nature* 2001; 413.

Walsh J., Arora A. and Cohen W. The Patenting of Research Tools and Biomedical Innovation Science. Technology and Economic Policy Board of the National Academy of Sciences, 2000.

Chapter 10

ARE WE ON OUR WAY IN THE NEW ECONOMY WITH OPTIMAL INVENTIVE STEPS?[1]

Ove Granstrand

Chalmers University of Technology, Department of Industrial Management and Economics, Göteborg, Sweden

Chapter contents:

Abstract: As the economy is shifting weight from physical to intellectual capital dominance, accompanied by the emergence of the pro-IP era, it is natural to try to reassess the traditional challenges, trade-offs and operating standards of the IP system. There is no change in the fundamental nature of information and technology with its associated legal and economic difficulties in arranging for property rights, investment and trade, but the proportions of various difficulties increase with the increasing role of information in the economy. This

[1] I want to thank John Barton, Lars Björklund, Tom Ewing, Jakub Gubanski, William Kingston, Joseph Straus and Hanns Ullrich for helpful discussions and comments on this chapter. The competent research assistance of Ola Küller is greatly appreciated. The help from patent offices and examiners interviewed in Japan, US, Denmark and Sweden is also gratefully acknowledged. This chapter is a partial result from a study of patentability criteria, especially the inventive step requirement. The financial support from The Romanus Fund and the Research Fund of the European Patent Organisation is also gratefully acknowledged.

O. Granstrand (ed.), Economics, Law and Intellectual Property, 223-258.

chapter addresses the causes and consequences of the anti-commons problem with fragmentation of interdependent IPRs in complex technologies and the associated problems for IP assembly and technology trade. In particular the chapter analyses patentability criteria and the possibilities to use the inventive step or non-obviousness standard as one out of several policy remedies. Raising the minimum inventive step standard will reduce transaction costs, invent-around costs and hold-up problems in commercializing innovations, but will also reduce incentives to innovate under certain conditions. While an optimal inventive step standard exists in principle, and uniquely so in certain cases, its empirical determination is obviously a non-obvious matter. However, a low inventive step standard may be instrumental for incumbent "evergreening", i.e. prolonging effective patent protection, and bridging technology transitions. The patent system could finally be studied as a decentralized taxation scheme in a governance context, taking total governance costs into account.

Keywords: Patents, IPR, anti-commons, IP assembly, inventive step, transaction cost, technology markets

10.1 Purpose and Outline

If the economy is gradually shifting weight from physical to intellectual capital dominance, it is natural to try to reassess the traditional challenges, trade-offs and operating standards of the IP system. The purpose of this chapter is to ask, first, how the IP system is challenged by a new type of economy, and how transaction costs (or more generally governance costs) could be taken into account when analysing the economics of IPRs. In particular the chapter elaborates upon the causes and consequences of difficulties in assembling the necessary IPRs in complex technologies with many agents, possibly resulting in excessive and/or deterring transaction costs. A subsequent purpose of the chapter is to discuss how this problem could possibly be mitigated by raising the inventive step requirement in granting patents. A first attempt is thereby made to address the issue of optimality of an inventive step requirement in a static framework and then in a dynamic situation involving sequential innovation and a technology transition. In that connection the chapter cannot answer the question raised in its title, but just elaborate upon it a bit. Finally, the chapter briefly views the patent system in a governance context, in which total governance costs with both transaction costs and management costs have to be taken into account.

10.2 Are We on Our Way into a New Economy?

There are several sound reasons to be skceptical about much ado over the so-called new economy. Is the concept of a new economy just another management fad, boosted by a new generation of impatient entrepreneurs, opportunistic consultants, exaggerating media, pro-active stockbrokers and the like? Is it a product of the propensity to announce deep-running new changes in connection with the advent of a new decade, century or millennium?

In the early heyday of the concept of a new economy it was certainly costly to be stigmatized by financial markets as belonging to the old economy with its old industries and old, large companies run by old-fashioned managers. When the stock market bubble burst, it became even more costly to be associated with the new economy. Opinions were then frequently voiced that there was no such thing as a new economy and, if anything, there was "just" a gradual change in connection with emergent new technologies, infocom technologies (ICTs) in particular.

So, what is the factual basis underlying any sharp distinction between an old and a new economy and any claimed transition? No doubt, there has been a significant strengthening of capitalist economic systems around the globe after the downfall of the Soviet empire, and the spectacular and sustained resurgence of the US economy in the 1990s. Equally clearly, there has been a significant emergence of new ICTs (Internet, PCs, mobile communications, digital media etc.) in recent decades. On a grander time scale, economic growth and transformation have been spurred for centuries by cumulative new technologies, with technology-based firms increasingly becoming their main repositories, at the same time as markets have expanded through international economic integration.

In one sense it is now justified to speak of the emergence of a new economy, namely that intellectual capital rather than physical capital has come into dominance. This is a standard argument by proponents of the new economy. However, definitions and classifications of intellectual capital differ, and methods of measuring and accounting for intellectual capital are undeveloped to say the least.[2] Nevertheless, a number of indicators suggest that

[2] Here intellectual capital is taken to comprise all non-material (or intangible) resources that could be considered as capitalizable assets of an economic agent. Intellectual capital can be decomposed from the point of view of a firm into intellectual property (in patents, databases, trade secrets, trademarks etc.), relational capital (related to qualities such as trust in internal relations, constituting organizational capital, and qualities such as goodwill and reputation in external relations, constituting network capital) and human capital (related to competencies of various kinds).

there is a growing importance of different types of intellectual capital, and that there has been a cross-over to its dominance by some measures in the last few decades (see e.g. Granstrand 2000).

In addition, one can observe not only a growing share of intellectual capital in traditional firms, markets, products and professions, but also a growth of "pure" intellectual-capital firms, markets, products and professions.

Thus, there is in this sense a shift to a new economy (which consequently could be dubbed "intellectual capitalism"), in a mostly gradual and evolutionary manner. One main driving force behind this transformation or shift is technological change with the accumulation of new technologies in general, and in particular infocom technologies or ICTs. Through a number of key functionalities (enhancing e.g. codifiability of information and connectivity and excludability among agents), ICTs enable faster, more inexpensive and differentiated production and distribution of various old and new types of information that are of value to larger sets of users. ICTs also enable information to be commercially transactable at lower average transaction costs. Most importantly, ICTs enable more privatization of gains from production and distribution of information on a commercial basis, by embedding communication in "the world's largest machine" with possibilities to build electronic fences and locks, possibly reinforced by legislation (sometimes overly so). The traditionally recognized failure of information markets specifically due to appropriability problems thereby becomes mitigated.[3] Human communication then becomes linked through as well as to various machines, and thereby potentially becomes more easily commodified and commercialized through these various ICT functionalities. However, it would obviously be overly techno-centric to argue that ICTs in themselves are the only driving force behind the emergence of a new type of economy.

10.3 What Role has the Intellectual Property System Played?

If we are on our way in a new type of economy, what role has the IP system played and what is its role ahead? This must be left largely as an open question here, apart from a few observations. First, the IP system has historically been neither necessary nor sufficient for either technological or economic progress, e.g. in the first industrial revolutions (see Granstrand 2000). This is hardly a surprising statement but is nevertheless important to keep in

[3] For a classic work on market failures in information markets, see Arrow (1962), giving three general reasons for failure – uncertainty, indivisibility and inappropriability. For further interpretations, see e.g. Cheung (1986), Winter (1989), and David (1993).

mind, especially since technological progress is increasingly seen as necessary for economic progress.

Second, the IP system does not appear to have significantly fostered the specific technological progress in form of ICTs, at least not in their early stages up till the pro-patent era emerging in the 1980s. A few examples will illustrate. The transistor was patented at Bell Labs but licensed out generously, and the subsequent emergence of the semiconductor industry was significantly spurred by public procurement and a lax IP regime (Mowery 1996). The same could be said about the emergence of Internet under DARPA. The software industry also emerged under a lax IP regime (Samuelson 1993). The telecom industry was largely nationally monopolized until the 1980s and 1990s, with little interest in IPR. Mobile telephony also emerged until the late 1980s under a lax IP regime (Granstrand 2000). Thus, although ICTs have contributed significantly to the emergence of a new type of economy, IPRs do not appear to have contributed significantly to the emergence of ICTs, at least not until the 1980s. In fact it may even be argued that lax IP regimes were instrumental for the emergence of several ICT industries.[4]

Third, the comparatively rapid emergence of a much stronger IP regime since the 1980s (the pro-patent era) has by and large been concomitant with the much grander emergence of the new type of economy (intellectual capitalism), the roots and trends of which stretch much further back in history. The strengthening of the IP regime may very well have strengthened some features of intellectual capitalism and speeded up the development of some of its components in the last decade or so, but with our limited knowledge at present about the feedback structure involved it is only safe to say that the pro-patent era was as much, if not more, a consequence of intellectual capitalism as a cause of it. In any case a strong IP regime is a feature of the new economy with a concomitant expansion of IPRs by volume, type, and value as well as strategic attention paid to them.

[4] History in general has plenty of examples of how pockets of open S&T have been instrumental for progress, at least temporarily. These pockets or pools of open S&T may be open also to the general public by design (as with open standards or the open source movement) or by default. Commonly, they are closed or semi-closed with some kind of entry condition (e.g. granting back of improvements or agreeing not to take certain actions).

10.4 What are the Challenges to the IP System?

10.4.1 General fitness problems

The IPR system has certainly not lacked skceptics, critics and reformers during its many years of existence. Consequently there are a number of old challenges like international harmonization, rationalization of IPR organizations, high litigation costs, alternative dispute resolution schemes, monopolistic abuses, protectionist abuses, as well as effectiveness relative to alternative incentive schemes and means of appropriation. These challenges are still valid, and mostly increasingly so, as the IPR institution has become more important and expansive. Some of the challenges that seem to have emerged as particularly relevant or somewhat newly recognized will be focused upon here. No attempt is made to be exhaustive. Most likely there are further challenges ahead, still to be recognized, in the ongoing fitting of the IP system to the evolving new type of economy.

The rapidly changing character of technology easily creates misfits between technology and the more inert legal framework designed to foster it. This could be called the *IP-technology fitness problem.* It is an inherent tendency that changes in legislation lag behind changes in technology, legislation being by tradition and design more reactive and reluctant to *sui generis* approaches than pro-active and anticipatory when facing uncertainty. However, lags between new technologies and new legislation created to adequately deal with these technologies tend to become more common and conceivably more costly to society. Contemporary technology is advancing fast, perhaps faster than ever in absolute terms, with an entire array of new technologies emerging and combining into even newer ones. Some of these new technologies challenge fundamental concepts in the intellectual property system, and it is not clear at the outset whether and how they could be given intellectual property protection under the prevailing IP regime. Well-known examples are software and biotechnology. Less well known examples involve new surgical methods, new teaching methods, new business methods or even new athletic techniques.[5] As the cost and/or prospective value of new

[5] New business methods have become patentable in the US after a court decision in the so-called State Street Bank case in 1998. By now, prominent examples are Amazon's patent ("Internet-based Customer Referral System", issued as US Patent on Feb. 22, 2000) and Priceline's generic auction patent ("Method and Apparatus for a Cryptographically Assisted Commercial Network System Designed to Facilitate Buyer-Driven Conditional Purchase Offers", issued as US Patent on Aug. 11, 1998). This type of patents has stirred up a debate about what should be patentable subject matter, standards of patentability, proper scope of

technologies and inventions increase, the push for and disputes over IP protection will increase.

A related challenge is how to make the IP system better fit different industries or, more generally, how to make the IP system better fit the need to stimulate production and distribution of information and knowledge in different industries in light of available incentive systems and appropriability conditions. This could be called the *IP-industry fitness problem.* Tailoring of the IP system to fit the situation in different industries has been suggested from time to time (see Thurow 1997 for a recent example). A certain amount of tailoring does occur (e.g. through confinement of patentable subject matter, prolonged patent protection term in pharmaceuticals or industry-specific adjustment of patent scope plus through other IPRs) but has traditionally been done only to a limited extent. However, such tailoring is costly and, despite the fact that misfits are costly as well, significant industry tailoring is likely to be difficult and exceedingly costly. This is so primarily because of the complex and dynamic nature of the increasingly many-to-many correspondence between products and technologies, that is, the emergence of multi-product (generic, general purpose) technologies and multi-technology products (see below).

Another separate but related fitness problem is the *IP-nation fitness problem.* Needless to say, nations have widely different mixes of technologies and industries, and widely different needs for new technologies and industrial developments. As IP systems are tailored to stimulate innovations and their diffusion for the world as a whole, based on criteria not especially catering to nation-specifics (such as the novelty criteria), fitness problems are to be expected. International harmonization (for which there is also a need) aggravates this fitness problem when taken in a narrow sense of equalization, especially when primarily tailored ready-made to fit nations that are advanced or in other ways unrepresentative of the world spectrum. There is, of course, much to be said about this fitness problem, a problem that has been well recognized and debated over the centuries, but recently magnified and heated up with the advent of the pro-IP era, especially in connection with TRIPs and WTO. (See e.g. Mansfield and Mansfield 2000, and Maskus 2000.)

---

patent protection and proper cost/benefits of patent office operations (see e.g. Merges 1999). Some critics claim that such obvious but generic inventions, requiring almost no R&D, could jeopardize the development of e-commerce.

A fourth challenge is how to interface or harmonize different IP regimes. Different co-existing IP regimes have evolved over time, linked to different sectors of society and their institutions, organizations, norms, etc. Science and universities constitute one, technology and industry another, military and government another, culture and artists a fourth, and religion and churches perhaps also a fifth. These IP regimes are partly overlapping and interdependent, of course, but increasingly so as technology and economic concerns continue to penetrate modern societies. Thus, clashes between IP regimes occur more frequently, e.g. in industry/university collaborations. Pressures thereby arise to align different IP regimes with each other, and to find regime designs that are in some sense preferable on the whole. In this context one may note that universities, US ones in particular, have become economic institutions (Rosenberg and Nelson 1994, Nelson 1996 and Rosenberg 2000). Many public knowledge institutions in general have also become more business and proprietary knowledge-oriented, offering yet another indication of intellectual capitalism.

In this ambience the question must be asked whether there exists a single superior IP regime or a superior mix of complementary IP regimes for different economic and quasi-economic sectors of society. These sectors tend to gather creative and knowledge-producing people with different motivation structures and different propensities to be incentivized by standard utilitarian-based IPRs. This could be called the *IP-regime fitness problem.*

Finally, an *IP-criteria fitness problem* could be added as a separate category, even if it is closely related to the other categories. Tailoring of IPRs to fit their purposes could be done with regard to the whole set of IPRs as well as with regard to each IPR type, as to its scope of protection and criteria for being granted. While various IPR types are tailored very differently, each IPR type is fairly ready-made in terms of scope and granting criteria with fairly few variants. Rights-granting criteria easily create fitness problems as they are applied in a binary way, with a causal link to rights purposes easily becoming inadequate as the criteria set is stretched, mended, amended and adjusted to changing circumstances as time goes by.[6] This will be illustrated in the next section.

---

[6] Attempts to increase fitness in some area may also give rise to fitness problems in other areas, as unintended consequences might accrue. See Kash and Kingston (2001) for an illustrative view of this.

10.4.2 The IP-criteria fitness problem

As registered IPRs are granted based on a set of criteria, specific for each type of IPR, this set could become more or less fitting to the purpose of the IPR type in question as the criteria evolve and are applied over time. Patent rights provide a good example.

Patent rights are commonly granted for inventions on the basis of criteria regarding disclosure, unity of invention, usefulness or industrial applicability, novelties and inventive step or non-obviousness of inventions made in areas of patentable subject matter.[7]

A first question to ask is how well this set of criteria serves the purpose of the patent system, i.e. to stimulate innovation and diffusion when underinvestment could be expected. The criteria have been adopted fairly much the same across countries, but legal codes and administrative practices have evolved over long periods of time, while the nature of investment in innovation and diffusion has changed considerably, so some misfits could be expected. For example, in Europe patentable subject matter should have a "technical character". This limitation has a questionable basis in economic terms, since underinvestment in innovation and diffusion is not always present in or limited to technical fields. Besides, the boundary between what is technical and non-technical is fuzzy and changing. With this limitation the debate about patentability of e.g. software, allegedly lacking technical character, becomes too limited and distanced from economic considerations.

A second question is how to operationalize the different criteria and how to determine what level should be used for assessing whether they are fulfilled or not. For example, it is likely that, at some relaxed levels, a large volume of enforceable patents, dispersed among competing agents in an area, will become counterproductive due to potential or factual transaction costs and hold-up problems.[8] The area will simply be congested with rights, a danger that has been recognized since long ago. On the other hand, too hard-to-get patents in an area will reduce incentives to innovate to sub-optimal levels, given that there is an underinvestment in the area in the absence of patent rights.

The *volume of patent applications* increases at the applicant end with (a) the availability of technological opportunities perceived as profitable by

---

[7] These are the common major criteria. There are a few additional ones, usually of minor importance or subsumable under the major criteria and therefore left aside here (e.g. regarding reproducibility and non-obscenity).

[8] At one extreme, patents could just be granted without examination, as has been the case in some countries. However, weak enforcement of such rights mitigates transaction costs.

(mostly overoptimistic) agents; (b) R&D investments and their yield or productivity; and (c) the patenting propensity by inventors and companies (influenced in turn by patenting costs and benefits, alternatives to patents, and habits). The *volume of patents granted* for a given quantity and quality of patent applications increases with (a) expansion of patentable subject matter; (b) lowering of patentability requirements such as inventive steps; and (c) shortening of processing time (temporarily). The *number of patent-blocking encounters* for a given volume of (maintained) patents then increases with (a) the dispersion of patents in a business area among a number of agents; (b) the number of patents needed to market a new product or process; (c) the number of new product and processes marketed; and (d) the scope of the patents. The *transaction cost* for buying a given blocking patent license then increases with (a) uncertainty about the scope of validity of the patent; (b) unavailability of substitute suppliers; and (c) information asymmetries and opportunistic behavior. In addition, the price of the license increases when the seller is a direct competitor and when the seller has a hold-up position.

Suppose we would like to redesign the criteria for patentability in order to reduce the sheer number of granted patents, so as to reduce transaction costs without reducing R&D incentives and payoffs too much. Then one can first observe that the set of criteria for patentability has a missing link to the purpose of the patent system. There is no explicit requirement to show that R&D efforts have been spent or are needed.[9] There is some, but not sufficient, correlation between the need for R&D investments and what are traditionally defined as areas of patentable subject matter, i.e. typical areas in engineering departments in industry and in technical universities. Thus, requiring in some sense substantial R&D efforts for patentability is one possibility.

Turning from missing to existing criteria, the *disclosure criterion* is probably a fairly functional criterion, although it has to be qualified as to how much should be disclosed ('enabling disclosure') and when.[10] The *unity of invention criterion* is somewhat fuzzy but probably not giving rise to severe dysfunctional effects.[11]

---

[9] This is in some contrast with the criteria for database protection in Europe.

[10] The timing of disclosure is highly important for its functionality. This brings in issues regarding consequences of late disclosure, e.g. in the form of so called submarine patents, generally seen as dysfunctional (see Granstrand 2000), and consequences of early disclosure, e.g. in a grace period. (For a good recent review of the grace period issue, see Straus 2001.)

[11] Apart from being a natural requirement regarding coherence in some sense, the criterion has been motivated by the need to prevent applicants from lumping applications together in order to lower application fees.

The *usefulness criterion* is the only criterion with some explicit economic bearing, but this criterion has been applied in a very weak sense if at all, though perhaps strengthened recently (Domeij 2000).

The *novelty requirement* induces a race and as such may have mixed effects. It is not clear that the best trade-off is when the winner takes all as in the patent system. Besides, novelty as well as usefulness is a matter of degrees and, without a qualification, congestion of rights easily obtains.

In fact the *inventive step requirement* was formed in Europe as a qualification or derivative of the novelty requirement, since novelty alone was perceived to allow uneconomically many patents to be granted. A criterion of this sort seems necessary, since taking it away would require some instrument for filtering out inventions with little usefulness or novelty that would anyway likely be generated without patent rights and would generate excessive transaction costs with patent rights.[12]

10.4.3 The IP assembly problem

At the level of innovations rather than at aggregate technology and industry level, a most challenging problem for the intellectual property system is what can be called the *IP assembly problem.* This problem constitutes an important source of transaction costs. Different technologies, old and new ones, have always been interacting with each other in complex and interdependent ways. However, this is increasingly so in the new economy with its increasing dominance of information (being highly recombinant and cumulative) and innovations (being new combinations of things in the economy). Opportunities to combine various technological advances can simply grow very fast. As a result, new products and services become not only increasingly based on new technologies, but increasingly based on many different technologies. That is, products and services become more multi-technological, or "mul-tech" for short, which is different from becoming "hi-tech" in the sense of using some specific advanced, new technology. At the same time more generic technologies appear, so in this sense technologies become also more multi-product or multi-process. All in all, the cross-links between new products and technologies proliferate. This means that patents and businesses become more cross-linked and interdependent, with each new

[12]The inventive step or non-obviousness requirement is in fact a fairly new one in the US. For its assessment in the US, see e.g. Adelman *et al.* (1998); in Europe, Cornish (1981), Domeij (2000) and Knesch (1994); and in Japan, JPO (1995) and JPO (2000). For the history of the inventive step requirement in various countries in North America and Europe, see Barton (2001), Beier (1985), Bochnovic (1982) and Ullrich (1977).

business becoming reliant on an increasing number of inventions and patents, and more new inventions and patents having an impact on a wide range of businesses.

Moreover, the sources of new technologies proliferate as more firms and nations invest in R&D, and firms also increasingly internationalize their sourcing and exploitation of new technologies. Thereby the number of firm-to-firm encounters increases as both factor input and product output markets become more global. The IP assembly problem is further aggravated by the recent trend in some fields, notably biotechnology, to grant patent and other IPRs (e.g. database protection) to research tools, i.e. inputs to the R&D process itself rather than to the downstream production process.

Thus, in a new technology as well as in a product area, there will be not only more agents on average, but increasingly interdependent agents in a mixture of cooperation and competition ("coopetition" or "competeration"). Technology trade, e.g. through licensing and cross-licensing, then becomes increasingly necessary. This is because IPRs to sustain a business become increasingly fragmented among players who are ready to enforce or otherwise exploit their rights, thereby creating transaction costs and possibly dynamic efficiency losses through a web of hold-up problems.[13]

The factors mentioned so far put increasing demands on the well-functioning of technology markets, which at the same time is actually facilitated by the IP system by design. What further complicates the functioning of technology markets is strategic firm behavior in using and abusing the intellectual property system. Some inventors and small firms without manufacturing act as "patent extortionists". Large corporations aggressively build up patent portfolios and employ various patent strategies. Moreover, they combine them with various other IPRs into a kind of multi-protection strategy, and thereby build up bargaining and retaliation power. IP management skills also develop in general. As IP-based bargaining powers are accumulated in industry, asymmetries in bargaining powers become more likely to appear – between new and old firms, between small and large firms, as well as between companies adapted to strong and weak intellectual property regimes in different sectors and countries. These asymmetries in bargaining powers create increasing risks in innovation and entrepreneurship, risks that become more and more difficult to absorb, especially for small manufacturing firms. (New kinds of insurances are being tried but with expensive premiums.)

[13] This would then be analogous to the anti-commons problem described in Heller (1998) with department stores in Moscow being unable to assemble all the necessary rights for their operations.

Thus, the intellectual property system may slow down, misdirect or hold up innovation and diffusion, although not necessarily discouraging all R&D investments. Consequently, there is, as there always has been, a mixed verdict over whether the intellectual property system promotes technological innovation and diffusion, but perhaps the doubts in the mix are increasing, not least due to increasing transaction costs. The pendulum continues to swing between trust in and suspicion of the intellectual property system.

10.5 What Remedies are there to the IP Assembly Problem?

There are a number of possible remedies to the IP assembly problem that can be considered, such as (a) more effective filtering out of insignificant patents through raising the standards of non-obviousness and usefulness, reducing the patent scope, steepening the renewal fee schedule, and implementing more efficient patent examination procedures; (b) using a two-tier structure with patents and utility models; (c) improving mechanisms for technology markets and transfer, including more liberal attitudes towards patent pooling and technology sharing, schemes for collecting rights and clearing-house procedures, cross-licensing and block-licensing incentives; (d) control of monopolistic abuse through reducing scope and length of protection and/or more consistent use of compulsory licensing; (e) reduction of legal uncertainty through faster and cheaper validation of rights and dispute resolution; and (f) facilitating the internalization of the necessary R&D through organizational integration, e.g. through consortia, joint ventures, mergers and acquisitions. Finally, IPRs could be abandoned altogether and replaced by alternative institutional arrangements (with their specific problems). For a summary of possible remedies, see Table 10-1, which also shows the available options or response strategies for a company encountering blocking patents.

Thus one possibility to mitigate the IP assembly problem is to raise the required level of invention (or level of non-obviousness) for patentability and to narrow the effective scope of a patent, especially in emerging technologies. This is done in order to decrease the hold-up problems and blocking power of many minor patents, as well as the blocking power of major patents in wide applications remote from their original ones.

Table 10-1: Remedies for the IP assembly problem (in the case of patents)

Society level	Company level
1. Filter out patents (reduce volumes) by raising: • Fees (base + renewal fees) • Examination quality • Standards of non-obviousness and usefulness	1. Invalidate blocking patents
2. Filter out patents by reducing: • Patent scope • Patentable subject matter • Length of patent protection	2. Invent around blocking patents
3. Improve technology markets by enabling: • Patent pooling and technology sharing • Block licensing and cross-licensing • Open source licensing • Rights collection and clearance	3. Obtain blocked technologies through acquisition, joint ventures or licensing
4. Reduce strategic behavior and abuse by: • Compulsory licensing • Injunctive reliefs	4. Cross-license or pool patents (e.g. through fencing-in or counterblocking in some other area)
5. Reduce legal uncertainty regarding: • Validation • Dispute resolution	5. Build up bargaining position, e.g. through partnering, purchasing power, patent power, and create credible threats
6. Enable integration and internalizing of interdependent R&D	6. Ignore or infringe blocking patents
7. Employ alternatives to private rights approaches, e.g. procurement contracts or public finance	7. Wait until blocking patents expire
	8. Stop relevant R&D and related commercial operations

The costs of patent processing and patent litigation, too, could be lowered in this way. Future patent flooding may also increase considerably when (rather than if) countries like China and India start patenting on a broad scale. Moreover, it is probable that something such as "computer-aided patenting" (or more broadly computer-aided invention) will come into play. That is, computers and expert systems can generate certain types of inventions (e.g. based on combinatorial alterations of inventive elements) or inventive inputs that form the basis for patent applications.[14] Such computer-

[14] This may appear a preposterous scenario to some, but is in fact quite feasible. Computer-generated musical compositions, art pieces, poems, visual patterns, logos, trade marks etc. are improving, as is the understanding of creative processes. So-called genetic algorithms also develop, with increasing capabilities to find optimal technical design configurations.

generated inventions are likely to be minor, at least in the beginning, and non-obviousness requirements must reasonably exclude such inventions. The impact on R&D and innovation efforts, as well as on diffusion of technical information, would probably not be significantly weakened in total by raising required levels of invention and limiting patent scope, but this issue requires further analysis.

An additional rationale for studying whether the inventive step requirement could and should be raised is that interviews with patent examiners and patent managers in leading countries (US, Japan and Europe) indicate that the inventive step requirement has become less stringently applied in recent years in some areas. Everything else equal, this would contribute to the proliferation and fragmentation of rights and their associated transaction costs, thereby magnifying the problems of fitting the IP system to the new type of economy.

10.6 Could the Inventive Step Requirement be Raised?

To assess whether the inventive step requirement is fulfilled, a suitably operationalized scale of non-obviousness and measurement procedures are needed.[15] Currently the scale in use is a binary one, with measurement commonly based on comparing a best reference document (BRD) (resulting from prior art search) and the claimed invention (CI), the comparison being done by a simulated synthetic person skilled in the art (PSA), who is specified in a certain way, and has to be distinguished from the inventor I. The mental step (effort) required for the PSA to move mentally from BRD to CI is then judged by the patent examiner (assisted by guidelines, experience and sometimes colleagues) as obvious or non-obvious or having a sufficient level of invention or inventive step, as the statutory language goes in some countries.[16] The final judgement is typically done after an exchange of requests,

[15] This assessment is related to assessing the size or radicalness of an invention, something that has been attempted by several authors over the years in different contexts (see e.g. Green *et al.* 1995). The presentation in this section is very stylized in an attempt to provide a formal representation as a first approximation, an attempt which by far does not capture all complexities involved in actual assessments of inventive step. The primary purpose here is to indicate how the requirement can be raised and lowered in principle.

[16] Note that the term 'non-obvious' refers explicitly to a mental process of the PSA, while 'inventive step' and some of its related present and earlier concepts in other languages (e.g. 'Fortschritt' and 'Erfindungshöhe' in German) refer more explicitly to the relation between the invention and prior art.

evidence, arguments and modifications between the examiner and the inventor, in which the burden of proof is shifted around, very briefly expressed.

There is now a technological distance TD between the BRD and the CI that has to be "travelled" by the PSA, as illustrated in Figure 10-1.[17] It seems impractical to adjust the amount of protection continually to the mental effort of the PSA (which however could be taken as an indicator of the amount of R&D and productivity needed in creative work). Retaining a binary outcome would still need a more structured scale if the inventive step or non-obviousness criterion is to be useful as a policy variable. At least a metric scale, if not normed, is then needed.[18] Lengths of inventive steps or amounts of non-obviousness then have to be defined in some way. One possibility is to have empirical reference points. Still, a theoretical foundation of measurement is needed. For this, a suitable operationalization of the concept of technological distance TD is needed for measuring the distance between the CI and the BRD, plus a mapping D of technological distances to mental efforts of a PSA, the latter suitably specified as a vector of attributes defining capabilities (knowledge, skills and equipment). An operationalization of the concept of mental efforts (or mental step) is then also needed.[19] The level of (mental) inventive step at time t (date of patent application) is then determined by $\tilde{D} = E^{i}_{t+\Delta}\,\{D[TD(BRD_t(CI),CI),\, PSA_t]\}$, where $E^{i}_{t+\Delta}$ is the estimation of D made at time $t + \Delta$ by patent examiner i.[20] The amount of protection awarded could then be related to $\tilde{D}$. Retaining the binary approach means specifying a level (vector) of possibly binary requirements (conditions) $\underline{D}$ and granting a patent to CI if, and only if, the corresponding $\tilde{D} \geq \underline{D}$ (for some order relation). A change in the non-obviousness or inventive step re-

---

[17] For simplicity, the claim structure of the invention and the inherent nature of problems and solutions associated with the invention are not explicitly considered here. Also for simplicity reasons the CI, BRD, PSA and I are all represented just by points in a technology space, spanned by technology characteristics variables or invention attributes T_1 and T_2.

[18] A partially or even totally ordered scale of obviousness is not sufficient.

[19] Here one could conceive of a compound measure of technological and mental distances (or equivalently proximities) as well, but strictly speaking a measure of mental effort does not necessarily fulfill the triangle inequality as required for distance measures, basically saying that a detour can never be a short-cut. The latter is often the case in learning something new, however.

[20] It may appear an unnecessary exercise to use a symbolic expression like this. However, it captures in a compact way many of the elements involved (although without being complete here). Besides, any attempt to craft AI tools and decision-support systems for patent examination would involve symbolic representations. Note that features of the inventor are and should be irrelevant to the estimation.

quirement could then be achieved by changing D and/or re-specifying BRD, PSA, TD or D (e.g. by upgrading the PSA).

The question then is whether there is an optimal inventive step requirement D and how to characterize and find it.[21] The question is complicated by several facts. One is that inventive step is not assessed independently of other criteria. Thus considerations of novelty and usefulness and indirectly R&D efforts enter. This problem could be reduced to just considering D by assuming that there are monotonically increasing mappings from R&D efforts to technical performance T (i.e. the so-called effort curve in engineering) and from T to a utility function, plus a monotonically increasing mapping from T-differences to mental efforts. There is then a one-to-one relation between inventive step, R&D efforts and usefulness (utility). Equivalently we could then consider a minimal R&D effort R corresponding to D.

Considerations of patent scope are more difficult to handle for two reasons. First and foremost, it is not clear how patent scope should be represented. Gilbert and Shapiro (1990) use the patentor's ability to raise price, Klemperer (1990) the impact on close product substitutes, and Lerner (1994) the number of side classifications of a patent. The probability of infringement or the invent-around costs could conceivably also be used. Second, there is an association of a certain patent scope with a higher inventive step (see Barton 1995), but its nature is not clear. However, with a given representation a reasonable specification could probably be made for joint optimization purposes (apart from the complexities involved).

Leaving the scope issue aside and optimizing with respect to R instead of D, a formulation of the problem in the most simple case is given in the next section.

---

[21] There is a significant amount of literature on the optimal length and breadth (scope) of patent protection, as is well known, but to my knowledge almost nothing on the optimal inventive step (except for Hunt 1999). This is just a first attempt to deal with the question.

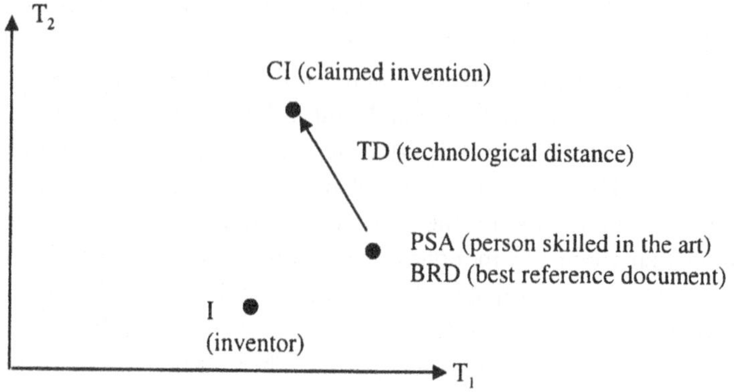

Figure 10-1: Positions in a technology-characteristics space for determining inventive step (non-obviousness) of an invention (represented by points for simplicity).

10.7 Optimal Inventive Step in the Simplest Case

Now let us turn to some formalized illustrations. The following variables and notation will be used below:

c	cost (variable cost $c = c(q)$)
p	price
q	quantity sold at price p, i.e. the demand function is $q(p)$ with an inverse demand function $p(q)$
r	discount rate
π	innovator's operating profit = $p \cdot q - c(q)$
R	total technology investment in in-house R&D and externally acquired technologies, with $\underline{R}$ = minimal R requirement; $\hat{R}$ = local, interior optimum; R_{opt} = glocal optimum; R_0 = value s.t. $V = 0$
B	transaction cost (incl. bargaining cost), with fixed and variable costs F and β
t	time (considered continuous)
V	total value discounted to time $t = 0$, i.e. present value; V^p producer surplus; V^c consumer surplus
W	Welfare = $V^p + V^c$

T	technical performance variable
L	length of period of patent protection
$\tilde{D}$	height of inventive step
$\underline{D}$	minimum inventive step as required for patentability
K, k, α	constants

All cash flow variables are functions of time corresponding to instantaneous cash-flow intensities, i.e. cash flows per unit of time.

The innovator's total discounted value V derived from a new product or process invention is then (with investments in production and marketing included in R):

$$V = \int_0^\infty \pi(t)e^{-rt}dt - \int_0^\infty R(t)e^{-rt}dt = V^P$$

To be able to aid R&D investment decisions in principle, the dependence of π upon R must be specified. This could be done by introducing a function T=T(R) (sometimes called the effort curve in engineering), a customer utility function U=U(T) and a T-specific cost function c=c(q,T). Considerations of T could also be bypassed by linking c directly to R through specifying c=c(q,R) instead.[22] One approach (Nordhaus 1969) is to introduce an "invention possibility function" for constant unit costs c (i.e. c(q) = c·q), being reduced from c_0 to c_1 by a cost-reducing patented invention derived from spending total R on cost-reducing R&D, according to:[23]

$$c_1 = c_0(1 - kR^\alpha) \;\; ; \; k > 0, \alpha \in (0,1), R \geq 0, c_0 > 0, c_1 > 0$$

Assume that the invention is sufficiently minor so that the pre-invention price $p = c_0$ and output q_0 remain the same until competition after patent expiration forces the price to fall to post-invention cost c_1 (assumed to occur immediately) with a corresponding expansion of output from $q(c_0) = q_0$ to $q(c_1) = q_1$. Then in the Nordhaus type of model, operating profit $\pi = 0$ when there is no patent protection and $\pi(t) = q_0(c_0-c_1)$ during patent protection.

---

22 Here, as is common, the symbols for variables and functions are used with differing connotations. Thus, the function c is not the same in the cases c(q), c(q,T), and c(q,R), but no misunderstandings are likely to derive from this convenient practice.

23 An alternative specification is $c_1 = c_0\,(1\text{-}e^{-\alpha R})$. Compare the specification in Wright (1983).

Inserting c_1 and assuming that q(p) is linear in p and that all investment expenditures occur at t=0 gives:

$$V^p = q_0 c_0 k R^\alpha (1 - e^{-rL})/r - R = KR^\alpha - R$$

The benefit to society of this invention then equals the producer surplus V^p, plus the additional consumer surplus V^c generated after patent expiration by the cost savings from the invention. Then (assuming the same discount rate r for consumers and producers):

$$V^c = \int_L^\infty q_0 (c_0 - c_1) e^{-rt} dt + \int_L^\infty \left(\int_{q_0}^{q_1} (p(q) - c_1) dq \right) e^{-rt} dt$$

The second term then corresponds to the dead-weight loss during patent protection being turned into consumer surplus after patent expiration when competition forces the price down to c_1. Now for q(p) linear in p:

$$V^c = (c_0 - c_1)(q_0 + q_1) e^{-rL} / 2r = (k_1 R^\alpha + k_2 R^{2\alpha}) e^{-rL}$$

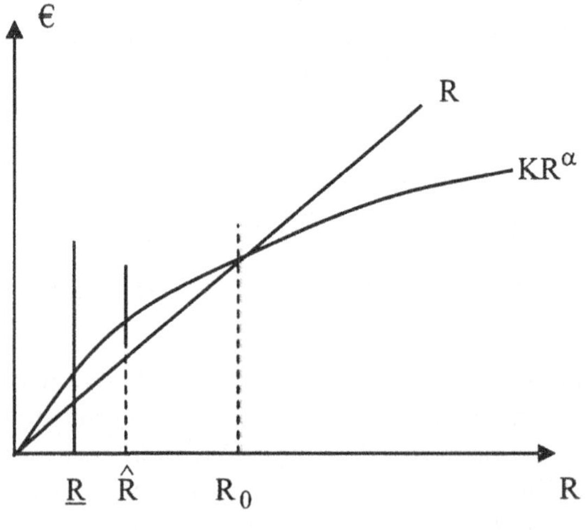

Figure 10-2: Optimal amount of R&D = $\hat{R}$ and minimal inventive step requirement, corresponding to $\underline{R}$, in the simple case of minor cost-reducing invention with linear demand.

Now, in order to simplify, include all productive investments in R, including costs for externally acquired technologies. Let transaction costs B that are borne by the company have two components, one fixed transaction cost F and one variable transaction cost ß(R), varying with R, i.e. B=F+β(R), as long as R > 0. Let B = 0 for R = 0. B includes patent fees and expected litigation costs as well as the company's bargaining costs for externally acquired technologies. If a certain share of new technologies needed by the company is externally acquired, and bargaining costs are proportional to the cost of these, we can let variable transaction costs be proportional to R as an approximation. That is, we can write β(R) = βR, where β is now a constant.

Thus, we have:

$$V^p = KR^{\alpha} - (1+\beta)R - F \qquad \text{for } R \geq \underline{R} \geq 0$$

$$V^c = (k_1 R^{\alpha} + k_2 R^{2\alpha})\, e^{-rL}$$

First, we study how β and F impact the optimal $R = \hat{R}$ and the maximal $V^p(\hat{R})$, and then how the inventive step requirement impacts β and F. Finally we look at impacts on V^c and total welfare $W = V^p + V^c$.

Differentiating V^p with respect to R gives an interior $\hat{R}$ as:

$$\hat{R} = (K\alpha/(1+\beta))^{\frac{1}{1-\alpha}} \qquad \text{and}$$

$$V^p(\hat{R}) = \hat{R}\,(1+\beta)(\alpha^{-1}-1) - F = (K\alpha)^{\frac{1}{1-\alpha}}\,(1+\beta)^{\frac{\alpha}{\alpha-1}}\,(\alpha^{-1}-1) - F$$

Since $d^2V^p/dR^2 < 0$, $\hat{R}$ is optimal if $\hat{R} > \underline{R}$ and $V^p(\hat{R}) > 0$.

If $V^p(\hat{R}) \leq 0$ then $R = 0$ is optimal.

For $\hat{R} < \underline{R}$, $\underline{R}$ is optimal as long as $V^p(\underline{R}) > 0$, that is, the inventive step requirement constraint is binding. If $V^p(\underline{R}) \leq 0$ when $\underline{R}$ is binding, then $R = 0$ is optimal.

Now we can see that in the case $\hat{R} > \underline{R}$ and $V^p(\hat{R}) > 0$, the following holds (see also Figure 10-2):

1) With no fixed but only variable transaction costs (i.e. F = 0, β>0), an increase in these through increasing marginal transaction cost β decreases $\hat{R}$ to $\underline{R}$ and V^p to zero.
2) With no variable but only fixed transaction costs (i.e. F > 0, β = 0) an increase in these through increasing F leaves $\hat{R}$ unchanged until V^p is decreased thereby to zero.

3) With both fixed and variable transaction costs increasing, V^p is decreasing for two reasons – partly since $\hat{R}$ is decreasing, and partly since V^p decreases for any fixed R.

Now what happens if we increase the minimum inventive step (patent height) requirement? The invention possibility function translates this requirement into a minimum technology investment requirement $\underline{R}$, so we can consider increases in $\underline{R}$ instead. From the above and Figure 10-2 we then see that if $\underline{R}$ increases from zero without increasing any transaction costs and $V^p(\hat{R}) > 0$, nothing happens until $\underline{R}$ increases beyond $\hat{R}$, in which case $\underline{R}$ becomes optimal and a loss in producer surplus is incurred since $V^p(\underline{R}) < V^p(\hat{R})$. Eventually $\underline{R}$ increases beyond R_0 in which case $V^p(\underline{R})$ becomes negative and R = 0 is optimal. Thus, the minimum inventive step requirement may become so high that it does not pay off on the whole to invest in new technologies, which require patent protection to pay off at all. Figure 10-3 depicts this case.

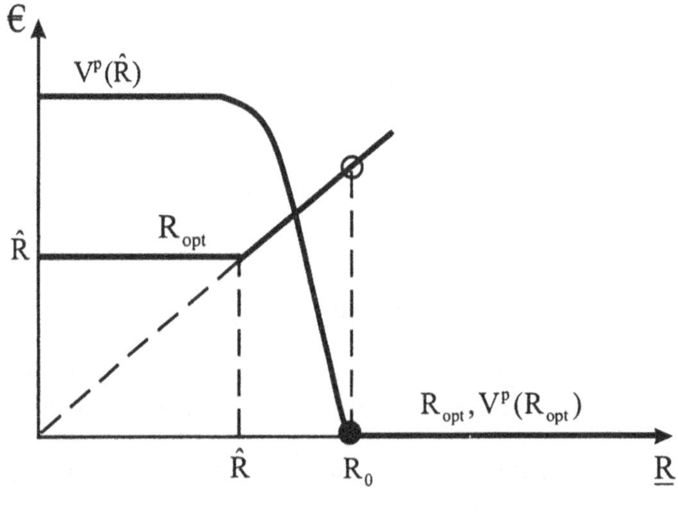

Figure 10-3: Impact of inventive step requirement $\underline{R}$ on technology investments R and producer surplus V^p.

However, changes in $\underline{R}$ will affect transaction costs. Transaction costs include patent fees and expected litigation costs.[24] With higher $\underline{R}$ there will be

[24] The classification of patent fees as transaction costs is not essential for the analysis here.

fewer possible patents per R&D dollar and fewer possible patent litigations, everything else equal, so these cost elements in B can be assumed to decrease in $\underline{R}$. Bargaining costs depend on the number of patent licenses acquired and this number goes down as $\underline{R}$ is increased, assuming that external technology acquisition cost is unchanged and that the transaction cost per license is constant. (The latter assumption could be replaced by the assumption that variable transaction costs depend only on the total acquisition cost (total in-licensing cost), not on the number of licenses, in which case $\underline{R}$ does not affect variable transaction costs, just fixed ones. In this case F decreases in $\underline{R}$, while β is unchanged, so $\hat{R}$ is unchanged within the range ($\underline{R}$, R_0) while V^p is increasing and so is R_0.)

If $\underline{R}$ is lowered, more patents can result per R&D dollar. Of course firms have the option to apply for patents with a higher than minimal inventive step requirement, or they can try to lump applications together. However, the unity of invention requirement has to be fulfilled. Besides, firms often use a patent strategy to apply whenever possible. (This strategy can be further analyzed in itself, of course.)

With more patents on average, the firms will have to pay more patent fees per R&D dollar and also higher bargaining costs for acquired technologies, being covered by more patents. Thus one can assume that variable transaction costs $\beta(R)$ are proportional to $R/\underline{R}$ at least as an approximation, i.e. $\beta(R) = bR/\underline{R}$, where b is a positive constant.[25] Thus, in the case where both fixed and variable transaction costs decrease when $\underline{R}$ increases, V^p increases as long as it is positive and so does $\hat{R}$ and then optimal $R = \underline{R}$ when $\underline{R}$ is binding. Again for sufficiently large $\underline{R}$, technology investments do not pay off and optimal R is zero, together with V^p.

With this specification we have for the company's problem:

$$V^p(R,\underline{R}) = KR^{\alpha} - (1 + b/\underline{R})R - F, \text{ for } R > \underline{R}$$

$$\hat{R}(\underline{R}) = ((1+b/\underline{R})/K\alpha)^{\frac{1}{\alpha-1}}; \qquad \lim_{\underline{R}\downarrow 0} \hat{R}(\underline{R}) = 0^{+}$$

$$V^p(\hat{R}(\underline{R}),\underline{R}) = \hat{R}(1+b/\underline{R})(\alpha^{-1} - 1) - F = (K\alpha)^{\frac{1}{1-\alpha}}(1+b/\underline{R})^{\frac{\alpha}{\alpha-1}}(\alpha^{-1} - 1) - F = \overline{V}^p(\underline{R})$$

[25] Here one may object that firms rationalize bargaining costs by cross-licensing, block-licensing and patent pooling, and also that the dispersion of relevant patents among firms is not proportional to the number of patents. Moreover, the propensity to acquire technologies

From this we see that $\hat{R}(\underline{R})$ and $\bar{V}^P(\underline{R})$ increase in $\underline{R}$ (with unrestricted R up to its optimal value without transaction costs), while the boundary $V^P(\underline{R},\underline{R})$ first increases, then decreases. In other words, increasing the minimal inventive step requirement will increase technology investments and producer surplus as long as the requirement is non-binding. If the require

$$V^P(\underline{R},\underline{R}) = K\underline{R}^{\alpha} - \underline{R} - b - F$$

ment becomes binding, increasing it will increase technology investments, but producer surplus then increases only up to a point, beyond which it will decrease. If the requirement is further increased, producer surplus will eventually turn negative. Relaxing the requirement almost entirely, i.e. letting $\underline{R}$ approach zero, will push technology investments towards zero, since almost all resources then will be spent on patent fees, litigation and bargaining.[26]

Now for society's problem, we have for welfare W and $R \geq \underline{R}$:[27]

$$W(R, \underline{R}) = V^P + V^c = KR^{\alpha} - (1 + b/\underline{R})R - F + (k_1R^{\alpha} + k_2R^{2\alpha})\, e^{-rL}$$

V^c increases in R for all R (also for major process innovations in the Nordhaus framework) and company-optimal R increases with $\underline{R}$ (until it drops to zero). Thus, an optimal $\underline{R}$ has to be found among values where V^P decreases, which only happens when $\underline{R}$ is binding.[28] Increasing $\underline{R}$ then serves to increase consumer surplus at the expense of producer surplus to the point where the net effect turns negative.

At some point V^P is reduced to zero and so is company-optimal R; thereby the whole welfare effect is lost. Thus, depending upon parameter values, there is an optimal $\underline{R}$ distinct from zero and not too small and not too large. However, for certain parameter values, giving high patent fees and other transaction costs (through high b) but low R&D productivity (through

externally may change as more minor inventions are being patented. These objections, however valid, can be ignored at this level of a first approximation.

[26] Litigation outcomes in terms of damages are assumed to leave V^P and V^c unaffected.

[27] A more formal and detailed discussion, also regarding major ("drastic") process innovations in the Nordhaus framework, must be left aside here.

[28] Note that for increasing patent length L, V^P increases since company-optimal R also increases, which in turn increases V^c but at the same time V^c is also decreased by a discount factor e^{-rL}. Increasing patent scope, simply in terms of amount of business applications, will increase company-optimal R and, through this plus a direct effect, increase V^P but decrease V^c through more dead-weight losses, although offset to some extent by increased R, so the impact on V^c is mixed.

low k and α close to 1), technology investments do not pay off at all to the firm. This holds when the patent lifetime L is held constant. (Note that several constants above depend on L.) However, L is also a policy variable and joint maximization of W with respect to both $\underline{R}$ and L involves a much more complicated analysis.

The analysis above is based on a stylized Nordhaus type of model, which leaves much room for discussion. Still, the analysis indicates that even in a simple but plausible case, an optimal inventive step requirement exists. However, how to find it is obviously non-obvious, requiring novel and inventive approaches for practical applications.

10.8 "Evergreening" by Incumbents

The analysis of a cost-reducing invention in a Nordhaus type of framework indicated the existence of a socially optimal level of inventive step requirement distinct from zero in certain parameter ranges. Raising the requirement from suboptimal levels would increase the available producer surplus and incentivize companies to invest more in R&D and new technologies, without having to spend most resources on patent fees and other transaction costs.

But if so, are there any reasons for companies to object to raising the inventive step requirement from already low levels without going too high? The analysis gives no such reason, as long as the requirement is non-binding; and any such requirement being binding on total R seems to be far from current reality.

Here, however, the limitations of the analysis must be taken into consideration. Neither R&D and technology acquisition, nor patenting, are decided and carried out as one-shot affairs in firms but take place intertwined in a process over time.[29] In such a process it may very well pay off to patent wherever and whenever possible, as witnessed in some industries and technologies with strong early mover advantages, e.g. in new, generic technologies with much uncertainty. A sequence of "small" patents granted at various steps in a process may then be more profitable (gives more producer surplus) to a firm than a single "large" patent granted at some specific step in the process, although difficult to assess *ex ante*. In fact, if an incumbent already has strong market, technology and patent positions in a certain product gen-

[29] The important issue of the role of patents in sequential invention has recently gained considerable attention; see Scotchmer (1991) for a pioneering article. See also Hunt (1999) for a study of the role of the non-obviousness requirement in a formal model of sequential patent races.

eration, continued follow-up patenting of even small product and process improvements and new applications serves to perpetuate or "evergreen" these positions. In other words, the effective patent protection is prolonged from a continually renewed patent portfolio. A new entrant trying to enter at some stage in this process will face unfavourable asymmetries regarding invent-around costs, transaction costs and bargaining power. This is not to say that it is always easy to evergreen through follow-up patenting, or that incumbents have always been good at it (which many of them have not), but lowering inventive step requirements opens up possibilities for once-innovative incumbents to maintain market power.

To clarify further, suppose there is an incumbent who has a major product patent A being complemented over time by a number of minor B-patents for product improvements, various add-on features, process steps and applications, as in Figure 10-4.

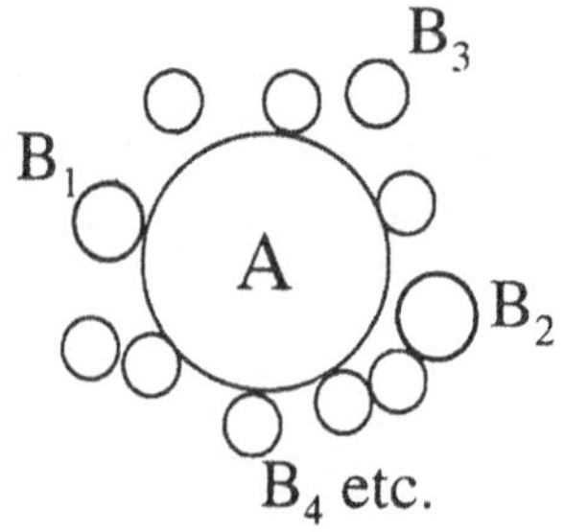

Figure 10-4: Major product patent A, being surrounded over time by follow-up minor B-patents B_1, B_2 etc.

Any new entrant wanting to invest in the A-technology when the A-patent expires also has to invest in or invent around B-patents. However, since product and process improvements derive much from learning by doing (learning by producing and using), the incumbent properly doing follow-up patenting is a likely source of many B-patents. The new entrant could of course invest more heavily than the incumbent in B-patents and succeed in doing so to the extent that the incumbent misses out in follow-up patenting.[30] However, the incumbent is well positioned on a set of learning curves and thereby likely to be relatively more efficient in this improvement type of

[30] A well-known alleged case of this is described in Spero (1990). DuPont's patenting of nylon is a classic case of attempted but not entirely successful follow-up patenting (see Scherer 1980, p. 451).

R&D.[31] Thus, a low inventive step requirement allows the incumbent to sustain its market power through incremental innovations without having to recreate market power through more radical innovative R&D. The incumbent can then engage in patent protection of vertical as well as horizontal product differentiation. (The latter is also aided by large patent scope, as dealt with by Klemperer 1990.) Consequently the prospective new entrant has an incentive to focus on major innovations based on new technologies, and in particular with an initial business application not focused on by the incumbent. In fact, technology transitions and substitutions have historically typically provided new entry possibilities through major innovations, forming the basis for a new product generation. The issue for the incumbent is then how market, technology and patent positions in the old generation can be leveraged to the new generation. The subsequent issue here is how lowering the inventive step requirement is likely to influence incumbent leveraging and new entry possibilities. Figure 10-5 depicts the situation.

Figure 10-5 illustrates the patenting behavior of different competing companies A, B and C in two subsequent product generations, each with a technology base (portfolio of technologies), denoted I and II. These technologies may be partly competing (substituting), partly complementary. The shift from one product generation to the other typically involves a transition to new technologies, with some old technologies still being used and some rendered obsolete. The technical performance of the two product generations typically improves over time, as shown by the schematic S-curves in the figure.

The incumbent company B holds a major patent for technology base I and concentrates its R&D on further improvements in that area, while the incumbent company A builds patent positions in both technology bases. Company C is a new entrant in the area and focuses only on technology base II. The competing companies gain different patent shares in the different technology bases for the competing product generations, just as they may gain different market shares.

---

[31] Learning by using and learning by producing do not solely result in cost reductions through minor process innovations but also in improvements of product performance through minor product innovations (see in particular Sahal 1981 and Rosenberg 1982 for several illuminating empirical studies). The amount of these (mostly) minor innovations is correlated with cumulative production and stock of products in use (i.e. customer-installed base). Incumbents typically cumulate production experience (even in the case of outsourcing) as well as cumulating user experience through links to their customer base (see in particular von Hippel 1988).

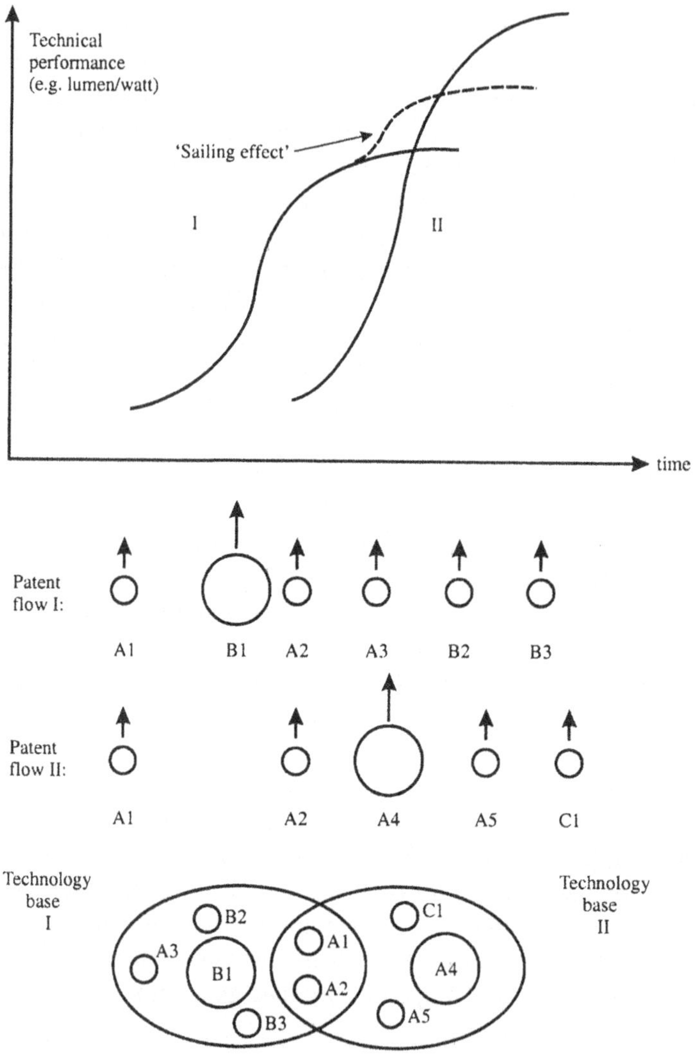

Legend: A1, B2 etc = Company A's first patent in the area, Company B's second patent in the area etc.

I, II = Two technical performance curves, corresponding to technology base I and II, represented by two overlapping sets of technologies, being partly protected in technology space by two patent flows over time. The 'sailing effect' refers to improvements in old technical performance in response to threats from new technologies.

Circles denote scope of patents

Arrows denote patent granting dates

Figure 10-5. Patenting strategies in the case of competing or subsequent product generations.

Established companies with high market and patent shares for an established product generation are then well positioned to build up strong patent positions for a new product generation if this generation is technologically similar to the old one. Thus, incumbents are favoured by large overlaps (small technological distances) between the technology bases and patent portfolios for the old and new product generation, while new entrants are favoured by large degrees of substitution of old technologies for new ones. Both incumbents and new entrants are in addition favoured by technology overlaps offering possibilities to leverage their technologies in their other product areas, thereby reaping economies of scale as well as scope. This of course favors existing diversified companies rather than start-ups.

In addition, incumbent companies are better positioned to influence the rate and direction of technological changes. For example, an incumbent may introduce a "gap filler" which increases the technology overlap between the old and new generations, but at the possible expense of increased cannibalization. An incumbent may also influence standard-setting, as well as the adaptation to complementary products.

Now with the increasing multi-technology (multi-patent, multi-invention) nature of new products and processes and the emergence of generic technologies (multi-product technologies, general purpose technologies), the technology overlaps between different product generations as well as the technology overlaps between related but different product areas tend to grow over time. Increased possibilities to patent, enabled by lower inventive step requirements, then help companies in their technology leveraging. This circumstance helps incumbents to bridge over from an old to a new product generation. It also helps existing companies hitherto outside the product area to bridge over or diversify into the product area, using their technology base in other product areas as a technology platform or technology springboard. This is particularly so in situations of technological convergence or confluence (as in computers and communications), where the direction of technological changes may asymmetrically favor the diversifying new entrant.

The only category of firms that are not favored at all by this type of technology diversification at product level are young start-ups having to build up technology positions from scratch. But even if they are successful at that, they are most likely not able to become, let alone remain, technologically self-sufficient due to high R&D costs, boosted partly by invent-around costs from dense patent nets.[32] Thus, in their innovation process they will become

[32] The cost of inventing around a single patent (i.e. the cost of inventing a substitute technology for the patent) typically increases with its scope and inventive step but depends on many

dependent upon acquisitions of some technologies from incumbents and other existing companies and then subjected to transactional hazards and uncertainties. Their possibilities to make a significant entry depend on (a) the amount of technological substitutions imposing on incumbents costly and time-consuming scrapping of old technologies, and/or (b) technology management failures of incumbents (including omissions in patenting for evergreening) or (c) the possibilities to find alliances with firms trying to diversify or catch up. In the latter process, the start-up entrant could very well be acquired fully or find its role reduced to that of a technology sub-supplier, lacking complementary resources.

What has been described so far is, of course, not a direct and definite outcome of a low level of an inventive step requirement, but lowering this requirement is likely to contribute to such an outcome. Thus, an argument could be made that it is in the interest of incumbents to have a low inventive step requirement when sequential invention and patenting is considered.[33]

10.9 Alternatives to Patents

Finally, when addressing the optimality of the inventive step requirement for patent protection, one could address the optimality of patent protection for innovation and diffusion inducement as well. This is a large and important topic for which a new angle of analysis will be given here and then left to further research.

Competitive markets could be expected to fail to generate adequate private investments in R&D and new technologies due to problems of e.g. appropriating returns on costly new information (Arrow 1962). Information has the standard properties of public goods, with non-excludable, non-rival consumption, as well as low variable and high fixed costs in production, therefore justifying some form of public provision and finance.[34] David (1993) distinguishes three approaches to such public provision – property, procure-

more factors, e.g. its position in the technology landscape and the skills of the parties involved. The cost of inventing around several related patents could be expected to increase far more than proportionately to the number of patents to circumvent.

[33] It is not immediately clear that this is welfare-reducing. To the extent that cross-licensing among incumbents functions, the situation could be seen as a form of "oligopolistic prospecting" to which the prospect theory of Kitch (1977) could possibly be extended. However, the standard counterarguments to Kitch's theory (see e.g. Kaufer 1989) apply as well and with even greater strength. In addition, cannibalization and strategic gaming and defection among the incumbents weaken the coordination or governance of the prospecting.

[34] Information has specific characteristics in addition, such as being cumulative and interactive (in the words of David 1993), thus making information a specific type of public goods.

ment and patronage (e.g. public grants or prizes to research) in his terms.[35] All approaches are used in a mixed approach in reality, but it is not clear that an optimal solution would be a mix and it is far from clear how to find it.[36] However, information and knowledge are uncertain and highly heterogeneous and so are the conditions under which they are produced and diffused, justifying a combined variety of approaches to foster suitable conditions. The heterogeneity could be roughly characterized in terms of a few variables related to the public goods characteristics used to assess the various approaches. Thus, using the property approach means decentralizing decision-making about scarce resources to agents with unique access to localized information for proper decisions, and incentivizing them to exercise their capabilities by providing them with access to a share of the extra surpluses they then generate. The latter is done by allowing the property holder to charge prices higher than marginal cost in order to help cover fixed investment costs.

Such monopolistic pricing is a drawback of the property approach, as it incurs a certain loss of consumer surplus apart from a shift of some surplus from consumers to the producer. However, in order to assess the property approach, this drawback has to be compared with corresponding drawbacks of other approaches. If the right to exercise certain monopolistic pricing is seen as a decentralized right to tax consumers, it corresponds to the right to impose a targeted sales tax administered by private agents. The administrative cost (transaction cost) could then be fairly low in comparison with public forms of taxation, be they targeted (selective) or general.[37] Of course, taxes could be more than minimally distorting and over-taxation could occur, as it could with any form of tax. (Few people seem to disagree on this.) The real virtue as well as drawback of the property approach, I would argue, is its amenability to flexible decentralization as well as to over-decentralization in the sense that too many and costly agent interdependencies will arise, resulting in too high transaction costs, eventually high enough to outweigh incentive effects and other efficiency gains. In addition, recentralization is usually more difficult (costly) than decentralization.

---

[35] To these three approaches could be added a fourth – private prizes (e.g. the Nobel Prize).

[36] A pioneering article here is Wright (1983), showing when patents, prizes and contracts are optimal.

[37] Just to mention one comparable alternative, consider the popular use of R&D tax credits or tax deductions for stimulating innovation, based on the idea to subsidize R&D inputs through targeted cuts in general taxes. This tax arrangement has significant limitations and hardly qualifies as a minimally distorting tax arrangement (see Mansfield 1982). It could be modified of course, e.g. to cover commercial activities as well, not just R&D, but it will still be inherently limited (see Granstrand 1998).

This view of the property approach is actually an organization-theory view, in which the handing out of private property rights is comparable to handing out or decentralizing responsibilities and accountabilities in an organization, applying management by objectives, dealing with principal-agent and information asymmetry problems, intervening for conflict resolution and so on. There are many organizational principles, some of which are that decentralization should be aligned to the information structure, incentive structure and structure of interdependencies, and should not be carried so far that the management cost of coordination outweighs benefits, e.g. from entrepreneurial motivation and economies of scale from division of labor. The adoption of the so-called M-form of organization, that is, a form of organization of a firm being decentralized into product divisions, is a recognition of stronger interdependencies within product-related activities than e.g. within functionally related activities (i.e. activities within R&D, production and marketing functions). Handing out patent rights to product inventions is then comparable (but not equivalent) to adopting an M-form of decentralization. If, however, inter-product interdependencies become more costly to coordinate than intra-product ones, the M-form has been carried too far, with too many small interdependent divisions with internal transfer pricing problems (transaction costs), conflicts and costly higher management intervention (the organization's internal court system). Thus, using a property approach is largely a matter of how far decentralization should go along what organizational principles, in order not to let transaction costs outweigh innovative and efficiency gains by handing out too many small interdependent property rights.

Finally, a few remarks on the other approaches are in order. With very generic, uncertain and interactive information, especially interactive without being embodied, more efficient forms of financing and taxation than through the property approach are conceivable. This could for instance be the case for basic scientific research. With specific, more certain and embodied information, targeted public procurement financed by public taxes could be a proper approach. This could be and often is the case for large, infrastructural development projects. (See again Arrow 1962.) If fame and prestige, and ex-post financing, are relatively more important incentives for producing information, then prizes might be a proper approach. Behaviors like defensive publishing and open source licensing provide other cases for similar analysis. The point is that, in considering demand and supply conditions when judging the various approaches to provide for innovation and diffusion and how they can complement and substitute each other, one should also take into account: (a) the nature of information (knowledge), e.g. in terms of genericness, uncertainty and interactivity, and (b) the nature of conditions surrounding information production and diffusion, e.g. in terms of information asymmetries, incentives and financing needs, costs of taxation and other transactions, and licensing conditions.

10.10 Summary and Conclusions

A new type of economy has gradually emerged, much as a result of a long-running cumulation of once new and still valuable technologies, not least ICTs, which have dual roles as generating value and enabling the privatization of value. Intellectual capital – including human capital, relational capital and IPRs – has come to dominate in some sense over physical capital. A pro-patent or pro-IP era has rapidly emerged since the 1980s, embedded in the much slower emergence of a new type of economy, apparently more as a consequence than a cause to it. Reassessments of old problems associated with IPRs and identification of new or recently magnified ones are then called for. The chapter briefly describes the increasing problems of fitting the IP system to technology, industry and country specifics in the new economy, and then focuses specifically on the IP assembly problem, magnified by congestion of various IPRs. Thereby intellectual resources become fragmented ("the anti-commons problem"), thus magnifying transactional problems, calling for more attention paid to transaction cost analysis of IPRs in the new type of economy.

Transaction costs arise from many sources, e.g. emergence of generic (general purpose) technologies and multi-technology products and processes, combinatorial growth of new technologies, growth of IPRs by types, numbers and scope and strategic use of IPRs by firms. The chapter briefly describes a number of remedies to the IP assembly problem and the role of patentability criteria, especially the non-obviousness criterion or inventive step requirement. This requirement was once introduced as a qualification of the inventive novelty requirement in order to reduce the congestion of patents. Interviews with industry and patent examiners indicate that the requirement has become less stringently applied at places and/or that it could be too low for its purposes. The chapter makes a first attempt to analyze the optimality of the inventive step requirement, taking transaction costs into account. The analysis of a simple, single invention framework of the Nordhaus type shows the unique existence of an optimal minimal requirement level, below which too many resources are spent on bargaining and patent fees, and above which R&D investments become sub-optimal. A qualitative analysis of sequential invention in a dynamic framework supports the argument that a low inventive step requirement favors incumbents, who then can engage in "evergreening" more efficiently to sustain market power in connection with technological transitions. Such transitions otherwise offer a window of opportunity for new entrants, especially if they involve bridging large technological distances.

Further research is warranted on the macro- and micro-economic implications of this micro-legal issue, e.g. regarding the IP assembly problem and its remedies, transaction cost analysis of inventive step and related patentability criteria, and empirical research on patent examination procedures. At a higher level, further research is warranted on optimality conditions for various institutional arrangements for innovation, diffusion and S&T governance in general, patents included, taking total governance costs into account.

In summary, there are reasons to be concerned that transaction costs make patents sub-optimal in certain areas, e.g. in basic research and generic technologies, and that the inventive step requirement should be increased. This, however, also raises the questions whether patents, even with optimized patentability criteria, are optimal in comparison with other institutional arrangements, such as prizes or contracts.

10.11 Literature References

Adelman, M.J., Rader, R.R., Thomas, J.R. and Wegner, H.C. (1998). *Cases and Materials on Patent Law.* American Casebook series, West Group.

Arrow K. J. (1962). 'Economic Welfare and the Allocation of Resources for Invention'. In *National Bureau of Economic Research,* 1962. *The Rate and Direction of Inventive Activity: Economic and Social Factors.* Princeton Univ. Press, pp.609–626.

Barton, J.H. (1995). 'Patent scope in biotechnology', *IIC, International Review of Industrial Property and Copyright Law,* 26 (5), pp. 605-618.

Barton, J.H. (2001). *Non-obviousness,* unpublished mimeo. Stanford University, Law School.

Beier, K-F. (1985). "Zur historischen Entwicklung des Erfordernisses der Erfindungshöhe". *GRUR,* Heft 8, pp. 606-616.

Bochnovic, J. (1982). 'The Inventive Step: its Evolution in Canada, the United Kingdom and the United States', *Studies in Industrial Property and Copyright Law,* Vol. 5, Weinheim: Verlag Chemie.

Cheung, S.N.S. (1986). 'Property Rights and Invention'. In Palmer (1986), pp. 5-18.

Cornish, W.R. (1981). *Intellectual Property: Patents, Copyrights, Trade Marks and Allied Rights.* London: Sweet & Maxwell.

David, P.A. (1993). 'Intellectual Property Institutions and the Panda's Thumb: Patents, Copyrights, and Trade Secrets in Economic Theory and History.' In Wallerstein *et al.* (1993), pp. 19–61.

Domeij, B. (2000). *Pharmaceutical Patents in Europe.* The Hague: Kluwer Law International.

Gilbert, R. and C. Shapiro, (1990). 'Optimal patent length and breadth', *RAND Journal of Economics*, 21 (1), 106-112.

Granstrand, O. (1998). *R&D Tax Credits – Why they mostly do not work and how they perhaps could be designed to work.* CIM Working Paper No 1998:02, Chalmers University of Technology, Göteborg, Sweden.

Granstrand, O. (2000). *The Economics and Management of Intellectual Property.* Cheltenham, U.K: Edward Elgar Publishing Ltd.

Green, S.G., Gavin, M.B. and Aiman-Smith, L. (1995). 'Assessing a Multidimensional Measure of Radical Technological Innovation', *IEEE Transactions on Engineering Management,* 42 (3), pp. 203-214.

Heller, M.A. (1998). 'The Tragedy of the Anticommons: Property in the Transition from Marx to Markets', *Harvard Law Review,* 111 (621), pp. 622-686.

Hunt, R.M. (1999). *Nonobviousness and the incentive to innovate: An economic analysis of intellectual property reform.* Working Paper No 99-3, Research Dept., Federal Reserve Bank of Philadelphia. Philadelphia: Federal Reserve Bank.

JPO (1995). *Practices in Examination and Appeals under 1994-revised Patent Law in Japan.* AIPPI, Japan.

JPO (2000). *Examination Guidelines for Patent and Utility Model in Japan.* Guidelines, JPTO, Tokyo, Dec. 2000. (Downloadable also from JPTO homepage.)

Kash, D.E. and Kingston, W. (2001). 'Patents in a world of complex technologies', *Science and Public Policy,* 28 (1), February, pp. 11-22.

Kaufer, E. (1989). *The Economics of the Patent System.* New York, NY: Harwood Academic Publishers.

Kitch, E. (1977). 'The nature and function of the patent system', *Journal of Law and Economics,* 30 (1), pp. 265-290.

Klemperer, P. (1990). 'How broad should the scope of patent protection be?', *RAND Journal of Economics,* 21 (1), pp. 113-130.

Knesch, G. (1994) 'Assessing Inventive Step in Examination and Opposition Proceedings in the EPO', *EPI Information,* 3, pp. 95-99.

Lerner, J. (1994). 'The importance of patent scope: an empirical analysis', RAND *Journal of Economics,* 25 (2), pp. 319-333.

Mansfield, E. (1982). 'Tax Policy and Innovation', *Science,* 215 (12), pp. 1365-1371.

Mansfield, E.D. and Mansfield, E. (guest eds.) (2000). 'Intellectual Property Protection and Economic Development', *Int. Journal of Technology Management,* Special Issue, 19 (1/2).

Maskus, K.E. (2000). *Intellectual Property Rights in the Global Economy.* Institute for International Economics, Washington DC. August, 2000.

Merges, R.P. (1999). *As Many as Six Impossible Patents Before Breakfast: Property Rights for Business Concepts.* Mimeo, UC Berkeley School of Law.

Mowery, D.C. (ed.). (1996). *The International Computer Software Industry. A comparative study of industry evolution and structure.* Oxford: Oxford University Press.

Nelson R.R., (1996). *The Sources of Economic Growth.* Cambridge, MA: Harvard Univ. Press.

Nordhaus, W.D. (1969). *Invention, Growth and Welfare.* Cambridge, MA: MIT Press.

Palmer, J. (1986) (ed.). 'The Economics of Patents and Copyrights', *Research in Law and Economics*, Vol. 8, Greenwich, CT: JAI Press Inc.

Rosenberg, N. (1982). *Inside the Black Box: Technology and Economics.* Cambridge, MA: Cambridge University Press.

Rosenberg N. and Nelson R.R. (1994). 'American universities and technical advance in industry', *Research Policy* 23, pp. 323–348.

Rosenberg, N. (2000). "American universities as endogenous institutions", published as Ch. 3, pp. 36-57, in Rosenberg, N. (2000). *Schumpeter and the Endogeneity of Technology*, Routledge, London.

Samuelson P. (1993). 'A Case Study on Computer Programs'. In Wallerstein *et al.* (1993), pp. 284-318.

Scherer, F.M. (1980). *Industrial Market Structure and Economic Performance.* Chicago, IL: Rand McNally.

Scotchmer, S. (1991). 'Standing on the shoulders of giants: cumulative research and the patent law', *Journal of Economic Perspectives,* 5 (1), pp. 29-41.

Sahal, D. (1981). *Patterns of Technological Innovation.* Reading, MA: Addison-Wesley Publ.

Spero, D.M. (1990). 'Patent Protection or Piracy – A CEO Views Japan', *Harvard Business Review*, 68 (5), pp. 58-67.

Straus, J. (2001). *Grace Period and the European and International Patent Law – Analysis of Key Legal and Socio-Economic Aspects.* IIC Studies in Industrial Property and Copyright Law, Vol. 20. München: Verlag C.H. Beck.

Thurow, L.C. (1997). 'Needed: a new system of intellectual property rights', *Harvard Business Review* Sept-Oct, pp. 95–103.

Ullrich, H. (1977). *Standards of Patentability for European Inventions – Should an Inventive Step Advance the Art?* IIC Studies in Industrial Property and Copyright Law, Vol. 1. München: Max-Planck-Institut.

Wallerstein, M.B., M.E. Mogee and R.A. Schoen (eds.) (1993). *Global Dimensions of Intellectual Property Rights in Science and Technology.* National Academy Press, Washington, D.C.

Weil, V. and J.W. Snapper (eds.) (1989). *Owning Scientific and Technical Information: Value and Ethical Issues.* New Brunswick and London: Rutgers University Press.

Winter, S.G. (1989). 'Patents in Complex Contexts: Incentives and Effectiveness'. In Weil and Snapper (1989), pp. 41-60.

von Hippel, E. (1988). *The Sources of Innovation.* New York, NY: Oxford University Press.

Wright, B.D. (1983). 'The economics of invention incentives: patents, prizes, and research contracts', *American Economic Review*, 73 (4), pp. 691-707.

Chapter 11

ON COPYRIGHT AND PATENT PROTECTION FOR SOFTWARE AND DATABASES: A TALE OF TWO WORLDS

Bronwyn H. Hall[1]
University of California at Berkeley, Department of Economics, Berkeley, CA, USA; National Bureau of Economics Research (NBER), Stanford, CA, USA

Chapter contents:

Abstract: Several recent evolutions in intellectual property policy have occurred that have raised policy concerns for the conduct of basic scientific research. These are the (possibly) increasing commercialization of the university following Bayh-Dole, the European database directive, which increased the level of IP protection on databases considerably, and the rise in the patenting of software and business methods. This paper considers the impact of increased copyright and patent protection for software and databases (that is, for "pure" information goods) on scientific research communities. The central issue discussed is the tension between the two worlds of commercial innovation and scientific research with respect to the twin goals of appropriating and diffusing knowledge. These two worlds have developed very different incentive systems for rewarding the production of information, and problems develop when the two

[1] An earlier version of this paper was presented at an ESF-IIASA-NSF Science Policy Workshop entitled "Building the Virtual 'House of Salomon': Digital Collaboration Technologies, the Organization of Scientific Work, and the Economics of Knowledge Access", held at the International Institute for Applied Systems Analysis in Laxenburg, Austria on 3-5 December, 1999. I am grateful to Paul David for very helpful discussions and Ove Granstrand for extensive comments on the earlier version.

O. Granstrand (ed.), Economics, Law and Intellectual Property, 259-277.

worlds move closer together, as they have recently in much of the world. Examples of this tension from university patenting in the United States and from increases in database protection are given. The paper argues that a useful distinction between the necessary incentives for the production of pure information goods (which require little complementary investment to make them useful) and industrial innovations (which require a great deal) might lead to a lesser need for intellectual property protection in the former case.

Keywords: software; database; scientific research

11.1 Intellectual Property Protection and Open Science

At least since the work of Nelson (1959) and Arrow (1962), economists have understood that the production of knowledge and information may be at an insufficient level from the point of view of society due to the relative ease and lower cost of using rather than producing knowledge, which leads to free-riding by others in its provision. In the absence of intellectual property protection, not only is the producer unable to cover his production costs in the presence of free entry of imitators, but he is also typically unable to charge for the benefits that his product (knowledge or information) confers on other producers whose knowledge production builds on his.

Intellectual property (IP) protection is often introduced as a second-best solution to the incentive problem; the obvious cost of this solution is that such protection creates at least a temporary monopoly and may lead to higher prices for the good that embodies the information in question. When the product itself is intangible "information", as in the case of scientific output, software, or databases, the tension between the benefits of IP protection to guarantee appropriability and the costs of restricted access to the product by those who wish to build on it is particularly acute. This is because the costs of imitation (and the marginal cost of production) in the case of pure information goods are quite low and therefore the IP protection required to prevent entry creates a larger deadweight loss, ceteris paribus. For the same reason, these types of goods are more likely to generate the spillovers that we would like to encourage, and we would therefore prefer not to have them subject to monopoly pricing.

With respect to the decision to undertake research and/or development, economists generally argue that the incentive problem creates a gap between the private and social returns to research that will vary depending on imitation costs and on the generality of application of the results of the R&D, with the gap being smaller for R&D leading to commercial products and larger for basic scientific research. For this reason, the "optimal" tradeoff between policies designed to ensure appropriability of research and those designed to promote spillovers will necessarily be different in the two arenas. In fact, since in reality R&D environments display a continuum between the most extreme private industry settings and the "open science" community, there ought to be a wide variety of policies, institutions and informal arrangements for both ensuring appropriability and facilitating the diffusion and sharing of research results.

When considering how the desire of the economic agents to encourage the spillovers from which they benefit plays out in a setting where there are also appropriability mechanisms in place, it is useful to distinguish between conventional R&D that is embodied in commercialized products and the production of such items as scientific knowledge, research tools, software, and databases. In the former case, diffusion of the "knowledge" created by the R&D can often be achieved separately from the sale of the product in which it is embedded, via information disclosed on the patent or reverse engineering. In the latter case, the "product" itself is the knowledge that will be used as an input to the creation of future products. In this case, there is nothing else to sell besides the output of the R&D, and therefore private provision of the knowledge will inevitably mean that its use is restricted or limited in some way if the knowledge is subject to strong IP protection.[2]

A second characteristic distinguishes many, but not all, pure information goods: they are often produced by creative individuals using few inputs other than "sweat of the brow". Such products include software of various kinds, books, musical compositions, games, some types of research discoveries, and some video and audio productions. For such goods, very little in the way of complementary investment is required to make a fairly attractive and useful product. For many of these producers, the utility and fame from invention and/or creation is its own reward, and requires little incentive of the conventional IP type. Because such goods do not require large financial outlays to others to produce, they are likely to be produced even in the absence of strong IP protection, although in many cases incentives in the form of priority or fame to the first mover may be important. For these types of goods, alternative systems that both ensure knowledge spillovers and provide appropriate (but not necessarily financial) incentives have often developed.

[2] Once again, this is a question of degree, not absolutes. Clearly firms that produce software and databases have devised a variety of ways to ensure that their products are not "merely" information, by providing attendant services, publishing in a convenient physical format, etc.

An important example of such a system is the "republic of science". Obviously the scientific research community primarily produces pure information goods, where the tension between appropriability considerations and the need for the sharing of information to increase researcher productivity and secure scientific advance is the greatest. As others have argued (David 1998; Dasgupta and David 1992; David 1992), this community has evolved a rather different approach to rewards for and spillovers from the production of information goods than that suggested by a conventional economic property rights analysis, one based on rapid publication and dissemination in order to achieve a prior claim as the inventor.[3] "Priority" thus acquired is an important input to the career and sometimes the financial reward structure faced by scientists, but because there is no direct sale of the information, there is no attempt to restrict its diffusion. The cultural and institutional norm in this sector is therefore to maximize the dissemination of research results, in order to establish priority in as wide an arena as possible. As Liebeskind and Oliver (1997) argue, because the quality of "new" information is frequently difficult to judge, exposing it early and often via publication serves an additional purpose: by allowing replication and verification, it increases the "trust" placed in new results from the same researchers. If the norm were secrecy instead (at least for a limited time), the progress of science would be substantially impeded.

Of course it is possible that the free diffusion of the "public goods" knowledge created by R&D might also be industry welfare-enhancing in some private industry settings, provided that there remain sufficient avenues to capture the returns to the investment via the production of private goods for sale.[4] That is, one can imagine an equilibrium with weak IP rights where firms were willing to allow diffusion of their own knowledge in exchange for low-cost absorption of the knowledge of others. Such an equilibrium might have transaction costs enough lower than those incurred in a setting with strong IP rights, large amounts of cross-licensing, and aggressive patent enforcement strategies that aggregate innovative effort would not suffer even though incentives of the conventional economic kind were weakened. It is

[3] Also see Arora, David, and Gambardella (1999) for empirical evidence on the "increasing returns" nature of the reward system in science, sometimes known as the "Matthew" effect.

[4] For example, Hicks (1995) finds that researchers in private firms often publish scientific articles in an effort to link to the scientific community and to signal the possession of tacit knowledge that will enable these researchers to participate in the "open science" community. The same idea is suggested by Cockburn and Henderson (1996, 1998) using evidence on research productivity in the pharmaceutical industry.

possible to argue that this was the situation in the U.S. semi-conductor and electronic computing industries prior to the strengthening of patent protection both statutorily and via legal precedent in the early 1980s.[5] Certainly it appears to be the model underlying the open source software movement.[6]

The difficulty is that such an equilibrium in the private (profit-maximizing) sector is unstable if IP protection is in fact available to the participants, and also that an equilibrium based on a tacit *quid pro quo* may discriminate against new entrants who are not part of the "club." For an example of the first difficulty, consider the aggressive litigation strategies of Texas Instruments in the 1980s, which appear to have been destabilizing in the case of the semiconductor industry. For the second, Hall and Ziedonis (2001) found that one of the primary arguments given in favor of strong IP protection in the semiconductor industry by the participants was that the possession of key patents helped start-ups to obtain financing for entry into the industry. Because external finance is essential to entry in industries that require high upfront investments, and because investors require an *ex ante* signal that the firm has a potentially rent-generating asset, obtaining IP protection becomes important when the only thing an entrepreneur possesses is a good idea. Once again, it is the need for *complementary* investment that suggests the importance of IP rights.

A couple of implications follow from this brief review of the "two worlds" of research and development: First, we might expect particular tensions to arise in settings where the conventions of one world (private industry) come up against the conventions of another (public R&D and university science). The design of appropriate incentives at the boundary is difficult but important. Second, as highlighted above, the area where we might want to be particularly careful to ensure that the policies we adopt to secure appropriability do not discourage spillovers is in the production of "pure" information goods and research tools. The remainder of this brief paper discusses these two aspects of IP protection in the scientific research setting in somewhat more detail and suggests avenues for future research on the management of IP policy to ensure continued coexistence of multiple reward systems.

---

[5] See Grindley and Teece (1997) and Hall and Ziedonis (2001), *inter alia*, for a discussion of changing IP protection in this industry.

[6] See Lerner and Tirole (2002) for a discussion of the role of "signaling" programming competence in the production of open source software and Kuan (2002) for an argument that open source represents the backward integration of consumers into production.

11.2 IP Issues on the Boundary

The tension between IP protection and the desire for the promotion of spillovers can be seen in a couple of examples from the recent U.S. experience with policy efforts to increase the ties between academic science and industry, and to speed the commercialization of inventions made in the university.[7] These efforts have been somewhat successful: shows a tripling of the share of university research funding that is paid for by private industry in the United States between 1970 and 2000 (although the fraction is still fairly low, just above six percent). Yet a number of problems and potential problems have arisen, which are mainly due to the collision between the reward structures of academic science and those of private industry.

Table 11-1: R&D performance in U.S. universities and FFRDCs

Funding for University R&D	1960	1970	1980	1990	2000 (est.)
% Federal government-funded	76.6	77.5	76.7	68.7	64.9
% Industry-funded	3.9	2.0	2.8	5.3	6.1
% Self-funded	6.2	7.9	9.9	14.2	16.6
% Other (non-profit/state&local)	13.3	12.6	10.6	11.8	12.4
Total spending ($1996B)	4.61	10.45	18.76	24.46	33.75

The first example is that of university-industry research centers in the United States. Cohen, Florida, and Goe (1994) conducted a survey of 437 universities that covered more than 1000 University-Industry Research Centers (UIRCs) in 1991. These centers are the principal vehicle for industry support of academic science and engineering in the United States. One of the findings from their survey was that industrial participants were often able to restrict information flow and delay publication of the results from the academic research that they were supporting, suggesting a conflict between the university's open science goals and those of industry. Whether we should be concerned about this deviation from the cultural norm of science depends

[7] The examples in this paper are largely drawn from the U.S. experience, with which I am more familiar and for which there have been a number of policy experiments and attendant studies in the recent past. See Cassier and Foray (1999a,b) for a discussion of this issue in Europe.

somewhat on whether the research conducted in these centers was "additional" to that normally conducted by the university. On this question, the study is fairly silent. However, more recent survey evidence due to Hertzfeld, Link, and Vonortas (2001), based on a small sample of firms involved in university research partnerships, suggests that companies are now beginning to find ways to accommodate the open science need to publish early.

The second example concerns the effects of attempts to increase university commercialization by granting them rights to their discoveries. In the United States, most basic scientific research is conducted within universities or within federal laboratories managed by universities. The Bayh-Dole Act of 1980 was one of several measures adopted in response to a perceived threat of Japanese technological competition that were designed to accelerate and enhance the commercialization of research results from the university community. This act allowed universities to obtain patents on technology developed by using federal research funds so that the technology could be licensed to private firms for development.[8]

One might expect that adding such a goal to the university agenda would have an impact on university behavior and there is some evidence that it did. University patenting, which had been growing prior to 1980, accelerated after 1980 from a 0.7% share in domestic U.S. patents in 1979 to 3.6% by 1999.[9] The share of new invention disclosures in universities that are patented rose from 26 percent in 1991 to 49 percent in 2000.[10] Henderson, Jaffe, and Trajtenberg (1998) found that universities increased their overall patenting per R&D dollar rate, with an apparent drop in patent quality, suggesting the harvesting of lower quality outputs of their research.

Mowery and Ziedonis (2001, 2002) provide more nuanced evidence on this point, finding little decline in importance or generality of the patents taken out by the University of California and Stanford University following the passage of Bayh-Dole. These two universities were two of the heaviest patenters both before and after the passage of this act and therefore dominate the statistics on "incumbent" universities. Entrant universities, those who began patenting in response to Bayh-Dole, account for the overall decline in

[8] Universities had been patenting some inventions before this time, but the Bayh-Dole Act replaced a series of individually negotiated agreements between particular universities and federal agencies.

[9] Mowery and Ziedonis (2001, 2002).

[10] Association of University Technology Managers (AUTM) Survey data, as reported in Graff (2002).

patent quality observed by Henderson, Jaffe, and Trajtenberg. Mowery and Ziedonis conclude that the primary effects of Bayh-Dole are increases in the marketing of innovations by incumbent universities and the entry of universities new to patenting, rather than an actual change in research strategy.[11] However, along with Mowery *et al.* (2001), they caution that other trends in scientific research and patenting, particularly the rise in biomedical research and the 1980 U.S. Supreme Court decision in *Diamond v. Chakrabarty*, which upheld the validity of a broad patent in biotechnology, make it difficult to attribute the entire effect to the Bayh-Dole Act.

In contrast, Argyres and Liebeskind (1996) found that university efforts to commercialize biotechnology innovations following the Bayh-Dole Act of 1980 were impeded by the academic institution's traditional commitment to the "intellectual commons" and absence of secrecy, suggesting that the tension goes both ways. Yet Mowery and Ziedonis (2002) do report that the majority of technology licenses granted by UC Berkeley and Stanford are exclusive, suggesting that those agreements that are reached are structured to satisfy the desires of industry. In a survey of university-industry partnerships that were partly funded by the U.S. Advanced Technology Program (ATP), Hall, Link, and Scott (2003) found that intellectual property issues were one of the main areas of conflict between the universities and industry partners, although in this case the dispute was over the allocation of rights rather than the diffusion of the information.[12] For their subsample of 25 ATP projects where there was no university partner, over half reported that IP issues had been an insurmountable obstacle to reaching agreement with a university partner. Hertzfeld, Link, and Vonortas (2001) surveyed a range of industry Research Joint Venture (RJV) participants and found that the most problematic area for RJV negotiations was those with universities, especially university technology transfer officers, who were perceived by industry participants as being overly aggressive and "greedy" in approaching IP issues.

The conclusion from this brief survey of the effects of changes in IP protection during the past 15-20 years on the university-industry research relationship in the United States is that "harvesting" of patents from inventions has increased greatly in the university, but with relatively little effect on actual research (this is similar to the trends in industry; see Ziedonis and Hall 2002). At the same time, the growth in partnerships with industry has led to

[11] This view is also supported by Thursby and Thursby (2000), using survey evidence from 65 universities that license innovations for commercial use and the businesses that license from them.

[12] See also Hall, Link, and Scott (2003).

increased tension over IP rights and the ability to publish freely. However, it is likely that the current trends in patenting (especially in software and genomics) and in database protection are probably more threatening to the university research environment than the effects of 1980s policy changes in joint venturing and university patenting.

11.3 IP Protection for Software and Databases

Recent trends in biotechnology (gene sequencing) and information technology (the internet) have brought to the forefront a set of issues in the law and economics of intellectual property that were first brought to the attention of economists by Scotchmer (Green and Scotchmer 1996; Scotchmer 1996). These issues have to do with the problem of rewarding multiple inventors in a setting with cumulative innovation. That is, is it possible to provide optimal incentives for innovation simultaneously to the producers of a first-generation product and a second-generation product that builds on it? The answer in general is no. At least two problems arise:

1. The first invention creates an externality for the second inventor and therefore may be worth developing even if the expected cost exceeds its value as a stand-alone product. However, broad patent rights for the first inventor to ensure innovation do not leave enough profit for the second inventor. One solution to this problem is "internalizing the externality" via licensing. Scotchmer (1996) shows the following:

    - *Ex post licensing agreements*, entered into after the cost of first innovation is sunk, can increase the profits available for the two innovators, but cannot achieve the first best, because it is impossible to give the total surplus to each party separately by using this (or any other) mechanism, as would be required to incent each of the innovators separately.
    - *Ex ante cooperative R&D investment (RJVs)*, entered into before the R&D cost is sunk, generally will achieve a more efficient outcome (in terms of total welfare), but it is very difficult to identify potential partners *ex ante* in practice.[13]

[13] See Headley (1995) for an interesting discussion of the political/legal history of the idea of extending *droit de suite* to cover scientific inventions during the earlier part of the twentieth century. This idea essentially foundered on a reluctance to impose compulsory licensing on inventors into the far future and the consequences such a move might have for the publication of the results of scientific research.

2. Where the first invention is the pure outcome of scientific research, that is, where the value is only the information, it cannot be sold without revealing it, which makes a sale moot, unless strong IP protection or legally enforceable non-disclosure agreements (NDAs) are in place. In the case where such measures (IPR or NDAs) are only partially effective, Anton and Yao (1998) show that a signaling equilibrium exists with partial disclosure of the idea that gives an indication of its quality. This essentially means that the inventor will receive a "lemons" discount for his innovation, because he gives away some of it as a signal. The discount, which can be large, will clearly reduce the provision of ideas unless non-financial motivations come to the fore (such as priority of the open science kind).

As discussed earlier, a characteristic of information goods such as software that differentiates them from industrial R&D products is that, once the invention exists, very little complementary investment is necessary to make it useful, so that without some form of IP protection, conventional economic incentives for their production would essentially not exist. Unlike physical products that merely embody the results of R&D, in the case of information goods, the R&D itself is what is for sale. It is this feature that makes the tension between IP protection, which gives incentives for production but restricts the subsequent use of the information, and measures to promote spillovers from the current generations to those which build on them particularly acute.

The insights of Scotchmer and Anton and Yao suggest the difficulty of contract design for optimal cumulative innovation in a setting where each innovation builds on the last, and where subsequent innovators are many, geographically diffuse, and hard to identify. This description characterizes the production of both software and databases in the scientific research community. The origins of database and software packages in common use are often "lost in the mists of time".[14] See Maurer (1999) for some examples.

[14] One widely diffused statistical package for the social sciences with which the author is familiar was originally developed by a set of graduate students in their spare time in the 1960s. The approximately 50,000 lines of code now contained in the package probably include at most 100 lines of the original code, but the basic design of the syntax has changed little over the years and its origins are clear. Some of the earlier development was financed on research grants, but most of the value added in the past twenty years has been financed by sales of the product. In spite of this, the package retains a strong link to the academic community and is typically sold to them at a substantial discount from the commercial price. This type of situation is very common in the scientific software world, where the primary product being sold back to the academic community from the private sector is service and support

In other cases, they are public and non-protected, but have been developed and augmented by private researchers or research firms.

Given the recent trends toward stronger IP protection in the commercial world, it is sensible to ask both whether there is an argument for extending these protections in the scientific community and also what the unintended impact of the changes already made might be on that community. In the case of databases, the issues, particularly those raised by the new European Union Database Directive, have been well discussed by David (1999) and Maurer and Scotchmer (1999). Maurer (1999) also discusses a large number of example databases and reviews the policy options available for ensuring their production.

At a practical level, two questions confront us:

1. Are the current incentives for the production of scientific software adequate?

2. How will changes in the patentability of software impact the academic establishment?

The answer to the first question is probably a qualified yes, primarily because the producers of such software have been very creative in funding its production and improvement. Although the priority system ensures that there are rewards for the original ideas that are the product of research activity and their rapid diffusion throughout the science community, it is less good at ensuring the production of "second generation" developments from the original research ideas. That is, the novelty requirement for research output tends to be too high to allow improvements to or even the creation of software or databases to qualify. In some cases, the implication of the scientific reward system has been that it is difficult to induce researchers to support and improve existing software rather than creating it anew. The same argument applies to updating and improving databases. On the other hand, it is difficult to measure and quantify the extent to which there is a real lack here, because scientists and researchers would almost always like updated and improved data and software if they could obtain it at zero cost. The crucial willingness-to-pay test is rarely applied.

For these reasons, there may be good reasons to consider other incentives for their maintenance and improvement such as IP protection. In fact, historically copyright protection has served this function when coupled with

---

rather than programming code. Were the algorithms in the code protected by strong patents, it is likely that these packages would command much higher prices than they do now.

limited privatization of the software production. That is, some individuals within or adjacent to scientific communities have chosen to fill the gap between commercial and academic software by supplying packages that incorporate some of the outputs of the research endeavor in their continuing, ongoing development and that are accompanied by improved efforts in both documentation and service.

Simple economic analysis can help us to identify situations where the provision of software to the scientific community might be either insufficient or at a price which researchers are unwilling or unable to pay. The most important characteristic of software or database production is that its cost structure consists of high fixed costs for the first copy coupled with very low marginal costs for subsequent copies. We know that a monopolist faced with this kind of cost structure will find it particularly advantageous to price discriminate if he can, since producing additional units costs so little. If he is able to segment the market into commercial and academic sectors successfully, and *if the demand in the academic sector is more price-sensitive than in the commercial sector,* we will obtain the outcome which prevails in several disciplines: provision of the good at two widely differing prices, often differentiated in a variety of ways to ensure that the markets remain segmented.[15]

The academic disciplines where this strategy is likely to work well and provide a sufficient supply of these types of information goods are those where the commercial sector generates demand for similar goods, such as economics, law, finance, business, computer science, and perhaps biotechnology. In some cases, a monopolist who expects to receive related research spillovers from academia in the future may even elect to charge a zero price for the good. This will be particularly true when the software is subject to ongoing development that depends on the latest research results in the field.

However, problems will arise in at least two situations: first, when the demand of academic researchers for the good is highly price-inelastic, as it will be when the good in question is essential to the research endeavor and when the price is not a large share of the overall research budget. In this case, market segmentation will not work, and the monopolist will choose to offer the product at a relatively high price to both markets. Second, the

[15] For example, the academic product may not have the most recent data, or may be somewhat more difficult to use (less investment may have been made in "user-friendly" characteristics, or support may be minimal). This strategy is very similar to the sale or distribution of "non-professional" versions of certain software products in order to build market share where there are network externalities (see Chen 1998 for a discussion of this strategy in the context of software piracy).

commercial market for some products may fail to exist altogether. In this situation, demand at the price charged may be so low that the producer of the software or database may be unable to cover his or her fixed costs. Of course, this is no different from the difficulty typically faced by basic scientific research and the policy solution is the same: fund the generation of the product as a public good using criteria similar to those used for ordinary research. For the first problem, which may obtain in some scientific disciplines (e.g., satellite data, see David 1999), there is no simple solution. The existence of a private sector solution, even at a high price, makes it difficult politically to fund a public sector solution.

The second question posed above has arisen because of the recent evolution of IP protection for software in the United States, and increasingly in Europe. Up until around twenty years ago, the standard advice given by patent attorneys to their clients was that it was possible to copyright software but not to patent it. The implication of this advice was that the functions of software could be imitated by reverse engineering so long as one did not simply copy the code directly. In general, algorithms themselves were viewed as not protectable.

All this changed during the 1980s as a result of a series of court decisions, beginning with *Diamond v. Diehr* (1981).[16] Today there is a new "land rush" as firms compete to obtain patents on things that were viewed as unpatentable in the early days of computing. Patents are now routinely being issued both on algorithms that may have been available for decades in published works and on "business methods" or "business models" especially when these are incorporated into the Internet. This has naturally led to an increased fear on the part of scientific researchers that they may be forced to pay for the use of software "concepts" and algorithms that were formerly regarded as free for the taking.[17] Figure 11-1 contains an example of such a patent (issued to Lucent Technologies). It describes a software and hardware

[16] Diamond v. Diehr, 450 U.S. 175 (1981).

[17] For an amusing example, see the discussion in Kasdan (2001) of *In re Pardo* [684F.2d 912 (CCPA, 1982)], where Court of Customs and Patent Appeal (the predecessor to the Federal Circuit Court of Appeal) overturned a rejection by the U.S. Patent and Trademark Office Board of Appeals of an application for a patent on a method of solving equations. A reader of the patent would recognize it as the repeated substitution method he or she is familiar with from a first course in algebra, with the equations arranged in the order that would be convenient for a computer. The Court produced an argument claiming that although it was an algorithm, it was not a "mathematical algorithm", and hence could be patented. This particular patent, like so many since, would seem to fail both the "prior art" test and the "nonobviousness" test of patentability.

implementation of a method for looking up the sine or cosine of an angle in a table of sines and cosines by using an "algorithm" that should be familiar to anyone who has taken elementary trigonometry. Some may question whether this patent passes the nonobviousness test.

5,937,438 – Sine/cosine lookup table filed June 1997
– cites 2 prior patents, and nothing else

1. A lookup table, comprising a complementer adapted to selectively complement a subset of bits of a multibit designation of an angle based on a most significant bit of the multibit designation to produce an address signal; a memory addressed by the address signal and adapted to produce two values; and a switching element adapted to receive the two values from the memory and selectively output the values based on the most significant bit.
2. A lookup table as recited in claim 1, wherein the multibit designation contains n bits, and wherein the memory is an array containing 2^n-1 rows.
3. A lookup table as recited in claim 2, wherein each of the 2^n-1 rows corresponds to an angle between zero degrees and 45 degrees.
4. A lookup table as recited in claim 3, wherein each row contains sine and cosine values associated with the corresponding angle.
5. A lookup table as recited in claim 3, wherein each row contains sine and cosine values associated with an angle between the angle corresponding to the row and an angle corresponding to an adjacent row.
6. A lookup table as recited in claim 5, wherein the sine and cosine values are associated with an angle substantially centered between the angle corresponding to the row and the angle corresponding to the adjacent row.

And 13 more claims of a similar nature.......

Figure 11-1: Lucent's patent on sine/cosine table lookup

The validity and enforceability of patents like the one in Figure 11-1 have yet to be fully tested in the courts, although the principle of patenting the computer implementation of a commonly used process seems to have been upheld in State Street Bank case.[18] Clearly the existence of such patents may make some researchers apprehensive. It could be argued that widespread enforcement of patents on the implementation of common mathematical algorithms might have a chilling effect on the research that uses and builds on them.

On the other hand, it is difficult to see a financial motive for the assertion of patents against academic researchers, because there are no product sales on which to collect royalties. Nevertheless, it is clear that this issue is of some concern, especially among university administrators.[19]

11.4 Concluding Thoughts

The central issue highlighted by this paper is the tension between the two worlds of commercial innovation and scientific research with respect to the twin goals of appropriating and diffusing knowledge. Recent developments in the protection of Intellectual Property, especially in the U.S., together with the increasing closeness of public and university research to commercialization in several major research areas, have heightened this tension, causing concern in the academic community and elsewhere that, in the race to ensure that the incentives to create new forms of information such as databases and software are in place, we may have also slowed their diffusion in ways that will harm the very enterprise that was responsible for generating the innovations that underlie the IT revolution to begin with (the "digital boomerang", in Paul David's phrase).

Of course, from an economic theory perspective, the policy question and remedy are relatively simple and not new: if society benefits from researchers having access to some forms of information at low cost, and there exists private sector willingness to pay for that information, then subsidies to researchers so that they can acquire the information would be socially beneficial, and at the same time, would leave the incentives to produce the information intact. Because private sector firms would still be charged the "market" price, these subsidies would not have to be as large as they would need to be if the government funded the entire activity.

---

18 State Street Bank and Trust Co., Inc. v. Signature Financial Group, Inc., 149 F.3d 1368 (Fed. Cir. 1998).

19 See the American Association of Universities website, http://www.arl.org/scomm/iptoc.html.

The problems with the simple economic solution in this situation are manifold:

1. The politics of government granting organizations usually exhibit considerable reluctance to finance the acquisition of easily reproducible software and/or databases at prices above marginal cost. In practice, there seems to be a bias towards funding the creation of new databases rather than simply purchasing them on the open market.
2. The transaction costs of this kind of solution can be substantial. In the software case, consider the difficulties faced by participant(s) in a small computer science research project with little administrative overhead that might have to license various pieces of software from a series of organizations in order to pursue its research agenda.
3. Imposing administrative and pecuniary costs on researchers who wish to use others' research tools as inputs, even if reimbursement is theoretically possible, tends to discriminate against new and young scientists without grants and also against "outsiders" with radical ideas who cannot get past a peer review. It is hard to quantify this idea, but there are repeated historical examples which suggest that the unpredictability of the sources of new ideas means that they are best encouraged when the costs of entry into the research or innovation endeavor are kept as low as is practicable.

Clearly it is beyond the scope of this brief paper to offer definitive solutions to the problem of reconciling the "two worlds" and their varying institutional and cultural approaches to the IP protection of information. I prefer to conclude by suggesting some unanswered questions and avenues for future research on this topic. The first need is empirical: beyond the work of Maurer (1999) on the effects of the European Database Directive, Bessen and Maskin (2002) on the broad effects of introducing software patents, and Kuan (2002) on the productivity of the open source software model, we actually have relatively little evidence on the impact of different forms of IP protection on the incentives to produce databases or software. In particular it would be helpful to know more about the needs of scientific researchers with respect to databases and the costs of filling these needs. What models of database provision have worked in the past and how have they been funded? On software, is there actual evidence of patent holders asserting rights against academic researchers? Or do computer science researchers avoid areas where IP rights are particularly dense, as in Lerner (1995)? If so, should we be concerned?

On the theoretical side, I am unaware of modeling that focuses specifically on the determination of the social welfare outcomes in the two worlds limned here. That is, it would be useful to develop a model of knowledge production in a game-theoretic setting with spillovers, but both with and without strong IP protection, for use in welfare analysis. Such a model should take explicit account of the transaction costs incurred under the two systems, as well as the features of the production function for new information goods that I have emphasized here, such as the important role played by the necessity for complementary investment in the choice of which goods to supply when the supplier is not primarily motivated by financial considerations.

11.5 Literature References

Anton, James J. and Yao, Dennis, A. *The Sale of Intellectual Property: Strategic Disclosure, Property Rights, and Incomplete Contracts.* U. of Pennsylvania: Duke University and the Wharton School, photocopied, 1998.

Argyres, Nicholas S. and Liebeskind, Julia Porter. Privatizing the Intellectual Commons: Universities and the Commercialization of Biotechnology. Journal of Economic Behavior and Organization. 1998; 35: 427-54.

Arora, Ashish; David, Paul A. and Gambardella, Alfonso. Reputation and Competence in Publicly Funded Science: Estimating the Effects on Research Group Productivity. Annales d'Economie et de Statistique. 1999; 49/50: 163-98.

Arrow, Kenneth, "Economic Welfare and the Allocation of Resources for Invention". In *The Rate and Direction of Inventive Activity,* R. R. Nelson, ed. Princeton, NJ: Princeton University Press, 1962; 609-25.

Bessen, James, and Maskin, Eric. Sequential Innovation, Patents, and Imitation. MIT and Princeton University, working paper, 2002.

Cassier, Maurice and Foray, Dominique. Connaissances Publiques, Propriete Privee et Role des Consortia de Haute Technologie. CNRS Cahiers de l'Innovation. 1999a; 99060.

L'Economie des Consortia de Haute Technologie: Etudes de Cas dans la Recherche Biomedicale. CNRS Cahiers de l'Innovation. 1999b; 99059.

Chen, Stephen, When is Piracy Beneficial: Some Applications of Game Theory in the Entertainment Industry. City University Business School, 1998: photocopied.

Cockburn, Iain M. and Henderson, Rebecca M. Absorptive Capacity, Coauthoring Behavior and the Organization of Research in Drug Discovery. Journal of Industrial Economics. 1998; 46/2: 157-82.

Cohen, Wesley; Florida, Richard and Goe, W. Richard. *University Industry Research Centers in the United States.* Carnegie Mellon University, 1994: photocopied.

Dasgupta, Partha and David, Paul A. *Toward a New Economics of Science.* Stanford University: CEPR Publication No. 320, 1992.

David, Paul A. The Digital Technology Boomerang: New IPR Protection, Privatization and the Enclosing of the Open Science 'Information Commons'. All Souls College, Oxford University and Stanford University, 1999: photocopied.

Knowledge Spillovers, Technology Transfers, and the Economic Rationale for Public Support of Exploratory Research in Science. A Background Paper for the European Committee for Future Accelerators Working Paper on Technology Transfers, 1998.

Knowledge, Property, and the System Dynamics of Technological Change. Proceedings of the World Bank Annual Conference on Development Economics, 1992; 215-47.

Graff, Gregory. University Research and Offices of Technology Transfer. Chapter 2, PhD Thesis, Department of Agricultural and Resource Economics, University of California at Berkeley, 2002.

Green, Jerry and Scotchmer, Suzanne. On the Division of Profit Between Sequential Innovators. Rand Journal of Economics. 1996; 27: 322-31.

Grindley, Peter C. and Teece, David J. Managing Intellectual Capital: Licensing and Cross-Licensing in Semiconductors and Electronics. California Management Review. 1997; 39: 1-34.

Hall, Bronwyn H., Link, Albert N. and Scott, John T. A Note on Universities as Research Partners. Review of Economics and Statistics. 2003, 85, 2.

Barriers Inhibiting Industry from Partnering with Universities. Journal of Technology Transfer. 2001; 26: 87-98.

Hall, Bronwyn H. and Ziedonis, Rosemarie Ham.The Determinants of Patenting in the U.S. Semiconductor Industry, 1980-1994. Rand Journal of Economics. 2001; 32: 101-28.

Headley, Weston. Minerva's Property: An Economic-Legal History of Proposals for the Patenting of Science's Discoveries. Stanford University, 1995: photocopied.

Henderson, Rebecca; Jaffe, Adam B. and Trajtenberg, M. Universities as a Source of Commercial Technology: A Detailed Analysis of University Patenting 1965-1988. Review of Economics and Statistics. 1998; 119-27.

Henderson, Rebecca and Cockburn, Iain. Scale, Scope, and Spillovers: The Determinants of Research Productivity in the Pharmaceutical Industry. Rand Journal of Economics. 1996; 27/1: 32-59.

Hertzfeld, Henry R.; Link, Albert N. and Vonortas, Nicholas S. Intellectual Property Protection Mechanisms and Research Partnerships. George Washington University and UNC Greensboro: working paper, 2001.

Hicks, Diana. Published Papers, Tacit Competencies, and Corporate Management of the Public/Private Nature of Knowledge. Industrial and Corporate Change. 1995; 4: 401-24.

Kasdan, John. Obviousness and New Technologies. Fordham Intellectual Property Law Review. 2001.

Kuan, Jennifer, Open Source Software as Lead User's Make or Buy Decision: A Study of Open and Closed Source Quality. Stanford, CA: Stanford University, 2002.

Lerner, Josh. Patenting in the Shadow of Competitors. Journal of Law and Economics. 1995; 38/2: 463-96.

Lerner, Josh and Tirole, Jean.Some Simple Economics of Open Source. Journal of Industrial Economics. 2002; 50/2: 197-234.

Liebeskind, Julia P. and Oliver, Amalya L. "From Handshake to Contract: Trust, Intellectual Property, and the Social Structure of Academic Research". In *Trust Within and Between Organizations*, C. Lane, and R. Bachmann, eds. Oxford: Oxford University Press, 1997.

Maurer, Stephen M. Raw Knowledge: Protecting Technical Databases for Science and Industry. Report prepared for the NRC's Workshop on Promoting Access to Scientific and Technical Data for the Public Interest, 1999.

Maurer, Stephen M. and Scotchmer, Suzanne. Database Protection: Is It Broken and Should We Fix It? Science. 1999; 284: 1129-30.

Mowery, David C. and Ziedonis, Arvids A. Academic Patent Quality and Quantity before and after the Bayh-Dole Act in the United States. Research Policy. 2002; 31: 399-418.

Mowery, David C. and Ziedonis, Arvids A. Numbers, Quality, and Entry: How Has the Effects of the Bayh-Dole Act Affected University Patenting and Licensing? Innovation Policy and the Economy. 2001; 1: 187-220.

Mowery, David C.; Nelson, Richard R.; Sampat, Bhaven N. and Ziedonis, Arvids A. The Growth of Patenting and Licensing by U.S. Universities: An Assessment of the Effects of the Bayh-Dole Act of 1980. Research Policy. 2001; 30/1: 99-119.

Nelson, Richard R. The Simple Economics of Basic Scientific Research. Journal of Political Economy. 1959; 67: 297-306.

Scotchmer, Suzanne. Protecting Early Innovators: Should Second Generation Products be Patentable? Rand Journal of Economics. 1996; 27: 322-31.

Thursby, Jerry G. and Thursby, Marie C. Who is Selling the Ivory Tower? Sources of Growth in University Licensing. National Bureau of Economic Research Working Paper No. 7718 (May), 2000.

Ziedonis, Rosemarie Ham and Hall, Bronwyn H. "The Effects of Strengthening Patent Rights on Firms Engaged in Cumulative Innovation: Insights from the Semiconductor Industry". In *Entrepreneurial Inputs and Outcomes: New Studies of Entrepreneurship in the United States*, Gary Libecap, ed. Vol. 13 of Advances in the Study of Entrepreneurship, Innovation, and Economic Growth, Amsterdam: Elsevier Science, 2001.

Chapter 12

EXPLORING THE TAIL OF PATENTED INVENTION VALUE DISTRIBUTIONS°

Dietmar Harhoff*, Frederic M. Scherer**, Katrin Vopel***
* *University of Munich, Munich School of Management, Munich, Germany*
** *Harvard University, John F. Kennedy School of Government, Cambridge MA, USA*
*** *Centre for European Economic Research (ZEW), Mannheim, Germany*

Chapter contents:

Abstract: We explore the tail of patented invention value distributions by using value estimates obtained directly from patent holders. The paper focuses on those full-term German patents of the application year 1977 which were held by West German and U.S. residents. The most valuable patents in our data account for a large fraction of the cumulative value over all observations. Several tests are conducted to pin down more precisely the nature of the high-value tail distribution. Among the Pareto, Singh-Maddala and log normal distributions, the log normal appears to provide the best fit to our patented invention value data.

Keywords: Patents, skew distributions
JEL Classification: O34, O31

° The research underlying this paper was supported by grants from the Sloan Foundation and the ZEW. The authors are also grateful for the invaluable research assistance of Jörg Kukies, Marc Dehoust, Teri Elniski, Renate Häßler, Sascha Karrassek, Stephan Seeberger, Stefan Schmidt, Suzanne Sheldon, and Jesus Viejo Gonzalez, and for helpful comments from Bronwyn Hall and Jenny Lanjouw.

O. Granstrand (ed.), Economics, Law and Intellectual Property, 279-309.

12.1 Introduction

Many industrialized nations charge invention patent holders periodic maintenance or renewal fees. Failure to pay causes the patent permanently to lapse. This phenomenon has been discovered (or rediscovered[1]) by economists and exploited to estimate the economic value of patent protection.[2] The lower the incremental fee at which payment is discontinued, the smaller is the patent right's estimated value. Recent patent renewal studies reveal a highly rightward-skewed distribution of values, with the weight of evidence favoring a log normal distribution of individual patent values, although an even more skew Pareto-Levy distribution has not been ruled out conclusively. However, for the sizeable fraction of patents that remain in force to their full term, the distribution parameters must be derived by extrapolation from patterns for patents allowed to expire earlier. This paper draws upon two new surveys to estimate directly the value of right-hand tail inventions whose patent renewal fees were paid to full-term expiration.

Exploring the distribution properties of the tail is important, because with skew distributions, outlying tail values account for a large fraction of the cumulative value over all observations. Lanjouw *et al.* (1998), for example, estimate that within four technology groups, the most valuable five percent of German patents – all presumably renewed to full term – contributed 22 to 31 percent of the total value of all cohort members. The longer and thicker the distribution's right-hand tail, the more difficult it is for business managers to achieve stable average returns through portfolio strategies. Indeed, if the distribution of values is Pareto-Levy and the distribution parameter $\alpha < 1$, the distribution has neither finite mean nor variance asymptotically, which implies that sample means fail to converge (under the weak law of large numbers) toward a stable value.[3] Extreme skewness of invention values (as distinguished from the value of covering patents) can also have macroeconomic implications. Assuming a Pareto distribution of high-value inventions with $\alpha = 0.8$, Nordhaus (1989) found through a simulation study that, aggregating across the entire U.S. economy, invention-based productivity effects fluctuated widely over time as a result of unusually favorable or unfavorable Monte Carlo simulation draws. His simulated patterns corresponded remarkably closely to actually observed productivity growth fluctuations.

---

[1] For an earlier but less rigorous analysis, see Dernburg and Gharrity (1961).

[2] See e.g. Pakes and Schankerman (1984), Schankerman and Pakes (1986), Pakes (1986), Lanjouw (1998), and Lanjouw, Pakes and Putnam (1998).

[3] See e.g. Johnson *et al.* (1994), Chapter 20.

12.2 Methodology

12.2.1 Sampling and Survey Questionnaire

The German patent renewal fee system provided for us a crucial wedge into the full-term patented invention value question. Germany was chosen because its patent examination system is unusually rigorous, screening out applications of low inventive content, and because its renewal fee schedule is one of the most progressive in the world. Figure 12-1 shows how renewal fees escalated for patents on which applications were filed in 1977. Beginning with DM 100 for the third year, the fees keeping the patent in force over incremental years rose to DM 2,700 for the 18th year. Over the maximum possible term of 18 years, cumulative renewal fees of DM 16,075 had to be paid.[4]

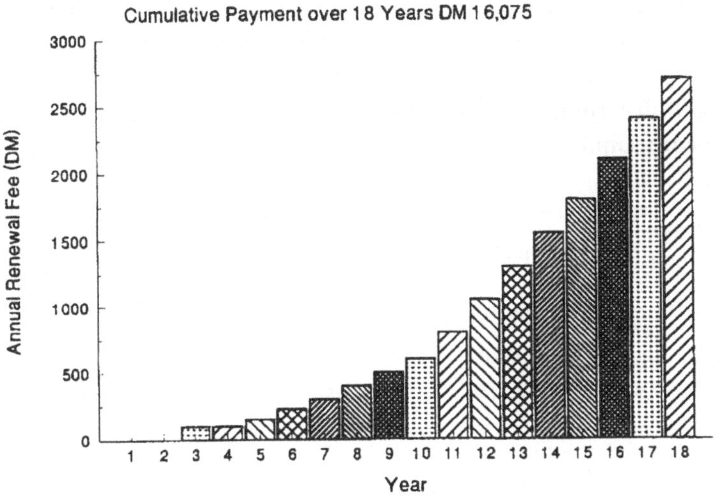

Figure 12-1 Progression of German patent renewal fees over time

[4] The maximum term was extended to 20 years after 1977. For patents declared available for non-exclusive licensing, renewal fees were reduced by 50 percent. Interviews revealed that firms sometimes chose not to pay their fee for the last year because patents are cancelled for non-payment only after half the year has passed.

[5] Most of our U.S. sample patents had 1976 U.S. priority dates, but their German counterpart patent expiration dates were geared to 1977 German applications. Some German patents in our sample had application dates (Nachmeldungen) later than 1977, but were entitled to a 1977 German priority.

Our survey was targeted toward the Class of 1977 – i.e. applications with a 1977 priority date, leading to patents expiring at full term during 1995.[5] Since the survey was conducted in 1996, only a year after the final year's fees were paid, memories concerning survey patents' value remained reasonably fresh. Beginning in 1978, inventors seeking patent protection in Germany enjoyed the option of filing patent applications with the European Patent Office. The emergence of two parallel systems complicates the tracking of inventions, and so the Class of 1977 was the last one for which a relatively clean research design could be implemented.

The total number of German patent applications filed in 1977 was 57,782, of which 27,954 were from applicants residing in West Germany and the remaining 29,828 from foreign applicants.[6] The lag from application to issue was bimodal, with mean of 6.5 years, median of 6 years, and modes at three years (16.9 percent of all issues) and nine years (11.2 percent of all issues). Of the 22,903 patents that were issued and not revoked in subsequent opposition proceedings,[7] 4,349, or 19.0 percent, were renewed to full term. For the six leading invention-originating nations, the number of patent applications, full-term patents, and full-term renewal rates as a percentage of applications are summarized in Table 12-1.

Table 12-1: Patent applications and full-term renewals by nation, 1977

Country of Origin	Applications	Full-Term Patents	Full-Term Patents as Share of Applications
Germany	27,954	1,431	5.12%
United States	10,207	900	8.82%
Japan	4,469	936	20.94%
France	2,675	221	8.26%
Switzerland	2,509	214	8.53%
Great Britain	2,451	166	6.77%
Other	7,517	481	6.40%
All Nations	57,782	4,349	7.53%

[6] Approximately 6,900 of the 57,782 applications were withdrawn by applicants before the 18-month initial publication deadline.

[7] See Harhoff, Scherer and Vopel (2003) for a discussion of opposition proceedings and their possible use as an indicator of patent value.

Full-term renewal rates are considerably higher for foreign patent recipients than for German residents, consistent with the finding of Putnam (1996) that inventors seek patent protection outside their home jurisdictions mainly for their most promising inventions. The extraordinarily high renewal rate for Japan suggests a more aggressive approach to maintaining patent portfolios; see IVA (1993).

The research for this paper focused on the full-term patents held by West German and U.S. residents. For the German patents, a two-stage methodology was pursued. A preliminary telephone and telefax screening elicited patent value estimates and identified the most valuable patents, about which on-site interviews were then sought to develop more detailed historical information. For the U.S. patents, only an extended first stage was executed.

Of the 1,431 full-term German patents, it was possible to trace 1,325, or 92.6 percent, to surviving firms or individual inventors. Most of the untraced patent owners were individual inventors or firms too small to be located through standard business directories. The 684 firms or individuals owning the 1,325 traced patents were contacted by telephone to identify the most appropriate respondent, and a questionnaire was dispatched, usually by facsimile, on each relevant patent. Its essence was a single substantive counter-factual question,[8] translated as follows:

> "If in 1980 you had known how its contribution to the future profitability of your enterprise would unfold, what is the minimum price for which you would have sold the patent, assuming that you had a good-faith offer to purchase?"

This asset value approach (consistent with the view of patents as intellectual property) was chosen over a question asking for the accumulated flow of profits following pilot interviews with German patent-holders testing both approaches. The team contacting patent owners had a more detailed written protocol answering the most common queries posed by recipients.[9] Respondents were asked to place their patent within one of five broad minimum

[8] On the use of counter-factual questions, see Tetlock and Belkin (1996).

[9] On the basis of early experience, the question posed in the U.S. survey instrument was altered slightly, conforming to the guidelines used in the German contact team's protocol: "If in 1980 you knew what you now know about the profit history of the invention abstracted here, what is the smallest amount for which you would have been willing to sell this patent to an independent third party, assuming that you had a bona fide offer to purchase and that the buyer would subsequently exercise its full patent rights?"

selling price ranges: less than DM 100,000, DM 100-399,999, DM 400-999,999, DM 1-5 million, and more than DM 5 million.

Our approach adopts a distinctly different counter-factual assumption than the one implied by previous patent renewal studies. Failure to renew a patent means that the covered subject matter will move into the public domain, allowing it to be used by both the original patent holder and others. Erosion of the original inventor's profits due to non-renewal is often constrained by first-mover advantages shown by Levin *et al.* (1987) to be more potent on average than patent protection. In our approach, on the other hand, sale of all rights in a patent to a third party implies that the buyer can prevent the original patent holder from practicing the subject invention or demand license fees approaching the value of profits foregone. Conversely, in studies using the renewal value of patents, the patent that is not renewed lapses into the public domain so that the former patent holder can still employ the formerly patented technology. For broad patents that covered key features of products or processes – a case found in interviews to be common for the most valuable patents – the sale of rights to a competitor puts at risk the whole stream of quasi-rents realizable from a product or process. Or at minimum, the sale of rights can impose upon the seller the profit sacrifice from foregoing key patented features or the cost of inventing around them. Therefore, higher valuations are expected under our approach than under the renewal approach.[10]

12.2.2 Response Rates

After extensive follow-up, positive responses were obtained on 772 patents (58.3 percent of the total 1325 on which contacts were initiated) held by 394 organizational entities and individual inventors (including ten unaffiliated inventors). Table 12-2 reports probit regressions of a binary survey participation variable on the characteristics of respondents and non-respondents for 684 full-term patent-holding firms and individuals. Three explanatory variable groups are introduced: firm size (or a dummy variable for independent inventors), industry or (for independent inventors) organizational affiliation, and the professional specialty of the principal contact person. The base (intercept) case is a firm with 50 or fewer employees in the machinery industry, with a patent counsel as the principal contact person. The firm size ef-

[10] We elaborate on this issue in a companion paper where we use a simple formal model to contrast the renewal and the asset approaches to defining the value of a patent. See Harhoff, Scherer and Vopel (2003).

fects are significant and generally rising with employment when they are considered in isolation, but fail to be significant with respondent and industry effects included. The respondent effects are highly significant, with responses being particularly likely when an inventor or patent attorney was the principal contact. Pseudo-r^2 values reveal that the three sets of characteristics explain at most only modest amounts of response variance.

Table 12–2: Probit analysis of German patent-holder response behavior*

Characteristic	Number of Cases	Firm Size Model	Full Model
Individual inventor	55	-0.282 (0.078)	-0.441 (0.080)
Firm Size (employees):			
<50	115	(reference group)	(reference group)
50-249	129	0.056 (0.061)	0.041 (0.066)
250-499	77	0.010 (0.072)	-0.010 (0.076)
500-999	87	0.083 (0.066)	0.055 (0.074)
1000-4999	112	0.192 (0.058)	0.104 (0.072)
5000 or more	52	0.122 (0.075)	-0.002 (0.097)
No. of employees unknown	57	-0.038 (0.080)	-0.131 (0.087)
Firm Size Dummies χ^2		14.4	8.2
p-value (df)		p=0.025 (6)	p=0.223 (6)
Respondent Function:			
Patent counsel	179		(reference group)
R & D Executive	142		-0.056 (0.064)
Inventor	63		0.074 (0.082)
General management	181		-0.250 (0.061)
Legal counsel	13		-0.057 (0.155)
Marketing / PR	21		-0.371 (0.097)
Function unknown	30		-0.490 (0.063)
Respondent Type Dummies χ^2			51.5
p-value (df)			p=0.001 (6)
Industry Group Dummies χ^2			14.6
p-value (df)			p=0.101 (9)
Number of observations		684	684
χ^2 (df)		38.82 (7)	107.2 (22)
Pseudo-R^2		0.042	0.116

* Standard errors are reported in parentheses. The dependent variable is participation in the survey (0/1).

A separate analysis reported in Harhoff, Narin, Scherer and Vopel (1999) revealed that the economic valuations elicited in our survey were positively and significantly associated with the number of citations in German patents subsequent to the survey patents. Companies holding four of the most highly cited Class of 1977 full-term patents chose not to participate in the survey. Inspection suggests that those non-responding patents would have reported relatively high economic values. However, a formal test was unable to reject the hypothesis that citation frequency did not differ between responding and non-responding patents. Thus, there appears to be no evidence of selection biases in our first-stage survey responses.

The U.S. survey, added as a by-product of the German survey, used a stratified sampling approach. All U.S.-resident holders of two or more full-term German patents (totalling 630) were included in the starting sample, as were 89 holders of a single full-term patent, including 70 patents held by U.S. corporations known to remain in existence and 19 by New England-based individuals and small companies. A manual search of these 719 German patents was conducted to identify U.S. patent application priority serial numbers for the U.S. patent applications on the basis of which, under international rules, a priority filing date is accepted in foreign jurisdictions. From those 719 German patents, 632 could be linked to valid U.S. application serial numbers – sometimes several per patent. Eighty-seven others dropped out because the priority claims were to nations other than the United States (e.g., when the invention came from a foreign subsidiary of a U.S. multinational enterprise) or because no non-German priority claims were reported. The U.S. application serial numbers for the remaining 632 German patents were linked to 485 U.S. patents, which comprised the basis of our U.S. sample.[11] For the 23 percent of cases with no link to a U.S. patent, the most likely explanation was rejection of applications by the U.S. Patent Office, although there are gaps in the underlying records, and a few parallel U.S. patents may simply have been missed.[12] For 20 of the 485 U.S. sample patents, no questionnaires were dispatched, in 11 cases because no address could be found for the patent holder and in nine other cases because linking

[11] The U.S. serial numbers for entities with two or more German patents were linked by the U.S. Patent Office, for which the help of Jane Myers and William Brown is gratefully acknowledged. The link for the single German patent subsample was accomplished using the Boston Public Library's computerized patent data base.

[12] Roughly two-thirds of patent applications filed in the United States during the 1970s resulted in issued patents. That only 23 percent of the linked applications failed suggests a positive correlation between the probability of issuance in the two jurisdictions.

errors were discovered (e.g., the U.S. application was filed too early or too late to support a 1977 German application).

Of the 465 U.S. questionnaires sent, usually after a preliminary telephone contact, 225, or 48.4 percent, were completed by a total of 78 companies or (in three cases) individual inventors. [13] There was a clear bias in the returns. For 12 companies with eight or more linked patents, the response rate was 37 percent of relevant patents despite intensive follow-up; for firms with fewer than eight patents, the rate was 54 percent, even though follow-ups for the companies with fewer than four patents were less thorough. Two main reasons were given for non-response by the companies with extensive patent holdings: unacceptable compliance burden, and fear that response would reveal too much about the profitability of individual company divisions.

12.3 Results

12.3.1 The First -Stage German Survey

Table 12–3 reports the distribution of estimated values for 772 German patents on which first-stage responses were obtained. Ninety-nine patents were valued in the highest range, at more than DM 5 million. Figure 12–2 plots the cumulative distribution function on doubly logarithmic coordinates. If the distribution of values were Pareto-Levy of the simplest form, it would plot as a straight line on the coordinates chosen, i.e., with $\log N = \log k - \alpha \log V$, where V is the reported patent value (in thousands of German Marks) and N is the number of patents with value V* or greater. An ordinary least squares regression fitted to the data is (with standard deviations in brackets): [14]

$$(1) \qquad \underset{[0.116]}{\log N = 3.481} - \underset{[0.043]}{0.385} \log V; \qquad R^2 = 0.963, \; n = 5.$$

[13] For some extensively restructured corporations, divisions were treated as separate companies.

[14] Since we are particularly interested in the right-hand tail of the patent value distribution, we use in this preliminary characterization an unweighted regression of group geometric mean values and ranks, rather than weighting by group patent counts. The slope from observation-weighted maximum likelihood estimate (e.g., in Table 4, Part A) is smaller than the unweighted estimate of regression (1). The lower-bound value for the "less than DM 100,000" group was set at DM 23,000, which approximates the cost of initial patent application plus full-term renewal payments. Logarithms are taken to base ten here.

[15] Similar results emerged with ordered probit regressions. That is not surprising given that the log value thresholds were chosen such as to induce interval scaling in the variable VALUE.

Adding a quadratic value term increases R^2 by 0.034, which is significant at the 5 percent level in an F-ratio test. If a log linear regression is fitted to the three highest-value classes (with one residual degree of freedom), the estimated slope is 0.518. Both slope estimates fall into the range of α values at which Pareto distributions lack asymptotically finite means and variances. Thus, a high degree of skewness is suggested.

Table 12-3: Distribution of full-term German patent values

Estimated Value Range	Number	Percent
More than DM 5 million	99	12.8 %
DM 1-5 million	121	15.7 %
DM 400,000 - 999,999	149	19.3 %
DM 100,000 - 399,999	200	25.9 %
Less than DM 100,000	203	26.3 %
Total	772	100.0 %

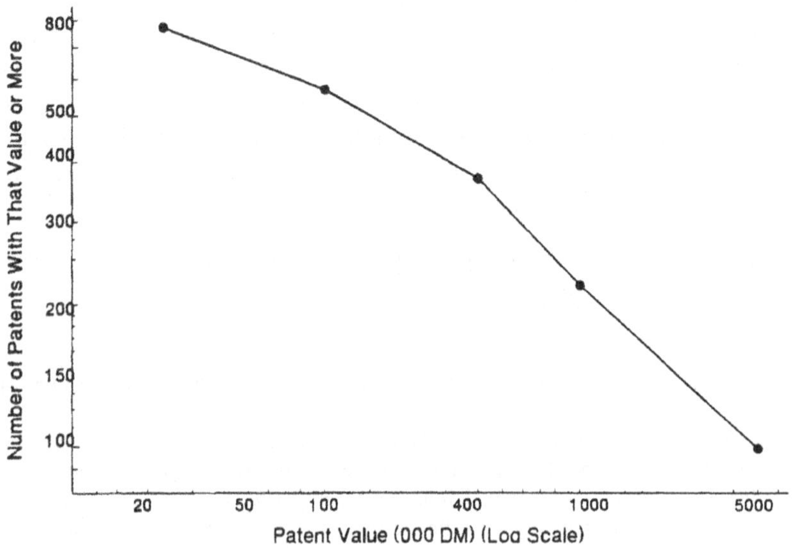

Figure 12-2: Pareto plot of surveyed German patent values (N = 772)

In a disaggregated regression over 772 patent responses, the five value reporting classes were characterized by a dependent variable VALUE, ranging from 1 (for the least valuable inventions) to 5 (for the most valuable). Zero-one dummy variables were defined for patents originating from electrical industry firms (ELEC, 226 cases), chemical industry firms (CHEM, 131 cases), and machinery makers (MACHY, 203 cases); and for responses from patent counsel (PAT, 426 cases), research and development executives (RDEXEC, 128 cases), and inventors (INVENT, 77 cases), with all other industries and responses from other occupational specialties serving as the base or intercept case. Other variables were the logarithm of company employment (EMPLOY) and a one-zero dummy GAP for 64 cases with no employment data. The resulting regression, with standard errors in brackets, was as follows: [15]

$$
\begin{aligned}
(2)\quad \text{VALUE} = {} & \underset{[0.167]}{2.491} + \underset{[0.133]}{0.004}\ \text{ELEC} + \underset{[0.159]}{0.626}\ \text{CHEM} + \underset{[1.475]}{0.200}\ \text{MACHY} \\
& - \underset{[0.136]}{0.372}\ \text{PAT} - \underset{[0.147]}{0.157}\ \text{RDEXEC} + \underset{[0.165]}{0.358}\ \text{INVENT} \\
& + \underset{[0.050]}{0.063}\ \log \text{EMPLOY} - \underset{[0.250]}{0.010}\ \text{GAP};
\end{aligned}
$$

$$R^2 = 0.0441, \quad n = 772.$$

The value responses of patent counsel are found to be on the conservative side, ceteris paribus, while inventors lean toward relatively generous estimates of their contributions. Chemical industry inventions are more valuable on average by nearly two-thirds of a choice interval, possibly because (as Levin *et al.* (1987) show) patents provide a particularly strong appropriability regime. The analysis reveals no significant firm size effects. Adding a quadratic employment variable (not separately reported) left both size variables insignificant. Industry, respondent, and company size variables together explain only a small fraction of the variation in patent value responses, suggesting that most of the variation was invention-specific.

12.3.2 The German Interview Survey

Interviews were sought with all 69 firms owning the 99 patents whose value was estimated at DM 5 million or more in the first-stage questionnaires. Fifty-five on-site interviews were conducted, supplemented by one telephone interview and five cases in which patent holders completed a detailed questionnaire without a face-to-face interview. [16] The interviews covered a wide range of topics, including the history of the inventions patented, the number of nations in which patents were sought, the extent of licensing (domestic and foreign), the incidence of infringement disputes if any, and most importantly for the present paper, a detailed exploration of the subject patents' value. Interviewees were asked to supplement the minimum patent-rights sale-price range answers to the questionnaire's counter-factual question with a point estimate, surrounded when appropriate by a range of uncertainty. In addition, they were asked to estimate the annual sales (including foreign and export sales) and profits, cost savings, and/or royalty receipts attributable to the patented invention, the fraction of profits that would not have been achieved without the patent (usually, the source of the greatest estimation uncertainty), and the role patent protection per se played in sustaining the profits.[17] Interviewees often had detailed records on which to base their answers because of a German law requiring employers to compensate employee inventors for their inventions using a formula including revenues, profits, the fraction of sales attributable to subject inventions, and the degree of initiative exercised by the employee.[18] The estimates analyzed here focus in most cases on the profit sacrifice that would have resulted if the firm were precluded from using the patented invention, not on the role patent protection played per se, although in some cases the two questions were disentangled only with difficulty. Some interviews were able to cover in detail only one high-value invention among several held by a respondent. Careful analysis of one (usually the most valuable) was considered preferable to superficial examination of several.

Useable value responses were obtained on 69 patents originally valued at DM 5 million or more. Estimates for ten other patents were considered too unreliable to include in the formal analysis.[19] Among the 69, profit flow estimates were available in 54 cases; counter-factual asset sale price estimates were available in 38 cases; and in 23 cases, both flow and asset sale estimates were obtained. In those 23 cases, the geometric mean value was DM 11.1 million per invention with flow estimation and DM 19.1 million in the

---

16 The interviews were conducted primarily by Jörg Kukies and Katrin Vopel.

17 The interviews explicitly tallied the value of both domestic and foreign rights. On average, patents covered by interviews were patented in 10 nations other than Germany, with a standard deviation of 9.9.

18 See *Patent- und Musterrecht* (1995, pp. 92-109).

19 The estimated average value per patent in those cases was DM 22.6 million.

asset sale counter-factual. Although the differences appear sizeable, they are not significant at the 0.05 level (t = 1.21) in a test of logarithmic means.

The flow value estimates were computed from annual sales and profit ratio data, with all values converted to 1995 price levels and then discounted back to the year 1980 at a 0.05 real discount rate. In what follows, flow value estimates are used in all but the 15 cases in which they were unavailable and counter-factual estimates were substituted. In 57 cases, best-estimate values were accompanied by an error range, whose average single-side magnitude was 25.1 percent of the best estimate, with a median value of 22.7 percent.

Thirteen of the best estimates, all based upon flow data, were below DM 5 million. In five of those cases, counter-factual asset value estimates were elicited also at the interview stage. All five were greater than or equal to DM 5 million. Discrepancies resulted in these and other cases for complex reasons – e.g., because a high counter-factual value was placed on the blocking role of patents or on ultimately unrealized, but in 1980 plausible option values, because it was difficult to disentangle the role of the invention in a complex systems product or because multiple patents covered the invention, and because respondents estimated surprisingly low profit margins on product sales. We have opted to err on the side of accepting the more conservative flow values when conflicts existed.

Altogether, the best-estimate values ranged from less than DM 1 million (in five cases) to well over DM 1 billion. The mean value was DM 38.8 million if all 69 observations are averaged and DM 15.1 million if the most lucrative invention, with a point estimate roughly 15 times that of the second most valuable invention, is excluded. Figure 12–3 introduces the values for individual high-value patents into the cumulative distribution function of Figure 12–2, multiplying each interview patent's rank by 1.45 to reflect the fact that only 69 of the 100 first-stage high-value patents yielded useable estimates, and aggregating interview estimates below DM 5 million into appropriate lower-value groups. Relative to Figure 12–2, the overall distribution becomes considerably more concave downward. The straight-line fit associated with a Pareto distribution is plainly absent. However, the large jump between the largest and second-largest patent values leaves considerable uncertainty concerning the distribution's form. If a function linear in the logarithms is forced by ordinary least squares on all 56 observations of DM 5 million or more, the slope is -0.874, with standard error of 0.033. If the billion-DM outlier is excluded, the estimated slope steepens to -1.040, with standard error of 0.027.

Several tests were conducted to pin down more precisely the nature of the high-value tail distribution. A graphical test attributable to Bryson (1974) solidly rejected the hypothesis that the distribution for patents valued at DM 5 million or more was negative exponential, Weibull, or any less skew variant. See also D'Agostino and Stephens (1986, Chapter 2).

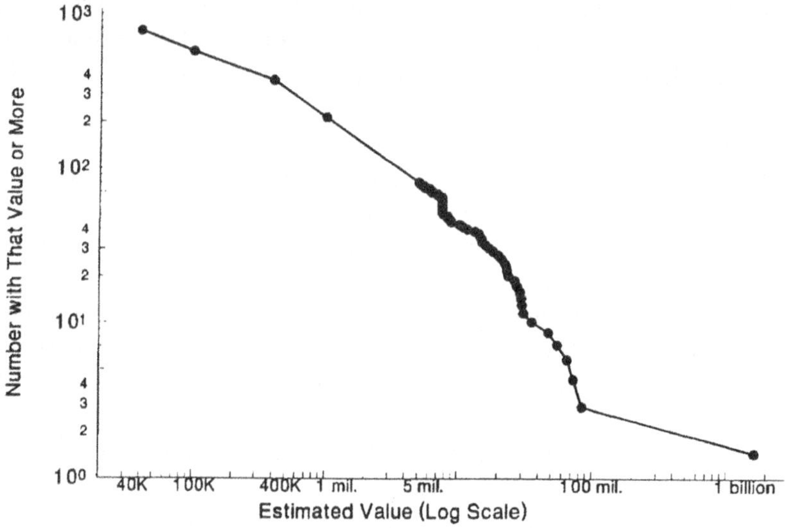

Figure 12–3: Plot of all renewed German patent values on Pareto coordinates

A difficulty with any test is that our data relate only to the right-hand tail of a wider patented invention value distribution. Figures 12-4a and 12-4b provide a simple graphic test of log normality attributable to D'Agostino (1986, pp. 23-29). Where V is mean log patent value and *s* its standard deviation, we plot the standardized log normal variate $Z_i = (V_i - V)/s$ actually observed against a theoretical log normal distribution (from published tables) with the same mean and standard deviation. A necessarily arbitrary assumption is that the total number of observations in the high-value half of the theoretical distribution consists of the 69 patents with originally reported values exceeding DM 5 million plus 69/100^{ths} of the lower-valued full-term observations.[20] Thus, the high-value cases with useable point estimates are

[20] Because the complete distribution is not known, the means and standard deviations are ambiguous. Where Z* is the theoretical standardized normal variate derived on the basis of a

assumed to be a sample from the hemi-distribution. Not surprisingly, the theoretical log normal variates over-predict the high-value distribution extremity when the single billion-DM outlier is excluded (Figure 12-4a) and under-predict it when that outlier is included (Figure 12-4b). For a quantitative comparison with the Pareto-Levy distribution, theoretically predicted values of V_i were derived from the relationship $V_i^* = V + s\,Z_i$. The sum of squared deviations SSD between those predictions and the actual V_i was computed and compared to the equivalent SSD from fitting a one-parameter Pareto-Levy regression.[21] The resulting SSDs (in logarithms to base 10) are as follows:

	Log Normal	**Pareto-Levy**
All patents with V > DM 5 mil.	0.6634	0.7215
Largest outlier excluded (n = 55)	0.2345	0.3128

In both cases, and especially when the largest outlier is excluded, the fit is better with a log normal distribution than with the Pareto-Levy.

Maximum likelihood techniques provide a more general approach to the goodness-of-fit problem, permitting *inter alia* extrapolation of the fitted distribution function to all patents, including those not renewed to full term, and hence excluded from our survey. Three highly skew alternatives were evaluated by maximum likelihood techniques: the two-parameter log normal, the one-parameter Pareto-Levy, and the three-parameter Singh-Maddala distribution. The third of these alternatives, whose high-value tail approximates the Pareto-Levy but does not impose log-linearity on low-value observations, has been used with success in characterizing income distributions. See Singh and Maddala (1976), McDonald (1984), McDonald and Ransom (1979), and Esteban (1986). The likelihood functions used to estimate distribution parameters are summarized in an appendix. Here we focus on the results and their interpretation.

---

patent's value rank, best-fitting values were estimated using the transformed regression log $V_i = V + s\,Z_i + \varepsilon_i$, with V and s as parameters.

[21] For comparability, and unlike regression (1), the sum of squared deviations was minimized in the patent value direction.

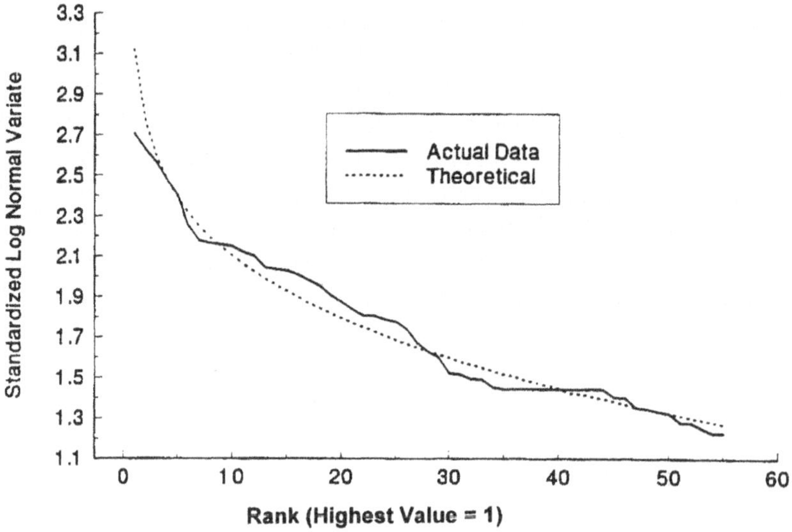

Figure 12–4a: Log normal plot of high-value German patent values (highest value excluded, N=55)

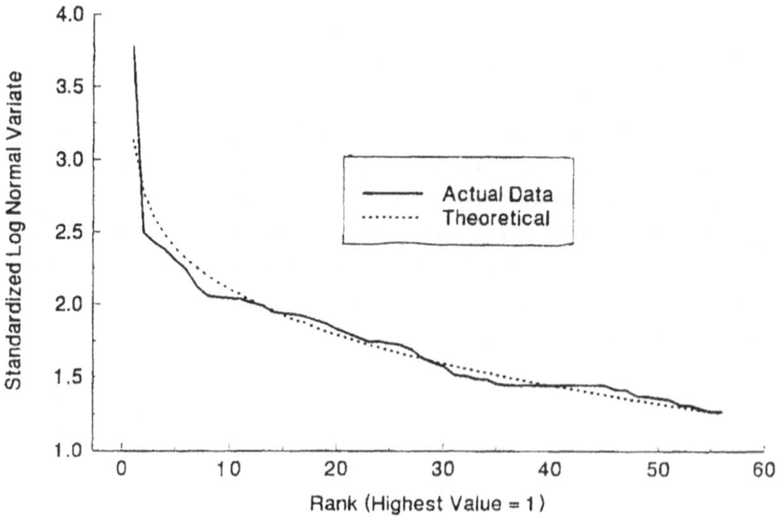

Figure 12–4b: Log normal plot of high-value German patent values (all values included, N=56)

Table 12–4 summarizes the estimation results and goodness-of-fit tests. Part A focuses only on the patents in our response group, i.e., excluding German-origin patents not renewed to full term and truncating the lower-bound value of the full-term patents at DM 23,000.[22] Patents valued above DM 5 million were divided into three discrete groups. Both with and without the most valuable outlier, the log normal form provides a distinctly superior fit. Part B reports maximum likelihood estimates when the distribution includes 9,282 non-renewed German-origin patents, assumed to be generally less valuable than the renewed patents but constrained to have positive values.

Table 12–4: Maximum likelihood estimates for three alternative distributions

Table 12–4 Part A: German patent survey responses only*

Distribution	Pareto	Pareto	Log Normal	Log Normal
Sample	N = 772	N = 771 (largest value excluded)	N = 772	N = 771 (largest value excluded)
Parameters	$\alpha = 0.341$	$\alpha = 0.342$	$\mu = 12.09$ $\sigma = 2.428$	$\mu = 12.14$ $\sigma = 2.366$
χ^2 (df)	175.3 (7)	179.6 (6)	22.4 (6)	26.0 (5)

* Lower-bound patent value truncation at DM 23.000

Table 12–4 PartB: Including non-renewed German-origin patents

Distribution	Pareto	Pareto	Log Normal	Log Normal	Singh-Maddala	Singh-Maddala
Sample	N = 772 + 9282	N = 771 + 9282 (largest value excluded)	N = 772 + 9282	N = 771 + 9282 (largest value excluded)	N = 772 + 9282	N = 771 + 9282 (largest value excluded)
Parameters	$\alpha = 0.216$	$\alpha = 0.216$	$\mu = 4.028$ $\sigma = 5.463$	$\mu = 4.061$ $\sigma = 5.433$	a = 10.02 b = 62.39 q = 0.034	A = 10.19 b = 63.83 q = 0.037
χ^2 (df)	565.6 (9)	573.0 (8)	192.7 (8)	199.5 (7)	325.2 (7)	333.5 (6)

[22] Estimates for the Singh-Maddala distribution could not be obtained with truncation, since the numerical optimization routine did not converge. For the log normal and Pareto distributions, we experimented with other truncation points, e.g., by analyzing only patents with reported values greater than DM 1 million or DM 5 million. In all cases, the log normal distribution provided a better fit, but the differences between the two became quite small and sensitive to omission of the most valuable patent.

Both with the most valuable outlier included and excluded, the log normal distribution provides by far the best fit, with the Singh-Maddala distribution placing second and the Pareto form third. Chi-squared values rise dramatically relative to those for estimates confined to our right-hand tail sample observations, reflecting the larger number of groups and the difficulties of extrapolating outside the range of high-value observations.[23] Estimated means and standard deviations for the log normal form also deviate considerably between the truncated and all-patent analyses.[24] However, graphic inspection reveals that the shape of the right-hand log normal tail changes little between the truncated and all-patent cases. It seems clear that the log normal distribution provides a quite good fit, especially for the high-value tail.[25]

12.3.3 The U.S. Survey

While the German data can be considered reasonably representative for the 1995 group of patents, our U.S. survey does not allow us to test for the overall distributional properties with the same confidence as with the Ger-

---

[23] Formally, the Chi-squared values are sufficiently high to reject even the log normal distribution hypothesis. The rejection of distributional assumptions is a common result in large samples, e.g., in the income distribution literature. See McDonald (1984) and Kloek and Van Dijk (1978).

[24] The parameter estimates here, unlike other parts of the paper, are in logarithms to base e.

[25] We conducted additional tests to determine how Paretian slope estimates and coefficients of skewness (estimated in the logarithms) were affected by plausible individual patent valuation errors. The estimates are fairly insensitive to changes in patent values within the reported range of uncertainty.

[26] Inflating for the less than full sampling of entities holding only one full-term German patent, the total number of U.S. counterpart patents must have been approximately 604, or 1.5 percent of the 41,252 U.S. patents issued to U.S. residents in 1978 – the median year of issue for linked U.S. patents.

man data. Nonetheless, the U.S. data can be used to generate some interesting insights.

The 485 linked U.S. patents with which our U.S. survey began comprised an even smaller fraction of their applicable universe – less than two percent – than the patents in our German survey.[26] They were in effect thrice-screened – once by being applied for both at home in the United States and in Germany, once by having applications approved in both relatively stringent jurisdictions, and again by being renewed to full term in Germany.[27]

Because field interviews were not contemplated, the range of values among which respondents were asked to choose was elaborated and expanded to include at the upper bound a category, "more than \$100 million". Table 12–5 reports the distribution of outcomes. One respondent placed all three of his company's patents in the "more than \$100 million" group and added explanatory comments (invited on all questionnaires) showing a clear misinterpretation of the requested counter-factual question. Those three patents are excluded from subsequent analyses, leaving 222 valid responses.

Table 12–5: Distribution of full-term U.S. patent values

Estimated Value Range	Number	Percent
More than \$100 million	22	9.8
\$50-100 million	6	2.7
\$20-50 million	10	4.4
\$5-20 million	34	15.1
\$1-5 million	41	18.2
\$500,000 to \$1 million	30	13.3
\$100,000 to \$499,999	45	20.0
Less than \$100,000	37	16.4
Total	225	100.0

Figure 12–5 plots the cumulative value distribution on doubly logarithmic coordinates, assuming the minimum value of the least profitable inventions to have been \$40,000. The ordinary least squares log linear regression equation is given by:

$$\text{(3)}\quad \text{Log N} = \underset{[0.074]}{2.945} - \underset{[0.021]}{0.322} \log V; \qquad R^2 = 0.976,\ n = 8.$$

[27] Among other things, they were cited much more frequently in subsequent U.S. patents. See Harhoff, Narin, Scherer, and Vopel (1999).

where estimated patent value V is scaled in thousands of dollars, standard errors are given in brackets, and logarithms are to the base 10. Modest concavity is evident in the plotted points. When a quadratic value term is added, the 0.022 increase in R^2 is significant in an F-ratio test at the 0.01 level. When a linear regression is fitted only to the top four value categories (i.e., \$5 million and higher), the estimated slope is -0.429, consistent with the tail of a highly skewed Pareto-Levy distribution. However, if that right-hand tail segment is extrapolated, it implies that the single most valuable patented invention would be valued at approximately \$90 billion.[28] This is an order of magnitude greater than plausible values associated with the most profitable "blockbuster" drugs, although close to the 1997 stock market value of Microsoft (whose fortunes were based upon multiple innovations, none covered by patents in our sample). It seems probable that within the "more than \$100 million" open interval, the distribution function must become more concave, as it does within the "more than DM 5 million" interval for the German patent data.

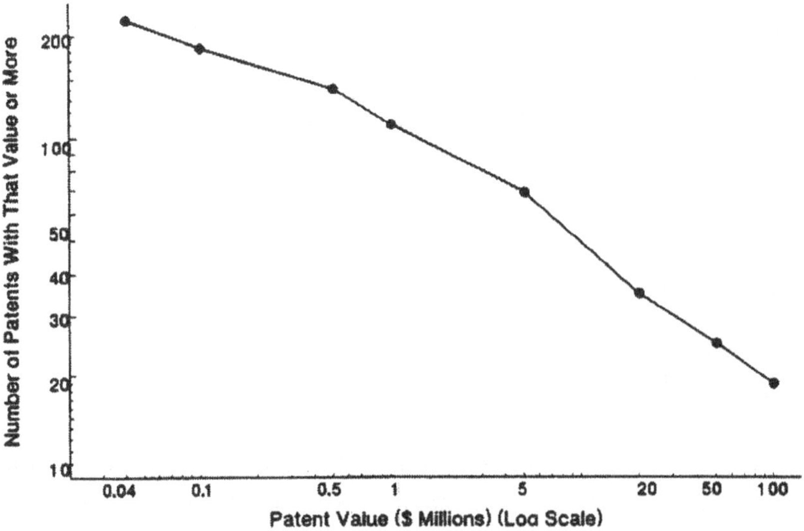

Figure 12–5: Pareto plot of U.S. patent values (N = 222)

While we do not apply the distributional tests to the U.S. data that we have used before, we can combine the patent value data from our U.S. sam-

[28] For the second to fifth most valuable patents, the predicted values are \$17.3 billion, \$7.3 billion, \$3.57 billion, and \$2.12 billion, respectively.

ple with data on R&D expenditures and other variables. For 48 sample companies with 165 linked full-term patents, it was possible to obtain the 1976 company-financed research and development expenditures which presumably gave rise to the surveyed patented inventions and their estimated value, aggregated to the company level.[29] For the closed-end intervals, values were estimated as the geometric mean of the interval bounds. For the open "more than $100 million" interval, the average patent value was assumed to be $250 million.[30] This seems a conservative estimate, considering the evidence from our German study that the average value of the most valuable patents was three to seven times the top-value interval's threshold.[31] Letting VALSUM be the estimated value of a company's patented inventions and R&D its 1976 R&D outlays, the resulting OLS regression for companies with data of acceptable quality was:

$$\text{4) } \log \text{VALSUM} = \underset{[0.553]}{-1.174} + \underset{[0.314]}{1.193} \log \text{R\&D}; \qquad R^2 = 0.239, \; n = 48;$$

with logarithms taken to base 10 and standard errors given in brackets. The relationship between value and R&D is positive as expected, and highly significant statistically. A ten percent increase in R&D outlays was accompanied on average by a 12 percent increase in the value of linked patented inventions. There is considerable "noise" in the relationship, however. The standard error of estimate is 1.07, which means that individual company profits deviated upward or downward by as much as two orders of magnitude from central tendencies implied by the regression equation. Lowering the assumed average value of the above-$100 million inventions to $200 million reduced the regression coefficient to 1.170; the t-ratio remained at 3.80. In a multiple regression including the logarithm of 1976 company sales along with R&D outlays, the sales variable had a negative sign, suggesting that larger companies do not realize higher profits from their inventions, ce-

---

[29] The source of R&D data was "What 600 Companies Spend for Research", *Business Week*, June 27, 1977, pp. 62-83.

[30] However, in one case, a lower $100 million figure was used as a result of additional information provided by the company.

[31] Inflating for sample response rates, one might predict from our results approximately 157 inventions valued at more than $5 million in the United States and 167 inventions valued at more than DM 5 million in Germany. Adjusting for market size differences and purchasing power parity exchange rates, the two most valuable cohort counts do not appear wildly inconsistent.

teris paribus[32], but both the sales variable and the increment in R^2 fell far short of statistical significance.

For the 48 companies with complete data, company-financed research and development outlays in 1976 totalled $4.82 billion, 27.6 percent of the reported $17.44 billion aggregate for all of U.S. industry in that year. Assuming an average value of $250 million for inventions valued at more than $100 million, the total value of those companies' inventions was $5.16 billion. That the estimated value of linked full-term renewed inventions, which comprised only a small fraction of all the inventions patented by responding companies, exceeded (or at least approximated) total company-financed R&D outlays suggests that on average the profit rewards to industrial R&D were appreciable.[33]

Going beyond the response limitations of our sample, 1976 R&D expenditure data were available for a total of 97 U.S. companies with U.S. patents linked to full-term renewed German patents. Those 97 corporations spent $10.69 billion on company-financed R&D in 1976 and obtained approximately 11,087 U.S. patents in 1978, including 381 patents (3.4 percent of their total 1978 patent receipts) linked to full-term German patents.[34] The OLS regression of all patents received in 1978 by the companies on their R&D spending, with standard errors in brackets, was as follows:

$$(5)\quad \text{Log ALLPATS} = \underset{[0.107]}{0.570} + \underset{[0.060]}{0.726} \log \text{R\&D}; \qquad R^2 = 0.604,\ n = 97.$$

The more R&D the companies performed, the more patents they received. However, the relationship between U.S. patents linked to German full-term renewed patents and R&D exhibits much more noise (standard errors in brackets):

$$(6)\quad \text{Log LINKPATS} = \underset{[0.112]}{-0.090} + \underset{[0.063]}{0.298} \log \text{R\&D}; \qquad R^2 = 0.191,\ n = 97.$$

---

32 See also Cohen and Klepper (1996).

33 That substantial benefits are realized from unpatented technology and run-of-the-mill patented inventions is shown by Hollander (1965).

34 The total patent counts were derived using the U.S. Patent Office's annual Index of Patents for 1978. Since the counts for subsidiaries receiving patents in other than the parent's name were undoubtedly incomplete, the 11,087 estimate is biased downward.

Indeed, the relationship is of about the same strength as regression (4), relating (for a sub-sample of companies) the *value* of linked patented inventions and R&D.

We return now to survey data disaggregated to the level of individual linked patents. For most of the patents, information was available on the professional specialty of the questionnaire respondent, the industry from which the invention originated, and the nature of the invention. These data allowed us to explore three questions that have been of considerable interest in the economic analysis of patents and innovations.

We first considered the question whether patented products are more valuable than patented processes. Among other things, 202 inventions could be coded as pertaining primarily to a product sold by the company or to a production process used by the company. Of those 202, 27.7 percent were process inventions – a figure closely comparable to estimates from earlier studies.[35] We could not detect any strong evidence that process inventions are less valuable – the differences were not statistically significant. Being subject to less market risk than product inventions, process inventions may also have less variable values, although the group variances fall just short of significance at the 0.05 level in an F-ratio test.

Secondly, as with the German data, we also tested for respondent biases and industry effects. We summarize the main results here without presenting the full regression tables. Controlling for industry effects, process inventions are found to be two-thirds of a value group less profitable on average. Drug and surgical supply inventions are significantly more profitable; electronic inventions nearly a category group less profitable. As in the German sample, patent attorneys appear to make relatively conservative estimates, all else equal. Unlike the German results, however, inventors reported relatively less valuable inventions, probably because few of the inventor respondents were employed by companies with a strong commercial orientation.

Finally, we considered the impact of patent protection on the profitability of intrinsically valuable inventions. To determine whether the strength of patent protection was contributing importantly to our survey results, indices from the so-called "Yale Survey" of the effectiveness of patents in protecting the competitive advantages from product and process inventions in narrowly defined industries were linked to our patent data, depending upon the line of

[35] See e.g. Scherer (1982).

business in which an invention arose.[36] Since separate Yale survey indices existed for products and processes, the coding reflected that distinction. To avoid collinearity with the variables used in the Yale coding, the PROCESS dummy was excluded, as were industry-specific dummy variables. Where YALE is the matched Yale survey appropriability index, the resulting regression was (standard errors in brackets):

$$(7)\quad \underset{[0.731]}{\text{VALUE} = 3.245} + \underset{[0.139]}{0.276\ \text{YALE}} + \underset{[0.639]}{0.301\ \text{RDEXEC}}$$

$$+ \underset{[2.120]}{0.636\ \text{INVENT}} - \underset{[0.398]}{0.991\ \text{PAT}};$$

$$R^2 = 0.080,\quad n = 194.$$

Greater effectiveness of patent protection in appropriating the benefits from innovation is found to increase the reported value of our survey inventions, although only by about one-fourth of a value group. Evidently, most of the value differences are specific to the inventions and not the result of generalized patent strength variations. The conservative bias in patent attorneys' responses is also apparent in regression (7).

12.4 Implications

Previous studies have found the distribution of patented invention values to be highly skew. We confirm that conclusion, but also contribute a new insight: when patent values are measured relative to the counter-factual of being deprived of an invention's use, rather than having the invention lapse into the public domain (as in patent renewal studies), much higher extreme values emerge. Analyzing the renewal of German patents applied for between 1952 and 1972, Pakes (1986, p. 777) estimated the *maximum* patent value to be roughly $420,000 (in 1980 dollars). Our surveyed maxima are several hundred times greater. Subdividing German patent data into industry groups, Lanjouw (1998, Table 4 estimated an average value per patent for the top 0.1 percent of patents to lie between DM 191,000 and DM 433,000 (at 1975 price levels). Since resident German patent recipients obtained

[36] See Levin *et al.* (1987). The indices varied from 6.88 (in agricultural chemicals) and 6.53 (in pharmaceuticals) down to 2.00 (in electric batteries). Higher values denote greater effectiveness of patents in appropriating the benefits from innovation.

9,826 patents in 1980, the comparable top 0.1 percent cohort for our sample period includes ten patents. We find the average value of those patented inventions to have been DM 48 million if the most extreme observation is excluded or DM 193 million if it is included – at least two orders of magnitude larger.

Among several plausible alternative skew distributions, a two-parameter log normal distribution appears to provide the best fit to our patented invention value data. Although the log normal distribution has better-behaved asymptotic properties than the Pareto-Levy alternative, the observed distribution remains highly skew. The most valuable five percent of all renewed German patents accounted for 46 to 61 percent of total sample patent value, depending upon whether the largest outlier is excluded or included. In the U.S. sample, the 19 patents valued at more than $100 million (8.5 percent of the sample by number) accounted for 76 to 80 percent of total sample value, depending upon whether the average value of those patents is assumed to be 2.0 or 2.5 times the threshold value. The facile convergence to stable means sought in R&D risk-hedging through portfolio strategies operates at best imperfectly. Investing in technological innovation must be viewed as intrinsically risky, even if (as our U.S. value sums suggest) profitable in the aggregate.

Given the highly skewed nature of patent values, it has also become clear that simply counting patents in an attempt to measure the "intellectual capital" of corporations is a futile undertaking. Mere counts are likely to reveal very little of the underlying value of a patent portfolio.[37] In related research (Harhoff, Scherer and Vopel 2003), we have investigated an alternate route – we discuss correlates of patent value that can be used to weight patents in order to approximate the value of patent portfolios. It turns out that the researcher's problem of assessing patent value *ex post* can be resolved to some extent; it should not be surprising that those correlates which help to identify patent value typically have a highly skewed distribution themselves. In the absence of such *ex post* measures, assessing patent value *ex ante* remains a daunting task.

In combination with other evidence on new pharmaceutical compounds and the outcomes of high-technology venture investments (Scherer 1998), we now possess a clear picture of the range of profit or quasi-rent distribution shapes resulting from investments in innovation. Those distributions are

---

[37] Griliches (1990) also comments on the measurement question and is sceptical about counts of patents as measures of knowledge capital. See also Lanjouw, Pakes and Putnam (1998).

the result of stochastic processes played out as the menu of technological possibilities is tapped, market prospects are tested, and competitive forces impinge. In related research[38], the data employed in this paper have been used to identify likely stochastic processes consistent with the observed profit distributions.

A final conclusion is noteworthy. In a world with skew-distributed outcomes of the R&D and innovation process, there is very little room for "picking winners" – either at the business or the public policy level. First, managers in large corporations seeking to reach some degree of risk-hedging within the firm will be forced to build relatively large portfolios of R&D projects. Second, society at large will be better off conducting contests among many projects, e.g. in the form of newly founded technology-oriented firms, than with trying to assess the value of an invention or a startup firm early on. We can also learn from these results that a high rate of failing projects is not necessarily a signal of failure of policy – one cannot escape the fundamental distributional properties of R&D and inventions.[39] Hence, a large share of failures or low-value projects is the natural concomitant of having a few outstanding successes.

---

[38] See Scherer, Harhoff and Kukies (2000).

[39] Other policy implications of the skewed distribution of innovation returns are discussed in Scherer and Harhoff (2000).

Technical Appendix

Estimation of Distribution Parameters

Using the data described in the body of the paper, we estimate the parameters of Pareto-Levy, log-normal and Singh-Maddala distributions. The distribution function for the Pareto-Levy is given by:

$$\psi(x|\alpha) = \left(\frac{X}{X_0}\right)^{-\alpha} = x^{-\alpha}$$

where $x = X / X_0$ is defined over the interval $[1,\infty]$. X is the actual valuation for the patent, and X_0 corresponds to the minimum valuation for a patent in the sample. The parameter α determines the slope of the distribution function in a log(value)-log(rank) plot.

The Singh-Maddala function is a three-parameter distribution with cumulative distribution function

$$\Sigma(a,b,q) = 1 - \frac{1}{\left(1+(y/b)^a\right)^q} \quad .$$

where b is a scale parameter and a and q determine the shape of the distribution function.

The third function under consideration is the log-normal whose probability function is given by the standard normal cumulative function evaluated at $(\ln X - \mu)/\sigma$ where μ is the mean of the log-normal distribution and σ is the corresponding standard deviation.

To obtain the estimates in Part A of Table 12–4, we used the 772 patents for which we obtained valuations in our survey to estimate parameters from truncated distributions. We assume that the value of the patent right is bounded from below at DM 23,000, i.e. the group for which respondents gave a minimum counter-factual sales price of less than DM 100,000 is assumed to have values in the interval [23000,100000]. The choice of the lower bound is somewhat arbitrary, but approximates the discounted sum of renewal fees in 1995 currency units (in order to be consistent with our patent value estimates).

Each observation enters the likelihood function as the probability of observing a patent right's value to be in a known value interval. The interval observation comes either from the first-stage survey, or it has been obtained in the second-stage interviews. In cases where the interviews elicited only a point estimate, we assume that the interval is defined by the point estimate minus or plus 10 percent of the point estimate.

Thus, instead of observing the actual values X_i, we actually observe an upper bound B_{Ui} and a lower bound B_{Li} such that $B_{Ui} \leq X_i < B_{Li}$. Hence, the likelihood function (neglecting constant terms) is given by

$$log\,L(\theta) = \sum_{i=1}^{N_1} log\left(\frac{F(B_{Ui},\theta) - F(B_{Li},\theta)}{1 - F(T,\theta)}\right) + \sum_{i=N_1+1}^{N_1+N_2} log\left(1 - \frac{F(B_{Li},\theta)}{1 - F(T,\theta)}\right)$$

Here $F(\cdot)$ is the cumulative distribution function, θ denotes a vector of parameters, and T is the truncation point, assumed to be equal to DM 23,000. The values of observations $(1,\ldots,N_1)$ fall into intervals that are bounded from above and below, while the values of observations $(N_1+1,\ldots,N_2)$ are bounded from below, but no upper bound has been established. The latter case occurs whenever we do not obtain detailed interview information on patents with first-stage valuations of greater than DM 5 million.

In the case of the Pareto-Levy distribution, the above expression simplifies considerably, since the truncated Pareto-Levy is again a Pareto-Levy distribution. Therefore, the likelihood is given by

$$log\,L(\alpha) = \sum_{i=1}^{N_1} log\left(b_{Li}{}^{-\alpha} - b_{Ui}{}^{-\alpha}\right) + \sum_{i=N_1+1}^{N_1+N_2} log\left(b_{Li}{}^{-\alpha}\right)$$

where $b_{Ui} = B_{Ui}/X_0$ and $b_{Li} = B_{Li}/X_0$ and constant terms are again neglected.

We estimate the parameters by implementing the likelihood function in a non-linear optimization routine, using Newton-Raphson numerical techniques to obtain numerical solutions. The standard errors are computed from a variance-covariance matrix obtained by multiplication of the score vectors. For each distribution, we perform the estimation with and without the most valuable patent in our sample in order to explore the sensitivity of our results to that particular observation. This is an informal test of robustness, since the estimated parameters of the distribution should not change much if a particular observation is taken from the sample, assuming that the distributional assumption is correct.

In Part B of Table 12–4, we take into account that the actual number of German-owned patents not renewed to full term is actually known. For the

Singh-Maddala and the log-normal distribution, we assume that patent values are non-zero and positive. The likelihood function is now given by

$$\log L(\theta) = \sum_{i=1}^{N_1} \log\left(F\left(B_{Ui},\theta\right) - F\left(B_{Li},\theta\right)\right) + \sum_{i=N_1+1}^{N_1+N_2} \log\left(1 - F\left(B_{Li},\theta\right)\right) +$$

$$+ \sum_{i=N_1+N_2+1}^{N} \log\left(F\left(B_{Ui},\theta\right)\right)$$

where the third group describes the patents that were not renewed to full term – in their case, we only know the upper bound of DM 23,000. For estimating the parameters of the Pareto-Levy distribution, we assume that patent values in the latter group range from DM 1 to DM 23,000. Note that the lower bound can in principle be estimated, but we have relied thus far on the assumptions described here.

For computing a goodness-of-fit measure, we use up to 11 value intervals which are defined by the threshold values DM 23000, DM 100000, DM 400000, DM 1 million, DM 5 million, DM 10 million, DM 20 million, DM 40 million, DM 80 million and DM 120 million. The Pearson Chi-Square is computed as

$$N\sum_{j=1}^{J}\left(\frac{n_j}{N} - P_j\left(\hat{\theta}\right)\right)^2 \Big/ P_j\left(\hat{\theta}\right)$$

where *j* denotes the interval, n_j/N is the actual share of patents observed to be in interval *j*, and $P_j\left(\hat{\theta}\right)$ is the predicted share of observations in the interval. This statistic is distributed as a Chi-Squared random variable with *J-k-1* degrees of freedom, where *k* is the number of distribution parameters estimated.

12.5 Literature References

Bryson, M.C. (1974). 'Heavy-tailed Distributions: Properties and Test', *Technometrics*, Vol. 16, pp. 61-68.

Cohen, W.M. and Klepper, S. (1996). 'A Reprise of Size and R&D', *Economic Journal*, Vol. 106, pp. 925-951.

D'Agostino, R.B. and Stephens, M.A. (1986). *Goodness-of-Fit Techniques*. New York: Marcel Dekker.

Dernburg, T. and Gharrity, N. (1961). 'A Statistical Analysis of Patent Renewal Data for Three Countries', *Patent, Trademark, and Copyright Journal*, Vol. 5, pp. 340-361.

Esteban, J.M. (1986). 'Income Share Elasticity and the Size Distribution of Income', *International Economic Review*, Vol. 27, pp. 439-444.

Griliches, Z. (1990). 'Patent Statistics as Economic Indicators: A Survey', *Journal of Economic Literature*, Vol. 28, pp. 1661-1707.

Harhoff, D., Scherer, F.M. and Vopel, K. (2003). 'Citations, Family Size, Opposition and the Value of Patent Rights', *Research Policy*, Vol. 32, No. 8, pp. 1343-1363

Harhoff, D., Narin, F., Scherer, F.M. and Vopel, K. (1999). 'Citation Frequency and the Value of Patented Inventions, *Review of Economics and Statistics*, Vol. 81, No. 3, pp. 511-515.

Hollander, S. (1965). *The Sources of Increased Efficiency: A Study of DuPont Rayon Plants*. Cambridge: MIT Press.

IVA (1993). *Profit from Innovation: A Comparison of Swedish and Japanese Intellectual Property Management*. Stockholm: Royal Swedish Academy of Engineering Science.

Johnson, N.L., Kotz, S. and Balakrishan, N. (1994). *Continuous Univariate Distributions*. Vol. I, 2nd ed.. New York: Wiley.

Kloek, T. and Van Dijk, H.K. (1978). 'Efficient Estimation of Income Distribution Parameters', *Journal of Econometrics*, Vol. 8, pp. 61-74.

Lanjouw, J.O. (1998). 'Patent Protection in the Shadow of Infringement: Simulation Estimations of Patent Value', *Review of Economic Studies*, Vol. 65. pp. 671-710.

Lanjouw, J.O., Pakes, A. and Putnam, J. (1998). 'How to Count Patents and Value Intellectual Property: Uses of Patent Renewal and Application Data', *Journal of Industrial Economics*, Vol. XLVI, No. 4, pp. 405-433.

Levin, R.C., Klevorick, A., Nelson, R.R. and Winter, S.G. (1987). 'Appropriating the Returns from Industrial Research and Development', *Brookings Papers on Economic Activity*, No. 3, pp. 783-820.

McDonald, J.B. (1984). 'Some Generalized Functions for the Size Distribution of Income', *Econometrica*, vol. 52 (May 1984), pp. 647-663.

McDonald, J.B. and Ransom, M.R. (1979). 'Functional Forms, Estimation Techniques and the Distribution of Income', *Econometrica*, Vol. 47, pp. 1513-1525.

Nordhaus, W.D. (1989). 'Comment', *Brookings Papers on Economic Activity: Micro-economics*, pp. 320-325.

Pakes, A. (1986). 'Patents as Options: Some Estimates of the Value of Holding European Patent Stocks', *Econometrica*, Vol. 54, pp. 755-784.

Pakes, A. and Schankerman, M. (1984). 'The Rate of Obsolescence of Patents, Research Gestation Lags, and the Private Rate of Return to Research Resources', in Zvi Griliches, ed., *R&D, Patents, and Productivity*. Chicago: University of Chicago Press, pp. 73-88.

Patent- und Musterrecht (1995). 3rd edition; Munich: Beck-Texte.

Putnam, J. (1996). 'The Value of International Patent Protection', Unpublished Ph.D. Dissertation, Yale University.

Schankerman, M. and Pakes, A. (1986). 'Estimates of the Value of Patent Rights in European Countries during the Post-1950 Period', *Economic Journal*, Vol. 97, pp. 1-25.

Scherer, F.M. (1982). 'Inter-Industry Technology Flows in the United States', *Research Policy*, Vol. 11, pp. 227-245.

Scherer, F.M. (1998). 'The Size Distribution of Profits from Innovation', *Annales d'Economie et Statistique*, Vol. 49/50, pp. 496-516.

Scherer, F.M. and Harhoff, D. (2000). 'Technology Policy Implications for a World with Skew-Distributed Outcomes', *Research Policy*, Vol. 29, pp. 559-566, 2000.

Scherer, F.M., Harhoff, D. and Kukies, J. (2000). 'Uncertainty and the Size Distribution of Rewards from Technological Innovation', *Journal of Evolutionary Economics*, pp. 175-200.

Singh, S.K. and Maddala, G.S. (1976). 'A Function for Size Distribution of Incomes', *Econometrica*, Vol. 44, pp. 963-970.

Tetlock, P.E. and Belkin, A. (1996). 'Counterfactual Thought Experiments in World Politics', *Social Science Research Council Items*, Vol. 50 (December).

Chapter 13

UNLOCKING THE POTENTIAL OF INTELLECTUAL PROPERTY

William Kingston
School of Business Studies, Trinity College, Dublin, Ireland

Chapter Contents:

Abstract: Intellectual property's development has been retarded by restrictions, which effectively shoehorn new ways of inventing and new kinds of information into a dual paradigm of patent and copyright law, no matter how badly they fit. However, repairs to the system are possible, and include means of bringing patents into line with contemporary innovative reality; a practical solution to the notoriously excessive cost of resolving disputes; and adding a financial dimension to time in the measurement of grants.

Keywords: Innovation protection; measurement of grants; compulsory dispute arbitration

13.1 Introduction

Intellectual property protection has never been so much used as it is today, and at the same time it has never been so widely criticised since the nineteenth century controversy which all but destroyed the patent system in

O. Granstrand (ed.), Economics, Law and Intellectual Property, 311-329.

Europe (cf. Machlup and Penrose 1950). There is an increasingly influential body of writing, which argues that the system is progressively less capable of meeting the demands which are being made on it. One of the earliest diagnoses was the following:

> "The nineteenth century vision that subdivided world intellectual property law into discrete and mutually exclusive compartments for industrial and artistic property has irretrievably broken down. The theory that the classical patent and copyright models coherently address the way intellectual creations behave has been discredited by its inability to deal adequately with the behavior of many commercially valuable, cutting-edge intellectual creations". (Kronz 1983, pp. 178, 180)

In endorsing this, Reichman, an equally perceptive later critic, stressed that

> "These recent technological creations account for an ever-growing share of the gross domestic products of both developed and developing countries." (Reichman 1994 p. 2500)

Intellectual property, it seems, is "frozen" into a dual patent-copyright paradigm, into which new ways of inventing and new kinds of information have to be fitted somehow if they are to receive protection. There is no shortage of evidence that this process is becoming more and more difficult, and that the results are correspondingly less satisfactory. In Thurow's summing up,

> "The world's one-dimensional intellectual property system must be overhauled to create a more differentiated one. Trying to squeeze today's developments into yesterday's system of intellectual property rights simply won't work. One size does not fit all." (Thurow 1997, p. 103)

Not alone is intellectual property doing a poor job of protecting information that should be protected, and leaving all other information free to be used by all; its cost is escalating rapidly. Just how serious this is, has been recognized in an official U.S. Report, which stated that

> "patent litigation has become an increasingly inefficient, ineffective and undesirable means of resolving patent related disputes...The Commission fears that, unless the problems of cost and delay in patent litigation are addressed now, the central purpose of the patent system to provide an effective incentive for development and commercialization of new technology will be seriously eroded. Such an erosion could well prove a threat to the very existence of the patent system..."
> (Commission on Patent Law Reform 1992 pp. 78, 76).

13.2 Failure to Develop

This progressive divergence between new ways of producing information and new kinds of information, on the one hand, and ways of protecting them, on the other, is evident in each of the main types of intellectual property and their respective subject matter. These originated in Enlightenment thinking, and reflect a particular view of the nature and value of individual human rights. According to this, invention, for example, is the act of an individual, and the protection which patents were designed to provide relates to *individual* invention. However, during the nineteenth century, invention became a corporate matter, the result of large-scale, purposive investment in research and development. This change was so radical as to require a new kind of patent protection. What actually happened was that the divergence was allowed to grow until the traditional system became all but unworkable through judicial recognition of its incoherence. The special need to protect the results of pharmaceutical research associated with the antibiotic revolution was then dealt with by introducing the "inventive step" or "non-obviousness" criterion. (The full story of this is in Kingston 2000a.) This operates through the pretence that invention through investment remains invention of the kind for which the patent system was originally designed. But because it was no more than a "running repair" and not the radical overhaul which was needed, it has resulted in an entirely new set of problems, so that the system is once again "in crisis" (Vaver, 2000).

13.2.1 Copyright

Modern copyright was originally designed to protect individual creative works. Much of what it is now used for, however, is the result of large-scale investment, as in the motion picture and television industries. In the same way, computer software developed from being a simple adjunct to mainframe computers and from individuals tinkering with the early microcomputer kits of Steve Jobs, into the huge international industry that it is today. As well as being different in scale from what copyright was intended to protect, computer software is also a new type of information. Certainly, this is in the form of text, but it differs crucially from other kinds of text in that it "*performs*" (Reichman 1994). As such, its need for protection is quite different from that required by authors and artists. It needed (and needs) its own special form of protection which recognises this, and almost an entire issue of the Columbia Law Review rehearses only a few of many sets of proposals for the shape this ought to take (cf. Reichman 1994). Instead, protection of software was forced into copyright, with all kinds of unfortunate results. The most articulate critic of copyright protection of software is Aharonian (2001) His case against it rests on legal grounds. The economic case is reflected in the way firms, which produce computer programs, or motion pictures typically use payback periods of between 5 and 10 years for their investments in these. It is consequently quite absurd that their copyright protection should last for up to 120 years.

13.2.2 Patents and biotechnology

Biotechnology has some analogies to software (DNA can be considered as a cell's "operating system"). It, too, produces a quite new kind of information, which clearly called for its own special type of protection. However, just as software was forced into copyright, biotechnology has been forced to use patents. It is widely considered that in this case, the patent system's criteria come far too close to protecting pure science, with the ability to patent research instruments being a cause of particular concern.

Patent protection in its present form is inappropriate for genomics for three main reasons. Firstly, immediate application of the criteria for patenting pre-empts the careful consideration, which should precede any decisions about what information is to be protected and how this is to be done. Should protection be available as early as possible (as the genomics firms want) or further downstream in the drug-discovery process (which would suit the pharmaceutical firms) or only when an actual product has been produced? Or, indeed, should biotechnology not be protected in any sense akin to patents at all, as many – especially in Europe – think? In an entirely new field such as this, there are indeed grounds for caution, lest whole areas of development in the life sciences might be under threat of monopolisation by individual firms. This would also carry with it the danger of slower development through lack of stimulus from competition.

Secondly, commercialization of the results of genomic research may require the use of a number of gene fragments, so that the holder of a patent on a single one of these can be in a classical "blocking" position. As Heller and Eisenberg (1998) have pointed out, this can make the patent system an impediment to innovation rather than a stimulus to it. The third reason why patents are particularly unsuitable for biotechnology is that so much of the research is publicly funded, and it is impossible to be precise about the balance between the public and private contributions in any disclosure for which a patent is granted.

13.2.3 Implications for University Research

Indeed, this is only one aspect of widespread concern about a growing tendency to grant intellectual property rights "on what used to be considered as 'science' and introduced into the public domain" (Mazzolini and Nelson 1998). It is all the stronger because so much of this research is publicly funded. It is widely held that information, which is the result of such funding, should instead be made available as quickly and extensively as possible, as happens with the traditional practice of journal publication. Also, to the extent that university research is funded by parties which intend to patent the results, they naturally want to place restrictions on the researchers lest patentability should be endangered by prior disclosure. These restrictions can even go so far as preventing them from telling their colleagues what they are working on. This is undermining the free discussion and exchange of ideas and information, which is the traditional basis of the Academy.

13.2.4 Databases

Yet another new kind of information is what is included in electronic databases. It, too, needed its own appropriate type of protection, and it fact did get it in Europe through Commission Directive 96/9. This partially broke out of the traditional paradigm, by accepting for the first time the important principle that investment *per se* was a sufficient basis for the grant of protection. Unfortunately, the benefit of this has been overshadowed by a disastrous provision (inserted as a result of lobbying by publishers) which offers these publishers the potential to obtain perpetual monopolies on their data. A database developer is to be given a 15-year monopoly initially, but indefinite renewals are possible as a result of "substantial new investment to improve the database". This Article 7 (3) has rightly been described by Reichman and Samuelson as "a monstrous caricature of intellectual property laws" (1997 p. 164). Incidentally, there is no better guide to the bizarre way in which changes in intellectual property laws are brought about, than Samuelson's 1997 article on the WIPO Diplomatic Conference. This describes the efforts of publishers to obtain the same type of database protection in the United States as the European Commission has so generously provided for them.

There is also a disturbing link to biotechnology in this development. The same firms as are building up portfolios of biotechnology patents are also developing biotechnology databases. Pharmaceutical firms are already subscribing heavily for access to these, whose developers will certainly make "substantial and continuing investments" to improve them. This could extend their protection indefinitely. What are the implications of private tend their protection indefinitely. What are the implications of private firms consequently having monopolies forever on their collections of genetic information?

13.2.5 Complex technologies

Kash and Roycroft (1998) contrast these with simple technologies (which are characterized by being capable of being fully understood by a single individual) and have demonstrated how rapidly their economic importance has been growing. Empirical research has also shown that they use intellectual property in an altogether different way than that for which it was originally designed. It is now much more a bargaining currency to prevent "lock-out" from use of state-of-the-art components developed by competitors, than it is a stimulus to R&D. For example, when applied in a complex technology, the inventive step criterion allows huge numbers of patents to be granted for changes which merit no special protection (cf. Kash and Kingston 2001). In the hands of a firm with powerful resources for litigation, however, even technically worthless patents have to be treated respectfully. In complex technologies, patents are also being increasingly used to bargain with standards regulators, so as to have an industry standard incorporate as much as possible of a firm's technology – yet another use which diverges from their economic justification. Indeed, the large firms that are characteristic of complex technologies already have so much of other kinds of market power that they could easily innovate without any intellectual property at all.

13.3 Protecting Innovation Directly

These and other problems with intellectual property will persist and even become more severe, until the shift from individual to corporate generation of information is adequately recognised in the law. The logic of this recognition points towards protection of invention and innovation on the basis of no other criteria than *commercial* novelty and investment, as argued by Kronz and myself in *Direct Protection of Innovation* (1987). This requires bringing market factors into the test for whether protection is to be given or not, and relating this test specifically to investment.

Such a reformed type of protection would have innovation rather than invention as its subject matter. A further advantage of this approach is that it means that whatever protection is granted also captures some of the *tacit* information in the marketed innovation. Kronz (1983) had proposed direct protection of innovation for doing this through the grant of "Innovation Patents" and I suggested the slightly different "Innovation Warrants" (Kingston 1981, 1987). The criterion for grant, which is the strictly commercial one of "non-availability in the ordinary course of trade", is common to both.

13.4 Reducing the Cost of Resolving Disputes

The cost of obtaining intellectual property is only a minor deterrent to investment in innovation compared with the cost of enforcing it. In addition to the measurable costs of litigation, there are many others that are very substantial and that certainly have important social implications. These are the burdens in terms of distraction, diversion of energy, and misdirection of creativity that any intellectual property dispute imposes on innovatory firms. Worst of all, litigation costs are destructive of the exceptionally valuable contributions to innovation that smaller firms have proved they can make. It is obvious that the measurable costs of prosecuting or defending an action for infringement of intellectual property are far beyond the resources of all but the largest firms, apart from the fact that the burden of the costs that cannot be measured (such as distraction from more immediately paying tasks) falls most heavily on smaller ones (Kingston 2001, *passim*).

As to the underlying cause, an EU expert group reported recently that it was "convinced that the main element in the excessive cost of resolving IP disputes is the use of the *ordinary* Courts to deal with what are essentially technical matters" (ETAN 1999 p. 26). In other similar areas of economic life, inappropriateness of litigation has led to growth in use of alternative dispute resolution mechanisms of which the most widely used is expert arbitration. It is only very rarely that disputes over technical contracts end up in the Courts, because they invariably include clauses providing for this. However, arbitration is almost never used in intellectual property, because large firms do not wish to give up their advantage in terms of ability to intimidate competitors through the threat of litigation costs. Arbitration arrangements established by the World Intellectual Property Organization some years ago, for example, have been scarcely used at all for patents. If the advantages of arbitration are to be achieved, therefore, it will have to be made compulsory. Also, since the TRIPs section of the World Trade Organization agreement requires that there should be access to Courts of Justice for settlement of intellectual property disputes, there would have to be the right of appeal to a Court from an arbitration decision.

Both requirements could be reconciled through the provision of legal aid for the respondent party (i.e. the party which accepts the arbitrator's decision) in the event of an appeal. This would cost very little in practice, because the likelihood of getting a decision of expert technical arbitrators changed by appeal to a Court is so low. The International Chamber of Commerce, which handles what is probably the biggest arbitration portfolio in the world, reports only a 1% rate of successful appeals. For intellectual property specifically, there is compelling evidence from the records of the "Interferences" system in the United States Patent and Trademark Office. This is precisely a system of compulsory arbitration of pre-grant intellectual property issues by experts, and it provides an actual large-scale working precedent or model for what is now proposed. The expert Board of Patent Appeals and Interferences delivers between forty and fifty final decisions of this kind each year. Just over one-third of these are appealed to the courts, but *only 5 percent* of them are either wholly or even partially reversed (Calvert and Sofocleous, 1989, 1992, 1995).

This performance of compulsory expert arbitration in the U.S. Interference procedure is therefore a good augury of how well a similar system could work for the settlement of disputes *after* grant of exclusive privilege. Claims for legal aid should be very few. No financially weaker firm would ever appeal, because to do so would be to move the conflict on to ground where its stronger opponent already has the advantage; on the other hand, it is likely that the financially stronger firms would appeal only in rare cases. This is both because they would have a poor chance of winning (having lost the expert arbitration) and because legal aid for their weaker opponent (because he has not appealed, not because he is weaker) would have deprived them of power to intimidate (cf. Kingston 2000b).

13.4.1 Voluntary initiatives

In the United States, the National Patent Board has recently been established by a number of large firms in an attempt to deal with the high cost of resolving intellectual property disputes. Members agree to go to expert arbitration in the first instance, and a party which appeals from an arbitration decision to the Courts, has to pay all the accrued arbitration costs of both sides.

Large-scale empirical research for the EU on small-firm patentees in Europe has revealed considerable support for a "Patent Defence Union". Membership of this would require acceptance of arbitration of any dispute with another member, and the Direction of the pool would have funds to litigate selected cases when a member is in dispute with a non-member and the non-member refuses arbitration. It is believed that the cumulative effect of such cases should significantly lessen intimidation through the threat of litigation costs (Kingston 2001).

13.5 A Financial Dimension in Measuring Grants

Direct protection of innovation and compulsory arbitration of disputes would go a long way towards providing a much wider range of firms than at present with the level of protection for high-risk investment in research and development, which they need. These changes could hardly fail to improve investment incentives greatly. Direct protection of innovation need not interfere in any way with existing patent arrangements for chemical inventions, since these work well, and the proposals for resolving disputes could be applied immediately with advantage to all types of intellectual property. Their success would then enable a more radical reform of intellectual property law to be undertaken.

This is to bring money into the measurement of any privilege granted. The proper measure of any economic privilege, in fact, can only be money – time is only a surrogate, and a poor one at that. No doubt when the different kinds of intellectual property originated, any measure other than time was out of the question, since accounting techniques were undeveloped. But it is not only in respect of science that Kelvin's principle that "we advance according to the precision of our measures" operates, and to persist with such a poor measure as time today is simply to ignore all the achievements of Accountancy since. It can only be sheer accident that any period of time, which is the same for all technologies (as the 20-year patent term is today) could provide just the incentive that is required to bring about a particular investment at high risk. Many of the problems of intellectual property rights, especially in new fields such as biotechnology and information processing, can be shown to be actually *caused* by using time on its own as the measure of a patent or copyright grant. The accounting techniques are now available to change the measure of the grant of exclusive privilege from time, to time calibrated by money, without reducing incentives to invest in R&D, and with strengthened support for innovation, through a system which combines compulsory licences with *capital* payments (Kingston 1994).

Compulsory licencing may be objected to by users of patents on the ground that it would deprive them of the essence of a patent grant, which is a monopoly right. In fact, it is ironic that if the existing patent system actually worked in practice as it is supposed to do in theory, there could be even less innovation than there is. Empirical research has shown that in contrast to a

U.S. patent's former nominal 17-year monopoly term, the average period of effective protection is no more than three years (Levin *et al.* 1987). Worse still, the cost to an imitator of producing a competitive product within that period has been shown to be less than what the invention had cost the originating firm (Mansfield *et al.* 1981).

Instead of relying for innovation diffusion on the failure of the patent system to deliver the protection it promises, therefore, it would clearly be better to use a compulsory licence system to get the process of diffusion started as early as possible. This would open the way for competitive firms to explore several different trajectories of incremental change, to the undoubted benefit of product quality, employment and economic growth. Of course, there would be no point in doing this if it meant reducing the incentive to invest in inventing, since in that event there would be fewer or even no inventions worth diffusing. The problem is therefore to reconcile the need for the quickest and widest possible diffusion of inventions to the market, with maintaining, indeed improving, incentives to invent and innovate.

13.5.1 Practical measuring arrangements

Ideally, any exclusive privilege should last until its possessor has made profits from his innovation which amount to some socially acceptable multiple of the investment, which was made in it at high risk. However, *ex post* measurement of this kind has been found to be impractical. Measuring *ex ante,* i.e. establishing what it had cost to produce an innovation, is much more practical and less susceptible to fraud. If combined with compulsory licencing, it would open the way to allowing a competitor to share the use of any information generated by an innovator, provided that he also shares retrospectively in both the investment which the originator had to make in order to bring the information into being, *and the risk of that investment.*

Socially acceptable "multiples" of the investment, which had been made to produce the information that is to be the subject of the licence, would be officially prescribed for the relevant capital payments. These multiples could be varied according to the needs and risks of different industries and according to the stage of invention or innovation reached when the licence is taken out, but of course there would be no question of adjusting the multiple to individual firms, any more than a term of intellectual property would be adjusted today. The cost to which the multiple applies should be that of a firm's entire portfolio of R&D projects, since a single success is certain to reflect many failures, whose costs should also be taken into account. It should not be difficult to establish this figure, since if obtaining protection is going to depend upon keeping precise records, firms will make sure that this is done. As Merges has pointed out, proving such costs

> "will not be difficult or burdensome. Patent applicants and patentees collect this information anyway for a variety of reasons, including 1) tax benefits, 2) internal cost accounting, 3) use in project evaluation, 4) use in licensing negotiations and the like. Patentees appear to have no trouble showing research expenditures at the damages stage of a patent infringement suit, and...such information has been introduced in some cases to show the nonobviousness of the invention involved. Simply adding one more reason to collect data on the cost of a research project does not appear to pose a major problem" (Merges 1992, p. 55).

It is also the case that analysts of high-tech stocks on the Nasdaq market are increasingly paying attention to price/R&D ratios, which in itself must be forcing innovatory firms towards more precise recording of their investments in research.

13.5.2 Capital payments, not royalties

The feature of the proposal that payment for licences would be in the form not of royalties but of *capital* is an important one. It is an essential part of the arrangements, which ensure that compulsory licencing does not reduce the incentive to undertake the high risk of investment in invention and innovation. Given this condition, enabling a competitor to use information, which another has generated, carries with it an absolute requirement for retrospective sharing of both investment and its risk. The investment is now a sunk cost for the originator. There is no reason why sharing in this by a licencee should be dependent on that licencee's future success in using the information, as would be the case with royalty payments.

The more important any information is seen to be by competitors, the more licences will be requested for it, and as each licence would earn a capital payment, the originator could find that his risky investment was very well rewarded indeed. This reward might be much greater than could have been achieved with a patent monopoly, because several trajectories of incremental development would be exploited simultaneously.

It is in the public interest that the information should be exploited along as many such trajectories as possible. A licencee who has made a capital payment for access to information is more likely to be motivated to get the best possible value out of the information, which this has bought, by doing the necessary development work on it. This motivation is not necessarily present to the same extent when payment for the licence is contingent, i.e. through royalties. Firms which can licence information on a royalty basis, may be content simply to produce clones of the originator's product, which would reduce the returns, not only to the originator, but also to all his licencees. The public interest is best served when the firms, which do obtain compulsory licences, are those which will themselves do R&D to exploit independent trajectories of incremental innovation. Having invested a significant capital sum for the licence adds to the incentive for this. Another incentive is the knowledge that this will give them an advantage when they have to face competition from firms which are copiers and nothing else once the period of exclusive privilege ends (which perhaps should be earlier than for a patent today).

13.5.3 Empirical research

To investigate this idea empirically, it was possible to calculate the risks and degree of success of investments in 23,000 cases of the U.S. Small Business Innovation Research Programs, stage by stage from ideas to products on the market (Kingston 1994). The results suggest that if both parties are to be put on an equal footing, a competitor who takes a licence from an originator at the prototype stage should pay a multiple of 8 times the originator's investment to that point. If the licence is sought only when the invention has actually become a product on the market, the risk for the newcomer has been very greatly reduced. The figures indicate that the multiple might then be 4 times the originator's investment, but as this of course would have grown very considerably in the interim, the total capital payment for a licence would be correspondingly greater.

All that is claimed for these figures is that they indicate that *some* multiples could be worked out that would combine better incentives for investment in inventing and innovating than those offered by the patent system now, with the earliest possible and widest diffusion of the results.

13.6 Some Advantages of this Proposal

Adding money to time as the measure of protection would face up frankly to the reality that modern invention and innovation depends primarily upon investment. Compulsory licencing with capital payments would shift the emphasis away from the abstract considerations – rooted in an outdated image of the importance of the individual inventor – which are dominant in the minds of intellectual property administrators as well as judges throughout the world. Bringing money into the measure of any exclusive privilege granted, combined with compulsory licencing, promises the multiple sources of innovation which optimum development requires.

By measuring grants in the way proposed, there is also likely to be much less infringement and waste of time, energy and money in litigation. Competitors are likely to calculate that it is in their interest to pay the capital sum required for a licence and get into production quickly, rather than take the risk of losing "early mover advantage" in the market as well as an infringement action. Also, it would be reasonable to expect the Courts to treat infringers more severely than they do now, because infringers would have had an option to take a licence, which they had not exercised.

13.6.1 Innovation protection in complex technologies

Patents as currently issued are indeed intended to bestow *temporary* monopolies, but for individual or stand-alone patents, the empirical evidence is that (except in the chemical industry) these are weak and consequently do not often erect barriers to entry to a new technology that are so strong as to inhibit technological development (Cohen *et al.* 2000). It is an entirely different matter when groups of firms in complex technologies obtain a large number of patents which are used as currency for trade between themselves, but which form an insuperable barrier to entry to their markets by newcomers. Such policies of "saturation patenting" by firms in complex technologies could not even have been envisaged when the first patent laws were passed. Indeed, there was no need for them until patent "pools" were outlawed by the Federal Trade Commission in the United States. These formal institutional arrangements for cross-licencing had been set up in many industries involving cumulative systems technologies of which the most important were aircraft, automobiles and semiconductors. Holding of intellectual property rights on parts of such systems by different firms was no drag on technological development once patent pools were set up for their transfer (sometimes with the encouragement of the Department of Defense, so that it would be able to obtain better equipment). The downside of such pools is their inherently anti-competitive nature, in that they keep out newcomers and effectively bar entry to all smaller firms. This is why they came under Federal Trade Commission disfavour. But a pool is a much less expensive way of arranging technological transfer between firms in complex technologies than patenting "every blade of grass" to build up a store of bargaining chips. This is what they now have to do to ensure that they are not denied the ability to use some improvement made by a competitor. It is surely significant that the United States Patent and Trademark Office has recently published a set of arguments from an Expert Group for establishing patent pools for biotechnology (USPTO 2001). All the advantages of a patent pool would be provided by what is now proposed, since any firm, which wanted access to information, could licence and use it immediately.

13.6.2 Publicly funded research

By bringing money into the measure, many of the problems of university- and publicly funded research, actual and looming, would be resolved. Without reversing the encouragement now being given to universities to use intellectual property, generous licencing of it is clearly desirable. Indeed, the world's biggest royalty-earner from university research, the Cohen-Boyer patent, has been very widely licenced. This, of course, is exactly what would happen with all inventions if the changes now proposed were in force. Completely free access to the earliest stages of scientific research has traditionally been the norm, and those who work in basic science are naturally on their guard against any erosion of this freedom by those who would extend the range of proprietary protection. The changes proposed would protect this freedom of access through eliminating monopoly rights.

In the particular case of biotechnology, because publicly funded genome data is made available freely, it is impossible to know how far the private firms' patent applications result from this work or from their own; but irrespective of the relative proportions, any valid patents which are granted on these applications will benefit only the actual patentee. In contrast, with a financial component in the measurement of grants, it would be possible to establish how much *investment* a firm has made to turn both the publicly funded information and its own into whatever can be protected. The prescribed multiple of this for biotechnology, payable to such a firm by others which want a compulsory licence to use its information, could provide any level of incentive that could be needed for investing at high risk, without allowing patentees to capture rewards from information which has come into existence through public funding.

This would provide a basis for ending the battle between those who want exclusive privileges in respect of biotechnology to be as strong or as weak as possible. Present arrangements can provide no common ground between one group which holds that patents for gene sequences should be issued with broad claims, and another group which wants distribution of all relevant information to be so free as even to be on the Internet. But with money as well as time in the measure of protection, the first group would get the incentive for risky investment which it wants, and the second one would be able to use all the information it needs, subject only to the reasonable condition of sharing retrospectively in the investment and risk which produced it. The legitimate grounds for concern on the part of those who oppose biotechnology patents in their present form would be removed.

13.6.3 World Free Trade in Information

The World Trade Organization was brought into being in 1994 as a new and extended version of the General Agreement on Tariffs and Trade. However, TRIPs (the Trade-Related Intellectual Property Section of this) has met with enormous opposition from poorer countries, which regard it as a vehicle for Western technological imperialism (cf. Hamilton 1996, Oddi 1996, Kingston 2000c). Not unreasonably, they ask why they should give monopolies for numbers of years in their countries to Western brands, inventions and media productions, when they themselves produce nothing similar, which could benefit from reciprocal protection in Western countries.

Changing from time to "time mediated by money" as the measure of intellectual property rights could do much to resolve these tensions. The survival of TRIPs could even depend upon it. The violent demonstrations at Seattle, Stockholm and elsewhere, which have disrupted WTO meetings, show a quite unusual depth and breadth of antagonism. Since the multiple in a money measure of intellectual property would only apply to investment in R&D in each individual country, it would instantly remove what is seen as the "imperialistic" aspect of the monopolies granted under the present system and defuse this world-wide anger.

13.7 Conclusion

Many of the contemporary problems of intellectual property can be diagnosed as resulting from failure to keep pace with new kinds of information and new ways of generating it. In particular, the authorities have failed to come to grips with the reality that most of what intellectual property exists to protect now comes into being through large-scale investment and not from independently exercised creativity. This confusion has caused a major escalation, both in numbers of disputes and in the costs of resolving them.

These problems could be diminished in importance by introducing:

- direct protection of innovation;
- compulsory expert arbitration of disputes, with legal aid for the party which does not appeal to the Courts from an arbitration decision; and
- a financial dimension to the existing time measure of grants.

13.7.1 Further Research

The first two of these proposals have already been the subject of considerable research (e.g. Kingston 1987, 2000b). That to introduce a financial dimension to measurement of intellectual property has been recommended for official investigation by the EU Expert Group referred to earlier (ETAN 1999, p.28). This would obviously need to involve Accounting as well as intellectual property experts. Achieving precision about the costs of doing R&D should not be difficult: the main challenge for this research would be to develop multiples of these costs to give prices for compulsory licences whose incentives for risky investment in R&D are at least as good as those provided by the present system of intellectual property.

A second topic for research is why intellectual property has so much difficulty in adjusting to new kinds of information and new ways of producing it. A promising hypothesis, however surprising it may be to some, is that the root cause is in the Constitution of the United States. Article I.8 of this gives power to Congress to legislate "to secure for limited times to authors and inventors the exclusive right to their writings and discoveries", and Congress has used this power to provide a copyright law for authors and a patent law for inventors. But because Article I.8 gives Congress *nothing more than* this power, and because there is such respect for the Constitution, it is extremely difficult for U.S. authorities to do anything other than try to fit protection of new kinds of information into the traditional dual paradigm. It is surely significant that in 1889 the Supreme Court struck down the first Federal Trademark Act on the ground that Trade Marks are monopoly rights, and the only monopolies sanctioned by the Constitution were those which could be granted to authors and inventors under Article I.8. And in 1989, it did exactly the same with a Florida State Act to provide a new kind of protection for yacht design.

Because American example and influence are so powerful in intellectual property matters internationally, restrictions which may originate in the U.S. Constitution also inhibit the development of intellectual property in other countries as well. A cogent illustration of this is that Japan was well on the way to establishing a *sui generis* system for software, but came under heavy U.S. pressure to protect it through traditional copyright. The EU followed suit in its 1983 Directive. The history of the World Intellectual Property Organization has always revealed strong United States influence, and of course TRIPs, the intellectual property part of the World Trade Organization agreement, was almost entirely a U.S. initiative.

13.7.2 Teaching innovation

Intellectual property lawyers need to know more about business, and business men and economists need to know more about intellectual property. Unfortunately, the education which both groups receive tends to be compartmentalised, so that most students are only partially equipped when they enter upon their careers. The unifying concept, which both groups need to be taught, is that of market power, the power to impede the operation of market forces, and consequently make economic innovation possible. Every type of this can be shown to depend upon some provision of positive law (cf. Kingston 1984).

The first of these types, Capability, is achieved through investment in productive assets, and relies on the law of Limited Liability. Persuasive market power is built up through investment in psychological assets ("reputation") to develop Brands on the basis of Trade Mark Registration Law. In the third kind, Specific market power, the barriers to market entry are to be found in explicit legislation or government edict by which the State formally defines the entry barrier, as in an exploration licence, an airline route franchise or in the legislation which generates intellectual property. Derived market power, made possible by Trades Union and similar laws, enables management specialists and labour to capture some of the primary rents arising from the other types of market power, and is the basis of discretionary income. All these types of market power are to be found in every firm, although in different proportions, and the role of intellectual property can only be properly understood when it is seen in this broad context. This "market power paradigm" deserves to be taught in both law and business schools.

13.8 Literature References

Aharonian, G. (2001). *Deconstructing Software: 30 Years of Bad Logic*. Accessible at: <www.bustpatents.com/aharonian/softcopy.htm>

Arundel A, van de Paal G., Soete L (1995). *Innovation Strategies of Europe's Largest Industrial Firms*. EIMS Publication No. 23, European Commission.

Calvert I.A., Sofocleous M. (1989). 'Interference Statistics for Fiscal Years 1986 to 1988'. *Journal of the U.S. Patent and Trademark Office Society* 71: 399-410.

Calvert I.A., Sofocleous M. (1992). 'Interference Statistics for Fiscal Years 1989 to 1991'. *Journal of the U.S. Patent and Trademark Office Society* 74: 822-6.

Calvert I.A., Sofocleous M. (1995). 'Interference Statistics for Fiscal Years 1992 to 1994'. *Journal of the U.S. Patent and Trademark Office Society* 77; 417-22.

Cohen W., Nelson R.R., Walsh J.P. (2000). *Protecting their Intellectual Assets: Appropriability Conditions and Why U.S. Manufacturing Firms Patent (or Not)*. Mimeo: Carnegie Mellon University.

ETAN Report (1999). 'Strategic Dimensions of Intellectual Property Rights in the context of S&T Policy', SBN 92-828-7309-9. Brussels: European Commission, D-G XII.

European Commission (1996). Directive 96/9/EC of the European Parliament and of the Council of 11 March 1996 on the Legal Protection of Databases, 1996 O.J. (L. 77) 20.

Hamilton, M.A. (1996). 'The TRIPs Agreement: Imperialistic, Outdated and Overprotective'. *Vanderbilt Journal of Transnational Law* 29: 613-34.

Heller, M.A., Eisenberg, R. (1998). 'Can Patents Prevent Innovation? The Anticommons in Biomedical Research'. *Science* 280: 698-701.

Kash, D.E., Rycroft, R. (1998). 'Technology Policy in the 21st Century: How Will We Adapt to Complexity?' *Science and Public Policy* 25, (2 April): 71.

Kash, D.E., Kingston, W. (2001). 'Patents in a World of Complex Technologies'. *Science and Public Policy* 28, (2 February).

Kingston, W. (1981). 'An Investment Patent'. *European Intellectual Property Review* (7): 207-12.

Kingston, W. (1984). *The Political Economy of Innovation*. Dordrecht, Kluwer Academic Publishers.

Kingston, W. (ed.) (1987). *Direct Protection of Innovation*. Dordrecht/Boston: Kluwer Academic Publishers for the European Commission.

Kingston, W. 1994. 'Compulsory Licencing with Capital Payments as an Alternative to Monopoly Grants for Intellectual Property'. *Research Policy* 23 (5), pp. 1275-89.

Kingston, W. (2000a). 'Antibiotics, Invention and Innovation'. *Research Policy* 29 (6) pp. 679-710.

Kingston, W. (2000b). 'The Case for Compulsory Arbitration – Empirical Evidence'. *European Intellectual Property Review* 22 (4), pp. 154-8.

Kingston, W. (2000c). 'A spectre is haunting the world – the spectre of *global* capitalism'. *Journal of Evolutionary Economics* 10 (1, 2), pp. 83-108

Kingston, W. (2001). *Enforcing the Patents of Small Firms. Results of a research project commissioned by the European Commission,* Luxembourg, EU Official Publications. ISBN 92-894-0633X.

Kronz, H. (1983). 'Patent Protection for Innovations: A Model'. *European Intellectual Property Review* No. 5: 178-83.

Levin, R.C., Klevorick, A.K., Nelson, R.R., Winter, S.G. (1987). 'Yale Study of R&D Appropriability Methods'. *Brookings Economic Paper.*

Machlup, F., Penrose, E. (1950). 'The Patent Controversy'. *Journal of Economic History* 10: 1-29.

Mansfield, E.M., Schwartz E., Wagner S. (1981). 'Imitation Costs and Patents: An Empirical Study. *Economic Journal*: 904.

Mazzolini, R., Nelson, R.R. (1988). 'The benefits and costs of strong patent protection: a contribution to the current debate'. *Research Policy* 27: 273-84.

Merges, R. (1992). 'Uncertainty and the Standard of Patentability'. *High TechnologyLaw Journal* (7), pp. 1-70.

Oddi, A.S. (1996). 'TRIPS – Natural Rights and a Polite Form of Economic Imperialism'. *Vand. J. Transnational Law* 28.

Reichman J.H. (1994). 'Legal Hybrids Between the Patent and Copyright Paradigms'. *Columbia Law Review* 94: 2442-558.

Reichman J.H. and Samuelson, P.A. (1997). 'The U.S. Digital Agenda at WIPO'. *Virginia Journal of International Law* 37 (2): 360-440.

Samuelson, P. (1997). 'Intellectual Property Rights in Data?' *Vanderbilt Law Review* 50: 52-166.

Thurow, L.C. (1997). 'Needed: A New System of Intellectual Property Rights'. *Harvard Business Review*, September/October: 95-103.

United States Patent and Trademark Office (1992). Commission on Patent Law Reform: Report. Washington, D.C.: U.S. Government Printing Office.

United States Patent and Trademark Office (2001). 'White Paper. *Patent Pools: A Solution to the Problem of Access to Biotechnology Patents?* Accessible at: <www.uspto.gov/web/offices/pac/dapp/opla/patpoolcover.html>.

Vaver, D. (2000). 'Patently Absurd. *Oxford Today*: 21-2.

Chapter 14

ECONOMICS OF PATENTING AN INPUT ESSENTIAL TO FURTHER RESEARCH

Bonwoo Koo* and Brian D. Wright**
International Food Policy Research Institute, Washington DC, USA
***University of Californi at Berkeleya, Berkeley, CA, USA*

Chapter Contents:

Abstract: Recent developments in intellectual property rights in the areas of biotechnology and computer science have resulted in patenting of elements of innovation sequences, within which one invention makes further innovation possible. In this context, the sophistication of patent life as a policy instrument, especially when innovators who use the invention are competitive, has been insufficiently appreciated. This study takes a closer look at the dynamic implications of the patent instrument when an innovation granted for patent is an essential input to further innovation in a research sequence. In a highly stylized model, we show that a limit on patent life can induce subsequent innovation that would be precluded under infinite patent life, and reduce rent dissipation in such innovation. On the other hand, an increase in a finite patent life T can advance the date of innovation when its cost is in an intermediate range.

14.1 Introduction

The current revolutions in biotechnology and information technology have generated sequences of innovations that culminate in a final consumer product. The concurrent revolution in intellectual property rights has resulted

O. Granstrand (ed.), Economics, Law and Intellectual Property, 331-346.

in patenting of intermediate elements of these innovation sequences. In this context, it has been recognized that the effects of a specific patent policy constitute a tradeoff between encouragement of prior innovation and reduction of incentives for subsequent research. Some studies (e.g., Heller and Eisenberg 1998) emphasize the negative effects of patenting initial inventions on subsequent innovations, while others endorse stronger protection of early innovators who opened new fields of research (see, for example, Kitch 1977 and the critiques in Merges and Nelson 1990).

Often discussed patent policy instruments include patent scope (or breadth) and patent life. While several studies have analyzed the role of patent scope in the design of an optimal patent system (Green and Scotchmer 1995, Chang 1995, O'Donoghue 1998), the implications of patent life itself in the context of a competitive dynamic research sequence have been relatively neglected (with an exception by Gallini 1992). Indeed, the sophistication of the patent instrument with finite life has been insufficiently appreciated in the current literature. This study takes a closer look at the dynamic implications of the patent instrument (especially, patent life) via a positive analysis of patenting when innovations form a dynamic sequence.

The standard analysis of optimal patent life is based on the Nordhaus (1969) model of an independent, stand-alone innovation that reduces the production cost of a consumer good. His derivation of a finite optimal patent life balances the gain in size of the cost-reducing innovation from an increased period of monopoly granted by the patent against the associated deadweight loss from higher cost to consumers due to an extension of the period in which royalties must be paid. However, his model assumes no competition in the innovative process so that the lone innovator is guaranteed a patent once she makes an innovation. Subsequent studies introduce competition in the innovative process and analyze the effect on optimal patent life (Kamien and Schwartz 1974, DeBrock 1985). Unrestricted R&D competition in the innovation race may result in the rent dissipation familiar in open-access resource models (Gordon 1954, Barzel 1968), and this can have significant implications for social welfare and optimal patent life. Wright (1983) demonstrates in a one-stage model that the social loss associated with rent dissipation by competitive innovators can dominate the deadweight loss from monopoly awarded by a patent.

This paper is a positive (rather than normative) explanation of the implications of patenting in a model of sequential innovations. In particular, we focus on the case where an initial innovation is an input essential to a subsequent innovation that in turn lowers the cost of producing a consumer good.

We construct a two-stage sequential innovation model by assuming an exogenous first-stage innovation is necessary before the search can begin for a second-stage innovation. We assume away the static consumption inefficiency addressed by Nordhaus, by assuming a fixed size of the cost-reducing innovation and a perfectly inelastic demand, with no income effect, for the consumer good ultimately produced using the patented second-stage process. To further restrict the dynamics to the innovation process itself, we assume final demand and input supplies are static, in contrast to Barzel (1968). In this simplified framework, we analyze the innovation incentive for a second-stage innovation under different patent lives and derive the socially optimal patent life.

The paper is organized as follows. Section 2 introduces a two-stage sequential model and discusses the licensing equilibrium and the efficient royalty for licensing a patent for use by a subsequent innovator. Assuming a first innovation has already been successfully made, we analyze in section 3 the incentive for the second innovation race under perfect competition and derive the optimal patent life, which maximizes social welfare. The implications of finite patent life and the importance of licensing agreements are considered in this dynamic context. Concluding remarks follow in section 4.

14.2 A Two-Stage Sequential Innovation Model

14.2.1 Assumptions

We adopt a two-stage model in which the second innovation is dependent upon the first innovation. The first innovation does not impart any direct externality other than that it enables the search for the second innovation.[1] If the first innovator could achieve the second innovation efficiently, then she would produce both innovations, and the issues discussed here would not arise. Thus we address the case in which the first innovator cannot compete for the second innovation. A simple example is a small firm, which has obtained a patent for a research input but does not have the capacity to conduct the follow-on research efficiently. We assume that, if it has no patent, the first innovator cannot negotiate an efficient takeover (or merger) by a potential second-round innovator without losing control of its technology, pro-

[1] The embodied idea essential for initiation of the search for the second innovation is generated by the first innovation. When the first innovation is patented, the idea is completely revealed in the patent and becomes common knowledge, and can costlessly be embodied by others, absent the prior patent.

tected only by trade secrecy. Thus the first innovator always patents its innovation. The associated disclosure means that all potential second innovators share the information crucial for competing for the follow-on patent. Thus a takeover by any potential innovator before he patents the second innovation would be injudicious. A takeover after committing the sunk costs of research offers no advantage. Thus the second innovator remains a separate entity and must obtain a license to commercialize his innovation.

To emphasize the dynamic implications of the patent system itself, we assume demand is static for the final product of innovation. The flow value of the completed innovation sequence to consumers is v per period, accruing indirectly as a result of a reduction in the cost of a consumer good after achievement of the second, dependent innovation. We avoid the potential static inefficiency of the patent monopoly that justifies patent life limitation in the Nordhaus model, by assuming a perfectly inelastic consumption demand curve, with zero income effect, for this product. Under our assumption, the optimal patent life would be infinite in the Nordhaus single-stage model because the deadweight loss is zero with perfectly inelastic demand curve. In this paper, we will show that the optimal patent life can be finite in a sequential model of innovation, even if the patent monopoly incurs no static deadweight loss. We assume that the first innovation is exogenously given and focus on the incentive for the second innovation.

An innovation patented at time zero is, by assumption, fully protected till the end of the patent life, T. The scope of the patent is assumed to be infinite in the sense that it cannot be "invented around" by producing a substitute. The second innovation always infringes the first and a licensing agreement is required for commercialization of the second innovation before T. This assumption contrasts with some studies (e.g., O'Donoghue 1998, Hopenhayn and Mitchell 2001) in which the second innovator effectively "invents around" the first and provides a substitute with lower production cost or other superior attributes, rendering the first innovation obsolete. Delay of the second innovation can increase the first innovator's expected profit by extending her stream of revenue in those studies. In our model, by contrast, delay of the second innovation reduces the first innovator's expected profit because the expected stream of licensing revenue is shorter and starts later. The royalty rate $\alpha \in [0, 1]$, which is the share of the profit transferred from the second to the first innovator, is determined through an *ex post* efficient Nash bargaining process.

Firms in the race for the second innovation are assumed to be identical and atomistic, and in the aggregate produce the Poisson hazard rate $\lambda \in R^+$.

We assume the flow marginal cost of λ for the industry is constant at c. We also make a technical assumption that firms in the race commit to a given rate of flow investment for a period Δ in advance, where Δ may be arbitrarily small. An alternative assumption with equivalent implications is that there is a lag Δ between a successful innovation outcome and the arrival of this news to research administrators including competitors. During this lag period, research effort is of no social value, since the discovery has already been achieved.

Our specification can be compared with that of Loury (1979), which implies that the commitment period Δ is infinite and that research expenditures are an infinite-lived investment with the capacity to produce a constant flow of research effort. Furthermore in our model the research technology is scale-neutral, whereas Loury's model has first decreasing and then increasing marginal cost for each firm. Our specification allows us to make an analytic study of this dynamic problem, including the possibility of competitive rent dissipation. It can be viewed as the limit of a sequence of models with finite rates of response to innovation incentive similar in general specification to the model that one of us has analyzed numerically (Koo 1998). Firms are risk-neutral, and the discount rate is r.

14.2.2 Licensing equilibrium

We assume the *ex ante* agreement addressed in the two-firm world of Green and Scotchmer (1995) is not feasible in this world of a countable infinity of potential second innovators. Each has equal chance of winning the race for the second patent, so a contract would have to be made with each potential innovator. Any positive transaction cost would make *ex ante* agreement infeasible. The first patent holder can block commercialization of the second innovation until her patent, received at date zero, expires at date T. The second patent holder can similarly block commercialization of the second innovation, awarded at date t^* and expiring at $t^* + T$. Thus, the second innovation is vulnerable to the "double-holdup" problem (Merges and Nelson 1990). The surplus to be divided between the two patent holders is the flow gross value v from the date of issue, t^*, of the second patent (assumed identical to time of discovery) until T, the date of expiration of the first patent. Assuming Nash bargaining with equal bargaining power, the solution is a 50-50 share of v until date T. Here we assume a royalty rate $\alpha = 0.5$.

The cost of achieving to second innovation is not observable by the first innovator, and communications from the second innovator are not credible *ex ante* or *ex post*, due to moral hazards associated with cost information.

Should joint returns to follow-on innovation actually turn out to be less than α, the first innovator would prefer to make a credible offer of a lower royalty rate to render the second innovation more attractive to potential innovators. However, her inability to observe costs prevents her from committing to a royalty rate *ex ante*, and the non-verifiability of costs prevents her from committing to do so *ex post* via an *ex ante* contractual commitment conditioned on the realization of cost information. Competitive innovators who anticipate a fifty percent share of revenue will not pursue the second innovation if the profit margin on the second innovation is less than one half the present value of costs. An *ex ante* royalty rate below fifty percent, proclaimed unilaterally by the first innovator, is not credible *ex post*.

One credible alternative could be a compulsory royalty rate set by the government, a possibility under the patent laws of many countries. Another credible means of increasing the gross share of expected present value appropriated by the second patentee above 50 percent of the total social value is a finite patent life. If the second innovation has positive net social value, it can be induced, with a lag, by restriction of patent life to some value $T \in R^+$, even if the royalty rate α stays at its equilibrium level of 0.5.

14.3 Social Welfare and the Optimal Patent Life

14.3.1 Hazard rate of the second innovation

Assume that the market for the search for the second innovation is perfectly competitive with free entry, facilitated by common knowledge of the essential idea revealed by the patent on the first innovation. The expected revenue of a successful second innovation that occurs at time t ($\leq T$), where the first patent occurs at time 0, is

$$V(t) = (1-\alpha)\int_0^{T-t} ve^{-r\tau}d\tau + \int_{T-t}^{T} ve^{-r\tau}d\tau . \qquad (1)$$

Before the first patent expires, the successful second innovator receives a part of the revenue after paying a royalty fee to the first during the overhang period $[0, T-t]$, the first term on the right-hand side (RHS) of equation (1). He then receives full revenue beyond the overhang and before his own patent expires (the second term on the RHS). Firms in the race decide their timing of entry, and the intensity of innovation, by comparing the expected marginal revenue, net of royalty, with the cost of innovation. The following lemma characterizes the hazard rate of the second innovation, in a sequence of models in which the industry marginal cost is constant and the cost commitment period Δ approaches zero:

***Lemma 1**: Hazard rate of the second innovation and rent dissipation*

Assume expected profits are completely dissipated through competition. If the value of the innovation V(t) at time t exceeds the flow cost of search c, in the limit as the cost commitment period Δ approaches zero, the innovation is made (almost surely) instantaneously at t.

Proof. When atomistic identical firms compete for a follow-on innovation at date t, producing an aggregate hazard rate λ, the industry-wide expected profit, under the assumption of Δ-period commitment, is

$$\Pi(t) = \int_0^\infty \left[V(t) - c - c\lambda(1-e^{-r\Delta})/r\right]\lambda e^{-(r+\lambda)\tau} d\tau, \quad \tau < T.$$

The first term of the integrand in square brackets is the expected revenue evaluated as a one-time present value accruing at date t, which is, for finite T, increasing as the timing of innovation is delayed, reducing the duration of overhang of the first patent, $T - t$. The second term is the expected research cost flow incurred per unit of the hazard rate λ, until a successful innovation is achieved. The third term is the extra pre-commitment cost incurred by follow-on innovators during an additional period Δ after success is achieved by some innovator, accruing as a one-time present value at date t – representing, for example, the cost of resources expended during the time delay of news of a successful innovation.

Since innovators have the option of setting $\lambda = 0$, $\Pi(t)$ is bounded below by zero. If λ is positive, the integrand is non-negative. The zero profit condition implied by free entry and constant marginal cost of search ensures that

$$\left[V(t) - c - c\lambda(1-e^{-r\Delta})/r\right]\lambda = 0$$

for all $t \geq 0$. Thus, the flow of innovative effort at t is

$$\lambda = \max\left[\frac{r\left[V(t)-c\right]}{c\left(1-e^{-r\Delta}\right)}, 0\right].$$

For a positive rent gross of commitment cost ($V(t) - c > 0$), $\lim_{\Delta \to 0} \lambda = \infty$.

Q.E.D.

As the commitment period goes to zero, lemma 1 shows that the industry innovation rate approaches infinity, and the time t^* before the innovation succeeds goes to zero almost surely. Thus, our model yields both dissipation of the second innovator's total rents in the innovation process, and instantaneous innovation after entry, in the case of constant marginal cost of innovation. While models in the tradition of Loury and Lee and Wilde can explain rent dissipation under competition, there is an expected delay between resource commitment and the discovery of innovation in their model. The instantaneous innovation in our model enables us to address analytically the timing and welfare effects of second-stage innovation, which heretofore have been addressed in numerical simulations (e.g., Koo 1998). We are also able to study the fully competitive, constant-cost scenario without the complications of increasing and decreasing returns to innovative efforts of individual firms, which limit entry in previous models.

14.3.2 Timing of the second innovation

To simplify the analysis, we express the marginal cost, c, of the hazard rate as a fraction of the present value of the flow of benefit from the innovation upon success, i.e., $c \equiv kv/r$, where $k \in [0, 1]$ is the cost coefficient. The statements about timing in this section apply, with probability one, in the limit as the innovation commitment period Δ goes to zero. When the marginal cost is less than the expected revenue immediately after the first patent, i.e., $c \leq V(0)$ or $k \leq (1-\alpha)(1-e^{-rT})$, then the second innovation follows, given competition, immediately after the first innovation is achieved and patented, and the second innovator pays royalties for the entire life of the first patent. On the other hand, the second innovation is never made if the marginal cost of search exceeds the value of the second patent after the expiration of the first (i.e., $c > V(T)$ or $k > 1-e^{-rT}$).

For an intermediate range of marginal cost, i.e., $(1-\alpha)(1-e^{-rT}) < k \leq (1-e^{-rT})$, the second innovation is made, in the limit as Δ goes zero, within the first patent life at the almost sure equilibrium time t^* when $V(t^*) = c$ or $(1-\alpha)+\alpha e^{-r(T-t^*)} - e^{-rT} - k = 0$. Thus,

$$t^* = \frac{1}{r}\ln\left(\frac{e^{-rT} + k - (1-\alpha)}{\alpha e^{-rT}}\right) \qquad for\ (1-\alpha)(1-e^{-rT}) < k \leq (1-e^{-rT}) \quad (2)$$

For cost lower than the range indicated, the second innovation is instantaneous, and for higher cost it is never achieved. Figure 14-1 illustrates the timing of the second innovation under perfect competition, given a fixed patent life *T*. If cost is too high to allow immediate innovation upon patenting of the first innovation but low enough to allow innovation if there were no obligation to pay royalties to the first innovator, the timing of the second innovation is an increasing function of the cost coefficient *k*. With free entry in the race for the innovation, any potential rents are completely dissipated through competition. Clearly, the timing of innovation depends on the patent life.

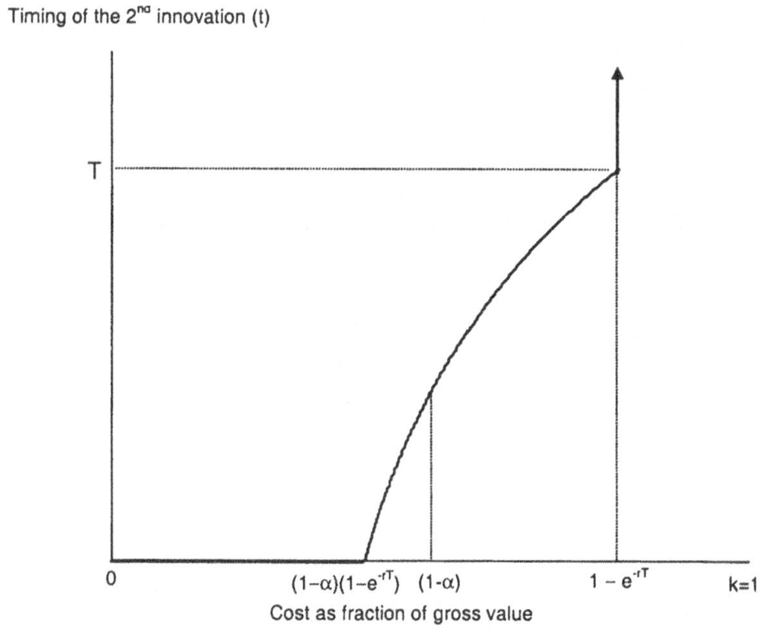

Figure 14-1: Timing of the second innovation

***Proposition 1**: Patent life and the timing of the second innovation*

If the second innovation yields positive total return at given T ($k \leq 1 - e^{-rT}$) but innovation at time zero is unprofitable in expectation to potential second innovators ($k > (1-\alpha)(1-e^{-rT})$), an increase in patent life delays the second innovation, if and only if the marginal cost of search is greater than the second innovator's share of royalty.

Proof. Differentiation of (2) yields

$$\frac{dt^*}{dT}=\frac{k-(1-\alpha)}{e^{-rT}+k-(1-\alpha)}.$$

The sign of the denominator is positive since $k>(1-\alpha)(1-e^{-rT})$, so the sign of this expression is the sign of the numerator. Proposition 1 implies that if the second innovation occurs at $t \in (0, T)$, it can be advanced with a shorter patent life if $k > (1 - \alpha)$. The second innovation occurs closer to the expiration of the first patent, but the expiration date T is advanced. The net effect is earlier second innovation. Consumers capture the surplus only after both patents have expired, and a shorter patent life can advance the onset of the flow of consumers' surplus.

When the patent life is infinite and $k \geq (1 - \alpha)$, the revenue flow, net of royalty, from the second innovation is less than the cost and thus the second innovation will never be made. Though a low enough royalty rate would induce the second innovation, the first innovator cannot *ex ante* identify the cost k, nor can she credibly commit to a royalty conditional on the realized cost, due to the non-verifiability of the cost *ex post*, which precludes legal enforcement of such conditional commitment. If the patent life becomes finite, however, any second innovation that offers a positive profit stream at that patent life, net of marginal cost c, will be pursued by competitive innovators at some time before (or at) the end of the life of the first patent. Thus, proposition 1 implies that a finite patent life may provide a credible assurance that the first innovator's share of the present value of the second innovation will decline monotonically with time, to zero at $t = T$. A second innovation that is unprofitable to the second innovator under infinite patent life might thus become possible at some finite $t \leq T$.

14.3.3 Socially optimal patent life

Given an inelastic (i.e., exogenous) first innovation achieved with no rent dissipation and a perfectly competitive race for the second innovation, social welfare from the second innovation consists of the royalty paid to the first innovator and the consumers' surplus after the patent expires. All second-innovation rents are dissipated. In the limit as Δ goes to zero, expected social welfare is thus:

$$S = \frac{\alpha v}{r}\left(e^{-rt^*} - e^{-rT}\right) + \frac{v}{r} e^{-r(t^*+T)}. \qquad (3)$$

Substituting t^* from equation (2), the size of expected social welfare under different levels of cost is summarized in equation (4).

$$S = \begin{cases} \dfrac{v\left[\alpha + (1-\alpha)e^{-rT}\right]}{r} & \text{if } 0 \le k \le (1-\alpha)(1-e^{-rT}) \\ \dfrac{\alpha v e^{-rT}(1-k)}{r\left[e^{-rT} + k - (1-\alpha)\right]} & \text{if } (1-\alpha)(1-e^{-rT}) < k \le (1-e^{-rT}) \end{cases}. \qquad (4)$$

Figure 14-2 illustrates the social welfare of equation (4), given a fixed patent life. For a low marginal cost $0 < k \le (1-\alpha)(1-e^{-rT})$, the second innovation is made immediately after the first and the social welfare is independent of k. The potential rent to the second innovator decreases as k increases in the range, but this is completely dissipated (except for the royalty flow) with free entry. As the cost coefficient k increases above $(1-\alpha)(1-e^{-rT})$, the social welfare decreases since the second innovation is delayed with the high cost of innovation, and the present value of both royalty and consumer surplus decreases. If the cost is very high $\left(k > \left(1-e^{-rT}\right)\right)$, there will be no second innovation and the social welfare is zero.

The change in patent life changes social welfare when it changes in the timing of the second innovation. Thus, we can derive the socially optimal *finite* patent life under a competitive market for the second innovation.

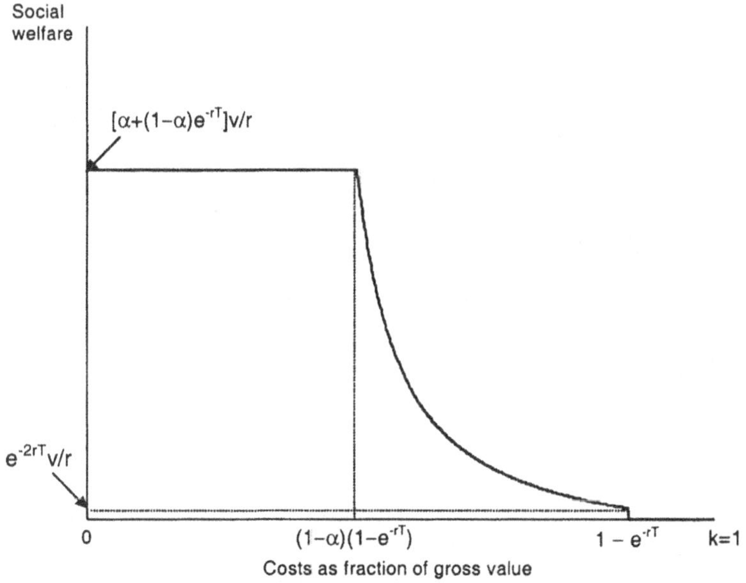

Figure 14-2: Social welfare for a given patent life

***Proposition 2**: Socially optimal patent life*

Under perfect competition in the innovation market, there exists a socially optimal finite patent life T^*, which depends on the level of the marginal cost of the second innovation.

Proof. Differentiation of (4) with respect to the patent life yields:

$$\frac{\partial S}{\partial T}=\begin{cases} -v(1-\alpha)e^{-rT} & \text{if } 0\leq k\leq(1-\alpha)\left(1-e^{-rT}\right) \\ \dfrac{\alpha v e^{-rT}(1-k)}{\left[e^{-rT}+k-(1-\alpha)\right]^{2}}\left[(1-\alpha)-k\right] & \text{if } (1-\alpha)\left(1-e^{-rT}\right)<k\leq\left(1-e^{-rT}\right) \end{cases} \tag{5}$$

When the cost is sufficiently low $\left(0<k\leq(1-\alpha)\left(1-e^{-rT}\right)\right)$, the sign $\partial S/\partial T$ of equation (5) is negative. An increase in patent life delays the flow of consumer surplus, and all rents generated (net of royalty payments) are dissipated by competition. The minimum patent life that enables the second

innovation within this range at $t = 0$ is $T^* = -\ln\left[(1-\alpha-k)/(1-\alpha)\right]/r$. If the cost is in the intermediate range, $(1-\alpha)\left(1-e^{-rT}\right) < k \leq \left(1-e^{-rT}\right)$, then the sign $\partial S/\partial T$ of equation (5) is ambiguous: it is positive if $k < (1-\alpha)$, and negative if $k > (1-\alpha)$. Thus, the patent life that maximizes social welfare within this range is

$$T^* = \begin{cases} -\dfrac{1}{r}\ln\left(\dfrac{1-\alpha-k}{1-\alpha}\right) & \text{if } 0 \leq k \leq (1-\alpha) \\ -\dfrac{1}{r}\ln(1-k) & \text{if } (1-\alpha) < k \leq 1 \end{cases} \tag{6}$$

Q.E.D.

Figure 14-3 illustrates the socially optimal patent life derived in proposition 2. For $k < (1 - \alpha)$, the socially-optimal patent life allows the share $(1 - \alpha)$ to precisely cover the expected minimum cost of follow-on innovation, leaving no expected surplus to be dissipated by rent-seeking second-round innovators. As the cost coefficient k increases, the socially optimal patent life increases accordingly to a limit of infinity at $k = (1 - \alpha)$. For costs up to this limit, the second innovation occurs immediately after the first patent. As the cost increases further, the optimal patent life drops to a finite level, allowing the second innovator to just cover his costs in expectation if he innovates at the expiration of the first innovation, leaving no royalty for the first innovator (assumed to be unresponsive to incentives at the margin). For higher levels of k parent life increases again to a limit of infinity at $k = 1$. The figure shows that although the optimal patent life can be very long when the cost share is almost as large as the revenue share, net or gross of the royalty α, it is much shorter in most other ranges of cost k.

One implication of proposition 2 is that, for a low-cost second innovation, allowing the first patent holder to have a patent that controls subsequent innovation through a licensing agreement can be welfare-improving under perfect competition, even if the first innovation needs no incentive. For example, if the cost of the second innovation is low $\left(0 < k \leq (1-\alpha)\left(1-e^{-rT}\right)\right)$ and no licensing agreement is necessary (due, for example, to insufficient patent scope), then the second innovation follows immediately after the first and all the expected revenue from the second innovation is completely dissipated through competition with free entry. With a licensing agreement, on the other hand, part of the revenue from the second innovation is transferred to the first innovator as a royalty payment.

Therefore the size of dissipated rent, when there exists a possibility of licensing agreement, is smaller. Given the royalty rate, a reduction in patent life T can increase the present value of consumer surplus received after the second patent expires. When costs are higher, a finite patent life makes the second innovation feasible (in general before the first patent expires), and allows consumers to benefit after the second patent expires.

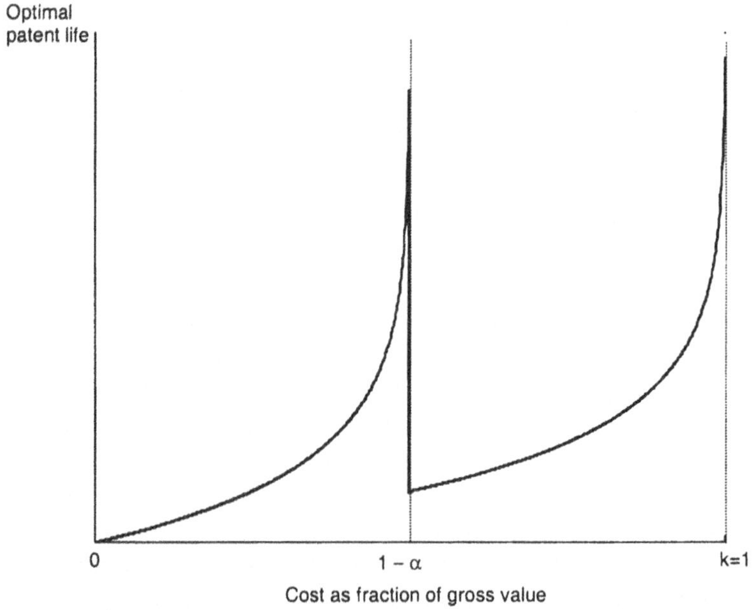

Figure 14-3: Socially optimal patent life

14.4 Conclusion

In this paper, we have examined the role of the patent protection when granted for an innovation that is an essential input to further innovation in a research sequence. In a highly stylized model, we have found a richness in the implications of patenting not evident in one-stage models or models restricted to two firms.

The analysis reveals benefits from patent life limitation quite distinct from those related to distortion in consumption (Nordhaus 1969) or rent seeking in innovation (Barzel 1968, Wright 1983, 1984). Where the gross profit margin is modest, the limit on patent life can induce subsequent innovation that would be precluded under infinite patent life. At the optimal patent life, the second innovation yields zero net profit and occurs on expiration of the first patent. But if the patent life is set too long, the cost in delay of innovation is moderated in a polar competitive innovation market because the subsequent innovation begins before the patent life expires. The patent life limitation acts as a means of (partial) commitment against excessive exploitation by the holder of the innovation essential to further innovation.

Where the second innovation is highly profitable, a patent on the first innovation and the requirement for a licensing agreement can be welfare-improving. Both the royalty flow to the first innovator and the patent life limitation reduce the rent dissipated in second-innovation rent-seeking. If the rents from the royalty flow are not dissipated in search for the first innovation, both the patent life limitation and the requirement to pay a royalty to the first innovator increase social welfare. Together, they make the social welfare generated by a two-stage patent sequence much less sensitive to the choice of patent life.

The assumptions we have made here are extreme, in order to facilitate the analysis and exposition, but they are not crucial for the qualitative results. But we believe, based on numerical results in modifications of the model not reported here, that if we introduce the possibilities of duplication in research approaches, less responsive market entry by second-stage researchers, finite elasticity of supply of research, or finite elasticity of demand for the final product, the model would yield similar qualitative conclusions. Introduction of a lag between research effort and results would lengthen optimal patent length in some cases, but would not otherwise change our findings on the general advantages of finite over infinite patent life, and of the benefits of licensing when patented innovations are themselves essential research inputs to further patented innovations in a competitive environment. The implications of a different market structure for follow-on innovation, and of relaxing the assumption of exogenous innovation of the research tool, are interesting topics for further investigation.

14.5 Literature References

Barzel, Y. 'Optimal Timing of Innovations'. *Review of Economics and Statistics* 50, 1968: 348–55.

Chang, H. 'Patent Scope, Antitrust Policy, and Cumulative Innovation'. *RAND Journal of Economics* 26, 1995: 34–57.

DeBrock, L.M. 'Market Structure, Innovation, and Optimal Patent Life'. *Journal of Law and Economics* 28, 1985: 223–44.

Gordon, H.S. 'The Economic Theory of a Common-Property Resource: The Fishery'. *Journal of Political Economy* 62, 1954: 124–42.

Green, J. and S. Scotchmer. 'On the Division of Profit in Sequential Innovation'. *RAND Journal of Economics* 26, 1995: 20–33.

Gallini, N.T. 'Patent Policy and Costly Imitation'. *RAND Journal of Economics*, Vol. 23, 1992: 52–63.

Heller, M.A. and R.S. Eisenberg. 'Can Patents Deter Innovation? *The Anticommons in Biomedical Research*'. Science 280 (May 1) 1998: 698–701.

Hopenhayn, H.A. and Mitchell, M.F. 'Innovation Variety and Patent Breadth'. *RAND Journal of Economics*, Vol. 32, 2001: 152–66.

Kamien, M.I. and N.L. Schwartz. 'Patent Life and R&D Rivalry'. *American Economic Review* 64, 1974: 183–7.

Kitch, E.W. 'The Nature and Function of the Patent System'. *Journal of Law and Economics*, Vol. 20, 1977: 265–90.

Koo, B. *The Economics of Plant Genetic Resources: The Effects of Alternative Intellectual Property Protection Systems and Advances in Biotechnology.* Unpublished Ph.D. dissertation, Department of Agricultural and Resource Economics, University of California, Berkeley, December, 1998.

Lee, T. and L. Wilde. 'Market Structure and Innovation: A Reformulation'. *Quarterly Journal of Economics* 94, 1980: 429–36.

Loury, G. 'Market Structure and Innovation'. *Quarterly Journal of Economics* 93, 1979: 395–410.

Merges, R.P. and R. Nelson. 'On the Complex Economics of Patent Scope'. *Columbia Law Review* 90, 1990: 839–916.

Nordhaus, W. *Innovation, Growth, and Welfare.* MIT Press, 1969.

O'Donoghue, T.A. 'Patentability Requirement for Sequential Innovations'. *RAND Journal of Economics* 29, 1998: 654–79.

Wright, B.D. 'The Economics of Invention Incentives: Patents, Prizes, and Research Contracts'. *American Economic Review* 73, (4) 1983: 691–707.

Wright, B.D. 'The Resource Allocation Problem in R&D'. In *The Economics of R&D Policy*, G. Tolley, J. Hodge and J. Oehmke, eds. New York, NY: Praeger Press, 1984: 41–69.

Chapter 15

IS UNIVERSITY PATENTING NECESSARY OR SUFFICIENT TO MAKE UNIVERSITY RESEARCH VALUABLE ECONOMICALLY?

Richard R. Nelson
Columbia University, Department of International and Public Affairs, New York, NY, USA

Chapter contents:

Abstract: There once was widespread belief that there was a clean divide between science and technology. Science was advanced through a system in which new research results and theories were open public knowledge. Technology was advanced through a system driven by the lure and reward of proprietary rights on new technological knowledge. In fact, science and technology have overlapped for a long time, but today the overlap clearly is considerable. Many research results occur in the overlap area. Should they be treated as public knowledge, or allowed to be made proprietary? What are the issues at stake? In this essay I try to illuminate the problem, if not find clean solutions.

15.1 Introduction

The contribution of American university research to technical progress in American industry clearly has been significant over the past quarter century,

O. Granstrand (ed.), Economics, Law and Intellectual Property, 347-361.

especially in biotech and medicine-related fields more generally, and in electronics and software. These contributions have been accompanied by a surge of university patenting. Several universities have been earning significant sums from licensing. There is a strong tendency today in the United States to presume that the universities' contribution to technical progress can be measured by, and largely has been driven by, their patenting. It is quite natural that external observers, in Europe and Japan, have taken a similar point of view. A number of countries are in the process of implementing their equivalent of the Bayh-Dole act, which is widely assumed to be the key factor behind the recent strong patenting of American universities, in the belief that patenting is the key to enabling and spurring universities to contribute to technical progress.

However, the message of this essay is that it probably is a mistake to focus on the recent patenting activity of American universities either as a measure of their contribution to industrial innovation, or as a necessary support for their clearly strong ability to contribute to technological advance and economic development. Such a perspective neglects the fact that American universities have been contributing to economic development for more than a century and that, until relatively recently, they patented little. Rosenberg and Nelson (1994) and Mowery and Rosenberg (1989) give good general accounts. Long before the passage of Bayh-Dole, American universities were contributing significantly to technological advance in agriculture; they were the source, for example, of the hybrid revolution (see Griliches, 1957). Their research contributed to important advances in drugs (Henderson, Orsenigo, and Pisano, 1999), and medical devices (Gelijns and Rosenberg, 1999), well before Bayh-Dole. American university research created the first electronic computer (Bresnahan and Malerba, 1999) and did much of the early work leading to the Internet (Mowery and Simcoe, 2002). For the most part these contributions did not involve university patenting, and where it did there is little evidence that patenting was a necessary part of technology transfer.

Indeed, I want to argue that the university patenting activity that is so visible recently may not be as important an aspect of what makes American universities so productive in the creation of new and widely used technologies as now seems commonly believed. More, to focus on patenting runs the risk of overlooking the basic factors behind that strong performance. And the patenting itself has some very problematic elements.

15.2 Patenting and Technology Transfer: The Era Since the Passage of Bayh-Dole

The following broad patterns are well known (see e.g. Mowery, Nelson, Sampat, and Ziedonis, 2001). The number of patents issued to U.S. universities more than doubled between 1979 and 1984, more than doubled again between 1984 and 1989, and more than doubled again over the 1990s. The number of universities with technology licensing and transfer offices increased from 25 in 1980, to 200 in 1990, and by the turn of the century virtually every American research university had such an office. While the numbers here are more difficult to calculate, over the period between 1980 and 2000 a very large number of startup firms were established based on university research, with many university researchers playing pivotal roles as consultants to those firms, or as members of their board of directors, and a number of well-known academics left their university settings to work full-time in those firms.

What lies behind these developments? I report here on the judgments I and my colleagues reached, based on a detailed study we undertook of recent developments at Stanford University, the University of California, and Columbia University, the three universities that stand at the top of the list regarding license revenues (Mowery *et al.*, 2001). The widespread impression is that the rise of university patenting and licensing occurred as the direct consequence of the Bayh-Dole Act, which established the presumption that universities would take out patents on inventions resulting from the publicly financed research that they did, and virtually eliminated the need for universities to gain permission from the research-funding agency to do so. This piece of legislation, in turn, legitimated and motivated policies at universities to claim patents on inventions coming out of non-government-funded research, unless bound by contract not to do so. Thus many observers today are drawing a strong causal chain from passage of legislation like Bayh-Dole, to increases in university patenting, to increased university contribution to technological progress in industry.

However, after studying in detail the time series and the structure of patents and licensing at our three universities, my colleagues and I have come to a more complex explanation for the rise in American university patenting. First of all, this period saw the development and maturation of certain new fields of science, in particular the rise of biotechnology, where research results often seem to promise significant commercial value down the road. Over this period, biomedical research rose significantly as a fraction of overall university research, and a large share of that research involved biotechnology in one manner or another. There also was increasing employment of computers and specialized software in the undertaking of research across a broad front, and in a number of cases the techniques employed, or the results, or both, looked commercially promising.

Second, as a result of Court and Patent Office decisions, many of the research results in these fields became patentable. The lion's share of patenting in all three universities we studied was concentrated in these areas, but particularly in the biomedical arena. The increasing ability to patent in these fields was part and parcel of a broader movement in the United States toward strengthening intellectual property rights. The passage of Bayh-Dole itself can be regarded as one aspect of this broader movement.

At Stanford and the University of California, one can see significant increases in patenting, largely in biomedical fields, before the passage of Bayh-Dole; both universities had technology transfer offices prior to Bayh-Dole. The Cohen-Boyer patent, of Stanford and the University of California, precedes Bayh-Dole. Columbia's most lucrative patent was applied for prior to Bayh-Dole, and there already had been several discussions at Columbia about setting up a technology transfer office, prior to Bayh-Dole. Given the broad developments discussed above, a significant increase in university patenting and licensing was going to happen in any case. The passage of Bayh-Dole legitimated and reinforced these trends, almost surely speeding them up and magnifying them. The particulars of the legislation and government policies to implement the act had a significant effect on how the new patenting and licensing activity was institutionalized, in particular on the nature of the university technology transfer offices that have become so common (see Sampat and Nelson, 2002). But in our view, the broad developments were inevitable, in the absence of policies and decisions to head them off or to temper them.

Whatever have been the basic causes of the dramatic increase in university patent, it clearly is important to try to understand the consequences. The dominant view, of course, is that increased patenting has greatly facilitated technology transfer.

The theory behind Bayh-Dole was that technology transfer from universities to industry would be greatly facilitated if universities got patents on their research results, and licensed these patents to industry, generally on an exclusive basis. Both implicitly, and sometimes explicitly, it was argued that, when universities publish their results and place them in the public domain, as contrasted with patenting them, companies have little incentive to use them. In the hearings that led to the passage of Bayh-Dole, the focus of discussion was on university inventions that were embryonic pharmaceuticals, requiring lots of testing and development work before their utility could be fully known. It was argued that companies would not have incentives to do this follow-on work unless they had assurance that they would reap the returns if that work were successful, and they could only have those assurances if they had an exclusive license.

I and my colleagues have only begun our detailed inquiry into the nature of the inventions made by our universities. (For a preliminary report see Colyvas, Crow, Gelijns, Massoleni, Nelson, Rosenberg, and Sampat, 2001.) It does appear that a number of them are *embryonic inventions* in the sense above. Among the set of university inventions that we are studying are several potential pharmaceuticals, but one can see embryonic inventions in other areas as well, for example instruments of various types. Our scrutiny of these cases does reveal several where companies indicated that they would be interested in follow-up development only if they had an exclusive license.

However, we also have observed several cases of embryonic university inventions in which companies were interested in taking the work further, even if they did not have an exclusive license. They clearly expected that, if they were able to develop something useful from what the university had to offer, they would be able to patent it, or otherwise reap returns on their investments. They did not need an exclusive license to induce them to make the investments they thought would lead them to a profitable product.

In some of the cases we studied, the information dissemination efforts of the university technology transfer offices seemed to play an important role in getting industry informed and interested, and the efforts of these offices surely were motivated by their interests in getting licensees and license income, and this required that the university hold property rights. But in most of the cases we looked at that involved effective technology transfer, companies were well aware of what was coming out of university research without any advertising or pushing from university offices. In these cases, the holding of intellectual property rights by the university is unlikely to have facilitated technology transfer, but actually may have made it more difficult by imposing positive transaction and financial costs on firms that wanted to further develop that technology.

Also, several of the most important inventions made by our universities were most certainly not embryonic inventions, but rather were techniques ready for use. The two most important university inventions that we have looked at, that by Cohen-Boyer at Stanford and the University of California, and that by Axel at Columbia, were fundamental techniques of gene splicing, gene expression, and protein production that were widely applicable in drug development and other research, rather than embryonic pharmaceutical products. It is noteworthy that these inventions were picked up by companies almost immediately after they became known. The activities of the university technology transfer offices, therefore, basically amounted to trying to collect revenues from companies that already were using the technique.

Several of our case studies involved the birth of new firms. But most of them did not. For example, the two inventions mentioned above were widely licensed to established firms. Most of the embryonic pharmaceutical inventions in our sample were taken on for further development by large established companies.

My colleagues and I do not yet have enough cases for statistical analysis, and several of the cases we have studied are very difficult to classify in any simple way. However, my strong suspicion is that a good share of the technology transfer that has occurred would have proceeded as widely and as rapidly as in fact it did, even if there had been no claiming of intellectual property rights by the university. And in some cases, it would appear that such claiming probably has made technology transfer more costly and time-consuming for the firms involved.

15.3 The Economic Contribution of Research at American Universities: The Long-run Basics

I would like to go back to my opening observation that, long prior to Bayh-Dole, the American university research system had a well-known record of strong performance in doing research that contributed to technical progress and industrial development, and strong efforts in technology transfer. The latter almost always was accomplished without the university claiming any intellectual property rights.

Agricultural experimentation stations, associated with land-grant universities, have been contributing importantly to technical change in agriculture for over a century. Important advances coming out of those research stations, for example the tested principles of hybrid corn, and the pure breeds of seeds that seed companies worked from to develop commercial hybrid seed varieties, were made freely available. Many of the state universities long have had strong engineering departments, interacting closely with local industry. Much of their research and consulting was oriented to helping firms improve their products and produce more efficiently; while there were exceptions, there appears to have been little patenting of research results by the universities involved. Academic medical centers long have been the locus of important research contributing to the solution of medical problems, often through providing the necessary knowledge inputs for private firms to develop appropriate products. Until quite recently, many of the most prominent American medical schools had rules that forbade patenting of research results.

Under sponsorship from military agencies, university researchers were very active in the early history of the computer, later the Internet, and more broadly across a wide range of technologies that now have great economic importance. In many of these cases there were specific mechanisms to facilitate communication between the university and potential civilian users of the research output. Often the results that were of general interest were placed in the public domain. In the case of the first electronic computer, the inventors did take out a patent, which was ignored by most firms in the industry, and eventually was overturned by the court. Hardly any of the contributions which made the Internet were treated as proprietary.

Nathan Rosenberg has pointed out that American universities were particularly rapid and flexible in developing and building into their structure the new engineering disciplines that were formed to support new technologies when they arose. Thus while German universities clearly were far stronger than the American in research and training in organic chemistry, American universities pioneered in chemical engineering (Rosenberg, 1998). Similarly, while Germany pioneered in the development of scientific knowledge bearing on aircraft performance, American universities led in the development of aeronautical engineering (Rosenberg, 2001). The results of university research in these fields were published and open for use by industry. In both cases American firms were the principal beneficiaries.

I want to note, and highlight, that these contributions of university research to economic growth in the United States were not the product of a few elite universities, but rather involved many universities, many of them providing service to local industry and agriculture. As Mowery and Rosenberg (1989) have argued, one of the strengths of the American university system has been the decentralization of decision-making, and the dependency of many universities on the support of regional economic interests.

There has been a tendency to think of the last several decades as marking the birth of a new kind of *knowledge-based* economy, and there is no denying that many of the leading industries today are strongly research-intensive, and draw significantly from universities for both their highly trained people and the scientific understanding that underpins their own R&D efforts. However, it is arguable that science-based technologies emerged more than a century ago, with the birth of the organic chemical products industries and the electrical equipment industries. And as the examples above tell, university research has been contributing to technological advance in industry for a long time.

Reflection on this record suggests that many contemporary analysts of how universities contribute to innovation in industry have bought into myths. One myth is that effective technology transfer almost always requires university patenting and licensing; a somewhat weaker version is that patenting and licensing greatly facilitate technology transfer. Historical analysis of the sort summarized above, and analysis of a number of recent cases, suggest that this is generally not true. Industry has eagerly picked up and employed university research results it found useful when these were placed in the public domain. While in some cases an exclusive license was useful to gain the interest of industries, this certainly has not been the general case.

On the other hand, while the hearings that led to the Bayh-Dole Act tended to stress the theory that firms needed an exclusive license in order to pick up university research results and develop them, the principal positive effect of Bayh-Dole probably has been to augment the incentives for universities to reach out more to industry. As I noted above, in some cases, this reach-out has been important and productive. However, as I also noted, in several of the cases we have studied such reaching was not necessary; open publication and information dissemination were sufficient to spread the news. And the historical record shows that in agriculture, medicine, and the engineering fields, American university researchers were reaching out, without any significant patenting, in the era prior to Bayh-Dole.

The current conventional wisdom clearly has it that the principal way that university research contributes to technological progress in industry is by providing embryonic inventions. A recent survey study by Cohen, Nelson, and Walsh (2001) asked respondents in industry to identify the kind of output of university research they found most valuable. Many more of the respondents listed *research findings* than listed *prototypes*. The same study asked respondents to rate the importance of different channels through which they gained access to university research results. Publications, conferences, and informal meetings were rated as far more important than licenses by respondents in most industries. Belief that technology transfer from universities to industry takes place largely through patent licensing of prototype invention takes attention away from the more general importance of research findings that enable firms to solve problems, and the traditional pathways that are used by industry to benefit from university research. Worse, a strong proclivity on the part of universities to try to patent and license can hinder or even block these other pathways.

Another current myth is that universities can expect a lot of money to result from their patenting and licensing activities. In fact, our three universities have done quite well financially. However, there are strong reasons to believe that they are in a small minority. Very few university inventions garner significant license incomes. It is almost a sure thing that many universities are paying significantly more to run their patenting and licensing offices than they are bringing in license revenues.

15.4 The Down-sides of University Patenting: Potential Trouble Ahead

In this section, I focus attention on several potential down-sides of the new proclivity of universities to patent and license. One possibility that has disturbed a number of analysts is that the new regime is squeezing out basic research at university, and leading to a decline in appreciation of first-rate scientific work.

My colleagues and I see little evidence at our three universities that the new climate, where patenting and licensing now are welcomed and encouraged, has in itself significantly changed the allocation of university research efforts. In particular, it has not tilted away from fundamental research, and towards research that is deemed applicable in the short run. Federal funding of academic research has increased very rapidly in the biomedical research area, and that research increasingly involves biotechnology. The use of computers and specialized software is strong in these areas, and across university research more generally. Research in these areas is in what the late Donald Stokes (1997) called *Pasteur's Quadrant*, fundamental in its orientation to basic understanding, if potentially useful as well and intentionally so. In the three universities I and my colleagues looked at, we have picked up no evidence that research has become any less fundamental than it used to be. Each of these three universities places a very high premium on the scientific reputation of its faculty, and that reputation still is largely tied to the importance of their scientific reputation as judged by their peers. That has not changed. What has changed is that the results of fundamental research in expanding fields of university research have become patentable and are being patented by universities, where earlier such research results were simply published and placed in the public domain.

On the other hand, there are clear signs that the new regime is generating a certain amount of internal university conflict. This is not necessarily bad in itself, but some of the areas of new conflict have the potential of being associated with real troubles.

The new surge of patenting and licensing is leading to greater intra-university inequalities in salary and perks. Only a few areas of the university are engaged in patenting and licensing. While we have yet to do detailed empirical work, there is good reason to believe that the incomes of university researchers and the funding of their labs have become more sensitive to royalty income, and to research funding by business firms, than used to be the case. American universities, much more so than European or Japanese, have accepted considerable dispersion among faculty members in their salaries and other remunerations. But large across-department differences clearly are a source of tension. Among other things, there is a tension between the research groups and departments that have had big winners, and the university central administration that wants to use a significant share of that revenue to support activities elsewhere at the university and to prevent inequalities from getting out of hand. These tensions are real. To the extent that those parts of the university generating the license revenues have their way, universities will tend to divide into communities of the *haves* and a large community of the *have-nots*.

There also are issues of conflict of interest when faculty have a financial interest, as well as a scientific interest, in certain activities like research on the efficacy of a new medical treatment. Managing these issues isn't easy. Many American research universities have established faculty committees to deal with such conflict-of-interest problems, and these committees can have full agendas.

While put in place in the name of increasing the flow of research results from universities to industry, the new policies carry the risk of increasing the areas of conflict between universities and industry. We already see a number of companies, which had been active supporters of university research, becoming increasingly angry about universities claiming and trying to profit from intellectual property. There have been a number of noteworthy squabbles regarding who has property rights on the results of research that the company finances at universities. Companies are complaining that universities are now much more aggressive about this. And companies have complained about universities charging them royalties for the use of research results that the government financed.

The new belief that university researchers and universities ought to make money from university research clearly poses the risk of alienating various beneficiaries of that research. Traditionally, the articulated goals of university research have been to advance scientific knowledge and to benefit various publics. As noted earlier, in many cases those publics have been associated with particular economic or industrial groups. But in these activities, the university traditionally was viewed as a service organization, rather than an organization trying to make money on what it was doing. The perception that universities are in the business of research to make money can cause a significant change in public attitudes, and perhaps in public policy.

I noted above that the new proclivity to patent research findings whenever possible runs the risk of, among other things, downplaying and at least partially blocking the traditional pathways through which university research results get picked up by industry. Here I want to flag an area where I think that problem potentially is particularly serious.

As I noted earlier, the last quarter century has seen the intrusion of intellectual property rights into what used to be the domain of public open science. This largely has been the result of Patent Office and Court decisions that have extended the range of what is patentable. Research results, particularly techniques, or conceptions of a line of attack on a practical problem that may prove fruitful, now often fall within the realm of the patentable. That is, patents are now being given on the results of research whose use is mainly in additional research, with a long and uncertain path ahead before anything of actual practical use may be discovered or created. Thus, firms, and universities, are now often in the position where they need to get permission, or even to obtain a license, in order to do research of certain kinds. The issue of patents on research tools has received considerable attention in the United States. For the most part, the patent-holding organizations whose actions are proposed to be increasing the transaction costs of doing science have been for-profit companies, not universities. But in a number of cases recently, those entities have been universities. Consider the recent announcement of the University of Wisconsin of its control of stem cell patents, and the concern among researchers caused by that announcement..

When the custom develops of placing patents on research results, the consequences may not only be to restrict access to use of those results, but also to hinder the openness of research activity in the area more generally. Research groups become more reluctant to exchange preliminary research findings with each other. This is not just a theoretical possibility. While the effects of patenting, and hopes of patenting, on the communication patterns in basic research fields where patenting has become the norm have not been systematically studied, there are a sufficient number of anecdotes to indicate that there is real cause for concern.

I believe it is extremely important to preserve a large domain for open public science, and to resist encroachments of private property rights into that domain, even if one believes the central purpose of science is to increase human material well-being, and even if one believes that for-profit firms are almost always the appropriate vehicles not only for delivering goods and services but also for doing the end-stage work of designing and developing new products. Under the latter presumption, patenting inventions that are close to commercial use is a reasonable thing to do, although I note a series of empirical studies which have found that, except in a few industries, patents are not the central vehicle that firms use to appropriate returns from their R&D.

But what of the upstream body of knowledge and technique that is widely used in R&D? I am concerned in particular with the body of understanding and technique that is far distant from any easily specifiable commercial application, but which provides valuable starting points and inputs to activities of a wide variety of shapes and forms that may bring applications more clearly into view.

I think there are strong arguments for keeping much of this kind of understanding in the public domain, available for anyone who thinks they see a promising research road that builds from or uses it, and free of the encumbrances associated with the need to take out a license before use. The range of potential uses is too wide, the gains to be made in use too uncertain; and even after further success in research, the path to travel to something of practical use is still too long and poorly mapped for commercial markets to work well in this arena. There are strong reasons why it desirable for the research opportunities to be open to any competent scientist or scientific team who sees excitement and promise in exploring a particular path and, in turn, for the results to be open for others to work from, to the extent that they largely are inputs to further research. (For a similar argument see Dasgupta and David, 1994.)

While university patents are becoming important in this arena, there is good reason to believe that the university system will arrange matters so that university researchers can use the patented results of other university researchers' work without too much hassle and expense. On the other hand, there may be an undesirable tendency of university technology transfer offices to restrict or make cumbersome the ability of industry labs to work with patented university research results, even for relatively fundamental explorations.

It would appear that traditionally companies have not bothered to go after university researchers who are using their patented processes or inputs, so long as that research was fundamental in nature and the patented item was not something where the company expected to gain significant money from licensing researchers (as with a research tool). Thus there has been a de facto *research exemption.* However, the new proclivity of universities to patent their own research results, and to try to push these towards commercial applications, clearly is causing some companies to change their minds on this. To the extent that universities are seen as commercially oriented entities, and their research a potential threat to companies whose research outputs they are using, they may lose their research exemption.

There is no persuasive evidence that the basic research enterprise has been seriously encumbered by these problems, as of yet. However, the problem here is potentially serious. The major achievements of American research universities have been made in an environment of open public science. It is in their interest not to have these norms and customs erode. This means, it seems to me, that when universities get patents on research findings and products that are important inputs to future research, their licensing policies should be designed to ensure that all potential research users have more or less automatic access with low costs of transaction and use. These may often not be the licensing policies that universities see as maximizing their expected revenues. But it is vitally important that universities, in this arena and in others, not confuse their legitimate roles and objectives with those of private for-profit business firms.

15.5 The Important Elements

So, what have been the most important factors behind the major contributions that American research universities have been making to technological and economic development, for more than a century? The research effectiveness of universities could not have happened if the quality of the researchers had not been high, and if they had not been well supported in the areas that mattered to industry and to the other publics that were drawing from university research. By and large, public finance of university research in these areas has been generous. The university contributions didn't come for free.

American universities have been flexible and pioneering in their ability to support research in Pasteur's quadrant. When the American chemical industry began to develop, American universities pioneered in the field of chemical engineering. Electrical engineering arose at several American universities in response to the needs of the new electrical equipment industry. American universities pioneered in aeronautical engineering. They quickly embraced the new fields of material science and computer science. American medical schools were quick to pick up on the promise of molecular biology. This creative adaptation to new scientific fields and opportunities, and new practical needs, has been a hallmark of the American university system, and an area where the European and Japanese university systems have fallen short.

And American research universities have, by and large, welcomed contacts with industry, and more generally with those that were the target beneficiaries of their research. This was the case long before Bayh-Dole, and until recently it has proceeded without the universities claiming any patent rights or taking royalties of any magnitude.

The patenting and licensing activities of American universities in the era since Bayh-Dole may well have facilitated technology transfer in certain cases. But my central argument in this essay is that this is not the heart of the capability. It is a mistake to think that it is.

I want to conclude by acknowledging that the basic argument I have put forth in this essay is what I believe, based on my reading of piecemeal evidence. The part of my argument to the effect that university patenting seldom is a necessary ingredient for effective technology transfer is controversial, and I admit that my evidence for it is limited. Obviously, exploring this issue on a wider front, and in more depth, is a high-priority item for research in this field.

15.6 Literature References

Bresnahan, T. and Malerba, F. (1999).'The Computer Industry'. In *The Sources of Economic Leadership*, Mowery, D. and Nelson, R., (eds.) Cambridge: Cambridge University Press.

Cohen, W., Nelson, R., and Walsh, J. (2001). *Links and Impacts: The Influence of Public Research on Industrial R and D.* Manuscript, Carnegie Mellon University, April 2001.

Colyvas, J., Crow, M., Gelijns, A., Mazzoleni, R., Nelson, R., Rosenberg, N. and Sampat, B. (2001). 'How Do University Inventions Get Into Practice'. *Management Science*, 48, pp. 61-72.

Dasgupta, P. and David, P. (1994). 'Towards a New Economics of Science'. *Research Policy.*

Gelijns, A. and Rosenberg, N. (1999). 'Medical Devices'. In Mowery and Nelson (1999).

Griliches, Z. (1957). 'Hybrid Corn: An Exploration in the Economics of Technological Change'. *Econometrica.*

Henderson, R., Orsenigo, L. and Pisano, G. (1999). 'Pharmaceuticals'. In Mowery and Nelson (1999).

Mowery, D. and Nelson, R. (1999). *The Sources of Industrial Leadership.* Cambridge: Cambridge University Press.

Mowery, D., Nelson, R., Sampat, B. and Ziedonis, A. (2001). 'The Growth of Patenting and Licensing by U.S. Universities: An Assessment of the Effects of the Bayh-Dole Act of 1980'. *Research Policy.*

Mowery, D. and Rosenberg, N. (1989). *Technology and the Pursuit of Economic Growth.* Cambridge: Cambridge University Press.

Mowery, D. and Simcoe, T. (2002). 'The Origins and Evolution of the Internet'. In Steil, B., Victor, D., and Nelson, R. (eds.). *Technological Innovation and Economic Performance,* Princeton: Princeton University Press.

Rosenberg, N. and Nelson, R. (1994).'American Universities and Technical Advance in Industry'. *Research Policy.*

Rosenberg, N. (1998).'Technological Change in Chemicals: The Role of University-Industry Relations'. In *Chemicals and Long Run Economic Growth,* Arora, A., Landau, R. and Rosenberg, N. (eds). NY: John Wiley.

Rosenberg, N. (2001). *Engineering Knowledge.* Manuscript, Stanford University, Sept. 4, 2001.

Sampat, B. and Nelson, R. (2002). 'The Emergence and Standardization of University Technology Transfer Offices: A Case Study of Institutional Change'. In Ingram, P. and Silvermn, B.S. (eds.), *The New Institutionalism in Strategic Management,* Boston: JAI Press.

Stokes, D. (1997). *Pasteur's Quadrant.* Washington: Brookings.

Chapter 16

PATENTS AS STRUCTURAL CAPITAL – TOWARDS LEGAL CONSTRUCTIONISM

Ulf Petrusson
Center for Intellectual Property Studies, Chalmers University of Technology and Göteborg University, School of Law, Göteborg, Sweden

Chapter contents:

Abstract: This paper analyses the intellectual property and intellectual property right concepts and their interaction with the transformation of industrial society. Its main aim is to increase the understanding of how the concept of patent and the concepts which underlie the Patent Institute are integrated with technological and industrial development. This aim involves not only a questioning of the intellectual property concepts within jurisprudence, but also a more radical questioning of concepts of law and how law interacts with an increasingly knowledge-oriented economic system. A marked feature of the analysis is an endeavor to capture the complexities of intellectual property as a phenomenon and to contribute to a constructionistic understanding of law.

O. Granstrand (ed.), Economics, Law and Intellectual Property, 363-394.

16.1 Introduction

In 1958, Fritz Machlup made an important remark about the concept of intellectual property in his well-known examination of the economic impact of the patent system. He concluded: "The meaning and object of 'property' and 'property rights' are shrouded by confusions, which, however are more troublesome to lawyers than to economists. But it is almost embarrassing how often the controversial idea of property right in invention is confused with the noncontroversial idea of a property right in a patent".[1] Machlup, as I see it, realized that there exists a fundamental uncertainty, as well as lack of awareness, regarding the intellectual property concept. Now that we are entering an era of globalization, which is more information- and knowledge-orientated, it seems increasingly important that there should be, if not a common understanding, at least an awareness of the different views of the concept. If one is not even aware of the confusion, how can it be possible to determine or question whether the concept actually stimulates the development of new inventions and innovations, the establishing of new high-tech firms, and the structural transformation of an emerging knowledge-orientated market economy? Of course, it is particularly difficult for those who are to make use of the intellectual property and intellectual property right concepts when they are creating the structures of a firm, conducting business and concluding transactions.

From a Scandinavian perspective, I would argue, the confusion is graver than ever. Hence, the more important intangibles as commercial phenomena become, and the more we have to use the concepts in commercial transactions and agreements, the greater the confusion becomes. If we do not know how to handle intellectual property concepts in the traditional "patent sphere", how are we to treat new phenomena relating to the Internet, telecommunication and biotechnology? Especially troublesome is the unawareness among specialists in IPR, who too often do not realize that confusion exists. It is not unusual that lawyers draft license agreements without clarifying the object of the license; there is confusion about whether it is the patent or the invention, and/or whether it is the wider technical invention or the more narrow patentable invention, which is licensed. It is even possible that the same contract includes clauses which state that the licensee is granted permission to act in a specific way, that is, the license does not place any

[1] Machlup, Fritz, "An Economic Review of the Patent System", Study of the Subcommittee on Patents, Trademarks and Copyrights of the Committee on the Judiciary, United States Senate, 85th Congress, 2nd Session, 1958, p. 53.

property at the licensee's disposal. These rather common confusions regarding license agreements are, in my opinion, the result of a prevailing unawareness regarding the intellectual property concept.[2]

The obvious question following Machlup's conclusion is whether it is possible to treat inventions as intellectual property, or whether it is only the patent that may be subject to commercial transactions as property. Another traditional question within jurisprudence is whether the patent should be handled as property and property rights at all. Perhaps it is more correct to describe patents as monopolies – a position upheld by trade regulation? The patent could then be described as a government "permit" giving the patentee the right to prohibit or sanction the market behavior of others within a specific technical field.

If it is possible to treat intangible inventions as property, however, should then only patentable inventions be regarded as property? Perhaps it is also possible to use a wider concept of invention as property; if that is the case, is it then also possible to consider phenomena like computer programs, databases, know-how, R&D results, homepages and broadband as property? If it is possible to use these wider concepts, it also becomes obvious that we have to question the meaning of "rights" when handling intellectual property concepts. Is it, for instance, possible to assign rights to intellectual assets which are not directly related to patents and copyrights but still construed as intellectual property?

It should be emphasized that a structural transformation is taking place in which intellectual properties are becoming the most important and valuable commercial assets of many firms, despite the fact that even specialists seem to be unaware of the meaning of intellectual property or intellectual property rights.[3] The overall trend suggests that the market economy is shifting towards a system based on license control, in which the individual company's ability to master intellectual property will determine competitiveness.[4] Pat-

---

[2] An example would be the Block Exemption on technology transfer, EC Reg. 240/96. Art 1.1 (1) speaks of licensed technology. Art. 8.2 stipulates that the regulation applies to exploitation of inventions. Art.10 speaks of "[p]atents where a license under the patent is necessar[y]".

[3] There are many studies on this topic. See for example Petrusson, Ulf, *Patent och industriell omvandling*, Stockholm: Norstedts Juridik (1999), pp. 125-130.

[4] Compare Petrusson, Ulf, "Structural transformation towards license-based R&D-structures", in Workshop Report on IPR aspects of Internet collaborations, European Commission, fifth framework program (2001), pp. 36-39. Compare also Merges, Robert and Nelson, Richard, "Market Structure and Technical Advance: The Role of Patent Scope Decisions", in Jorde and Teece, *Antitrust, Innovation and Competitiveness*, New York: Oxford University Press (1992), p. 201. Compare also Sherman, Brad, "Governing Science – Patents and Public Sector

ents, for example, constitute not only important assets, but also vital strategic means in the struggle for high-tech competitiveness.[5] The increasing strategic interest that we now experience could be seen as the result of a process of transformation in which business and industry have become more knowledge-orientated. One of the key changes is that it has become more important to transform knowledge not only into general corporate assets but also into virtual products and other commodifiable intellectual capital.[6] This structural transformation, though, seems to be the result of a more or less uncontrolled evolution, which is ironic given its economic significance.[7]

If we consider the consequences of this state of unawareness and confusion of the intellectual property and intellectual property right concepts, it would not necessarily lead to a negative and destructive development. A case could be argued that it actually stimulates the structural transformation of society. On the other hand, it might also be one of the important factors which contribute to our lack of control over such a transformation. It could even be one of the most important risk factors which could lead to recession or, eventually, even to a collapse of the economy.

However, it is reasonable to assume that the confusion is destructive, especially in the commercial process in which patents are used to create new business structures. I would stress that when one is developing strategies on how to use the concepts of property and property rights – which will be discussed below as "structural tools" – it is very important to be aware of their complexity. This is equally important when one makes operational use of the concepts – which will be discussed below as "structural bricks" – for the creation of the firm itself, as well as for the creation of products and services, and even in the creation of markets. Unawareness and confusion of property concepts would probably result in inferior structural tools, and subsequently the "structural bricks" would be of poor quality as well. Naturally this need not lead to a structural collapse.

Research in the United Kingdom", *International Review of Industrial Property and Copyright Law*, Vol. 26, No.1 (1995), p. 22.

[5] See for example Merges, Robert and Nelson, Richard, "On the Complex Economics of Patent Scope", *Columbia Law Review* (1990), p. 908. IVA-M 281. *Profit from Innovation – A Comparison of Swedish and Japanese Intellectual Property Management*, Stockholm: Royal Swedish Academy of Engineering Science (1993), p. 19.

[6] See, for example, Computer Science and Telecommunication Board, National Research Council, *The Digital Dilemma: Intellectual Property in the Information Age*, Washington D.C.: National Academy Press (2000), pp. 152-198. Harris, Lesley Ellen, *Digital Property – currency of the 21st century*, McGraw-Hill Ryerson (1998), pp. 37-47.

[7] *The Digital Dilemma: Intellectual Property in the Information Age*, p. 54, op.cit.

Who, then, is responsible for this lack of common understanding of the intellectual property concept? It would be easy in a civil law tradition to accuse the legislature, since the legislature is the body which should clarify how the intellectual property concept is to be understood. But is it justifiable? Should the responsibility perhaps lie upon legal theorists to examine the law and explain to others how to understand and use such concepts? Or should it lie upon the judges, who clarify the concepts by interpreting the law? What if it is not the legal profession that stipulates what should be regarded as property? Could it be that the use of the property concept in management actually determines the concept and the legal profession must follow suit? If that is the case, should we argue that companies not only are responsible for the existence of their own structures, but also have to assume self-regulatory responsibility for the creation of new intellectual properties, and thereby also for the transformation of legal constructions?

Even though the confusion and lack of awareness still could be described as a practical legal problem in a national legal system, where the severity of the problem differs depending on which nation is focused upon, we ought to recognize the problem as theoretically fundamental and, thus, should realize that it is a global question. For a knowledge-based company, devoted to commercializing knowledge, it is crucial that intellectual capital which is recognized as property in one country also is recognized as such in other countries. It is reasonable to assume that confusion, unawareness, insecurity, and even explicit national differences concerning what a company can govern as properties, have a structurally destructive effect on the transformation to an intellectualized economy.

The purpose of this paper is to analyze intellectual property from a conceptual perspective in general, and as a structural phenomenon in the "patent sphere" in particular. What is to be considered property, and how legal concepts are to be understood and used in the emergence of a new global, knowledge-based economy, will be discussed. The main aim is to increase the understanding of how to govern intellectual property concepts and intellectual property right concepts in legal argumentation. The ambition is to contribute to a constructionist approach in legal argumentation. Important to illustrate is the interaction between legal concepts and concepts in management and also in economics.[8] It is important that we within jurisprudence

[8] As will be argued at the end of this article, I think that a constructionistic approach will increase the possibilities for integration between law, economics and management. David makes the following remark about economic studies of intellectual property: "They should take more pains not to allow familiar, simplifying abstractions to obscure a central fact about

question how intellectual property concepts interact with the usage and application of the concepts in a specific technological and financial context.[9] Especially important for progress towards legal constructionism is the normative development of intellectual capital concepts, used by theorists as well as managers.[10] It opens up a path whereby we can analyze as well as govern patents, patentable inventions, technical inventions etc as structural capital: on the one hand as intellectually substantial concepts (structural tools), and on the other hand as applied commercial phenomena (structural bricks) used to construct commercial reality.

It is important to acknowledge that if we are to be able to understand the inherent complexity of intellectual property, we must question our understanding of law as well. Perhaps the chief conclusion to be drawn in this article is that neither law nor intellectual property exists in itself, and that law, as well as intellectual property, is nothing else than the beliefs which are communicated between different actors/governance structures. This means that property is a concept, and that the concept is nothing else than what we individually, and collectively, believe it to be. Thus, from this point of view it is necessary to look at intellectual property in a global as well as in a more interdisciplinary context. The article will hopefully contribute to ridding us of a naïve legal formalism and to fostering a perspective that not only ac-

---

the nature of the world for which they would prescribe institutions reforms, namely that the complex of body of law, judicial interpretation, and administrative practice that one has to grapple with in this field was not created by some rational, consistent, social welfare-maximizing public agency. What one is faced with, instead, is a mixture of the intended and unintended consequences of an undirected historical process on which the varied interests of many parties, acting at different points (some widely separated in time)... So, it would be really quite remarkable if the evolution of legal institutions concerning patents, copyrights, and trade secrets had somehow resulted in a set of instruments optimally designed to serve either public policy purposes or the private economic interests of individuals and firm seeking such protections". David, Paul, "Intellectual Property Institutions and the Panda's Thumb: Patents, Copyrights, and Trade Secrets in Economic Theory and History", in Wallerstein, M.B., M.E. Mogee and R.A. Schoen (eds.)., *Global Dimensions of Intellectual Property Rights in Science and Technology*, National Research Council, National Academy Press (1993), p. 21.

[9] Compare Bruun, Niklas, *The Role of The Patent system in the Protection of Intellectual Property*, NIR (1992), p. 206.

[10] See for example Kaplan, Robert S. and Norton, David P., "Why Does Business Need a Balanced Scorecard?" *Journal of Strategic Performance Measurement*, February/March 1997, Vol. 1, No. 1, pp. 5-11. Edvinsson, Leif and Malone, Michael S., *Intellectual Capita*, New York, N.Y.: Harper Business (1997). Sveiby, Karl Erik, *The New Organizational Wealth: Managing and Measuring Knowledge-based Assets*, San Fransisco, CA: Berrett-Koehler (1997).

cepts that intellectual property is a social construction, but also allows us to handle the construction process with an open mind.[11] I am of the opinion that legal realism, with critical analysis of intellectual property and rights as metaphysics, is the way to increase such awareness.[12]

16.2 Property and Property Right Status – a Brief Historical Exposé of the Patent Concept

A central supposition is that the patent institution is in a state of continual change in its interaction with industrial transformation. We are becoming aware of an increasing strategic interest which alters the concepts of patent law, not only within the economic sphere but gradually also within the legal profession. The obvious subject for analysis is therefore how patentability criteria, patent-claim theory etc, are influenced by industrial transformation. From an overall, legal-realist perspective, however, it is even more interesting to speculate on how ideas relating to patents and inventions themselves may be changing.

From the point of view of legal history the patent institution is a relatively new construction which, during its brief existence, has presented a theoretical challenge to academia. By analyzing patent theory one can get a good picture of how the institution has been altered over time. Especially interesting is whether, and how, the understanding of the patent was altered when new legal theories emerged – theories with fundamental implications for the understanding of law itself. This survey of patent theory and jurisprudence, however, is only a brief exposé.

---

[11] A remark made by Nelson, Winters *et al.*, that "patents do not always work in practice, as they do in theory", points toward a more evolutionary patent theory in which we ought to analyze the meaning of the property concept in a structural transformation process, where the firms are competence-based. Levin, Klevorick, Nelson and Winter, "Appropriating the Returns from Industrial Research and Development", *Brookings Papers on Economic Activity* 3, (1987), p. 784.

[12] The Danish realist Alf Ross said that law is of magical nature: Ross, Alf, *Virkelighed og Gyldighed i Retslæren – En kritik af den teoretiske retsvidenskabs grundbegreber*, Copenhagen: Levin and Munksgaard (1934), p. 19. The Swedish realist Karl Olivecrona described legal phenomena as fantasy-beliefs: Olivecrona, Karl, *Lagens imperativ*, Lund: Gleerups (1942), p. 5.

16.2.1 A monopoly based on public regulation – the mercantilist origin

The patent construction has its origin in the mercantilist era and the systems of privileges.[13] Philosophically the ideas of the patent emerged from what we today would describe as an economic discussion.[14] This was an epoch where legal philosophy became more and more separated from theology, giving room to economics as a discipline. In the theoretical and political discussions dominated by free trade ideology, the patent was mainly discussed as a monopoly granted to the inventor.[15] The patent was a permit from the state, which gave the holder the sole right to carry on a certain type of enterprise. In the English Statute of Monopolies from 1624 the patent was a "grant of monopoly power by the state over the commercial exploitation of an invention for a limited time".[16] The patent provisions were exemptions from the general rule that prohibited monopolies. The patent was thereby primarily understood as a means to prevent others from using a specific technology.[17] Consequently, we could argue that in the beginning neither the patent nor the invention created any notion of property.

---

[13] The common opinion is that patent theories originated in the view of society referred to as mercantilism. The first regulation which made the protection of inventions possible is said to have been instituted in 1474 in Venice. See for example Machlup, Fritz, "An Economic Review of the Patent System", Study of the Subcommittee on Patents, Trademarks and Copyrights of the Committee on the Judiciary United States Senate, 85th Congress, 2nd Session (1958). Neumeyer, Fredrik, *Patent i omvandling, en översikt över svenska och internationella patentfrågor*. Stockholm: Studieförbundet Näringsliv och Samhälle (1977), p. 7. Neumeyer confirmed the earlier view of the origin of patents in 17th-century England.

[14] See Godenhielm, Berndt, *Patentskyddets omfattning på basen av patentanspråkets funktionella innehåll*, Juridiska Föreningen, Finland, Publication series no. 20 (1950), p. 10.

[15] Smith advocates the patent system and argues that it is essential for the inventor, during a limited period of time, to be able to receive compensation for work done, in particular since such compensation would depend on the commercial success of the invention in accordance with the principles of supply and demand. Smith, Adam, *Lectures on Jurisprudence*, Oxford at the Clarendon Press (1978, original from 1762-63), p. 83.

[16] Walterscheid, Edward C., "The Early Evolution of the United States Patent Law" (Part 1), *Journal of the Patent and Trademark Office Society*, Vol. 76, No. 9 (1994), p. 700.

[17] Concerning the early aversion to monopolies in England, see Fox, Harold, *Monopolies and Patents. A Study of the History and Future of the Patent Monopoly*, Toront: University of Toronto Press (1947), pp. 127-145.

16.2.2 Inventors' right to their inventions – the influence of the natural law tradition

The influences of different liberal traditions created ideas which emphasized the need to "both recognize and protect a property right in invention".[18] It was also important that it was "the true and first inventor" who would receive the patent. Only in France, however, were patents looked upon as "rights of natural law". In other countries the emergence of the notion of property was more gradual. According to the tradition of natural law, property was the inventors' ideas, as they understood them. Important for this development was of course John Locke's "labor theory", according to which the natural right to property emanated from the idea of everyone's right to enjoy the fruits of their labor.[19] The concepts of natural rights changed the attitudes towards patents. Now the patent represented the inventor's natural right to his invention. This meant that it became the inventor's possession. Even if one did not accept the natural rights position, it nevertheless became common to regard both patents and inventions as property.

One influential philosopher who developed the concept of property right was David Hume, who defined property right as "a relation between a person and an object as permits him, but forbids any other, the free use and possession of it, without the laws of justice and moral equity".[20] Hume's theory was an important contribution to the understanding of patents both as property rights and as property.

16.2.3 Patents as property – the utilitarian approach

As liberal ideas developed, the transformation of the legal system was characterized by the vision of a private sphere in which individuals should

---

[18] Bernitz describes the period with a starting-point in the notion of the acknowledgement of a system of private law. Bernitz, Ulf, *Marknadsrätt*, Stockholm, Jurist och samhällsvetareförbundets Förlag (1969), pp. 118-119. A similar view can be found in Machlup, Fritz, and Penrose, Edith, *The Patent Controversy* (1959), p. 2. Compare Undén, Östen, *Översikt över den svenska patenträtten*, C.W.K., Lund: Gleerups Förlag (1915), p. 1. Walterscheid, Edward C., "The Early Evolution of the United States Patent Law: Antecedents" (Part 1), *Journal of the Patent and the Trademark Office Society*, Vol. 76, No. 9 (1994) (1959), p. 699. Dutton, H. I., *The patent system and inventive activity during the industrial revolution 1750-1852*, Manchester, Manchester University Press (1985).

[19] Locke, John, *Two Treatises of Government* (1980, orig. 1690), Cambridge University Press, pp. 304-308.

[20] Cairns, Huntington, *Legal Philosophy from Plato to Hegel*, Baltimore, The Johns Hopkins Press (1949), p. 385.

be free and able to control private property without government interference.[21] In Anglo-American development, which was more utilitarian, it was seemingly more common to regard patents as property. Bentham, being a prominent figure in the utilitarian tradition, had argued that there was no existing natural property; property was a result of regulation, court decisions etc.[22] A granted patent was the most obvious result of such regulation. The patent holder ought, therefore, to have the right to sell, and in other ways dispose of, his patent as private property.

16.2.4 Theories of the objectively defined invention as property

The late 19th century was the heyday of theories which argued that the invention should be understood as property. In Germany an object theory emerged which implied that the invention, as something objectively determinable, generated legally defined property that could be the object of patenting. The legal philosopher Josef Kohler was especially important for this development.[23] According to Kohler the object which was protected by the patent was the invention. The basic idea was to make it objectively possible for anyone to determine what the invention was. By studying the patent claims one should be able to see the patented invention. Thereafter it was possible to relate to the invention as an intellectual object, which could be defined from the patent claims. The late 19th century was very dynamic when it came to understanding patents as private property rights. The prevailing notion was that the patent could not be systematized in the same way as ownership to material property, but could be understood as a right related to that of the property concept.[24]

---

[21] H Habermas, Jürgen, *Borgerlig offentlighet*, Lund: Arkiv Förlag (1984; orig. "Strukturwandel der Öffentlichkeit", 1962), p. 99.

[22] Bentham, Jeremy, *Manual of Political Economy*, pp. 263-265. In Stark, W., *J. Bentham's Economic Writings*, Vol. 1, The Royal Economic Society (1952, orig. 1793-1795).

[23] Important works of Kohler are Kohler, Josef, *Urheberrecht an Schriftwerken und Verlagsrecht*, Stuttgart: Ferdinand Enke (1907), Kohler, Josef, *Forschungen aus dem Patentrecht*, Mannheim: Beusheimer (1888)

[24] Ekeberg points out that neither the theory of possession nor the theory of vindication has been considered relevant as an argument that rules of property could not be applied, at least indirectly. Ekeberg, Birger, *Studier i patenträtt*, Uppsala: Almqvist and Wicksells Boktryckeri (1904), p. 42.

16.2.5 Scandinavian legal realism and the critique of the property concept

During the 20th century there emerged a critique against those legal theories that regarded inventions as property. Developments in Scandinavia took a different turn in connection with the realist current of ideas. Scandinavian realism, mainly through the theoretical work of Ross, came to have a marked influence on the theory of intellectual property rights, giving a unique character to the debate in the Scandinavian countries. Ross claimed that the only properties one can speak about are material products.[25] According to Ross, the intellectual object is nothing more than an individual experience, and cannot as such be regarded as a reality.[26] Ross thereby returned to the original standpoint in which patents were looked upon as a position where one could forbid certain behavior by others. Ross' critique was radical, though accepted by many Scandinavian legal theorists specialized in IPRs.[27]

16.2.6 All the different concepts are to be found in today's legal argument

The controversies which we can discern historically, concerning the theoretical significance of the patent institution, reflect differences of opinion in relation not only to the area of intellectual property rights, but also to law as an intellectual phenomenon and, logically, to jurisprudence itself. The debate, however, did not attain to clarity and, on the contrary, complexity and uncertainty are more evident than ever, which among other things is connected with the fact that realism never achieved a substantial breakthrough into intellectual property rights theory. The influence of other traditions such as that of object theory is still obvious.

As I see it, our situation today is a result of all these different theories. It is important to stress that the impact of all of them can be found in Swedish patent law. When the criteria of inventive step and technical effect, for example, are described, the invention is understood as a wider technical phenomenon than the patentable invention (Art. 1, Swedish Patent Act

---

[25] Ross, Alf, *Ophavsrettens grundbegreber*. TfR, 1945, p. 340.

[26] Ibid. p. 345.

[27] Koktvedgaard, belonging as he does to the more radical and realist-oriented intellectual rights theoreticians, follows Ross in emphasizing the importance of understanding the Patent Institute in an openly functional perspective. Koktvedgaard, Mogens, *Immaterialretspositioner*, Stockholm: Juristforbundets Forlag (1965). See also Bergström, Svante, *Uteslutande rätt att förfoga över verket. Studier över upphovsmannarättens föremål och innehåll enligt det s.k. nordiska förslaget*, Uppsala, Sweden, Universitetets Årsskrift 1954:8. Uppsala, Sweden.

1967:837). The approach to the invention as an objectively definable object can be traced in, for example, rules stating who the inventor is and deciding the scope of the patent. The regulations of the relationship between employers and employees are focused on the rights to patentable inventions (Art. 1, The Swedish Act on the Right to Employee Inventions 1949:345). The regulations on pledge, however, are focused on the patent and the patent applications (Art. 94, Swedish Patent Act 1967:837). Concerning patent infringement, the patent is described more as a right to forbid the behavior and actions of others (Art. 57-58, Swedish Patent Act 1967:837).

There will always be confusion concerning the concept of property and property rights due to the national and international complexity of the issues both in theory and in practice. We have to realize that it is an impossible task to make sure that there will exist no confusions or uncertainties. It will, for example, never be possible for a national legislature to draft an act that would resolve these problems – especially not as long as the confusion is a result of different approaches to law and jurisprudence. For me it is important to make clear that the patent institution, as well as law itself, is primarily a communicative notion, which is constantly changing. Communicatively it becomes obvious that the function of a specific legal construction is not separable from the construction in itself.

16.3 A Functional Concept of Property and Rights – the Path of Scandinavian Realism

If we are to grasp the complexity of intellectual property it is of utmost importance to understand the different concepts that comprise the construction process, and how these concepts are transformed. The next step in this article is to further penetrate Scandinavian legal realism and its functional concept of property right.

16.3.1 The "concept of rights" in Scandinavian realism

The Scandinavian realists Hägerström and Lundstedt declared, in their polemic against the prevailing legal tradition, that the judicial system is nothing more than social machinery in which the cogs are people.[28] Ross displayed a similar way of thinking when, in his earlier work, he analyzed

[28] Hägerström, Axel, "En straffrättslig principundersökning", *Svensk Juridisk Tidskrift* (1939), p. 214.

law as a totality of governance.[29] A characteristic of the Scandinavian realists is that they describe law, and concepts of rights, as a false conceptual world which conceals real considerations. However, in their early analyses of the legal concepts of property and ownership, Lundstedt, Olivecrona and Ross were all relatively advanced at a practical, functional level. It was probably Lundstedt who was most advanced in his sociological discursions at a more comprehensive theoretical level. Lundstedt described functional rights as *favored positions*.[30] The belief that there exists a right gives anyone who claims proprietorship a position, which can activate the legal machinery. A proprietor could then activate intervention.[31] Olivecrona, who very much agreed with Lundstedt, stated that the belief in the existence of the right constituted a feeling of power and strength.[32] This feeling would become obvious in situations of conflict and potential conflict.[33] He also showed that the belief in a property right creates *consequential beliefs*.[34] The belief that someone has proprietorship creates the consequential belief that the government would intervene if another person were to use that property without permission. Another consequential belief is that contractual transactions would be upheld in court. [35]

Ross developed a functional concept of rights.[36] He accepted the realistic standpoints as they were put forward by Hägerström and, in the same way as Lundstedt, he focused on how the belief in a right could generate "favored positions". [37] His theory of how property rights are the result of self-assertive interests is especially interesting.[38] Ross' theories open the way for an understanding of the concept of rights as a belief. This belief is based on market power and the ability of those with specific interests to persuade others to accept property claims. Here Ross is very much in line with Lundstedt, who

---

[29] Ross, Alf, *Virkelighed og Gyldighed i Retslæren,* Copenhagen: Levin & Munksgaard, (1934), p. 113.

[30] Lundstedt, Vilhelm, *Obligationsbegreppet.* Senare delen. Första häftet. A.-B. L Norblads bokhandel (1930), p. 107.

[31] Ibidem.

[32] Olivecrona, Karl, *Rätt och dom,* Stockholm, P.A. Norstedts and Söners Förlag (2nd edition, 1966), p. 99.

[33] Ibid.

[34] Ibid p. 104.

[35] Ibid p. 110.

[36] Ross, Alf, *Ejendomsret og ejendomsovergang,* Copenhagenn: Levin and Munksgaard (1935), p. 13.

[37] Ross, Alf, *Om ret og retfærdighet,* Köpenhamn, Nyt nordisk Forlag, Arnold Busck a/s (3rd edition, 1971 [1953]), p. 213.

[38] Ibid p. 214.

explicitly explained that concepts of rights are façades, which serve to veil interests that ought to be discussed. Late in his career Ross was influenced by modern semantic research and focused on the function of the rights concept in legal argumentation. Ross himself considered that the realist discussion regarding the rights concept had gone through two major stages, and that it was entering into a third.[39] In the first stage Hägerström developed his theory of rights as metaphysical notions. In the second stage Lundstedt developed his theory of rights as beliefs with different functions, which together constituted a favored position. The third stage, according to Ross, was characterized by an attempt to demonstrate the functions of the rights concept in legal argument and judicial proceedings. Both Ross and Olivecrona tried to include the two earlier lines of development in their later, more linguistically influenced studies. Olivecrona argued that a right, as a term, does not express anything in itself. It is instead the consequential beliefs that have directive effects on judges etc. [40] Ross argued in much the same way – that the rights concept is only an aid in legal argumentation.[41]

It is obvious that we still have much to learn from the Scandinavian realists. However, a number of conclusions can be made at this point. Especially important is the conclusion that patents as well as patentable inventions are fictitious or illusionary. We can conclude that there exist several theoretical beliefs regarding patents, which still are communicated and used. At the same time we have to recognize that these beliefs have functions in a market and company context, as well as in a more legal context. An interesting question to ask ourselves is then to what extent these functions differ regarding the different beliefs/concepts. A realistic functional approach makes it possible to ask how the different concepts generate "favored positions". If we choose to describe a patent as a property, a number of consequential ideas will follow. The question is then how these consequential ideas would differ if we were to see the intellectual invention as a property and the patent as a property right. Crucial, however, is the presupposition that we understand how patents and patentable inventions, as illusions, are based upon self-assertive interests.

---

[39] Ross, Alf, "Status i Rettighedsdiskussionen", *Svensk Juridsk Tidskrift* (1953), p. 532.
[40] Olivecrona, *Karl, Rätt och dom* (2nd edition, 1966), p. 125.
[41] Ross, Alf, *Tü-Tü, Festskrift for Henry Ussing*, Juristforbundet (1951), p. 478.

16.3.2 Patents as communicated self-assertive interests

A realistic approach shows us the importance of making a distinction between a descriptive and a normative approach. Legal constructions are by their character normative and value- or interest-based. They do not have any existence in themselves. From a descriptive point of view they are nothing more than communicative actions – shared individual beliefs and individual actions.[42] Normatively the communication is, to a great extent, hidden. This has been described by the conclusion that the legal system is normatively closed.[43] Normatively intellectual property concepts are decided by the use of legal sources. Thus the patent concept is decided by the interpretation of legal sources, and the specific patent is decided by the interpretation of the patent claims. Actors in the legal profession who have not accepted a realistic standpoint and do not differentiate between a descriptive and a normative approach are consequently unwilling to lift the formalistic and normative veil that hides self-assertive interests.

The patent construction and especially the patent application procedure is however a good example of when self-assertive interests, at least to some extent, already today can be recognized from a normative perspective. A common normative understanding is that the patent claim, as put forward in the application, is an expression of the applicant's will, but when the patent is granted, it is instead an expression of the will of the patent authority.[44] The drafted patent claim constitutes an explicit self-assertive element in the administrative decision process. Patent claims, descriptions, drawings and other items, which emerge from the standpoint of the technology, are transformed into normative elements in the patent grant. Descriptively we can see the patent grant as a communicative process that differs depending on to what extent the Patent Office forms an opinion on the concrete invention or through examination of previous applications in the area. Consequently, pat-

---

[42] A descriptive communicative understanding of patents is more thoroughly described in Petrusson, Ulf, *Patent och industriell omvandling – en studie av dynamiken mellan rättsliga och ekonomiska idésystem*, Stockholm: Norstedts Juridik (1999).

[43] Niklas Luhmann is often described as one of the important theorists in social constructionism. Luhmann has a functional approach to law and describes it as on the one hand cognitively open and on the other hand normatively closed — "[t]he unity of the system is produced by the system itself". Luhmann, Niklas, "Operational Closure and Structural Coupling: The Differentiation of The Legal System", *Cardozo Law Review*, Vol. 13, No. 5 (1992), p. 1420.

[44] Godenhielm, Berndt, *Patentskyddets omfattning i europeisk och nordisk rätt*, Helsinki: Juristförbundets förlag (1994), p. 150. See also Godenhielm, Berndt, *Patentskyddets omfång på basen av patentanspråkets funktionella innehåll*, Stockholm: Nord. bokh (1950), p. 129.

ent applications, patents and patented inventions could descriptively be considered as inter-subjective concepts – continually communicatively transformed.

The fact that we can descriptively regard the patent construction as a communicative process based on self-assertive interests is also clear if we consider an infringement case. In the judgment on the scope of protection, beliefs/concepts will be selected from the administrative patent application process. In addition, beliefs regarding the functions of the patent in a commercial context will be selected. Judges will also be affected by descriptions of the inventions as technological phenomena in a competition-related context. Legal counselors will translate their clients' self-assertive interests into arguments that they on the one hand think will affect the judges in the "search process" and on the other hand think that the judge can use in the "justification process". If the judges in the cognitive "search process" are affected by commercial arguments, profit arguments etc, the patent-claim theory will have the effect of giving a façade of legitimacy. It is therefore possible to assert that patent-claim theory does not make it possible to fulfill the ambition of providing a judge with ready-formulated rules on when a patent infringement shall be deemed to have occurred.[45]

More controversial but still even more important to emphasize is that the intellectual property constructions in themselves are constantly changing communicative actions or concepts – to a large extent as a result of hidden self-assertive interests. Criteria regarding patentability are constantly changing as new technological phenomena are created. Patent agents, legal counselors etc create a constant normative pressure on the Patent Office, courts and, of course, the legislature to modify specific provisions. Self-assertive interests are transformed into legal arguments in order to secure investments in information technology, biotech etc.

As described above, the patent concept is under communicative pressure – i.e. there are a number of competing approaches. Even on a theoretical level we can talk about self-assertive interests. Scholars in law as well as economics bring forward normative standpoints on the patent concept as if they were descriptions of reality. Today we work with three different concepts of what constitutes intellectual property and a competing property-less perspective.[46] A view of the invention as an intellectual object increases the

[45] Koktvedgaard, Mogens, *Immaterialretspositioner*, Copenhagen: Juristforbundets forlag (1965), p. 147. Koktvedgaard, Mogens, *Patentloven*, Copenhagen: Juristforbundets forlag (1971), Copenhagen, p. 163.

[46] See above in section 2.

prospects of the patent being regarded as an unlimited protection of the idea, while a view of the invention as first and foremost a "materializable" technological phenomenon tends to limit the patent idea to a concept of protection on the use of a certain product. In my opinion, it is reasonable to assume that the increasing strategic patent interests in business and industry will result in the concept of the invention as an objectively determinable object becoming more widespread. Self-assertive interests to capitalize knowledge and inventions will communicatively strengthen the understanding of the invention as well as the patent as property and capital. Advancements in this respect are directly related to a development in which licensing agreements are given ever greater importance.

16.3.3 Patents as a "favored position" based upon "consequential beliefs" and prognoses

From a traditional realist/pragmatic standpoint, the law is nothing more than what the courts decide it to be.[47] Thus, from a realist viewpoint, a patent can also be described as a "position of governance" (a favored position) based on the prognosis of when a court would rule against someone.[48] The prognosis of when the courts would declare a violation creates the image of an exclusive right. Because judges relate to certain legal sources such as patent regulation, case law and patent documentation when making their considerations, it is also possible to use these sources when we develop our prognosis.[49] The insight into their communicative character, however, tells us that it is too risky to relate only to "legal sources" when making the prognosis. The more we know about the specific judicial behavior and actual considerations etc, the better prognosis of "the law" we can deliver.

It is important in this context to distinguish the normative standpoint that the validity of law is based on court behavior – that is, that the law is made of normative constructions upheld by the courts. From my point of view this normative approach among legal realists has primarily had the function of

---

[47] This notion was discussed by most realists. It had a special impact among American realists and pragmatists. Important early contributors were Pound, Roscoe; see for example Law in "Books and law in action", *American Law Review*, Vol. 44 (1910), p. 12, and Llewellyn, Karl, "A realistic jurisprudence – the next step", *Columbia Law Review*, Vol. 30 (1930), p. 431. Regarding the Scandinavian realists see Ross, Alf, *Om ret og retfærdighet* (3rd ed. 1971), p. 41, Copenhagen: Nyt nordisk Forlag.

[48] Lundstedt, Vilhelm, *Obligationsbegreppet*, (1929), p. 107, Uppsala: Norblad. Ross, Alf, *Ejendomsret og ejendomsovergang* (1935), Copenhagen: Levin & Munksgaard, pp. 536, 540.

[49] Ross, Alf, *Om ret og retfærdighet*, Copenhagen: Nyt nordisk Forlag (3rd ed. 1971), p. 47.

reconstructing law as a coherent and normatively closed system where legal sources are used to "find the law".

The descriptive analysis of the patent as a "governance position" based on prognoses of court behavior is something different. Here we are talking about a specific patent (the patent as a structural building brick), not of the patent concept as a legal construct (as a structural tool). From a company point of view it is obvious that the behaviors in the patent office and in court are the most concrete. Without the patent application you are not even part of the game. After filing for a patent, the favored position is dependent on the prognosis of court behavior. It is therefore possible to argue that the favored position that will be upheld by the courts is the one that should be considered in making business decisions. The favored position upheld by courts is thus the basis for the governance position of the patent in commercial relations – the basis for whether clients, competitors etc are going to be loyal to that patent.

The knowledge of which normative questions or factors the judges will feel bound to makes it possible to create a descriptive infringement-prognosis model of the "governance position" – a model that can be used to evaluate the patent as a "favored position" (as a building brick in the structural creation of commercial reality). The purpose of the evaluation could be to handle a specific infringement situation, but it could also be to analyze a license proposition, a merger, an R&D cooperation etc. What is the real "governance position"? The prognosis of the favored position creates a number of consequential beliefs, for example regarding the licensable object, the company assets, the potential innovations etc.

The analysis of the governance position (i.e. favored position) ought, in consequence, to start with an evaluation of the factors a court would take into consideration in an infringement case. We should now, however, acknowledge that our descriptive analysis also includes a normative element, where we will evaluate the functions of specific normative legal beliefs. In the prognosis we analyze the function of a number of concepts, criteria etc. One should bear in mind that the relevance of the different questions in a model like this depends on the actual behavior of the judges; thus, posing these questions serves no normative purpose in itself.

If a patent has been granted we could use the following simplified model:

1) Would the court consider the patent valid?
2) Would the patent protection be considered to cover the technology in question?

3) Would the court consider the patent holder's behavior to be of an unlawful character?
4) Are there any circumstances, in this particular case, which the court would consider to be an exemption?
5) What would the sanctions be?

The first step would be to determine if and to what extent the court considers that protection actually exists. The fact that there is a patent granted can only lead to a presumption of patent protection. In an infringement situation it is not uncommon that the infringing party claims that the patent is void. The most common ground for repealing a patent is that the patent has been issued without complying with the prerequisites of patent law (Art. 52, Swedish Patent Act 1967:837, EPC Art. 100). Consequently we have to examine the discussion regarding patentability of the invention in the Patent Office. The best information would probably be found in the patent documentation, although it is not the only source. The more we know of what different circumstances and facts actually affect the examiner, the better prognosis we can make. From there we have to consider the risks that the patent will be declared void – completely or in part. If, for example, we know that the information has been made public before the patent application, we know there exists a concrete risk of invalidation.

The next step would be to determine if it is likely that the court would consider the patent to provide coverage in a given situation. The formalistic approach would be to ask if the patent claims block the use of the suspected infringing technology (Art. 39, Swedish Patent Act 1967:837, EPC Art. 84). Once again, the most central source of information would be patent documentation, but information about which factors really influence the decision of the patent examiner would be essential. With better information about what actually influences a judge, the formalistic argument of semantic analysis of patent claims aside, a more accurate prognosis could be made about the outcome of the case. For this purpose, analysis of the market and competition would be useful. It is clear, however, that knowledge about the process of determining the extent of patent protection is elusive. This is explained by the fact that the judges themselves find the question of "scope" elusive, and that different people are likely to come to different conclusions. Still, we have to recognize the importance of the patent claims as a communicative instrument. From a normative point of view, it would be so much more constructive if we could rely on our interpretation of the claims. A descriptive realistic conclusion, however, is that we often cannot.

As a rule, the third question causes less trouble; what commercial behavior would be considered unlawful or not permitted? It is clearly stated in patent regulations what actions, concerning patented products or methods, would be considered violations (Art. 3, Swedish Patent Act 1967:837). With a starting-point in the enumeration of activities not permitted – for example, manufacture, import, marketing and use – the patentee could estimate who would be a potential party to a conflict.

The fourth question is whether there are any circumstances indicating that the court would make an exception in this particular case. A number of legal concepts, such as "right of prior use" (Art. 4, Swedish Patent Act 1967:837), exhaustion of right (Art. 3, Swedish Patent Act 1967:837) and non-commercial use (Art. 3, Swedish Patent Act 1967:837), have been codified. It is important to analyze the impact of these limitations before making prognoses of the outcome of an infringement suit.

The fifth step in the model is a somewhat different question. The exercise is no longer to try and foresee what the court would consider an infringement, but to determine the consequences of certain behavior. This type of estimation is brought to the fore in many contexts when it is necessary to determine the position of governance. The significance of such an estimate is obvious, for example, if a company is considering infringement and judges the risk of sanctions to be negligible or the sanctions to be bearable.

The position of governance is thus estimated after making prognoses about the expected behavior of the court in a number of hypothetical commercial situations. Prognoses of these scenarios create an idea of which actions are permitted or not permitted. Together they create a notion of the patent as an exclusive right. It is this exact notion which makes it possible for the patentee to grant others permission to act in a way which otherwise is perceived or described as unlawful behavior. The understanding of the "governance position" creates consequential beliefs and norms, e.g. consequental beliefs in the patententable invention and the patentent as licensable properties.

16.3.4 Patents in the interaction between a substantial and a functional approach

The realist approach to property rights, as being what the courts decide them to be, is often described as functional, while the more ideological approach where one talks about the subject matter of a property right, content of the right etc is described as substantial.[50] According to a substantial approach based on an "objective theory", the invention is defined by the patent claims. (If we instead have a substantial approach to the patent as the property, the patent claims define the patent.) By applying the criterion of inventive step, the Patent Office decides what is the legal invention. This also means that it is possible to decide what is the patentable invention. Since the inventive step is foreseeable, it is also possible to see how the patent claims are to be decided and one could conclude what the legal invention actually is. Of course it is possible to call such formalism naive. It is also possible, of course, to look at it as an ideal normative picture which we use, at the same time as we are aware of its being too simplistic. However, as long as the normative, substantial model does not work, but we see it as something real, it will shroud the real processes taking place. Thus, substantial formalism tends to be a facade. It is possible to show that it is not a formal interpretation of the inventive step which is the sole basis for the granted claims. Neither are the granted claims the only grounds for the strength of the patent. There are even those who would argue that the claims are, more or less, without importance when the court decides whether or not there is an infringement.

When from a descriptive point of view it becomes obvious that the substantial approach is not applied in the cognitive process – i.e. the substantial patent concept is only used in the justification process – it becomes necessary to argue for another normative substantial model. Another solution would be that we need to develop the realist approach to the concept of right and property – that is, we need to develop a legal constructionist approach.[51] It is important, I believe, to recognize that the Scandinavian realists failed to accept the normative consequences of their own insights. They maintained a

[50] For a thorough analysis of the interaction between a substantial and a functional approach, see Doublet, David R., *Rett vitenskap og fornuft*, Bergen: Alma Mater Forlag (1995).

[51] Other legal theories which have opened the way for progress in a constructionalist tradition are those theories linked to the sociologically orientated views of law, which are expressed in the work of Habermas, Luhmann and Teubner. See Habermas, Jürgen, *Between Facts and Norms – Contributions to a Discourse Theory of Law and Democracy*, London: Polity Press (1996; the original *Faktizität und Geltung* is from 1992). Compare also Habermas, Jürgen, "Law as a medium", in Teubner, *Dilemmas of law in the welfare state*, Berlin/New York: Walter de Gruyter and Co (1986). Habermas is particularly interesting when he describes law as both 'system of knowledge' and 'system of action'. See also Luhmann, Niklas, "The Self-reproduction of Law and its Limits", in Teubner, *Dilemmas of law in the welfare state*, Berlin/New York: Walter de Gruyter and Co (1985); Luhmann, Niklas, 'Operational closure and structural coupling: The differentiation of the legal system', *Cardozo Law Review*, Vol. 13, No. 5 (1992).

monistic attitude, keeping to legal sources as, in principle, the only sources of knowledge, and they still considered systematizing codes of law an important task. We are on relatively safe ground in criticizing the Scandinavian realists for failing to formulate a normative understanding of law that could replace the understanding of law as an ideology (i.e. a existing system of preordained rules). The strength in the realists' approach is found in their descriptive analysis of law in terms of real concepts and conduct in society. To continue to explore this realistic approach, we must once and for all abolish the normative construction of law as a unity in and of itself – as a coherent system – which can be found by studying legal sources. I stress that any furtherance of realism will require us to adopt a more communicative and pluralistic attitude towards law in terms of both concepts and conduct. We have to switch between a pluralistic substantial normative approach and the reality of intellectual concepts as communicative action.

16.4 A structural understanding of intellectual property – towards legal constructionism

The main reason for a legal constructionist approach to intellectual property and rights is the increasing necessity to be able to understand as well as handle the complexities of a knowledge-based and intellectualized structural transformation.[52] The foundation of this approach is, as stated above, that intellectual property and intellectual property rights are societal structures built on nothing more than the collective beliefs shared between persons.[53] In effect they are illusions that have no independent existence; only in their communication are they given substance. Thus, the more people who accept and trust a given intangible phenomenon or concept, the more possible it is that there will develop common consequential beliefs. This will in turn mean that the risk of confusion decreases. If there exists a number of different concepts that are not shared and do not result in the formation of consequential beliefs, there will be no trust, which will probably have destructive commercial effects.[54]

---

[52] The complexity in the "post-industrial era" should at least to some extent be regarded as a result of "a failure to understand complex systematic effects of regulatory interventions". See Sunstein, Cass R., *After the Rights Revolution*. Cambridge, MA: Harvard University Press (1990), p. 91.

[53] Compare the description of 'institutional facts' in Searle, John, *The Construction of Social Reality*. London: Allen Lane (1995).

[54] *The Digital Dilemma: Intellectual Property in the Information Age*, pp. 54-60, op.cit.

The situation where lawyers rhetorically argue that law has an existence of its own is perhaps the single most important factor that hinders the development of awareness of the complex, pluralistic nature of intangibles. The normative concept of law as a coherent and normative closed system must be abandoned, as it is a social construction that unnecessarily blinds us. It is also important to realize that an open acceptance within the legal profession of the role of communicative processes will not result in chaos and the sudden loss of the common understanding of legal constructions. On the contrary, it will most likely increase the possibility that more people will share the same concepts. An increased awareness that intellectual properties are abstractions resulting from self-assertive interests etc will promote an open discussion of which values and interests are stimulated by the creation of favored positions. At the same time it will also become more obvious how important it is that we share the same concepts and consequential beliefs.

Hence I argue that we need to develop a legal constructionist approach to intellectual property. This normative approach should on the one hand promote intellectual property as structural constructions (illusions), and on the other hand always strive to explain the communicative reality. An important task then is to describe the lack of communicative unity instead of stipulating that law is an existing unity, such as the normative standpoint that we as lawyers can interpret the valid patent concept. It is therefore important, in the frame of legal argumentation, to shed light on how the patent, as a structural construction, can be and has been regarded as a property, a property right or an exclusive position. We establish a normative pressure on ourselves to explain how patent constructions, as different substantial concepts, are the results of communicative actions, power struggles and self-assertive interests, internalization and externalization etc. A development like this, of course, has to be collective, and it cannot be separated from the reconstruction of the concept of law and the role or identity of the lawyer.[55] This is clearly an enormous normative project; still, I think it is inevitable.

16.4.1 Acknowledging the illusion of patents and other social constructions

The fact that patent concepts as well as the specific patents themselves are social constructions is obvious for most. A legal constructionist approach,

[55] Compare Petrusson, Ulf, *Den rättsvetenskapliga forskningens roll – Vad bör den rättsvetenskapliga forskningen syssla med och varför?* (Report from Legal Symposium on November 22-23, 2001.) *SvJT* No 3 (2002).

however, requires that we also acknowledge this normatively. Patents have no existence in themselves and cannot be described other than as communicated beliefs and actions. We must always, as stated above, be willing to switch between a substantial approach and an approach where we try to capture the real communicative process.

A legal constructionist approach also shows how important these illusions are. It is not too pretentious to argue that our collective skills of designing society's structures are the essence of civilization. When we focus on patents and other legal phenomena as social constructions and try to develop a theory of legal constructionism, it is only natural to use the construction-metaphor. We can talk about design, construction, reconstruction, creative destruction and deconstruction. The concept of structure has also regained its potential as an important concept to capture the character and function of patents and other legal illusions. Today more and more people speak of "structural capital".[56] The concept of structure clarifies how human relations can be transformed into the experience of a social reality. We experience structural persons such as companies, organizations, universities and public authorities. We also experience structural objects. In the financial sector, money, company shares, promissory notes, stock options, insurance etc are examples of important structural objects. It is evident that this financial make-believe world has a great impact on our lives. To be able to see the impact with open eyes we must recognize that these structures are illusionary – based on beliefs, communicative actions and trust.[57]

When actors in industrial relations experience a knowledge-oriented transformation, the structural (illusive) phenomena become more and more important. For knowledge-oriented business, structural capital manifests the capitalization of human resources. Patents, for example, proprietize relational knowledge processes. It therefore becomes more and more appropriate to talk about developing, designing, governing etc structural capital. Especially interesting are innovations in ICT (information and communication technologies) oriented businesses, as ICT has become the most important medium to transform human resources into structural capital. Together with concepts of copyright, patents and other legal constructions, information technology makes it possible to relate to virtual products, features, Internet

[56] Sveiby, Karl-Erik, "Designing Business Strategy in the Knowledge Era", *The Knowledge Advantage*, Capstone Publishing (1999), p. 177.

[57] Compare Searle, John, R., *The Construction of Social Reality* (1995), pp. 113. op.cit.

services, knowledge markets and other new structural objects.[58] The line between code solutions and legal constructions becomes more and more difficult to distinguish.[59] Thus information technology increases the difficulty in drawing the distinction between reality and fantasy.

In a knowledge- and information-oriented economy it is more and more urgent that we collectively understand and govern those processes that generate the conceptualization of structural persons, structural objects and even structural relations. Patent applications, granted patents, and patentable innovations could in this context be described as structural building bricks that can be used to construct new knowledge innovations, virtual products, license relations, joint ventures, strategic alliances, start-ups, knowledge markets etc. The substantial patent concepts are then best described as structural tools. They are concepts that can be used regarding a specific knowledge process to generate the conceptualization of a specific patent into a building brick. The internalization of tools makes it possible for us to externalize the specific patent. The more people who internalize a common substantial concept, that is, the more real unity that is created, the greater the potential of a specific patent as a structural brick. Communication is a decisive factor, which can create the trust needed for value creation.

16.4.2 Substantial patent concepts – evolution and social construction

A constructionist approach means that we analyze to what extent a substantial patent concept is communicated, accepted and trusted. An important issue is to determine whether there are several concepts – that is, concepts that have different communicative origins – which may be in conflict. Perhaps even the same actor uses several concepts, as described above, unaware of the confusion.

From a substantial point of view, constructions expressed in legislation are of special importance. Democratic loyalty requires that especially judges, but also other actors, strive to internalize legislated substantial constructions.[60] However, from a company point of view those substantial construc-

---

[58] *The Digital Dilemma: Intellectual Property in the Information Age* (2000), op.cit. Stefik, Mark, *The Internet Edge*. Cambridge, MA: MIT Press (1999).

[59] Lessig, Lawrence, *Code and Other Laws of Cyberspac,*. New York, N.Y.: Basic Books (1999), p. 3. Lessig, Lawrence, *The Future of Ideas*. New York, N.Y.: Random House (2001), pp. 4-6.

[60] Regarding the concepts of internalization and externalization, see Berger, Peter and Luckmann, Thomas, *The Social Construction of Reality*, Garden City, N.Y.: Doubleday (1966), pp. 78-79.

tions applied by the patent office and the courts are of more obvious importance.[61] If different patent concepts are applied, it is normally most important to make a prognosis of which concepts are applied in the first instance.

The internalization process, based on learning, often means that we take the existence of structural phenomena for granted. Instead of questioning and trying to deconstruct the intellectual property concepts, we just accept them as something that exists. Our lack of awareness regarding this internalization process generates an evolutionary process, where the legal profession lacks structural control. It is therefore important to question communicative origin to discover the historical reason for the existence of several patent concepts. However, it should be underlined that the existence of several patent concepts in itself does not lead to destructive confusion. It is the lack of awareness and the existence of conflicting beliefs that create problems.

The constructionist approach shows that sophisticated structural phenomena, such as the patent, also have to be regarded normatively as pluralistic substantial concepts. As a structural phenomenon the patent has different functions in different communicative contexts, i.e. the communicative reality of the patent concepts differs. A patent in the Patent Office is an experienced grant based on an evaluation of an application, that is, a grant based on the applicability of the substantial criteria – novelty and inventive step. In an infringement case, the patent is a position where the proprietor can forbid specific behaviors. From the infringing party's point of view, the substantial patent represents those behaviors that are criminalized and can result in damage claims. From the proprietor's point of view, the substantial patent can be described as a right – a right on the one hand to forbid others from these behaviors, and on the other hand to perform them by oneself. The infringing behaviors can be described as the substantial content of the patent.

We can see how the concept of the patent generates different consequential beliefs depending on the context. Especially interesting is the understanding of the patent as an asset in a firm – an asset that you can sell, license and in other ways commercially use.[62] It is in this context that confusion and lack of awareness regarding the substantial patent concept become obvious. Perhaps it is possible to accept normatively that the technical invention as a substantial construct, the patentable invention as a substantial construct, and the patent as a substantial construct all can be regarded as property. If the patentable invention is regarded as property, the consequential

---

[61] See above, Section 3.3.

[62] Compare Merges, Robert P., "Uncertainty and the Standard of Patentability", *High Technology Law Journal*, Vol. 7:1 (1992), p. 5.

belief is that the patent is a right to a patentable invention, that patent claims are defining the scope of the patentable invention, etc. If, on the other hand, the substantial understanding of the patent is that there is no property at all, but only a right to permit others to behave in a certain way that otherwise would be a criminalized infringement, the consequential beliefs regarding the capitalization of patent assets will also be altered. Patent claims are then describing what technical behaviors are possible to forbid.

16.4.3 Internalizing and externalizing patents as a result of communication in three structural arenas

A constructionist approach means, as stated above, that we can both recognize and switch between the substantial approach and the communicative reality. Contextually we know that patent concepts, as communicative means, have different receivers. The patent as a substantial concept means different things to the patent examiner, the judge in an infringement case, the judge in a contract-related case, the manager in a knowledge-oriented firm etc. As said above, however, this does not necessarily result in confusion. It could be the result of a sophisticated structural order, where different actors have different roles in the construction process.

Consequently, it becomes obvious that the patent claims as structural phenomena are going to have different communicative functions, and therefore can be regarded as different structural phenomena. The patent examiner as well as the applicant can see the claims in the patent application as a communicative prospect. The actual patent becomes the granted claim(s). In an infringement case, the patent claim is the communicative medium that decides which behaviors are possible to attack, while in a more contractual context it can be said to communicate the actual transferred property. A constructionist approach also shows us how these different concepts are dependent on each other. This includes how they result from a structural order, that is, an order where we communicatively have constituted three different structural arenas: an administrative arena in the patent office, a judicial arena in the courts, and a commercial arena.

The constructionist approach consequently means that we normatively accept the structural complexity of the patent institution. We see how patent regulation etc creates structural persons such as Patent Offices, courts etc. We also see how these different structural actors apply substantial patent concepts when they create/grant specific patents, when they declare patents void, declare the scope of patent, consider patents as licensed objects etc. From a constructionist point of view we can separate, on the one hand, *de-*

signed patent concepts from *applied patent concepts*, and on the other hand, the patent concepts (patents as structural tools) from the specific patent (patent as a structural brick). We have a public authority, the patent office, which applies the patent concepts and grants the specific patent. The internalization of the patent concept together with the actual grant of the patent office results in the communicative externalization of the patent. When it comes to copyright, it is the author, manager etc that decides how to apply the substantial copyright concept concerning a specific phenomenona. In the courts, the copyright concept is used to question whether the phenomenon is really copyrighted. The internalization of copyright concepts together with a prognosis of court behaviors results in the communicative externalization of the copyright. Because the courts have the power to invalidate or partly invalidate the patent, the externalization regarding patents is also dependent on a prognosis of court behavior.

If a court has tried the validity or the scope of a specific patent, this will of course have a direct normative effect on what is the externalized patent or patented invention. Otherwise it is primarily the patent grant that has a direct normative effect. The knowledge of how the courts apply the patent concept has an indirect normative effect, in that it helps us to perform prognoses of what the court behavior will be regarding a specific patent. Constructively, we can see how it is all based on communicative action.

Regarding inventions as structural phenomena, we can see how the communication within firms results in concepts that try to capture the technological phenomena. By using and applying the concept of the patentable invention (i.e. the structural tool), it is for example possible for an employer to conceptualize a specific work result as a patentable invention (a structural brick). Before the patent application it is consequently possible to externalize a patentable invention by communicatively internalizing the concept of the patentable invention and performing a prognosis of future behavior in the patent offices as well as in the courts. When the patent examiner communicates what she considers to be patentable and finally decides to grant a patent, this will have a direct normative effect on what is going to be considered to be the patentable invention and finally the patented invention. Here we must also include the indirect effect of court behavior regarding the application of the invention concepts.

16.4.4 Patents as structural capital – the metaphor of structural tools and structural bricks

It is important to understand that when a company successfully communicates the image of an extensive substantial concept of property and property right, the customers' willingness to pay license fees increases, as does the competitors' willingness to avoid certain behaviors and instead enter into alliances. There are long-term advantages in communicating such an image, such as when the company tries to impose licensing agreements. The chance of success is greater if they have built trust based on a realistic prognosis of how the court would react. If there is little trust in the company's ability to uphold its claim, then there is a high risk of conflict. Consequently it is best to project an image that is in line with a future court ruling. Simultaneously, communication is part of the process of staking a claim; if one is successful in projecting an image of a strong position of control, it might very well influence the opinion of the court. Consequently, if the company has the competence needed to communicate with the court, it has greater chances of communicating with competitors, thus making them accept the company's claims.

The constructionist approach leads to an understanding of intellectual property and intellectual property rights as structural phenomena – on the one hand as inter-subjective concepts (structural tools) and on the other hand as externalized concepts in a specific situation (structural bricks). Specific patents are best described as structural capital – internalized ideological processes resulting in the conceptualization of externalized objects. Patents, patentable inventions and other intellectual properties become "structural bricks" when designing tangible products, virtual products, license agreements, standards, strategic alliances, companies, markets etc. We are also entering an era where it becomes more and more obvious that it is not only society as a superstructure that is the result of a communicative (ideological) process, but that this applies to the products/assets as well. Patenting is increasingly becoming a means to define the invention as an asset and also create the conceptualization of the product. When products become less materialized, drafting of patent claims cannot in the same way be separated from the understanding of the invention. Communicatively we have to be prepared for an increasing normative pressure of self-assertive interests that strive for the capitalization of knowledge, whereby patents are one of the important means in the quest for 'privatization of knowledge'.

I believe that as an overall structural hypothesis we could posit a development towards markets for virtual products and commodified knowledge.

In many areas patents are being used more and more among major companies to establish cross-license relationships, which increases the importance of strategic alliances. The fact that standards are increasingly patented is a structural expression of how markets as external structures become more controlled by private structural persons, i.e. companies. In a process where the tendency is towards an even more constrained diffusion of technology, there is also reason to ask whether the patent institute acts, and will increasingly come to act, as a means of excluding the developing countries from participation, and thereby from economic development. The more we understand and deconstruct structural complexity, the more we are able to see that it is not the patent institute in itself, but rather our ability to govern patents and patentable inventions as building bricks when designing and constructing societal structures, that determines social reality. Thus, patents can in fact be used to create constructs for open technology diffusion etc. Patents can be structural bricks in collective constructions, where the purpose is to transfer knowledge to as many actors as possible, etc.[63]

16.5 Conclusions

The more collective awareness we generate about how communicative internalization processes, actions in patent offices, judicial decisions etc result in conceptualized intellectual property and property rights, the less confusion we will have. A legal constructionist approach means that we are constantly trying to deconstruct structural phenomena. The ever-present striving to deconstruct is based on the insight and acknowledgement that patents and patentable inventions have no existence in themselves. One normative approach can be to see it as our obligation in legal argumentation to deconstruct patents as structural tools and as building bricks. Necessary, however, is to be able to switch between a substantial approach where we talk about content, scope etc and an approach where we describe communicative actions, including both internalization and externalization processes. Collectively we can create an understanding of how patents can be understood as (1) possibilities to enforce infringement claims, (2) a communicative process, (3) property, property rights and ownership, (4) structural capital etc.

Consequently I argue that the confusion regarding patents is largely the result of the lack of awareness of law as a structural phenomenon. This con-

[63] Compare discussions in Lessig, Lawrence, *The Future of Ideas* (2001), op.cit., and Feller, Joseph and Fitzgerald, Brian, *Understanding Open Source Software Development*, Harlow: Addison-Wesley (2002).

fusion makes it more difficult for companies and other users, as well as for politicians, to stimulate, govern and control knowledge and information processes. The purpose of the constructionist approach is to increase structural awareness and increase responsibility. Legal constructionism is, according to my point of view, one of the most important factors in the quest to collectively govern structural transformation. In the long run we can collectively free ourselves from structural captivity and with open eyes govern development. We acknowledge and question our role as designer of structural reality – our role as social engineer – meaning that we must constantly strive to deconstruct structural phenomena as well as consider the design implications. By always deconstructing the design process of structural reality, it becomes an important value to avoid façade legitimizations, to openly declare our self-assertive interest, to discuss the favored positions we generate, and to question the structural results of different consequential beliefs.

Theoretically this constructive development of legal realism opens the way for the possibility of a common agenda with the more evolutionary approach in economics. Institutional and evolution-directed economic theories are already of significant interest in order to understand the reality of legal constructions in an economic context.[64] This applies, for example, to the recent theories of Nelson[65] and North[66], the older theories of Schumpeter[67] and

[64] An illustrative example of this "cross-fertilization" is Merges, Robert and Nelson, Richard, "On the Complex Economics of Patent Scope", *Columbia Law Review*, Vol. 90, No. 4 (1990), pp. 839-916.

[65] Nelson, Richard and Winter, Sidney, *An Evolutionary Theory of Economic Change*, Harvard University Press (1982). Nelson, Richard, "Economic Growth via the Coevolution of Technology and Institutions", in Leydesdorff, Loet and Besselaar, Peter van den (eds.), *Evolutionary Economics and Chaos Theory*, London: Pinter Publishers (1994). Nelson, Richard, "National Innovation Systems", in Dosi, Giovanni and Malerba, Franco, *Organization and Strategy in the Evolution of the Enterprise*, Houndmills, Basingstoke: Macmillan Press (1996).

[66] North, Douglass, "The Evolution of Efficient Markets in History", ewp-eh/9411005. North, Douglass, "Where have we been and where are we going?", ewp-eh/9612001. North, Douglass, "Economics and Cognitive Science", ewp-eh/9612002. North, Douglass, "Institutions, Organizations and Market Competition", ewp-eh/9612005.

[67] Schumpeter, Joseph, *Business Cycles – A Theoretical, Historical, and Statistical Analysis of the Capitalist Process*, Vol. 2, New York: McGraw-Hill Book Company (1939). Schumpeter, Joseph, *Capitalism, Socialism and Democracy*, 3rd edition, New York: Harper and Brothers (1950).

Hayek[68], and also the classical theories of thinkers such as Marx and Engels. In the future we can see a common normative agenda where economists as well as legal scholars question and deconstruct their own roles as well as the participation of others in the structural transformation. Theoretical discussions regarding patent concepts and other intellectual property concepts have had, and probably will have even more, important normative consequences regarding what in the future are going to be considered assets, capital, property, companies, markets, standards, financial instruments etc. The constantly present ambition to deconstruct and to take responsibility for design consequences among economists and legal scholars, as I see it, will be a decisive factor in a process where we collectively strive to free ourselves from structural captivity.

---

[68] Hayek, Friedrich, "Use of Knowledge in Society", *American Economic Review* Vol. 35, No. 4 (1945). Hayek, Friedrich, *Individualism and Economic Order*, London: Routledge and Kegan (1949). Hayek, Friedrich, "Competitions as a discovery procedure", in Kirzner, Israel M., *Classics in Austrian Economics, Vol. III. The Age of Mises and Hayek*, London: Pickering (1994, orig. 1969).

Chapter 17

INFORMATION TANGIBILITY

Margaret Jane Radin
Stanford University, Law School, Stanford, CA, USA

Chapter contents:

Abstract: Information is being assimilated to the physical world. Digital information is a physical state of a hard drive; genetic information is a chemical molecule. This assimilation of information to the physical world is proving useful for those who want to expand the scope of information property. One expedient is just to find that more things count as tangible objects in which information can be fixed; e.g., determining that when information exists in RAM it is a "copy" for purposes of copyright. A second expedient is getting people to accept real estate analogies, with their connotations (at least to lay people) of absolute control. A prime example here is "cybersquatting"; another is the prevalent analogy (inscribed in the DMCA legislative history) between using information without permission and stealing a physical object. Finally, the latest expedient is simply to redescribe the information as a physical object, or to collapse the distinction between information and physical object. This expedient is seen in a range of cases, described in this paper, including the patenting of computer programs, the patenting of genes and DNA fragments, and the use of trespass to chattels doctrine to protect databases. Information propertization has traditionally been considered a matter of balancing: determining the right amount of monopolization, with the understanding that there is always a necessarily

O. Granstrand (ed.), Economics, Law and Intellectual Property, 395-418.

uncontrolled public domain. The strategy of assimilating information to the realm of physical objects and to physical property enables proponents of propertization to bypass this traditional balancing rhetoric and to expand the scope of propertization without having to argue explicitly about the benefits of control on the one hand versus the benefits of free competition and flow of information on the other.

The collapse of the distinction between information and physical objects is also having an effect on contract. Traditionally a contract has been conceived of as a text about a transaction in goods or services, where the goods or services are a separate entity from the text. In the networked environment, the terms under which goods or services are distributed are becoming indistinguishable from the goods or services themselves, and the distinction between goods and services is itself collapsing. Terms are part of the product/service, not a text about it. Terms propagate along a chain of distribution and the proponent of the terms intends them to bind everyone who comes into possession of the product/service. Moreover, terms become technological, rather than textual, constraints when digital rights management systems are implemented. These developments are further problematizing the traditional conception of contract as based on voluntary agreement on textual terms.

> "I say to you that the VCR is to the American film producer and the American public as the Boston strangler is to the woman home alone."[1]

17.1 Introduction

"Information tangibility" sounds paradoxical, because we are used to thinking of information as intangible. One reason to think we have embarked on an Information Age, however, is that our conceptual world is rearranging itself: the distinction between tangible objects and intangible information is in the process of breaking down. Digital information can be understood as intangible. That is the way we are used to thinking about information. But it can simultaneously be understood as tangible, by considering physical states of a computer. The bits, the information, are also physical positions of electrons in printed circuits. Genetic information can be understood as intangi-

[1] Testimony of Jack Valenti, President of the Motion Picture Association of America, at a Congressional hearing entitled "Home Recording of Copyrighted Works" before the Subcommittee on Courts, Civil Liberties, and the Administration of Justice of the Committee on the Judiciary of the House of Representatives dated April 12-14, June 24, August 11, September 22-23, 1982

ble, but at the same time also tangible, a chemical molecule made up of physical atomic building blocks. The notion of tangible information is not so paradoxical now as it might at first seem in light of our received categories of understanding. That it is not so paradoxical is just a way of saying that the categories are breaking down. In this process of disintegration of old categories, technological developments lead. Language and culture follow, and with them, the law.

The distinction between tangible objects and intangible information is a distinction upon which much of our modern understanding of the world was built, and hence, from which a great many legal categorizations derive. What will be the consequences for legal regimes when this distinction can no longer construct and order them? This general question generates the research program I begin here. Efforts to assimilate information to the physical world have recently been playing out in intellectual property law, and in other areas as well. These efforts are causing tensions and distortions (or, at least, surprising results). In this essay, I want to survey some of what is happening in order to set the stage for exploring new understandings that might replace the old dual rhetoric of tangibility and intangibility (corresponding to machines vs. texts). Assimilation of information to the category of tangibility is fostering commodification; that is, a great increase in the scope of intellectual property and allied regimes of privatized information control. I also think that the notion of agreement or consent that underlies contract law is now seriously problematic, with no replacement normative principle yet on the horizon.

17.2 Traditional Dichotomies

The law of information as we have received it owes much to the "modernist" dichotomies of the Enlightenment – between subject and object, between autonomous persons and heteronomous things. As Richard Rorty has put it, this worldview posits a basic disjuncture between what is "in here" to be created and expressed (in the mind, subjective, part of the person) and what is "out there waiting to be found" (the pre-existing physical world).[2] We can take Kant and Hegel as emblematic of this prevalent worldview. Kant and Hegel argued that "property" must exist in order for the will of the person to manipulate and have control over objects and thus extend to the fullest the reach and capacity of the will and its freedom. Thus "property"

[2] Richard Rorty, *Philosophy and the Mirror of Nature* (Princeton University Press, 1981).

belongs firmly to the object realm in late eighteenth and early nineteenth century theory. This is an understanding of property that is still strong.

In light of this dualistic metaphysics, both Kant and Hegel in their jurisprudence had trouble with the concept of intellectual property. "Intellectual property" seemed to bridge the unbridgeable gap: the "intellectual" part belonging to the autonomous interior subjective category of the person, and the "property" part belonging to the heteronomous exterior objective category of things. Kant and Hegel each constructed an uneasy compromise with their core principles in order to admit the concept of intellectual property, in the form of copyright, to the realm of market exchange. The compromise marries information to the external realm of objects. The structure of the compromise involves the process of externalizing the internal ideas and embodying them in an object – a book.[3] That is, the creative work starts out internal to the person, hence unpropertizable, but becomes embodied in an external object, hence propertizable. Central to this understanding of intellectual property is the notion that works are embodied in tangible objects.[4] It is this metamorphosis – from internal to external, from person to object – which makes possible commodification (market exchange of embodied creative works). In a sense, what we are seeing today is the end result of this eighteenth-century compromise. My question in this essay, at its broadest, is whether this compromise is still serviceable in the information age, or whether it has finally been exhausted.

17.3 Physical Invasion and the Power of Property Rhetoric

The distinction between the physical world and the internal world of personhood also has another (and in some sense opposite) kind of traditional importance. A specific category of grave legal injury to personhood has always existed for invasions of the realm of the person by outside physical objects, when other persons set the invasions in motion. Physical assault on another without justification or excuse is a core offense. Trespass to another's land was assimilated to the notion of physical invasion of the person because of the postulated close connection (in theory) between a person and his land. Trespass rests on the notion of invasion by physical objects into

[3] See Margaret Jane Radin, *Reinterpreting Property* (University of Chicago Press 1994); Margaret Jane Radin, *Contested Commodities* (Harvard University Press 1996).

[4] Abraham Drassinower, "Labour and Intersubjectivity: Notes on the Natural Law of Copyright", available at http://papers.ssrn.com/sol3/papers.cfm?abstract_id=275470.

protected physical space (invasion of land by nonphysical intrusions, such as noise or smoke, instead comes under the law of nuisance). In the common law the idea of trespass was extended to physical invasions of other owned objects besides land – chattels – that could be understood as assimilable to the person. As I will shortly mention, in the United States this ancient doctrine is now being applied to computers invaded by software.

Part of the power of the concept of property, in legal discourse but especially in the lay imagination, is the sense of a right to insulation from entrance of persons and objects from outside.[5] It is this conceptual power that undergirds the notion of trespass. In contrast, in the United States, the concept of information has no such conceptual force. Indeed, because of the strong tradition of free speech expressed in the broad interpretations of the First Amendment, even very hurtful information directed at others is not treated as a redressable wrong to the victim.

The U.S. Supreme Court extended the powerful understanding of property when it declared the right to exclude others to be one of the prime rights in the bundle of sticks, even in situations where personhood was obviously not involved. The same Court regularly declares harm that can be characterized as caused by speech to be without remedy (even if the harm is caused by conduct interpreted as speech); it regularly reminds us that the remedy for harmful speech is more speech. Thus, Nazis are permitted to march in communities of holocaust survivors, but a state is not allowed to permit a cable TV box to be placed on a building without the owner's permission.[6]

In the United States, therefore, the notion of physicality has a double valence. When owned items are physical, they are imbued with a very broad panoply of property rights, including a very strong right to exclude others. And when physical objects enter an owned item without permission, that is much more likely to be an event triggering legal redress than if information enters an owned item (or a person's consciousness) without permission.

17.4 Property Metaphors (Rhetorical Capture)

Even physical property is not absolute – we don't have the right to discharge noxious fumes on our land, and we can't charge passersby for the benefit they enjoy in smelling our roses. But the mythology of property, the rhetoric of property, has an absoluteness that has not attached to information,

[5] See Reich, "The New Property", 73 *Yale L.J.* 733 (1964).

[6] See *National Socialist Party v. Skokie*, 434 U.S. 1327 (1977); *Loretto v. Teleprompter Manhattan CATV Corp.*, 458 U.S. 419 (1982).

and could not attach to information so long as information has one foot in the realm of communication, the world of free speech between persons. Partly because of the dual valence of information, intellectual property is not constructed with the mythological absoluteness of tangible property; instead it is constructed as a giant balance between the public domain needed for communication and innovation, and the amount of ownership and control needed to provide incentives for the same.[7] Against this backdrop, it is understandable why those who wish to establish control over information assets – to make them more fully into market commodities – do everything they can to assimilate such assets into physical property.

I will call this the "expedient" aspect of the coalescence of physical and non-physical in the realm of information. For those who seek to establish control over, or reap profit from, information as an asset, it is expedient to assimilate information to the physical. Often in the past it has been simply a matter of invoking a powerful metaphor, of capturing the rhetoric. The powerful word "property" was apparently not applied to information assets until the mid-19th century.[8] Since that time, analogies to physical property, and invasion of physical property, have regularly substituted for the "official" balancing arguments, because they are showstoppers of persuasion. Consider what Jack Valenti said about the VCR twenty years ago, quoted in the epigraph for this essay.

Fast forward to the legislative history accompanying the Digital Millennium Copyright Act, in which the House committee report says: "The act of circumventing a technological protection measure put in place by a copyright owner to control access to a copyrighted work is the electronic equivalent of breaking into a locked room in order to obtain a copy of a book."[9] The analogy to trespass supports a legislative enactment that extends copyright beyond protection of information to prohibiting certain technologies and uses of technologies; and supports that enactment's extension of copyright beyond its previous limits by allowing owners to prevent the public from copying parts of works that are in the public domain.

---

[7] See generally Ove Granstrand, *The Economics and Management of Intellectual Property*, Edward Elgar Publishing Ltd. (1999) (describing the "dispossession impossibility" feature of information that importantly distinguishes knowledge from physical property, therefore limiting the application of traditional property concepts to possession of knowledge).

[8] See William W. Fisher III, "The Growth of Intellectual Property: A History of Ownership of Ideas in the United States", in *Eigentum im Internationalen Vergleich* (Vandenhoeck and Ruprecht, 1999), 265-91.

[9] Section-By-Section Analysis of H.R. 2281, House Committee on the Judiciary, 105th Congress (Comm. Print 1998)

My favorite example of legal victory by rhetorical capture (so far) is the term "cybersquatting". Squatting on physical property sends shivers up the spines of landowners. By applying this term to the practice of speculating in valuable Internet domain names, trademark owners were able to convince courts (without ever having to argue for it) that domain names consisting of words similar to someone's trademark come into being always already owned by the trademark holder (or one of the trademark holders, since many owners can have similar marks if they are geographically separated or in different industrial categories).[10] The word "squatting" had so much power that it succeeded in completely begging the baseline question: when a new asset comes into being, does it come into being pre-owned by someone holding a (conceptually) neighboring asset?

A real analysis of whether (some) trademark owner should also be deemed the owner of any corresponding Internet domain name would no doubt have involved some thought about how these valuable assets should initially be allocated and how transfers should be structured – what are the needs of the public and the various commercial and non-commercial interests. Even in a state of nature with unowned land available, a physical landowner would not be deemed the owner of adjoining physical property just because it is valuable to her. The debate might in the end have arrived at the result that domain names sounding like someone's trademark should be awarded free to some trademark owner. But – at least in my opinion – all of this debate was finessed by the simple use of a word that called to mind a threat to physical property. Real estate metaphors are of course rife on the Internet. Perhaps the "squatting" metaphor would not have been so powerful if the asset had not been called a "domain" in the first place. Previous communications revolutions apparently did not bring forth such assimilation to real estate. We don't speak of telephonic "space" the way we speak of cyberspace. We don't speak of radio "sites" the way we speak of web sites. A web site is not a "site" – it is a set of electronic document files maintained on a computer server, consisting of text with formatting information provided by HTML codes, that can be accessed from a client computer via the Internet using the HTTP protocol, which causes the files to be transmitted to the client computer and displayed graphically on a monitor. These real estate

[10] See, e.g., *Panavision Int'l, L.P. v. Toeppen*, 141 F.3d 1316 (9th Cir. 1998). The result is that speculation in domain names corresponding to words in trademarks makes you a criminal, but speculation in domain names that cannot be trademarks because they are generic (e.g., cars.com, passover.com, asseenontv.com) makes you an entrepreneur. See, e.g., www.greatdomains.com.

analogies undergird the claims of information owners. They imply that owners should have fee simple absolute, not just limited rights for limited times.

On behalf of plaintiff Eric Eldred, an online publisher of classical literature, Professor Lawrence Lessig of Stanford Law School argues that the 1998 Sonny Bono Copyright Term Extension Act violates the text of the U.S. Constitution (specifically, the "limited time" clause of the Article I, Section 8, Clause 8, and the First Amendment) and also subverts the Framers' original intent to grant *limited* monopoly protection for creative works. The staying power of these real estate analogies might explain why Professor Lessig has an uphill battle trying to put teeth into what would otherwise look like apparent plain meaning of constitutional limitations on the legislative power to enact copyright and patent protections.[11]

17.5 Reductionism

The process of digitization has immensely aided expedient strategies involving assimilation to physical property, and made possible some new ones. The metaphor of physicality, of object-ness, has become ever more rhetorically literal. Consider, for example, the issue of whether computer software should be treated as tangible or intangible property for the purpose of taxation. Most states and other taxing jurisdictions in the United States impose sales taxes on tangible goods sold in the jurisdiction, and they impose use taxes on tangible goods sold elsewhere and brought into the jurisdiction. The City of New Orleans sought to tax computer software (switching programs) that the local telephone company had licensed from out-of-state vendors. Against a claim that the software was exempt because it was intangible ("incorporeal") intellectual property, the state court held that the software was tangible ("corporeal") personal property and thus taxable for sales and use tax purposes.[12] The court was able to arrive at this expedient (for the City) decision by noting that software is "physically manifested in machine readable form by arranging electrons, by use of an electric current, to create either a magnetized or unmagnetized space".[13] The software is physical. It is a

---

[11] *Eldred v. Ashcroft*, pending, case documents available at http://eldred.cc/.

[12] *South Central Bell Telephone C. v. Barthelemy*, 643 So.2d 1240 (La. 1994).

[13] Perhaps the court was adhering to some interesting "precedent". Legend has it that when a politician inquired as to the usefulness of 19th-century scientist Michael Faraday's pioneering findings on electricity and magnetism, Faraday responded: "Why sir, there is the probability that you will soon be able to tax it!" Unfortunately, the remark is probably apocryphal. See "Who Said That?", *Physics World* (2002), at http://physicsweb.org/article/world/15/6/2.

"set of instructions" for a computer, but it is not "mere knowledge"; rather, it is "a certain arrangement of matter" that will make a computer perform a desired function.[14] Many other taxing jurisdictions, though not all of them, similarly have held that computer software is tangible and therefore taxable.

Expedient assimilation of information to the realm of the tangible has displaced the law of intellectual property in an important emerging body of law. Copyright law treats "facts" as unoriginal and therefore not protectable. Here copyright adheres to pre-20th-century philosophy; for copyright, facts are "out there waiting to be found", unrelated to human constructions. Hence database protection under copyright is at best "thin" (covering only the organization, if it is original, but not the facts themselves).[15] In the United States, therefore, databases are in the public domain if not organized in an "original" manner, and in any case, the facts they contain are in the public domain.

This feature of copyright law is posing a problem for those whose information assets consist of valuable databases, or (to speak more accurately) databases that are costly to compile and that would be valuable if they could be kept secret from competitors or if they could be legally protected from competitors. The United States has not yet enacted *sui generis* database protection; although it is widely expected that it will do so, there are in fact constitutional obstacles to propertization of databases[16].

Several recent cases have bypassed the federal intellectual property regime by resurrecting the old common law doctrine of trespass to chattels, that is, state tort law, to grant recovery for incursion into databases.[17] In *eBay, Inc. v. Bidder's Edge, Inc.*, eBay, a large online person-to-person trading site, wanted to prevent Bidder's Edge, a firm that posted data from numerous online auction sites, from using robot programs to gather data about eBay's ongoing auctions for the purpose of posting them on its site in order to enable potential purchasers to make comparisons. The defendant claimed that it would lose about one-third of its users if it could not cover the eBay auctions. The court found that eBay was entitled to an injunction against Bidder's Edge based on the common law doctrine of trespass to chattels. In

---

[14] See *South Central Bell*, supra note 12, at 1246-1247.

[15] *Feist Publications v. Rural Telephone Service, Co.*, 499 U.S. 340 (1991).

[16] See Yochai Benkler, "Constitutional Bounds of Database Protection: The Role of Judicial Review in the Creation and Definition of Private Rights in Information", 15 *Berkeley Tech. L.J.* 535 (2000).

[17] See *eBay, Inc. v. Bidder's Edge, Inc.*, 100 F. Supp. 2d 1058 (2000); *Register.com v. Verio, Inc.*, 126 F. Supp. 2d 238 (2000).

persuading the court to apply this doctrine, eBay successfully argued that there was no distinction between an ongoing trespass to real property and the trespass committed by the continual access of Bidder's Edge's software robots to the eBay site.[18] The rationale for the court's decision was that the electrons of the opponent's robot program were physically invading and taking up space on the computers owned by eBay.[19] According to the court, this invasion would harm eBay's system performance in numerous ways – ultimately leading to the decreased satisfaction of eBay's customers, and a corresponding loss in profits. While the court found that eBay had demonstrated "tangible" harm that justified the "trespass" finding, many have criticized this decision as inappropriately attenuating the harm requirement. Relying on this unwarranted lower standard of harm in electronic trespass to chattels cases could lead to dramatic over-propertization of the Internet.[20]

The injunction won by eBay enjoined the defendants "from using any automated query program, robot, web crawler or other similar device... to access eBay's computer systems or networks, for the purpose of copying any part of eBay's auction database".[21] The injunction makes explicit what was clear in any case: that what eBay was seeking here was database protection. The injunction prevented the defendant from copying the valuable eBay auction database.

Since what eBay wanted to prevent was copying of information, why did eBay not proceed directly under copyright law? Because, in the United States, databases are not covered by copyright.[22] Why didn't eBay rely on the causes of action it had duly pleaded for misappropriation of information or unfair competition under state law? Because these would have most likely been pre-empted by the federal law of copyright. It was only by translating the cause of action from the realm of information to the realm of the physical that eBay was able to protect its database. In my opinion, the court's much-criticized application of the trespass to chattels doctrine to remedy eBay's

[18] Though the court did not specifically adopt this analogy, eBay claimed the virtual trespass was equivalent to sending "an army of 100,000 robots a day to check the prices in a competitor's store". See *eBay,* supra note 17.

[19] *Id.* Although the tort of trespass to chattels requires physical harm to the chattel, the court in this case thought it sufficed for eBay to claim that if Bidder's Edge could get away with its crawling, other firms would follow suit, and if that happened, "eBay would suffer irreparable harm from reduced system performance, system unavailability, or data losses". *Id.* at 1066.

[20] See generally Dan L. Burk, "The Trouble With Trespass", 3 *J. Small & Emerging Bus.* L. 1 (1998), available at http://www.isc.umn.edu/research/papers/trespass-ed2.pdf

[21] See *eBay,* supra note 17, at 1073.

[22] See *Feist,* supra note 15.

alleged harm is best read as expedient pretext. The court believed that eBay's database ought to be protected and found the way to do so without fear of pre-emption by federal intellectual property law.

Using the doctrine of trespass to chattels expediently in this way treats the computer equipment housing the database as tangible property that is being invaded by incoming tangible electrons. It sidesteps the crux of the problem, which is that the injury for which recovery is sought is for loss of intangible information, not for damage to tangible objects by other tangible objects. What should we make of this development in the case law? Certainly it is undermining the regime of copyright and the legal treatment of information generally, by finding a method of coming up with database protection that copyright precludes – i.e., it is a transfer of certain kinds of factual compilations from the public domain to the ownership of the compiler. In doing so, moreover, it is also furthering the breakdown of the role of tangibility as a meaningful legal category.

17.6 Functionality and Tangibility: The Impact of Digitization

As the cases imposing taxes and protecting databases show, construing computer information as physical can be expedient for those parties for whom categorization as physical "property" would be advantageous. Is the breakdown between the categories of tangible and intangible merely an artifact of legal argument, a vehicle for interest-group struggle that happens to be made possible by digitization? Or does it have deeper implications? This is a topic for further research. At minimum, I want to note (and will mention later) that the breakdown of categories is taking place not just with digitized information but also with biological information: DNA as a physical molecule and as a form of information. The breakdown seems to be a reconceptualization in progress, one that will eventually have profound effects on the law, given how dependent the law is on the old dichotomies.

Digitization caused trouble for copyright as soon as it became clear that all kinds of different works – literary texts, computer software, movies, and musical recordings – are now collections of digits. Copyright law previously treated these various categories of works differently, but with digitization, it has become difficult to see why, or how the different categories can ultimately be maintained. Why should the soundtrack recording of a movie be treated differently from some other recording, when both are a collection of digits? But the trouble for copyright goes deeper than the coalescence of its categories.

True to the philosophy of the Enlightenment, copyright is built on a fundamental distinction between tangible objects and intangible information. A "copy" is a tangible physical object, and "fixation in a tangible medium of expression" is the prerequisite for copyright protection.[23] Commodification is linked to embodiment in a physical object. Adaptation to the digital environment has caused this basic assumption to be, at minimum, distorted, if not erased. Courts and commentators in the United States have adopted the notion that the momentary arrangement of electrons in a computer memory, which we might have thought of as intangible information, amounts to a tangible physical object, a copy.[24] Almost everything that a computer does involves copying in this sense. Because of this, a great many activities that were not covered by copyright in the offline environment are being brought under copyright – that is, under control of an owner – in the online environment. More information is assimilated to the tangible, hence assigned to an owner and removed from the public domain. Tangibility fosters commodification.[25] Even if a landowner cannot prevent passersby from smelling her roses, copyright owners want to be able to prevent passersby from even glancing at their works without paying. The physical analogy to browsing in a bookstore is obliterated by the more powerful assimilation of the activity involved to a physical object – production of physical "copies" by a computer.

Copyright (especially in the U.S.) is also built on the distinction between functional production and non-functional expression. The fundamental notion here is that authorship, artistic production, is essentially non-functional. The aesthetic is understood to exclude the utilitarian. To my knowledge it has not been remarked on, at least in the legal literature, that this embeds a pre-20th century theory of art: in copyright law, the more that form and

[23] 17 U.S.C. §102(a). ("Copyright protection subsists, in accordance with this title, in original works of authorship fixed in any tangible medium of expression, now known or later developed, from which they can be perceived, reproduced, or otherwise communicated, either directly or with the aid of a machine or device".)

[24] See, e.g., *MAI Sys. Corp. v. Peak Computer*, 991 F.2d 511 (9th Cir. 1993); Jane C. Ginsburg, "Putting Cars on the 'Information Superhighway': Authors, Exploiters, and Copyright in Cyberspace", 95 *Colum. L. Rev.* 1466, 1476 (1995); U.S. Copyright Office, Digital Millenium Copyright Act, Section 104 report (2001), available at http://www.loc.gov/copyright/reports/studies/dmca/sec-104-report-vol-1.pdf.

[25] See Neil Netanel and Niva Elkin-Koren, *Commodification of Information*, Kluwer Information Law Series (2002).

function are melded and inseparable, the less that copyright protection can attach.[26]

More important for my project, perhaps, is the anomalous inclusion of computer programs under copyright as literary works – anomalous because the value of a computer program is its functionality. Computer programs are both text and machine. They are text when considered as code statements; they are machines when considered as devices for accomplishing a task. Copyright law reflects the text perspective (programs are considered literary works);[27] patent law reflects the machine perspective (a programmed computer is a "new machine").[28] The fact that computer programs are both copyrightable and patentable is awkward for the structure of intellectual property law. Copyright is supposed to exclude works that are functional; patent is supposed to focus on functionality and exclude texts.[29] Computer programs are the only large area covered both by patent and copyright.

This anomaly is obscured to some extent by the fact that copyright and patent regard programs differently. Patent focuses on the protocol for accomplishing the task, however the programmer chooses to code it, whereas copyright focuses on the code statements. But copyright also attaches to the structure, sequence and organization of the code, so long as those more abstract features can be determined to be at the level of "expression" rather than "idea".[30] The difference between structure, sequence and organization (copyrightable), and useful algorithm, protocol or method (patentable) is, however, conceptually difficult to maintain. Once structure, sequence, and organization collapses into protocol or algorithm, the categories of text and machine have coalesced.

The text aspect is sometimes emphasized outside of copyright law. Those who write code sometimes genuinely feel that it is their speech and should

[26] See *Brandir Int'l, Inc. v. Cascade Pacific Lumber Co.*, 834 F.2d 1142 (2d Cir. 1987) (bike rack held not copyrighted).

[27] See, e.g., *Apple Computer, Inc. v. Franklin Computer Corp.*, 714 F.2d 1240, 1249 (3d Cir. 1983) (quoting the definition of literary work in 17 U.S.C. § 101—which includes expression comprised of 'numbers, or other . . . numerical symbols or indicia'—and holding object and source code to be literary works).

[28] *In re Alappat*, 33 F.3d 1526, 1566-67 (Fed. Cir. 1994) (Archer, C.J., concurring and dissenting).

[29] See, e.g., Patent and Trademark Office, United States Department of Commerce, *Examination Guidelines for Computer-Related Inventions: Final Version*, *available at* http://www.uspto.gov/web/offices/pac/dapp/oppd/pdf/ciig.pdf (distinguishing between sometimes patentable "functional descriptive" subject matter and categorically unpatentable "non-functional descriptive" subject matter).

[30] See, e.g., *Computer Assocs. Int'l, Inc. v. Altai, Inc.*, 1992 U.S. App. LEXIS 14305 (1992).

be protected by the First Amendment. Because U.S. legal culture is extremely respectful of free speech rhetoric, U.S. courts have been willing to declare that code is speech for First Amendment purposes.[31] At the same time, because those same courts are also extremely respectful of property rhetoric, sometimes the property side trumps the speech side in specific disputes.[32]

The United States legal system has not yet come fully to grips with the conflict between information as freedom of expression, and information as property.[33] The type of information that can be owned under copyright law is called "expression" (that is, "expression of ideas", as opposed to "ideas" themselves, which are not propertizable); copyrightable expression must be non-functional, as I have mentioned. The type of information that must be free under the First Amendment is also called "expression" (as opposed to "conduct" or "acts"); there is some crossover in situations where communicative elements predominate; the category of "functionality" is not highlighted in this discourse. (It seems that protected expression can be functional, as in making a promise, or non-functional, as in expression of an opinion.) Freedom of "expression", and the legal discourse of the First Amendment, are associated with both non-commercial and commercial speech: a public domain of politics and self-constitution (primarily non-commercial) and a public domain of competitive free markets (primarily commercial). Ownership of "expression", and the legal discourse of copyright, are associated with a privatized domain of monopolies – incentives created by establishing non-competitive markets for the purpose of benefit internalization.

At any rate, in spite of programmers' experience of code writing as expression, and in spite of some judicial sympathy for this understanding, it is clear that the primary *raison d'etre* for programs is their technological function, their ability to accomplish a task. The law is in an unstable position, where programs are machines in view of one kind of property law (patent),

---

[31] See *Universal City Studios, Inc. v. Corley*, 273 F.3d 429, 445-448 (2d Cir. 2001) ("Communication does not lose constitutional protection as "speech" simply because it is expressed in the language of computer code".).

[32] Sometimes commercial free speech wins against claimed individual property rights: see *U.S. West v. Federal Communications Commission*, 182 F.3d 1224 (10th Cir. 1999); but often propertization wins against claimed individual free-speech rights: see *Corley*, supra note 31.

[33] It has been argued that the two systems (freedom of information, information propertization) are harmonized by copyright's fair use doctrine, or by copyright's idea/expression dichotomy. I don't think these doctrines solve the conflict, but I will not argue about them right now. A lot of further thought is needed in this area.

but expression in view of another kind of property law (copyright), and in another meaning of expression, also expression for free speech law (First Amendment, the communicative realm).

Patent is different from copyright because it does not depend upon embodiment of intangible creative work in a tangible object called a "copy". But it does depend upon instantiation of ideas in useful and concrete technology. Patent, too, is built on the distinction between tangible and intangible and the allied distinction between functional and non-functional. Patentable subject matter is a functional machine or method, under the doctrine of utility (which is called industrial applicability outside the United States). The notion of functionality separates the domains of patent and copyright – what is functional is patentable, what is non-functional belongs in copyright or some other doctrine, such as trademark. In spite of the functionality of computer programs, patenting programs gave the courts trouble, because programs were thought to be algorithms that were too intangible to come under patent protection. Eventually the courts found doctrinal "fixes" to get around the dilemma – first by considering the computer as part of a concrete physical process,[34] later by considering the programmed computer itself as the tangible apparatus, the "new machine".[35] The program, the information, was collapsed into the computer, the physical machine, and the whole package was assimilated to the physical.

Now that the algorithm for a program is patentable, and now that business methods are patentable, the Court of Appeals for the Federal Circuit (the U.S. Court charged with appellate decisions in patent cases) is still saying that a "useful, tangible result" is the touchstone of patentability. But it is hard to know what meaning is left for "tangible" when the input is a number and the output is another number.[36] Because computer programs are both copyrightable (assimilating them to the law governing production of original texts) and patentable (assimilating them to the law governing invention of new and useful machines), difficulties have arisen with respect to the traditional dichotomies.

When the Federal Circuit held, a number of years ago, that a programmed computer is a new machine, because the arrangement of electrons in its circuits is a new physical state, a dissenting opinion quite cogently pointed out that when music is inscribed in digital form on a hard drive or disk, it too

---

[34] *Diamond v. Diehr*, 450 U.S. 175 (1981).

[35] See *In re Alappat*, 33 F.3d 1526 (Fed. Cir. 1994).

[36] *State Street Bank & Trust, Co. v. Signature Financial Group*, 149 F.3d 1368 (Fed. Cir. 1998); *AT&T Corp. v. Excel Communications, Inc*, 172 F.3d 1352 (Fed. Cir. 1999).

creates a new physical state, so, by the majority's logic, it could also be patented. This observation nicely illustrates the breakdown of the traditional categories and the conceptual dilemma it causes. The U.S. Patent Office subsequently issued guidelines for its examiners saying that, whatever is "functionally related to the medium" is patentable, and whatever is "merely carried by the medium" is not.[37] No one understands what this means in the context of digitized information, so the guidelines are unlikely to help the examiners much.

In biotechnology, too, arguably parallel difficulties arose with patenting. The court insisted that genes are merely chemical molecules, physical objects, which (if synthesized rather than found in nature) are patentable.[38] Genes are at the same time a repository of information, and it is the information that makes them valuable. But patent law did not have a way of recognizing this, and complete propertization was the result. That is, whoever owned the chemical molecule owned the information it coded for, and could therefore control the activities of all others who needed to use the information.

Commentators have criticized this result in both economic and non-economic terms. In economic terms, the result was arguably propertization of research tools too far upstream in the chain of innovation, with the inefficient result that too many licenses would need to be acquired before a downstream innovator could build upon the information. In non-economic terms, it is thought by some to be inappropriate commodification. Whatever one makes of cases in which a patent on a DNA sequence allows a patentee to control distribution of the protein for which it codes, Rebecca Eisenberg points out that the patent system – with its assimilation of information to tangible physical matter – is even less appropriately applied to propertization of the current generation of biotechnological research tools.

As DNA sequence discovery has moved beyond targeted efforts to clone particular genes to large-scale, high-throughput sequencing of entire genomes, new questions have emerged. The DNA sequences identified by high-throughput sequencing look less like new chemical entities than they do like new scientific information. From the perspective of patent claimants, the chemical analogy is of little value as a strategic guide to exploiting this information as intellectual property. From the perspective of the PTO and courts, claims to these discoveries raise unresolved questions that strain the

---

37 1996 Examination Guidelines for Computer-Related Inventions, 61 F.R. 7478.

38 See, e.g., *Amgen, Inc. v. Chugai Pharm. Co.*, 927 F.2d 1200, 1200 (Fed. Cir. 1991) ("A gene is a chemical compound, albeit a complex one".).

chemical analogy. The result is profound uncertainty concerning how to apply the doctrinal tools of patent law for determining what may be patented and for drawing boundaries between the rights of inventors and the rights of the public. [39]

17.7 Contract Collapsing Into the Objects of Exchange

Contract law is no less profoundly affected by the digital revolution than intellectual property law. The basis of contract is voluntary commitment – "agreement", or "consent", or "assent" to terms that govern use of a product or service. "Assent" to "take-it-or-leave-it" transactions erodes the notion of "agreement" and the notion of "consent", but in any event, these core contractual indicia, even if attenuated to the notion of "assent", assume at minimum that the contract is a separate conceptual entity from the product or service being sold. The conceptual picture is that the contract is a text about something; the something that the text is about is a useful functionality (either or product or a service that the buyer values and wishes to acquire through exchange).

Even before the advent of digitization, the prevalent economic view of contract had already blurred this dual conceptual picture, that is, the dualism of an agreement, formerly thought of as a document or text, and a product or service being sold, formerly thought of as a functional object or a collection of functional features. Although this view of contract actually predates the digital revolution, in the online environment it is becoming more powerful. In a previous article I called this view "contract as product", and contrasted it with the view of contract as consent or agreement.[40]

In the "contract as product" view, the contract is part of the product, part of the collection of functional components, and not a separate text about that collection. For example, suppose you buy a cell phone that contains a chip that will wear out within a year, and the phone comes with a set of fine print terms including a clause that says in the event of any dispute arising out of the transaction you must litigate in California under California law. Both the chip and the clause operate in the same way from the economic point of view: if you know that they are there, they will help determine what you are

---

[39] Rebecca Eisenberg, "Re-Examining The Role Of Patents In Appropriating The Value Of DNA Sequences", 49 *Emory L.J.* 783, 784-85 (2000)

[40] Margaret Jane Radin, "Humans, Computers, and Binding Commitment", 75 *Ind. L.J.* 1125 (2000).

willing to pay for the phone. How the product will work, how long it is going to last, what kind of warranties it comes with, what limitations on remedies it comes with – all of these are exactly the same from the economic point of view. The product you are buying is not just the phone – it is the phone *plus* the terms. The contract is not a text about a product, but part of a product.

This contract as product view is suited to adhesion contracts because in such a take-it-or-leave-it transaction there is no dickering over terms and no dickering over the components either. You can buy this product that is going to wear out in a year, over which you will be forced to litigate in California if a dispute arises, or you can walk away and buy something else more to your liking. (In order for the market to function efficiently, in this view, one must suppose that other products and/or other terms are available.) You are not able to request, "I wish you would remanufacture this so it will not wear out in a year", and you also cannot suggest, "I wish you would rewrite the contract so that I can litigate in my home state".

Although I have been calling this view of contract "contract-as-product" to emphasize the collapse of text into a tangible object, the collapse is conceptual only (until we come to digitized contracts mixed together with digitized products, which I will mention later). Moreover, the situation is more complicated because the conceptual collapse can involve a service (intangible) rather than a product (tangible) – that is, the contract (text) can collapse into a service (intangible functionality being contracted about) as well as a product being contracted about. And the situation is more complicated still in the digital environment because the distinction between product and service is itself collapsing.

Many transactions in the digital environment will involve digitized products (or services). When a digitized product, for example a computer program, is the product or service being marketed, and a digitized license laying down the terms of the transaction is an integral part of the product or service, it becomes easy to understand the two things as one, and difficult to maintain the conceptual separation that makes possible the idea of contracts being "about" some object separate from themselves. Both the license and the program consist of code, implemented through physical connection with a machine.

In the digital environment, the distinction between product and service is blurred or obliterated. When I subscribe to a paper newspaper that is delivered to my front yard or physical inbox, we are used to thinking of it as a product; but when I subscribe to a digital newspaper that is transmitted to my digital inbox, is that a product or a service? Purchasing a video is purchasing a product. Renting a video also seems like a transaction about a product. But what about paying to see a video online? What about paying to use programs online, which might be paid for per document produced using the program or per hour? (Is this a product or service?)

This blurring of the distinction between product and service seems to relate in a complex way to the point I am making about the assimilation of information to categories of physicality. It seems that things that were formerly unequivocally products can now be seen as services, which at first glance seems like a transition from tangibility to intangibility rather than the other way around. Yet it also seems that this migration is swallowed up by the larger tendency to consider everything digitized as an object. The service is an object (a program consisting of physical electrons that alter the physical state of a computer) and so is the package, product/service cum contract.

The advent of machine-made contracts – the use of programs to create binding commitment – is hastening the breakdown of the distinction between text and machine. I am thinking particularly of the context of "B2B" e-commerce. Manufacturing is becoming ever more automated, and the advent of the machine-made contract completes the picture by automating the supply process. If some computer processor "realizes" that more supplies are needed at a certain part of the assembly process, it can also search certain suppliers and see which can most readily supply what is needed, and it can give the go-ahead for the supplies to be delivered. Computers at each end of the transaction could be programmed with sets of terms. When the buyer computer encounters a seller computer, the two computers could enter into a computerized handshake protocol, and if they determine that they have a set of terms in common they could arrive at a commitment, without needing a human being to sign off on it.[41] I think this procedure is going to turn out to be so efficient that it will in fact become the contracting norm in B2B transactions. When (or if) this transformation does occur, it will further undermine the distinction between the text and the machine, because computerized contracting will be seen as integrated with general computerized management of manufacturing processes.

Perhaps the process of integration of text and machine is even clearer in the case of what I call viral contracting. Viral contract (or purported viral contract, because the legal validity of this procedure is not yet determined)

[41] This will work for many run-of-the-mill transactions. Sometimes, however, human intervention will be needed, and it may be difficult to program computers to "know" when to call in a human. See *id*.

occurs when a digital product[42] has digital terms integrated with it, and the product-plus-terms propagates down a chain of distribution, with the intent that the terms be binding on whoever comes into possession of the package. The digital product could be a software program or some other kind of content that someone wishes to propagate. Integrated with such a digital product could be digitally programmed terms that purport to constrain use of the digital product – for example, prohibition of criticism of the program, or prohibition of reverse engineering. The economists' contract-as-product view is here brought to fruition. The digitized product and the digitized terms are literally (not just conceptually) the same in kind and part of a package. Not only does such a package undermine the distinction between text and functionality, it seems difficult to maintain the distinction at all. That is, at this point it seems arbitrary to call one set of programming statements a functional product and another set of programming statements a text.

It also seems that digital rights management systems (DRMSs) are doing their part to undermine the distinction between text and machine. A DRMS is a program that limits distribution and use of some piece of digitized content; it is essentially next-generation copy protection. That is, a DRMS could prevent content from being copied, or allow it to be copied once and sent to one recipient, but deleted from the original recipient's computer; or it could delete the content after a set time period; and many other permutations. DRMSs give rise to many policy problems that I am not discussing here, in particular the problem of overreaching by content owners who can use technological protection to prevent activities that are otherwise the right of the user (for example, copying of material that is not protected by copyright).[43] At least it seems that DRMSs are also contributing to the undermining of the idea that a contract is a text, separate from and "about" (accompanying) some machine or functionality. The DRMS is itself a machine or functionality, and it is not at all clear whether to think of it as a contract; to me it seems like non-contractual technological self-help. In this case the product, whether "content" (e.g., music) or "machine"(e.g., computer program), has become so integrated with the terms governing it (the DRMS) that it is difficult to

[42] In light of the blurring of the distinction between products and services online, I will use the term product to cover both.

[43] Protecting DRMSs is the purpose of the Digital Millennium Copyright Act, and it is this grant of protection beyond copyright that is engendering a lot of complaint by law professors. See Pamela Samuelson, "Intellectual Property and the Digital Economy: Why the Anti-Circumvention Regulations Need to Be Revised", 14 *Berkeley Tech. L. J.* 519 (1999).

find a foothold for the notion of contract at all. I am not sure that the traditional notion of agreement is going to help us when it comes to working out how far the law should allow unfettered operation of DRMSs, but so far another paradigm has not emerged to substitute for it. This is a field in which further research is urgently needed.

Against my labeling DRMSs as technological self-help, one could say that the consumer chooses whether or not to purchase the content-plus-DRMS package, and that this decision is contractual. At minimum, construing the transaction as contractual in this way underlines the coalescence of contract into the product, or, as I am arguing, the transition of contract from text to machine, from intangible information to tangible object. In order to think that the consumer is subject to the terms contained in the package because the consumer chose to be bound by them, we are remanded to familiar empirical questions about the market: whether the same content is available in the market without the DRMS attached to it, whether the consumer is aware of the operations of the DRMS, and so on.

Probably the advent of DRMSs, and the law's extraordinary solicitude for them, is my best evidence about the blurring of contract into machine. Before concluding, however, I want to mention another development that seems to fit into the general pattern of absorbing contract into machinery: computerized identifier languages such as XML. XML is a language that can tag significant functional digitized texts.[44] The purpose of XML is to make possible efficient searches in electronic commerce. For example, if every web store that had an umbrella for sale used codes that tagged the item as an umbrella, it would be possible to use my browser to search directly for umbrellas, and receive a listing of all umbrellas for sale. An analogous tagging procedure could be used for digitized texts that represent legal terms. For example, a code at the beginning and end of the fine print could designate it as a "contract". More usefully, perhaps, a code at the beginning and end of a particular clause could designate it as a "choice of law clause". With these tags, my browser could be used to search for all choice-of-law clauses.

The result of widespread deployment of XML-type tags would be that one could search for the exact products needed and, in the very same way, one could also search for the exact clauses desired. Here again there is no difference between functionality (desired attributes or features of a product) and (what was formerly conceived of as) text. The result, if it comes to pass,

[44] See Jane K. Winn, "Making XML Pay: Revising Existing Electronic Payments Law to Accommodate Innovation", 53 *SMU L. Rev.* 1477, 1480-81 (2000).

will be that consumers could search for products they like and warranties they like in exactly the same way.

Using XML-type tags, attorneys could search all clauses used by others and replicate the ones they like. This will broaden legal modularity – the practice of constructing documents out of prefabricated clauses or sections. This is one of a number of reasons why I believe that in the digital environment, it is likely that standardized transactions will occupy even more of the transactional universe than in the offline world.[45] (Other reasons include easy proliferation of standardized sets of terms that authorities and the market find acceptable; and the need for standardized terms in machine-to-machine contracts, which I think will become prevalent in B2B e-commerce.) In online standardized transactions, the nature of the transaction is more transparent than it was in the past, because the fine print that comes with the (other) features being purchased is more accessible to everyone. These are the main reasons I believe that the lay conception of consent will at least become more difficult to maintain.

17.8 Conclusion and Suggestions for Further Research

Commodification is socially constructed as involving objects separate from the self. Information has traditionally been understood as knowledge and communication, intertwined with personhood. In this conceptual universe, commodification of information was made possible by marrying information to the physical; e.g., in copyright, by conceiving of the information as commodifiable because (a) externalized and (b) embodied in a tangible object. As long as commodification of information was conceived in this way, there seemed to be a realm of noncommodified information too, which was not externalized and not embodied in tangible objects.

Information commodification has increased through various expedients. One expedient is just finding that more things count as tangible objects in which information can be embodied; e.g., that computerized information in ephemeral memory can amount to a "copy" for purposes of copyright. Technology has provided the tools for increasing the universe of tangible objects in which information can be embodied. This expedient is buttressed by analogies that get us to think of information as if it were real estate, so that the attributes of the myth of physical property can attach to information.

---

[45] There are pressures that I think will lead to greater standardization; but greater customization is also possible. See Margaret Jane Radin, "Online Standardization and the Integration of Text and Machine", 70 *Fordham L. Rev.* 1125 (2002).

Another expedient, and the one that interests me most right now, is simply to bypass the traditional kind of information commodification – by linkage of information to the external world and embodiment in a physical object – and instead move directly to redescribe the information itself as a physical object from the outset. Technology has also made this redescription possible. The redescription tends to make obsolete the former understanding of information as knowledge and communication inextricably bound up with personhood.

In thinking for the future, we should consider the impact of tangibility and the growing link between information and physical objects. In particular, we should think about how this redescription may undermine "free" expression – by moving free communications in the direction of propertization, away from our traditionally unpropertized discourse.

The more that information can be divested of its links with personhood and assimilated to the categories of objects (machines, tangibility, functionality), the more it can be commodified. In the examples I have looked at, the assimilation to tangibility is for the purpose of accomplishing commodification (e.g., in the case of genetic information protected by patent, or databases protected under trespass to chattels). Assimilation of information to categories of tangibility (information "objects") also recasts our understanding of information toward seeing it as fully fungible. The further ramifications of this redescription of information have yet to be explored.

One likely ramification will be in the realm of contract: here redescription of information impacts both our traditional notions of consent and contractual enforceability. As I have discussed, legal relationships, binding commitment, and consent may be rendered obselete by new technologies. Here an urgent question will be: what should become of contract in the face of the challenges posed by assimilation of the agreement and the product/service being transferred thereby? This redescription of information will also impact individual privacy: if data become more readily understood as physical objects, the ownership claims made by data gatherers will presumably be more cogent. Future research might consider what protections should be erected to stave off the encroachment of information tangibility on individual privacy.

Expediency is at least part of the reason for the assimilation of information to the realm of the physical; in light of stubborn background assumptions about property, it is easier for those who wish to control information assets to get broad rights under the rubric of physical property. Thus commodification has moved from powerful analogies to physical property to assimilation into "literal" physical property. At the same time, it may be that the physicalist reductionism of early and mid-twentieth century philosophy has only now thoroughly permeated the law. Here is a topic for students of the history of ideas. As physicalist reductionism has usually been thought to foster increasing commodification, the use of assimilation to tangibility as an avenue of increasing information commodification seems to fit well within that general view.

Chapter 18

COPYRIGHT AND CULTURAL POLICY FOR THE CREATIVE INDUSTRIES

Ruth Towse
Erasmus University, Faculty of History and Art Studies (KCW), Rotterdam, The Netherlands

Chapter contents:

Abstract: Copyright, which was initially introduced for the encouragement of authors of literary and artistic works, is not able to offer artists sufficient economic incentive to create. Royalty payments to all but the top artists are typically small and firms in the creative industries are typically large, making for a very unequal bargaining situation. Already, though, digital delivery of cultural products is beginning to change this scenario and we can consider possible effects on markets and the implications for copyright and cultural policy.

18.1 Copyright and Cultural Policy for the Creative Industries

18.1.1 Introduction

To most economists, the term Intellectual Property (IP) has until recently been largely synonymous with patents, whose economic effects are studied in the context of innovation, technical progress and growth. Copyright and the creative industries in which it is crucially important have until lately attracted little attention. In this Chapter, I put the spotlight on copyright law in the creative industries that comprise the cultural sector, and on artists' labour markets. I therefore adopt an instrumental and empirical approach to copy-

O. Granstrand (ed.), Economics, Law and Intellectual Property, 419-438.

right law, viewing it as an incentive to cultural production. In this chapter, I give a brief introduction to the economics of copyright and to the creative industries and then go on to discuss the impact of the digitalisation on incentives and rewards to creators in the creative industries and the implications for copyright and cultural policy, making a plea for more institutional and empirical analysis in this area.

18.1.2 Copyright law

Copyright law was first enacted in England in 1709 with the Statute of Anne and gradually adopted in other countries. In the USA, the principle was embodied in the Constitution in 1776 and the first Federal Copyright Act was passed in 1790. It gives authors the right to exclude others from copying their work without permission, the so-called exclusive right of authorisation. The basic right conferred on the author is that of controlling or restricting the acts of copying, that is, reproducing the work, issuing copies to the public, performing the work in public, broadcasting it by wire or satellite and including the work in a cable programme, playing and showing the work in public and renting or lending it to the public. The threshold requirement for copyrightable works is originality. However, independent creation is allowed by the scope of copyright law but it is subject to limitations and exceptions; the fair use exception is discussed in the next section.

Copyright in what is now called the Anglo-Saxon tradition is essentially conceived of as an economic right that enables trade to take place in information goods. From the start, it applied to publishers as well as to authors. In Continental European countries, influenced by the Kantian concept of the author, copyright is an author's right (droit d'auteur) attached to the personality of the author; it embodies droit morale, what are now called moral rights, the right to attribution, integrity, disclosure and withdrawal, and these rights are inalienable. The underlying rationale for this concept of copyright is natural justice rather than to facilitate transactions. With the globalisation of the cultural industries and increasing standardisation of copyright worldwide, however, the distinction between the civil law countries' emphasis on moral rights and copyright in the common law tradition is eroding. Moral rights have been incorporated into Anglo-Saxon law and European countries have extended copyright to neighbouring rights (rights neighbouring on copyright) to performers and to firms producing information goods. In Anglo-Saxon law, statutory rights such as performers' property rights are also called neighbouring rights. For the sake of convenience (and at the risk of offending European lawyers), I shall refer throughout this paper to copyright in a generic way to cover both authors' and neighbouring rights and in the discussion below of the creative industries, to authors and performers as creators.

Copyright applies to a wide range of literary, dramatic, musical and artistic works in various media, such as films, recordings, broadcasts, computer software and the like. It does not require any proven artistic or innovative merit and accepts authorship on the basis of creative effort; thus arrangements, compilations, listings, databases, etc are protected by copyright separately from the original material embodied in them. The author may license, assign or sell these rights outright or in part or transfer them to an agent; only the author's moral right in the work may not be sold or transferred. As techniques for reproducing and copying creative work have developed and the hardware for applying them has become cheaper, making it possible for the average household to own several copying devices (aural and video tape recorders, photocopiers, computers), the scope and degree of protection of copyright law have increased. In addition, changes in social attitudes to creativity and 'high' and 'low' culture and to the status of artists have led to extensions of copyright law, such as droit de suite for visual artists (artists' resale rights)[1] and performers' rights. As to the administration of copyright, royalties for sales and other primary use are usually administered by the publisher; remuneration for secondary use, such as photocopying and public performance of recorded works, is licensed by co-operative collecting societies (see Towse, 2001a).

18.1.3 Economic features of copyright

In general, the economic case for copyright for author is the same as that for patents for inventors: it creates statutory property rights that overcome free-riding problems of information goods and therefore provides an incentive mechanism for rewarding creators and for the disclosure of their works. While patents protect ideas, however, copyright protects only the expression of ideas (works), which must be fixed in some form (written down, recorded, filmed, electronically stored, etc) to be eligible. Works by literary authors, visual artists, composers, choreographers, film-makers, performers, and so on, in all media are protected by copyright law, as well as those by publish-

[1] The right of the artist to a share of the increase in value of her work of art in subsequent sales (usually public auctions). The *droit de suite* was established in France and spread to many European countries and to their dominions. At the time of writing, *droit de suite* was part of the European Union harmonisation programme and was due to be introduced into countries where it had not formerly existed – among them UK, Ireland and the Netherlands.

ers, record, broadcasting and film companies and the like. Copyright confers a monopoly to the copyright-holder of 70 years after the death of the author (or that of the last surviving one in the case of joint authorship) and 50 years from the date of fixation in the case of a sound recording, broadcast or the like; this monopoly applies work by work. This is now the case throughout the European Free Trade Area and in North America (and elsewhere), following various harmonisation policies (see Towse and Holzhauer, 2002). Both patents and copyrights are monopolies, but copyright is a much weaker monopoly and is more of the nature in economic terms of a Chamberlinian monopolistic good.

Landes and Posner (1989) provide a definitive economic analysis of the doctrines of copyright law. One of these, fair use, is particularly important to the discussion in this chapter; indeed, through legal cases like Napster, it has shot into the news. The rationale of fair use doctrine lies in the public interest in balancing the incentive to create that copyright provides with that of ensuring users' access to the works that are created. The exclusive right of authorisation is therefore limited in copyright statutes and exceptions made for certain types of 'fair use' – the use of copyrighted material by consumers and producers (authors and publishers) without the author's consent and without payment. With the advent of cheap office- or home-based copying devices, such as photocopiers, home video recorders, DVD and MP3, unauthorised use by consumers has increased considerably, some of which is fair use but much of which is illegal. Fair use also influences creativity; 'standing on the shoulders of giants' is a familiar phrase to patent analysts but the equivalent concept in relation to copyright is not so well known. Fair use doctrine recognises, notwithstanding the Romantic view of creativity, that most new works are derived from existing material in some way or another – through inspiration, reference, imitation, shared language and cultural values etc. Therefore, the problem copyright law has is to find a balance for creators between giving them access to protected extant work without excessive transaction costs and royalty payments and providing an incentive to create new works; this balance is sought by fair use. As Landes and Posner demonstrate, a too strong copyright regime that tolerated little fair use would raise transaction costs and copyright-based earnings, transferring rents to creators from users; it would, however, raise the costs of creation. A too weak regime, on the other hand, would not provide sufficient incentives to look for means of charging, and therefore would reduce transaction costs and earnings but would ease what Landes and Posner called 'productive' (as compared to 'reproductive') fair use of copyright. In economic terms, fair use can be justified by the transaction costs of obtaining authorisation for each and every use of copyrighted material. Markets may not develop if transaction costs exceed the value of copies to individual users (possibly the case with online music delivery).

In the creative industries, notably music, the market is served by private collective copyright organisations, collecting societies, that use blanket licensing to reduce costs of individual transactions; in other areas, such as administering public lending rights and photocopying charges, governments are involved, often using compulsory licensing. The problems that these copyright collecting arrangements overcome are the cost and bother to individual authors, publishers and users of clearing and paying for the use of copyright material and that of enforcing copyright in private homes and offices where infringement, often on a large scale, takes place. Collecting societies are particularly important for licensing secondary use of copyright material, where 'third parties' are involved – those not a party to contracts between authors and publishers. Secondary use of recorded music in public performance in broadcasting and as an ancillary service by a large number of private enterprises (hotels, restaurants, shops, aircraft, discos, sports halls – to name a few) and of printed matter for photocopying is very widespread, and collecting societies' revenues run to millions of dollars (see Towse, 2001a; 2002). As we shall see later, digitalisation may or may not exacerbate these problems.

18.2 The Creative Industries

From the above discussion, it can be seen that the main forum for the application of copyright law in practice is in the creative industries. The term 'creative industries' is new, though the industries it covers are not. It seems to be a British invention that parcels together what were previously known as the arts ('high' culture) and the cultural industries (mass-produced 'low' culture). There is a certain amount of semantic confusion here, as with terms such as the 'Information Age', the 'Digital Age', the 'New Economy', and the 'Creative Economy'. To make matters worse, it is sometimes necessary to distinguish between the creative industries (the whole cultural sector) and the cultural industries (those which mass-produce 'recorded' cultural products).

The creative industries have come to be defined in a number of countries as the 'traditional' creative and performing arts (visual arts, literature, music, dance, opera, drama) and the cultural industries (film, radio, television, sound recording, publishing, multi-media). In most countries the arts and heritage are supported by some form of government intervention, whether state provision, government subsidy or indirect support via tax breaks and the like, depending on cultural policy. The cultural industries too may be publicly or privately owned, subsidised, assisted through the tax system and, in the case of the press and broadcasting, regulated. There is considerable divergence of practice on this in different countries (Towse, 2001a). Other industries that are entirely private, such as fashion, advertising and computer software, depend strongly on creative input (by people we call artists) and they have come to be regarded as part of the 'creative' industries as well. Whatever we call it, this is a development of and reflects the increasing significance in post-industrial economies of intangible production (the stage of human capitalism, to use Granstrand's (2000) term). What is important is that in all these industries producers rely upon copyright law to establish property rights and protect revenues, and this has therefore become a unifying feature of the creative industries. At their core is creativity protected by copyright. This recognition has led in some countries to viewing copyright as the basis for official definition of the creative industries.

It is only recently that the economic importance of the creative industries has been recognised. This recognition came about in two ways: one, when estimates were made of the economic size of the cultural sector, under the heading of the economic impact of the arts; the second was a similar exercise in social accounting, the measurement of the economic effect of copyright protection. The task has been a difficult one, as National Income statistics do not classify the creative industries as such. It is even more difficult to make international comparisons, and estimates should be taken with a liberal pinch of salt (Towse 2001a). Nevertheless, the figures are interesting. As can be seen from Table 1, the items listed there are ones covered by copyright.

The identification of copyright and the creative industries has certain policy implications. Policy on copyright implicitly becomes part of cultural policy, though the full implications of this are not always recognised. That is the case in the UK. The broader approach to cultural policy has brought the arts and the cultural industries together under the remit of the Department for Culture, Media and Sport (DCMS). The cultural industries were transferred to DCMS from the Department of Trade and Industry (DTI), which previously was responsible for policy in the commercial cultural industries. Copyright, however, is still dealt with by the Patent Office under the DTI. In the Netherlands, by contrast, there is not the same emphasis as in the UK on the cultural industries having common cause with the traditional subsidised arts, and copyright policy is divorced from cultural policy, being handled by the Ministry of Justice; and though it is clear from policy statements of the Ministry of Education, Culture and Science that copyright is regarded as important for cultural policy, the two tend to be viewed as separate entities. In Australia, however, matters have been taken further with the formation of the Department of Communications, Information Technology and the Arts, which is responsible for copyright as well as for cultural policy. This could become the model for copyright policy in other countries.

Table 18-11.: Global creative industries 1999 market size, in US $ billions

	Global	US	UK
Advertising	45	20	8
Architecture	40	17	2
Art	9	4	3
Crafts	20	2	1
Design	140	50	27
Fashion	12	5	1
Film	57	17	3
Music	70	25	6
Performing Arts	40	7	2
Publishing	506	137	16
R&D	345	243	21
Software	489	325	56
Toys and Games	55	21	2
Television & Radio	195	82	8
Video Games	17	5	1
Total	2,240	960	157

Source: Howkins (2001)

18.3 Economics of the Creative Industries

Most people associate creativity with the arts. Creativity is also central to the cultural industries and studies of artists' labour markets have shown that many artists work in them. I do not attempt to define creativity here (for a brief survey, see Howkins, 2001); suffice it to say that it leads the economist into uncharted territory of what is art and who is an artist. Most cultural economists have avoided the issue (as with tastes), and rely on self-definition or on social statisticians who draw up questionnaires for labour market and occupational surveys. Another approach, which I favour, is to take the implied stance of copyright law – anything that is original for the purposes of copyright is creative. As indicated earlier, this does not imply a very high threshold of artistic creation.

Creativity plays the equivalent role in the creative industries to that of innovation in other sectors of the economy. Just as firms in manufacturing have outlays on research and development (R&D), so firms in the creative industries search for new ideas and talented workers to supply them. And, as with innovation, we may distinguish product and process innovation. New products are very important in the cultural industries, with a stream of novelty being demanded and supplied. It is misleading, however, to focus only on product innovation because there has been enormous process innovation in the creative industries as well. Indeed, the cultural industries are the product of technical developments – sound recording, film, video, television and computers. The Internet and digitalisation are now beginning to have a considerable impact on the creative industries. As with all technological revolutions, these changes have altered the pattern of demand for workers, reducing the employment in the cultural sector of some types of artists and increasing it for others. They also have implications for the location of industry. The post-industrial economy has been called the 'weightless economy' and the creative industries epitomise that tag. If we were to apply Weberian location analysis to this sector, we would think of the 'weight' now being at the consumer downloading end, rather than packaging the content for delivery in tangible form – you supply the paper to print my articles, not I! (Indeed, paper may soon no longer be a necessity for reading if e-publishing develops.)

Features common to all the creative industries are high set-up costs for content and low/negligible marginal costs of delivery (Shapiro and Varian, 1999; Acheson and Maule, 1999). These are the classic economic characteristics of natural monopolies. These features are responsible, at least in an analogue environment, for market concentration into an oligopolistic industrial structure with a few large firms dominating the industries (Disney, Sony, Seagram, Time Warner, to name a few international conglomerates; for a detailed analysis, see Bettig, 1998). We also observe tacit price-fixing (the price of CDs has been investigated by the UK antitrust body, the Monopolies and Mergers Commission). Another feature is the tolerance of small independent companies in these oligopolised industries. It seems they are necessary to the large corporations as a source of artistic R&D (in the music business this is known as A&R – Artists and Repertoire) because large, bureaucratic organisations apparently lack the ability to spot talent at an early stage.

A second feature of creativity that has an economic interest is the incessant search for novelty and uncertain demand on the part of consumers, making the creative industries highly risky: 'nobody knows' is how Caves characterises them (Caves, 2000). In my opinion, this ought to be revised to 'some people know more than others' – that individual creators who supply the novel content face radical uncertainty, whereas the firms in the creative industries 'know more'. Firms can pool risk by holding a portfolio of copyright assets of different ages and riskiness and have access to capital markets; individual creators can rarely do either. Thus there is an inherent asymmetry between creators and firms and that is unintentionally exacerbated by copyright law, which not only establishes property rights but also creates assets – a case of unintended consequences. Those consequences are a matter of concern for both cultural and copyright policy. These points are developed later in the chapter.

An aspect of this new economy and its dependence on copyright that has attracted less attention from economists is that risk-bearing is reallocated. This is most easily seen in relation to royalty payments for copyright. Under typical present arrangements of publication, creators and publishers share risk in a royalty arrangement, with the creator typically bearing the fixed costs of creating the primary content (writing the book or music, acquiring the necessary human capital etc). But though the fixed cost of creation is relatively high, it is difficult for the vast majority of artists to earn an adequate income. Firms in the creative industries are able to 'free-ride' on the willingness of artists to create, and the structure of artists' labour markets, characterised by short-term working practices and oversupply, makes it hard for artists to appropriate rewards.

The complex interaction of copyright and artists' labour markets and the incentives and rewards to creators are explored in detail in Towse (2001a). Here, I use some results of that work as the basis for a further enquiry, the reward of creators (or artists: the workers responsible for creativity) as digitalisation advances. In order to make this case, it is necessary to start with a brief analysis of what cultural economists have had to say about artists' labour markets.

18.3.1 Economics of artists' labour markets

Cultural economics has developed over the last 30 years as a subdiscipline of economics analysing markets for the arts, heritage and the cultural industries[2]. A central area of interest in cultural economics has been the study of artists' labour markets, the response by artists (meaning all kind of creative and performing artists and craftspeople) to earnings, and the mirror image, the role of artists' labour costs in cultural production. The latter featured in the analysis of Baumol's 'Cost Disease', which attributed the increasing costs of producing the arts (and other labour-intensive service industries) to the limited scope for growth in labour productivity, causing the prices of artistic products to rise above the general price level; thus markets would be increasingly unable to support high-quality art.[3] This widely accepted argument throws the spotlight on artists' incomes and labour markets and on artists' supply behaviour, and that has given rise to empirical studies of artists' employment, earnings and career development. Work is difficult in this area because there are so few official statistics (also the case with the creative industries); thus researchers have had to rely on surveys, which are not always satisfactory. In particular, it is difficult to deal with problems of defining artists (or creative workers); often researchers have to rely upon self-definition rather than on a 'market' test of success. Nevertheless, there is now a body of work that allows some generalisations about artists' labour market behaviour and experience (Towse 2001a).

The distribution of artists' incomes is highly skewed, with a few superstars having very high incomes from fees, sales and royalties. Research in a number of countries has shown that the 'typical' (that is, non-superstar) artist is a multiple job-holder, working longer than average hours in arts and non-arts work on short-term contracts with no career structure and earning a variable and lower than average income, despite being highly educated. One of the results that is of particular interest in the present context is that many artists work both in 'high'-culture subsidised organisations and with commercial 'low'-culture firms in the creative industries. With respect to supply behaviour, artists respond to increases in income from both arts and non-arts work by spending more time on their chosen art form. The elasticity of artists' labour supply to rewards is important for cultural policy, as the creativity and talent of artists are at the root of arts provision; thus understanding incentives to artists, whether pecuniary or non-pecuniary, is necessary in order to achieve policy objectives of innovation and high-quality art.[4]

Copyright plays a role in artists' labour markets by protecting property rights to artistic creation and by providing both a financial incentive in the

---

[2] See Towse (1997) for a collection of articles in the field.

[3] See Towse (1998) for the collected works of Baumol in this and related areas.

[4] See Towse (2001b).

form of royalty earnings and a non-pecuniary incentive through moral rights and the recognition of artistic status. But while copyright law creates rights, it cannot guarantee rewards, notwithstanding the rhetoric of lawyers and artists' organisations; the value of copyright royalty rates is decided in the marketplace, and it is therefore artists' bargaining power with firms in the creative industries that determines copyright earnings. Artists' bargaining power is, however, considerably weakened by the persistence of excess supply of creative workers to the creative industries. That is one of the universal findings of research on artists' labour markets. As with artists' earnings from other arts sources, the individual distribution of copyright earnings is highly skewed, with a few top stars earning considerable sums but the median or 'typical' authors earning only small amounts from their various rights.

Cultural economists explain general oversupply in the creative industries in terms of inherent radical uncertainty. A derivative of Caves' 'nobody knows' theorem is that there is oversupply in the creative industries. As in Nature, so in art: all forms of life produce millions of seeds and eggs, far in excess of the amount needed to reproduce the present population, in order to ensure the continuation of the species under conditions of uncertainty. The comparable phenomenon in art is overabundance of trainees in all the creative and performing arts and of trained artists trying to make it professionally. Unsurprisingly this leads to two related phenomena (which Adam Smith observed in the legal profession of his day – 'the lottery of the law', as he called it in the *Wealth of Nations* Book 1) – very low rewards to the majority of those who work in these industries and very high rewards to the few, whom we nowadays call superstars. It is radical uncertainty that drives this lottery; 'no-one knows' so they latch on to the famous to provide information about quality. The internal dynamic is that the chance of success is a lure to risk-taking artists, who flock to take their chances. The result is a highly skewed distribution of income.

18.3.2 Digitalisation, copyright and rewards in the creative industries

The foregoing analysis has set the scene for considering the effects of digitalisation in the creative industries. If digitalisation is a threat to copyright, a question that at present has considerable importance for lawyers and economists as well as for those whose livelihood depends upon it, nowhere will it have greater impact than in the creative industries. Throughout its 300 years' history, copyright has adapted to technological change while retaining essentially the same legal and economic principles. The very origins of copyright are tied up with the technical ability to copy, as illustrated in the clever title of Goldstein's 1998 book *Copyright's Highway: from Gutenberg to the Celestial Jukebox.* Until digitalisation, however, copies of most types of art products were inferior to the original; with digital copying, it is only a figure of speech to make a distinction between the original and copies in relation to some products – printing and recorded music being prime examples. Works in many media can easily be reduced to a digital signal and, with existing technology, delivered through telephone lines and fibre optic cable to home-based computers, by satellite if distances are great; developing broadband technologies promise far more. Thus works of art and entertainment, as well as a host of more mundane services, become 'content' to be delivered, along with the take-away dinner, on demand. This presents a challenge to legal analysts and to economists as to how these services can be charged for, as, unlike the dinner, there is no physical product that can be withdrawn upon non-payment.

It may be that these developments present a greater challenge to firms in the creative industries than they do to the artists and other creators of content. Indeed, they have empowered some artists to free themselves from dependence on publishers for the marketing of their products, enabling them to retain effective control over their IP. Some professional pop groups and stars have already taken advantage of this turn of events. Thousands of *wannabees* are vanity-publishing in all media on the Internet. It will be interesting to observe the changing role of literary publishing, film, TV and radio companies in the Information Age. To survive, they will almost certainly have to follow the example of music publishers, who, with the advent of computer programmes for music printing, changed to handling rights rather than copy.

Such technical developments call for new ways of organising markets in the creative industries: the development of e-commerce, which will lead to changes in the industrial organisation of the supply of content and delivery; a switch to far more licensing/franchising arrangements as a substitute for outright sales; and more market segmentation as price discrimination becomes easier with e-commerce.

E-commerce will clearly alter the costs of production. Take the case of books: even a simple e-mail ordering system such as that of Amazon Books removes the need for shops on high-street locations and transport to them; substitutes are warehouses on cheap land with postal delivery. There are still costs of printing and paper. But when books and other reading material are downloaded from the Internet, the customer pays for the paper and the printing while the publisher markets the list and administers the copyrights; when authors learn how to market, or new firms develop providing information services about authors and their output, there is no need for publishers in their present role.

It is easy to see from the above that rights management is likely to become more and more important for content delivery. Whereas the older literature on the economics of copyright considered the welfare case for its existence, the recent literature deals with issues such as automated rights management (Bell, 1998) and licensing fees.[5] The choice of trading methods – sales, licensing, franchising, to name the obvious possibilities – becomes the digital marketplace equivalent of the 'make or buy' decision of firms, which determines the structure of industries. The different pricing procedures of these ways of doing business are a new application of modern price theory. Moreover, new sources of revenue become possible; Meurer (1997) explores price discrimination and fair use with respect to digital works, arguing that digitalisation may encourage the demand for excerpts of copyright material, for example, for creating multimedia products, and revenues could accordingly rise. This would make the formation of digital collecting societies economically feasible and enable copyright-holders to charge even small amounts and so cut down the amount of 'free' use, which would inevitably result if no mechanism for charging exists.

Although there is a lot of pessimism in some industries, especially the film and music industries, about the feasibility of charging for Internet delivery, the bottom line is that 'there has to be some way of arranging payment': where there is effective demand for information content – and we know that people are even willing to pay a price for material they can download from the Internet – there must be some method of payment that makes it happen. Indeed, the developments in the music industry since the Napster case point in that direction.

It is now well understood that online delivery facilitates greater opportunities for price discrimination, which increases revenues. There is a variety of market and non-market price regimes, each with a different set of incentives and rewards to economic agents on the supply side and to consumers of products containing copyright material on the demand side. The question is how much of this is reaped as reward by creators of content and how much accrues to the firms in the creative industries.

The creative industries, in fact, offer a wide range of reward systems for copyright owners. They suggest a variety of ways in which payment may be

[5] For applied studies of both legal and economics aspects of copyright, see a collection of conference papers in Towse (2002).

made for content supplied via new delivery channels. At present, the following methods of payment are to be found in the cultural industries:

- spot prices charged to consumers (users) by producers; first sale doctrine allows the consumer freedom to enjoy use (e.g. to share or resell) indefinitely but copyright law restricts copying;
- discriminatory spot prices charged to consumers;
- spot prices paid to the creator for unlimited use of specific copyright material (buy-out);
- flat rate licences to users for specified uses of copyright material for a limited time period;
- licences to users for metered use of specific copyright material;
- future payments – royalties (a percentage of revenues) to copyright-owners based on sales;
- present payments of future prices paid to creators of copyrighted work, e.g. advances on royalties;
- profit-sharing between copyright-owners, such as star performers' and directors' shares in musicals and films;
- flat-rate share of revenues between copyright-owners, such as those from blanket licences issued by copyright collectives for unlimited use;
- pro-rata share of revenues between different copyright-owners based on itemised uses of material, e.g. licence income from public performance sound recordings, which is shared between composers, performers and record companies;
- legal enforcement of the share of resale value, e.g. droit de suite for visual artists;
- site licence model, i.e. blanket licences for unlimited use of a bundle of copyrights negotiated between owners and organisations on behalf of multiple users, such as software licences for business employees/university members; photocopying licences;
- state regulation of contractual licensing arrangements, as above; for example, regulation of music and photocopying licences by the Copyright Tribunal in the UK;
- compulsory licences with equitable remuneration for some purposes embodied in copyright law, as with performers' rights in the public performance of sound recordings;
- compulsory licences organised by the state, e.g. state-controlled TV licences;

- state-organised collection and distribution of remuneration for copyright-owners, for example, the UK Public Lending Right;
- replacement of prices by taxes as compensation for use, for example, the blank tape levy.

This list is not intended to be comprehensive but rather to suggest that there are many ways of organising transactions. All these methods of payment and reward are currently in operation and they are models that may be applied to digital delivery in one way or another. As Granstrand has suggested, where excludability problems cannot be solved for a particular item, bundling non-excludable with excludable elements would be a solution (Granstrand, 2000). Markets have proved to be capable of resolving such problems. However, as may be seen from the list above, some arrangements can be made by contracts between buyers and seller, whereas others rely on institutional arrangements, such as collectives, government agencies and copyright law.

What is particularly interesting for economists is whether the 'new' price system will emerge spontaneously or whether, as, for example with photocopying, it needs to be engineered by a government agency. Markets can find a way; for example, they solved the incredibly complex problem of administering music royalties by setting up private, co-operative collecting societies, and that suggests that artists and other creators will be paid for creating content in new media.[6] In order to better understand these issues, economists need to do detailed institutional analysis of the pricing and administration of copyrights to assess the role of copyright law in assisting rather than replacing the market, the option that seems to be favoured by lawyers.

Policy-makers sometimes assume that the market cannot do the job and should be replaced. An instance of the tendency of law-makers to come up with non-market legal solutions to perceived problems is the 1992 EU Rental Directive, which laid down that certain rights be made unwaivable. That is the case with visual artists' right to droit de suite and some performers' rights, for example rental rights and the entitlement to equitable remuneration for the public performance of sound recording (think of a radio play of a CD). The last-named right requires that a pro rata payment for each individual performer's contribution track-by-track on a CD be 'fairly' compensated for public performance. What this piece of law-making expressly forbade

[6] In the UK there are over 20 such societies and the number increases all the time as new rights and sources of royalty income are created.

was the payment of a flat rate fee for the artists' services that bought out their future rights – what I called above, in line with music industry practice, a buy-out. This assumes two things: one, that, a buy-out cannot be 'fair', that is, actuarily equivalent to the present value of a stream of future royalty payments;[7] secondly, that artists have a preference for risk-taking by being tied in with the publisher in a royalty deal rather than being paid a certain price upfront. However, it ignored the transaction costs of such a move, which can easily exceed the payment due to most performers. This was a case of applying legal principles regardless of potential market incentives and outcomes. The problem this legislation attempted to tackle was the uneven bargaining power between creators and firms in the creative industries, but legal solutions are not appropriate; markets always find a way round them, for example, by discounting future calls on rewards and reducing present payments. This has been the experience of the droit de suite, which though unwaivable and inalienable, is frequently not exercised by artists.

The vastly stronger bargaining position of these firms is rooted in the economies of scale and scope and network economies of the creative industries, which has led to large oligopolies and, by contrast, weak organisation of creative and performing artists in highly competitive labour markets characterised by patterns of short-term employment and casualisation[8]. However, what we do not yet know is what the market structure of the creative industries in the digital age will be. This is something that economists should address. It seems likely that the primary creative content-providers will still be individual artists and small start-ups, while the firms that deliver information goods to markets could grow ever bigger. But there is no inherent reason why, in the changed circumstances of the digital era, firms that deliver content should not more highly reward those creating it by a range of new payment methods. If content is in shorter supply than delivery channels, we would expect that result.

18.4 Copyright as an Asset

The asymmetry of market power between artist/creator and publisher/firm in the cultural industries is further exacerbated by the role of copyright in turning a work of art into a durable asset long out of the control of the original author – the unintended consequence of copyright law men-

---

[7] This may be the case, however, for other economic reasons; see Towse (2001a).

[8] See, for example Caves, 2000, on the effects in the film industry of the demise of the Hollywood studio system.

tioned above. This process could not happen without the requisite copying technology, such as sound recording and photocopying, but once that is in place, copyright magnifies the effect on artists' labour markets. Indeed, I would argue that copyright has enabled mergers to take place in the cultural industries through this asset-creating role. These mergers are currently about delivery buying up the rights to content. This effect of copyright is a result of the frequently held idea that 'strengthening copyright' means increasing its duration and scope. The longer copyright lasts, the greater the chance that the market for the work will change in ways that could not be predicted at the time of the original contract. We have seen this with back catalogues of films, TV programmes and sound recordings, for which new delivery techniques and exploitation of markets worldwide have provided a large demand. Economists usually argue that such unpredictable events lead to losers as well as winners. The point is that the winners are assisted by copyright law in their gains. These are not assets traded in a free market but ones that get pure economic rent from statutorily created property rights.

Access to capital markets is another crucial feature of asymmetry between creators and firms in the creative industries. Large firms have the ability to obtain capital and to pool risks by holding a broad portfolio of assets (for example, Seagram; see Bettig, 1996). By contrast, creators initially have only their human capital as collateral. Having copyright on your works does not help if you have to sell it to finance basic living costs.

18.5 Copyright Policy and Cultural Policy

The earlier discussion of copyright law stressed the problems for striking a balance between the strength of protection for authors and publishers and the effect on the circulation of information for citizens and also for other creators. The scope and breadth of copyright law, from the economic point of view, weigh up the costs and benefits of incentives and rewards and transaction costs. It is also the case that copyright law has become a means of regulating the uneven bargaining position between individual creators and the firms in the creative industries who hire them. These aspects of copyright law make it important in cultural policy.

Various solutions have been suggested to strengthen the position of artists: strengthening copyright to enable creators to trade on the open market; state organisation of royalty and other copyright payments so that the state bears the transaction costs; state grants to artists and other creators, which reduce the necessity for them to sell their work cheaply; state-organised capital loan schemes to enable artists to exploit their works themselves; state-organised loan guarantee schemes combined with private finance (like the US student loan scheme); competitions and prizes to reward successful creators. The first solution, as I argued above, has the opposite of the desired effect as it increases the asset value of copyrights and thus the tendency to oligopolisation of firms in the creative industries; the second has resulted in very high transaction costs in those countries where it has been adopted; and the remainder are essentially means of rewarding individual creators as an *alternative* to copyright law.

There is one superior policy, however, which is to reduce the term of a copyright to 15–20 years and make it renewable so that the market can re-value copyrights. This suggestion was put forward by Plant (1934) and has been proposed by, among others, the International Managers' Federation, the pop group managers' interest group, to the UK Monopolies and Mergers Commission (MMC as it was called at the time) in their submission to the enquiry on the Performing Rights Society monopoly (MMC, 1996). The copyright (or neighbouring right) would revert to the original creator who could therefore capture its current market value during her lifetime as well as being able to benefit descendants.

18.5.1 Summary and conclusions

As with patents, economists have queried the case for copyright as a necessary system for incentive and reward and have questioned its economic consequences. Plant, for example, thought that copyright encourages moral hazard in publishers (firms in the creative industries) without sufficiently rewarding authors (creators) who supply the creative input. He believed that the publishers could rely on the temporary monopoly of lead time to establish new products on the market. Although the development of copying technologies has considerably reduced lead time as an effective business strategy in the creative industries, it nevertheless still has a role to play (because 'nobody knows'). As to moral hazard, it is now accepted that over-reliance on copyright protection on the part of the creative industries (as witnessed by heavily financed anti-piracy campaigns nationally and internationally via the World Trade Organisation, World Intellectual Property Organisation and the like) has reduced their incentive to adopt new technologies, for example by developing legal digital downloading of cultural products.

The current debate about copyright is not whether or not it should exist but whether it will work with digitalisation. This is a debate in which economists should have a strong voice. It is not only a matter of legal principle but also of economic pragmatism. The creative industries, those most likely to be affected by digitalisation, have evolved a range of pricing methods and strategies for organising the delivery of creative content to the market; they need the incentive of contestability to continue to do this. These topics merit further study by economists in order to anticipate the effects of digitalisation, and of changes to copyright law, on industrial organisation and on artists' labour markets. The most serious problem of copyright policy is an economic one – the tendency to oligopoly in the creative industries. For copyrights not only reduce competition; they appear also to encourage mergers of firms based on copyright assets (for example, the AOL/Time Warner merger[9]). This has important consequences for cultural policy and, as a result, I believe that copyright policy (so often in the hands of lawyers) should explicitly take cultural issues into consideration. It can be argued that that is the purpose of fair use doctrine, but this is particularly under threat from digitalisation. Although the economists' approach to fair use emphasises the balance of costs and benefits, this is at bottom an empirical question; but little empirical work has been done on copyright at all.

The empirical work that has been done is in the context of artists' labour markets, looking at the distribution of artists' earnings from copyright and other sources (royalties appear to contribute very little to the 'ordinary' artist's income). In artists' labour markets there is also a tendency to concentration – the superstar phenomenon. The selection of superstars, however, relies upon a pool of artists (creators) and encourages oversupply with the result that rewards are depressed. Creators often work alone or in small 'craft' firms and, though their work is protected by copyright when it is sold on, these small operators are very vulnerable to economic pressures, reflecting the uneven bargaining power with purchasers in the creative industries. The vicious circle, however, is that strengthening and extending copyright does not solve the problem; it may indeed exacerbate it. Thus copyright policy cannot alone solve this problem. It is a matter for cultural policy too. Work by cultural economists versed in copyright law and its administration, and in industrial organisation in the creative industries, is needed to streamline copyright and cultural policy.

[9] At the time of writing, several mergers of content and delivery firms were underway: AOL/Time Warner was agreed and Bertelsmann/Napster and Vivendi/MP3 were being discussed.

18.6 Literature References

Acheson, K. and Maule, C. (1999). *Much Ado About Culture – North American Trade Disputes*. Ann Arbour: University of Michigan.

Bell, T. (1998). 'Fair Use vs 'Fared Use': the Impact of Automated Rights Management on Copyright's Fair Use Doctrine'. *North Carolina Law Review*, 761, pp. 558–619.

Bettig, R. (1996). *Copyrighting Culture*. Boulder: Westview Press.

Caves, R. (2000). *Economics of the Creative Industries*. Cambridge, MA: Harvard.

Howkins, J. (2001). *The Creative Economy: How People Make Money from Ideas*. London: Penguin.

Goldstein, P. (1998). *Copyright's Highway: from Gutenburg to the Celestial Jukebox*. Cambridge, MA: Harvard.

Granstrand, O. (2000). 'The Shift Towards Intellectual Capitalism – The Role of Infocom Technologies'. *Research Policy*, 29, 9, pp. 1061-1080.

Landes, W. and Posner, R. (1989). 'An Economic Analysis of Copyright Law'. *Journal of Legal Studies*, 18, pp. 325–66.

Meurer, M. (1997). 'Price Discrimination, Personal Use and Piracy: Copyright Protection of Digital Works'. *Buffalo Law Review*, 45, pp. 845–98.

Monopolies and Mergers Commission (1996), *Performing Rights*. Cm. 3147. London: HMSO.

Plant, A. (1934). 'The Economic Aspects of Copyright in Books'. *Economica*, May 1, pp. 167–95.

Shapiro, C. and Varian, H. (1999). *Information Rules*. Boston: Harvard Business School Press.

Towse, R. (ed.) (1997a). *Cultural Economics: the arts, the heritage and the cultural industries*, 2 vols. Cheltenham: Edward Elgar Publishing.

Towse, R. (ed.) (1997b). *Baumol's Cost Disease: The Arts and Other Victims*. Cheltenham: Edward Elgar Publishing.

Towse, R. (2001a). *Creativity, Incentive and Reward: an economic analysis of copyright and culture in the Information Age*. Cheltenham: Edward Elgar Publishing.

Towse, R. (2001b). 'Partly for the Money: Rewards and Incentives to Artists'. *KYKLOS*, 54 2/3, pp. 473-90.

Towse, R. (ed.) (2002). *Copyright in the Cultural Industries*. Cheltenham: Edward Elgar Publishing.

Towse, R. and Holzhauer, R. (eds.) (2002). *Economics of Intellectual Property*. Cheltenham: Edward Elgar Publishing.

Chapter 19

LEGAL PROTECTION OF INNOVATIVE TECHNOLOGIES: PROPERTY OR POLICY?

Hanns Ullrich
Bundeswehr University Munich, Faculty of Economic and Organisational Sciences, Neubiberg, Germany;
College of Europe, Brugge, Belgium

Chapter contents:

Abstract: In the European Community, a new body of intellectual property law has been built up that lends itself rather well for an examination of whether the development of IPR-protection for new technologies follows sound principles. There is, indeed, a number of current legal issues of intellectual property protection which appear to be almost entirely untreatable, such as defining the proper conditions for access to technological information under copyright law and database protection schemes, the determination of spare-part protection under design law, and the treatment of international exhaustion of intellectual property rights; and there is a widespread unease about the scope of available protection (biotechnology, business methods). These problems do not only result from the difficulties of adapting the IPR-system to new technological realities. Rather they also mirror changes in our perception of what the IPR-system should do and can be expected to do. IPR's are no longer considered as entitlements granted for merit, but as a means to obtain optimal economic results. The institutional perception of IPR as private property has given way to an instrumental approach using IPR for specific macro- and microeconomic purposes. Where such purposes are in conflict, it is impossible to solve them by systemic value judgements. The task ahead is to return to a systems understanding that allows us to solve such conflicts on the basis of overarching prin-

O. Granstrand (ed.), Economics, Law and Intellectual Property, 439-487.

ciples. The purpose of the paper is to explain the problems, not to develop the principles that bring the solution to the problems.

The paper starts with some examples of the failure of the IPR-system vis-à-vis conflicts of protection. As most of these conflicts also raise problems of competition law, and as most confidence is placed in competition law as a way to solve the conflicts, a short digression is made into competition law. The purpose of this digression, however, is only to show that competition law does not bring the answers. However, it well explains the relationship between intellectual property protection and competition. It is against this background that the "instrumentalization" of IPR for purposes of economic and commercial policy may best be examined and criticized. In a concluding section, a number of problems will be dealt with that economic IPR-theory poses for the administration and the application of IPR-law within the broader legal system, in particular within European Community law.

19.1 Introduction

This contribution is about intellectual property protection being used as a – misguided – tool of economic policy, be it innovation policy or trade policy, and the need to rethink it as a legal system of individual property in technological information. Such a proposition may be out of tune with the currents underlying our pro-IPR era. Indeed, legal protection of innovative technologies, such as patentable inventions, utility models, technical designs, computer programs or databases, is developing rapidly. Even though protection by the law of torts or by the rules on unfair competition is still available, in particular for secret know-how, the trend is to provide protection in the form of property rights including copyright, the latter being even reinforced by technical control devices and contracts of adhesion.[1] This is a movement

[1] See Art. 6 Directive on Copyright in the Information Society OJEC 2001 L 167, 10, transforming Art. 11 WIPO Copyright Treaty of 1996 into Community law; K. J. Koelman, "A Hard Nut to Crack: The Protection of Technological Measures", *Eur. Int. Prop. Rev.* 2000, 272; P. S. Marks, B. H. Turnbull, "Technical Protection Measures. The Intersection of Technology, Law and Commercial Licences", *Eur. Int. Prop. Rev.* 2000, 198; B. Hugenholtz, "Code as Code, Or the End of Intellectual Property as We Know It", 6 *Maastricht J. Eur. Compar. L.* 308, 1999.

Contracts of adhesion have reappeared rather forcefully with the practice (and its legalization) of shrink-wrap and click-wrap licenses, a matter which is beyond the scope of this paper (but see infra III.2).

of federal law in the U.S.A.,[2] it is a movement of harmonization and modernization in the EU[3] bringing all Member States on a legal par, and it is an international movement within the framework of WIPO[4] and, due to the TRIPs Agreement, of WTO. The basic features of these movements are a permanent extension of the subject-matter that qualifies for protection, an accompanying lowering of the thresholds for access to protection for any given subject-matter, a gradual narrowing of the built-in exceptions to available protection,[5] a targeted broadening of the scope of protection, in particular as regards all forms of contributory infringement,[6] and a reinforcement of enforcement against and sanctions for infringement. Thus, it would appear that the system of technology protection is flourishing and particularly healthy, at least in industrialized countries. Occasional disruptions, such as the refusal to grant utility model protection for inventions to chemical or pharmaceutical compounds or processes,[7] might represent minor incidents at worst.

Yet, one may wonder whether, as a legal system following a rule of law, intellectual property protection by patents really is all that sound. In the

---

[2] See A. B. Jaffe, "The U.S. patent system in transition: policy innovation an the innovation process", 29 *Res. Pol.* 5, 2000; R. Merges, "Uncertainty and the Standard of Patentability", 7 *High Tech. L.J.* 1, 8 et seq., 1992.

[3] See H. Ullrich, "Die gemeinschaftsrechtliche Gestaltung des Wettbewerbsrechts und des Rechts des geistigen Eigentums", in P. Müller-Graff (ed.), *Gemeinsames Privatrecht in der Europäischen Gemeinschaft*, 2nd ed. Baden-Baden 1999, 403.

[4] Though within WIPO progress has been made much more in the copyright area due to the "digital revolution" (as to the WIPO Copyright Treaty and the WIPO Performances and Phonogram Treaty, see Reinbothe, Martin, Prat, v. Lewinski, "The New WIPO-Treaties: A First Resume", *Eur. Int. Prop. Rev.* 1997, 171) than in the area of industrial property, where international agreement is limited to simplification of forms (see e.g. WIPO Patent Law Treaty of June 2, 2000, WIPO-Doc. PT/DC/47).

[5] See the narrow exception in Art. 5, 6 EC-Directive 91/250 on the legal protection of computer programs (OJEC 1991 L 122, 42); Art. 5, 8, 9 EC-Directive 96/9 on the legal protection of databases (OJEC 1996 L 77, 28) as compared to general copyright principles; see J. Spoor, "General aspects of exceptions and limitations to copyright: general report", in Association Littéraire et Artistique Internationale (ed.), *The Boundaries of Copyright*, Sydney 1999, 27 and the companion reports dealing with the risks of modern technology for copyright exclusivity. These worries, in turn, tend to put the exceptions into casuistic straightjackets; see Art. 5 Proposed Directive on Copyright in the Information Society, supra n. 1.

[6] See Art. 7 (2) "Directive on the protection of computer programs" (supra n. 5); Art. 6 (2), 7 (1) Directive on copyright in the information society (supra n. 1), following Art. 11 WIPO Copyright Treaty and Art. 18 WIPO Performances and Phonograms Treaty.

[7] See Art. 4 lit. b, c "Amended Proposal for a Directive on the protection of inventions by utility model", COM, 1999, 309/fin 2.

USA,[8] a good part of the strengthening of the system is due not to amended legal rules, but to a simple reorganization of the judiciary, namely to the centralization of patent litigation in one federal court, which, within a few years, brought the invalidation rate for patents down from over 60% to about 45%, i.e. by roughly 1/3. At the same time, the affirmation rate for infringement holdings increased and the concept of patentable subject-matter has been broadened beyond the realms of technology. Similarly, in the EU, the fate of a Community Patent seems to largely depend on that litigation being centralized in one court, at least in one or very few courts per Member State, or else there will never be sufficient trust in the proper operation of the system.[9] Of course, it is not unthinkable that courts, like administrations, simply are held under some sort of bureaucratic capture, but that can hardly be the full explanation of the problem. Rather, there seems to be a considerable number of problems of intellectual property law, which, if not left to specialized courts and their ability to deal with them on technical insider-terms within the IPR-community,[10] are no longer manageable on the basis of generally acceptable legal principles.

Indeed, in addition to the systematic divergences of national intellectual property systems, which are hard to overcome because deeply rooted in national legal and cultural tradition – such as the first-to-file/first-to-invent controversy, the copyright/droit d'auteur alternative, the reluctance of some countries to admit compulsory-licensing rules or the various concepts of claim construction, to name just a few examples of different importance – there is disagreement even in or among industrialized countries over whether protection should at all be extended to certain subject-matter and/or certain acts of its exploitation. Thus, within the relatively homogeneous European Union, harmonization of the rules of design law relating to the protection of

---

[8] See Jaffe, loc. cit. 29 *Res. Pol.* at 533, 2000; J. P. Allison, M. A. Lemley, "Empirical Evidence on the Validity of Litigated Patents", 26 *AIPLA Qu. J.* 185, 1998.

[9] See Commission, "Promoting Innovation through Patents – Follow-up on the Greenbook on the Community Patent and the Patent System in Europe", COM (1999) 42 final of Feb. 5, 1999, sub. 2.3 id., "Proposal for a Council Regulation on the Community Patent", COM, 2000, 412 final, sub. 2.4.5; Ministerial Conference of Member States of the European Patent Organisation held in Paris on June 24 and 25, 1999, Mandate, as reprinted in GRUR Int. 1999, 722, sub. 2; J. Schade, "Gerichtliche Regelung der Patentstreitsachen in Europa", GRUR 2000, 101 with references; id., "Das Streitregelungssystem zum Gemeinschaftspatent nach dem Verordnungsvorschlag der Kommission", GRUR Int. 2000, 827; Leith, "Revision of the EPC, the Community Patent Regulation and 'European Technical Judges'", 2002, Eur. Int. Prop. Rev. 250.

[10] For this IPR-Community see P. Drahos, "Biotechnology Patents, Markets and Morality", *Eur. Int. Prop. Rev.* 1999, 441.

spare parts has proven to be impossible for lack of overarching guiding principles[11]. The courts of the neighbouring Roman law countries of France and Italy have taken opposite stands on the matter. The Court of Justice, the consensus-building institution of the Community, rightfully refused to settle the question[12] or to at least prevent hardship by imposing effective minimum rules of conduct in the matter on the basis of the rules on competition.[13] Similarly, the question whether the exclusive right of distribution is exhausted by the first sale of the goods covered by an intellectual property right not only with respect to domestic trade, but with respect to international trade, has been left unresolved by the WTO Agreement on the Trade Related Aspects of Intellectual Property Rights, even though this is *the* trade issue of international protection of intellectual property. Within the European Union, after extensive hearings, it turned out to be impossible to find a common position on that matter following the Court of Justice's negative ruling in the Silhouette case.[14] Again, the competition rules have been called upon to solve at least the worst cases,[15] but whether they really do so remains yet to be seen. Finally, the seemingly logical step, which the Community has taken when complementing copyright protection of databases by a new *sui generis*

---

[11] Comp. Art. 14, 18 Directive 98/71 on legal protection of designs (OJEC 1998 L 289/28) and the Declaration Relating to Art. 18 made by the Commission (ibid. at p. 35) to the effect that the spare-part issue is to be settled directly by the interested industrial circles in a consultation process, which the Commission coordinates with a view to reaching a voluntary agreement by the interested circles. This agreement has not yet been reached. As a consequence, the Commission has been compelled to submit a "Modified Proposal for a Regulation on the Community Design" (COM, 1999, 310 final) which renounces on regulating the matter (Art. 10a), i.e. the Community legislature is impeded from introducing a fully developed Community IPR-title; see Recital 13 Council Regulation 6/2002 of December 12, 2001 on the Community Design, OJEC 2002 L 3, 1.

[12] CJEC of May 11, 2000, case C-38/98, Renault/Maxicar; for divergent national law see Opinion Adv. Gen. Alber of June 22, 1999, in case C-38/98, Renault/Maxicar, not yet officially reported; Corte di Cassazione of July 24, 1996, GRUR Int. 1997, 650 annot. Zorzi; P. Frassi, "Der Schutz modularer Erzeugnisse im italienischen Recht", GRUR Int. 1999, 698; see also OLG Düsseldorf of Dec. 23, 1996, GRUR Int. 1997, 646.

[13] Comp. CJEC of Oct. 5, 1988, case 53/87, CICRA/Renault, Rep. 1988 I 6039; of Oct. 5, 1988 case 238/87 Volvo/Veng, Rep. 1988 I 6211; Ullrich in U. Immenga, E. J. Mestmäcker, *EG-Wettbewerbsrecht*, Munich 1997, 1253 et seq.

[14] See CJEC of July 16, 1998, case C-355/96, Silhouette International Schmied/Hartlauer, Rep. 1998 I 4799; of July 1, 1999, case C-173/98, Sebago/G.-B. Unic, Rep. 1999 I 4103; Communiqué from Commissioner Bolkestein on the issue of exhaustion of trademark rights of June 7, 2000, http://europa.eu.int/comm.internalmarket/en/intprop/indprop/comexhaust.htm.

[15] See Trib. 1st Inst. of Dec. 16, 1999, case T-198/98, Micro Leader Business/Commission, Rep. 1999 II 3989.

right, which affords protection for data-based information services merely on the ground that the investment needs protection,[16] apparently will not be (fully) followed by its major trading partner, the USA.[17] In fact, the Community itself seems to have been all but sure of the benefits of its initiative, since its Directive expressly provides for a permanent monitoring of possibly anticompetitive effects of the protection granted for databases.[18]

This paper submits that these examples may not sufficiently be explained as problems resulting from the classical dilemmas which intellectual property protection raises, namely, first, the dilemma between the exclusivity necessary as an incentive for the creation of new technology, and competition as the best way to ensure its optimal exploitation and dissemination (the "horizontal" dilemma), and, second, the dilemma between the incentive for the creation of technology as an output, and its use and accessibility as an input for the further development of the same or of dependent technologies (the "vertical" dilemma).[19] Rather, they also mirror systemic difficulties in the development of intellectual property protection as a legal system. These have their causes not so much in the evolution of technology, which is generally designated by the indeterminate catch-words of science-based industry and information society, but in the way we deal with the protection of these technologies. We have, indeed, come from using exclusive rights as part of a legal property system following a rule of law in constituting, attributing and

---

[16] See Art. 7 et seq. Directive 98/9 on the legal protection of databases, supra n. 5, and recitals 7 et seq. 40, J. Gaster, "La protection juridique des bases de données dans l'Union européenne", *Rev. Marché Unique Eur.* 1996 (4) 55, 66 et seq.; see also the discussion of the legislative reasons by O. Bensinger, *Sui generis Schutz für Datenbanken*, Munich 1999, 85 et seq. 94 et seq.

[17] The matter has not been included in revisions of the Copyright Act nor have specific bills passed the legislature; see M. Glazier, "Legislation under consideration by the Congress of the USA regarding the protection of databases", 11 (6) *World Tr. Arb. Mat.* 7 (1999); J. Gaster, "Die draft U.S. database legislation und die EU-Datenbankrichtlinie – ein Vergleich", *CR* 1999, 669; M. J. Davison, "Proposed U.S. Database Legislation: A Comparison with the U.K. Database Regulation", *Eur. Int. Prop. Rev.* 1999, 279; for a critical approach see J. Reichman, Uhlir, "Database Protection at the Crossroads: Recent Developments and Their Impact on Science and Technology", 14 *Berkely Tech'y L.J.* 793, 1999.

[18] See Art. 16 (3) Directive 96/9, supra n. 5.

[19] For the well-known first proposition see only P. David, "Intellectual Property Institutions and the Panda's Thumb: Patents, Copyrights and Trade Secrets in Economic Theory and History", in Wallerstein et al. (eds.), *Global Dimensions of Intellectual Property Rights in Science and Technology*, Washington 1993, 19, 32 et seq.; for the latter proposition Y. Benkler, "Free as the Air to Common Use: A Political Economy of the Public Domain", in R. Dreyfuss *et al.* (ed.), *Expanding the Boundaries of Intellectual Property*, London 2000 sub. I.A.

limiting these rights to preferring an instrumentalist approach, whereby the rights are developed, designed, and eventually re-designed in accordance with more or less immediate objectives of industrial and/or commercial policy. In order to better understand the resulting difficulties, and the need for conceiving new ways out of them – a return to the old property approach is both historically impossible,[20] and socially undesirable – I shall, first, examine whether the application of competition rules may help to overcome the difficulties. Intellectual property protection has, indeed, always been conceived of, at least implicitly, against the background of a free market economy. The principles governing IP-antitrust law may, therefore, be revealing as to the ideal relationship between intellectual property and industrial competition as legal systems. The reality, however, is different. It is this difference which creates the problems. In a second part, therefore, I shall attempt to analyze the specific difficulties which a political, instrumentalist approach to intellectual property protection necessarily creates for the well-functioning of intellectual property as a legal system.

19.2 Exclusive Rights and Market Exclusivity

19.2.1 Exploitation of the legal monopoly by contract

The IPR-reward and the licensing dilemma

Conventional antitrust analysis of intellectual property-related restraints of competition seems to be concerned with the same fundamental dilemma that is at the root of intellectual property protection in general, namely the balance between the exclusive exploitation of protected subject-matter as a "monopoly privilege", and competition for the uses of new technology. However, whilst the intellectual-property dilemma is about the right definition of the exclusivity, the antitrust dilemma is about maintaining competition in the face of the exclusivity as defined by the legislator. In a perspective of intellectual property protection, this appears to be a matter of guaranteeing the lawfulness of restraints, which are inherent in the monopoly right; in a perspective of competition, this appears to be a matter of limiting the exercise of the exclusivity to what is necessary for it to serve its reward-rationale. This dichotomy is based on the idea that, as such, the intellectual

---

[20] In Germany, at least, conceiving of patents as private property was the royal avenue to the legislature's enacting intellectual property protection for inventions; see R. Walz, *Der Schutzinhalt des Patentrechts im Recht der Wettbewerbsbeschränkungen*, Tübingen 1973, 120 et seq., 138 et seq.

property right excludes some competition, namely competition with the goods embodying the protected subject-matter. Consequently, whilst it was commonly recognized that agreements which competitors conclude as to the exploitation of their respective intellectual property are subject to the same antitrust rules that generally apply to horizontal restraints of competition, a seemingly endless controversy arose as to which restraints of competition should be tolerated in agreements by which the owner of intellectual property licenses other enterprises in some limited way to exploit the protected subject-matter.

For a good part, this controversy mirrors yet another dilemma, which is the licensing dilemma. It results from the risk that the owner of intellectual property will refuse to hand out licenses, which ultimately enable the licensee to compete with him, unless the licensor is allowed to contractually keep the licensee at some distance on the market. The controversy, however, was understood as resulting from a basic antagonism between exclusive intellectual property rights and competition. This antagonism rests on two assumptions. The first is that intellectual property protection is granted as an incentive or a reward for the creation of new technology, which entitles the proprietor to impose on licensees whatever restrictions of competition they accept as a "market price" for the grant of the license.[21] The second assumption is that, as a matter of law and competition analysis, the proprietor, by granting the license, voluntarily accepts some kind of intraband competition, which he is entitled to exclude. Any interference by antitrust law with the way the proprietor chooses to contractually exploit his title to exclusivity would, therefore, amount to a curtailment of his legitimate claim to control the reward he may extract from the market, provided always that the proprietor does not overspan his monopoly and/or his reward interests. The tension inherent in this approach – what is an undue extension of the "monopoly claim" – tended and tends to be resolved, at least since the wild years of antitrust have passed,[22] by relying on another pair of assumptions. These are, first, that, in the long run, the legal monopoly will be eroded anyway by the effects of dynamic competition, and, second, that, in the short or medium term, the incentive functions of the exclusive right and of licensing restric-

---

[21] See W.S. Bowman, *Patent and Antitrust Law*, Chicago 1973, 1 et seq., 53 et seq.

[22] For an account and a critique of the development of approaches, see Ullrich, "Lizenzkartellrecht auf dem Weg zur Mitte", GRUR Int. 1996, 555; also A. Heinemann, "Intellectual Property Rights and Competition Policy – The Approach of the WTO Working Group on Trade and Competition", in R. Zäch (ed.), *Towards WTO Competition Rules*, Berne 1999, 299, 302 et seq.

tions must be given full effect in order to make the licensor willing to grant and the licensee willing to seek and take a license.[23]

Intellectual property protection and competition

The problem with this approach is that, by an equation of the protected intangible subject-matter with its tangible embodiments, it creates a confusion between the reasons justifying the exclusivity (on the technology market) and an alleged right to restrain competition (on the product market). Therefore, it assumes an antagonism where there is none. The reason justifying the grant of an exclusivity is not the need to provide an incentive or a reward for a meritorious economic effort, which, like research and development, may easily be annulled in competition, nor is the property right as such the incentive or the reward. There are many economic activities, the fruits of which may easily be reaped away by others in competition.[24] The reason for protecting new technologies resulting from costly research and development (and requiring costly production and marketing) is that technologies, by their very nature, cannot be exposed to competition unless they are protected against imitation in one way or the other. This precisely is the teaching of information economics. Technologies, such as patentable inventions or copyrightable computer programs, represent informational goods – technical teachings, data processing instructions etc – that are in the nature of public goods. They are not naturally appropriable, and they are not subject to con-

[23] Licensor restrictions necessary to make an enterprise seeking licences traditionally have been neglected (see Sect. 17 (ex-Sect. 20) German Act Against Restraints of Competition). Yet they are common practice, e.g. exclusivity requirements or most-favoured-licensee promises. It is by focussing on its enforcement policy on territorial exclusvities in patent and know-how licences that the European Commission has triggered a rethinking of the antitrust approach to licensing restrictions; see Ullrich, loc. cit. GRUR Int. 1996, 558 et seq.

[24] Thus, not only business ideas, such as distribution by franchising or offering cars for rental (instead of offering them for sale), may be adopted by competitors; more generally "free rides" on other enterprises" achievements are inherent in the proper operation of a free market economy; e.g. the first to discover a new business opportunity or to enter a new market is not protected against others developing that same opportunity whatever the merits or the advance investments of the first mover may have been, and enterprises advertising their products are not protected from consumers buying precisely those kinds of products from competitors, etc. Competition is, indeed, expected to precisely do both: provide the incentives (which also mean the pressure) to make such risky first moves (competition as a discovery process), and provide for conditions of optimal exploitation of whatever profit potentials are discovered. The concept of "free rides", therefore, is meaningless (if not a treacherous misnomer), unless it has first been established by a normative judgement whether, in which way, and to what extent a profit opportunity ought to be attributed to individual enterprises.

sumption (though to obsolescence). Once created, they may be used simultaneously and at no additional cost by others. This means that there is no rivalry in use. Therefore, there is no use in investing in their creation in the first place. Consequently, rivalry of use must be introduced artificially. This is done by the grant of exclusive rights, which transform well-defined informational items into individually appropriable goods. These, then, may be traded, may be valued in terms of market prices and scarcity relations, and accordingly, will be produced efficiently with a view to the profitability of the investment. All this is very well known.[25] What it means in terms of competition law is two things.

Protection for, not from, competition

First, intellectual property is in no way functionally different from any other property.[26] It is not the reward, but a naked right. As such it allows the individual collection of a reward from the market, be it directly via the sale of the protected subject-matter or via its offer for use, be it indirectly via the sale of the embodiments of the protected subject-matter. It is the market, i.e. competition existing on both the side of demand and the side of supply, which determines both the incentive and the actual reward. Holders of intellectual property, therefore, have no special claims whatsoever to any particu-

---

[25] See David in Wallerstein et al. (eds.), loc. cit. at 25 et seq.; N. Harabi, "Determinanten des technischen Fortschritts: eine industrieökonomische Analyse", in Harabi (ed.), *Kreativität, Wirtschaft, Recht,* Zürich 1996, 61, 85 et seq.; H. J. Schalk, U. Täger, *Wissensverbreitung und Diffusionsdynamik im Spannungsfeld zwischen innovierenden und imitierenden Unternehmen,* Munich 1999, 16 et seq.; D. Foray, "Production and Distribution of Knowledge in the New Systems of Innovation: The Role of Intellectual Property Rights", *STI-Review* 14 (1994) 119, 122 et seq.; for more references see Ullrich, "Technologieschutz zwischen Wettbewerbs- und Industriepolitik", in Th. Dreyer, A. Kur, *Geistiges Eigentum im Dienste der Innovation,* Baden-Baden 2000, 83, 90 et seq. and extensively O. Granstrand, *The Economics and Management of Intellectual Property,* Cheltenham: Edward Elgar Publ., 1999, 82 et seq.

[26] This seems to become a generally accepted starting point of antitrust analysis, see US Department of Justice, Federal Trade Commission, Guidelines For Licensing of Intellectual Property, 4 Trade Reg. Rep. (CCH) 13.132 = 49 BNA-PTCJ 714 (1995), sub. 2.0, 2.1; Heinemann in Zäch, loc. cit. at 403. However, it is not always clearly realized that it is really no more than a starting point, meaning that, just as with respect to tangible property (see European Commission of March 11, 1998, Van den Bergh Foods Ltd., OJEC 1998 L 246, 1), property as such does not yield any justification for restrictive agreements or practices. For a broader analysis see Ullrich, loc. cit. GRUR Int. 1996, at 562 et seq.; id., "Intellectual Property, Access to Information and Antitrust: Harmony, Disharmony and International Harmonization", in R. Dreyfuss, H. First *et al.* (eds.), *Expanding the Boundaries of Intellectual Property,* London 2000, 365 sub. II A.

lar reward. All they may claim is equal treatment in competition. The objective of the grant of the exclusivity is precisely to allow enterprises to respond to the opportunities offered by the market, not to control the market. Intellectual property offers protection for, not from, competition. It is a means intended to enable the proprietor to enter into competition. As such it confers upon the inventor or upon the author precisely that autonomy of decision and of contract regarding the exploitation of protected subject-matter which any property offers as part of the general autonomy of doing business and competing for profit. Consequently, when proprietors of intellectual property enter into restrictive agreements, be they horizontal or vertical,[27] they must be subject to the same rules, which generally apply to the kind of restraint in question. Competition policy, not intellectual property, determines which restrictions are acceptable and which are not.

Market regulation by intellectual property protection

Second, however, whilst an understanding of intellectual property as a legal artefact, which merely allows us to collect the rewards offered by the market, but does not promise any reward, goes a long way to explain why patent protection does not yield many results in non-market environments such as public science[28] or planned economies, it does not mean that protection of intellectual property is neutral vis-à-vis competition. Quite to the contrary, precisely because it allows competition to take place, its institution and the definition of its terms do not only modify the conditions of existing markets as new kinds of products may be introduced, namely all those information-dependent products which make up technological innovation. In that sense, but only in that sense, intellectual property may be at the root of dy-

[27] While the distinction matters for antitrust analysis, it is particularly hard to make in a licensing context where the contradistinction of technology markets and product markets (see U.S. Dept. Justice, FTC Guidelines, loc. cit., sub. 3.2) tends to obscure the fact that the licensee frequently is at least a potential competitor of the licensor. The licensee takes the license as a result of a technology make-or-buy decision, the license enables the licensee to compete, and the licensing agreement, therefore, contains restrictive clauses precisely in view of keeping the licensee at a distance from the licensor; see also H. Johannes, "Technology Transfer Under EEC Law", 1982 *Fordh. Corp. L. Inst.* 65, 74 et seq. (B. Hawk, ed. 1983); W. Alexander, "The Horizontal Effects of Licensing a Technology as Dealt With by EEC Competition Policy", 1988 *Fordh. Corp. L. Inst.* 11-1 (B. Hawk ed. 1989).

[28] For the difficulties of making the patent system work in the non-market, non-demand-driven environment of public R&D-financing in general, and of public science in particular, see European Commission (ed.), "ETAN Working Paper: Strategic Dimensions of Intellectual Property Rights in the Context of Science and Technology Policy", Brussels 1999, sub. 1.7.

namic competition and contribute to technological progress.[29] Rather, the introduction of intellectual property, by its transforming public goods into private goods and by its profit-rationale, may altogether change a non-market environment into a market-place, a fact that is relevant not only for judging claims for patenting science, but also for the relationship between biotechnology patents and ethics[30]. The important point regarding competition law, however, is that, because it has to safeguard all possible competition, it may not interfere with the terms and conditions of intellectual property protection. The intellectual property system, by defining what may become merchandisable goods on which terms and conditions, and by affording autonomy of their exploitation, constitutes a framework regulation of the market, which determines the conditions, the terms and the development of competition. Competition policy must respect this framework regulation.

19.2.2 Exploitation of the legal monopoly by monopolies

Such respect of the intellectual property system by competition policy is, of course, too beautiful to be true. In particular, as competition policy does not necessarily protect competition as such, but may itself pursue specific political objectives, it frequently uses intellectual property protection as an instrument for some of these goals, e.g. when it comes to promoting innova-

---

[29] The patent community, therefore, generally overstates its case; see typically F.-K. Beier, "Die Bedeutung des Patentsystems für den technischen, wirtschaftlichen und sozialen Fortschritt", GRUR Init. 1979, 227; id., "Patentschutz – weltweit Grundlage des technischen Fortschritts und industrieller Entwicklung", in K. H. Oppenländer (ed.), *Patentwesen, technischen Fortschritt und Wettbewerb*, Berlin 1984, 29; the equation of or the confusion between a (non-existing) incentive function and the (real) function of protecting promising markets becomes clear in P. Braendli, "Europäisches Patentrecht als Instrument zur Förderung spezifischer Wirtschaftsstrategien", in Harabi (ed.), *Kreativität, Wirtschaft, Recht*, Berne 1996, 275.

[30] See in particular Drahos, loc. cit. *Eur. Int. Prop. Rev.* 1999, 441; consequently, justifying the grant of patents for biotechnological inventions on the – correct – ground that patents convey only a negative right to exclude, not a positive right of exploitation, largely misses the point, and it is also at odds with the objective the patent community assigns to the patent system, contra: R. Singer, D. Stauder, *Europäisches Patentübereinkommen*, 2nd ed. Cologne 2000, Art. 53, annot. 7; U. Schatz, "Zur Patentierbarkeit gentechnischer Erfindungen in der Praxis des Europäischen Patentamts", GRUR Int. 1997, 588, 593. More than such formal arguments are needed to overcome the argument, provided it is accepted in the first place, that the subject-matter in question should not become subject to trade, since making the protected subject-matter a merchandisable good is precisely what patent protection is all about.

tion and competitiveness of industry by facilitating technology transfer and cooperation in research and development,[31] or by granting direct financial support.[32] Even more important is the question how much respect the intellectual property system owes to competition as the system whose well-functioning determines the outcome of the protection granted. It is precisely in view of that question that the issue has been raised more frequently in recent times of how seriously competition law should take the respect for an intellectual property system, which, due to its expansion and nivellation, seems itself to stand in the way of achieving its goals. This is the issue of whether access to protected information should be granted on the basis of the antitrust laws.

IPR-pooling

The problem may arise, first, when intellectual property is pooled by two or more enterprises. Such arrangements have found new advocates, who see them as a way to reduce the transaction costs resulting from quantitative or qualitative overprotection of new technologies.[33] Whatever transactional vir-

---

[31] See in the first respect Commission Regulation 240/96 of January 31, 1996 on the application of Art. 85 (3) of the Treaty to certain categories of technology transfer agreements (OJEC 1996 L 31, 2), Recitals 3, 8; and Ullrich in Immenga, Mestmäcker, *EG-Wettbewerbsrecht*, München 1997, 1276 et seq.: in the latter respect see H. Hansen, "Die wettbewerbspolitische Behandlung von Forschungs- und Entwicklungskooperationen zwischen konkurrierenden Unternehmen", *WuW* 1999, 468 ff.; Monopolkommission, Hauptgutachten 1988/89, Baden-Baden 1990, Nr. 972 et seq., critical Ullrich, "Antitrust Law Relating to High Technology Industries", in Zäch (ed.), *Towards WTO Competition Rules*, Berne 1999, 261, 266 et seq.; Whereas Commission Regulation 418/95 of Dec. 19, 1984 on the application of Art. 85 (3) of the Treaty to certain categories of research and development agreements (OJEC 1985 L 53, 5 as amended by Reg. 151/93, OJEC 1993 L 21, 8), though triggered by the Community's Research and Technology Policy, establishes its own claims to promoting technological progress (see recital 4), the recently proposed Draft of a Regulation of the Commission on the application of Art. 81 (3) of the EC Treaty to certain categories of R&D agreements (OJEC 2000 C 118, 4) clearly states the complementary relationship between RandT-policy and competition policy (recital 2) as it always formed its historical background (see Ullrich, *Kooperative Forschung und Kartellrecht*, Heidelberg 1988, 103 et seq., 129 et seq.). It also expressly recognizes in recital 14 one of the IPR-rules of the Model Contract the Commission applies in its RandT-policy exercise with a view to enhancing technology transfer and exploitation; for these rules see Council, Decision of December 22, 1998, OJEC 1999 L 26, 46 and Commission Regulation 996/1999, OJEC 1999 L 122, 9.

[32] See Commission (ed.), "Strategic Dimensions of Intellectual Property Rights in the context of Science and Technology Policy", Final Report (ETAN-Working Paper) 1999.

[33] See R. Merges, "Institutions for Intellectual Property Transactions: The Case of Patent Pools", in Dreyfuss, First, *et al.* (eds.), *Expanding the Boundaries of Intellectual Property*,

tues pools and cross-licensing may have, since they constitute collective arrangements, they raise only general problems of antitrust law, rather than problems which specifically relate to the interrelationship between intellectual property protection and competition policy. What one may legitimately question, however, is the legislative wisdom of allowing so much overcrowding of technology that it needs to be disentangled by collectivization, and, vice versa, the wisdom of a competition policy which allows so much group-building, e.g. by way of cooperation in research and development, that collective intellectual property protection becomes a problem of competition. After all, much of the justification of R&D-cooperation is based on the fact that it allows the internalization of knowledge externalities [34]. Thus, in these cases intellectual property protection serves no longer to enable competition, but to allow knowledge distribution among the members of the group, and protection of the group against non-members, i.e. as a reinforcement of the group's impact on competition.[35]

Market domination and intellectual property

By contrast, the safeguard of the exclusivity as such seems to be in question, when market-dominating enterprises unilaterally use their intellectual property rights as a defense against claims for access to technological information raised by third parties, possibly even by competitors. Such claims directly address the general dilemma that intellectual property protection, which is granted as a matter of allowing the economically profitable creation

---

London 2000, 123. Notable recent examples are Commission, Press release of Oct. 9, 2000 (IP/00/1135)-DVD-patent licences, Commission, "Notice on notification of case COMP/37920 – 3G Patent Platform", OJEC 2000 C 227, 1b.

[34] See J. Ordover, W. J. Baumol, "Antitrust Policy and High-Technology Industries", 4 *Oxford Rev. Ec. Pol'y* 4, 26 et seq. (1988); Th. Jorde, D.J. Teece, "Rule of Reason Analysis of Horizontal Arrangements: Agreements Designed to Advance Innovation and Commercialize Technology", 61 *Antitrust L.J.* 579 (1993); D. J. Teece, "Information Sharing, Innovation and Antitrust", 62 *Antitrust L.J.* 465 (1994); Monopolkommission 1988/89, loc. cit. sub. 967 et seq., 970; D. B. Audretsch, "Intellectual Property Rights: New Research Directions", in H. Albach, S. Rosenkranz (ed.), *Intellectual Property Rights and Global Competition*, Berlin 1995, 35, 58 et seq. with references.

[35] This is acknowledged in extreme cases only, and only with respect to members of the group by the Commission (see draft Guidelines on the application of Art. 81 EC Treaty to agreements on horizontal cooperation, OJEC 2000 C 118, 14 sub. 64), but it really is a general problem: see A. Fuchs, *Kartellrechtliche Grenzen der Forschungskooperation*, Baden-Baden 1989, 447 et seq.; J. Temple Lang, "European Community Antitrust Law: Innovation Markets and High Technology Industries", 1996 *Fordh. Corp. L. Inst.* 519, 570 et seq. (B. Hawk, ed. 1997).

of new technological subject-matter as an output, may obstruct the sufficiently broad availability of the subject-matter as an input for the development of improvements, of implementing and of complementary technology, or as a tool for further research[36]. However, these cases are less unique than they appear to be. Thus, claims for information access may be raised also with respect to non-protected, though arguably proprietary, information on innovation plans or simply on production plans.[37] More generally, they may be raised not for imitation, but for the purpose of supplying value-added services or products.[38] Both situations mostly relate to enterprises operating on after-markets or on markets related to that of the proprietor of the technology or of the information. It is this divide between monopoly extension to or maintenance of competition on neighbouring markets, which these cases have in common with the well-known spare-part cases in antitrust law.[39] After all, claims for information access with a view, for example, to provide maintenance services are only the reverse side of infringement claims brought by the owner of information against spare-part suppliers, or against

[36] See Benkler, in Dreyfuss, First, loc. cit., 267, sub. IA; R. Eisenberg, "Patents and the Progress of Science: Exclusive Rights and Experimental Use", 56 *U. Chi. L. Rev.* 1017, 1070 et seq.; The problem is exacerbated by the narrow definition of experimental use under most European patent laws following the model of Art. 27 lit. b Community Patent Convention (OJEC 1989 L 401, 1), which has been taken over to Art. 9 lit. b Draft Community Patent Regulation. Even though it is an old problem (e.g. improvement of complementary parts always required experimental use with, not only of the other parts), it has come to broad attention only recently; see J. Straus, "Intellectual Property in Human Genome Research Results", in German-American Academic Council (ed.), *The Changing Character, Use and Protection of Intellectual Property*, Washington 1999, 85, 96.

[37] See, as to the claims for innovation pre-disclosure, Berkey Photo v. Eastman Kodak, 603 F.2d 263 (2d Cir. 1979), and as to the IBM and Microsoft cases Ullrich, "Intellectual Property, Access to Information, and Antitrust, Harmony, Disharmony and International Harmonization", in Dreyfuss, First *et al.*, loc. cit. London 2000, 365, sub. IIB2; J. E. Lopatka, "United States v. IBM: A Monument to Arrogance", 68 *Antitrust L.J.* 145 (2000). For examples of claims to access to information on current or forthcoming production, see CJEC of April 6, 1995, cases C-241/91P and 242/91P, RTE and ITP/Commission, Rep. 1995 I 743; OLG Hamburg of May 15, 1997, WuW E OLG 5861 (Pro 7/TV Today).

[38] This is also true of Trib 1st Inst. of June 12, 1997, case T-504/93, Tiercé-Ladbroke/Commission, Rep. 1997 II 923.

[39] See for the EU the CJEC case law supra n. 13; for the US see e.g. Image Technical Services v. Eastman Kodak, 125 F 3rd 1195 = 44 USPQ 2d 1065 1077 et seq. (9th Cir. 1997), both lines of cases differing, though, in that the European cases relate to infringement defences, the US case to an IPR-based defence of a refusal to supply. Note that the vertical relationship existing in all the cases mentioned may make the difference to the recent IMS Health-case, Court 1st. Inst. of October, case T-184/01R, IMS Health/Commission, not yet officially reported.

enterprises supplying such services by using software which the owner seeks to keep under control, either contractually or by virtue of the intellectual property exclusivity.[40] However, there is not only an economic and legal difference between, on the one hand, the simple exposure to infringement by third parties, i.e. to the risk of "theft", which one may eventually seek to escape by proper means such as technical controls or secrecy, and, on the other, an obligation to actively disclose proprietary knowledge. Rather, due to the pervasive, cross-sectoral use of electronic data-processing, owners of proprietary data may be exposed to claims for access to information as a matter of enabling competition on upstream or on downstream markets which they do not supply themselves. [41] In all these types of situations, however different, the threat to exclusivity is the same in terms of the legal safeguard of the intellectual property, and in both situations the same principles of antitrust law apply.[42]

Exclusivity in the absence of competition

First all these claims are relevant only when the proprietor of the exclusive rights holds a dominant position on the market, the exclusivity as such constituting neither a monopoly nor an indicium of monopoly power. Second, the proprietor of an exclusive right, who dominates a relevant market, may nevertheless exploit his exclusivity and use it fully against infringers just as any other enterprises may do. It is only the abuse of market power which is controlled by the antitrust laws. This means that, even though in the case of market domination the market is not competitive, so that intellectual property protection might be devoid of the purpose it is intended to serve, the exclusivity is maintained as a matter of protecting property, i.e. competition policy still respects the intellectual property system as a framework regulation of the market. Again, however, it will control the exercise of the individual right as to its conforming with principles of competition. Two approaches are typically chosen. One is, again according to general, not IPR-

---

[40] Comp. BGH of February 24, 2000, CR 2000 656 (error rectification in computer programs justifies program disclosure to independent maintenance firm); but see Data General Corp v. Grumman Systems, 36 F 3rd 1147 = 32 USPQ 2d 1385 (1st Cir. 1994) as discussed by L. A. Sullivan, W. S. Grimes, *The Law of Antitrust: An Integrated Handbook*, St. Paul 2000, 848 et seq. (852).

[41] See OLG Munich of September 17, 1998, *WuWE* DE-R 251.

[42] See for the following I. Govaere, *The Use and Abuse of Intellectual Property Rights in E.C. Law*, London 1996, 110 et seq., 129 et seq., 154 et seq.; Ullrich in Immenga, Mestmäcker, loc. cit., 1250 et seq.; id., "Intellectual Property, Access to Information and Antitrust", in Dreyfuss, First, loc. cit. sub. IIB2.; Sullivan, Grimes, loc. cit. at 848 et seq.

specific, rules of competition, that the proprietor is held to an obligation of non-discriminatory treatment of the enterprises with whom he deals, including an obligation to deal on equal terms with all enterprises, which are in a similar position as are his clients (licensees etc). The other is that he may not use the exclusivity to unduly impair whatever "residual" competition still exists. He may even be obliged to enable enterprises to enter into competition either directly or at least on related markets, if there are no other feasible ways of market entry than via access to his technology.

Whilst the non-discrimination rule for market-dominating enterprises is relatively easy to apply in cases of discrimination by reference to the terms of existing business relations, or in cases of non-admission to otherwise generally accessible business relations, subjecting these enterprises to a duty to enter into transactions which are not their business is an exceptionally difficult legal exercise. Courts have accepted such claims only very reluctantly and under strictly and narrowly defined circumstances.[43] Even then, they have earned more criticism than applause.[44] As regards access to protected information in particular, the Court of Justice, when granting access to copyrighted information in its famous Magill case,[45] really did so by relying on considerations which are common to many intellectual property systems, namely the grant of compulsory licenses in cases where the development of a innovation depends on the availability of subject-matter which the proprietor himself does not exploit or does not exploit fully. Thus, the competition rules only served to bring principles to bear which intellectual property may itself incorporate as a matter of ensuring its compatibility with competition. Yet its ruling is beset with problems, not the least being that the license which the Court imposed seriously devaluated the licensed information for its proprietor.[46]

---

[43] See the narrow definition in CJEC, supra n. 13, the refusal by the Trib. 1st Inst. supra n. 38, and see also Intergraph Corp. v. Intel Corp., 195 F 3rd 1346 (Fed. Cir. 1999).

[44] See references supra n. 42, and inter alia A. B. Lipsky, Jr.; J. G. Sidak, "Essential Facilities", 51 *Stanf. L. Rev.* 1187, 1218 et seq. (1999), Th. F. Cotter, "Intellectual Property and the Essential Facilities Doctrine", XLIV *Antitrust Bull.* 211 (1999).

[45] CJEC of April 6, 1995, cases C-241/P and C-242/P, RTE and ITP/Commission, Rep. 1995 I 743.

[46] See Ullrich, "Intellectual Property, Access to Information and Antitrust", in Dreyfuss, First, loc. cit. sub. IIB 2b) with references.

Access claims for protected subject-matter

The point of interest, however, is not the difficulty of these cases, but their common characteristics. First, they are limited to the exercise of intellectual property by enterprises dominating their markets. Second, they do not generally allow access to the technology of such enterprises, but only exceptionally when competition is endangered beyond the existence both of market power and of the exclusivity. Third, they are entirely a matter of competition policy as it may be applied under the specific circumstances of a given case. Fourth, neither are they IPR-specific nor may IPR considerations affect their outcome.[47] The latter point is important in that it means that intellectual property may not justify anti-competitive conduct by monopolistic enterprises. However, it is also a self-evident point, because the control relates to the exercise of market power, not to the exercise of the exclusive right, which merely is its instrument.

19.2.3 Systems interaction

Returning to the point of departure of this short inquiry into the competition background of intellectual property protection, the answer to the question, whether the antitrust laws may contain "excessive" protection within "reasonable" limits, appears to be somewhat disappointing. It is true that protection of intellectual property has been conceived of as a way of bringing informational subject-matter into the realm of market rules with a view to optimizing their creation. It is also true that, to operate properly as a system, intellectual property protection depends on the well-functioning of competition on these markets for information or information-based goods. Nevertheless, competition policy, in reality, largely must take a neutral stance vis-à-vis the definition of the terms of intellectual property.

However, depending on how competition policy is defined, intellectual property protection will produce different effects. Thus, when an instrumentalist concept of competition is put into operation with a view to achieving such purposes as promoting international competitiveness of industry by enhanced technology transfer and increased R&D-cooperation, i.e. when Art. 81 EG Treaty is so applied,[48] then intellectual property protection as well

---

[47] See Sullivan, Grimes, loc. cit. at 848/849 et seq.

[48] See supra n. 31, The full measure of "politicization" of the application of the EU competition rules cannot be detailed here; suffice it to cite Commission, "Green Book on Innovation", Bull EC, Supp 5/95 sub 9 (at 23 et seq.); id., "Growth, Competitiveness, Employment", Bull. EC Supp 6/93 sub. 2.3 (at 67 et seq.); Commission, "Draft Guidelines on the application of

will become so instrumentalized, however tacitly this may be done. Conversely, where competition policy is limited to ensure the basic functioning of the market system – as is the case with respect to Art. 82 EC Treaty – no correction of the general operation of the intellectual property system may be expected or justified. In short, the intellectual property system cannot be better than the competition system upon which it is based. And vice versa: as the terms of intellectual property protection determine which competition may take place on the markets for informational goods or for information-based goods, competition policy cannot be better than these terms allow. Being a regulatory framework of the market, the operation of the intellectual property system simply may not produce or benefit from more or different competition than the design of the system admits. In sum, the intellectual property system and the competition system of markets are not only interdependent, but they are also mutually determining their operation and their results. This is what brings so much tension into their cooperation. It is also what allows us to make policy choices on how to influence and direct the functioning of the system so as to achieve mutual control and reinforcement. The question then is whether, instead of a relationship of mutual instrumentalization of protection and competition with a view to predetermined objectives, there might also be a more open-ended form of systems interaction.

19.3 The Rules of the Market and the Rules of Law

19.3.1 Systems synthesis

There is, indeed, a fundamental question in intellectual property law: which competition does the system of protection need in order to function so as to achieve its objectives? Clearly, the answer depends on the nature of

---

Art. 81 EC Treaty to agreements on horizontal cooperation", OJEC 2000 C 118, 14 sub. No. 2; as to the policy concepts underlying EC competition policy in general see Commission, "The Competitiveness of European enterprises in the face of globalisation – How to promote it", COM (1998) 718 endg. of Jan. 20, 1999; K. van Miert, "Die Wettbewerbspolitik der neuen Kommission", *WuW* 1995, 553; E. Kantzenbach, H. Krüger, "Wettbewerbspolitische Leitbilder für Europa", in B. Gahlen *et al.* (ed.), *Europäische Integrationsprobleme aus wirtschaftswissenschaftlicher Sicht*, Tübingen 1994, 191; W. Kerber, "Zur Wettbewerbskonzeption im europäischen Wettbewerbsrecht", in H. Gröner, A. Schüller (ed.), *Die europäische Integration als ordnungspolitische Aufgabe*, Stuttgart 1993, 279; J. Schmidt, "Die europäische Wettbewerbspolitik nach dem Vertrag von Amsterdam", *WuW* 1999, 133; Pantz, "Les politiques communautaires d'ajustement structurel des marchés: concurrence, compétivité, et contestabilité", *Rev. Marché Unique eur.* 1999 (4) 103; M. Furse, "The Role of Competition Policy: A Survey", *Eur. Comp. L. Rev.* 1996, 250.

these objectives. However, there can be no doubt either that relying only on so much competition as the antitrust law may safeguard is not enough, since this is only the legal minimum. Information access, for example, is at the root of the vertical IPR-dilemma in general.[49] It must be solved at any level, not only with respect to market-dominating enterprises or technologies.[50] In fact, the intellectual property system itself has always been designed so as to allow for the kind and scope of competition that seemed necessary for its functioning as a system.

The definition of protectable subject-matter and the thresholds for obtaining protection, which both limit the nature and the scope of appropriable knowledge; the disclosure requirements, or the exceptions to protection, such as experimental use and fair use; the time limits set to protection, at least as regards patents and design rights – all serve this purpose. The question, therefore, is not whether there is a need for competition to be built into the system, but what kind of and how much competition is inherently necessary for the optimal operation of the system. Again, this question may be examined in two different perspectives. The intellectual property lawyer may investigate the conditions of competition which are suited to make the protection achieve its purpose. The competition lawyer, by contrast, would want to determine the terms of protection which are best suited to have competition meet its goals. As both systems have multiple and not necessarily identical objectives,[51] the answers need not be the same. However, as set forth above, both systems really are interrelated and interdependent. Intellectual property protection as a legal system, and competition as an economic system, simply are integrated elements of the organization of the market in that they fulfill complementary functions. Intellectual property protection determines the conditions of competition by providing new parameters of market conduct. Competition determines the market incentives and rewards intellectual prop-

---

[49] See supra text at n. 19.

[50] This, rather than difficulties of application, is the reason for non-reliance on antitrust law as a way to solve frictions, which are due to the very design of the system, contra Cotter, loc. cit. XLIV Antitrust Bull. at 235 et seq. (246 et seq.) 1999.

[51] Thus, the patent system is not as one-dimensional as many economists and even lawyers would like to have it, but follows principles of justice that are not always easily reconciled with goals of efficient innovation (e.g. first-to-file v. first-to-invent controversy; attribution of employee inventions; determination of co-inventorship; scope of protection of "meritorious" pioneer inventions; scope of – punitive?! – damages etc), not to mention the moral and social dimension of copyright (from control over first publication to participation even in profit opportunities the author couldn't even imagine, let alone develop himself, and this even for the benefit of his grandchildren, if not great-grandchildren).

erty may secure to its owner. In order to better determine this interrelationship, how it is affected by the present trend to increased protection, and what these changes mean for intellectual property protection as a legal system, it may be useful to return to some basic considerations, which are at the origin of granting intellectual property rights.

Protection and competition: the discovery process

As economists teach us,[52] granting intellectual property rights is not the only way of solving the problem of "underinvestment" in the production of socially desirable knowledge, which results from the public-good nature of information. An alternative would be direct subsidization of the creation of new technologies to the extent necessary to induce a sufficient level of innovation, as is done with respect to public science. However, even assuming that the results actually obtained through subsidized research would be put to use sufficiently[53], this approach suffers from a double disadvantage. Its administrative burdens are enormous, and it requires an *ex ante* knowledge of just how much subsidy is necessary for just which activity R&D. However, due to the indeterminate outcome of creative activity, this knowledge is available only *ex post*, once the desired results have been obtained. It is precisely because of these drawbacks of subsidization that the intellectual property system is so attractive a mechanism. It combines the private interest in creating knowledge, which will be socially accepted, with the virtues of competition so that, instead of a centralized process of subsidization, a decentralized process of discovering new knowledge for new (and old) uses is institutionalized.[54] Market forces determine which activities are necessary for which profit opportunities. Intellectual property allows us to exclusively exploit these opportunities. If the property is well-defined and competition

[52] See W. F. Baxter, "Legal Restrictions on Exploitation of the Patent Monopoly: An Economic Analysis", 76 *Yale L.J.* 267, 273 (1966); David in Wallerstein et al. (eds.) (1993), loc. cit. at 32 et seq.; B. Wright, "The Economics of Invention Incentives: Patents, Prizes, and Research Contracts", 73 *Am. Ec. Rev.* 691 (1983); H. Klodt, *Grundlagen der Forschungs- und Technologiepolitik*, Munich 1995, 36 et seq.

[53] This is not only a problem of public science (see supra n. 28), but a general and fundamental one: subsidies do not set incentives of individual interest; i.e. even if all other problems, in particular the information problem mentioned in the text, were overcome, their motivational value simply is too low, precisely because they lack the lottery-game aspect of exclusive rights; see infra sub b) (ii).

[54] I.e. Hayek's "Competition as a discovery process", see F. A. Hayek, *Der Wettbewerb als Entdeckungsverfahren*, Kiel 1968.

works well, the costs of innovation will be as optimal as the level of innovation.

Equal-opportunity protection

What is meant by a well-functioning of both systems is no more and no less than is generally expected for a market system to work satisfactorily. It simply means, on the one hand, that competition in the market not be distorted or restricted, in particular that it be "open" as regards access and outcome. On the other hand, it assumes, that intellectual property protection operates evenly, i.e. is equally available for any kind of knowledge which is not appropriable by itself,[55] but which society expects to be both produced and turned into full use on a private-profit rationale.[56] Asymmetric availability of intellectual property protection will of necessity distort the discovery process. Hence, in this concept, intellectual property must be subject to a rule of neutrality vis-à-vis competition. Translated into legal terms, this means that, as a system, the intellectual property should follow some sort of rule of equal access and equal opportunity. Evidence of the existence of such a principle is the high degree of differentiation of intellectual property, at least on the Continent.[57] In part, this differentiation follows from the different nature of protected subject-matter, e.g. patentable inventions and copyrightable works; but in order to give equal access for all industries, the differentiation also concerns the form of protection of related types of subject-matter (utility models, trade secrets, design protection, unfair competition remedies against misappropriation).[58] Similarly, the terms of protection, such

---

[55] As may be the case due to first-mover advantages such as head start in production, distribution and service, learning effects, and, of course, due to secrecy or other knowledge barriers such as lack of skilled labor force, quality instruments etc; see in general Harabi, in loc. cit. at 95 et seq. with references; id., "The appropriability of technical inventions – an empirical analysis", 24 *Res. Pol.* 981 (1995); Audretsch in Albach, Rosenkranz, loc. cit., at 53 et seq.

[56] It is due to its profit rationale (not due to the utility requirement of patentability) that all IPR-protection has a bias towards inducing the exploitation of those market opportunities which are the most promising in commercial terms; see the early remark by A. Plant, "The Economic Theory Concerning Patents for Inventions", *Economica* 1934, 30, 46.

[57] It may be noted *en passant* that, due to their being impregnated by the US system of IPR, most economists miss much of the legal IPR-reality as regards both the variety and the operation of the system; for the simple bi-polarity of patent and copyright protection in the US, see the implicit assumptions made by Reichman, "Legal Hybrids between the Patent and Copyright Paradigms", 94 *Col. L. Rev.* 2432 (1994), and the critique by W. Kingston, "Unlocking the Potential of Intellectual Property", this publication, Ch. 13 (sub. 2 et seq).

[58] In fact, even within IPR-systems, a high degree of differentiation has evolved, particularly in copyright law, where the differences of protected subject-matter have resulted not only in

as the definition of protectable subject-matter, the criteria for granting protection, or the period of protection, are defined in the abstract and independently of the alleged or true needs of an industry so as to avoid a bias in favor of specific industries or technologies. The equal opportunity/non-distortion rationale of these notions is frequently misunderstood, when standards are proposed which directly link the grant or the scope of protection to the commercial or social value of a given kind of subject-matter.[59] Conversely, it is surprising to see how frequently the differing proclivity of specific industries to protection, for example to patenting, is noted, but how rarely it is analyzed as a – probably unintended – bias of the system, which may or may not need to be rectified in favor of the disadvantaged industries.[60]

---

the distinction between copyright proper and copyright-related rights (of various nature), but also in different definitions of basically common concepts, in particular as regards the new technological subject-matter of computer programs and databases; see Ullrich, "Die gemeinschaftsrechtliche Gestaltung des Wettbewerbsrechts und des Rechts des geistigen Eigentums", in Müller-Graff (ed.), *Gemeinsames Privatrecht in der Europäischen Gemeinschaft*, 2nd ed. Baden-Baden 1999, 403, 444 et seq.; H. Cohen, Jehoram, "The EC Copyright Directives, Economics and Authors' Rights", 25 *IIC* 821 (1994).

[59] See recently e.g. K. J. Boyd, "Nonobviousness and the Biotechnology Industry: A Proposal for a Doctrine of Economic Nonobviousness", 12 *Berkeley Tech'y L.J.* 311 (1997); A. S. Oddi, "Beyond Obviousness: Invention Protection in the Twenty-First Century", 38 *Am. Univ. L. Rev.* 1097, 1128 et seq. (1989); for a critical approach see R. Merges, "Commercial Success and Patent Standards: Economic Perspectives on Innovation", 76 *Cal. L. Rev.* 803 (1988); H. Ullrich, *Standards of Patentability of European Patents*, Weinheim 1977, 84 et seq., 105 et seq.

[60] As to the factual differences of the use made of the patent system see European Patent Office (ed.), *The Use Made of Patent Protection in Europe* (Eposcript Vol. 3), Munich 1994; Schalk, Täger, *Wissensverbreitung und Diffusionsdynamik im Spannungsfeld innovierenden und imitierenden Unternehmen*, Munich 1999, 33 et seq.; the link with the specific legal design of a patent system is mainly based on more or less plausible assumptions (see e.g. Erickson, "Patent Law and New Product Development: Does Priority Claim Basis Make a Difference?" 36 *Am. Bus. L.J.* 327 (1999)). It is even unclear whether the system really "fits" some industries better than others (e.g. the pharmaceutical industry due to full coverage of new products by patent protection as distinguished from isolated coverage of elements of complex technologies), since industries have developed highly sophisticated strategies and tactics of optimizing patent protection (see Granstrand, loc. cit. at 209 et seq.), and since advantages in obtaining patents may be offset by disadvantages in enforcement (the pharmaceutical industry is most exposed to the principle of exhaustion of patent protection upon first sale of a patented product). Thus, the competitive neutrality of an IPR-system may precisely depend on its not being tailor-made for a specific industry, see text infra sub. 2.

Strategic protection

The market-neutrality of the system of intellectual property protection is not necessarily affected when the conditions and the terms of protection are revised with a view to expand protection to new subject-matter, to make protection more easily available by lowering standards to what is called sub-patentable inventions or low-authorship works[61], or to strengthen protection by reducing exceptions. The system still serves a decentralized, market-based discovery process. However, the nature of competition will change as more intellectual goods become subject to market rules. To the extent that the proliferation of property rights results in mutual dependencies and risks of blocking situations, such "overprotection" may become excessive to the point of resulting in an essential change of the quality of the entire IPR-system. This then will reduce rather than enhance dynamic competition for innovation. In any case, such dependencies and blocking situations are in themselves a disincentive for the individualistic-minded entrepreneur. At the very least, in order to unblock the stalemate, license exchanges become necessary, which may entail additional costs, frequently including high transaction costs.[62] A major problem of all these costs is that their amount is unpredictable at the time of investment into new creative activity, and that the profitability of these costs is just as unpredictable as the technical and/or the commercial success of the creative activity for which they have been incurred.[63] Moreover, the need to resolve dependencies by transactions almost always carries with it the problem of unequal bargaining power, a problem which could be avoided if intellectual property protection were conceived so

[61] See J. Reichman, "Charting the Collapse of the Patent – Copyright Dichotomy", 13 *Cardozo Arts and Entertainment L.J.* 475, 489 et seq. (1995); id., "Solving the Green Tulip Problem" in Dreyfuss, First *et al.* (eds.), *Expanding the Boundaries of Intellectual Property*, London 2000, 23 et seq.; J. Ginsberg, "U.S. Initiatives to Protect Works of Low Authorship", in Dreyfuss, First *et al.* (eds.), loc. cit., 55 et seq.; the European examples are the low thresholds established for the protection of computer programs and databases (both under copyright and *sui generis* protection); see Art. 1 (3) Computer Programme Directive (supra n. 5) and Art. 3 (1), 7 (1) Database Directive (supra n. 5).

[62] See supra II2a; additional transaction costs are particularly likely in cases of intransparent protection, such as copyright protection.

[63] Another problem results from the fact that there is no correlation between the costs of invention and its market value under a patent, which means either party to the transaction may take a disproportionate benefit from its contribution. This may be both dysfunctional and "unjust", and, consequently, endanger the transaction.

as to favor the development of independent technologies. This, indeed, ought to be one of its primary aims as a title of property.[64]

In sum, in the presence of a protectionist system of intellectual property, competition will no longer be for innovative market opportunities as such, but either for obtaining a strong, intellectual property-based bargaining position or for obtaining technological independence by virtue of intellectual property protection. This means that, rather than merely serving as a tool of knowledge appropriation for competition, the acquisition of intellectual property protection becomes itself a goal of competition. This is more obvious for registered rights than for rights accruing by operation of the law, the catchword being "strategic patenting" in view of license exchanges, cooperation, strategic alliances, safe home markets etc. Such strategic approaches do, of course, have a self-reinforcing effect in that they increase the need for protection. But this is only one reason for the race to protection.

Compensation and competition: the jackpot-rationale

Whilst a differentiation of the intellectual property system may enhance equal access to protection, it may also result in unequal treatment, which needs justification in order to be acceptable under a rule of law. An example is utility model protection, which, under national and future European law, is refused to processes and chemical and pharmaceutical compounds.[65] One of the reasons given is the risk of overcrowding the technology with non-examined property rights. The risk of overcrowding increases, of course, as thresholds of access to protection are lowered, and it may even worsen as, due to easy applicability, lower standards tend to create legally safer rather than uncertain titles to protection.

Access for all

The trend toward this kind of over-protection, and the ensuing potential for blocking rights, is not only a companion of the information society.[66] It may as well be a result of the tendency of equal-access rules to mutate into rules of access for all. The claim is that any informational goods need protection in view of the risks of free rides, which are due to the ease of imitat-

---

[64] See infra b) (ii).

[65] See supra n. 7 and the reasons given in Commission, Proposal of December 12, 1997 for a Directive on the approximation of the rules relating to protection of inventions by utility model, COM (1997) 691 final, at Art. 4.

[66] See supra n. 61.

ing the good at no comparable cost. Although this claim rests on a circular argument – there is no free ride unless it has been first determined that protection should be granted[67] – it is widely accepted as legitimate. It is, indeed, the major rationale underlying low-authorship protection of computer programs, databases, non-registered designs of fashion wear, and many other non-commonplace product configurations.[68] Again, such an extension of the protection influences the concept of competition underlying the system as it moves from markets for staple goods to innovation markets. But since, at the same time, the risks and dangers of overprotection increase, the mode of protecting informational goods by property rights comes to be put into question. The alternative would be a liability system.[69] Whichever way such an alternative is construed – compulsory licenses, licenses of right, collective rights management, individual compensation claims – the change would be fundamental, and so are the questions it raises. Inherently, a liability system compensates only for investments made, not for profits lost, or else the argument becomes circular. Any profit distribution requires rules of attribution, which define who is entitled to how much profit. While a liability system very well corresponds to the principle of granting protection for all and to all, it undermines competition for profit opportunities. This precisely is the goal of protection by property, which, by allowing the appropriation of knowledge, enables control over market opportunities[70].

---

[67] See supra n. 24.

68 See the "ease of imitation" argument in recital 2 Computer Programme Directive (supra n. 5) and recital 7 Database Directive (supra n. 5), and, more particularly, the German law against unfair competition as applicable to acts of "slavish imitation" and "misappropriation of the industrial achievements of others", A. Baumbach, W. Hefermehl, *Wettbewerbsrecht*, 21st ed. Munich 1999, § 1 UWG, annot 439 et seq.; P. Sambuc, *Der UWG-Nachahmungsschutz*, Munich 1996, 6 et seq.; A. Beater, *Nachahmen im Wettbewerb*, Tübingen 1995, 395 et seq.

[69] See in particular P. Samuelson, R. Davis, M. D. Kapor, J. Reichman, "A Manifesto Concerning the Legal Protection of Computer Programs", 94 *Col. L. Rev*. 2308, 2365 et passim (1994); Reichman, loc. cit. 94 Col. L. Rev. 2432, 2504 et seq. (1994).

[70] See the reaction by R. Merges, "Of Property Rules, Coase, and Intellectual Property", 94 *Col. L.J.* 2655, 2664 et seq. (1994) to the Manifesto approach (supra n. 69); note also that it is only due to the exclusivity that prices are set pursuant to market rules, and, accordingly, costs controlled by competition. A liability system, by contrast, is inherently inefficient as regards the economic production of knowledge.

Property for freedom

Whilst it may very well be that liability systems yield more for everybody, the property system being plagued by risks and costs of enforcement, the latter provides all the advantages of taking chances individually. It is the only mechanism that allows us to individually reap the full market price, and possibly even a true monopoly price. As has been stated more than half a century ago,[71] intellectual property protection, more specifically patent protection, follows a jackpot-rationale. Recent economic analysis of the skewed distribution of the profit potential of invention and innovation seems to confirm the legitimacy of this approach.[72] It also corresponds to the understanding of property rights as safeguards of economic freedom.

This, indeed, may be the point the European Court of Justice[73] had in mind, when it held that protection of intellectual goods by exclusive property rights is a matter of public interest equal to the safeguard of the fundamental right to do business. The issue arose as the Community harmonized national copyright law by introducing a separate rental right, which is not exhausted by the first sale of the embodiment of a copyrighted work. In Germany, this meant the abolition of a liability rule of copyright law, because the rental was only subject to an obligation to compensation. As a result of the change of law, enterprises had to close shop which were in the business of letting audio or video discs for rent that they had bought on the market, because the copyright owners no longer had to tolerate their business. The Court, nevertheless, dismissed the defendant's fundamental-rights argument by holding that, in view of the high risks and the ease of copying protection, an exclusivity right is the most efficient form of protection against copyright infringement. It was impressed by the danger that the reward due to those who invest in the production of such works would no longer be adequately safeguarded, which in turn would have negative effects on the activities relating to the creation of new works. This is not the place to discuss the validity of the Court's ruling. After all, the problem of piracy is not one of protection, but one of detection and enforcement. However, the Court's ruling is remarkable in two respects. First, the Court does not refer to its case law concerning non-exhaustion of intellectual property rights when the sales have been made under a compulsory licence or as a matter of a general obligation

[71] See M. Polanyij, "Patent Reform", XI *Rev. Ec. Stud.* 61, 62 (1944).

[72] See F.M. Scherer, "The Innovation Lottery", in Dreyfuss, First *et al.* (eds.), *Expanding the Boundaries of Intellectual Property*, London 2000, 3 et seq.

[73] CJEC v. 28.IV.1998, case C-200/96, Metronome Musik/Music Point Hokamp, Rep. 1998 I 1953, No. 22 et seq.

to supply the market.[74] Yet it is precisely in these cases that the Court put so much emphasis on the circumstance that the right of a proprietor of intellectual property to freely decide upon when, where and how to exploit is the very essence of intellectual property, as indeed it is. It is this freedom which allows competitive conduct on the market in accordance with individual preferences.

Second, the Court expresses its opinion in precisely those terms of the general intellectual property dilemma which economists use, but it fails to fully state it. The dilemma is between, on the one hand, the need to restrict the use of new knowledge for the sake of stimulating its creation, and, on the other, the public's interest in having the knowledge put to optimal use by virtue of competition.[75] As the Court neglects this latter aspect, it also fails to ask the real question, which is whether the substitution of a compensation scheme by a system of exclusive property rights is proportionate in relation to the objective of protection. This, in turn, would have required examining whether such substitution is the means which represents the least intrusion on the fundamental right to free enterprise, a matter which the Court, as already mentioned, simply put aside by raising intellectual property to the equal, if not superior, level of public policy.

19.3.2 Interventionist systems

Owning markets

The consequences of the Court's approach are considerable. It is true that intellectual property represents a constitutive element of competition rather than a restriction. Therefore, it would appear to be undervalued if assessed only as an exception to competition, which needs justification. But it is equally true that the competition system is made up of more elements than merely property. It is, indeed, based, inter alia, on such fundamental rights as freedom to do business and to select a business of one's own choice, autonomy of contracting, free movement of goods, services, persons and capital. The claim which the defendant in the Metronome Musik case may have had to continue his business unaffected by legal changes of market conditions[76]

---

[74] CJEC of July 9, 1985, case 19/84, Pharmon/Hoechst, Rep. 1985, 2281 (No. 25); of December 5, 1996, cases C-267/95 and C-268/95, Merck/Primecrown *et al.*; Rep. 1996 I 6285 (No. 48 et seq.).

[75] See supra n. 19.

[76] See as to the requirement and the limits of transition rules CJEC of June 29, 1999, case C-60/98, Butterfly Music/CEMED, Rep. 1999 I 3939.

may be inherently weak, as markets change due precisely to competition. However, if property rights may be installed in favor of competition, which deprive enterprises of their business opportunities without it being necessary to subject that kind of market regulation to a proportionality test, which brings the various rights to competition into balance, then there is only little left for judicial control of the adequacy of a given system of intellectual property protection.

Property as principle

Indeed, if the market-rationale which underlies intellectual property protection is taken as being self-sufficient, other countervailing goals of that same market system are referred back to the level of exceptions, whose legitimacy needs yet to be established. The perspective is no more the functionality of the entire system of competition with its various, interrelated elements, but that of a system of protection by property. Property is property, a legal value in itself. Experimental use is no longer a right of equal standing that flows out of the right to free competition, but a burden on property. It then requires some specific, additional justification, and such justification may be established only in terms of a tribute the proprietor owes to society.[77] In this perspective, expansion of intellectual property protection is a natural tendency, limitation, however, an incursion on well-acquired rights or on the legal promise to grant protection. In fact, as standards lower and protectable subject-matter expands under the threat of ease of imitation, the traditionally accepted principle, that the exclusivity is an exception from a general principle of free competition, which needs to justified, has been permanently weakened, if not abandoned.[78] As intellectual property is a legal system, such

---

[77] See BVerfG (German Constitutional Court) of May, 10, 2000, GRUR 2001, 43-clinical experiments; comp. also A. Fechner, *Geistiges Eigentum und Verfassung*, Tübingen 1999, 192 et seq., 240 et seq.

[78] A good example is the expansion of the misappropriation doctrine under German law against unfair competition (see references supra n. 68) and the attempt to introduce such a principle into European law via an extension of Community Design Protection; see Art. 1 (2a), 11, 20 (2) Council Regulation on Community Designs, supra n. 11, and see A. Kur, Ansätze zur Harmonisierung des Lauterkeitsrechts im Bereich des wettbewerbsrechtlichen Leistungsschutzes, GRUR Int. 1998, 771. Even in the USA, the constitutionally mandated patent-copyright dichotomy (see supra n. 57) and the preemption doctrine have not really contained this development; see references supra n. 61, and note specific federal legislation such as the Semiconductor Chip Protection Act (17 US 901) or the Vessel Hull Design Protection Act, 17 U.S.C. §§ 1301 – 1332 (1999); as to the latter see W. Fryer III, "The Evolution of Market

changes have not only doctrinal, but direct practical, implications. Every lawyer knows that a shift of the burden of proof, and *a fortiori* an inversion of the principle/exception dichotomy, really means a turn of tides as regards the economic effects of legal rules.

Protecting competitors from property

There are, of course, good reasons explaining the Court of Justice's reluctance to enter into an examination of the legislator's choice of a property rather than a liability system for protecting intellectual goods. After all, such an examination ultimately may not stop before the alternative between the two types of protection, but would have led the Court into the problems of determining the conditions which might make one of the systems legally superior; i.e. the Court would have had to resolve questions which economists discuss under the heading of optimizing the trade-off, which determines the necessary and sufficient reward at any desired level of innovation.[79] In this respect, the problem is not so much that lawyers and judges shun economics – I am not going to dabble in this field either – but that such a determination involves precisely the kind of prognostic and discretionary judgement that is reserved for the legislature. Indeed, the due reward for the inventor or for the author,[80] as determined by the length and breadth of protection, must be as-

---

Industrial Design Protection: An International Comparative Analysis", *Eur. Int. Prop. Rev.* 1999, 618.

[79] See David in Wallerstein et al. (eds.), loc. cit. at 36 et seq. with references; E. Kaufer, "Die Ökonomik des Patentsystems", in Bombach (ed.), *Industrieökonomie – Theorie und Empirie*, Tübingen 1985, 53, 61 et seq.; R. Merges, R. Nelson, "The Complex Economics of the Patent Scope", 90 *Col. L. Rev.* 839 (1990); R. Mazzoleni, R. Nelson, "The benefits and costs of strong patent protection: a contribution to the current debate", 27 *Res. Pol.* 273 (1998) with references; Schalk, Täger, loc. cit. at 33 et seq., 107 et seq.; as regards copyright see the summary by Audretsch in Albach, Rosenkranz (ed.), loc. cit. at 44 et seq.; extensively G.S. Lunney, Jr., "Reexamining Copyright's Incentives Access Paradigm", 49 *Vanderbilt L. Rev.* 483 (1996), and see infra n. 80.

[80] Due to the constitutional mandate (Art. 1 Sect. 8 Cl. 8 ... To promote ...), US doctrine of copyright largely follows the incentive rationale of protection (see W.M. Landes, R.A. Posner, "An Economic Analysis of Copyright Law", 18 *J. Leg. Stud.* 325, 361 et seq. (1989); for more differentiated, though still economic, approaches see W. A. Gordon, "An Inquiry into the Merits of Copyright: The Challenges of Consistency, Consent, and Encouragement Theory", 41 *Stanf. L. Rev.* 1343 (1989); J.E. Cohen, "Lochner in Cyberspace: The New Economic Orthodoxy of 'Rights Management'", 97 *Mich. L. Rev.* 462 (1998); and for an even broader view N. Weinstock Netanel, "Copyright and a Democratic Civil Society", 106 *Yale L.J.* 283 (1996)), whilst Continental copyright largely follows less utilitarian approaches not only as a matter of legal argument: see Fechner, loc. cit. at 48 et seq., 68 et seq., 105 et seq., 121 et

sessed by reference to what level of inventions or creation a society desires, and it must be defined in the abstract and in advance, although a "just" assessment can be made only individually and *ex post*.[81]

The discretionary and prognostic nature of intellectual property legislation, as well as the abstention by courts from examining the equities of the balance of interests the legislature establishes, mean that there will never be a legal principle of substantive equality of protection, let alone one of just remuneration by reference to the social utility of protected subject-matter.[82] However, it is precisely in view of this deficit that there should at least be a principle protecting enterprises against being unduly burdened by their competitors' intellectual property. Whilst such a rule may exist, at least *in nuce*, it has again been formulated as an exception based on countervailing claims rather than as a built-in limit. Thus, tort law and antitrust law may, within narrow limits at least, prevent the owner of intellectual property from making unwarranted claims to exclusivity by threatening competitors with infringement actions.[83] Once infringement is established, however, sanctions may not only reach beyond the reward interest of the proprietor in that – due to a property rationale – the profits made by the infringer must be handed over to the proprietor (instead of that only the profits lost by the proprietor be restituted).[84] Rather, the market covered by the exclusivity is itself con-

---

seq.; Schricker in Schricker (ed.), *Urheberrecht,* 2nd ed. Munich 1999, Einleitung No. 11 et seq.; P. Götting, in F.-K. Beier, P. Götting, M. Lehmann, R. Moufang, *Urhebervertragsrecht*, Munich 1995, 59 et seq.; W. Cornish, *Intellectual Property: Patents, Copyrights, Trademarks and Allied Rights*, 4th ed. London 1999, 9 – 42; G. Davies, *Copyright and the Public Interest*, Weinheim 1993, 7 et seq.; A. Quadvlieg, "Copyright's Orbit Round Private, Commercial and Economic Law – The Copyright System and the Place of the User", 29 *IIC* 420 (1998). The problem is that copyright has become a catch-all protection obfuscating the distinctions, which ought to be made according to the protected subject-matter. Technological subject-matter, whose production is subject to economic principles of innovation, simply is misplaced under the copyright laws as regards the nature of the exclusivity (definition of infringement), its scope and its term (see infra n. 94).

81 See B. Mackaay, "Legal Hybrids: Beyond Property and Monopoly?" 94 *Col. L. J.* 2630 2635 (1994).

82 See E. Mansfield, J. Rapoport, "The Social and Private Returns from Industrial Innovations", 91 *Qu. J. Ec.* 221 (1977); Klodt, loc. cit. at 37.

83 See for German law K. Bruchhausen in G. Benkard, *Patentgesetz*, 9th ed. Munich 1993, vor §§ 9 – 14, No. 13 et seq.; for US antitrust law see Sullivan, Grimes, loc. cit. at 833 et seq., for EU antitrust Ullrich in Immenga, Mestmäcker, *EG-Wettbewerbsrecht*, loc. cit. at 1258, all with references.

84 See R. Rogge in Benkard, loc. cit. § 139, annot. 72 et seq.; and expressly § 97 (1) (2) German Copyright Act, see G. Wild in G. Schricker, loc. cit. § 97 annot. 67 et seq. (annot. 69 et

sidered to be the property. Thus, Dutch courts have held not only that submission of pharmaceuticals to official testing for marketing approval constitutes an infringement, but that the appropriate remedy is to enjoin the "infringer" from making and selling the generic drug upon expiry of the intellectual property right, for a period equal to that which he would have needed had he applied for drug approval only once the exclusivity expired; i.e. he has to return the market to the proprietor. The Court of Justice of the European Communities[85], in one of its few less enlightened moments, has accepted the Dutch case law as a matter of sovereign national intellectual property policy, rather than holding it to be disproportionate by reference to the objective of intellectual property protection. Again, it is protection for its own sake, property as property.

Attributing markets

The tendency to define the protection of intellectual goods in a perspective of protecting property, rather than in a perspective of promoting competition, and to identify this property by the appropriation of markets, results from more than an isolated and extreme judgement or a doctrinal simplification. It mirrors a general understanding, which largely underlies present intellectual property legislation. Intellectual property is not granted as a matter of legal principles which ensure equal opportunity of competition on the merits with a view to maintaining competition as a guarantee of individual freedom. Rather, it is granted as a way of directing competition so as to achieve predetermined economic and social goals, a matter which, of course, largely depends on the evaluation of the competitive strength of the economy under control, i.e. of the perceived need of strengthening and, if necessary, sheltering it. Property is protected not as a matter of law, but as a matter of policy, however well disguised by legal rules.

Technology protection for technology policy

In fact, this policy approach hardly ever is made in disguise. Thus, in most countries the legislative initiative for and the administrative control of technological property belongs to the departments of industry and/or tech-

---

seq. also as regards tendencies to enhance claims for damages: multiple and punitive damages etc); annot. 75 et seq.: damages for non-pecuniary losses).

[85] CJEC of July 9, 1997, case C-316/95, Generics/Smith Kline and French Laboratories, Rep. 1997 I 3929.

nology rather than to the department of justice.[86] More important, almost any measure of intellectual property harmonization in the European Union has been motivated at least as much by concerns of strengthening the industrial development and the international competitiveness of European industry as by the need to avoid distortions in internal trade. This follows not only from the preparatory green books;[87] it is in the recitals of the directives themselves,[88] i.e. it is raised to the level of a binding rule of statutory interpretation. In addition, the attainment of these objectives, though in no way specified, is subject to regular monitoring by periodical reviews of the operation

---

[86] Germany used to be and still is an exception, but nowadays both the Ministry of Education and Science and the Ministry of Economy and Technology take an active interest at least in "patent policy", the former attempting to shape IPR so as to better serve its R&D-policy and technology transfer (e.g. university patent policies; status of employed researcher/inventor; IPR-rules in international science cooperations), the latter seeking to develop IPR as a component of its innovation policy in general (thus, the Schalk, Täger study, loc. cit., has been commanded by the Ministry of Economy with a view to developing a "New Approach for Innovation Policy").

[87] See for a general policy approach Commission, "Green Book on Innovation", EC-Bull Supp 5/95 at No. 9 (p. 25 et seq.) referring to the harmonization initiatives regarding the protection of designs, plant varieties, biotechnological inventions, utility models and copyright in the information society; see in particular Commission, "Promoting innovation through patents – Green Paper on the Community patent and the patent system on Europe", COM (97) 314 final, p. 1, which was part of the Community's "First action plan for innovation in Europe" (COM (96) 589 final).

[88] See recital 2 et seq., Directive 87/54 on the legal protection of topographies of semiconductor products (OJEC 1987 L 24, 36); recital 2, 3 Computer Programme Directive (supra n. 5); recital 2, Reg. 1768/92 on the creation of a supplementary protection certificate for medicinal products (OJEC 1992 L 182, 1); recital 3 Reg. 1610/96 on the creation of a supplementary protection certificate for phytosanitary products (OJEC 1996 L 198, 30), both providing protection for R&D "within the Community and in Europe"; recital 1 Directive 98/44 on the legal protection of biotechnological inventions (OJEC 1998 L 213, 13) stressing the "fundamental importance for the Community's industrial development", recital 7, 9 – 12 Database directive (supra n. 5) noting in particular a deficit of investment in database development by reference to leading third countries, recital 1, 4, 5, 13 Amended proposal for a directive approximating the legal arrangements for the protection of inventions by utility model, COM (1999) 309 final; recital 4 Directive 2001/29 of May 22, 2001 on the harmonisation of certain aspects of copyright and related rights in the information society (OJEC 2001 L 167, 10) aimed at "growth and increased competitiveness of European industry"; surprisingly enough, such language is missing in the Commission's Proposal for a Regulation on the Community Patent, COM (2000) 412 final. Even more surprising is that CJEC of October 9, 2001, case C-377/98, Netherlands/Parliament and Council (not yet officially reported), while recognizing such objectives, has not deemed it necessary that they be taken into account as a matter of determining the legal basis for the Community's legislative action.

of the harmonized rules of protection.[89] Correspondingly, though generally not with a view to achieving such purposes, the terms of protection have become ever more "interventionist" in that protection has become increasingly specific as regards subject-matter – computer programs, databases, semiconductor topographies, biotechnological inventions, additional certificates, technical control devices – and in that standards of protection have been ever more banalized: simple individual creation, non-commonplace topography, substantial investment etc.[90]

The extent to which intellectual property protection is made the instrument of an interventionist innovation policy may be illustrated by a few examples. Thus, according to Recitals 10, 11 and 18 of the Directive on biotechnological inventions, patent protection is expected to promote progress, especially in areas such as protection of the environment, combating diseases and improving cultivation, the two latter problems regarding, more particularly, developing countries. In line with such specification, it is also stated that, as regards the development of orphan drugs, patent protection is an insufficient incentive, which must be complemented by other systems of promoting progress. Whilst part of such language may be "symbolic politics"[91] – which doesn't make the approach any better – the interventionist intention results even more clearly from the experimental nature of the legislation. Thus, according to Art. 16 of the Directive, within two years of entry into

[89] See art. 16 (3) Database directive (supra n. 5); Art. 16 Directive on biotechnological inventions (supra n. 88); Art 18 Directive on the legal protection of designs (OJEC 1998 L 289, 28); Art. 28 Proposed directive on utility models (supra n. 88) requiring the Commission to report on whether the directive "should be adapted in order to safeguard, in the context of utility models, the proper functioning of the internal market and innovation by Community undertakings"; Art. 12 Directive on copyright in the information society (supra n. 88) requiring inter alia to examine whether the directive "confers a sufficient level of protection (regarding technical anti-copying devices) and whether acts which are permitted by law are being adversely affected by the use of effective technological measures"; Art. 12 also establishes a specific "Contact Committee" charged, inter alia, with the tasks "to facilitate the exchange of information on relevant developments in legislation and case law, as well as relevant economic, social, cultural and technological developments" (lit b), and "to act as a forum for the assessment of the digital market in works and other items, including private copying and the use of technological measures" (lit c). By comparison, Art. 62 Proposed Regulation on the Community Patents (supra n. 88) looks harmless as it addresses mainly the issue of patenting costs and the effects of the litigation system in the field of infringement and validity (but what if there are many patents held invalid? Comp. supra text at n. 8).

[90] See Art. 1 (3) Computer Programme Directive (supra n. 5); Art. 1 (1), 7 (1) Database Directive (supra n. 5); Art. 2 (2) Directive Semiconductor Topographies (supra n. 88).

[91] See M. S. Edelmann, *The Symbolic Uses of Politics*, German edition (*Politik als Ritual*), Frankfurt 1976.

force of the Directive, a report has to be given by the Commission to Parliament and Council assessing the implications for basic genetic engineering research of failure to publish, or late publication of papers on subjects which could be patentable. Similarly, pursuant to Art. 10 of the Database Directive, a specific report must be given within 3 years on whether the protection of databases, in particular *sui generis* protection, has resulted in abuses of dominant positions on the market or in any other impairment of free competition that would mandate corrective measures, such as compulsory licensing. The Design Directive also provides that the Commission must "submit an analysis of the consequences of the provisions of this Directive for Community industry, in particular the industrial sectors which are most affected, particularly manufacturers of component parts, for consumers, for competition and for the functioning of the internal market" (Art. 18). This means that after years, in the case of the Biotechnology Directive after a gestation period of almost a decade, the legislator still has no precise idea of the effects of the proposed legislation, but undertakes some sort of a pilot experiment, e.g. as regards *sui generis* protection. This cautious approach may be somehow explained by the complete failure of another form of specific protection, namely that of protecting semiconductor chips.[92] Nevertheless, it clearly is evidence of the interventionist character of the legislation. Even more important is the fact that the risk is virtually unmanageable: if, for example, database protection proves to be excessive, it cannot simply be repealed, but must be counterbalanced by other measures[93]. Indeed, rights which have been granted too easily thereafter do exist and become well-acquired rights. Standards may be tightened or the term of protection may be reduced only for the future, i.e. with full effect only after 15, 20 or 25 years, in the case of copyrighted databases or computer programs only with effect for the third

[92] This is generally recognized; for the low number of applications, see Deutsches Patent- und Markenamt, Annual Report, Munich 1998, 28 (55 applications, of which 2 from the Netherlands, 52 from Japan, none from Germany); id., Annual Report 1999 (Bl. PMZ 2000, 89, 110; 64 new applications). Apparently, the legislation became obsolete due to technological development (reduction of risks of simple copying) at the very time it entered into force. This is particularly ironic in view of the fact that it had been introduced as a reaction to reciprocity pressure, and with much insistence on the indispensability of such protection.

[93] Which, then, must withstand constitutional scrutiny; see supra n. 73, 76, 77. However, excessive protection by technical measures under Art. 6 Directive on Copyright in the Information Society (see supra n. 88) may be more easily remedied, as arguably there is no property right in the protection of such measures, and as the issue is only one of enforcing already recognized limits of protection (as distinct from the question whether such protection is necessary at all, and whether the exceptions have been defined too narrowly in the first place).

generation succeeding the living generation of programmers.[94] The intervention thus tends to be irreversible. In addition, what kind of incentive for the creation of databases is it, anyway, that is granted with a caveat that, later on, compulsory licensing may be introduced? Or is that merely symbolic politics as well?

It is, indeed, not unlikely that the interventionist intentions of the Community legislator reach beyond its determination to exercise a control over its effects. Thus, the duty to monitor the general development and impact of the intellectual property directives is sanctioned by an obligation of the Commission to submit annual, or tri-annual, reports to the Council and to Parliament. Such reporting certainly is useful and legitimate as a way of controlling the impact of legislation on legal practice and societal reality, provided that the legislation's target may be identified in reality, and that the impact may be determined with some precision.[95] But what, in addition to a review of the practice of the law as developed by the courts, and possibly some complaints by industry, can be put into such a report with a view to determining the IPR-legislation's impact on the economy?[96] Increases of in-

[94] See Art. 1, 11 Directive on the Harmonization of the terms of protection of copyright and related rights (OJEC 1993 L 290, 9) with recital 5 and the critique by Ullrich in Müller-Graff (ed.), loc. cit. at 449 et seq.

[95] See Th. Dreier, *Gesetzesfolgenabschätzung und Gesetzungsevaluierung im Urheberrecht, Festschrift Dittrich*, Vienna 2000, 49. A major concern of the assessment of legislation is whether it correctly translated the reality it is intended to regulate into legal rules. Therefore, Art. 62 Proposed Community Patent Regulation (supra n. 89) addresses at least the right issues: access to protection and efficiency of judicial enforcement. By contrast, Art. 11 Directive 2001/84 of September 27, 2001 on the resale right for the benefit of the author of an original work of art, (OJEC 2001 L 272, 32) is more ambivalent. It makes the future of the resale right dependent upon the uncertain analysis of the "competitiveness of the market" in modern and contemporary art. Apart from the issue of substantive law whether this is a proper approach to the resale right at all, the point simply is that, if possible at all, it is rather difficult to identify increases or decreases of the resale right as factors that appreciably affect the trade's competitiveness.

[96] The only report that exists (and which is due not to a formal requirement, but to a political promise made in the legislative process; see J. Gaster, *Der Erfahrungsbericht zur EG-Computerprogrammrichtlinie*, CR Int 2000, 11, 12) concerning the Computer Programme Directive (supra n. 5); see Commission, Report on the transformation and on the effects of Directive 91/250/EEC on legal protection of computer programs, COM (2000) 199 final. It is largely an account of how Member States adopted the Directive, and states some concern of industry of a legal nature, to which it adds, on less than one third of a page, that, as regards the effects on the software industry, piracy has gone back from 78 % to 36 %, that employment has increased as well as turnover and that there is a marked tendency to open systems. There is not a shadow of a shade of an attempt to show, in the report, whether and how the

novation rates, advances of industrial development, and the strengthening of international competitiveness of industry are hard to measure, are long-term tendencies, and they are a permanent concern. This is so, because they are part of an evolutionary process, and because rival countries will develop equally, if not at a faster pace. Therefore, it is hard to imagine how, upon an "economic review of any intellectual property system",[97] let alone an annual review, a revision of the system may be made which is fine-tuned to predetermined goals of innovation, industrial development or international competitiveness. Rather, what may be expected is a spiral movement of protection, a "race to the top" and/or (eventually) a serious legal breakdown.[98] This is the more likely as the – increasing – need to provide incentives for innovation can be satisfied only by broadening and banalizing intellectual property protection.

Trade policy for technology protection

There is, indeed, a profound misunderstanding underlying the tendencies of intellectual property protection just described, namely the assumption that the economic-policy rationale, which motivates the protection of intellectual goods by exclusive rights, may also be made a yardstick which would allow us to more or less precisely control its actual operation. The misunderstanding is quite obvious. Whilst intellectual property may be used in a relatively short term to positively influence innovation by strengthening and/or broadening the exclusivity, it may not be thus used conversely by narrowing, reducing or repealing protection other than in the very long term. Therefore, even leaving aside the question, introduced earlier, whether the intellectual

---

increase in employment and turnover is causally linked to protection. This, however, is precisely what is necessary to justify the interventionist claims made by the legislation (and it is only these claims that raise concerns). In fact, even less ambitious monitoring attempts are open to question; see Dreier in Festschrift Dittrich, loc. cit. at 65 ff. questioning the Commission's statements regarding a decrease of piracy.

[97] Paraphrase of Machlup F., "An Economic Review of the Patent System", Study No. 15, U.S. Congr., Senate Subcomm. on Patents, Trademarks, and Copyright, 85th Congr., 2nd Sess.

[98] This is the concern underlying the "Manifesto", supra n. 69, or the anti-commons debate in biotechnology patenting as triggered by M. A. Heller, R. Eisenberg, "Can Patents Deter Innovation? The Anticommons in Biomedical Research", 280 *Science* 698 (1998); see also R. S. Eisenberg, "Bargaining Over the Transfer of Proprietary Research Tools: Is the Market Failing or Emerging?" in R. Dreyfuss, H. First *et al.* (eds.), *Expanding the Boundaries of Intellectual Property*, London 2000, 223 et seq. The background of such a legal crisis is, of course, formed by the IPR-dilemmas (see supra text at n. 19) that underlie the debate on patent breadth and duration (see supra n. 79).

property system may at all lend itself as a way to "instrumentalize" competition as a mechanism of decentralized organization of markets, controlling the level of innovation by intellectual property protection with a view to achieving specific goals easily leads into the political lock-in of the "race to the top" just described. This is not only a risk, which may result from a vulgarization of industrial economics of the intellectual property system in that this invites us to adopt its teachings as instructions for legislation without taking due account of the *ex post* character of the theoretical analysis, and of the irreversibility of the IPR-dilemma.[99] Rather, intellectual property policy has already made its way far into that one-way street.

The reason for this pessimistic assessment is the complementarity which exists between, on the one hand, the instrumentalist concept of intellectual property as a means of innovation policy, and, on the other, the support which international intellectual property protection has obtained from national trade policies. On a conceptual level, this complementarity results from the economic assessment of intellectual property in terms of market exclusivity. When innovation policy relies on intellectual property protection as an incentive, then, what it really does is to hold out promises or expectancies for market shares on the innovation market. This is in full accord with the system. But it means that, whenever the incentive needs to be upgraded, the market potential of the exclusivity must be enlarged. This may be done by lowering the thresholds to protection or by broadening the substantive scope of protection, and it may also be done by extending the monopoly to more markets then simply the relevant subject-matter market. Spare-part protection by design rights, or copyright protection of the interfaces of computer programs, allows one to control the after-markets for repair and maintenance, or the sub-markets for peripheral equipment. Limiting the scope of the exhaustion rule by widening the objective of trademark protection[100] enhances control over trade, and granting protection to mere discoveries[101] brings downstream markets of all kinds within the realm of the exclusivity.

---

[99] Note that harmonization of the national copyright terms by the EC-Directive (supra n. 94) through increasing rather than levelling-off of the various copyright terms was motivated precisely by the fact that as a matter of law – the constitutional protection of well-acquired rights – such levelling-off was impossible or would have resulted in an excessively long period of transition; see recital 9 Copyright Term Directive (supra n. 94).

[100] See CJEC of November 4, 1997, case C-337/95, Parfums Christian Dior/Evora, Rep 1997 I 6013, Ullrich, "International Exhaustion of Intellectual Property Rights: Lesson from European Economic Integration", *Mélanges Waelbroeck*, Brussels 1999, 205, 238 et seq.

[101] For this controversy relating to biotechnological inventions see Art. 5 and recitals 22 et seq. Directive on Biotechnological Inventions (supra n. 88); N. Machin, "Prospective Utility:

Trade policy allows one to extend the incentive of exclusivity to more territorial markets than the proprietor of national intellectual property could have expected to obtain under the individual-property rationale of the classic conventions of Paris and Berne. Two points are important in this respect. One is simply the equation of intellectual property protection with markets, which would otherwise be lost to "free(-rider)" competition. This equation results from the fact that not only bilateral trade policy, but also its multilateralization by the TRIPs Agreement is by no means a matter of free trade, but one of controlling markets. The TRIPs Agreement, by its origin as well as by its operation, is based on the principle of territoriality, i.e. it is based on the protection of nationally defined markets and, more precisely, on the protection of the aggregation of so-defined markets. It is the result of trading access to product markets against control over technology markets, and it is administered with a view to maintaining a balance of trade interests.[102] The other important point is that intellectual property protection has not been put on the agenda of international trade negotiations as a matter of fairly regulating global markets (which, in the mid-eighties, were not all that global), but as a matter of redressing an allegedly failing international competitiveness of US industry.[103] Whilst this may have been only the element triggering negotiations, which then resulted in some true North/North deals on intellectual property, and the imposition of these deals on all other nations, it nevertheless is evidence of the instrumentalist approach to intellectual property.[104]

A New Interpretation of the Utility Requirement of Section 101 of the Patent Act", 87 *Cal. L. Rev.* 421, 423 et seq. (1999); B. Looney, "Should Genes Be Patented? The Gene Patenting Controversy: Legal, Ethical and Policy Foundations of an International Agreement", 26 *Law Pol'y Int'l. Bus.* 231 (1994); G. Smith, D.M. Kettelberger, "Patents and the Human Genome Project", 22 *AIPLA Qu. J.* 27, 51 et seq. (1994). The issue is, of course, precisely that which the authors, supra n. 79, discuss on the basis of E. W. Kitch, "The Nature and Function of the Patent System", 20 *J. L. Ec.* 265 (1977), see also as to related problems of disclosure and enablement J.C. Todaro, "Enablement in Biotechnology Case After In Re Goodman", 5 *Fordh. Intellec. Prop. Media Ent.-ment L.J.* 1 (1994); J.M. Lucas, "The Doctrine of Simultaneous Conception and Reduction to Practice in Biotechnology: A Double Standard for the Double Helix?" 26 *AIPLA Qu. J.* 381 (1998).

[102] For more details see Ullrich, "Technology Protection According to TRIPs: Principles and Problems", in F.K. Beier, B. Schricker (ed.), *From GATT to TRIPs – The Agreement on Trade-Related Aspects of Intellectual Property Rights*, Weinheim 1996, 357, 372 et seq.

[103] See references in Ullrich, "GATT. Industrial Property Protection, Fair Trade and Development", in Beier, Schricker (eds.), *GATT or WIPO – New Ways in the International Protection of Intellectual Property*, Weinheim 1989, 127, 131 et seq.

[104] In fact, concern for international competitiveness is still a major driving force; see, for the EU, Commission, "Green Book on Innovation", Bull. EC Supp 5/95, sub. 8 (at p. 25).

Both these points also go far to explain the impact which reliance on trade policy, as a way of enhancing intellectual property protection, does have both on domestic intellectual property policy and on the scope of intellectual property protection in general. Once that intellectual property had been made a trade issue, its international protection was bound to develop from a principle of national treatment based on the respect of national intellectual property policies to a principle of national treatment based on a principle of equal national protection, i.e. on substantive reciprocity. This, indeed, is the very purpose of TRIPs. And once that substantive reciprocity has been established, and its effect has been put to evaluation in terms not only of market exclusivities, but in terms of market volumes, as it has to be done for imposing and enforcing the TRIPs Agreement,[105] the determination of a nation's intellectual property policy becomes a matter of international rivalry. Rather than being a mere support of international intellectual property protection, trade policy will come to influence domestic policy. This is so because, under the principle of reciprocity, it is impossible to claim international protection which has not first been made available domestically, and it is so as a matter of "disguised retaliation",[106] and, most important, as a matter of strengthening one's own domestic position in technological competition by creating "safe" home markets.

Evidence of these spillover effects of trade policy relating to intellectual property protection on the very determination of intellectual property policy is that States have not been satisfied with developing trade policy instruments as a support to their nationals' claims to protection abroad.[107] Rather,

---

105 See references in Ullrich in Beier, Schricker (eds.), *GATT or WIPO*, loc. cit. at 138 et seq., 149 et seq.; id., in Beier, Schricker (eds.), *From GATT to TRIPs*, loc. cit. at 377 et seq.

106 See in the first respect recital 8 a Council Regulation on Community Designs, supra n. 11, stating that Community design protection would represent an incentive for the States representing the Community's most important export markets to introduce equivalent protection. In the second respect see the reciprocity requirement of Art. 11 Database Directive (supra n. 5) regarding the *sui generis* right, and comp. Gaster, loc. cit. *CR Int.* 1999, 669 ("retaliation" against the misguided Semiconductor Chip Protection Act 1984 and its reciprocity requirement).

107 See for the USA Sect. 301 Trade Act of 1974 as applied to impose intellectual property standards of US understanding (see M.Haedicke, *Urheberrecht und die Handelspolitik der USA*, Munich 1997, 61 et seq., 80 et seq.); Sect. 301 – practices remain possible notwithstanding its doubtful status under WTO law (see Jakob, "Die Zukunft US-amerikanischer unilateraler Section 301-Maßnahmen", GRUR Int. 2000, 715); for the EU see Reg. 3286/94 laying down Community procedures in the field of Common Commercial Policy in order to ensure the exercise of the Community's rights under international trade rules (so-called Trade Barrier Regulation, OJEC 1994 L 349, 7 as amended by Reg. 356/95, OJEC 1995 L 41, 3), and

they have become unable to independently define their intellectual property policies as it best fits their own interests, and so they have entered into a "race to the top of protection", and into interfering with their neighbours' intellectual property policies.

Thus, the U.S.A., though adhering to an incentive/reward rationale of copyright protection as mandated by their Constitution, have felt compelled to match the EU's 70 years p.m.a. term of protection rather than defending themselves against this kind of over-protection. Similarly, they struggle to match the EU's protection of databases by a *sui generis* right even though a less radical approach would facilitate legislation by Congress.[108] The European Union has locked itself into its own rules on internal exhaustion of intellectual property rights. Now, out of fear of losing international bargaining power, it is unable to liberalize its regime in accordance with legal principles, which would call for a differentiated approach to international exhaustion, as is commanded by the differing functions of the various intellectual property rights.[109]

In a global perspective, it is indeed difficult to imagine how a nation will ever be able to grant less protection domestically than other countries do. Under a principle of reciprocity, whether express or implied,[110] this will always mean disadvantaging its own nationals on foreign markets. They will enjoy no protection there, and even if they do, they will have to compete on less favorable terms as they cannot benefit from a protected home market,

---

D. Rose, "The EU Trade Barrier Regulation: An Effective Instrument for Promoting Global Harmonisation of Intellectual Property Rights?" *Eur. Int. Prop. Rev.* 1999, 313; C. Garcia Molyneux, "The Trade Barriers Regulation: The European Union as a Player in the Globalisation Game", 5 *Eur. L. J.* 375 (1999).

[108] See in the first respect the Sony Bono Copyright Term Extension Act, 56 BNA-PTCJ 696, 731 (1998); in the latter respect see supra n. 17.

[109] See CJEC of July 16, 1998, case C-355/96, Silhouette International Schmied/Hartlauer, Rep. 1998 I 4799; of July 1, 1999, case C-173/98, Sebago/GB Unic., Rep. 1994 I 4103; Communiqué Commissioner Bolkestein of June 7, 2000 on the issue of exhaustion of trademark rights (http://europa.eu.int/comm/internalmarket/en/intprop/indprop/comexhaust.htm) (of June 12, 2000), J. Gaster, "Die Erschöpfungsproblematik aus der Sicht des Gemeinschaftsrechts", GRUR Int. 2000, 571; C. Baudenbacher, "Erschöpfung der Immaterialgüterrechte in der EFTA und die Rechtslage in der EU", GRUR Int. 2000, 584; Th. Bodewig, "Erschöpfung der gewerblichen Schutzrechte und des Urheberrechts in den USA", GRUR Int. 2000, 597.

[110] See for examples of express reciprocity Art. 11 Database Directive (supra n. 5); Art. 3 (3) (7) Directive Semiconductor Topographies (supra n. 88); as to the reciprocity implied in the TRIPs Agreement's trading mechanism see Ullrich, in Beier, Schricker, loc. cit. 361 et seq. 372 et seq.

but must fight against competitors who precisely enjoy a protected home market. Conversely, it comes as no surprise that nations do seek to unilaterally impose their standards of protection on others by way of an extraterritorial application of domestic intellectual property rules, e.g. by seizing goods in transit which are protected under their laws, but not under the laws of either the country of origin or the country of destination.[111] At first glance, such disrespect for another country's intellectual property policy – abstention of protection does, indeed, represent a definite industrial policy in most cases, rather than simply an abstention or merely a free-rider approach – may be explained by deficits of the international legal order. Thus, in the European Union, for example, it is only due to the acceptance of a firm rule of free trade that it was possible to establish the principle of cross-border exhaustion or a limitation of intellectual property-based control over transit.[112] In reality, however, contrary to the TRIPs Agreement's claims of constituting a fair regulation of trade in technologies and technological goods, the true reason for all the excesses mentioned is to be found in the system itself, and in the policy interests that are at its roots.

19.4 Conclusion

19.4.1 Outlook

The influence of trade policy on national intellectual property protection is not only a matter of defining its terms in an international perspective.[113] Its more subtle, but also more far-reaching, effect is that which it has on the very concept and understanding of intellectual property, since it perfectly meets the instrumentalist approach described above. Both currents of legislative and judicial IPR policy converge into a new paradigm of intellectual

---

[111] See for a striking example, on the one hand CJEC of April 6, 2000, The Polo/Lauren Company v. Dwidua Langeng Pratama International Freight Forwarders, Rep. 2000 I 2519 = GRUR Int. 2000, 748; on the other CJEC of September 26, 2000, case C-23/99, Commission/France, Rep. 2000 I 7653, and see CJEC of May 11, 2000, case C-38/98, Renault/Maxicar, Rep. 2000 I 2973.

[112] For the link existing between the European Community's approach to market integration and the application of free trade principles to the exercise of intellectual property rights, see Ullrich in *Mélanges Waelbroeck*, loc. cit. at. 209 et seq.

[113] Which in itself is problematic enough; see S. Fitzpatrick, "Copyright Imbalance: U.S. and Australian Responses to the WIPO Digital Copyright Treaty", *Eur. Int. Prop. Rev.* 2000, 214, 226 et seq.

property as a pro-active, deterministic, if not quasi-interventionist[114] system of market regulation. The importance of this change cannot properly be assessed without taking account of the equally pro-active, deterministic competition policy which has developed over the last years or is about to develop at least in the European Union.[115] Indeed, as mentioned above,[116] the combined effects of the IPR system and the system of competition in the market place will reinforce each other. This parallel development in turn means that, whatever hopes of controlling IPR excesses by antitrust laws may have existed, they are bound to be disappointed. Antitrust law cannot be better than the competition policy it is intended to protect.

The problem, indeed, is more deeply rooted. It is not only that intellectual property protection and competition policy have entered into a marriage of convenience commanded by the interests of strategic policies of innovation and of trade. Rather, the equation of property with market exclusivities has resulted in an identification of State interests with industry interests. This not

---

[114] For the various forms of direct or indirect, industry-specific or cross-sectoral, but always result-oriented market intervention and their relation to the new industrial policy and to strategic trade policy, see Chr. Engel, "Europarechtliche Grenzen für die Industriepolitik", in W. Rengeling (ed.), *Europäisierung des Rechts*, Cologne 1996, 35; H. Feldmann, "Konzeption und Praxis, der EG-Industriepolitik", in 44 *Ordo* 139 (1993); for a general account of industrial policy and its instruments, see recently M. J. Seitz, *Staatliche Industriepolitik*, Baden-Baden 2000, 170 et seq.

[115] This profound change results from the combined effects of the Commission's new approach both to vertical restraints of Competition (see Commission, Notice on the application of the EC competition rules to vertical restraints, COM (1998) 544 final; Commission Reg. 2790/99 on the application of Art. 85 (3) of the Treaty to certain categories of vertical restraints, OJEC 1999 L 336, 21; Commission, "Guidelines on Vertical Restraints", OJEC 2000 C 291, 1; see R. Whish, "Regulation 2790/99: The Commission's 'New Style' Block Exemption for Vertical Restraints", 37 *C.M.L. Rev.* 887 (2000)), and to horizontal restraints of competition (Commission, Regulation of November 23, 2000 on the application of Art. 81 (3) EC Treaty to Categories of agreements on research and development, OJEC 2000 L 304, 7, and to specialisation agreements, OJEC 2000 L 304, 3; Guidelines on the application of Art. 81 EC Treaty to agreements on horizontal cooperation, OJEC 2001 C3, 2)) as well as from the Commission's reform proposals regarding the enforcement system; see Commission, "White Book on the Modernization of the rules on application of Art. 85 and 86 of the Treaty", OJEC 1999 C 132, 1; Commission, "Proposal for a Regulation on the Implementation of the Competition Rules laid down in Art. 81 and 82 of the Treaty", COM (2000) 582 final. These changes cannot be analyzed here; see only Cl. D. Ehlermann, "The modernization of EC antitrust policy: A legal and cultural revolution", 37 *C.M.L. Rev.* 537 (2000); W. Möschel, "Guest Editorial: Change of Policy in European Competition Law?" 37 *C.M.L. Rev.* 495 (2000); see also supra n. 48.

[116] Sub. II.3.

only renders a proper definition of government policy difficult.[117] It also makes the implementation and the translation of State policy into practice and reality dependent on the initiative of and acceptance by industry, be it only because all the necessary information must be obtained from industry, which best knows the markets and their development. This means nothing less than a loss of public control. This loss concerns not so much the control over how the individual right is exercised in actual business, but over the definition of the very contents and scope of the property, a circumstance which goes far to explain the continuous narrowing of general-interest exceptions to protection.[118] As a result, social responsiveness of private intellectual property tends to diminish.[119] Similarly, subjecting, by a functionalist approach,[120] the exercise of intellectual property to requirements of compatibility with the overall principles of a market system becomes a problem. In fact, binding it to the kind of deterministic competition policy which actually prevails on major national market places would only worsen things.

---

[117] See e.g. as to the breakdown of the spare parts-regulation supra n. 11; other examples are the protracted lobby battles over the decompilation issues in software protection and their doubtful results (see H. Ullrich in H. Ullrich, E. Körner (eds.), *Der internationale Softwarevertrag*, Heidelberg 1995, 74 et seq.) or the long-lasting stalemate regarding EC legislation on artists' resale right, which is due to industry's capture of parts of the legislative bodies (see supra n. 95, and Commission, Reply to a Written Question of the Parliament, as reported in GRUR Int. 2000, 182; Commission, "Statement for the Protocol of the Council on the Directive on Artists' Resale Right", OJEC 2001 C 208, 2.

[118] Unless, of course, the exception serves the interests of a powerful lobby; see e.g. the farmers' privilege in Art. 11 Biotechnology Directive, supra n. 88.

[119] See Fitzpatrick, loc. cit. *Eur. Int. Prop. Rev.* 2000, 214, and, taking a broad view, W. Kingston, "A Spectre is Haunting the World – The Spectre of Global Capitalism", 10 *J. Evolutionary Ec.* 83 (2000).

[120] See P. Drahos, *A Philosophy of Intellectual Property*, Dartmouth 1996, 199 et seq., 213 et seq., 220 et seq., contrasting a "proprietary" understanding of intellectual property protection with an "instrumentalist" one, meaning that the definition, interpretation and enforcement of intellectual property must remain tied to the socio-economic objectives (in a broad, moral sense) underlying the legislative grant of protection. Instrumentalist in this sense is more akin to a functionalist or to a teleological conception and application of the law than to the "instrumentalist" approach criticized in the text, which uses a proprietarian approach to achieve interventionist goals of economic policy. It is precisely the separation of the exercise of protection as a right of "property" from the interventionist policy goals pursued by the legislator which constitutes the camouflage of the intervention, and which produces social risks due to the absolute or abstract character of the exercise of the right.

Research perspectives

A simple return to traditional concepts of private property and to its embedment in an outcome-neutral system of competition as a discovery process is unlikely, and probably out of tune with the information society. Therefore, the research directions asked for by this seminar do not only point, as they do anyway as a matter of minimizing the risk of public IPR-policy, to a better integration of industrial economies, i.e. its teachings, its progress and its warnings, into the understanding of intellectual property protection. Rather, research should also go into a more critical analysis of the interaction of public policy and private property.[121] More particularly, what is needed is a fundamental reformulation of the purpose, the functioning, and the limits of private property as a way to allow the production and exploitation of an otherwise public good, technological information, under conditions of privately and publicly pre-established and/or pre-defined competition.[122] Ultimately, there is a dilemma which has to be overcome. Intellectual property protection has two different, but interrelated, functions. On the level of market regulation, it is defined so as to serve public policy objectives, whereas on

[121] An all too obvious case for analysis is the cumulative use of intellectual property protection and R&D subsidies, possibly even combined with the promotion of R&D-cooperation (see the critique by Ullrich, *Kooperative Forschung*, loc. cit. at 166 et seq.; Monopolkommission, Hauptgutachten 1988/1989 Baden-Baden 1999, at No. 1082). Another example might be the combination of the IPR-exclusivity with standardization in view of the public good-nature of standards as infrastructure and of the network effects to which they give rise; see for a discussion J. Liotard, "Normalisation, Droits de propriété intellectuelle et concurrence: L'exemple des télécommunications", *Rev. int. dr. écon.* 2000, 279.

[122] The Commission itself notes and favours the high degree of inter-enterprise cooperation and strategic alliances in innovation markets (see Commission, "White Book: Growth, Competitiveness, Employment", Bull. EC Supp 6/93 at 2.3 (p. 67 et seq. id., "Communication on Competitiveness of European Enterprises in the face of Globalisation", COM (1999) 718 final, sub II.5, II 6). In fact, the cooperative networks in industry have grown still further, so that the IPR-paradigm has to be readjusted: not only do we have the team invention rather than the individual inventor, not only are inventions a result of investment rather than of genius, and not only do patents not cover products (except in some instances of pharmaceuticals), but entire technologies by virtue of patent packages. Rather, the R&D process itself is no longer a matter of individual business activity, but of a group effort. Nowhere in the patent system is there any trace of these changes. Does the traditional model of the property approach really fit so well the interests of all industry, and does it fit the public interest in free competition? The question is the more intriguing as even economists generally do analyze the patent system on such idealistic assumptions, and then look at strategic R&D alliances as an alternative rather than as a synergistic combination of the patent system and cooperative competition. For a brief summary of the state of analyses and further references see H. Klodt, *Grundlagen der Forschungs- und Technologiepolitik*, Munich 1995, 44 et seq.

the level of competition it is an instrument at the service of the private interests of rivalling individual enterprises. These should be guaranteed a level playing field in terms of equal opportunity of protection, of equal chances of freedom, and of overall fairness; i.e. the system must be guarded by principles of law and equity. The question, therefore, is what the link between the two functional levels would have to look like in order to properly hold them in a productive balance. Clearly, the answer will not be easy, since much of the tendencies described in the text are due to broader political attitudes and economic mentalities, which defy a purely legal analysis.

Therefore, rather than setting up an ambitious research design, I would like to conclude with three less demanding suggestions, which might pave the way to a better understanding of the overall task.

First, intellectual property protection is not an isolated, self-contained system. Rather, it always needs to be properly put in context. As regards the international system of protection, for example, its claims to legitimacy, as enshrined in the TRIPs Agreement, are made with a view to avoid distortions of competition, to obtain a level playing field, and to have intellectual property recognized as a result of competition on the merits. These are claims for a free international trade order, to which the TRIPs system itself must live up. They imply that every country may pursue its own intellectual property policy in accordance with its own economic, technological and developmental objectives.[123] The interpretation and the application of the TRIPs Agreement, in particular of its indeterminate terms and openly defined exceptions, should follow a rule of substantive respect and active comity between member States. Such principles have yet to be developed on the broader basis of WTO as a legal order which is binding on all. This is a matter for all lawyers, in particular for business lawyers trained in regulatory principles which are aimed at fairness, freedom, and open markets, but less for trade lawyers, who mentally tend to analyze trade rules in terms of trade concessions.

Second, there is a need to rethink the relationship between the substantive legal principles governing intellectual property protection and its economic functions, i.e. between property granted for merit and property granted as an incentive. After all, intellectual property protection also is a matter of law and justice, not merely one of economics.[124] It might be worthwhile, therefore, to rethink the scope of protection granted to subject-matter which, in view of its engineering-like and/or programmable development, may only

---

[123] See Fitzpatrick, loc. cit., *Eur. Int. Prop. Rev.* 2000, 214; UNCTAD, *The TRIPs Agreement and Developing Countries*, Geneva 1996, 14, 21 et seq. et passim.
[124] Compare Drahos, supra n. 120.

need and justify protection against such unfair imitation, which is direct copying, but not against honest, innovative use, which is made with a view to supply value-adding or otherwise complementary products or services. Much of computer programs, databases or spare parts, which enjoy protection by a privilege of exclusivity on the basis of copyright or design rights, do so mainly because the law of unfair competition is not sufficiently developed in the European Union (and in the USA!). It is at least in these cases that the identification of intellectual property protection with markets, and, consequently, the inclusion of aftermarkets (for additional services, spare parts etc) and of upstream or downstream markets, tends to favor large enterprises having broad capacities and potential of knowledge exploitation along the full line of diversification over small enterprises. It also tends to allow pricing policies based on lock-in effects in that the "reward" will be captured on the aftermarkets, once entry on the primary market has been achieved by relatively modest pricing. Finally, it tends to favor numerous dependencies between equally low-level subject-matter, however commercially valuable, which result in avoidable costs and disincentives for the individualistic-minded entrepreneur. Therefore, a more prudent way of protection might be conceived of with a view to reinstalling the principle that protection should be awarded for merit rather than for markets.

Another line of investigation might focus on that, due to the banalization of protection and the investment-rationale, the creative mind – which determines the direction, the nature and the extent of the discovery process, be it in reaction to signals coming from the market, be it autonomously – has fallen almost into oblivion, and, if not, is about to be entirely disregarded (e.g. as regards the employed inventor and/or author).[125] The question, however, to whom the exclusivity of protectable subject-matter should be attributed, may hardly be decided properly without taking due account of this personal element (e.g. in determining the first-to-invent/first to-file controversy, in attributing employee creations, or in defining and dissolving joint ownership etc). Another question is whether the role of this personal element should really be limited to this basic function, or whether it should also come

---

[125] See Art. 2 (3) Computer Programme Directive (supra n. 5), Art. 3 (4) Database Directive (supra n. 5), and compare the preliminary hearing on reforming the law of employee inventors in Germany, GRUR 2000, 1000.

The question is one of which paradigm to follow (see supra n. 122), and of our concepts of industrial organization in general. However, the primary concern must be how to conceptualize the relationship between information and the person or organisation who created it and/or specified its utility and use. The economic nature of information as a public good should not make us forget that it is a product of the mind.

into play when determining the level of inventiveness/creativity required for protection or the scope of protection, e.g. in case of pioneer inventions. Re-adherence to principles of justice may also prevent excessive and instrumentalist uses of the intellectual property system, and it may help to properly address issues such as the free-rider problem, or the social and ethical implications of allowing intellectual property-based control over all kinds of biological resources and materials. It is true that many of these are old problems, but they should be addressed again in the new context of the expansion of intellectual property protection.

Third, as intellectual property becomes ever more diversified and as, at the same time, the scope of copyright protection expands into technological areas and the scope of patent protection tends to reach beyond the limits of technology, there is not only the question of whether the systems of protection, however diverse, do converge in fact. Rather, another question should be raised as well, namely whether all forms of intellectual property protection still follow the same theoretical paradigm of promoting progress of technology by restricting its exploitation in favor of the inventor/creator. This paradigm rests on the assumption that the protected subject-matter establishes a new manner or method of producing goods which, by being kept under an exclusivity, allows profitable exploitation of the technology, but which, thereafter, will be exposed to competition so that ultimately diffusion of the technology will be enhanced. However, this two-layer model of technology as a source of wealth on product markets does not fit where the protected subject-matter is itself the product, which is sold on markets as a matter of supplying services, as is the case for computer programs or databases. In these cases the exclusivity seems to have another function, and the concept of a trade-off between protection and competition, exclusivity and diffusion, seems to be misplaced. Rather than promoting the development of the supply of a service, the function of the exclusivity primarily is to define the service to be supplied, and to allow a determination of the terms upon which the service is supplied. The exclusivity is the basis of the contract, which fixes and limits the use that may be made of a computer program, or of a database which is offered as a service by the proprietor. Typically, the program or the database is let for rent rather than sold, and the exhaustion principle does not apply, whilst restrictions of use are commonplace. It is because of this different nature of the protected subject-matter that the thresholds of protection had to be and could be lowered, that protection is granted – explicitly or implicitly – for mere investment efforts, and that the term of protection is virtually infinite, i.e. greatly in excess of the slowest conceivable innovation rate. Carrying over traditional intellectual property concepts from the hardware- to the software-age may simply result in stretching the conventional terms where, in reality, new concepts are needed.[126] Probably, information economics can yield the insights necessary in order both to better understand the markets for information services, and to better explain and define the terms of protection needed for these services.

[126] In fact, we have generally not very well understood, at least as lawyers, the implications which the multifunctional and multi-use properties of information may or should have for the definition of property in such information. Probably, due to increased dependencies, the new approach of the revised European Patent Convention (Art 54 (4) (5)) to patent protection for successively discovered medicinal uses of pharmaceutical compounds will result in so much transaction cost that, instead of no less costly institutional arrangements (see supra n. 33), new concepts of property in information may need to be developed, which bring the respective profit potentials more directly to bear. Technological information, which is split up in pieces of separate property according to its multifunctionality, should produce rules of "good neighbourhood", which, though certainly different, would be analogous in purpose to those known and developed over centuries in the field of property in land; i.e. there may be some wisdom in accommodating the use of one property with the use others are entitled to make of their property, rather than to insist on the exclusivity. In fact, the idea that there is some relativity in the absolute exclusivity of property is not yet very much developed in the area of intellectual property. Compulsory licences are a very crude remedy, and not of much help in the long run, as ever more property titles to information of all kinds are likely to arise, either under existing or under new laws, to satisfy the needs of an ever-expanding information economy. As a consequence, there will be an increasing need not only to accommodate intellectual property with the public domain, but also to limit its exercise so as to avoid conflicts with "overlapping", "interrelated" or "concurring" rights to "exclusive" protection.

Chapter 20

INTELLECTUAL PROPERTY RIGHTS IN THE WORLD ECONOMY[1]

Bart Verspagen
Eindhoven Center for Innovation Studies (ECIS);
University of Technology, Department of Technology Management, Eindhoven, The Netherlands

Chapter contents:

Abstract: This chapter broadly summarizes some of the basic economic theory on the working of the patent system. It starts by outlining the role technology plays in economic development, and the way in which economic theory has approached the technology-economy relationship. It then reviews the basic economic motive for establishing a patent system: to solve the incentive problem that firms face when they develop new technologies with potential spillover effects to other firms and consumers. A discussion of alternatives to the patent system is also provided. From an economic point of view, however, a crucial aspect of patents is that they leave some opportunity for spillovers. In other words, patents should not provide a pure monopoly to the inventing firm.

[1] An earlier version of this chapter was presented at the WIPO Arab Regional Symposium on the Economic Importance of Intellectual Property Rights, Muscat, Sultanate of Oman, February 22-24, 1999. I thank participants at the conference and Eddy Szirmai for useful comments and discussions. The work for this chapter was sponsored by the Norwegian Research Council under the programme "Globalisering som transformativ kraft", carried out by TIK.

O. Granstrand (ed.), Economics, Law and Intellectual Property, 489-518.

The economic logic behind this argument is explained and some general (and abstract) theoretical guidelines are proposed to strike a balance between providing incentives (a legal monopoly for the inventor) and leaving opportunity for spillovers. The chapter concludes with a summary of the debates surrounding issues of patents (and IPRs more general) in an international context. The role patents may play in stimulating technology transfer is reviewed, but also critical remarks are made with respect to the ability of a strict patent system alone to achieve technological developments of the poorest nations.

20.1 Introduction

Intellectual property rights (IPRs) are high on the agenda of policy makers, academics and business firms. Now that knowledge and immaterial products are becoming more and more important in the world economy, IPRs are more crucial than ever. With rapid technological developments in many fields, policy makers are asking themselves how to adapt the existing systems of IPRs to the changing circumstances. What guidance can economic theory give them in this process?

Especially in the process of economic development, the role of knowledge can hardly be underestimated. The economic history of the world shows that, in the long run, only by applying new production techniques and introducing new products can the level of welfare be increased. The development of such new processes and new products is a goal that is actively pursued by both governments and private firms. In light of the development issue, technology transfer from developed to developing nations is a major topic of interest. IPRs are a major issue in this respect, with two potentially conflicting implications. On the one hand, IPRs are demanded by those who own the knowledge to be transferred, so that some control over where it is distributed remains in their hands. On the other hand, those who are on the receiving end of the knowledge transfer are afraid that (strong) IPRs limit the transferred knowledge and its beneficial applications.

It is the main question of this chapter to outline the chief economic arguments in this debate around the role of IPRs in the world economy. In order to provide a background to this debate, it is necessary to establish the economic function of patents. That will be the first task undertaken below. It will be argued that patents, more than other forms of IPRs (such as copyrights and trademarks), are important for the dynamic performance of the economy.

A fundamental question in this respect is how economic analysis can guide the design of a patent system. Here, issues such as the patent length (duration), breadth (scope of protection) and height (novelty requirements) are analyzed. Although there are many formal models of the patent system that can help in outlining the relevant economic processes, these do not offer, as will be argued below, very concrete guidance. The main reason is that these models are too abstract to be applied in practical terms. It will be argued that only detailed case studies of existing patents in combination with the study of technological systems can provide practical insights into how broad patents should be.

With this background in the economic theory of patents, one may address the issue of the role of IPRs in the global economy, and their implications for the prospects of developing nations. The discussions around this issue are dominated by the role of the main institutional arrangement that has emerged over the last decade: the so-called TRIPs agreement. This agreement, which has been interwoven into the talks on liberalizing trade and investment flows, sets a uniform minimum level of patent protection for all countries that participate in the World Trade Organization (WTO). Whether such a uniform level is beneficial from a global point of view, and whether or not the actually implemented minimum level is too high, has been a major point of debate ever since the first plans for TRIPs. It is the aim of this paper to discuss the economic theory around these issues, and to use this theory to derive some conclusions on where the debate could further develop.

The rest of this paper is organized as follows. Section 2 briefly outlines some developments in the economic theory on growth. It will be argued that patents play a crucial role in modern growth (theory). The section will also introduce the concept of technology spillovers. Section 3 will outline the economic functions of patents, and also introduce the concepts of patent breadth and patent length. Section 4 will come back to the issue of spillovers, and their link to patents. The issue of patent breadth will be analyzed, taking into account the economic importance of spillovers. Section 5 provides an overview of the main factors through which IPRs have an impact on development and technology transfer. This section also outlines the main developments at a practical level, i.e., how international IPR regimes converged into the TRIPs agreement that has been in effect since 1996. Section 6 provides a summary and discussion of the main arguments. Some specific recommendations will be made with regard to supportive policies in the field of international IPRs.

20.2 Technology and the Economy

The importance of technology for economic growth is obvious to anybody who has even a vague notion of the history of technology or the history of the world economy. The prolonged growth of GDP per capita (which, admittedly, is an imperfect measure of what matters for the quality of human life) since the (first) Industrial Revolution was made possible by a combination of entirely new processes and new products, which kept being introduced into the economy at what appears to have been an increasing rate (see, e.g., Landes, 1969, Maddison, 1991 and Freeman and Soete, 1997).

Despite the load of historical evidence, (mainstream) economic theory, however, until very recently, was not very comfortable with the relation between economic growth and technology. Formal theorists as economists are today, they were rather uneasy with the 'qualitative' work by 'pre-modern' economists such as Marx (1981) and Schumpeter (1939), who had kept closer links with the historical evidence and given technology a central role in their analysis.

The dominant theory of economic growth (Solow, 1956) was based on the cornerstone of all modern economic analysis, namely that of 'decreasing marginal returns'. This notion refers to the fact that if one keeps adding more and more capital (machines, buildings) to a production process, the additional value generated by this capital will keep falling, until it eventually becomes zero. This concept, which dates back to Marshall (1890), is very central in economic analysis because it enables the theorist to calculate the outcome of a rational decision-making process. For example, using this assumption, it is possible to derive an upward-sloping supply curve ('the higher the price that can be obtained in a competitive market, the more a firm will supply') as a result of profit-maximization by firms. Without the assumption of decreasing marginal returns, the supply curve would not be upward-sloping.

However, when marginal returns keep falling until they are zero, long-run economic growth is only possible if some 'exogenous' factor is assumed to be present. This could, for example, be technical change that falls as 'manna from heaven', or is given by 'God and the engineers'. Such exogenous factors, by definition, are not affected by economic decisions, and that is why economic models did not have very much to say about growth.

It was only recently (e.g., Romer, 1986, Grossman and Helpman, 1991) that economists were willing to admit that with technological change that is motivated by economic goals, the assumption of zero marginal returns in the long run was impossible to maintain. Investment in technology and R&D is a way to avoid them, and to keep returns to capital positive in the long run. This opened the way for a wholly new class of so-called 'endogenous growth models', in which long-run growth can be explained without resorting to exogenous technological change. In these models, firms' decisions on research and development (R&D) are explicitly modeled as profit-driven activities. Patents are always assumed to exist, and usually they are even assumed to hold forever. The large majority of the 'endogenous growth literature', however, does not analyze the institutional setup of the patent system (notable exceptions are Bucci and Saglam, 2000 and O'Donoghue and Zweimüller, 1998).

Although not all of the new growth models agree on this, some (e.g., Grossman and Helpman, 1991) argue that the mere existence of R&D by firms is not enough to solve the problem that decreasing marginal returns pose for economic growth. They argue that long-run positive economic growth is only possible when technological change displays so-called 'externalities' or 'spillovers'. By this notion, they refer to the idea that a technological invention is of use not only to its inventor, but also to other firms in the economy. The nature of technology, as will be argued in more detail in the next section, makes it possible that other firms than the original inventor can use (parts of) it as well.

Grossman and Helpman, as well as other 'new growth theorists', argue that without spillovers, long-run economic growth will cease. The intuition behind this finding is that while innovations keep occurring, there will be more and more competition and therefore profits for each (new) innovation fall. Spillovers provide a source of falling R&D costs, without which R&D becomes too expensive relative to the eventual pay-offs. Although their models, as well as this specific proposition, remain to be tested empirically (e.g., Jones, 1995), their assertion clearly illustrates the importance of the spillover concept for the economy. The question arises, however, why a firm would invest in R&D if other firms may reap (part of) the benefits of this investment. Obviously, this is where a system of intellectual property rights (IPRs), more specifically a patent system, comes in.

20.3 Patents as Incentives for R&D

20.3.1 The appropriability problem

In a sense, technological knowledge is an economic good in which firms (and governments) invest money. Competition between firms is based on product quality (including service) and price. In both of these aspects of the competitive process, technology plays an important role. The price of a good depends on productivity and the costs of inputs such as labour, raw materials, machines and buildings. By enhancing productivity, technological change may lead to a dramatic fall of the price charged by the firm that implements such process innovations. Other firms in the same business are then forced to drop their prices as well, or else they will be driven out of the market. How this may lead to dramatic price falls is illustrated well by an historical example quoted in Freeman and Soete (1997, p. 60). Over the period 1870-1898, the price of steel (in $ per ton) fell by 83%, or an average of almost 3% per year. This tremendous drop coincided with a period in which important innovations in steel-making (most notably the Bessemer process) were applied in the American economy.

Investment in technological change may also be aimed at product innovation. Moore's law is perhaps the most famous example of rapid product innovation. Gordon Moore, the co-founder and chairman of the Intel corporation, predicted in the 1960s that the complexity (measured as the number of components put on one chip) of so-called integrated circuits would double every 18 months. For the firm that was leading this development (i.e., Intel), this high rate of product innovation led to a dominant market position, which, nowadays, is challenged by only a handful of competitors.

It would thus appear from such anecdotal evidence that firms have more than enough reason to invest in research and development (R&D) in order to increase their competitive position. Why then is a system of intellectual property rights necessary to stimulate investment in R&D? The answer to this problem lies in the fact that technology has a number of special characteristics that are not often found in other economic goods. A normal economic good (say, an orange) is both rival and excludable. This means that only one person can consume or use the orange (rivalry), and the supplier of the orange can exclude persons from consuming it (i.e., those who are not prepared to pay for the orange). These two characteristics, which hold for the large majority of all goods in modern economies, ensure that these goods will be produced in a market economy. A farmer is willing to grow oranges because, due to the rival and excludable character of the orange, she is able to sell the oranges on the market and earn a profit.

Technological knowledge is a good for which the characteristics of rivalry and excludability do not hold perfectly. Imagine a situation without intellectual property rights. If a firm were to invest to develop a new chip, its competitors would be able to copy the knowledge embodied in this circuit by buying a single unit of the new product, and reverse-engineer it. In other words, the knowledge embodied in the chip is non-rival (the fact that one firm uses it does not imply that other firms cannot use the same knowledge), and is non-excludable (there is no way the inventor can exclude others from using the knowledge she developed, except for the trivial case that the knowledge is not used in any way).

There would thus be no incentive for a firm to invest in such knowledge. Without protection of its intellectual property, other firms can free-ride on the efforts of the inventor, and, hence, assuming that imitation is cheaper than developing the invention, put the new product on the market for a far lower price than the original inventor. This is why non-excludability pose a problem in terms of incentives to produce these goods. Non-rivalry (or spill-overs), however, implies at least a potential economic benefit: from the point of view of the economy as a whole it is rather desirable that something is produced by only one firm can be used by many.

Besides technological knowledge, there are a number of other goods that have the characteristics of non-rivalry and non-excludability. Examples are national defense and clean air (one cannot exclude individual citizens from either of those goods, and they can be consumed by numerous people at the same time). In economic theory, these goods are said to be characterized by market failure, i.e., a free market economy will either not produce these goods at all, or produce them in quantities far too small for the existing demand. National defense and clean air (as well as other examples one may think of) are goods that are usually supplied by public governments. This is why these goods are called public goods.

However, public provision is not the only way in which market failure of non-rival and non-excludable goods may be dealt with. The system of IPRs can be considered as an institution that tries to solve the problem of market failure by providing private producers with incentives to supply public goods. As such, a system of IPRs is thus one of the possible ways to solve the problem of market failures. The next section will provide an overview of all of these mechanisms, and discuss the advantages and disadvantages of IPRs (relative to the other remedies for market failure) in some detail.

20.3.2 Ways of stimulating invention

David (1993) discusses the three P's of trying to solve market failure in the area of technological change: Patronage, Procurement and Property Rights (or Patents). All three mechanisms are actually used to stimulate the development of new knowledge in practice, although they are related to different parts of the R&D infrastructure. The first P, Patronage, refers to the process where government finances a group of researchers to undertake R&D, and thus provide new knowledge. This is the system that is most widely used for basic science, where publicly financed universities or public research labs play a large role in pushing forward the frontier of knowledge. Note that this is similar to the solution of market failure in the case of standard public goods such as defense.

Procurement refers to the process where governments engage in contracts over the development of a specific piece of knowledge. Thus, public authorities may identify a specific problem for which a technical solution seems feasible, and they contract a specific group of researchers to develop this solution. Of course, often, the same researchers who work in universities or government labs are engaged in competitive bids for government-procured research projects, so that the two systems overlap in practice.

As David (1993, p. 32) notes, the procedures of procurement and patronage suffer from the problem of setting the prices right. How much should governments invest in research grants to universities, and how much should they be prepared to pay for a specific project undertaken to solve a predefined technical problem? These are questions that are difficult, if not impossible, to answer. The third P, Property rights, provides at least a theoretical way out of this problem, for a special class of technological knowledge.

A part of knowledge generated through research and development leads to possibilities for products and processes that have commercial value. With a system of property rights, i.e., a (temporary) legal monopoly granted to one firm, these goods can be supplied on the free market. Thus, a system of property rights leaves to the market to decide what a 'fair' price for technological knowledge embodied in a product or process is. The incentive problem is solved by legally excluding others than the inventor (or patent holder) from using the technical information. Thus the patent holder is enabled to make a profit on her research.

Obviously, there are also certain disadvantages to granting a monopoly. With 'normal' economic goods (i.e., rival and excludable goods), economic theory clearly shows that a market with many suppliers and many buyers produces more welfare than a market in which only one (monopoly) or a few (oligopoly) suppliers are active. Put in simple terms, monopoly firms charge too high prices from a societal point of view. This is why public governments often pursue an active anti-trust and pro-competition policy. The trade-off between the advantages of a monopoly provided by patents and the disadvantages is often discussed as the trade-off between static efficiency (stimulating competition) and dynamic efficiency (stimulating invention through patents) (see, e.g., Kamien and Schwartz, 1982). The trade-off also plays an important role in the tension between government policies aimed at science and technology and anti-trust policy. In the context of European integration, for example, strict rules have been set to technology policy in order to ensure that it does not intervene with competition policy.[2]

Besides the problem of monopolies charging too high a price, there are also a number of other disadvantages to the patent system. David (1993) discusses the so-called 'common-pool' problem. This refers to the notion that firms often compete for the same invention, which leads to so-called patent races, in which the winner typically takes all (see, e.g., Dasgupta and Stiglitz, 1980). The common pool problem presents two problems from the point of view of social benefits and costs. According to David (1993), first, "it is likely that from the viewpoint of society there will be too many contestants in the races for priority in discovery and invention. Those entering consider only what they individually stand to gain, and they do not take into account the effect of their participation on the expected outcomes of all the other competitors" (p. 33). These effects on the outcomes of other contestants are obviously negative, for the more competitors there are, the smaller the probability for each of them to be first. In other words, when potential inventors fish in a common pool of knowledge, resources will be spent in a wasteful way (from the point of view of the total economy). Second, again citing David (1993), "there is a tendency for private rents to be dissipated in the scramble for the prize of priority and all that it would bring. The private value of arriving at a new finding a little sooner than the second-place contestant is likely to exceed greatly the benefit that society would derive from the slight advantage in the date of discovery" (p. 33).

Thus, although patents do not only entail positive effects on welfare, most economic treatments of the subject would conclude that overall, the benefits of a patent system are positive (e.g., van Dijk, 1994, Scherer and Ross, 1990). For example, Mazzoleni and Nelson (1998, p. 281) conclude: "In some areas, patent rights certainly are economically and socially productive in generating invention, spreading technological knowledge, inducing innovation and commercialization, and providing some degree of order in the development of broad technological prospects. However, in many areas of technology this is not the case". This conclusion leaves, however, at least

[2] Business research sponsored by the European Commission is limited to the so-called pre-competitive phase.

two issues to be resolved. First, whether patents (or IPRs in general) are efficient means of reaching their goal (stimulating invention and commercialization thereof), and second, whether anything can be said about the design of patents.

With regard to the first question, it has been argued that firms have alternative options for appropriating the return to R&D investment, and that these alternative options are often used more than patents. Levin, Klevorick *et al.* (1987), in a survey among large firms in the U.S., and Arundel and Van de Paal (1995) for European large firms, found that secrecy, establishing a lead-time, an effective marketing campaign, and learning effects were measures of protecting knowledge that were considered to be more effective than patents by many (although not all) firms. Similar conclusions had been reached in earlier studies such as Taylor and Silberston (1973). Mazzoleni and Nelson (1998) argue that the above-mentioned studies which arrive at the conclusion that patenting is often only a minor tool in appropriating knowledge are biased towards large firms. Many of the ways in which these large firms appropriate knowledge are closely related to their size (marketing budget, learning effects), and hence small firms may have to rely more on patents.

Important differences in this respect exist between industries, or the knowledge bases underlying and the institutions surrounding them. For example, in the pharmaceuticals sector, due in part to the fact that copying of chemical substances is very precise and rather cheap, and given that authorities request detailed information about the contents of medicines, patent protection is considered to be very important. In the electronics sector, short product life cycles often make patents relatively inefficient, although most of the larger electronic firms hold large patent portfolios. Thus, the so-called 'propensity to patent innovations' differs considerably between different industries.

With regard to the issue of the design of the patent system, economic analysis has mainly analyzed the question how an 'optimal' patent should be designed. An optimal patent is one that maximizes the welfare of the invention it concerns, or, in other words, one that strikes the best balance between the positive and negative effects of patents as outlined above. In this respect, the issues of patent length (duration of the monopoly right) and patent breadth (scope of protection) have been widely analyzed.[3]

Increasing the length of a patent obviously increases the amount of profits the inventor may draw from her invention, but it also increases the welfare losses due to monopoly power. Nordhaus (1969) was the first to address

[3] Van Dijk (1994) also uses the concept of height, which refers to the novelty requirements.

the issue of patent length in a formal setting. In his analysis, the optimal patent length depends on the price elasticity of demand, and the elasticity of the extent of technical improvements with regard to R&D expenditures. With higher price elasticity of demand for the new product, the optimal patent length is shorter, because the high monopoly price implies a large welfare loss. If larger productivity increases are achieved with a given level of R&D, the optimal length of the patent will also be shorter, because R&D is cheap, and hence the incentive does not need to be very large.

Following Klemperer (1990), the formal literature mostly considers the issue of patent breadth in a context of so-called horizontal product differentiation.[4] In this approach, technological innovation is seen as a process that produces more variants of a consumption good. Because consumer tastes differ, each new variant creates its own demand, without fully capturing the market.[5] A broad patent then captures a large part of the horizontally differentiated product space. As in the case of patent length, the optimal breadth depends on a number of model parameters, such as various elasticities. Van Dijk's (1994, p. 113) conclusion that "the exact conditions for choosing an imitation or improvement strategy are not particularly important because they depend on specific modeling assumptions" in a strict sense refers only to his own model of patent height and breadth, but strikes me as reasonably valid for the field as a whole.

20.4 Patents and Technology Spillovers

The technological knowledge that is described in a patent application is useful not only to the patent applicant but also to other inventors in the same field. Although these other inventors are not allowed to use the patented knowledge in a product or process that will be used for economic purposes, the knowledge in a patent may still be useful to them in different ways. For example, this knowledge may give them new ideas for inventions. Also, the knowledge described in a patent often increases the general stock of knowledge in a field, such as would, for example, be the case if a patent describes

[4] With horizontal product differentiation, products are differentiated into variants that cannot be ranked in terms of some objective quality measure, but are nonetheless distinct (for example, the commodity fruits is horizontally differentiated into apples, oranges, etc.). With vertical product differentiation, product variants can be ranked according to quality, e.g., French wine has a higher quality than Norwegian wine. In the latter case, consumers will choose on the basis of quality-price ratios.

[5] In terms of the example in the previous footnote, some people will always prefer oranges to new (e.g., genetically engineered) variants of fruit.

that some technical procedure is possible to carry out. Also, some patent systems, such as the European one, require the patent applicant to reveal so-called non-claimable knowledge if this is relevant to the device or procedure described in the patent.

Thus, even if a patent precludes pure imitation of an invention, it does not rule out all externalities related to it. The patent provides the inventor with a monopoly that enables her to generate profits and hence provides an incentive for the research effort, but it leaves certain aspects of the technological knowledge to be exploited by others than the original inventor. How much is left to others to explore, and, thus, how much can be appropriated by the inventor, depends on the breadth of the patent.

The fact that patents, at least patents that are not too broad, leave open externalities is an important distinction with other types of IPRs. For example, trademarks and, perhaps to a lesser extent, copyrights do not induce any externalities, or at least not to the same extent as patents do. When a firm takes out a trademark, it basically seeks protection for its marketing activities. Obviously, marketing does not carry the same amount of spillovers as research and development, although, in some cases, it might be just as effective a means of strategic advantage for a firm. Given the economic importance of spillovers (or externalities) that was underlined above, this clearly establishes the special importance of patents as compared to certain other types of IPRs.[6] One could say that a patenting system has an important bearing on the dynamic efficiency (growth potential) of an economy, while this is less obvious for other types of IPRs.

This also implies that the breadth of patents has important consequences for the growth potential of the economy. Usually, however, the models of optimal patent design, which were discussed briefly in the previous section, do not consider these dynamic effects. They are limited to the static welfare effects of patents, i.e., they compare the welfare costs and benefits of a patent without taking into account the effect a patent may have on future innovation (through spillovers). Important exceptions to this are Scotchmer (1991) and Scotchmer and Green (1990), as well as the less formal, qualitative literature on patent breadth. The latter branch of literature started with

[6] Trademarks, for example, are mainly used for advertising, and this does not obviously generate externalities. Copyrights on, for example, computer code do not imply disclosure of the underlying 'blueprints' (source code) and hence also generate limited externalities. Clearly, this does not mean that copyrights or trademarks are not important for the economy. There are good economic, legal and other reasons for the existence of these forms of IPRs.

early contributions by Kitch (1977) and Beck (1981), while Mazzoleni and Nelson (1998) is a recent contribution.

Taking into account the spillover effect of patents on the productivity of future research, one is faced with a familiar trade-off. On the one hand, broader patents reduce spillovers to other firms than the inventor. Although in principle these spillovers could be 'internalized' by the patent holder, i.e., the beneficial effects on future invention could be captured by the patent holder, this internalization is unlikely to be complete. For example, in the case of a 'general-purpose technology', the scope of the firm that holds the patent is unlikely to cover the complete spectrum of possible applications of the spillovers, and/or transaction costs for licensing may be too high to allow efficient spread of the spillovers to other firms. Thus, broad patents are bad for spillovers, and, hence, bad for dynamic performance of the economy.

On the other hand, broader patents increase the (potential) pay-off to the patent holder, and hence the incentive for invention is increased. By increasing the number of inventions, obviously, also the amount of spillovers is increased. Whether broader patents increase or decrease the amount of knowledge available for spillovers thus depends on the various elasticities involved in this process.

How this trade-off turns out, and hence whether or not broad patents are good for dynamic performance of the economy, is hard to judge in a purely theoretical approach. Without an idea of the empirical facts, it is likely that such theory runs into the same problems as were signaled above for the 'static' models of patent breadth. The outcome depends on model parameters, and the models are too abstract to make empirical estimation of the parameters possible. Thus, case studies of specific sectors, technologies and countries are very useful with regard to the question of patent breadth.

For example, recent practical discussions in the field of IPRs focus on the scope of protection that should be offered on inventions in fields such as computer software, integrated circuit designs, and biotechnology (life) (see, e.g., Chapters 11-15 in Wallerstein, Mogee *et al.*, 1993, as well as Van Wijk and Junne, 1993). The general tendency of the discussion has been to offer more extensive protection for these technological fields than was possible on the basis of the legal arrangements some years ago (when these technologies were just coming into existence).

Mazzoleni and Nelson (1998) warn against such a trend of broadening patent protection. They argue that when technological change proceeds in "cumulative systems" (p. 281), broad patents are potentially hampering to the rate of invention. The danger they see is that an early, broad patent in such a field locks out firms who do not have access to this patent, especially if transaction costs for licensing are high. In other words, although they do not use the term 'spillovers' or 'externalities', they make exactly the same argument against broad patents as has been made above using the idea of spillovers. Merges and Nelson (1990) discuss a number of specific examples from the (recent) history of technology to support the case that broad patents hinder spillovers, due to, among other things, high transaction costs for licensing.

I tend to support the Mazzoleni and Nelson conclusion that broad patents are potentially dangerous. There is no need to use the patent system to aim to internalize all the spillovers of invention to a single firm (i.e., the inventor). This would essentially come down to eliminating a large part of the potential benefits to the economy at large, because no single firm is large enough to fully exhaust the possibilities of important inventions in key technology fields. The aim of a patent should be to provide a firm with the possibility to make a fair profit in order to earn back its R&D costs. It is therefore perfectly sound to leave a large part of the spillovers to outsiders, and thereby increase the overall benefits to the economy. As was argued in Section 2, this is the basic idea behind modern growth theory, a part of which argues that without such spillovers, long-run growth would converge to zero.

In many respects, the studies by Mazzoleni and Nelson (1998) and Merges and Nelson (1990) reach conclusions opposite to those in the early contributions by Kitch (1977) and Beck (1981). These authors were arguing in favour of broad patents, essentially to rule out inefficiencies in the coordination between many contestants in a patent race following an early basic patent in a field. They recommend that such an early basic patent should be broad, so that the firm that holds it may either explore the field on its own, or license the patent to the other firms that are most promising with regard to success in R&D. It is thus seen that no strong conclusion has yet been reached in this literature. Some recommendations for future research will be made below.

The World Bank (1998), finally, although it argues in general terms for increasing the breadth of patents on a worldwide scale (the so-called TRIPs agreement, see below), warns against too broad protection in the specific field of gene splicing, on the account that this is a technology with such a broad range of applications that patents run the risk of locking out too many spillovers.

20.5 Patents and Technology Transfer: a Short Review of the Debate

Intellectual Property Rights (IPRs) are an important factor in the debate on the role of institutions in technology transfer (Yankey, 1987, Van Wijk and Junne, 1993). As was already seen above, patents are the form of intellectual property rights most closely associated with technological inventions. By technology transfer, this paper will refer to the process in which technological knowledge developed and (first) applied in the developed countries (say, OECD countries) is transferred to countries with lower levels of technological knowledge (as embodied in their productive process). It has to be recognized that the latter set of countries is in fact a very heterogeneous group, including, for example, the so-called Newly Industrialized Countries (NICs), as well as countries with pre-industrial agricultural economies.

The twofold aim of the patent system – first, to protect an inventor from imitation and hence to increase the incentive for inventive activity, and, second, to stimulate the dissemination of technical information, so that it can be used in further inventive activity, thereby increasing the system-wide rate of invention – is again relevant for the debate here. Obviously, the second aim (diffusion) is closely associated with technology transfer, something that is actively pursued by both national governments and international organizations. However, just as in the general case for a patent system discussed above, there might be some tension between appropriation (first aim of the patent system) and technology transfer. Broadly speaking, the literature discerns four different ways in which patents have an impact on development and/or technology transfer (e.g., Yankey, 1987, Van Wijk and Junne, 1993):

1. Strong(er) patent protection in developing nations may increase the inventive efforts in the developing countries themselves, and thereby increase the rate of growth in these countries.
2. Patents allow for (international) licensing, so that firms in developing countries may buy technology from firms in (technologically) more advanced nations (technology transfer).
3. Strong(er) patent protection may be necessary to induce firms from developed countries to engage in one of many different economic transactions that may lead to technology transfer. One may think of Foreign Direct Investment (FDI), exports (to developing nations) of capital goods embodying technological knowledge, joint ventures between firms in developing and developed

countries, etc. Without some form of protection of their knowledge in the foreign markets, firms from developed nations may choose not to engage in these activities, because they run the risk of their knowledge being copied.

4. Developing nations that do not provide a system for protection of intellectual property of imported technology run the risk of retaliation in terms of trade restrictions. Especially the U.S. government has (recently) been active to enforce protection of intellectual property of U.S. firms by means of trade measures (Van Wijk and Junne, 1993).

All of these reasons are not only subject to academic debate by theorists, they were and are also subject of intense negotiations in international organizations such as the World Intellectual Property Organization (WIPO) and the World Trade Organization (WTO) (see, e.g., Mody, 1990, Van Wijk and Junne, 1993, and World Bank, 1998). Van Wijk and Junne (1993) describe how in the 1960s and 1970s, the large majority of developing countries began to oppose the implementation of a (strong) patent system in their own economies:

> "Developing countries did not deny that industrial property systems could encourage industrialization, but contended that in developing countries, due to the weak economic and technological structures, they did not bring the desired benefits. It was argued that in developing countries the privileges created by the industrial property systems failed both to stimulate inventions among their own nationals and did not encourage the rapid transfer, appropriate adaptation or widespread diffusion of imported technology" (p. 22).

Thus, the argument was twofold: first that the technological capabilities of firms in developing countries were too low to generate important new innovations (point 1 above), despite the existence of a patent system, and, second, that the desired technology transfer (points 2-4 above) did not materialize. In 1975, UNCTAD published a study (UNCTAD, 1975) that presented a lot of evidence in favour of this position. For example, the report outlined statistical trends illustrating the marginal role of developing countries in total patents granted in the world. Moreover, it showed that in developing countries, the large majority (typically, more than three quarters) of patents granted was controlled by foreign firms (from the developed world).

The argument that developing countries can hardly contribute to the advancement of the technological frontier remains valid, even more so today. This is related to the limited amount of resources available in these countries, in terms of human capital, funds to be invested in frontier research, and cumulated experience in research. Corporate R&D, and patenting, are a matter for the developed nations and, within them, mostly for the five or so largest countries (European Commission, 1998). Thus, without policy measures aimed at increasing the indigenous research capabilities of developing countries, a patent system can hardly be expected to be an efficient means of stimulating innovations in the poorer parts of the world, especially in a political climate where free trade is high on the agenda.

The role of licensing (factor 2 above) was also shown to be important only for a limited set of countries. In order to use licensed knowledge effectively, firms in developing countries need a certain level of technological sophistication of their own. Analogous to the point of indigenous research capabilities raised above, this is exactly what was often lacking, due to shortages of human capital etc. Some even went so far as to suggest compulsory licensing as a means to effectuate technology transfer, but this is extremely difficult, because mere licensing without the transfer of (tacit) know-how from the side of the patent holder cannot be expected to be efficient (Yankey, 1987). The ineffectiveness of compulsory licensing is also shown by the limited number of cases of such arrangements (typically less than 5 per country over the period of a decade; see Yankey, 1987, Table 2.1).

In practice, one observes that only certain countries are able to use technology licensing as an effective way of (inward) technology transfer. Typically, in these cases, technology licensing goes hand in hand with the build-up of domestic technological capabilities. Freeman (1994) discusses the case of the Korean firm Samsung, which effectively used licensing agreements with various Western European and U.S. companies to build up its own technological capability. Over time, Freeman observed a rapid tendency for Samsung to switch from reliance on licensing agreements to developing its own frontier technology. In fact, taking R&D intensity and patenting as indicators, Korea, as well as other South-East Asian NICs, can be seen to converge rapidly to the technology frontier in the course of the 1990s (e.g., European Commission, 1998, for recent data, and Soete and Verspagen, 1993, for a theoretical and empirical analysis). In general terms, the conclusion seems justified that technology licensing may be a useful part of a policy aimed at building up local technology capabilities, but it is only a part of such a policy.

Based on the arguments on the role of patenting in developing countries, a political discussion took place in the 1970s and 1980s between developing countries and developed nations, in which the issue of patent protection in developing nations was heavily debated. In broad terms, the developing nations argued for less strong patent protection in their own economies, while the developed world called for global strengthening of patent protection. Van Wijk and Junne (1993) provide an overview of this debate, as well as some of the finer (legal) details as they were discussed at various conferences organized by WIPO. They also describe how, at the end of the 1980s, the developed nations started to pull away this debate from WIPO, trying to integrate the issue of intellectual property rights with issues of free trade. This trend had started in the US in the first half of the 1980s (Granstrand, 1999, Ch. 2). In practical terms, this meant that negotiations about intellectual property rights were integrated into the Uruguay Round. This implied that negotiations about free trade were coupled with negotiations on IPRs, leading eventually to the so-called Trade Related aspects of Intellectual Property (TRIPs) agreement.

The TRIPs agreement is a part of the WTO, and sets minimum levels of intellectual property protection for the whole range of forms of IPRs (patents, copyrights, trademarks, industrial designs, etc.). It also requires signatories to establish certain basic legal measures to prevent infringement. Disputes over TRIPs are subject to the same settlement procedures as WTO in general. TRIPs became effective in 1996, but developing countries are granted several transition periods applying to specific parts of the agreement, so that it will become fully effective only in 2006.

The TRIPs agreement means that countries that do not respect the minimum levels of IPRs set can now expect retaliation measures in terms of trade restrictions (point 4 above). Van Wijk and Junne (1993) point out that this is an especially effective measure in combination with the trend found in many developing countries to switch from a policy of import substitution to export-led growth. Obviously, export-led growth crucially depends on access to world markets, and hence the pressure to respect the IPR levels set by TRIPs becomes larger.

Thus, in the late 1990s, the debate on the role of patents in technology transfer mainly focuses on points 3 and 4 of the above list. The first two points, i.e., the (direct) impact of a patent system on domestic inventive activity in developing nations, as well as the issue of technology licensing, were shown to depend crucially on domestic technological capabilities. These can only be built up by means of a broad policy which includes, besides IPRs, also elements such as (semi-)public research facilities, education and training of the labour force, and industrial and trade policies.

With the TRIPs agreement in effect, the consensus on the issue of IPRs and technology transfer seems indeed to converge to the points 3 and 4 listed above. The uniform and strong IPRs are generally considered to stimulate technology transfer by means of FDI, joint ventures and by stimulating international trade in general. Mansfield (1993, 1994, and 1995) provides some empirical evidence for this assumed relationship.

The first two of these papers by Mansfield analyzes survey data obtained for 100 U.S. firms in a range of industries. About half of the firms in this sample reported that strength or weakness of IPRs has a strong effect on whether or not direct investment will be made. This effect was found to be strongest in the chemicals and electrical equipment sectors, and to apply mostly to investment related to R&D facilities and facilities to manufacture complete products. The top countries that were reported as having too weak IPRs to permit investment in joint ventures with local partners were India (44% of respondents indicate IPRs are too weak), Nigeria (33%), Brazil (32%), Thailand (31%), Indonesia and Taiwan (28%). The same countries were reported to have IPRs too weak to permit transfer of the newest or most effective technology to wholly owned subsidiaries, or to permit licensing of the newest or most effective technology. Mansfield (1995) extends the survey to Japanese and German firms, and also undertakes more sophisticated econometric testing. The findings, again, show that weak IPRs may be an important barrier to technology transfer.

The World Bank, in its World Development Report 1998/99, also champions strong and uniform IPRs as in the TRIPs agreement. Their empirical evidence mainly consists of the Mansfield surveys mentioned above. Despite this apparent consensus, the academic debate on the issue of TRIPs is far from conclusive. Siebeck (1990) concluded that the theory did not provide any strong answers on how strong IPRs in developing countries should be, and that the empirical studies on the issue were too few to allow firm conclusions. In 1992, a conference was convened at the National Academy of Sciences in the U.S., which debated the issues. In the proceedings, which were published as Wallerstein, Mogee *et al.* (1993), no firm conclusion was reached on whether a uniform system of strong IPRs was to be preferred over a system with international differentiation in IPRs.[7] Since then, although the first of these two variants now seems the *de facto* situation since

[7] See, e.g., the contributed chapters by Sherwood (1993) and Frischtak (1993).

TRIPs came into effect, the theoretical debate has not supplied the final answer, as will be argued in the next section.

20.6 Discussion and Issues for Further Research

The debate on the strength and scope of IPRs briefly outlined in the previous sections is still largely unresolved, at least at an academic level, and more theoretical and empirical research is necessary to arrive at useful conclusions. This section will attempt to outline three angles from which further contributions may be made. These three points are all somewhat preliminary, and must be considered as starting points for further research, rather than finalized and testable propositions.

The first issue relates to the dynamic effects of patent breadth. The economic models we have available now provide a clear-cut, although admittedly somewhat abstract, argument about the static effects of patent breadth. From a static point of view, i.e., when looking at only one invention without taking into account the cumulative nature of inventions, and hence the effect that an individual patent may have on future technology, broader patents give up benefits for the consumer but they provide incentives for the inventor. An optimal point in this trade-off may be calculated under certain (abstract) assumptions. These models could be extended to take into account dynamic efficiency by analyzing how one invention may generate future inventions, and hence also what the welfare effects of these future inventions may be. The main challenge here is to find a satisfactory way of representing the dependence of one invention on previous ones. This dependence structure is often quite complicated and also usually quite impossible to predict. Hence the standard models of fully rational firm behavior may not be very useful here, and an alternative would have to be developed. In this respect, knowledge from the engineering sciences on how inventions are made, and which relevant sources of knowledge exist, as well as from practical studies on the use of patenting literature by engineers, are very relevant as inputs to more realistic economic models.

The second issue relates to the question of whether a patent regime with (more or less) uniform protection levels is desirable from a point of view of total world welfare (see Sherwood, 1993, Frischtak, 1993). As was seen above, microeconomic theory analyzes the length and breadth of patents. The length of a patent refers to its duration, while the breadth refers to the scope of protection. Nordhaus (1969) analyzed the 'optimal' patent length, and concluded that this depends on variables such as the price elasticity of product demand, and the elasticity of the extent of technical improvements with regard to R&D expenditures.

Following Klemperer (1990), the literature mostly considers the issue of patent breadth in a context of so-called horizontal product differentiation. In this approach, technological innovation is seen as a process that produces more variants of a consumption good. Because consumer tastes differ, each new variant creates its own demand, without fully capturing the market. A broad patent then captures a large part of the horizontally differentiated product space.

Van Dijk (1994, Chapter 7) presents a model in which two countries, which trade with each other, choose the optimal level of patent breadth. He arrives at the following conclusions:

> "[W]hen countries place equal weight on profits and consumers' surplus of their own citizens (...) patent breadths are too narrow. This result reflects the existence of a positive externality flowing from each country's patent breadth to the profit and consumers' surplus enjoyed by citizens of the other country. (...) [E]xcept in very special circumstances, equilibrium patent breadths are not identical in the two countries. (...) Further, if equilibrium breadths are sufficiently asymmetric, there is no symmetric patent policy that Pareto-dominates the original equilibrium" (p. 153-4).

In practical terms, these results establish three main points. First, in an international context, spillovers between countries are relevant decision variables in designing national regimes of intellectual property rights. More specifically, national governments may want to set the scope of protection at a broader level than they would if they based their policy just on national considerations. Second, there is not much theoretical support for the preference of a uniform worldwide level of patent protection (breadth) over a system with differentiated patent breadth. Third, international coordination of the scope of patent protection (breadth) does not necessarily lead to unequivocally 'better' results than a regime in which each country sets its patent policy independently of the rest of the world.[8] In fact, in discussing his results, Van Dijk makes the following, quite strong, statement:

---

[8] In the latter conclusion, the concept of 'Pareto-optimality' plays a large role in Van Dijk's analysis. This concept refers to the notion that it is difficult to weight individuals' welfare level. A so-called Pareto-improvement is one in which all individuals in the economy at least have the same level of welfare as before the improvement, and at least one individual has a

> "In terms of our model, one could say that the north has a high and the south has a low innovation density. The model predicts that asymmetric innovation densities lead to extensive patent protection in the innovation-intensive region and narrow protection in the weaker region. This situation can indeed be observed in the world (...). The proposal of northern countries, however, to extend their standards of protection to the south does not Pareto-improve the global welfare if innovation densities are too different (as they seem to be)." (p. 154-5).

Obviously, Van Dijk's model is but one in a large literature in this field. Other models of the role of international property rights regimes and international trade are, for example, Deardorff (1992), Diwan and Rodrik (1991), Helpman (1993) and Chin and Grossman (1990). All of these models are highly stylized theoretical constructs, for which one needs a great deal of imagination to apply them to practical situations.[9] Other models, such as the one by Deardorff (1991) and the one by Diwan and Rodrik (1991), are more positive towards the idea of strengthening global patent protection.[10] All in all, the conclusion reached by Primo Braga (1990), namely that economic theory does not provide a clear-cut answer to many questions in relation to technology transfer and intellectual property rights, still seems to be valid.

Nevertheless, one may draw some positive conclusions from the theoretical debate, despite its high level of abstraction and relative indeterminacy. First, it seems unlikely that the uniform and strong IPRs in TRIPs will prove beneficial from a point of view that takes into account the interests of both developed and developing nations. A case for differentiation of patent protection by levels of development can be made from an economic point of view as well as from a humanitarian or ethical (e.g., AIDS medicines) point of view. However, more empirical research is highly welcome in support of such a view. Second, it is clear that supportive measures in terms of technological capacity building may greatly increase the efficiency of technology transfer, and thus, in a way, make the TRIPs agreement (as it is presently outlined) more efficient.

---

higher level of welfare. Note that this is a rather strong requirement, because one may imagine situations in which a part of the welfare of a (small) group of individuals is 'sacrificed' for a larger improvement in the welfare of another (larger) group.

[9] See David (1993) for a general discussion of the difficulties of applying economic theory to the practice of intellectual property rights.

[10] I am afraid this is one of those situations where the (ironic) saying applies that one can always find an economist to defend one's position, no matter how outrageous this position is.

The debate of the 1970s and 1980s already clearly showed that in order for (strong) IPRs to be effective in developing countries, the domestic capability of these countries to generate and use new technologies needs to be enhanced (see above). Relatedly, the model by Van Dijk cited above points to the fact that a regime with uniform and strong worldwide IPRs may be more efficient (in terms of welfare) when differences between countries in terms of technological capabilities are small. In the above-mentioned World Development Report 1998/99, the World Bank also points to the importance of building local knowledge bases. Thus, I would argue that TRIPs is not to be considered as the final solution to problems of technology transfer and development, but rather as a most useful step in awareness of the importance of IPRs and technology in general. In addition to agreements of IPRs, the developed and developing world should continue to focus on building up domestic technological capabilities in developing countries. IPRs play an important role in this process, but there is more to it than just IPRs.

What role could international organizations such as the World Bank, WIPO and WTO play in this process? WTO, although it is the platform at which TRIPs was negotiated, and at which conflicts on TRIPs must be submitted, does not seem to be a likely candidate for such a role. Its nature as a body to enhance free trade does not easily conform to policy goals that concern domestic issues, such as the stimulation of R&D infrastructure. Moreover, IPRs are only of indirect relevance for WTO, since its main role is the promotion of free trade. The World Bank obviously has a task in this area, and the World Development Report contains many examples of how this organization attempts to help build up local knowledge infrastructures.

One may well argue that also WIPO may play a role in this process, despite the fact that one may argue that WIPO is an international platform, much like WTO, which should not 'intervene' in local issues. However, the issue of international IPRs, which is, of course, a main concern of WIPO, is indeed closely related to domestic technology capabilities, and thus the issue seems to be more at the heart of the matter for WIPO than for WTO. As I have tried to argue here, the new institutional environment (TRIPs) adds another dimension to this issue, rather than making it obsolete. Thus, given the increased need for international attention to technology capacity building in developing countries, one may imagine that WIPO would, in some way, address this issue.

The third issue that I want to address in this section builds, in a way, on the first one, because it considers the issue of patent breadth. In the econometric literature on international R&D spillovers, one of the 'hot issues' is the question whether or not such spillovers are embodied in traded goods and/or FDI. Coe, Helpman *et al.* (1997) have forcefully argued that R&D spillovers are indeed embodied in trade goods, while Lichtenberg and Van Pottelsberghe (1996) found that R&D spillovers are connected to FDI flows between countries. These papers do not investigate the causal effect between embodied (either in trade or FDI) spillovers and IPRs. Thus, a first line of research that may prove useful to the debate outlined in the previous section could be to incorporate IPRs in such models of spillovers.

However, Fagerberg and Verspagen (1998) also introduce into these models so-called disembodied spillovers. They follow earlier work by, among others, Cornwall (1977) and Abramovitz (1979) in relating these disembodied spillovers to the initial level of labour productivity in an industry. An estimated negative sign on this variable is interpreted as evidence of the hypothesis that relatively backward countries benefit from the international diffusion of technology. Because a variable taking into account trade-embodied R&D spillovers à la Coe, Helpman *et al.* is also present in the Fagerberg and Verspagen model, the effect related to initial labour productivity is interpreted as disembodied spillovers.

Fagerberg and Verspagen find that in a sample of 14 OECD countries for the period 1975-1995, disembodied spillovers have a much stronger impact on productivity growth than trade-embodied spillovers. In other words, the international diffusion of technology mainly takes place through other channels than international trade in goods. Admittedly, Fagerberg and Verspagen do not consider the effects of FDI embodied spillovers. Still, their results seem to underline the crucial importance of spillovers through other channels than embodiment (think of international mobility of labour, international contacts at conferences, scientific and technical literature, patent specifications, etc.).

One important caveat must be placed with regard to the application of these results to the relationship between technology transfer and patents. Verspagen (1991), in an empirical model that did not include any type of embodied spillovers, found that disembodied spillovers, of the type that Fagerberg and Verspagen estimate, tend to decrease with the level of the technology gap between two countries. In other words, for countries lagging far behind the world technological frontier, 'technological congruence' (Abramovitz, 1979) may be too low to allow them to benefit from disembodied spillovers. Thus, the results that Fagerberg and Verspagen find may indeed be rather specific to the set of countries included in their analysis.

Although much more research is necessary to extend the Fagerberg and Verspagen results to the issue of North-South technology transfer (e.g., extending the set of countries in the analysis, as well as taking into account FDI), the results do seem to indicate that, to a certain extent, free-riding on foreign knowledge is possible. Whether or not such a process involves substantial infringement on patent holders' rights is not clear from the Fagerberg and Verspagen analysis. However, it is well imaginable that making IPRs 'stronger', especially in those countries benefiting from the spillovers, i.e., the developing countries, reduces the scope for such disembodied spillovers. At the same time, according to the arguments set out in the previous section, such stronger IPRs may stimulate trade and FDI, and thereby increase technology transfer related to these factors. Whether or not the net effect on the amount of spillovers taking place is positive or negative is highly speculative, given the current state of the art in this field of research.

In the models discussed very briefly here, the patent system, licensing and trade in know-how do not play an explicit role. The models are rather abstract, although well-founded in historical research. A useful venue for further research seems to be a more explicit analysis of IPR systems. This could well start from an historical investigation of the role of these systems in development and catching-up-based growth, and from there be included in the existing (empirical) models.

The fourth and final issue that I would like to raise in this section concerns the topic of appropriate technology. As is well-known from the development literature, not all technologies developed in OECD countries can readily be used in developing countries. Many of these technologies, or at least their specific implementation, are specific to the (advanced) needs of the societies they are developed in, or depend on infrastructures that are not commonly found in many of the developing countries. Abramovitz (1994) has termed this 'a lack of technological congruence'.

This implies that not all R&D efforts by firms in OECD countries are relevant for the issue of technology transfer. In general, it is quite difficult to make a clear-cut distinction between sectors with more or less appropriate technology. For example, although much of the research in the electronics sector is obviously beyond the reach of many developing economies, the relatively high-tech field of mobile telephony is a well-known example of a field where diffusion potential is large in many developing countries, due to a low level of commitment to an installed base of wired communication.

However, one field for which the outcomes of R&D carried out in OECD countries clearly have large consequences for developing nations, is biotechnology (see, e.g., Acharya, 1995 and Van Wijk and Junne, 1993). The impact of biotechnology on developing countries is a vast area of research in which I cannot claim any expertise, but I would nevertheless like to conclude this paper with two observations on this field.

The first observation I would like to make is that in a field where the economic relevance of a technology is larger for developing countries than for the developed world (as one may argue biotechnology is; tropical diseases are another, perhaps even more clear case), the importance of IPRs in developing countries is especially high. Given that the market for products based on these technologies is small(er) in developed countries, strong IPRs in the developed world may simply prove to be too small an incentive to stimulate R&D (Van Wijk and Junne, 1993). This shows that generic policy recommendations may be misleading, and specific knowledge of technologies and economic, social or political circumstances is very valuable. In terms of the implications for further research, this means that case studies, well-formulated with both theoretical and policy concerns, remain of great value.

The second observation is that the 'old' concern that multinational companies from the developed world gain control over technologies that are crucial to the fate of developing countries is also especially great in those cases. The World Bank (World Development Report 1998/99, Box 2.6 and related text) discusses the issue of compensation when 'bioprospecting strikes gold'. Examples are mentioned of cases where large pharmaceutical companies from the developed world "appropriate valuable biomedical knowledge from indigenous peoples" (WDR, Box 2.6). However, a trend is also signaled in which companies provide compensation in the form of lump sum payments and/or royalty sharing to local communities. It seems to me that such a trend might well be formalized into international rules to prevent such 'reverse technology transfer' without adequate compensation.

20.7 Literature References

Abramovitz, M.A. (1979). 'Rapid Growth Potential and its Realisation: The Experience of Capitalist Economies in the Postwar Period'. *Economic Growth and Resources, Vol. 1: The Major Issues. Proceedings of the Fifth World Congress of the International Economic Association*. E. Malinvaud. London: Macmillan: 1-51.

Abramovitz, M.A. (1994). 'The Origins of the Postwar Catch-Up and Convergence Boom'. In *The Dynamics of Trade, Technology and Growth*. J. Fagerberg, B. Verspagen and N. Von Tunzelmann (eds.). Aldershot: Edward Elgar: 21-52.

Acharya, R. (1995). *The Impact of New Technologies on Economic Growth and Trade. A Case Study of Biotechnology.* Ph.D. thesis, Faculty of Economics. Maastricht, University of Limburg.

Arundel, A. and G. Van de Paal (1995). 'Innovation Strategies of Europe's Largest Industrial Firms'. Maastricht, MERIT, unpublished manuscript.

Beck, R.L. (1981). 'Competition for patent monopolies'. *Research in Law and Economics* 3: 91-110.

Bucci, A. and H.C. Saglam (2000). 'Growth Maximizing Patent Life-Time'. Discussion Paper no. 2000019, Université Catholique de Louvain, Institut de Recherches Economiques et Sociales (IRES), Belgium.

Chin, J.C. and G.M. Grossman (1990). 'Intellectual Property Rights and North-South Trade'. In *The Political Economy of International Trade. Essays in Honour of Robert E. Baldwin.* R.W. Jones and A.O. Krueger (eds.). Cambridge: Basil Blackwell.

Coe, D.T., E. Helpman, *et al.* (1997). 'North-South R&D Spillovers'. *Economic Journal* 107: 134-149.

Cornwall, J. (1977). *Modern Capitalism. Its Growth and Transformation.* London: Martin Robertson.

Dasgupta, P. and J.E. Stiglitz (1980). 'Uncertainty, industrial structure and the speed of R&D'. *Bell Journal of Economics* 11: 1-28.

David, P.A. (1993). 'Intellectual Property Institutions and the Panda's Thumb: Patents, Copyrights, and Trade Secrets in Economic Theory and History'. *Global Dimensions of Intellectual Property Rights in Science and Technology.* M.B. Wallerstein, M.E. Mogee and R.A. Schoen (eds.). Washington, D.C.: National Academy Press: 19-64.

Deardorff, A.V. (1992). 'Welfare effects of Global patent protection'. *Economica* 59: 35-51.

Denison, E. (1966). *Why growth rates differ.* Washington: Brookings Institution.

Diwan, I. and D. Rodrik (1991). 'Patents, Appropiate Technology, and North-South Trade'. *Journal of International Economics* 30: 27-47.

European Commission (1998). *The Second European Report on Science and Technology Indicators.* Luxembourg/Brussels, European Commission, DG XII.

Fagerberg, J. and B. Verspagen (1998). 'Productivity, R&D Spillovers and Trade'. ECIS Working Paper 98-1.

Freeman, C. and L. Soete (1997). *The Economics of Industrial Innovation.* 3rd ed. London and Washington: Pinter.

Freeman, C. (1994). 'Technological Revolutions and Catching-Up: ICT and the NICs'. In *The Dynamics of Trade, Technology and Growth.* J. Fagerberg, B. Verspagen and N. Von Tunzelmann (eds.). Aldershot: Edward Elgar: 198-221.

Frischtak, C.R. (1993). 'Harmonization versus Differentiation in Intellectual Property Rights Regimes'. In *Global Dimensions of Intellectual Property Rights in Science and*

Technology. M.B. Wallerstein, M.E. Mogee and R.A. Schoen (eds.). Washington, D.C.: National Academy Press: 89-106.

Granstrand, O. (1999), *The economics and management of intellectual property. Towards intellectual capitalism*. Cheltenham: Edward Elgar.

Griliches, Z. (1979). 'Issues in Assessing the Contribution of Research and Development to Productivity Growth'. *The Bell Journal of Economics* 10: 92-116.

Grossman, G.M. and E. Helpman (1991). *Innovation and Growth in the Global Economy*. Cambridge MA: MIT Press.

Helpman, E. (1993). 'Innovation, Imitation, and Intellectual Property Rights'. *Econometrica* 61: 1247-1280.

Jones, C. (1995). 'R&D based models of economic growth'. *Journal of Political Economy* 103: 759-784.

Jorgenson, D.W. and Z. Griliches (1967). 'Explanation of Productivity Change'. *Review of Economic Studies* 34: 249-283.

Kamien, M.I. and N.L. Schwartz (1982). *Market Structure and Innovation*. Cambridge, Cambridge University Press.

Kitch, E.W. (1977). 'The nature and function of the patent system'. *Journal of Law and Economics* 20: 265-290.

Klemperer, P. (1990). 'How broad should the scope of patent protection be?' *RAND Journal of Economics* 21: 113-130.

Landes, D. (1969). *The unbound Prometheus: Technological Change 1750 to the present*. Cambridge: Cambridge University Press.

Levin, R.C., A.K. Klevorick, *et al.* (1987). 'Appropriating the Returns from Industrial Research and Development'. *Brookings Papers on Economic Activity* 3: 783-820.

Lichtenberg, F. and B. Van Pottelsberghe (1996). 'International R&D Spillovers: A Re-Examination'. *NBER Working Paper 5668*.

Maddison, A. (1987). 'Growth and Slowdown in Advanced Capitalist Economies: Techniques of Quantitative Assessment'. *Journal of Economic Literature* 25: 649-698.

Maddison, A. (1991). *Dynamic Forces in Capitalist Development. A Long-Run Comparative View*. Oxford: Oxford University Press.

Mansfield, E. (1993). 'Unauthorized Use of Intellectual Property: Effects on Investment, Technology Transfer, and Innovation'. In *Global Dimensions of Intellectual Property Rights in Science and Technology*. M.B. Wallerstein, M.E. Mogee and R.A. Schoen (eds.). Washington, D.C.: National Academy Press: 107-145.

Mansfield, E. (1994). 'Intellectual Property Protection, Foreign Direct Investment and Technology Transfer'. International Finance Corporation Discussion Paper 19.

Mansfield, E. (1995). 'Intellectual Property Protection, Direct Investment and Technology Transfer: Germany, Japan and the United States'. International Finance Corporation Discussion Paper 27.

Marshall, A. (1890). *Principles of Economics*. London.

Marx, K. (1981). *Capital. Vol. 3*. Harmondsworth: Penguin.

Mazzoleni, R. and R.R. Nelson (1998). 'The benefits and costs of strong patent protection: a contribution to the current debate'. *Research Policy* 27: 273-284.

Merges, R.P. and R.R. Nelson (1990). 'On the complex economies of patent scope'. *Columbia Law Review* 90: 839-916.

Mody, A. (1990). 'New International Environment for Intellectual Property Rights'. In *Intellectual Property Rights in Science, Technology and Economic Performance*. F.W. Rushing and C. Ganz Brown (eds.). Boulder: Westview Press.

Nordhaus, W.D. (1969). *Invention, Growth and Welfare. A Theoretical Treatment of Technological Change*. Cambridge MA: MIT Press.

O'Donoghue, T. and J. Zweimüller (1998), 'Patents in a Model of Endogenous Growth'. Institute for Advanced Studies, Vienna, Economics Series no. 56.

Primo Braga, C. (1990). 'Guidance from the economic theory'. In *Strengthening Protection of Intellectual Property in Developing Countries. A Survey of the Literature*. E.W. Siebeck (ed.). Washington D.C.: World Bank Discussion Paper no. 112.

Romer, P. (1986). 'Increasing Returns and Long Run Growth'. *Journal of Political Economy* 94: 1002-1037.

Scherer, F.M. and D. Ross (1990). *Industrial Market Structure and Economic Performance*. Boston: Houghton Mifflin Company.

Schumpeter, J.A. (1939). *Business Cycles: A theoretical, historical and statistical analysis of the capitalist process*. New York: McGraw-Hill.

Scotchmer, S. (1991). 'Standing on the shoulders of giants: Cumulative research and the patent law'. *Journal of Economic Perspectives* 5: 29-41.

Scotchmer, S. and J. Green (1990). 'Novelty and disclosure in patent law'. *RAND Journal of Economics* 21: 131-146.

Sherwood, R.M. (1993). 'Why a Uniform Intellectual Property System Makes Sense for the World'. In *Global Dimensions of Intellectual Property Rights in Science and Technology*. M.B. Wallerstein, M.E. Mogee and R.A. Schoen (eds.). Washington, D.C.: National Academy Press: 68-88.

Siebeck, W.E. (ed.) (1990). 'Strengthening Protection of Intellectual Property in Developing Countries: A Survey of the Literature'. World Bank Discussion Paper 112. Washington D.C.

Soete, L. and B. Verspagen (1993). 'Technology and Growth: The Complex Dynamics of Catching Up, Falling Behind and Taking Over'. In *Explaining Economic Growth.* A. Szirmai, B. Van Ark and D. Pilat (eds.). Amsterdam: Elsevier: 101-127.

Solow, R.M. (1956). 'A Contribution to the Theory of Economic Growth'. *Quarterly Journal of Economics* 70: 65-94.

Taylor, C. and A. Silberston (1973). *The Economic Impact of the Patent System.* Cambridge: Cambridge University Press.

UNCTAD (1975). 'The Role of the Patent System in the Transfer of Technology to Developing Countries'. New York: United Nations.

Van Dijk, T. (1994). The Limits of Patent Protection. Essays on the Economics of Intellectual Property Rights. Ph.D. thesis, Faculty of Economics. Maastricht, University of Limburg.

Van Wijk, J. and G. Junne (1993). 'Intellectual Property Protection of Advanced Technology. Changes in the Global Technology System: Implications and Options for Developing Countries'. Maastricht, UNU/Intech.

Verspagen, B. (1991). 'A New Empirical Approach to Catching Up or Falling Behind'. *Structural Change and Economic Dynamics* 2: 359-380.

Wallerstein, M.B., M.E. Mogee and R.A. Schoen (eds.). (1993). *Global Dimensions of Intellectual Property Rights in Science and Technology.* Washington, D.C.: National Academy Press.

World Bank (1998). *World Development Report. Knowledge for Development. 1998/1999.* Oxford: Oxford University Press.

Yankey, G.S.-A. (1987). *International Patents and Technology Transfer to Less Developed Countries. The case of Ghana and Nigeria.* Aldershot: Avebury.

Chapter 21

SUMMARY AND REFLECTIONS UPON FURTHER DEVELOPMENTS[1]

Ove Granstrand
Chalmers University of Technology, Dept. of Industrial Management and Economics, Göteborg, Sweden

Chapter contents:

Abstract: This concluding chapter summarizes the preceding chapters, using a common structure, which throughout the chapters highlights their main focus, key/novel concepts, approach/empirical data, main findings/arguments, and suggestions for further research. The diversity of the chapters in these respects is rich, which is perhaps not so surprising, but there are also clear differences between the two groups of chapters representing economics and law. This observation gives reason to reflect over the past and future interaction between these two disciplines in the IP field. The need for pluralism in choice of research problems and methods, as well as the need for disciplinary perspectives complementary to economics and law, is pointed out. At the same time, the advent of the IP era has led to a rapidly growing research agenda, calling for some priorities. The chapter also reflects on some priorities for interdisciplinary research and teaching on the economics and law of intellectual property. The chapter ends with a speculative reflection about the future of the IP system and its interaction with the economic and legal systems.

[1] Helpful comments on this chapter have been received from Ulf Petrusson.

O. Granstrand (ed.), Economics, Law and Intellectual Property, 519-562.

21.1 Summary of Previous Chapters

What can be learnt from the foregoing chapters, viewed as a collection or sample of cases of discourses on IP? To summarize into a whole that becomes more than its parts is not easy. IP, with all its facets and pervasiveness, is hardly coherent enough to be coherently dealt with in the first place, let alone in a comprehensive way. This fact is reflected in the present book's intellectual variety, which has also been fertilized by a deliberate diversity in disciplinary perspectives. The variety pertains to focus, concepts, methods, empirical data, theory, findings and suggestions for further research. Table 21-1 attempts to give a summarizing overview of the chapters. A few observations will be made below regarding each of the headings in Table 21-1.

21.1.1 Main focus

All chapters focus on IP in one way or another. They are all written by economists or lawyers, coming by and large from industrialized Western countries. They focus on international conditions, but more on the US than any other part of the world. The focus is mainly on contemporary IP issues, although accompanied by several historic accounts. Thus extensions of time and space perspectives would have been possible, as well as extension of disciplinary perspectives.

Several papers focus on IP within the broader context of knowledge and information and the type of economy based on these entities. Most of these papers are by economists (e.g. Arrow, Arora *et al.*, Foray and Hall, among others) while this perspective is perhaps less represented among lawyers, with the notable exception of Radin. IP issues in connection with trade secrets, know-how and databases have scarcely been focused on at all in the law chapters. One may of course ask whether this difference is representative for economics and law of IP more generally, and whether trade secrets and databases need more attention in law.

In the general context of production and distribution of information and innovation, the relative effectiveness and efficiency (in a broad sense) of the IP system versus alternative economic and legal arrangements and policies (procurement, grants, prizes, taxes etc.) are focused on in several chapters. The clearest focus on a new alternative to the IP system, and the patent system in particular, is in William Kingston's chapter. However, it seems fair to say that more systematic comparative studies, empirical and theoretical, of the pros and cons of the IP system and its alternatives are needed in general.[2] (See also the suggestion for further research offered by Bronwyn Hall.) This applies not only to economics but to law as well. The identification of comparable alternatives (be they substitutes or complements) to the IP system is then influenced by the disciplinary perspective. The economist's traditional set of alternatives is defined in terms of public vs. private provision of knowledge and information, then mostly in financial terms, while the lawyer would look for alternatives in other areas of law, such as contract and competition law.

Closely related to a focus on alternatives to the IP system is a focus on various alternative IP regimes, a somewhat loose but frequently used concept. This concept is often further qualified as open or closed, mainly in order to contrast the IP regimes in university vs. industry settings. Several authors do this and then mainly in US contexts (e.g. Hall, Nelson, Colyvas *et al.*). This focus also relates to the long-standing issue of how – if at all – to tailor the IP system as codified in law to the variety of needs in different industries. As the university sector transforms more and more into an economic institution (for better or worse), the sector could be considered an industry in itself at some point with specific needs for a tailor-made IP system. The US university industry is internationally leading, highly market (rather than government) oriented, competitive and entrepreneurial. It also has a precursory role when it comes to IP and what could perhaps be considered a legal experiment like the Bayh-Dole Act.

The pervasiveness of IP leads to a variety of IP issues, in turn leading to a variety of tailoring needs for the IP system(s), which comes as no surprise. The tailoring of IP systems to various types of countries is focused on in the chapters by Anawalt, Barton and Verspagen. Harmonization and one-size-fits-all approaches reduce legal uncertainty and transaction costs (at least some types of them), but these savings do not come without other costs incurred, something which is well recognized. All countries are not equal and some are more unequal than others. If the one size has been chosen to fit some more than others, there are also legal issues of justice, human rights and cultural values involved beyond economic issues, as illustrated by Howard Anawalt. A critique from initially fairly silent academic quarters on the issue has been rising against the fitting of TRIPs and the WTO "costume" to the US size while misfitting many other types of countries, the developing

[2] Needless to say, many good studies are available, although mostly theoretical or qualitative. Pioneering ones are Arrow (1962) and Wright (1983). More recent ones are David (1993) and Gallini and Scotchmer (2002).

world in particular. The level of development is the key dimension for tailoring here, as argued by Bart Verspagen. Tailoring of this kind could provide not only for locally appropriate technologies, but also for increased competition globally, thereby enhancing welfare locally as well as globally, as argued by John Barton. The IP system could very well be used in a protectionist way, as it historically always has been used in periods and places, but now for a kind of protection of leading positions rather than protection to help catching up. Country-comparative studies, and studies in comparative law and comparative economics, are of course interesting in this connection. The chapter by Wesley Cohen *et al.* is a good example of such a focus. From this and other studies it appears as if country differences are larger than industry differences (the university industry being one possible exception). This suggests that IPR tailoring should focus on country differences in the first place (assuming costs of error are not too asymmetric). A certain country-tailoring has evolved historically, of course, so international harmonization should perhaps not be pushed too far too fast. A certain industry-tailoring of IPR features has also evolved over the years, but has not gone as far as country-tailoring.

Several chapters focus more specifically on some IPR type. Patents dominate the focus on this level (e.g. in chapters by Domeij, Granstrand, Harhoff *et al.*, Kingston, Koo and Wright, and Petrusson), but trademarks (Adams), databases (Hall) and copyrights (Hall and Towse) enter the picture as well. However, other IPRs (trade secrets, designs, utility models etc.) are not particularly focused on. Some chapters also focus on particular industries like pharmaceuticals (Domeij) and publishing (Towse), the latter being part of "copyright industries" and "cultural industries". The cultural sector with its idiosyncratic IP regime is also being transformed into an industry – just like the university sector – begging tailored IPRs, copyright being an old and perhaps increasingly obsolete example of an originally industry-tailored IPR.

At a higher level of resolution, particular features of patents and requirements for patentability are focused on, such as patent scope or breadth (Domeij, Verspagen), patent lifetime (Koo and Wright) and inventive step requirement (Granstrand, Petrusson). It is interesting to see how these features at micro-legal level could conceivably have a macro-economic impact.

Technological changes are finally focused on in a majority of papers, especially changes in infocom technologies but also in biohealth technologies, while less in more traditional ("mature", "old") technologies (like material and energy technologies). The challenges of these changes to laws and legal concepts are pointed out (e.g. by Peggy Radin). Views on their disruptive impact differ, however. John Adams views them as less disruptive in the context of e-commerce, while Ruth Towse views them as a major source of disruption in the publishing industry.

Thus, there is a wide selection of IP issues, representing a large space with large possible variations. Naturally, comprehensiveness is far away; several missing foci have been indicated above, and there are others as well (e.g. IP issues in environmental technologies, educational technologies and military technologies, and IP issues in different legal systems, nations, sectors etc.). Many IP issues are old but with enlarged proportions (such as cumulation of IPRs and IP power) and some are fairly new (such as IP impact on sequential innovation).

As to features of coherence in the collection of papers, there are no conceptual or logical inconsistencies in them, nor are there any clearly conflicting views or controversies. This is probably only on the surface, in light of the long history of academic controversies surrounding IP issues and the controversial nature of IPRs, being imperfect private solutions to public problems, with a number of difficult-to-handle side-problems, rapidly magnified in the pro-IP era. The controversies have also been magnified by the interdisciplinary relations between economics and law, as well as by intra-disciplinary relations around the IP field, a field traditionally being treated as some kind of minor stepchild. As new entrants from economics and law appear in the IP field, however, one could expect competition and controversies to grow. Not least, this is likely to be spurred by economists with competitive methodological tools, models and theories, probably providing "harder" armour and cutting edges of analysis than the traditional methods of legal analysis (see below), although basically dealing with the same soft and subjective matter of analysis. Hanns Ullrich's quest for IP theories with a unifying potential is indeed a justifiable goal, but there will be many contestants. Whether some economic or legal theories or some mixture will be best equipped is an open question. One may note in this connection that many, if not most, chapters are reformist in one way or another, with apparently no outright conservatists, advocates, revolutionaries or iconoclasts among the authors. In summary, there appears after all to be a great deal of convergence in the various foci on IP. Hopefully, unfruitful polarization can be postponed further.

Table 21-1: Overview of the chapters in the book

[1] "Economics and Law of Intellectual Property – an Introduction and Overview" *Ove Granstrand*	
Main focus	The role and development of intellectual property studies as an academic field of inquiry.
Key/novel concept	IP studies, science convergence
Approach/empirical data	Argumentative. Bibliometric analysis.
Main findings/arguments	Long-standing interaction between IP- related economic, legal and technological changes contrasts sharply with long-standing separation of economics and law in IP studies. Thus a need for more interdisciplinary IP research and teaching, especially since the emergence of the pro-IP era. Rapid growth of IP studies, dominated by US and by law with a "re-entry" of economists, with signs of science convergence.
Suggestions for further research	1. History of IP studies in economics and law 2. Review of recent IP studies 3. Further bibliometric analysis

[2] "E-Commerce: The Consumer, the Trade Mark and the Credit Card" *John N. Adams*	
Main focus	Consumer protection for Internet buyers and the role of trademarks and supplier/credit card company liability.
Key/novel concept	Distance contract, inertia selling.
Approach/empirical data	Argumentative. Law text analysis.
Main findings/arguments	Encountered problems in Internet-mediated e-commerce (e.g. with defective products, slow delivery and fraud) have market rather than government solutions, aided by the emergence of global trademarks and extended supplier/intermediary liability.
Suggestions for further research	1. History of IP studies in economics and law 2. Review of recent IP studies 3. Further bibliometric analysis

Table 21-1: Overview of the chapters in the book (cont.)

[3] "Patent Claim Scope: International Intellectual Property, Progress, and the Rule of Law" *Howard C. Anawalt*	
Main focus	Why and how to preserve national legal cultures in general in presence of unifying forces from technology, international business, multinational treaties and communication, and the specific role of IPR laws in this context. The historic evolution of IPR institutions and their recent rise to prominence and source of power in international relations, accompanied by international harmonization and support through WTO and TRIPs. Impact of TRIPs interventions on national legal structures.
Key/novel concept	Legal culture.
Approach/empirical data	Historic discourse. Interpretative and argumentative.
Main findings/arguments	Guidelines for future IP development should include: 1. Insist on non-interference of international IP agreements upon national cultures. 2. Disconnect international IP agreements from trade and taxation policies. 3. Limit IP laws to providing incentives for innovation and appropriate name protection. 4. Give nations freedom to curtail IPR claims advanced to achieve non-IP goals. 5. Limit scope, duration and excess agglomeration of IPRs.
Suggestions for further research	Study and analyze further: 1. Purposes and necessity of international IPRs and the functionality of different property institutions and capital formation mechanisms for innovation and diffusion. 2. Role of accompanying international IP access rights. 3. Functionality of links between IP requirements and membership in international communities.

Table 21-1: Overview of the chapters in the book (cont.)

[4] "Markets for Technology and Corporate Strategy" *Ashish Arora, Andrea Fosfuri, and Alfonso Gambardella*	
Main focus	The growing importance of licensing and technology trade in general and its implications for large and small firm strategies.
Key/novel concept	Technology markets missing markets.
Approach/empirical data	Data on transactions 1985-97 for all countries from Securities Data Corp., screened to include technology transfer, typically in form of licensing, excluding acquisitions of firms. Complementary data from web sites of leading corporations plus cases from previous research. Statistical analysis.
Main findings/arguments	Technology markets and trade have existed for a long time but have grown and become really important for companies in recent years. Buying and selling technology complements in-house R&D and product sales and thereby increases division of labor, e.g. between large and small firms, at the same time opening up more strategic options for them with more emphasis on technology monitoring and absorption. The role of technology as a source of competitive advantage may then be reduced, relative to distinctive resources without corresponding resource markets. Stronger IPRs may foster the development of technology markets, and their associated advantages from greater strategic options, specialization of R&D and wider diffusion of technologies.
Suggestions for further research	Collection of systematic data on markets for technology.

[5] "New International Arrangements in Intellectual Property and Competition Law" *John H. Barton*	
Main focus	Relations between IP and antitrust law and between static and dynamic competition in an international context. Exploration of three contexts in which IPRs sustain the market power of the developed world: (1) licensing, tying and leveraging; (2) research tools and broad patents; (3) oligopolistic licensing and market entry.
Key/novel concept	Oligopolistic licensing.
Approach/empirical data	Case studies. Argumentative.
Main findings/arguments	IPRs enable anticompetitive behavior and trade barriers in an international context. IP portfolio power offers doubtful research incentives in oligopolies. Need for WTO-type of code (not necessarily an international antitrust body).
Suggestions for further research	International comparative joint analysis of IP and competition law.

Table 21-1: Overview of the chapters in the book (cont.)

[6] "R&D Spillovers, Patents and the Incentives to Innovate in Japan and the United States" *Wesley M. Cohen, Akira Goto, Akiya Nagata, Richard R. Nelson, and John P. Walsh*	
Main focus	Patenting behavior in Japan and the US and the role of patents and patent information for appropriation and coordination of R&D and innovation.
Key/novel concept	Complex and discrete products/ industries. R&D coordination.
Approach/empirical data	International intra-industry comparative study of R&D labs in Japan and the US. Large-scale survey in 1994 of R&D labs in medium to large manufacturing firms (with sales at least 50 MUSD). 1478 US responses (response rate 54%) and 643 Japan responses (response rate 52%). 30 follow-up interviews in 2x9 Japanese and US firms. Statistical analysis.
Main findings/arguments	Relative to US firms, Japanese firms have more R&D and higher R&D share on product R&D, have greater intra-industry R&D information lags, rely more on patents for appropriation, and rely less on other means of appropriation (especially secrecy, which was the most important means in the US), and use patents more strategically. Publication, first to file priority and pre-grant opposition rules plus lower infringement costs in the Japanese patent system induce R&D information flows and spill-overs, as does technological interdependence through cross-licensing and less concentrated market structures. Cross-national differences are significant across industries and could be related to differences in patent systems, policies and cultures.
Suggestions for further research	Analyze empirically the welfare costs and benefits of patent information disclosure and its impact on R&D and technology diffusion in general, including its impact on R&D and patenting incentives.

Table 21-1: Overview of the chapters in the book (cont.)

[7] "Intellectual Property Rights and Academic Health Centers" *Jeannette Colyvas, Annetine Gelijns, and Nathan Rosenberg*	
Main focus	The role of academic health centers (AHCs in general) in university-generated new medical technologies (consisting of tools for research, diagnostics and therapeutics) and in particular in patenting and licensing. The role of patents on research tools.
Key/novel concept	Patents as research tools (cf. patents on research tools).
Approach/empirical data	Case studies (rDNA, FACS, cardiac catheter, MRI, PET), historical and statistical analysis. Data from top universities (Columbia, Stanford in particular).
Main findings/arguments	Role of AHCs is dominant and increasing as source of innovations, patents and licensing revenues. Research tools a critical output of AHC research. Analysis of patenting and licensing of research tools must consider their need and potential for further improvement, the needs of large and small firms, and the need for tradeoffs of various approaches. Patents on research tools could increase transaction costs as well as hampering the evolvement of research tools into diagnostic and therapeutic tools. Universities ought to consider a more nuanced approach in licensing, adapted to technology and industry characteristics.
Suggestions for further research	1. Further study of IP on research tools of various kinds, used by actors of various kinds. 2. Analyze cost/benefits of various approaches to university patenting and licensing, taking technology and industry characteristics into account.

[8] "Initial and Follow-On Pharmaceutical Inventions in the European Patent System" *Bengt Domeij*	
Main focus	The role of breadth and claim structure of pharmaceutical patents for the proper balancing and coordination of initial and follow-on inventors and their R&D. Comparison of economic explanation in patent claim interpretation and case law.
Key/novel concept	Follow-on inventions, broad claims, patent scope, R&D coordination.
Approach/empirical data	Qualitative legal case analysis, especially based on cases in German, Swedish, Danish and UK courts and EPO Board of Appeal, and EPO guidelines for examinations.
Main findings/arguments	Courts tend to limit patent scope on the basis of mostly implicit judgments of economic value of follow-on inventions, which could be seen as a process of inter-firm R&D coordination, comparable and complementary to intra-firm R&D management. More explicit consideration of the economic value of follow-on R&D and inventions rather than technical analysis, as is currently dominating, ought to guide courts in order to bring more valuable results of R&D to consumers.
Suggestions for further research	More legal/economic studies of initial and follow-on inventions and the role of dependent patents in research.

Table 21-1: Overview of the chapters in the book (cont.)

[9] "On the Creation of Fundamental Knowledge: Finding the Right Balance between the Public and Private Domains" *Dominique Foray*	
Main focus	The problematic nature of efficient production and distribution of knowledge as a special case of public goods and different public/private ways to deal with the different problems, ways such as IPRs, procurement, subsidies and consortia.
Key/novel concept	Anti-commons, property regime, coordination problem, collective production of public goods, innovation system.
Approach/empirical data	Argumentative, based on previous research and illustrative examples.
Main findings/arguments	The mechanisms designed to cope with the general problems with knowledge as public goods, tend to create three coordination problems: (1) excessive exploitation (tragedy of commons); (2) obstacles to exploitation (tragedy of anti-commons); (3) obstacles to cumulation (overly broad patent rights). For the latter problem, a private/public innovation system and/or a collective invention mechanism with a pool of managed common resources, as in a consortium, offer two types of potential remedies.
Suggestions for further research	

[10] "Are we on our way in the new economy with optimal inventive steps?" *Ove Granstrand*	
Main focus	Consequences of too low inventive step (non-obviousness) requirements in granting of patent rights and the notion of optimal inventive step
Key/novel concept	IP assembly problem, multi-technology products, technological distance, evergreening.
Approach/empirical data	Argumentative. Informal and formal economic analysis. Interviews.
Main findings/arguments	Low inventive step requirement together with multi-technology products and technological interdependencies lead to IP assembly problems with high transaction costs, possibly favoring incumbents. High inventive step requirement could lead to underprotection, indicating the existence of optimal requirement levels. Interviews indicate too low levels currently.
Suggestions for further research	1. Empirical research on IP assembly problems and their possible remedies. 2. Research on transaction costs related to inventive step and related patentability criteria. 3. Empirical research on standards and examination procedures for inventive step assessment. 4. Optimality conditions for different institutional arrangements for innovation and diffusion, taking total governance costs into account.

Table 21-1: Overview of the chapters in the book (cont.)

[11] "On Copyright and Patent Protection for Software and Databases: A Tale of Two Worlds" *Bronwyn H. Hall*	
Main focus	The basic incentive problems in a market economy for producing disembodied information such as software and databases and for producing information embodied in physical products. The tensions between appropriation and spill-overs (disclosure, diffusion) and between the incentive structures and the nature of information in the two worlds of university research and industrial R&D/commercial innovation when using private rights to information as remedies to the basic incentive problems. Policy issues when these two worlds (sectors) with their sector-specific IP regimes interact, especially regarding software, databases, university patenting and university research. Brief summaries of studies of university patenting in the US, and studies of database protection.
Key/novel concept	Spill-overs, pure information products, complementary investments.
Approach/empirical data	Mainly argumentative, based on secondary sources, mainly focusing on US. Economic policy analysis. Examples from US university-industry research centers and the Bayh-Dole Act, and from the software and database areas.
Main findings/arguments	Two important distinctions for incentivizing information production through IP protection are (a) the size of R&D investments vs. complementary investments necessary for marketing an information product, and (b) the extent to which embodiment of the information in a physical product or association of the information to the agent producing it could be used for appropriation of benefits from the information. Scientific research and industrial physical innovations differ in these respects, calling for different IP regimes, with need for complementary investments suggesting need for IP rights. Strengthening of IP protection in universities has not shown clear benefits, at least not yet.
Suggestions for further research	1) Study empirically the impacts of IP protection in various forms on incentives to produce software and databases in particular, with a survey of how database provision has worked in the past. 2) Model (theoretically) in a game-theoretic setting the knowledge production in science/university and technology/industry, accounting for spill-overs, transaction costs, and differences in production function and incentive structures, with and without strong IP protection. Welfare analysis of IP policies and multiple reward-systems.

Table 21-1: Overview of the chapters in the book (cont.)

[12] "Exploring the Tail of Patented Invention Value Distributions" *Dietmar Harhoff, Frederic M. Scherer, Katrin Vopel*	
Main focus	Nature of the value distribution of top-valued patents.
Key/novel concept	Value tail distributions, patent valuation.
Approach/empirical data	Asset value approach (in contrast to renewal value approach), obtaining value estimates from West German and US patent holders of German patents (with high renewal fees) held to full term, expired in 1995, using questionnaires (with one counterfactual question) and follow-up interviews. Data for 772 patents held by West Germans (58% response rate) and 225 patents with US patent holders (48% response rate). Econometric analysis.
Main findings/arguments	Top-value distribution extremely skewed. Although a log normal distribution provided best fit to the data, a Pareto-Levy distribution with neither finite mean nor variance could not be ruled out. The asset value approach used gives higher values and higher skewness than in previous studies. Top 5% of German-held patents accounted for 61% of patent sample value, while top 8.5% of US-held patents accounted for 80% of patent sample value. No particular value difference between product and process patents. Drug and surgical supply patents most valuable. Extreme skewness implies difficulties at firm level in stabilizing returns from patent portfolio strategies and in estimating patent portfolio value through simple patent counts and at policy level in "picking winners". A large share of failing or low-value projects is naturally concomitant to a few outstanding successes.
Suggestions for further research	1. Find patent weight correlates for patent portfolio valuation ex ante. 2. Identify underlying stochastic processes that generate observed value distributions. 3. Review of recent IP studies 4. Further bibliometric analysis

Table 21-1: Overview of the chapters in the book (cont.)

[13] "Unlocking the Potential of Intellectual Property" *William Kingston*	
Main focus	The misfits between the present international IP system and the evolving nature of creation, R&D and innovation and their effects on the world, on university research and on S&T progress in general.
Key/novel concept	Direct protection of innovation, innovation warrant, market power.
Approach/empirical data	Closely-argued policy analysis, drawing on previous works of the author and others, supported by short historical illustrations.
Main findings/arguments	Serious strains in the IP system have developed over long periods of time in face of the shift from individual invention to corporate R&D investments and the emergence of new technologies – software and biotech in particular – and increasing technological complexity. Favours *sui generis* arrangements, provides empirical support for arbitration proposal, and claims many advantages from improved measurement of grants.
Suggestions for further research	1. Develop accounting measures and procedures to enable the implementation of the proposed new form of protection. 2. Study the roots behind the limitations of the IP system in adjusting to new forms of information and information production.

[14] "Economics of Patenting an Input Essential to Further Research" *Bonwoo Koo and Brian D. Wright*	
Main focus	Welfare aspects of patenting and licensing in sequential innovation, especially regarding patent life as a policy instrument.
Key/novel concept	Sequential innovation, licensing
Approach/empirical data	Theoretical analysis of patenting in a two-stage sequential innovation model with an exogenously given first invention stage, followed by a second stage with perfectly competitive free entry. An invention (patent) from each stage as jointly necessary and sufficient for the innovation. Optimization of patent lifetime for maximal welfare.
Main findings/arguments	Limitations on patent lifetime may have benefits different from traditionally recognized ones (i.e. reduction of dead-weight losses), such as inducement of subsequent innovation and reduction of rent dissipation.
Suggestions for further research	Develop sequential innovation models further to explore the nature of the advantages derivable from patent lifetime limitations and various licensing schemes.

Table 21-1: Overview of the chapters in the book (cont.)

[15] "Is University Patenting Necessary or Sufficient to Make University Research Valuable Economically?" *Richard R. Nelson*	
Main focus	American research university system and the problematic nature of patenting and licensing. Causes and consequences of rise in recent decades of university patenting, licensing and start-up activities and the role of the Bayh-Dole act in this context. Pros and cons, myths and downsides of university patenting and licensing.
Key/novel concept	Ex post royalty collection.
Approach/empirical data	Essayic, based on ongoing research with primary and secondary data primarily from the top three universities regarding license revenues – Stanford University, University of California and Columbia University.
Main findings/arguments	Rise in university contributions to industrial innovations in the last decades even in absence of strong IPRs and technology transfer offices. Rise in university patenting and licensing mainly associated with rise of biohealth and infocom technologies and court and Patent Office decisions to enlarge patentability in these technologies. No evidence of shift away from fundamental research. Evidence that exclusive licensing not always necessary for embryonic inventions. University technology transfer offices important for dissemination in some embryonic cases while superfluous in other, and mostly acting as royalty collectors ex post of university inventions. University patenting and licensing give rise to intra-university tensions as well as to university-industry tensions (about unfair competition from universities), possibly giving rise to inefficiencies, especially in fundamental research, compared to an open, public science regime, e.g. regarding research tools.
Suggestions for further research	Explore further the role of university patenting in basic research and effective technology transfer.

Table 21-1: Overview of the chapters in the book (cont.)

[16] "Patents as Structural Capital – Towards Legal Constructionism" *Ulf Petrusson*	
Main focus	The evolutionary nature of legal systems and the IP system in particular in a Scandinavian legal realist perspective. The nature and role of the patent system in communication processes for legal, economic, technical, and managerial control purposes, particularly in the new type of knowledge-based economy.
Key/novel concept	Intellectual property vs. intellectual property right. Structural tool and structural brick. Governance position. Intellectual capital. Structural capital.
Approach/empirical data	Argumentative with a historical and philosophical discourse. Conceptual analysis.
Main findings/arguments	Considerable confusion surrounds basic IP concepts and institutions such as patents, which by and large are social constructions. A patent can be understood as a possibility to enforce an infringement claim; a process of communication; a property and a property right and a piece of structural capital. Confusion derives from lack of awareness of law as a structural phenomenon. Legal constructionism is decisively important for collective governance of structural transformation.
Suggestions for further research	To develop a legal constructionist approach to IP issues and to create a common research agenda with evolutionary approaches in economics.

Table 21-1: Overview of the chapters in the book (cont.)

[17] "Information Tangibility" *Margaret Jane Radin*	
Main focus	Tangibilization of information through new technologies and reconceptualizations.
Key/novel concept	Commodification / tangibilization /assimilation/propertization of information. Contract-as-product.
Approach/empirical data	Analysis of concepts, cases and examples in a legal-philosophical discourse, in a mainly US context of IPR and information control issues.
Main findings/arguments	Technology leads and law generally follows in conceptualizations, where old dichotomies and physical metaphors die hard. Assimilation of information to categories of physicality leads astray, e.g. when using real estate metaphors in cyberspace ('cyber-squatting', 'sites', 'domain', 'trespassing', etc.).
	Information commodification has increased through a number of expedients, especially generated by new technology for embodying information, reinforced by use of physical property analogies, giving better access to broad rights and rent control. Recent US case law indicate that information is not only increasingly commodified through linking it to physical embodiments and metaphors, but is being reconceptualized as being an inherently tangible or physical object from the outset, thereby alienating the concept of information from human personhood, linked e.g. to freedom of speech and privacy, and aligning it with property.
Suggestions for further research	1. To study the impact of growing links between information and its physical embodiments, and in particular how propertization of information enabled by such links will impact freedom of expression and free communication.
	2. To contribute to the history of ideas a study of how physicalist reductionism has permeated the law and in particular how it has fostered information commodification.

Table 21-1: Overview of the chapters in the book (cont.)

[18] "Copyright and Cultural Policy for the Creative Industries" *Ruth Towse*	
Main focus	The supply and demand characteristics of artists' labor markets, the role of copyright as an incentive to artists and as a vehicle for asset formation for publishers, and the role of new digital technologies and business models on these markets.
Key/novel concept	Creative (including cultural) industries, rights management, superstar phenomenon.
Approach/empirical data	Cultural economics applied to artists' labor markets with an empirical approach to copyright law, drawing upon the author's previous work.
Main findings/arguments	Copyright, essentially retaining its basic economic and legal principles over centuries, despite a long series of technological changes, is unable to offer artists in general sufficient economic incentive to create, while enabling intermediaries (publishers, distributors) to cumulate market power. The transition from analogue to digital technologies has a significant potential to change market structure and therefore poses challenges to copyright policy, being part of cultural as well as economic policy.
Suggestions for further research	1. Further study of the relation between copyright law and digitalization from both legal and economic points of view. 2. Analyze the artists' labor markets and the role of copyright, e.g. upon income distribution and concentration.

Table 21-1: Overview of the chapters in the book (cont.)

[19] "Legal Protection of Innovative Technologies: Property or Policy?" *Hanns Ullrich*	
Main focus	The nature of the IP system and its interaction with competition law and economic policy, especially technology/innovation policy and trade policy.
Key/novel concept	Horizontal and vertical dilemmas. Property vs liability vs policy.
Approach/empirical data	Argumentative, based on legal case analysis and a wide range of sources.
Main findings/arguments	The IP system is a misguided tool of economic policy and needs to be fundamentally rethought as a legal system, since the IP system creates problems beyond its classical problem of trading off static and dynamic efficiency, e.g. loss of public control.
Suggestions for further research	Overall task is the proper balancing of IP protection as an instrument for achieving public policy objectives and as an instrument for achieving private company policy objectives. Specific suggestions: 1. Develop operational legal-economic principles for WTO, on which TRIPs could be based. 2. Develop substantive legal principles governing IP protection and its economic functions as well as legal functions. 3. Develop a theoretical paradigm for promoting technological and economic progress, which could unify various forms of IP protection.

Table 21-1: Overview of the chapters in the book (cont.)

[20] "Intellectual Property Rights in the World Economy" *Bart Verspagen*	
Main focus	Main economic rationales for an IP system, especially for a patent system and how economic analysis can guide the design of a patent system, e.g. regarding proper patent breadth. Main arguments in the debate on the role of IPRs in the world economy, especially regarding the TRIPs and the relation between developed and developing nations, and the possible need for IP systems tailored to countries at different stages of development, with different technological infrastructures, technology transfer needs and possibilities, and trade situations.
Key/novel concept	Technology transfer, international trade, spill-overs.
Approach/empirical data	Mainly argumentative, based on secondary sources and history accounts. Economic policy analysis.
Main findings/arguments	Formal models developed so far of the patent system do not offer very concrete guidance for patent system design. The provision of technology spill-overs, e.g. by patent disclosures and limiting patent breadth, is a specific feature of patents among IPRs, and such spill-overs are important for growth and dynamic economic performance. IPR policies for developing countries have to be integrated with more comprehensive technology and economic policies. International differentiation of IP systems may be conducive to global welfare as long as economic and technological asymmetries between countries remain large, while reducing them may make a uniform IPR system optimal.
Suggestions for further research	1) More empirical research on the impact on global welfare of differentiated (country-tailored) IP systems, e.g. with differences in patent breadth. 2) Focus on the extent to which international technology spill-overs are product/FDI-embodied or disembodied, and incorporate IPRs in models of such spill-overs, especially north-south spill-overs. 3) Focus on the relation between IP systems and the generation and transfer of "appropriate technologies", i.e. technologies appropriate for specific levels of development of a country.

For structuring purposes, the macro-micro distinction between levels of foci as commonly used in economic analysis can be applied to legal analysis as well, either in its own right or in combination with economic analysis as illustrated in Table 21-2. Of course this is a crude distinction and more levels than macro and micro could be distinguished. For example, a trichotomy with a meso level inserted between the macro and micro levels can be more useful in many cases. The macro-micro distinction can be applied to and combined with other areas as well such as technology and innovations, and also combined with the distinctions between short and long term (or between short/medium/long term).[1]

Most authors focus on some combinations of or interactions between micro and macro levels of analysis. Such a type of focus is important since the macro-micro distinction easily creates a watershed in analysis. If the interaction between legal and economic changes at both micro and macro levels is focused upon, it moreover appears important to focus on the diagonal relations, that is, between micro/macro-economics and micro/macro-law, in order to attain a more adequate understanding of causal links and the aggregation/disaggregation problem. In the same spirit it is important to focus also on relations between transient microbehavior and long-term aggregate behavior.

[1] See Granstrand (1994, Ch. 19), for examples of combined use of macro/micro "lenses" in studying economics of technology.

Table 21-2: Principal levels of foci in economics and law of IP with examples

		Law: Micro	Law: Macro
Economics	Micro	• Extension of patentable subject matter (e.g. business method patents) • Bayh-Dole Act • Patent right adjustment for sequential invention	• Impact of litigation costs on IP legal developments in civil and common law systems • Specific companies lobbying for creation of *sui generis* rights (e.g. database rights) or stronger IP regimes • Shift from contract-as-consent to contract-as-product
	Macro	• Impact of patentability criteria on national industrial competitiveness • Impact of judicial changes on the development of technology markets • Macro-economic impact of key precedence cases or legislative acts	• TRIPs • Alternative incentive systems for innovation • Role of the IPR system in the new economy

21.1.2 Key/novel concepts

Needless to say, concept formation and new classifications are inherent in scientific progress. At the same time, it is a natural propensity in any science to utilize existing language. Some sciences are also for various reasons overly plagued by new concepts, or new terms rather, often vaguely defined. (Economists are said to use each other's toothbrush sooner than each other's concepts.) This contrasts with the strong propensity in law to preserve and stretch legal concepts, for both practical and more fundamental reasons. The chapter by Radin actually illustrates how this is done, not only to economize on the applicability of existing law in the public interest, but also to exploit existing law for private interests. As to concept formation in the collection of chapters there are fairly few novel (or recent) concepts, although a great deal of novel (or perhaps only magnified) phenomena are dealt with. Examples of novel or recent concepts are anti-commons problems, complex vs. discrete industries, innovation warrant, innovation system, intellectual capital, commodification, contract-as-product and cultural industry. As to key concepts, a general observation is that there is hardly (at this level of a general observation is that there is hardly (at this level of analysis) a severe language divide between economics and law of IP.

21.1.3 Approach/empirical data

While all chapters focus on the same topic, i.e. IP, their methodological approaches differ widely. The major divide is between economics and law. Judging from type of approach and frequency of its use, the interdisciplinary differences appear large compared to intradisciplinary differences. Still, there is a considerable overlap between the set of approaches used by economists and the set used by lawyers, an overlap which could serve as a common methodological ground. This common ground consists of approaches such as policy analysis, historical analysis and case analysis, apart from more general conceptual analysis (language or text analysis) and philosophical discourses. One could also add to the common "tool pool" a kind of industrial organization analysis, although not as explicit among the chapters (occurring mainly in the chapters by Barton and Towse). The approaches common to economics and law are mainly qualitative, although both policy analysis, historical analysis and case analysis could adopt quantitative approaches (cf. "cliometrics" and jurimetrics).

The case study approach is an interesting approach for interdisciplinary research (see e.g. the chapter by Domeij) as well as for teaching. Its uses in economics and law differ substantially, however. It is mostly used in business economics, but is (slowly) gaining ground in economics at large – especially when allowing for both qualitative and quantitative analysis. The latter requires samples of, say, at least 8-10 cases, in turn allowing for some case-based theorizing.[2] From a methodological point of view, the sampling of cases is usually more controlled (but not necessarily more controllable) in economics than in law, e.g. when it comes to court cases. The research-oriented analysis in law tends to be more sequential case by case, more language-oriented, qualitative and contextual, less quantitative and variable-oriented, less experimental (e.g. less oriented toward action research) and more influenced by the tradition of legal case analysis for practical purposes. Besides, key legal variables are more often binary, i.e. dichotomised. It is beyond the scope of comments here to pursue this theme further, except to

---

[2] Systematic case-based theorizing may in turn ultimately provide stronger links between common law and civil law systems through improvements in the codification process. However, case analysis is no panacea, either for research or for research-based developments of law, but has to be used as part of more comprehensive methodological approaches, e.g. as in triangulation.

point out the possibilities of developing more similar case study methodologies in economics and law, as there appear to be few inherent basic differences.

As to the dominating differences between approaches used in economics and law, one could crudely characterize them by claiming that approaches used in the economist chapters involve a wider variety of scientific methods, including quantitative techniques in statistics and mathematics besides qualitative techniques, and a wider use of empirical data bases. This is probably a crucial issue for future research in law in general, not only in IP law, and for the status of and relations between research in economics and law in terms of "scientific power". Supply and demand of economic and legal data from old and new sources will grow, as will techniques for database production and distribution, data mining and statistical data analysis, not least when full texts will be available on line with a variety of software tools for content analysis etc. In this general scenario with relevance for many disciplines, fields such as econometrics, jurimetrics, technometrics, scientometrics, bibliometrics, sociometrics etc. will develop. Considering the state (and status) of econometrics vs. jurimetrics prompts the question of how research in law will develop in response to this type of technological changes. Needless to say, these "X-metrics" do not replace but complement qualitative analysis. They are also likely to become an increasingly important complement, actually in line with an increasingly knowledge- and information-based society.

One may also note that empirical studies with large data sets are more team-oriented (with associated economies of scale, scope and speed). Several chapters by economists in the book are also co-authored, while all chapters by lawyers are single-authored.

A final comment in this context concerns the possibilities to use experimental approaches, which are very limited but still available in social sciences (besides counterfactual thought experiments). Experimental economics is a coined term, but hardly experimental law. Terminology apart, the question is whether a more experimental approach in law research and law-making is feasible (perhaps as an experiment in itself), especially when facing more rapid and complex changes. Law is traditionally built to last (as is mathematics grounded in logic, although discovery of contradictions cannot be excluded), i.e. to be cumulative with as little substitution or creative destruction as possible.[3] However, in the spirit of legal constructionism (as ad-

[3] Appeals notwithstanding, several legal doctrines and principles work for preservation, stability and cumulativeness and against substitution and creative destruction. The use of irrebuttable presumptions serves to preserve a set of facts, once established, by not permitting later

vocated in the chapter by Petrusson), an experimental approach seems natural, perhaps even as a legal realist extension.[4] Regardless of jurisprudence, one may claim that a closer interaction between law and technology would likely lead to more substitution of laws (i.e. legal obsolescence), just as there is a considerable rate of technological substitution, still in parallel to technological cumulation. New laws adapted to new technologies may become obsolete due to even newer technologies, at least partially.

21.1.4 Main findings/arguments

Eclectic variety, rather than coherence or convergence, characterizes also the main findings and arguments in the collection of chapters. This is quite natural for a rapidly developing field of inquiry into a rapidly changing, although old, phenomenon. Thus new as well as old research questions are opened or reopened. Some of these get new or altered answers based on new findings, but a fair amount of inconclusiveness and open questions remains, pointing out directions for further research as a companion finding. A fundamental and recurrent theme dealt with by many if not most of the authors concerns the differences and relations between knowledge and information on the one hand and physical goods and embodiments on the other, and the implications of these differences for the co-functioning of markets and rights. Here, a number of arguments, so far mainly theoretical and perhaps mainly economic, cumulate in a promising way. This hopefully leads both to a basis for a certain unification or integration of IPR rationales (as pledged for by Hanns Ullrich) and to a basis for differentiation of IP regimes and other alternatives for provision of information and knowledge in an economy (as pledged for by Foray, Nelson and others). Such a theoretically based integration and differentiation should preferably be robust and operational enough to accommodate a range of new technologies. This in turn would probably call for more economically oriented principles, requiring more empirical economic and legal analysis, sacrificing some legal certainty. The latter in turn is perhaps also fairly illusory in general, and not least regarding IPRs as claimed by Petrusson. Legal certainty is, moreover, volatile and severely limited by the impact of new technologies on basic conceptualiza-

---

evidence to the contrary. The "law of the case" principle serves to preserve the decisions of a judge in the event that the judges are replaced at the same level. The legal doctrine of precedence (*stare decisis*) has the presumption that legal principles established in previous court decisions are followed in similar subsequent cases (see e.g. Adams and Brownsword 1999).

[4] The legal areas most receptive to experimental approaches would probably be those with strong economic underpinnings, such as competition law and IP law.

tions, as illustrated by Radin. The empirical economic analysis needed for proper application of economic and legal principles may be quite costly, on the other hand. Such costs may even exceed transaction cost increases from increased legal uncertainty. For example, if the requirement that an invention should have technical character in order to be patentable is replaced by a more economically oriented requirement that the invention should be patentable if it otherwise would be underprovided, the latter requirement would conceivably be more costly to apply. A more grandiose example, in the same line of thought, would be to use the US constitutional language directly as a basis in the US for the wording of a requirement that an exclusive time-limited patent right is granted to inventors for their discoveries if it promotes the progress of science and useful arts.[5]

The relation between IPRs and new technologies – infocom technologies (ICTs) in particular but also bio-health technologies – is also a recurrent connected theme, dealt with by most authors. New technologies are normally conceived of (in a Schumpeterian spirit) as presenting challenges to and disruptions of legal and economic structures (as illustrated by Towse), but new technologies may have complex mixed effects, sometimes stabilizing and facilitating rather than destabilizing and misfitting. This is what John Adams finds regarding problems arising from a new form of trade, enabled by ICTs (e-commerce), problems which also have legal and economic solutions enabled by ICTs.

---

[5] The Constitution of the United States of America states that "The Congress shall have Power... To promote the Progress of Science and useful Arts, by securing for limited Times to Authors and Inventors the exclusive Right to their respective Writings and Discoveries;" (Article I, Section 8, the 8th clause in authentic wording, spelling and capitalization, unaffected by amendments (as of 2002).) This wording in the US Constitution from Sept. 17, 1787 can be interpreted as well as criticized in many ways, and has of course been a point of departure for formulating patentability requirements in the US. The point here is that as a legal framework develops in more detail, overall legal uncertainty is not necessarily monotonically reduced but may increase beyond some point, at which a movement *ad fontes* is called for. At the same time the use of empirical tests more or less on a case-by-case basis may be even more costly than an imperfect legal language test. It is notable that US constitutional language neither directly excludes scientific discoveries, nor requires any technical character. However, scientific discoveries may be excluded on the grounds that granting patents to them does not promote the progress of science and useful arts (e.g. due to excessive transaction costs associated with numerous transactions deriving from the generic nature of scientific discoveries and the existence of superior means for their provision). If this is judged to be valid in comparable cases, it may be cheaper to rule them out once and for all, depending upon the expected relative costs of the two types of possible errors, i.e. improper exclusion and improper inclusion.

The causes and in particular the consequences of the rapid emergence on a global scale of the pro-IP era are also a recurrent theme, quite naturally. This legal-economic change has magnified old phenomena like technology trade.[6] Thereby division of intellectual labor and its associated economic efficiency are increased, as argued by Arora *et al.* However, the advent of the pro-IP era also likely magnifies earlier less costly IPR misfits, especially since local judiciary changes rather than global legislative changes were behind its inception, changes subsequently reinforced by various self-interested actors. The many reformers among the authors, not least among the legal scholars, thereby acquire magnified reasons for reform. As mentioned, there are not really any conflicting findings about the nature of misfits but rather about their treatment.

An emerging but so far little researched theme is the relative effectiveness and efficiency of the governance mode or coordination mechanism in science and technology, induced by IPRs and their associated patent disclosures and court decisions. This theme in turn involves not only transaction cost analysis but management analysis as well. Although courts sometimes may picture themselves as a kind of "transaction cost engineers", they hardly refer to themselves as technology managers or "technology governors", which in fact they are to some extent as found by Bengt Domeij.

It remains to be seen whether the pro-IP era will revert, stagnate or continue, and what basic qualitative changes will occur if any. A quite conceivable scenario is that the pro-IP era will be accompanied by a pro IP-research era (to be distinguished from a pro-IP research era), which will contribute to qualitative change. This leads us into the next section.

21.1.5 Suggestions for further research

A major purpose of this book is to further research on IP, and the various chapters generate a multitude of more or less explicit suggestions for further research. It is inappropriate here to go on evaluating them and suggesting some kind of synthesized research program, not least since a rapidly developing field needs a variety of research strategies. The many misfits of IPRs and needs for IP reforms found in the chapters naturally call for further research on a number of frontiers. So does a more experimental and evidence-based approach to policy-making, as do legislative and judiciary processes facing increasingly complex interactions between economic, legal and technological changes.

[6] The pro-IP era could thus lead into a "pro-licensing" era as well (see Granstrand 2004).

Thus, the most obvious suggestion implicit in the book as a whole is that the rapid, many-faceted growth of pervasive IPR use should be accompanied by a corresponding growth of understanding of IP. This in turn needs a corresponding growth of IP studies with an intra- and interdisciplinary structure fitted to meet the need for understanding and action. As misfits grow larger and more costly, any uncoordinated growth of quasi-functional IP laws has to be disciplined by solid legal and economic principles.

Hence, interdisciplinary research seems needed. This is also a major suggestion for further research, explicitly made by several authors but implicit in the book as a whole.

Within the law discipline, unification of the various IPRs and integration of the relevant legal subsystems for IPRs, competition and contracts with a fair amount of international harmonization are old quests for research, growing strong in the pro-IP era. This is much in line with what Hanns Ullrich suggests. However, international harmonization of IPR laws and regimes is not naively advocated, either by legal scholars such as Anawalt, Barton and Ullrich, or by economists like Verspagen. Again, tailoring enters the research agenda, confronting standardization (harmonization, unification). Thus, complex and dynamic trade-offs have to be made in numerous dimensions. For some trade-offs legal principles are prime, for others economic principles are prime, and for still others no single discipline is clearly in charge. However, principles and flashes of insight do not come as manna from heaven but have to be patiently searched and researched. Experiments – natural and artificial – are necessary, as is realistic theory-building, especially in the face of complexity. Legal realism leads to legal constructivism, elaborated upon by Petrusson and probably accepted in principle if not in practice by many contemporary legal scholars. However, to push the development, constructivism leads further into relativism, experiments and theories. Will the ambition to build lasting law lead to experimental law, and perhaps even further to some kind of "mathematical law" (e.g. involving a search for legal "axioms", e.g. as in Rawls 1971)?[7]

Within the economic discipline, a number of suggestions for further research on IP are implicit in the more general quest for additional economic research on technology and innovation. Such research will spur a natural evolution from static to dynamic economics, including evolutionary economics and dynamic systems thinking. The inherently dynamic features of IPR

[7] Legal anthropologists have difficulties in empirically finding universally valid "natural" legal notions, something that should frustrate foundational searches, although without implying that universal foundations cannot exist naturally or artificially.

issues make them well suited for playing a prominent role in further dynamizing of economic models and theories, providing bridges to law and technology at the same time.

In the IP field, research on the economics of patenting over time (sequential patenting, sequential invention) is an example of evolution from static to dynamic analysis. This is a complex and demanding research area, still in its infancy, but its growth is simply necessary for understanding IP dynamics. Past and proposed research has mainly been theoretical as illustrated by Koo and Wright, proposing a class of staged models, as well as by Harhoff, Scherer and Vopel, proposing a continued search for stochastic processes generating increasingly skewed distributions over time. In this context it should be noted that economic valuation, which is a commonly suggested area for further IP research, involves dynamic analysis in an essential way.

Other, mainly intra-disciplinary, areas suggested for further research in IP economics concern a comparative analysis and more theory-based integration of the various alternative incentives and policy schemes for innovation and diffusion, as well as of various IP regimes. Within the latter category, more comparative and integrative research on the IP regimes in industry, academia and culture is clearly advocated. This calls for more economic welfare analysis of IP matters, which in turn could very well lead to new tools for economic analysis in the longer run. A particular type of analysis in this context is transaction cost analysis or, more broadly, governance cost analysis, well recognized but so far not much used in IP research, despite a long-standing quest (see e.g. Cheung 1986).

All in all, the IP field is in demand of much research but also supplies many promising opportunities to enrich received theories, models and methods. It is a fair bet that efforts to overcome the difficulties with information, knowledge, innovations and IP will eventually make economic and legal research in general more inventive, valuable and righteous.

21.2 Reflections upon Further Interdisciplinary Research

21.2.1 Economics and law

As seen from the collection of papers, there is a strong quest for more interdisciplinary research on IP. Thus, a few more arguments for further interdisciplinary research, and interdisciplinary interaction more generally, are justified, leaving aside a deeper discussion of nature of and rationales for interdisciplinarity in general. One can first observe that a long period of separation of two fundamentally related disciplines such as economics and law, as described in Chapter 1, promises new types of fruits from cross-fertilization. Second, if there is a fast-growing phenomenon of common interest such as IP and innovation, related problems and concerns are likely to grow in many quarters beyond the realm and capabilities of a single discipline. Third, there are standard arguments for interdisciplinary work referring to benefits (outweighing the considerable problems and costs involved) deriving from natural input/output relations among disciplines, usually mutual benefits but asymmetric and changing over time. For example, mathematics provides tools in physics and physics feeds problems back that can give rise to new offspring in mathematics. Physics has in fact been characterized as the mother (or engine, with a mechanical metaphor instead) of natural sciences, at least until the 21st century. Now the popular prediction is that biology will take over that role, also with respect to mathematics. This is to say that, in some sense, physics (so far) has by and large been feeding (exporting) more into other natural sciences than being fed by (importing from) them.

It is beyond the scope here to discuss natural input/output relations between economics and law in general. They are of course many and close, as could be expected from two social sciences that have, so to speak, grown up together. The movement referred to as "Law and Economics", with origins in the 1950s at the University of Chicago, should of course be mentioned in this context as a most visible attempt at bi-disciplinary work in analyzing legal issues in a market economy. The movement also illustrates some of the input/output relations between economics and law, and will therefore be briefly elaborated upon here. In this joint venture, economics provided concepts and objectives (economic efficiency in particular) that, in a revived utilitarian rationalistic spirit, promised to somewhat reduce the inherent indeterminacy of policy-oriented legal judgements. This legal indeterminacy had been disturbingly pointed out by the pre-war movement of legal realists in their criticism of earlier attempts to formalize law based on uncertainty-reducing scientific principles, much inspired by successful attempts in natural sciences.

Economics moreover provided tools and models for analysis of joint economic-legal problems (e.g. in the form of decision trees to support judicial decision-making). The analysis then often became formalized, just as economics became increasingly formalized and "mathematized" in the post-war era. To some extent it could summarily be said that economics exported to law more than it imported from law.

In the seminal article of the law and economics movement (Coase 1960), Prof. Ronald Coase in fact showed that in certain situations (involving e.g. no transaction costs) economic efficiency could be achieved by market mechanisms unaffected by the way certain property rights were allocated, as long as these rights were precise and proper damages would accrue in case of violations. In other words, multiple legal optima (equilibria) could exist, yielding the same maximal economic efficiency. Thus, legal reasoning in searching for a single best legal solution in a situation like this would not only be wasteful but futile, since none exists. Consequently there exist situations where legal indeterminacy is impossible to eliminate even in the presence of full and precise information and perfect judges. A reallocation of property rights between a buyer and a seller would change their objective functions and their surpluses but not total welfare (unless some constraints become binding). Still another way to put the result is that legal indeterminacy may follow from economic determinacy regarding the objective of a certain law simply because there may be several equally good solutions.

Once the objective of law becomes indeterminate – as when considerations of equity or justice are introduced and weighed imprecisely against efficiency – legal as well as economic indeterminacy of solutions rapidly grows.

Thus, the law and economics movement could help reduce legal indeterminacy (uncertainty) but only up to a point, depending upon the extent of economic determinacy (certainty) and the well-functioning of markets. The movement has grown and diversified, but has also aroused criticism on many fronts – of its pro-market ideology, of its focus (at least initially) on efficiency rather than equity and other values, of its conservative bias, of its overassimilation of stereotype economic assumptions and models, of its pretentiousness etc. In fact any interdisciplinary movement runs the risk of coming under cross-fire from interdisciplinary criticism (e.g. of economists by lawyers and vice versa) joining forces with intradisciplinary criticism (e.g. of neo-classical economics by evolutionary economists, or of legal formalism by legal realists). The point made here is that when a bi-disciplinary offspring such as the law and economics movement develops, it inherits and acquires certain features that typically do not represent the entire spectrum of desirable features of interaction between the two disciplines in question. As the movement attracts criticism as any scholarly movement will and should, there is always a risk that further bi-disciplinary cooperation inside as well as outside the particular movement will be hampered. This is not to say that the law and economics movement currently is right or wrong, but perhaps that it is too limited[8].

There are several principal ways to foster further research cooperation between economics and law on a broader front. One is to bring into common focus another discipline such as technology (engineering sciences) or management. Another is to bring into common focus a sub-discipline not much focused on by previous interdisciplinary research, such as intellectual property.[9]

21.2.2 Law, science and technology

The relation between law, (natural) science and technology (S&T) is interesting and deserves much serious attention. Law and S&T have of course frequently been focused upon in the book in relation to IP, and in relation to economics. However, law and S&T become more closely connected in other areas as well (such as environment, health, product liability, safety, privacy etc.), with different areas of law (criminal law, competition law, contract law, tort law etc.) becoming cross-connected to different areas of S&T (ICTs, BHTs, weapons technologies, transportation technologies, etc.). As to research (and teaching) in universities, centers or programs in law, science and technology are also emerging, perhaps more in law schools than at technical universities.

A number of justifications could be formulated for increased bi-disciplinary interaction between law and S&T. Four general ones will briefly be given here. First, science and technology penetrates virtually all aspects of society, including legal ones, at the same time as laws and regulations stimulate as well as constrain S&T progress. Many of these interactions are immersed in economic concerns, but far from all, and reductionist approaches rooted in economics are insufficient (e.g. in some areas of bioscience, medical technology and criminal law, or regarding ICTs and constitutional rights). Second, S&T and law change at different paces and with different logic. As misfits and time lags between them tend to become more severe, closer alignment becomes necessary, calling for closer communication and interaction and more upstream integration of technological R&D with "legal R&D" (i.e. research and development for new laws and legal

---

[8] A law and economics tradition in a more generic bi-disciplinary sense has existed for centuries in Europe.

[9] The law and economics movement has traditionally not focused particularly on IP. See, however, Besen and Raskind (1991) for an example. For a general work by a leading scholar in the movement, see Posner (1992).

processes and systems). This involves analysis of legal and technological conceptualizations, and timely reconceptualizations and redefinitions (including analysis of deceptive rhetorics used by interested parties). Various methods for technology analysis could also be useful, e.g. technological forecasting and technology assessment methods. As legal developments and legal research are organized differently in different legal systems, the interaction between legal R&D and technological R&D must be structured and financed accordingly.[10]

As to the logic of S&T and law changes, standardization and compatibility are important for both types of changes. However, backward compatibility in law is far more important. This is so for good reasons, but in certain areas it may have to be sacrificed to some extent for closer alignment of legal changes to S&T changes. Forward compatibility may also be used more frequently (e.g. through legal "platform solutions" or general clauses in new S&T areas).

Third, a closer interaction between law and S&T could be instrumental in internationalising law. S&T flies no flag but law does, as laws of nature apply across jurisdictions. New technologies will continue to push for international legal harmonization (compatibility) just as e.g. transportation technologies and communication technologies have in the past (with the Internet as a palpable recent example, largely unanticipated in the international legal community, despite being developed for years before breakthrough). As argued in the book, international harmonization could be carried out in wrong ways. More pro-active than reactive interaction at earlier stages of technological and legal developments across jurisdictions will lower such risks in view of increasing globalization prompting for some form of harmonization.

Fourth, current and future ICTs in particular have important applications in the legal system on the whole. One may argue that this creates a normal user/producer relation not in need of bi-disciplinary research. However, there are studies showing the importance of integrating user and producer R&D in certain cases.[11]

Finally, one can make the reflection that knowledge diversification into other disciplines rather proceeds step by step, and the route to more compre-

---

[10] Proper forms for the organization and financing of "legal R&D" in this context are important to analyze. For instance, solutions based on markets with slow feedback structures have limitations, which moreover may increase as litigation costs increase.

[11] See e.g. works by von Hippel, e.g. von Hippel (1988), on the importance of lead users as sources of innovation. (Legal researchers and practitioners being lead users in this case.)

hensive interdisciplinary research had better start with a bi-disciplinary stage.

21.2.3 Mathematics and law

Considering the key role of mathematics in S&T, and also the mathematization of parts of social science, what about the use of mathematics in law? Mathematics has a tendency to slowly creep into almost every discipline as it develops, despite resistance, backlashes, rejections etc. Sometimes parts of the discipline become hijacked by math and carried away beyond what are recognized as disciplinary borders. Bi-disciplinary labels such as mathematical physics, mathematical biology, economics, sociology etc. emerge. What, then, about the prospects for "mathematical law"? The term seems not to have surfaced yet. Certainly many if not most legal scholars would shiver or shrug at the idea (if they ever bother to take it seriously). No plea is made here for use of more mathematics in law, nor in economics, but for raising questions above and below. The rejection and absence of mathematically oriented models and representations (including graphs, diagrams etc.) in teaching and research in law are palpable. Content (information) representation in the form of text, and qualitative text and language analysis, have a monopolistic position, but for how long? Will some form of creative destruction set in on the further scientification of law, analogously to what has happened in economics (for better or worse)?[12]

21.2.4 Economics, law and technology

As far as IP and innovation are concerned, bi-disciplinary interaction is not sufficient. The contemporary IP systems are essentially utilitarian-based, and innovation is a utilitarian concept with technological innovations as a most important category. Thus, at least economics, law and technology have to be among the key disciplines in interdisciplinary research on IP and innovation.

Tri-disciplinary interaction in research involves far more dynamics (e.g. in catalyzing cross-fertilization or in checking reductionist tendencies) and

[12] The history of legal thought is clearly not devoid of attempts at scientification, leading to some form of legal formalism, depending upon the employed notion of science. Despite significant subsequent criticism of such attempts, they are likely to continue. It is interesting to note that law as an explicitly recognized academic subject (explicitly present in university curricula) is older than economics – which as an academic subject has roots in law – while economics has perhaps in modern times become precursory in certain academic respects. (See e.g. Strömholm 1985.)

uncertainties than bi-disciplinary (just like a three-body problem in physics). Adding a third discipline triples the number of binary relations, in which challenges and opportunities might accrue. As to economics, law and technology (engineering), the relations between economics and law and between law and technology have been dealt with above (and in the entire book for that matter), and the relation between economics and technology has been dealt with elsewhere in the literature (see e.g. Granstrand 1994). As is widely recognized in this literature, technology and innovation have for long penetrated our economies far more than economics, although economics of technology and innovation is now a rapidly growing field. The need for a closer interaction between economics, law and technology at different levels (legislation, practice, research, teaching etc.) has been emphasized at various places in the book, starting in Chapter 1, so there is no need to open up a new discussion here, but to reemphasize the need for this troika of disciplines in particular in pulling IP studies ahead.

A brief outlook on some additional disciplines is in place, however.

21.2.5 Behavioral science and management

Research relations between psychology and sociology on one hand, and economics and law on the other hand, have grown in general since fairly long ago, and their merits and justifications in general apply to studies of innovation and IP as well. Just to give a few specific illustrations, psychology may give valuable inputs to IP studies regarding the incentive structures and motivations of IP creators, i.e. inventors, researchers, authors, artists and creative individuals in general. Such knowledge is necessary in order to judge the relative effectiveness and efficiency of various IPRs and of different institutional arrangements for stimulating innovation more generally (IPRs, prizes, grants etc.) in the design of different incentive regimes.

Sociology and anthropology may give valuable inputs regarding IP notions in various communities and cultures; how innovators and imitators are treated; how reputation and fame matter; how codified IPRs interact with internalised norms etc. Criminology may throw light on piracy, counterfeiting and IP crimes in general and on the impact of IP criminalization and prospects of correction. Communication studies are needed of the impact of IP-based information trade on communication behavior. Many other examples could be given, of course.

As to management, there is definitely a need for further studies of IP management, as this has traditionally been a minor area indeed in industry and in management studies. With the advent of the pro-patent era and the pro-IP era more generally, IP valuation and IP strategies have come into focus, just to mention two examples. Studies of valuation and strategies are needed not only for integration of IP with other areas of management, but also for judging the impact of the IP system on company behavior and vice versa. A more general issue in relation to management is how to design proper governance structures for innovation and diffusion. For example, quasi-integrated organizational forms intermediate to management hierarchies and market organizations might be most conducive to innovation in many circumstances. This issue also involves network studies and organizational theory, incorporating rights allocation.

21.2.6 Arts and humanities

Arts and humanities are increasingly important to consider in IP studies. This must be said not just for the sake of completing an odyssey among disciplines, but because technology and IP issues increasingly penetrate these areas at the same time as these areas can provide many valuable inputs to IP studies, regardless of their main disciplinary orientation. A few examples may illustrate this. First, history studies provide an excellent way to integrate interdisciplinary studies. Second, foundational studies of IP notions and related notions (such as moral rights) are needed, calling upon philosophy. Third, ethical issues are also coming more to the front, especially in relation to IPRs and BHTs, calling upon humanities, involving not only philosophy and ethics but also e.g. religious studies. Fourth, a holistic and imaginative perspective, wherever needed, can also be provided by arts and humanities, being perhaps one of their defining characteristics. Finally, on a more mundane level, cultural innovations constitute a wide range of innovations important to all of us. Do we want more new sculptures, plays, poems, books, architecture, paintings, operas, songs, concerts, movies etc. and more new art forms in general and, if so, how to make best provision of them? Their provision is in transition being increasingly industrialized and "technofied", thus calling for research involving arts and humanities on one hand and economics, law and technology, behavioral sciences and management on the other. Thus, arts and humanities themselves seem to be in need of holistic studies.

21.3 Reflections upon Teaching Intellectual Property

The rapid growth of interest in and concern about intellectual property issues in many quarters naturally generates a need for learning about IP, and a concomitantly expressed demand for teaching of IP. Even the unlikely event of a major reversal of the pro-IP era in the short run would probably lead at most to a slowing of the growth of IP teaching and learning. The undercurrent towards a more innovation-oriented but still capitalist society pervaded by IP issues is simply too strong. (Compare also the changes and trends described in Chapter 1.) An illustration is the ambitious goal in Europe to approach an investment level of 3% of GDP for R&D and innovation by 2010. This will probably lead to educational efforts in technology and IP management regardless of whether the goal is achieved or not.

At the same time, growth in IP teaching and learning starts from a low point. Before the pro-IP era, IP teaching at higher educational levels (college and university levels) was at most a minor element in the teaching of law, business administration and engineering – and in fact an absent element in many places, just as it was and always has been at lower educational levels.[13]

At higher educational levels, the virtues of integrating teaching and research in the spirit of a "Humboldt university" are widely recognized.[14] The virtues of integrating various disciplines in higher education are less clear, however, at least in formal education. Considering the possible virtues of sequential specialist-generalist learning, and the sequential complementarities (dynamic economies of scope) between formal education and continued education with more opportunities to integrate different areas of expertise in on-the-job training, one could also argue in favor of differentiating formal and continued education with more specialist disciplinary formal education. On the other hand, this is a matter of making trade-offs, and strong socio-political tendencies in the university system towards intradisciplinary teaching create risks of too little interdisciplinarity. Looking at an "input/output matrix" of higher education, showing the inputs of various disciplines into the curriculum for higher professional education in economics, engineering and law, one sees fairly small off-diagonal shares. That is, typical education in economics (including business economics) has a minor share at most of

[13] A related concern may be the "under-teaching" of economics and law in general as distinct subjects in compulsory schooling. Some basic rules of economics and law of course enter very early in the education of children through various types of teaching, e.g. respect for physical property rights and quid pro quo principles, but not very much through formal teaching (and basically nothing about IP).

[14] The virtues could be expressed in terms of economies of scale, scope and speed accruing from integrating research and advanced teaching, sharing and cross-fertilizing similar knowledge and learning resources, as well as speeding up dissemination and application of new knowledge and ideas. Needless to say, diseconomies can accrue as well (e.g. in the form of distorted teaching and disturbed research).

law and nothing in technology; typical engineering education has at most a minor share of economics and almost nothing in law; and typical education in law has very little if anything in economics and technology.

It may now be argued – just as for research – that close interaction between rapid economic, legal and technological changes calls for a corresponding interdisciplinarity in teaching, starting already in formal education, in turn connected with research due to the pace of change.[15] Such arguments are not idiosyncratic of our times, however. This is in fact an old idea, succinctly expressed by Charles Babbage in his book "The Decline of Science" from 1830. Babbage, in his efforts to reform British science, also engaged in the related endeavor to reform university education, which he saw as necessary to link to science in general. One of his proposals was (Babbage 1830, pp. 5-6):

> "If it should be thought preferable, the sciences might be grouped, and the following subjects be taken together:
>
> | | |
> |---|---|
> | Modern History.
Laws of England.
Civil Law. | Political Economy.
Application of Science to Arts and Manufacture. |
> | Chemistry.
Mineralogy.
Geology. | Zoology, including Physiology and Comparative Anatomy.
Botany, including Vegetable Physiology and Anatomy." |

The essence of his proposal to combine law, economics and engineering with natural sciences, biology not least, and with humanities – represented by history – is surprisingly relevant for our times (just as his proposed computer is). Since the times of Charles Babbage, the Western university system has integrated research and teaching considerably and is currently integrating forwards into industrial activities to an increasing extent. At the same time, the system has developed considerable disciplinary specialization and separation, leading to e.g. separate institutions for professional education and separate professional disciplinary subcultures or epistemic communities.[16]

---

[15] To some extent such teaching is already in place, e.g. in form of "hybrid" engineering degrees, mixing engineering subjects with economics and management or (to a lesser extent) law, as a less demanding and more integrated alternative to dual degrees.

[16] See Snow (1930) for a classic treatise on the separation of S&T from humanities and social science. Features of disciplinary subcultures such as styles of thought and language have been

To accomplish interdisciplinary teaching is not easy. Here, one may reflect not only upon how to facilitate interdisciplinary teaching of IP, melting together e.g. management, economics, law and technology, but also upon how IP can be used as a focusing device to facilitate interdisciplinary teaching more generally. At least for the disciplines mentioned, various pervasive IP issues could be used as an interdisciplinary thread in teaching, as these disciplines develop broader interfaces with each other under labels such as technology management, law and technology, law and economics, economics of technology and innovation etc. IP issues have characteristics such as being not only pervasive but also being concrete as well as theory-based, being short-term as well as long-term oriented, demanding attention to detail as well as to "the big picture", being linked to various disciplines in an operational way etc., plus presently being interesting, engaging and novel to most students. For example, education and training in entrepreneurship could focus on IP issues and intellectual capital formation as a pervasive theme. Similarly, IP issues could provide an integrative teaching platform for more broad in-house competence development in an existing firm.

21.4 Technology and IP – A Final Reflection

On a concluding note it might be appropriate to put IP into a broader context, to remind ourselves of the risk of being overly IP-centric, and to offer some scenarios to prepare for change. One way to interpret at least the Western history of ideas is that mankind displays a ceaseless propensity to form ideas and seek greater insight for survival and well-being. Both religious and scientific ideas can be seen as expressions of this propensity, although these two sets of ideas have been mostly adversary with scientific ones steadily gaining ground over the centuries. Material incentives have obviously played an important role, but only up to a point, variable with periods and cultures. More narrowly but still in sweeping terms, economic incentives provided by codified IPRs have been neither necessary nor sufficient for progress, be it scientific, technological, economic, cultural etc. At the same time technological progress is and has been most decisive for economic progress and vice versa. The effects of the IP system are more localized, perhaps affecting the rate more than the direction of progress. Questions in this context are and

---

described in various writings, but an interdisciplinary comparative analysis is still largely missing. For illuminating writings of this sort, see e.g. Vandevelde (1996) and Adams and Brownsword (1999) on lawyers, Vincenti (1990) on engineers and McCloskey (1998) and Klein (1999) on economists.

will remain open, however, since the variation of "natural experiments" with different types of IP systems in different nations and periods throughout history is too small to permit any firmer conclusions on empirical grounds.

Thus, the long-standing debate about the extent and nature of impact of the IP system will continue. One could also argue that the extent or variability of the impact – good or bad – will grow as the importance of intellectual capital grows in the economy. To the extent that any convergence of IP systems in the world takes place, the variation of natural experiments decreases and the role of counterfactual analysis increases in the debate, which probably will add even more fuel to it.

In any case, the economic foundations of the IP system are not valid forever everywhere. Underinvestment in innovation and diffusion does not always take place, and there is always a risk of overinvestment if racing games rather than waiting games from time to time become dominant among investors, or if private returns to innovation exceed social returns. Private and social rates of return on innovation and the gap between them could also be expected to become more volatile in the new type of economy for various reasons, thereby creating more risks and needs for risk allocation schemes and, perhaps, liability rules rather than property rules. A devaluation of progress in parts of society could also occur if technological innovations are perceived to create more problems than they solve in the form of negative side and secondary effects. The nature of technological changes with inseparable, uncertain and skewly distributed good/bad, short/long-term consequences also makes technology as difficult as important to harness and steer by economic and legal institutions of various kinds. There already exist several more or less effective means besides IPRs to provide for innovation and diffusion (prizes, procurement etc.), and more means of provision may be invented, e.g. for financing open science or financing legal R&D.[17]

Similarly the legal foundations of the IP system are not built to last forever. Utilitarian foundations could perhaps be replaced by other areas of law (competition law, contract law etc.). At the same time, moral rights movements could be revived or appear in new forms, although they would hardly by themselves substitute for utilitarian justifications at societal level, especially not in a competitive corporativist world. One should not forget the

[17] It is even conceivable that a novel, useful and non-obvious incentive scheme for financing innovations could be patented as an institutional innovation – say a new contracting scheme invented by a team of university researchers, and licensed out as an alternative to the patent system. (The economic valuation of such a "meta-innovation" would probably call for some additional inventive approaches in turn.)

seemingly endless history of IP notions among humans in a broader sense than codified in law as rights. Thus one could claim that there are deeper cultural foundations for at least certain types of IPRs in line with the claim that there exist certain natural or moral rights in IP. To the extent that this holds, at least some foundations of the IP system could be seen as solid, if not *terra firma*. Even if parts of the economic and legal foundations of the IP system could conceivably be removed or replaced, it therefore seems that some fundamental IP notions could not. IP nihilism appears just as infeasible as IP-centrism.

However, the current issue is not whether the IP system could be abandoned altogether or not, but rather how far it should be allowed to expand. There are strong economic, legal and political forces supporting a strong IP regime. Criticism is growing but has perhaps not yet gained real momentum. There is a heterogeneous set of new entrants into the IP field, some being less than enthusiastic about many of its developments. A (re)entry of economists will certainly challenge many IP laws and practices from economic points of view, and so will many academics as well as practitioners who will find various IPR practices excessive and counterproductive. To the extent that the IP system is seen to limit rather than to foster dynamic competition, it will attract more serious criticism than the traditional one regarding static competition. The concentration of technology and IP power to large firms and to developed countries (the US in particular) will most likely sooner or later fuel criticism not only against the IP system but against capitalism in general. The "old-fashioned" tensions between capital owners and labor will take on a new and probably more potent dimension – a tension between owners (and controllers and managers) of intellectual capital and intellectual labor. Intellectual labor will also experience internal tensions with competition between high/low wage groups in the world as well as between young and old knowledge workers, perhaps to the point where intergenerational roll-over of knowledge becomes impeded by privatization. Besides, all sides will be penetrated by legal disputes over IP, so "frontiers" will be blurred. Nevertheless, "IP wars" could simply take on a new meaning of fighting for and against the IP system rather than fighting over specific IPRs among a mix of pro-IP reformers, IP revolutionaries, IP skeptics, etc.

A form of IP war is already taking place in cyberspace (see e.g. Lessig 2001). Another one is escalating in "biospace". While the former has gained widespread recognition and affected large parts of the public, not least the young generation, the latter will more likely be really crucial for the IP system as a whole.

There are several reasons – that can only be sketched here – in support of this scenario. First, collectivist utilitarian-based IPRs have a strong tendency to conflict with more basic individual rights notions, despite the fact that some IP notions have strong cultural and even biological foundations (e.g. identity marks and secrets). At a general level this type of conflict arises partly because IPRs constitute a capitalist institution, thus becoming a target for standard critique of capitalism (directed against e.g. inequalities, power concentration and exploitation of public resources). Conflicts also arise because IPRs influence the interface (or "social contract"), between the individual and society, capitalist or not (due to e.g. moral rights notions).

Second, at a technology-specific level, different technologies affect basic individual rights notions differently. Privacy and freedom of speech are affected primarily by ICTs, while e.g. rights to reproduction, bodily parts and genetic material are affected more by BHTs. Now, basic individual rights notions affected by BHTs are arguably stronger than those affected by ICTs. When people risk dying because they cannot afford a patented drug and are denied the use of a cheaper but illegal copy, the concept of deadweight loss becomes tragically more serious than if people cannot buy a book. To the extent that BHTs are lagging behind ICTs in their developments and impact, clashes in cyberspace could be seen as precursory to much stronger clashes around IPRs in biospace, reinforced by concern and critique over capitalism from other sources. When BHTs become more powerful not only in curing diseases and malfunctions but in performance-enhancing of species, including humans, will a kind of "bio-divide" arise among people in the world? What about distributional bio-ethics? Bio-piracy? Bio-crime? Etc.? Many BHT developments are as yet unrecognized and, more importantly, inconceivable. This is probably true for some basic individuals rights notions and BHT-related ethical issues as well. Bio-informatics is a particularly interesting area since it might become the nexus or focal point of rights and liability conflicts related to both BHTs and ICTs. What should rights to bodily parts include (parts in scarce supply, stem cells, an embryo, a foetus, right to death etc?) and should they extend to transferable rights to information about them? How should the production, distribution and use of such information be incentivized and controlled?

In this scenario of biospace conflicts, chances are that anti-IP movements, which certainly will brew in some quarters, will grow to proportions sufficient to transform and even reverse the pro-IP era. There are even chances that such movements allied with other forces (e.g. religious ones or forces against some kind of military-legal complex) could transform the capitalist development on a larger scale. A strength of a capitalist system is its feedback structure, enabling a fair amount of self-construction (Rosenberg 1992). The pro-IP era brought about as capitalism developed could grow out of proportions, jeopardizing itself as well as many features of its embedding system. However, the old but revived IP system with all its virtues and limitations and its embedding system could also be transformed in a more evolutionary way, perhaps even beyond recognition.

In other words, a *nova species* as the next generation changes.

21.5 Literature References

Adams, J.N. and Brownsword, R. (1999), *Understanding Law* (2nd ed.). London: Sweet & Maxwell.

Arrow, K.J. (1962), 'Economic Welfare and the Allocation of Resources for Invention'. In NBER (1962), pp. 609-25.

Babbage, C. (1830), *Reflections on the Decline of Science in England, and Some of its Causes*. London: B. Fellowes.

Besen, S.M. and L.J. Raskind (1991), 'An introduction to the law and economics of intellectual property', *Journal of Economic Perspectives*, 5 (1), 3-27.

Cheung, S.N.S. (1986), 'Property Rights and Invention'. In Palmer (1986), pp. 5-18.

Coase, R. (1960), 'The Problem of Social Cost', *The Journal of Law and Economics*, 3, 1-44.

David, P.A. (1993), 'Intellectual Property Institutions and the Panda's Thumb: Patents, Copyrights, and Trade Secrets in Economic Theory and History'. In Wallerstein *et al.* (eds.), 1993, Ch. 2, pp. 19–61.

Gallini, N. and Scotchmer, S. (2002), 'Intellectual Property: When is it the Best Incentive System?'. In Jaffe *et al.* (2002), Ch. 2, pp. 51-77.

Granstrand, O., ed. (1994), *Economics of Technology*. Amsterdam: Elsevier Science Publ.

Granstrand, O. (2004), 'The Economics and Management of Technology Trade – Towards a pro-licensing era?', *International Journal of Technology Management* (forthcoming).

Jaffe, A.B., Lerner, J. and Stern, S., eds. (2002), *Innovation Policy and the Economy 2*. Cambridge, Mass.: MIT Press.

Klein, D.B., ed. (1999), *What do Economists Contribute?* London: Macmillan Press.

Lessig, L. (2001), *The Future of Ideas*. Random House.

McCloskey, D.N. (1998), *The Rhetoric of Economics* (2nd ed.). University of Wisconsin Press.

NBER (1962), *The Rate and Direction of Inventive Activity*. National Bureau of Economic Research, Princeton, N.J.: Princeton University Press.

Palmer, J., ed. (1986), 'The Economics of Patents and Copyrights', *Research in Law and Economics*, Vol. 8. Greenwich, CT: JAI Press Inc.

Posner, R. (1992), *Economic Analysis of Law* (4th ed.). Boston: Little, Brown.

Rawls, J. (1971), *A Theory of Justice* (rev.ed. 1999). Oxford: Oxford University Press.

Rosenberg, N. (1992), 'Economic experiments', *Industrial and Corporate Change*, 1, 181-203.

Snow, C.P. (1930), *The Two Cultures* (2nd ed. 1964). London: Cambridge University Press.

Strömholm, S. (1985), *A Short History of Legal Thinking in the West*. Stockholm: Norstedts.

Vandevelde, K.J. (1996), *Thinking like a Lawyer, an Introduction to Legal Reasoning*. Boulder, CO: Westview Press.

Vincenti, W. G. (1990), *What Engineers Know and How They Know It*. The Johns Hopkins University Press.

von Hippel, E. (1988), *The Sources of Innovation*. New York, NY: Oxford University Press.

Wallerstein, M.B., Mogee, M.E. and Schoen, R.A. eds. (1993), *Global Dimensions of Intellectual Property Rights in Science and Technology*. Washington, D.C.: National Academy Press.

Wright, B.D. (1983), 'The economics of invention incentives: patents, prizes, and research contracts', *American Economic Review*, 73 (4), 691-707.

ABBREVIATIONS

AHC	Academic health center
AI	Artificial intelligence
ATP	Advanced Technology Program
AUTM	Association of University Technology Managers
B2B	Business-to-Business
BRD	Best reference document
CI	Claimed invention
DARPA	Defense Advanced Research Projects Agency
DRMS	Digital Rights Management System
EC	European Commission
EPO	European Patent Office
FDI	Foreign Direct Investment
GATT	General Agreement on Tariffs and Trade
GPS	Global positioning system
GSM	Global System for Mobile Communications (Originally "Groupe Special Mobile")
ICTs	Information and communication technologies, i.e. Infocom technologies
IP	Intellectual property
IPRs	Intellectual property rights
M&A	Mergers and acquisitions
NDA	Non-disclosure agreement
NIC	Newly industrialized countries
NRC	National Research Council
OECD	Organization for economic co-operation and development
OTL	Office of technology licensing
PSA	Person skilled in the art

R&D	Research and development
RJV	Research joint venture
S&T	Science and technology
SCI	Science citation index
SEF	Specialized engineering firm
SSCI	Social science citation index
TRIPs	Trade-related intellectual property section (of GATT)
UNCTAD	United Nations Conference on Trade and Development
USPTO	United States Patent and Trademark Office
WIPO	World Intellectual Property Organization
WTO	World Trade Organization
XIPO	Xerox Intellectual Property Office

INDEX OF SUBJECTS

This is primarily a guide to concepts and phenomena rather than proper names, the latter being extremely numerous in the book. It is also representative rather than exhaustive, mainly since the field of intellectual property has limited specific terminology as yet. While economic and legal terms predominate, many occur throughout the text with diverse contextual definitions, combinations and even spelling variants, whose full indexing could be pointless or misleading rather than helpful. Certain frequently used terms are marked *passim* instead of having numerous page numbers.

The manufacturer's authorised representative in the EU is Springer Nature Customer Service Centre GmbH, Europaplatz 3, 69115 Heidelberg, Germany. If you have any concerns regarding our products, please contact ProductSafety@springernature.com

Printed and bound by CPI Group (UK) Ltd, Croydon, CR0 4YY
10/10/2026
02231227-0010